Microsoft®
.NET E-Commerce
Bible

Don Jones

Hungry Minds™

Hungry Minds, Inc.

Best-Selling Books • Digital Downloads • e-Books • Answer Networks • e-Newsletters • Branded Web Sites • e-Learning

New York, NY ✦ Indianapolis, IN ✦ Cleveland, OH

Microsoft® .NET E-Commerce Bible

Published by
Hungry Minds, Inc.
909 Third Avenue
New York, NY 10022
www.hungryminds.com

Library of Congress Control Number: 2001091960

ISBN: 0-7645-4831-X

Printed in the United States of America

10 9 8 7 6 5 4 3 2 1

IB/RX/QX/QK/IN

Distributed in the United States by Hungry Minds, Inc.

Distributed by CDG Books Canada Inc. for Canada; by Transworld Publishers Limited in the United Kingdom; by IDG Norge Books for Norway; by IDG Sweden Books for Sweden; by IDG Books Australia Publishing Corporation Pty. Ltd. for Australia and New Zealand; by TransQuest Publishers Pte Ltd. for Singapore, Malaysia, Thailand, Indonesia, and Hong Kong; by Gotop Information Inc. for Taiwan; by ICG Muse, Inc. for Japan; by Intersoft for South Africa; by Eyrolles for France; by International Thomson Publishing for Germany, Austria, and Switzerland; by Distribuidora Cuspide for Argentina; by LR International for Brazil; by Galileo Libros for Chile; by Ediciones ZETA S.C.R. Ltda. for Peru; by WS Computer Publishing Corporation, Inc., for the Philippines; by Contemporanea de Ediciones for Venezuela; by Express Computer Distributors for the Caribbean and West Indies; by Micronesia Media Distributor, Inc. for Micronesia; by Chips Computadoras S.A. de C.V. for Mexico; by Editorial Norma de Panama S.A. for Panama; by American Bookshops for Finland.

For general information on Hungry Minds' products and services please contact our Customer Care department within the U.S. at 800-762-2974, outside the U.S. at 317-572-3993 or fax 317-572-4002.

For sales inquiries and reseller information, including discounts, premium and bulk quantity sales, and foreign-language translations, please contact our Customer Care department at 800-434-3422, fax 317-572-4002 or write to Hungry Minds, Inc., Attn: Customer Care Department, 10475 Crosspoint Boulevard, Indianapolis, IN 46256.

For information on licensing foreign or domestic rights, please contact our Sub-Rights Customer Care department at 212-884-5000.

For information on using Hungry Minds' products and services in the classroom or for ordering examination copies, please contact our Educational Sales department at 800-434-2086 or fax 317-572-4005.

For press review copies, author interviews, or other publicity information, please contact our Public Relations department at 317-572-3168 or fax 317-572-4168.

For authorization to photocopy items for corporate, personal, or educational use, please contact Copyright Clearance Center, 222 Rosewood Drive, Danvers, MA 01923, or fax 978-750-4470.

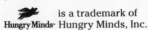 is a trademark of Hungry Minds, Inc.

About the Author

Don Jones (don@iridisconsulting.com) is the President of Iridis Consulting, LLC., an independent consulting firm providing training, software development, and systems design for high-end business technologies. Since 1989, Don has specialized in Microsoft technologies, most recently focusing on the .NET Server platforms, and has earned Microsoft's premier MCSE, MCDBA, and MCT certifications. Don has authored nationally recognized technical training courseware and is a frequent speaker at technical conferences across the country.

Don lives all across the country, fulfilling a lifelong dream to live and work in an RV while seeing this wonderful country. He travels with his partner and their four ferrets.

This book is lovingly dedicated to those closest to me, who had to put up with me while I was writing it: Buffy, Tigger, Clyde, Ziggy, and, most especially, Chris.

—DJ

Credits

Acquisitions Editor
Terri Varveris

Project Editor
Marcia Brochin

Technical Editor
Chuck Urwiler

Copy Editors
Rebekah Mancilla
Gabrielle Chosney

Editorial Managers
Ami Frank Sullivan
Kyle Looper

Project Coordinators
Emily Wichlinski
Ryan Steffen

Graphics and Production Specialists
Amy Adrian
Joyce Haughy
Stephanie D. Jumper
Gabrielle McCann
Jill Piscitelli
Betty Schulte
Kathie S. Schutte
Brian Torwelle
Erin Zeltner

Quality Control Technicians
Dave Faust
Andy Hollandbeck
Susan Moritz
Carl Pierce
Charles Spencer

Permissions Editor
Carmen Krikorian

Media Development Specialist
Gregory Stephens

Media Development Coordinator
Marisa Pearman

Proofreading and Indexing
TECHBOOKS Production Services

Preface

Just about everybody is "doing" e-commerce these days, and the Internet — and the technologies that it has engendered — has changed the way everyone does business, like it or not. Much of my work involves designing systems that in some way use e-commerce technologies, particularly Microsoft's e-commerce technologies. Getting individual products, such as Site Server or Internet Information Services, is rarely difficult. The challenge is getting all of them to work together to form a compelling, scalable, and reliable commercial product, and that's what this book is all about.

Over the past few years, Microsoft's product line has made amazing advances, and the company now offers an excellent set of software platforms for building e-commerce sites of almost any size or shape. These technologies include:

+ Site Server 3.0, Commerce Edition (and the newer Commerce Server 2000)
+ BizTalk Server 2000
+ Application Center 2000
+ Windows 2000 Server (and Advanced Server and Datacenter Server)
+ Visual Basic 6.0 and Visual Basic .NET
+ SQL Server 2000

Although each one of these products is by itself the subject of many books, making them all work together in a business environment is what makes e-commerce possible. Most e-commerce projects run over budget, miss deadlines, or fail altogether — not because the underlying technologies don't work, but because getting them all to work together to meet specific business goals can be tough! In this book, I've tried to lay out best practices for keeping things running smoothly, and I've made sure to address the common pitfalls so you'll know how to get around them before they happen to *your* project.

Who Should Read This Book

If you're building a Web site that uses e-commerce technologies — whether it's the latest dot-com smash hit or a site used only by members of your organization — you should definitely read this book. This book does assume that you're somewhat familiar with the previously mentioned technologies on an individual basis. This book is specifically written for:

- ◆ Senior software developers who have worked with one or more e-commerce technologies in the past
- ◆ Project managers working on e-commerce projects
- ◆ Technical leads and systems architects who are building e-commerce solutions

This book isn't intended to be a step-by-step tutorial for creating an e-commerce site. In fact, with so many e-commerce solutions out there vying for your attention, to create your site with a "wizard" or other template would be a huge mistake, because you would look just like everyone else! This book isn't intended to be an in-depth reference to any one product or technology, either. In fact, for every product or technology that I talk about, you'll find an entire book in this series dedicated to it. Instead of focusing on one technology, this book is designed to help you learn how *all* of these Microsoft products work together, and how to plan for an e-commerce site that makes the best possible use of their strengths while avoiding their weaknesses. This book is also about how to implement specific techniques and methodologies that will improve any Microsoft-based e-commerce site that you're working on — particularly techniques that give an e-commerce site an edge.

And although the specific technologies discussed in this book will continue to mature and change, the concepts and best practices that you'll learn from this book will always serve you well.

What You'll Learn From This Book

This is a "how-to" book, and you'll definitely have a lot of new knowledge when you finish reading it. Specifically, you're going to learn the best practices for implementing Microsoft e-commerce technologies to create scalable, reliable, and compelling Web sites. You're going to learn best practices for the non-technical trades that e-commerce Web sites depend on, such as marketing and product fulfillment, so that you can build Web sites that best meet the needs of those trades. And you're going to learn specific techniques for building those Web sites in as little time as possible, with as little fuss as possible.

Too many of the e-commerce sites that I've worked on had an incredible amount of thought put into them before the actual programming started — and yet, huge pieces of the final solution were still missing, because they hadn't been considered in advance. And as you are no doubt aware, "tacking on" major functionality to something as complex as an e-commerce Web site isn't anybody's idea of fun or efficiency. So I've taken pains to walk you through the planning process, and to point out areas that many e-commerce site designers forget or don't fully consider. This way, you'll be able to create a plan that addresses most of the site's critical needs — even the ones that aren't obvious.

Most importantly, my primary goal while writing this book was to anticipate the needs and problems that you probably haven't even thought of or run into, yet. When those problems do rear their ugly heads, you'll be able to flip through this book and find solutions that you can quickly put into place. Heck, just reading this book may give you enough advance warning to head those problems off at the pass—I certainly hope so!

Special Formatting

As with most computer books, you'll see that some text is highlighted by special formatting or with special icons. Here's a quick guide to the things you'll see in this book.

Note

Notes provide additional details and often contain information that you should read before trying to implement a reference technique.

 Notes look like this.

Tip

Tips inform you of little facts that may be useful to you as you work with the various technologies that I discuss. Tips provide helpful information that isn't always essential to getting things to work. Rather, Tips can be used to make them work *better*.

 Tips look like this

Caution

Cautions provide you with a warning about things that you should watch out for, or things that you shouldn't do. You should pay close attention to cautions when reading the text.

 Cautions look like this.

New Feature

The New Feature icon alerts you to features that are new to the latest version of a particular product. If you're familiar with older versions, these New Feature icons can help you identify features that can save you time or allow you to accomplish things that were formerly impossible.

 New Feature alerts look like this.

Cross Reference

The Cross Reference icon helps you quickly track down important information else-where in this book. I use this icon whenever I need to refer you back to an earlier portion of the book, or when I need to call your attention to a piece of information that I'll discuss in more detail later.

 Cross References look like this.

Source-Code Formatting

The text contains source-code listings as well is in-text references to objects, meth-ods, properties, and other source-code elements. Source-code listings in this book have several formats. Longer listings will appear in a traditional list, and I indicate which language — generally VBScript or Jscript — that I'm working with. For example:

Listing 1.1: VBScript: **The MsgBox Statement Sample**

```
'fire off a message box
MsgBox "Hello, world!"
```

In-text references to source-code elements are printed in a monospace font, so you'll know when I'm referring to the Redirect method of the Response object.

Support and Comments

Microsoft e-commerce design and development will always be evolving and changing in subtle — and sometimes drastic — ways, just like everything else in the technology industry. I'm always grateful to readers who take the time to point out new ideas and concepts, important new features, or decisions that have made a difference in their own projects.

I truly believe you'll find this book to be a valuable companion in your e-commerce development projects, and that it will find a permanent home on your shelf of refer-ence materials. And I hope you'll let me know what you think of it! E-mail me at don@iridisconsulting.com, or visit my Web site at www.iridisconsulting.com. I look forward to hearing from you, and wish you the best of luck on your e-commerce projects!

Acknowledgments

Writing any technical book is a difficult, time-consuming task. Writing one that deals with so many different technologies was especially challenging, and I couldn't have done it without the support of my friends, family, and ferrets. Special thanks goes out to the folks at Hungry Minds for their support, hard work, and patience while bringing this book to life. I'd also like to thank my keyboard for it's *extremely* hard work.

I'd like to acknowledge the support of my friends and contacts at Microsoft, who patiently answered questions when they could, and graciously listened to both my complaints and compliments about their products. And please give three cheers for the folks who gave me a "leg up" on e-commerce development: Micro Endeavors, Inc., Mark Scott, David Walls, Not Sold Separately, Inc., and the many fine authors of the other *Bible* books that have furthered *my* understanding of these complex technologies.

Finally, I'd like to thank my parents, John and Rhonda, for always having patience with me and encouraging me to succeed.

Contents at a Glance

Contents

• •

The Planning Phase

This part introduces the elements you should take into consideration when planning your e-commerce site. Planning is the most important and most overlooked step in creating a successful e-commerce site using the Microsoft platform. This part will walk you through each step in the planning phase, and help you make decisions that will set your e-commerce development on the right path.

Introduction to the Planning Phase

Once upon a time, implementing a Microsoft product involved simply running Setup and choosing a few configuration options. Unfortunately, those days are long gone. Before you can even begin to think about installing products and programming, you need to determine what specific products to install, what technologies you need, and how it all fits together. In other words, you need a plan.

In this and following chapters, I walk you through the planning process. My goal is to point out all of the decisions that you should be thinking about before any coding begins and before any products are installed. This way, you can start the actual development process with all of the difficult questions answered and with a clear blueprint of what the site should do. You'll be surprised at how much faster the actual development process proceeds when a clear blueprint is available to the technical professionals building the site. You'll also be surprised at how expandable, reliable, and scalable the final site is.

As you read through these first few chapters, start thinking about how you think your site should appear and function in six months. Or in a year — or in two years. Keep these thoughts in mind as you create your plan, because the plan must include a way for the site to grow toward those long-term directions. Obviously, implementing this growth is easier with access to the company's overall business plan for the site — yet another reason to make sure that the planning process involves business professionals from every department in your company, and not just the technical group.

Introducing the Planning Phase

In today's fast-paced, profit-oriented world, taking the necessary time to plan an e-commerce site can seem costly. After all, that's time that can be better spent actually getting the site online, right? Many companies deploy sites with this view, and find themselves struggling later — trying to implement features that they never thought would be important, reprogramming major portions of their site (instead of adding new functionality), and working hard to keep the site up and running for existing customers (instead of adding new customers). You can't underestimate the planning phase, and you definitely should not ignore it.

Strive to have a quality plan. If you're a technical professional, make sure that the plan answers *business* questions, and not just *technology* questions. See that your plan covers all the bases about what features are necessary and what growth is anticipated. Make sure that the people responsible for making your site a success — marketing professionals, managers, customer service personnel, and so forth — contribute to the site's overall plan. Getting "buy-in" (or input) from the entire management team ensures that the site is collecting the right data about your customers, delivering the right features, and creating a good impression from the first day.

Take the time to create a detailed *customer experience* plan. This plan spells out exactly what your customers (whether they are outside customers or other employees) will see and do when they're using the site. This type of plan is great for pointing out flawed designs and concepts, and for getting everyone to think about the most important aspect of any e-commerce site — the customer.

 Cross-Reference   I discuss how to design and plan the customer experience in Chapter 2.

Beginning a quality e-commerce site plan requires four major steps:

1. Create the vision that will guide the site's development.

2. Create a *scope,* which is a statement of what the first phase of the site should include.

3. Create formal documents to communicate the vision and scope, the technology decisions, a specification for the site, and a complete project plan to the rest of your company and your technical team.

4. Get that all-important "buy-in" from the entire technology and management teams, so that everyone is on the same page about how the site is to be built and what it should accomplish.

For small sites, these steps may take a couple of days. For larger, more comprehensive, or more complex sites, these steps may take weeks. Rest assured that the effort is an investment that will pay dividends in reduced development time and a superior end result.

I urge you to read the planning chapters in this book because the majority of the guidelines, cautions, and *bad* examples that I show you are from my actual experiences as an e-commerce architect and developer. Someone once said, "If we do not learn from history, we are doomed to repeat it." Read about my past experiences, and learn from the mistakes, so that you can avoid them in your future!

Starting the plan

The first step in the planning process is to create a *vision*. The vision should be a short, concise statement defining the overall goal of the project — in this case, an e-commerce site. Avoid using flowery language. Anyone, including non-technical people, involved with the project should be able to read and understand it. A good vision statement should embody the following qualities:

- ✦ Clear, concise language.
- ✦ Several sentences, if necessary.
- ✦ Specific, measurable, and achievable goals.
- ✦ Business-oriented goals rather than technical goals.
- ✦ Statements that convey the ultimate purpose of the site.

The vision statement should make the purpose and broad goals of the site absolutely clear to anyone who reads it.

The vision

I'll start right off with an example of a *bad* vision statement:

> Our site will utilize the latest technologies to produce a compelling customer experience, which will result in stickiness and increased sales.

First of all, at this point, you shouldn't care what technologies the site will use. The technology is supposed to be a means to a business goal, not a goal in itself. If you can build the site with ten-year-old technology, then you probably want to do so. Second, what is a "compelling customer experience?" Does this phrase refer to an experience that customers enjoy? If so, that should go without saying. If for some reason you want to create a site that customers don't enjoy, then put *that* in your vision. Finally, what do the phrases "stickiness" and "increased sales" really mean? Vision statements should be devoid of ambiguities. For example, consider the following revision:

> Our site will strive for repeat business, so that every customer returns within two weeks to make another purchase. The site will achieve sales that increase by 10 percent each month.

This vision statement is easy to understand, and its goals are clearly stated and measurable.

Your vision statement can also be used to state important philosophical goals, as demonstrated in the following example:

> Our site will utilize a minimum of extraneous graphics to produce the fastest possible response time for users. It will utilize friendly, understandable language to make users feel at ease. It will offer frequently updated information to compel the user to return several times each day.

This statement tells you that the site won't include a lot of graphics and animations, and that it's going to be mostly text. This text needs to be written in a casual style that users can understand. The site will be updated frequently, so making it data-driven is probably going to be important. Furthermore, the goal of frequently returning users may imply some kind of information "push" technology, or at least e-mail newsletters. This vision statement is already answering questions about how the site will look, the technologies it will use, and so forth. By stating everything so clearly, the folks developing the site can make every decision with these ultimate goals in mind. As new features are added, they can ask, "Is this feature going to help bring people back several times a day? Could this feature be made better if it were written differently?" Setting the tone for the site helps focus each decision on achieving these goals.

You may wonder if it's really necessary to nit-pick on something as simple as a vision statement. After all, "visions" are plentiful in today's business world, so why fret over one for a project? Is it really useful?

I believe it is. Consider "SuperDuper.com" as an example (a real company from my past, with the name changed to protect the innocent). Their vision statement read as follows:

> SuperDuper.com will strive to delight our customers with original content, beautiful layouts, and the most impressive names in our industry.

Delighting your customers is certainly a valuable goal, but one that is difficult to measure. The statement does contain some good descriptors, including "original content," which means that the site's creators must have a technological emphasis on ways to get this content online. Beautiful layouts means lots of graphics, and probably more advanced dynamic HTML techniques to present them. Indeed, this vision statement contains some great ideas, but do you see anything about making money? Getting customers to come back? You can't even tell what the site will try to sell.

Sadly, that particular "dot com" is no longer in business. I don't attribute its demise entirely to the lack of a solid vision statement for the site, but if we had been equipped with some formal statement confirming that the company was even vaguely interested in sales, we may have been able to guide the site in that direction. As it was, the company's internal focus was exactly what the vision stated — beautiful layouts, incredible graphics, and tons of original content. Employees spent hundreds of man-hours developing ways for editors to get content on the site fast and easily but relatively little time making the shopping cart easy for customers to use. The HTML pages were masterpieces of design, but customers often couldn't figure out how to sign up for SuperDuper.com's e-mail newsletter. In order to avoid having a site that doesn't meet all of your business needs and your customers' needs, develop a meaningful vision statement for your Web site to guide your every decision through the rest of the planning process.

Tip   The vision statement isn't intended to impress anybody — it's intended to guide the development and direction of the site.

Here is an example of a strong vision statement for Retailer.com, a fictional bricks-and-mortar retailer that is planning to launch a Web site in order to expand their market. Retailer.com is one of the many sample companies that I use throughout this book to demonstrate specific techniques and concepts. Their vision statement reads as follows:

> The Retailer.com Web site will entice customers to return frequently through creative promotions and targeted direct e-mail marketing. The site will entice customers to purchase by offering product suggestions based on customers' buying habits and preferences. The site will be compatible with the widest array of browsers and platforms possible, and will implement an uncluttered and intuitive user interface. The site's key operations will require a minimum of customer input, yet allow customers the maximum ability to customize their site experience.

With this vision in mind, the next step is to create a project scope.

The scope

The vision statement is intended to provide a broad, far-reaching statement of the site's goals and philosophies. You might even say that the vision statement presents the "sky's the limit" view of the site and what it will accomplish. The *scope*, by contrast, seeks to limit the site to a specific set of detailed criteria.

The scope is a "living" document that will constantly change and evolve. E-commerce site development should never be thought of as a single project, but rather a series of continuing, interconnected projects that result in a constantly evolving site. After each phase, the scope should be redefined to encompass the next phase of the site's evolution. Once defined, however, the scope for a particular phase of development can't change without certain consequences (see the sidebar, "The Physics of a Project").

The Physics of a Project

One of the nice things about the laws of physics is that they're fixed and unchangeable. Gravity, for example, won't let up on Monday because your boss isn't feeling well. And although an e-commerce site development project can constantly change and evolve, a simple set of what I like to call "project physics" never changes. Just about every project management methodology that I'm familiar with, including Microsoft's own Solutions Framework, defines these as three properties — time, features, and resources.

The term *time*, of course, refers to the amount of time in which a project must be finished. The term *features* refers to the things that the project will be able to do after it's finished. The term *resources* refers to the money and manpower required to complete the project.

The law of physics that ties these three properties together is simple: No one property can change without at least one of the others changing as well. You can add features to a project, but either more time or more people will be required to complete the project. You can take people away from a project, but either the feature set must shrink or the time must be expanded (or both) to compensate.

No amount of positive team attitude or creative management can change this physical law of the universe, and only good planning can prevent this give-and-take law from becoming a problem on your e-commerce project. Stick by your project documentation, and keep it up to date. By doing this, you can prevent features from "sneaking in," and you can show everyone why the project is behind schedule after half of the developers have moved to another project.

Because I began this discussion on vision statements with a deliberately bad example, I continue the tradition here by showing you what *not* to do in your scope:

> In its first phase, the site will implement complete personalization for all pages. The database will support all retail operations and business partner data exchanges. Fulfillment will be completely automated and first-line customer service will be provided by artificial intelligence routines drawing from a database of frequently asked questions.

Nothing like shooting for the stars in your first round, right? This scope is too vague, too broad, and too ambitious. Plus, it neglects to answer the important questions, including:

✦ Will some kind of checkout process be developed?

✦ Will people be able to actually buy anything?

✦ Will there be a catalog of products and services?

A good scope document should be short and to the point. You may prefer to list the things that the site *won't* include in the first phase. This way, you're acknowledging desired functionality while specifically relegating implementation to a later phase of the site's development.

Armed with a great vision statement, Retailer.com may create a scope that looks something like this:

> The site will support a product catalog of sufficient complexity to present our existing product line. No support for suggested add-on sales will be included in the first phase.
>
> The site will include support for simple text-file and EDI data exchange with trading partners over the Internet. We will be able to feed our product catalog to these partners, but we will not accept orders from them in the first phase.
>
> We will implement a navigation method that permits access to all of our product categories.
>
> We will implement a method for customers to sign up for various e-mail newsletters, and to specify their hobbies and other interests. We will use this information to generate mailing lists for targeted marketing e-mails on a weekly basis.
>
> Our checkout and shopping cart will be constructed to collect the minimum amount of information in the minimum number of screens. We will save as much information as possible and fill it in for customers on return visits. We will give the customer full control over our use of this information.
>
> Our site will be compatible with 4.0 and higher Web browsers on the PC, Unix, and Macintosh platforms.
>
> Our site will be designed to appeal to, and be intuitive to, our current marketing demographics — teenagers and young adults aged 17 to 30.

This scope establishes several important guidelines for the project. For example, the scope limits some of the vision statement's more far-reaching goals to a manageable level for the first phase by specifying the level of browser that will be the "lowest common denominator," the level of database complexity that will be developed, and so forth. Notice that the scope doesn't seek to make any technological decisions other than limiting the browser audience. At this stage, the project plan is still defining *what* Retailer.com wants to do — not *how* it's going to do it. Most importantly, the scope is completely in line with the vision statement (they don't contradict each other).

Your scope document should serve as a useful guide to the remainder of the development process. As you examine technologies and make decisions about what will be implemented, you can continually refer back to your scope document to make sure that your current line of thinking fits within the intended parameters. The vision statement helps you see where the site will *eventually* go, so you can make sure that your technology selections and decisions support that long-term direction while still restricting the actual development in this phase to the boundaries of the scope.

The next piece of this process is to write everything down.

Documenting the plan

The most important result of the planning phase is, of course, the documentation that explains what decisions were made and what the plan actually entails. The project's documentation should be more formal than some notes scribbled into your PDA, but not necessarily more complex than a few clearly-written Word documents.

Always keep the documentation's audience in mind, and make sure that the documentation provides enough information so that the entire audience can understand its intent. This project documentation is your blueprint for an e-commerce site, so it's critical that all the workers, technical or non-technical, be able to understand it. The documentation's audience may include:

✦ Technical professionals, such as systems architects, systems engineers, developers, and technicians

✦ Members of your company's management team

✦ Members of your company's board of directors

✦ Outside contractors, both technical and non-technical, brought in to help on the project

✦ Financiers and venture capitalists seeking to understand the company's plan or conducting due diligence processes

✦ Project managers of subsequent phases, who need to understand why certain decisions were made in prior phases

The fact that much of the documentation's potential audience is comprised of non-technical folks should make you want to spend some extra time explaining not just the decisions, but also the rationale behind the decisions.

A well-organized e-commerce development project includes five key pieces of documentation:

1. The vision and the scope
2. Technology decisions and selection

3. A functional specification

4. A complete project plan, including a timeline

5. An outline of the project team and the decision-making process used during the project planning

Documenting technology decisions and selections enables outsiders to understand the thought process that went into your decision to use, for example, Visual Basic instead of Visual C++, or Microsoft SQL Server instead of Oracle. You have specific reasons for selecting these specific technologies to build your e-commerce site, and you must document these reasons so they aren't forgotten in the future. In subsequent phases of the site's development, key decision-making factors like budget and product availability may change, and future project planners will need to understand which factors may be safely disregarded. Some factors, such as system compatibility or speed of development, may never change and future planners will appreciate knowing what led you to select certain products over others.

The functional specification essentially documents the decisions that I walk you through in the next four chapters; it is the heart and soul of your blueprint. The technical professionals creating your site will refer to this document again and again to see how the finished product should work and appear. If any document is worth laminating for protection against spilled coffee and soft drinks — the functional specification is it.

Finally, a listing of the project team and an explanation of how decisions were made are critical to the site's future success. This document isn't intended to be a way to prove fault in the future, but it can help determine where things went wrong in the decision process, and how to fix them. For example, suppose your project team spends six great weeks reviewing the business' needs and designing the perfect e-commerce site. The team spends six months developing the site to exactly the right specifications. Four months after the site goes live, everyone realizes that not a single bit of marketing data is being collected on your customers. Reviewing the original documentation, you realize that the Marketing department was nonexistent when the original plans were being built. You act quickly by adding your VP of Marketing to the project team for the next phase of the site's development, and you put a high priority on the features that she needs to do her job. Remember that with new people coming and going, this documentation provides the only consistency in the life of the e-commerce site.

For any of this documentation to be useful, it must contain the appropriate information in the necessary level of detail. In the next few sections, I show you examples of exactly what these documents should look like, using the fictitious Retailer.com as a guinea pig.

Documenting the vision and the scope

The vision and the scope are great starter documents for a more formal collection of documents. Consider getting a nice binder to keep everything in, so a hardcopy is available to employees for reference in the future. If you want, you can lend an additional sense of importance to the vision and scope document by printing it and having all of the company employees sign it (kind of like the "Declaration of Independence" of the e-commerce site to be built). Figure 1-1 shows Retailer.com's vision and scope:

Retailer.com

Our Vision

The Retailer.com web site will entice customers to return frequently through creative promotions and targeted direct e-mail marketing. The site will entice customers to purchase by offering product suggestions based on customers' buying habits and preferences. The site will be compatible with the widest array of browsers and platforms possible, and will implement an uncluttered and intuitive user interface. The site's key operations will require a minimum of customer input, yet allow customers the maximum ability to customize their site experience.

The Scope of our Project

The site will support a product catalog of sufficient complexity to present our existing product line. No support for suggested add-on sales will be included in the first phase.

The site will include support for simple text-file and EDI data exchange with trading partners over the Internet. We will be able to feed our product catalog to these partners, but in the first phase we will not accept orders from them.

We will implement a navigation method that permits access to all of our product categories.

We will implement a method for customers to sign up for various e-mail newsletters, and to specify their hobbies and other interests. This information will be used to generate mailing lists for targeted marketing e-mails on a weekly basis.

Our checkout and shopping cart will be constructed to collect the minimum amount of information in the minimum number of screens. We will save as much information as possible and fill it in for customers on return visits. We will give the customer full control over our use of this information.

Our site will be compatible with 4.0 and higher web browsers on the PC, Unix, and Macintosh platforms.

Our site will be designed to appeal to, and be intuitive to, our current marketing demographics, which is teenagers and young adults aged 17 to 30.

Figure 1-1: The Retailer.com project vision and scope

Documenting the technology decisions

As you continue planning your site, you will begin to make decisions about what technologies to use, what approaches to adopt, and what methods to employ in order to build the site. Document each decision as you make it, and include a brief example of the reasons behind the decision and who was involved in making it.

Create a standardized form for documenting major decisions. You can keep a Word template to fill in when necessary, or keep a stack of blank forms in a binder. The sample form in Figure 1-2 contains all the necessary information.

```
                        E-Commerce Site Technology Decision

Category (check one):

        [ ] Technology or product selection

        [ ] Methodology decision

        [ ] Design decision

        [ ] Feature/functionality decision


Decision refers to:_____

Decision made by (list names):




Decision (describe):
```

Figure 1-2: Sample technology decision form

By categorizing these decisions (as shown in Figure 1-2), you enable Web designers and software developers to easily refer back to these decisions in the future. This can save time and improve consistency, as well as prevent mistakes, when you're working entirely with staff developers and designers. The benefits increase a hundredfold when you're working with outside contractors, because a formal documentation of key decisions clarifies to everyone involved what the final product is expected to look like and do. Keeping these documents handy also makes your functional specification — generally a time-consuming document to create — easy to produce, because you can simply incorporate the decisions that have already been written down.

Many decisions will be made quickly in meetings involving several key company employees. Distributing the decision documents to the attendees allows them to confirm that the decisions reflect what they heard in the meeting. Again, this serves to improve consistency and ensure that the site turns out as everyone expects.

Figure 1-3 shows a product-driven decision document for Retailer.com.

Retailer.com Site Technology Decision

Category (check one):

> [X] Technology or product selection
>
> [ ] Methodology decision
>
> [ ] Design decision
>
> [ ] Feature/functionality decision

Decision refers to: Selection of database platform

Decision made by (list names): Joe Executive, Mary Technologist, Jim Accountant

Decision (describe): We will adopt Microsoft SQL Server 2000 as the database platform for the project. SQL Server provides the features we require, specifically clustering and replication. Its performance numbers are more than adequate for our needs. The cost of acquiring the software is lower than competing products.

Figure 1-3: Product-driven technology decision

Product selection is one of the most important items to document. If your company management ever needs to undergo a "due diligence" phase by potential investors, you must be able to provide them with the reasoning behind particular product selections.

Often, technology selections at e-commerce companies can be somewhat arbitrary, based on a particular person's favorite products. On the other hand, nobody really wants to write down "We picked XYZ product because Bob likes it best." The very process of documenting these decisions forces you to analyze them, and to make sure that they're being made for the right business reasons.

Figure 1-4 shows a methodology-driven technology decision form.

Methodology decisions are extremely important because in documenting *how* everything on the site will be done, you and your team are forced to think about the cost of these features in terms of "back end" development. For example, one e-commerce company that I worked with was given an estimate of 1,200 hours to produce the site they had designed. The site was actually completed in just over 1,300 hours, which was very close to the estimate. After the site was finished, however, they realized that the site contained absolutely no administrative interfaces. Because the default Commerce Server database schema had been modified, the default Commerce Server administrative tools were useless. They had no means of adding products to the catalogs, viewing orders, or changing content on the site unless they manually worked with the database in SQL Query Analyzer. Had they been thinking about how the company would interact with the site on the back end — and documented those decisions — they would have realized that the Commerce Server's tool set would also need to be modified and included in the original estimate.

Retailer.com Site Technology Decision

Category (check one):

       [ ] Technology or product selection

       [X] Methodology decision

       [ ] Design decision

       [ ] Feature/functionality decision

Decision refers to: Content production methodology

Decision made by (list names): Joe Executive, Mary Technologist, Paula Editor

Decision (describe): Content will be produced in plain text by editors within the company. HTML programmers will be hired to format that plain text into the actual web pages. The final page will be approved by the senior editor and will be posted to the web site automatically. Some form of administrative interface will allow the senior editor to review final pages and either approve them or send comments back to the HTML programmer. Approved pages will be automatically posted to the web site at a time determined by the senior editor and configured in the administrative interface.

Figure 1-4: Methodology-driven product decision

This decision by Retailer.com to use some form of automated interface for content production immediately points to additional custom software development, and you must have discussions about how this tool should work and who will be using it. This is absolutely the type of possibility you want to know about up front, before development begins.

Figure 1-5 details a design decision.

The technical team will refer most to design decisions as they are building the site to further clarify the project's scope document by stating exactly which navigation technologies will be allowed in the site's design, and which will not. You can also begin to imagine what the site will look like, and that it will include some form of shared navigation elements on every page, and perhaps a set of submenus that change as you move through the different areas of the site. By specifying to use a minimal amount of HTML, the project's developers are limited in their choices of layouts and designs to those which require a small amount of HTML to produce, which also has the benefit of keeping the individual Web pages small and fast-loading for users.

Retailer.com Site Technology Decision

Category (check one):

    [ ] Technology or product selection

    [ ] Methodology decision

    [X] Design decision

    [ ] Feature/functionality decision

Decision refers to: Site navigation design

Decision made by (list names): Joe Executive, Mary Technologist, Tim Designer

Decision (describe): Site will use minimal amount of HTML to produce navigation elements on each page. Absolutely no dynamic HTML will be used, and the only dynamic effect we will consider is rollover effects achieved through cascading style sheets. Each page will feature the same primary navigation elements, with secondary elements specific to the subsection of the site.

Figure 1-5: Design-driven technology decision

Figure 1-6 reflects a decision regarding the user experience.

Retailer.com Site Technology Decision

Category (check one):

    [ ] Technology or product selection

    [ ] Methodology decision

    [ ] Design decision

    [X] Feature/functionality decision

Decision refers to: Checkout process functionality

Decision made by (list names): Joe Executive, Mary Technologist, Arnold Marketer

Decision (describe): The checkout process will involve as few screens and clicks as possible. Our goal is to allow users to select a password to save their information for future visits, if they so desire. Users who do so should be able to check out in two clicks. Users who prefer not to do so, or new users, should be able to check out in a maximum of four clicks/screens, although more screens should be available for options such as gift wrapping. Our available e checkout features will be billing and shipping address and payment information. Optional features will include gift wrapping and a gift message. All users will be signed up for the main e-mail newsletter by default (a checkbox on the billing information screen will allow them to opt out of this signup).

Figure 1-6: User experience-driven technology decision

This decision provides guidelines for designing the user experience (something that I talk about in more detail in Chapter 2), and further clarifies the scope document, providing definite rules for how the site's checkout process will operate. The philosophy of a minimal, quick-moving checkout is emphasized, and the exact features that the checkout must implement, including allowing the user to select a gift message and gift wrapping for the purchase, are spelled out.

Keep in mind that e-commerce development is never set in stone. As the site evolves, many — if not most — of these documented decisions will change. Continue documenting new decisions, and reference older decisions that are affected. Consider the functionality change detailed in Figure 1-7.

```
                        Retailer.com Site Technology Decision

Category (check one):

        [ ] Technology or product selection

        [ ] Methodology decision

        [ ] Design decision

        [X] Feature/functionality decision

Decision refers to:  Checkout functionality extension for phase three

Decision made by (list names):  Joe Executive, Tammy Technologist, Arnold Marketer

Decision (describe):  Phase three development will include major extensions to the checkout process. In
addition to the existing feature set, we will modify the payment screen to accept a gift certificate or coupon
number. We will also add an "add-on sales" screen to the checkout, immediately following the
shipping/billing address screen. This add-on screen will offer the customer the opportunity to buy up to
four additional products related to the ones they are purchasing. They will also be able to purchase gift
certificates on this screen, and will be able to perform a product search from this screen. This decision ties
to earlier decisions in phase one and two regarding checkout functionality. We have agreed that the
checkout may now be extended to include additional screens in an attempt to boost sales, without risking
order abandonment because of the additional complexity. All of the new screens will be designed so that
the shopper can click a single button to continue past them if desired.
```

Figure 1-7: Changing a technology decision

This decision, which obviously comes later in the site's life cycle, contradicts an earlier decision to keep the checkout process as simple as possible. The document gives reasons for the decision, and explains how to mitigate the potential negative impact of the decision by providing the customer with an easy way to bypass the additional new screens.

Creating a functional specification

After you have collected your initial decisions on how the site should look and operate, start building your *functional specification*. The functional specification is a long, technically oriented document intended to describe in detail how the site should be built. The intended audience for the functional specification is the team of technology professionals who are building the site. The functional specification need not include detailed reasons for what it specifies, but simply provide the detailed blueprint of what to build.

The functional specification incorporates information from decision documents, and delves into the level of technical detail necessary to remove any ambiguity. Further, the functional specification should be treated as a "frozen in time" document. After the functional specification for a project has been approved and work has begun, no further changes to the functional specification should be allowed without serious consideration for the consequences (see sidebar, "The Physics of a Project.")

The functional specification should leave very little to the developers' imaginations — especially if your site is being developed by outside contractors. Items left open to question can result in lost time while an answer is sought, or may result in a developer "just deciding" on a process that will lead to inconsistencies, undesired features, and additional time spent backtracking and correcting.

Exactly how you organize your functional specification is up to you and the developers who are using it as their blueprint. I recommend that you try to group major functional areas, such as navigation, the shopping cart, the checkout, administrative tools, etc., into the same area of the document. Doing so will aid developers in locating the information they require.

A large, complex e-commerce site may have a functional specification of a hundred pages or more. Smaller sites, or functional specifications that only apply to a small phase of development, may be a few dozen pages. The length of the functional specification is irrelevant so long as the content is complete and detailed.

Consider the excerpt from Retailer.com's first-phase functional specification, shown in Figure 1-8.

This single page of Retailer.com's functional specification shows you exactly what a functional specification should do. Technical professionals are given a great level of detail about what to accomplish, what technologies to utilize, and how the final site should look and behave. Enough reasoning is provided so that developers can understand the intent of the functional specification in case questions arise about how things are supposed to look or work.

Understand the technologies that the developers will use. For example, writing about the design of the site navigation requires that you understand the things that a developer needs to know: Color selection, font selection, orientation on the screen, location on the page, and so forth. If you are not personally familiar with the technologies, hire a systems designer or architect to assist you with the functional specification. Simply telling a developer that the navigation buttons "should be located along the top of the page" is insufficient, because the developer won't know what colors or fonts to use, for example. You can always leave these selections up to the developer, but developers are not hired for their sense of style or aesthetics, so you may be less than pleased with their choices.

Another major purpose of the functional specification is to help you clearly classify and categorize the work that needs to be accomplished. The functional specification should be used to create an accurate estimate, and to break the tasks down according to technical disciplines, such as Web design, Visual Basic programming, systems engineering, and so forth. Having this information available is important for your next major piece of documentation — the project plan and timeline.

Retailer.com

First-Phase Functional Specification

Navigation (cont'd)

The major site navigation areas will be Widgets, Gadgets, Hodgets, and Mudgets. A navigation bar along the top of the page, immediately underneath the logo, will offer links to these four major areas as a single row of text.

Within each area, navigation sub-elements will be included in a vertical column, along the left-hand side of the page. The exact number of sub-elements will be determined by the number of product categories in the database. Rather than querying the database for these elements on each page display, we will write a utility that generates static left-hand navigation bars. These bars will be included at display time. The utility will be run nightly to update the include files with any changes.

Each navigation link must include the Customer Tracking information (see "Customer Tracking" elsewhere in this specification) that will be used to path customers through the site.

Exact color and font selections will be implemented in an included cascading style sheet for easy future modification. Initial CSS design will be submitted by the design department. Any background graphics or colors should either be driven from a static include file or in the CSS; we want the ability to easily and completely change the color scheme of the site to suit special holidays and events.

Customer Tracking

In accordance with our decision to completely forgo the use of cookies whenever possible, and in accordance with Marketing requirements to be able to build a "path" for any user as they travel through the site, we will implement customer tracking information in all URL's.

The path ASP code will be included at the top of each page. This code will reference an MTS component that will handle the actual business logic of the customer tracking. Whenever a customer hits their first page on the site, a random, unique number will be generated. This number will be embedded into all forms and hyperlinks used on the site. The same code at the beginning of each page will extract this unique number from the URL and update the customer tracking database with the appropriate information. In the database, this will build a "path" of what the customer clicked on while on our site. Each page on the site will be assigned a unique ID and only that ID will be stored in the database, to conserve space.

Database maintenance routines will run nightly. The routines will move a customer's "path" to one of two places. If the customer placed an order, their path will be attached to the order header so that we can see what clicks led the customer to place an order. If the customer did not place an order, the path will be moved into an archival database (which will be cleared each month). This will allow Marketing to analyze customer browsing patterns and make improvements to the site's design and flow.

Figure 1-8: First phase functional specification

Creating a project plan and timeline

Begin incorporating time and manpower estimates. After you have your estimates, you can construct your project plan and timeline.

Use your tool of choice to create the project plan and timeline. I prefer Microsoft Project because it simplifies the process of creating an easy-to-understand timeline. I can assign resources to specific tasks, track progress, assign task dependencies, and do a great job of managing the project. Figure 1-9 shows an excerpt from Retailer.com's Project file.

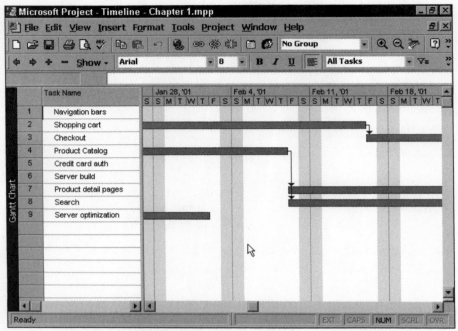

Figure 1-9: Sample project excerpt

Tip   You can certainly create an adequate project plan in Excel, but the investment in purchasing and learning how to use Project pays off in easier project management.

The timeline combines with all of your other documentation to form a complete project plan. Make this plan — especially the timeline — available to everyone in your company. Weekly status meetings should revolve around the timeline. Every department in your company should be aware of the timeline, the current status, their contributions to it, and so forth. Update the timeline every week or so, marking off completed tasks, updating the status of in-progress tasks, monitoring the resources assigned to each task, and so on.

The timeline helps upper management to understand the "physics of a project" (see the sidebar, "Physics of a project," earlier in this chapter). If they ask you to expand the feature set of the shopping cart, for example, you can pull up your project timeline and make the necessary modifications (by extending the time that the shopping cart takes to write, for example). If you use a tool like Project, you can instantly show them that even a minor decision has a cascading effect that can postpone the project's completion by weeks. Having the capability to defend the project's scope and timeline is worth the cost of Microsoft Project.

Documenting the project team and decision-making process

This is the last step in creating a complete, formal project plan. Each decision document should include the people who made the decision, so you don't need to repeat that information. Document the names and credentials of the people who are developing the project, even including a copy of their resumes if possible. Again, having this type of information handy will prove useful in the event of a management review or due-diligence review by potential investors.

The last step in documenting the decision-making process is to describe your final project approval process. In other words, who was involved in approving the functional specification and project timeline? Like the vision, this may be a great document to print and have upper management sign as a kind of formal approval for the project to begin. (If the vision was the "Declaration" for the project, then this document is the signature page of the project's "Constitution.")

I round out Retailer.com's project plan with their project team and decision process page as shown in Figure 1-10:

Retailer.com

Project Team

Joe Executive, CEO & President
Tammy Technologist, CTO
Jim Accountant, CFO
Arnold Marketer, VP Marketing

Dan Programmer, Sr. Developer
Maria Programmer, Developer
Kim Programmer, Developer
Yoki Layout, Web Developer
Greg Network, Systems Engineer
Nicole Helper, Technician

Decision-Making

The attached project plan, including the timeline and functional specification, was approved and the project began on February 9, 2002 by:

(signatures)

Good luck, team!

Figure 1-10: Retailer.com project team

Keep in mind that getting management to approve everything can be difficult. This is the process of buy-in that I've referred to throughout this chapter; in the next section, I discuss this process in more detail.

Buy-in

E-commerce management teams have many priorities to deal with, and they need to be comfortable knowing that their technical team is moving the company in the right direction when developing the actual e-commerce site. Communicating with management and letting them place their approval on the project is important because the project is going to need their support and assistance as the site is developed.

The potential problem, of course, is that the management team (or certain members of it) may want to spend a month bickering about minor details of the plan, thus preventing anything productive from being accomplished. Here are three strategies to make the buy-in process go smoothly, and by default, faster.

✦ Make sure you're getting buy-in from (and only from) the right people. (I'll discuss who the right people are in the next section).

✦ Clearly communicate your expectations for getting their approval.

✦ Keep the process moving quickly. Make sure participants are signing off by the deadlines you set. Check in frequently to make sure they're giving the project the appropriate amount of attention.

Who to get buy-in from

The short answer is to get buy-in from every member of your executive team. Other than the owner or CEO, you need to get buy-in from the people who depend on the site. Don't let them delegate their buy-in approval to subordinates; each executive should personally review the plan to make sure it fits their needs and expectations. Your buy-in list may include:

✦ The CEO

✦ Members of the board

✦ Chief Operations Officer

✦ Director or VP of Marketing

✦ CFO or Director of Finance

✦ CIO/CTO or Director of Development

✦ Whoever is in charge of developing content for the site

✦ Director of VP of Merchandising

Although this list is certainly not all-inclusive, and may vary significantly from company to company, you get the idea. With all of these high-powered personalities involved, you must clearly communicate your expectations for obtaining their approval.

Communicating for buy-in

I've found that the easiest strategy is to release a short memo and attach a timeline, as shown in Figure 1-11.

TO: Retailer.com executive team
FROM: Technology group
SUBJ: Project plan approval

The time has come for you each to review our final project plan, including the functional specification and most especially the timeline. We need you to either approve the plan or come back with a complete list of specific concerns or objections.

In order to complete this process as expeditiously as possible, we will adhere to the following timeline:

End of this week: Project plan will be in your hands.
End of next week: Approval or concerns will be back to me.
End of this month: We will have met to discuss any concerns and make any necessary changes.
Middle of next month: Final approval and project begins.

If I don't hear from you by the end of next week, I'll assume you have no concerns and that you approve the plan with no changes.

Thanks!
Tammy Technologist, CTO

Figure 1-11: Introductory memo for obtaining project buy-in

In the fast-moving world of e-commerce, a slightly Draconian approach to deadlines is justified. Obviously, the culture of your company should dictate exactly how this process begins and proceeds, but try to keep things as straightforward and clear as possible.

Keeping the buy-in process moving quickly

After you've set your deadlines, stick to them. Clearly indicate that the project must proceed, and that if any objections or concerns need to be aired, they must be aired in accordance with the published schedule. Make the buy-in process as much a part of the project's timeline as developing the shopping cart or product catalog.

Summary

Clear and abundant documentation is the key to a successful e-commerce project. Communication tools like a vision statement and scope document help focus the project and keep things moving toward a defined, business-oriented goal. Functional specifications translate those business goals into technical terms, and provide a blueprint for technical professionals to actually build the site. The project timeline communicates what functionality to develop, when to finish it, and in what order tasks need to be completed.

Taken together, these documents form a comprehensive project plan that can be used for a number of business purposes, including due-diligence investigations by potential investors, knowledge transfers between departing and newly-hired team members, and communications between your company and outside contractors.

In the next four chapters, I discuss the specific questions that you should be asking about your site's design, and the decisions you're going to have to make regarding technologies, products, methodologies, designs, and features. The following chapters form the basis for your decision documents and your functional specification.

✦   ✦   ✦

Designing a Look and Feel

The Web has become a visual medium, meaning that the "look and feel" of an e-commerce site is as vital to its success as the layout and merchandising is to a traditional bricks-and-mortar store. And because the Web is an interactive experience, "look and feel" carries a meaning that goes beyond mere graphic design, color selection, or page layout.

In a modern e-commerce site, the term *look and feel* refers to the appearance of the site, how customers move throughout the site, how information is presented to customers, and how information is collected from customers. Creating the look and feel of your site means thinking about the entire customer experience, from the design and layout of the front page to the navigation elements, from the presentation of advertising and promotion to the ways the site accommodates growth.

Designing the look and feel for a site is one of the most important parts of the planning process. The content of your site is important, but the look and feel determine how — and if — people access that content. The dynamic functionality of your site is important, but the look and feel determines how customers interact with and use that functionality. Your site's look and feel is the "wrapper" around everything that your site has to offer, so the wrapper should be attractive, intuitive, and useful.

Web Site Design Factors

You must consider several factors when deciding how you will design your site. These include:

   ✦ **Human factors** — You need to have an understanding of how people react to visual material on a screen. You should understand the metrics for placing important information in order to capture the most attention, and how to design navigation elements that are at once obvious and unobtrusive. Know how various graphics and symbols should and should not be used to help direct customers to the correct information on your site.

✦ **Enabling technologies** — You need to understand the pros and cons of various technologies that can be used to implement the look and feel of a Web site, including HTML, Dynamic HTML (DHTML), various scripting languages, and so forth. Define the technologies of your site's target audience to help determine which technologies are appropriate.

✦ **Target Audience** — Know how to define your target audience, and how to create a look and feel that caters to that target audience. Specific techniques may or may not be appropriate, depending on your target audience's language, age, familiarity with computers and the Internet, gender, and nationality.

✦ **Scalability** — Your e-commerce site *will* grow. You should fit all of the above factors into a design plan that includes room for growth and expansion, without having to redesign the entire site every time a new feature or function is added.

In this chapter, I define each of these factors, I explain how they impact your overall site design, and I talk about how you can fit each of them into the overall vision for your site. I also talk about some of my past experiences in helping e-commerce site creators choose the right design approach and technologies for their particular situations, and I present some case studies for fictional companies to demonstrate how specific situations and needs can drive you to certain design and technology decisions. I also make liberal use of screen shots to show you the "dos and don'ts" of various design techniques, and to demonstrate the best practices in designing a Web site for specific audiences and situations.

The answers to the following questions will drive your design and technology decisions and have a fundamental impact on your site's design, so you should implement these questions and answers into your formal project plan documentation.

1. What is your site's target demographic? In other words, who are your customers? Do they have considerable experience using the Internet? Do you expect your customers to be using an older Web browser or a more recent one? How old are they? Will they have any physical limitations, such as visual impairment, you will need to accommodate?

2. What is your site's browsing philosophy? Do you want customers to be able to jump to any part of your site from any other part, or do you want them to browse through a hierarchy — such as departments, categories, and groups — in order to access your products and services?

3. What are your goals for physically delivering your site's content? Do you want your Web pages to load as quickly as possible, or do you expect your site to be used by customers that have great network bandwidth, and for which larger pages won't present a problem? Do you want to let your customers make that decision, and offer a version of your Web site that's fast and a version with richer content?

4. Will customers access your site's content primarily from your home page, or will they be linking to various sections of your site from external sources, such as search engines or business partners?

Take a look at the following case studies from fictional companies and make a note of their answers to these questions.

Retailer.com sells high-end computer products in retail stores throughout the United States. Their Web site sells a wider range of computer products, including educational software and home productivity software. The site's target demographic includes everyone from video game-playing teenagers to grandparents shopping for their families. They want customers to browse their site much like they browse their stores — going to a particular department, looking for the right category, and then browsing through the available products. They know that their customers are accessing the site over slower dial-up connections, so quick page loads are important. They also know that their customers are using a huge variety of browsers, but they believe most of them are using at least a 4.0 browser or better. Customers can access the site's content from the main page, but they can also be linked from off-site to almost any portion of the site — both from search engines and from business partners' Web sites.

Services.com sells utility services over the Internet, including electricity, natural gas, long-distance and cellular phone service, and more. They expect their Web site to be visited by adults in their twenties to forties, and they anticipate that these adults have a varying level of experience with the Internet. They assume that most of their customers will be accessing the site from work, so network bandwidth is not a problem. Services.com also expects customers to access the site's content exclusively through the home page, and they want customers to be able to browse for different utility services no matter where they are on the site.

Great World, Inc. employs more than 60,000 people across the world. Company employees are accustomed to accessing the company intranet with their company-standard Web browser, and Great World's management wants to offer an online store to employees. The store will sell sundries like milk and bread, as well as gift items like small jewelry and clothing. Their idea is to make the store available so that employees can run errands over the company intranet, rather than rushing around during their lunch hours or leaving work early to get everything done. Employees will be able to pick up their purchases at a central location at each office campus. Because the store will only be available over the internal network, bandwidth is not a problem, and employees will always access the store's products from the home page. Great World wants to make the site as easy to use as possible, so employees will be able to jump from one portion of the store to another in order to quickly find the products that they need.

As I discuss the decisions that these companies will make as they move through the design planning process, you may want to refer back to their case studies, so put a bookmark on this page. The first item to design is your site's navigation.

Navigation

As you browse the Web, you will find sites that implement just about every type of navigation scheme you can think of — and then some. However, certain common factors do emerge:

✦ The use of menu bars, either horizontally or vertically oriented, are the most common way of allowing users to move through your site.

✦ Sites with a great deal of content often implement dynamic menu bars that change to present the most relevant options on each page.

✦ Sites often use some kind of "feedback" or special effect to let users know where certain navigation elements are located, such as graphics that change colors when the users point their mouse at them.

Although many Web sites have these navigation items in common, sites tend to differ in the presentation of the navigation items. Are they simple text links, or graphics? Does the page take a long time to load, or does it load quickly? Are there lavish special effects like pop-up menus, or no special effects at all? These differences reflect the diversities in the design philosophies and target audiences of the various companies.

You can use a variety of technologies and design elements to implement Web site navigation. In the following section, I explain and compare several of these methods, particularly those involving Microsoft technologies.

As you consider different navigation techniques, keep the following seven basic comparison factors in mind:

✦ **Visual** — Does the technique *look* like a navigation element that users are accustomed to seeing? In other words, is it a button or a menu that users will recognize as a navigation element?

✦ **Feedback** — Does the technique offer some form of feedback to indicate that a user has pointed at or clicked a particular navigation element? This type of feedback can be important because users often explore a site by moving their mouse around to see what happens. Navigation techniques that allow individual elements to respond to this activity make the overall navigation more likely to succeed.

✦ **Accessibility** — How does the technique work when a visually impaired person attempts to use the site with a specially equipped Web browser? If this demographic is important to your company, pay special attention to this capability.

✦ **Overhead** — Some techniques require the Web server to transfer more data to the Web browser than is required by other techniques. If your customers will be accessing the site over slower connections, then using techniques with a high overhead will result in slow page loads, and possibly bored customers who will give up and move on to the competition.

✦ **Scalability** — Does the technique offer any particular advantages to make growing the site easier? Some navigation designs may require you to redesign the entire site every time a new feature is added; others may simply require a few minor modifications to add several new departments to a menu.

✦ **Real estate** — Some techniques, combined with your site's browsing philosophy, require considerable space on the screen. Other techniques allow you to present a wider array of navigation choices while using less screen space. Keep in mind that your navigation elements should never occupy the majority of the screen (it's the content that your customers came for — not the menu bars).

✦ **Compatibility** — How well will this technique work within the available range of Web browsers? If one of your objectives is to have your site usable by as many customers as possible, pay attention to the techniques that offer a broad range of compatibility, and steer away from those that are limited to a smaller set of browsers.

In the following sections, I talk about specific navigation technologies, including Java, JavaScript, VBScript, static HTML, and Dynamic HTML (DHTML). I also talk about design techniques, including frame-based and no-frame navigation designs, text and graphical navigation elements, and the use of dynamic effects for navigation elements. I also talk about design "best practices" and explain some of the "human factors," such as how people respond to different types of visual presentations, which will affect how your site is used by your customers.

Navigation technologies

To implement Web site navigation, you can use one of four primary technologies:

✦ The oldest and simplest of these technologies is the basic, static HTML page.

✦ A step up from that is the static HTML page, which is dynamically generated on the Web server.

✦ Web pages can be given more interactive capabilities with Dynamic HTML (DHTML), whether programmed in VBScript or JavaScript.

✦ Java presents the opportunity to program a complete, standalone application to use as a navigational aid.

In the next section, I discuss the pros and cons of each technology, and provide a "scorecard" that shows you how they compare on the seven basic factors previously mentioned.

Static HTML

Static HTML links are the oldest and simplest form of navigation on the Web. They can be less exciting than their dynamic counterparts, but remain one of the most effective navigational techniques on the Web. Look at any major site that takes millions of hits per day, such as eBay.com, Yahoo.com, or Excite.com: All of these sites are built primarily around static HTML links for their navigation. Properly presented, HTML is an effective way to move around a Web site. Take a look at the Yahoo.com home page, shown in Figure 2-1. Every link on this page is a static HTML link. These links don't do anything fancy other than take you to another page when you click them. This page contains more than a hundred links, but they are laid out with careful use of white space and borders so that they're easy to understand and locate.

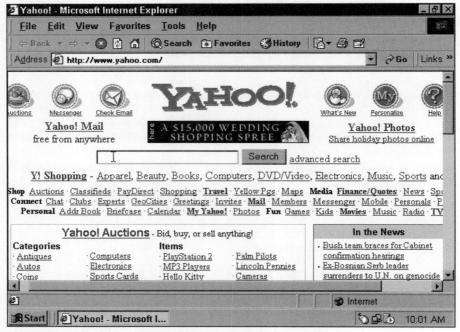

Figure 2-1: Yahoo.com home page

So how does static HTML stack up when judged by the seven basic factors?

✦ **Visual**—Unless you take pains to modify them, HTML links are immediately recognizable as navigation elements to the great majority of Web users, because they are in such widespread use. However, unless you're going to implement some dynamic effect, be careful to leave the link's color as the browser default, and make sure the link remains underlined. The link color and underlining is what users associate with the navigational aspect; without these, users may simply think your links are static text that won't do anything when clicked.

✦ **Feedback** — Browsers may or may not provide feedback for static HTML links. When you build the link in the HTML code, you can specify an ALT property. In most new browsers, the text of this property pops up in a small "tip" box when the user points the mouse at the link without clicking. An HTML link with an ALT property looks like this:

```
<a href="http://www.mysite.com" ALT="Go to the home page>
```

Some browsers also support the definition of an *active link* color, which causes the link to change colors when it has been clicked, letting users know they have successfully clicked the proper link. Browsers that support active link colors define the feature as red by default, and allow the user to customize it. You can also define your own active link color in the BODY tag of an HTML page:

```
<BODY ALINK="Yellow">
```

My advice is to always define this feature, and to make sure that the color is different from the regular or "visited" link colors, so that it stands out from your background colors. This is especially important if your background colors don't provide good contrast with most browsers' default link colors of blue, red and purple.

✦ **Accessibility** — Including the ALT tag also enables specially equipped browsers to read a description of the link aloud, helping visually impaired users understand what the link is for and where it leads.

✦ **Overhead** — Static HTML links can present the lowest possible overhead for any navigational technique, which is why busy sites like Yahoo! and Excite prefer them. Text-only links have the smallest overhead of all, but graphic links require additional overhead to transfer the graphic files to the users' computers.

✦ **Scalability** — The scalability of a static HTML scheme depends on your page design. If you've left room on the page for additional navigational elements, then you need only a few minutes to add them to the page when the time comes. On the other hand, scaling with static HTML requires manual work. Every time you add, change, or remove something on the site, you must manually edit the HTML files to update your navigation elements.

✦ **Real estate** — If you select reasonable font sizes for text links and reasonably sized graphics for graphical links, static HTML allows you to use as little screen space as you want. On the other hand, because you are limited by the size of text that your users are able to physically read (meaning you should make careful use of 8-point or smaller text), a large number of static links will require a large amount of screen space. In fact, this is the primary reason that other navigational technologies exist.

✦ **Compatibility** — HTML works with all browsers, and remains the "lowest common denominator" for building Web sites. Even older text-only browsers work properly with static HTML, and can often display the ALT text of graphical links if you include them.

The precise effectiveness of your static HTML links depend largely on the layout of your page and on your choice to use graphical or text-only links. (I discuss the pros and cons of text versus graphics later in this chapter.)

The advantages of using static HTML include being easy to work with, fast to load, and customizable in color and font (although you should limit the degree to which you tamper with default text link colors). You can apply some simple dynamic effects to static HTML links to make them more attractive and inviting, which I discuss later in this chapter.

Tip

If you want to force the HTML links on your page to be certain colors in order to fit the design of your site, be sure to use the same color set consistently for links throughout your entire site. I strongly discourage using text links that don't have the telltale underline—except in specific circumstances, and only when your site design places those links in a location that denotes a navigation element, such as a menu bar.

Figure 2-2 shows my own Web site, www.iridisconsulting.com. I use static HTML text links almost exclusively for their speed advantage. I've elected to make some changes to the default link colors to fit my site's color scheme, but I maintain the telltale underline on most links. The only links without underlines appear in the menu bar.

Figure 2-2: The author's Web site

Dynamically generated static HTML

The main disadvantage of static HTML links is that they can't change automatically. If your site is constantly growing and changing, static HTML will require a constant effort to keep the navigational elements in line with the site's growth. For example, a retail site that is constantly adding new product categories may find itself fighting a losing battle to keep the menu bars updated with the latest list of categories.

A common solution to this problem has been to dynamically generate the navigation elements when the page displays. By using Active Server Pages, for example, you can query the list of categories when the page loads, and dynamically build the menu bars with the current list of categories. I recommend against using this technique because by requiring a database query for every page load, you significantly reduce the overall scalability of your site. Customers should be able to browse your site with minimal database interaction. Instead, you may want to dynamically include the price of a product on a page because prices can change rapidly and the database must always have the correct price. Using this technique to generate navigational elements targets your database server as an immediate bottleneck in the performance and scalability of your Web site.

Tip   Only information that has the potential to change several times a day should be queried out of the database in order to display the information on a Web page. All other information should be taken out of static files kept on each Web server.

There is a "middle ground" between completely static and completely dynamic pages, sometimes called "dynamic static pages." Here's how it works: Write a Visual Basic application that runs every evening. This application queries all the information out of the database and writes out static HTML files to each Web server in your server farm. These static HTML files can then be included in the main pages that are viewed by customers. The result is a static menu bar that is regenerated from the database each evening in an automated process.

A similar technique uses the SQL Server Web Publishing Assistant to generate static HTML files based on the database content. I discuss the actual implementation of both techniques in chapters 10 and 11. I recommend that you use one of these techniques any time you need to display navigational information based on the contents of your database — provided the information does not change appreciably during the day.

Because this technique is essentially the same as static HTML — except that the HTML is produced by an automated process rather than by hand — its scorecard reads much the same as that of static HTML:

✦ **Visual** — Same as static HTML.

✦ **Feedback** — Same as static HTML.

✦ **Accessibility** — Same as static HTML.

✦ **Overhead** — Same as static HTML.

✦ **Scalability**—Similar to static HTML, but you don't have to manually update elements as the site grows, because an automated process regenerates the navigation elements as necessary, based on the information in a database.

✦ **Real estate**—Same as static HTML.

✦ **Compatibility**—Because any dynamic action happens on the Web server, this technique offers the same total compatibility as static HTML.

Keep in mind that dynamically generated static HTML is only useful when your navigation information can be gathered from the database. Building department or category menu bars is an excellent example of when this is useful. If you have other navigation elements that change frequently but are less product-related, consider building a set of database tables to hold that information so that you can use this technique.

For example, you may have a "Contact us" page on your Web site, with a left-hand menu bar listing your various offices throughout the world. This list of office names isn't likely to appear in your Commerce Server database, but there's no reason you can't add a table to hold it. Then your "Select an office" menu bar can be dynamically generated from the database, so you don't have to remember to manually update an HTML file when the information changes.

A general disadvantage to this technique is that it doesn't scale well as your site grows. For example, suppose that you designed a menu bar to hold two dozen product categories. Your company currently has only ten, so the list has room to grow more than twice its size. You set up a VB program to automatically create new menu bar pages every night, and you rest easy knowing that new categories will show up on the site the day after they are created in the database. After a couple of months of unprecedented growth, your merchandising department has added three dozen new categories, and now your menu bar looks horrible because it's so long. You can use other techniques to present such a large list in a small amount of space, and you can combine them with the dynamic generation technique.

For example, you can combine this technique with dynamic HTML (DHTML) techniques by using VBScript or JavaScript, thus allowing you to produce dynamic client-side menu bars. This can be useful when your navigation content exceeds the amount of screen space that you want to use for navigation, because DHTML lets you build hierarchical menu bar and pop-up menus to display an extended number of navigation elements. Dynamically-generated content is useful not just for navigation, but also for producing actual content pages on your site. For example, product detail pages usually contain a product picture, product description, pricing information, and perhaps an indicator of whether or not the product is in stock. Out of this information, only the pricing and in-stock information should be queried from the database each time the page displays. The rest of the information can be queried out of the database each evening by an automated process that creates static pages. This means that every product detail page that your site displays will only have to query two small pieces of information from the database, rather than querying a description, a picture, and other such "bulky" information. I talk more about the philosophy of hitting the database as little as possible throughout this book.

VBScript & JavaScript Dynamic HTML

DHTML is a technology that allows you to embed programming code in the Web pages that are sent to users' computers. DHTML code actually executes within the user's Web browser, and can change the appearance and content of the Web page in response to the user's actions on the page.

For an example, check out `www.Microsoft.com`. Microsoft's home page is shown in Figure 2-3 with one of its DHTML pop-up menus fully expanded onto the page.

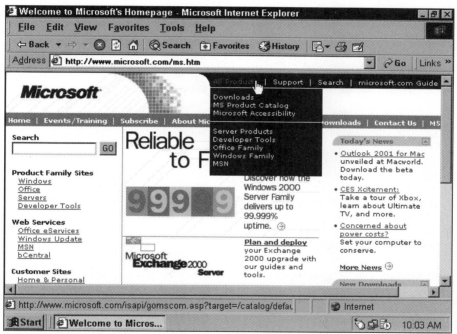

Figure 2-3: Microsoft's home page

Microsoft.com is a staggeringly huge Web site. Creating a feasible navigation scheme—without using every inch of available screen space just for that navigation—was a tough job. Microsoft decided to use pop-up menus throughout the site as a primary navigation technique, which works well because they simulate drop-down menus that users are accustomed to. The entire menu is downloaded into the Web browser along with the page, meaning that the pop-up menus don't require any additional time to load and display.

VBScript versus JavaScript

Although you may have "political" reasons for selecting one scripting language over another, you should also be aware of the technical differences between VBScript and JavaScript. After all, in an intranet environment, your client-side code can be whatever the company browser can support. Even on an Internet-based site, your *server-side* code can be written in whatever language you choose. So why choose one over the other?

The short answer, of course, is that you don't actually *have* to choose one or the other. Both client-side DHTML and server-side ASP code allow you to mix scripting languages. ASP actually supports any installed ActiveX Scripting Language, which can include PerlScript, REXX, and other third-party languages.

Most programmers prefer to work in a single language, however, and that preference should be a driving reason behind your choice. What does your programming staff prefer to use? If you don't have a staff yet, rest assured that VBScript programmers are easier to find than JavaScript developers.

If you need to make a technical distinction between the two languages to help make your decision, here's a list of the major differences:

✦ JavaScript is object-oriented, meaning that you can create reusable code objects in script. VBScript is object-based, meaning that it can use external COM objects but can't create its own.

✦ JavaScript's structure resembles the structure of a C program. VBScript resembles traditional Visual Basic.

✦ JavaScript is much pickier about formatting. Lines must end with a semicolon, and the entire language is case-sensitive. VBScript is case-insensitive and doesn't require any special formatting.

✦ Neither scripting language is appreciably faster than the other when executing equivalent code.

✦ Most of the examples that you can find on client-side scripting are in JavaScript; most examples for server-side scripting are either given in both languages or only in VBScript.

✦ VBScript has a more robust set of functions for manipulating string data; JavaScript is usually caught playing "catch-up" in this regard. Neither offers the string-handling power of Perl.

Many other sites use similar techniques, and I show you how to implement this type of menu in a later chapter. For now, you need to understand the technology behind this trick and how it affects the rest of your site.

By definition, DHTML requires programming. You must choose a programming language that the user's browser will understand, because the execution of that code takes place on the browser.

You have two basic choices in DHTML programming languages: VBScript and JavaScript (Microsoft's implementation of JavaScript is called *Jscript*; the industry-standard implementation is called *ECMAScript*). The choice between them is relatively straightforward: VBScript is supported on Microsoft's Web browser, Internet Explorer. JavaScript is supported on every browser that supports DHTML, including Internet Explorer. So JavaScript is your best bet if compatibility is a concern.

Note Although I usually use the term *JavaScript,* for the purposes of this book this term is interchangeable with Jscript and ECMAScript.

Why would you even consider VBScript? If you're in an intranet-only environment, and if your company has standardized on Internet Explorer as the desktop Web browser, then you'll find that it's easier to locate and hire VBScript programmers than it is to find JavaScript programmers. VBScript is also easier to learn if you already know VB (the basic language syntax is the same). For a complete comparison of JavaScript and VBScript, see the sidebar "VBScript versus JavaScript."

DHTML-based navigation requires significantly more time than static HTML-based navigation because of the required programming. Unless you're careful about how the DHTML code is included in the Web page, your code can be exposed to any customer or user who knows how to select "View Source" in their Web browser. Although you may not care if others have access to your DHTML programming code, some companies have strict policies about allowing that code to be seen — and potentially lifted — by the general public. Microsoft, for example, uses a technique (that I discuss later) to prevent the important bits of the source code from showing up in your browser window.

So how does DHTML do on the scorecard?

✦ **Visual** — Duplicating traditional non-Web navigation elements, such as buttons and drop-down menus, is often easier using DHTML, regardless of whether you use all-text navigation elements or mix text and graphics. Because DHTML provides precise control over the appearance of the Web page, you can use layout and color to greater effect, and you can use dynamic effects, such as changing colors, pop-ups, and so forth, to draw customers' attention to your navigation elements.

✦ **Feedback** — Again, DHTML's ability to dynamically change the appearance of the page in response to user actions lets you change colors, fonts, sizes, and even locations of elements as users move over them or click them, providing you with exactly the level of feedback that you desire.

✦ **Accessibility** — Not nearly as good as static HTML. Because dynamic elements like pop-up menus are actually in the Web page but hidden until you trigger them, browsers designed to assist the visually impaired are often unable to cope with advanced DHTML effects. On the other hand, implementing effects like changing colors to achieve feedback generally won't hurt. Used properly, DHTML can even make a Web site *more* accessible to the visually impaired by having their Web browser play sound effects (located in WAV or other file formats) when users position their mouse over certain portions of the page or click specific elements of the page. These techniques can be helpful to those who need them, but are generally regarded as annoying by those who don't, so don't plan on using them on a page for the general public.

✦ **Overhead** — Higher than static HTML. In fact, if you're using complex effects, the overhead can be *much* higher. Remember that all of your pop-up elements and the program code that makes them function must be downloaded to the customer's browser before the page can be displayed. For a complex, highly dynamic Web page, this means much longer download times. For example, Microsoft's home page, excluding the dynamic elements, is about a quarter the size of the full file that includes all the dynamic elements.

✦ **Scalability** — Similar to static HTML in that manual modifications are required. Of course, you can always use dynamic-generation techniques to improve the automation of page maintenance. Dynamic HTML can be more scalable than static HTML in the sense that it provides more screen space through the use of pop-up menus and navigation elements. By making more creative use of your available screen space, you can present more navigation information than you can with static HTML.

✦ **Real estate** — Depending on your design, dynamic elements can take up significantly less screen space than their static counterparts. For example, if you count all of the links on the various pop-up menus on Microsoft's home page, you'll see that they would almost require a page of their own if they were all implemented as static HTML links. On the pop-up menus, however, they conserve screen space and logically group the various links.

✦ **Compatibility** — Most browsers with a version number of 3.0 or higher can support DHTML to some degree, but you're not guaranteed a complete DHTML implementation in any browser with a version less than 4.0. If you cater to an audience of older browsers, make sure that you provide some alternate means of navigation. Microsoft does this on their site by making each item in a menu bar a hyperlink. If your browser can't display the pop-up window, you can still click the menu bar item to be taken to a static HTML version of the pop-up menu.

Java

Java is as different from JavaScript as English is from German — they're related, but not closely, and knowing one doesn't help much with the other. Java is a complete, robust application development language with the added benefit of being platform-independent.

Java applications, or *applets* as they are sometimes called, are written solely in the Java language. The applets are then executed within a Java Virtual Machine (JVM). The applet has very little awareness of the type of hardware or even the operating system on which it is being executed. The JVM translates everything that the applet does into the appropriate instructions for the operating system and hardware. JVMs are platform and operating system-specific, whereas applets will run on any properly written JVM.

As a navigation technique, Java applets present interesting possibilities. In fact, OpenCube Technologies has made an entire business of writing Java applets for Web site navigation purposes. Check out some of their offerings at `www.OpenCube.com`. Java applets can offer graphics, colors, animation, fast special effects, and a great deal more—while occupying relatively little screen space. A popular type of Java applet used for navigation is a *tree view* applet, where top-level menu items can be expanded to reveal nested sub-menu items, which can be further expanded to reveal more sub-menus, and so forth. An enormous variety of prewritten Java applets are available for navigation, ranging from simple menu bars to complex, animated affairs that can be customized to match your site's appearance.

Because Java is platform-independent and nearly every major 3.0 or higher browser supports a JVM, you have some assurance that your Java-based navigation is accessible to anyone who visits your site. Most Java applets are configured through the use of `Parameter` tags in a static HTML page, which means you can even use dynamic-generation techniques to configure a Java-based menu with a list of categories or other information from a database.

If Java sounds like the miracle answer to all your complex navigation needs, be aware that it does come with a few caveats. For one, some Web browsers ship with their JVM disabled, and many users either don't know how to enable the JVM or never bother to do so. Some users even turn off their JVM. Some corporations disable JVMs on their office computers out of a misplaced fear that Java applets can contain viruses (actually, Java applets can't usually perform any functions outside of the JVM, making them among the safer things you can download from the Web). If the user's JVM is disabled, a gray rectangle appears where your menu should be.

Java applets can also be quite large—especially those that are complex, flashy, or animated. This means that they take a while to download to the user's computer. Users with slow connections will stare at a gray square until your menu finally shows up. Unless you plan to write your own Java navigation applets, you are stuck with whatever functionality is included with the applet that you buy from third parties.

Finally, Java applets can only occupy a rectangular screen space. This makes them suitable for creating menu bars, but they can't duplicate the functionality of a DHTML drop-down menu, which covers a portion of the screen when it pops up. A Java applet must be given a dedicated rectangle of space that it can't dynamically resize or work outside of.

Take a look at how Java does on the scorecard:

✦ **Visual** — Among the better visual presentations, Java applets can literally look however you want them to.

✦ **Feedback** — Depends on the applet, but in general, Java applets can respond to a greater degree of user interaction. An applet can detect when the user is moving a mouse quickly or slowly across the applet's portion of the screen, and then react accordingly. If you're purchasing a prewritten applet, evaluate its use of user feedback before implementing it on your site.

✦ **Accessibility** — Because Java applets can't interact to any great degree with the operating system, they can't take advantage of any built-in services for the visually impaired. The specially equipped browsers that these users utilize to navigate the Web can't generally interact with Java applets, because there is no standard for doing so.

✦ **Overhead** — Potentially the highest of all the techniques discussed so far. Not only does the Java applet have to download in its entirety before it can be displayed and used, the user's browser has to initiate a Java Virtual Machine (JVM), which can be time-consuming on slower machines.

✦ **Scalability** — Similar to DHTML techniques, because most Java applets have their actual content customized through parameters embedded in the HTML. A dynamic process can be used to update these parameters on a regular basis, allowing for better scalability.

✦ **Real estate** — Depends on the applet, but be aware that the applet always consumes a fixed amount of screen space. Java is less flexible than DHTML in this regard, because DHTML has the capability to position pop-up menus and other elements "on top of" the other content on the page, creating an appearance that more closely resembles that of the computer operating systems your users are already familiar with, such as Windows.

✦ **Compatibility** — Compatible with just about any 3.0 or higher browser, but *compatible* doesn't always mean *available*. Many users disable or never enable the JVM function of their browser, causing heartache when your menu shows up as a plain gray square.

When used properly and with the right expectations, Java navigation applets can add a touch of pizzazz to your site, and allow you to include more navigational information that may fit on a plain screen. Java applets are platform-independent, and, if you choose to use prewritten applets, take much less time to implement than a DHTML script. Just be aware of their disadvantages if you plan to use them, and accommodate those drawbacks in your overall site design.

Choosing a technology

Given the pros and cons of the technologies discussed in the previous sections, what did the sample companies choose for their Web sites? In the real world, nothing is ever as simple as just choosing one technology, so — as you'll likely do — the sample companies chose a mix of navigation technologies.

Retailer.com will use dynamically generated static HTML for the portions of their navigation that involve product departments and categories, ensuring that the latest information is always on the site, and keeping them from querying the database constantly. Because so many of their customers will be connecting via modem, they won't use Java navigation applets. They will use dynamic HTML to create pop-up menus in order to leave more screen space for content and advertising than simple static lists of links.

Services.com wants a flashier-looking site, and because they aren't concerned about network bandwidth, they will use a couple of Java applets for navigation. They envision a hierarchical animated menu, with top-level menu items for each utility that they sell, and submenus for pages that explain rate information, offer special deals, and so forth.

Great World, Inc. will use dynamic HTML effects to create pop-up menus. Because everyone in the company uses the same browser, they are able to use advanced DHTML features that are only offered by that browser. Bandwidth is not a concern, so they will use more graphics and design elements in their pop-up menus than plain text. They will use dynamic-generation techniques to create the DHTML code so that the navigation menus always reflect up-to-date site content.

With an understanding of the base technologies for creating navigation, you can explore design techniques for creating navigation elements.

Design techniques

No matter which technology or technologies that you choose to implement into your site's navigation elements, the design of these elements has a drastic impact on how well customers use your site. These design techniques focus mainly on where your navigation elements are placed, what they look like, and how they react to customers' activities.

Go back and look at www.yahoo.com. Most links on this site are a simple word or phrase, with a few graphical links for special features. All of the links are presented on a single page, which changes completely as you move through the site. Take a look at www.microsoft.com for an example of a more structured site. A couple of menu bars appear across the top of each page, and navigation information specific to the page is located in a vertical bar on the left side. The result of this placement is that each page looks very similar, so learning how to use the site is easy.

You need to make three categorical decisions before beginning to implement navigation on your site.

✦ Will you use frames-based navigation or in-page navigation?

✦ Will you use text-based navigation, graphical navigation, or a mixture of the two?

✦ Will you use dynamic effects to provide navigational feedback to the user and, if so, what effects will you choose?

Frames versus no frames

HTML frames were first introduced in version 3.0 browsers from Microsoft and Netscape. The idea behind HTML frames is that they divide the browser window into multiple sub-windows, which can be laid out adjacent to one another. In effect, each sub-window becomes its own browser and displays a specific HTML page. Special HTML coding allows a link in one frame to change the content in another frame.

Frames quickly became one of the most popular navigation techniques on the Web. By creating a narrow frame on the left side of the window, Web designers could display a vertical menu bar. The links on the bar could then change the content of the larger, right side *window pane*. This allowed a single navigation page to be created for display in the left window pane, and all of the content pages could be created without any navigation elements at all. No matter where a user browsed on the site, the navigation elements would remain handy in the left pane.

Without extremely careful HTML programming, however, frames can cause problems. If a hyperlink in the right pane links to another Web site, then that entire Web site appears in the right pane, with the original site's navigation elements still showing in the left pane. Because the frame layout has to be set up by a special *frameset* HTML page, it is impossible to link to a particular page of content from another site; you must link to the home page so that the frames are set up correctly.

Very few major commercial sites use frame-based navigation today because of their one remaining drawback: Unless a user links to the frameset page, the site doesn't get laid out correctly in the browser window. Linking directly to a content page displays only the content and not the related navigation elements, which are supposed to appear in a separate frame.

Note   There are ways to use JavaScript to work around this problem, but they require that your users have Web browsers compatible with more recent versions of JavaScript. One such workaround can be found at http://www.pcdesign. com/harvillo/frames.html.

Many commercial sites, however, are still laid out as if they used frames. Visit www.microsoft.com again. Notice that the top portion of the page (the company logo and a site-wide menu) is the same on nearly every page of the site. This can be displayed in a pane that stretches across the top of the browser window. The bottom pane can then be split into two, with a narrow left side pane for navigation elements and a wider right side pane for the main content pages. Like many other sites, Microsoft chose not to use frames because of their limitations. Users can link to any page in the Microsoft site and have it appear correctly, no matter what.

Nonetheless, with careful attention to the proper HTML programming details, frame-based navigation can be quite effective — particularly if you don't plan on having other sites link to anything but your site's home page. Frames can be "nested," allowing for complex layouts that can meet almost any navigation need.

The borders between the frames can be made invisible so they don't detract from the content on the page. The exact size and position of the frames can be precisely controlled to achieve specific effects and layouts. The layout depicted in Figure 2-4 offers a navigation bar as well as an area across the top and bottom for a company logo or banner advertising.

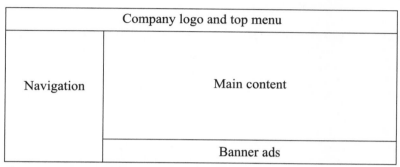

Company logo and top menu	
Navigation	Main content
	Banner ads

Figure 2-4: Sample frames layout

If you like the layout possibilities that frames offer and you don't need to have users link to anything but your home page, then frames may be for you because they present the easiest way to achieve many layouts. You can usually achieve these layouts by using other methods (discussed in Chapter 10), but more time is required to get them looking just right.

Without using frames, each and every page of your site must include all of your navigation elements. This presents two basic drawbacks. First, the size of each page increases considerably because every page must contain the navigation elements. Without using frames, unfortunately, you can't get around this. Second, you face the possibility of much more difficult maintenance. Because every page contains the navigation elements, a change to the navigation elements requires an update of every page. You can get around this by creating your navigation elements in a separate file, and then *including* that file in each and every page. Navigation changes can then be made to the one included file.

You can achieve complex layouts like the one shown in Figure 2-4 by using HTML tables with an invisible border. Although this significantly increases the complexity of each page's HTML code, it also allows for column-and-row based layouts that are very similar to those made possible by frames. The benefit of the table method over frames is that all of the layout information is contained within the actual content page, so anyone linking to the page from off site sees the page exactly as it is meant to be seen.

Cross-Reference   I discuss how to implement both table- and frames-based layout techniques in Chapter 10.

Framed navigation and non-framed navigation compare on the scorecard in the following ways:

✦ **Visual** — Both techniques offer similar visual effects, although frames certainly facilitate implementing navigation bars and menus. One advantage of frames over tables is that you can program your frames to be resizable by the customers, allowing them to make minor customizations to the appearance of your site.

✦ **Feedback** — The decision to use frames doesn't significantly impact your ability to provide navigation feedback. If you plan to use DHTML to change the appearance of a pane *other* than the pane where the navigation elements are located, the process becomes more complex (it's somewhat more complicated to write DHTML code that runs in one pane and modifies the content of another).

✦ **Accessibility** — Properly implemented, frames can actually allow your site to be more accessible and aesthetically pleasing. Many designs fall apart if users force their browsers to use a larger font size than the Web designer intended. Frames allow you to "contain" the amount of word-wrapping and other compensations that occur.

✦ **Overhead** — Generally speaking, frames require less overhead than an in-page navigation design because the elements in the navigation frame only have to download to the user's browser once. In-page elements, on the other hand, must download the navigation elements for every new page that the user views.

✦ **Scalability** — Choosing frames versus in-page navigation doesn't provide any significant scalability advantages or disadvantages.

✦ **Real estate** — Frames allow you to be slightly less creative in your use of screen real estate because the frame occupies an entire rectangular area of the screen. In-page navigation allows for more complex layouts where the navigation elements flow into the actual page content, making for better use of the screen space. Frames can also limit the use of DHTML effects like pop-up menus, because the menu pops up in the original pane, and can't "overlap" the content in other panes.

✦ **Compatibility** — Frames work well with almost any version 3.0 or higher browser. Two notable exceptions are television-based browsers like Microsoft's WebTV and America Online's AOL TV. The browsers use special techniques to ensure that Web pages never exceed the width of a television screen and, as a result, the browsers can modify your frame layouts. Be sure to test these browsers if you intend to use frames.

So which techniques did the sample companies choose?

Only Retailer.com needs to allow users to link to anywhere in their site from elsewhere on the Web, so of the three sample companies, it will definitely use a non-frame navigation method. Because they envisioned a layout similar to the one shown in Figure 2-4, they will use a table-based navigation layout, and will include the navigation elements in a set of included files to make maintenance easier. Retailer.com intends to use dynamic-generation techniques, so they will only have to dynamically update the included pages with new product departments and categories.

Services.com doesn't expect their users to link to anywhere but the main page. Because they plan on using Java applets for their navigation, frames present an excellent navigation strategy. By placing the Java applet in a frame, it can stay loaded in the users' browsers as they move from section to section in the site. Frames actually make Java a better alternative, because an in-page navigation design would require the applet to reload each time the user linked to a new page.

Great World, Inc. expects their users to link primarily to the home page. Because their navigation technique will rely heavily on dynamic menus, they don't want to use frames. A pop-up menu that appeared in a frame would not be able to "overlap" the content in another frame and would "disappear" behind the border of the frame in which it was created. Great World envisioned a site with navigation bars across the top of the pages, but not necessarily down the sides, so they may be able to achieve the design that they want with a minimum number of invisible tables.

Text versus graphics

The debate between text and graphics as the superior navigation element has been raging since the HTML language first included a way to display graphics on a Web page. Both sides of the argument have excellent points. Text links are small, but graphics are more aesthetically appealing, and most commercial sites settle on some mix of the two.

I worked with an e-commerce company that insisted on using graphics for nearly every navigation element — and every other kind of element, for that matter — on every page. They said that they simply couldn't guarantee that the user would see the exact look that they intended unless they used graphics. So, even their text links were actually graphic files. They did have a point: Users have the ability to configure a default font for their browser, and some browsers allow the user to override things like font face and size, no matter what you program the page to use. On the other hand, this company's home page was over 100k in size and took half a minute to download over even a moderately fast modem connection.

When you need a navigation element to have a particular look, use graphics. When you need a non-critical page element to have an approximate look, use text. The size of an average text link (for example, the word *Products*) is about 25-30 bytes. The smallest possible graphic you can use containing the word *Products* is at least 600 bytes. Whenever possible, start with the assumption that navigation elements will be text, and then you can determine if you really need to use graphics.

Text versus Graphics: A Browser Question

The debate over whether to use text or graphics as navigation elements takes on a whole new flavor when you bring America Online into the picture. America Online, or AOL, has millions of members that use the AOL network to access the Internet. Although AOL has invested heavily in their infrastructure and maintains connectivity to the Internet measuring in the hundreds of megabytes per second, the sheer number of users would still overwhelm their network if they didn't take special steps.

One of the special steps used by AOL is a *proxy server* (also called *proxy*). Proxies retrieve commonly requested information, especially graphics, and frequently check them for changes. Most major corporations use proxies on their networks because they are great for reducing the amount of data that must be transmitted over the network. Client computers requesting content from the Internet receive the proxy server's copy—instead of having a whole new copy transmitted over the network connection to the Internet.

AOL takes this a step further. Because the vast majority of their users access AOL via modem, AOL knows that large Internet graphics won't just transfer slowly, but will also create additional overhead on their beleaguered infrastructure. Therefore, AOL converts most graphics taken off of the Internet to the ART graphics format, which is highly compressed, before transferring those graphics to the actual members.

Unfortunately, ART uses a *very* aggressive, *lossy* compression algorithm, which can significantly reduce an image's quality The practical upshot of this is that your graphics look somewhat different to AOL members and are of lower quality. In the past, using a multipass JPG or GIF format prevented the conversion to ART, but AOL is updating their software to recognize these additional formats and convert them to ART.

From a design standpoint, this means that your carefully designed graphical navigation elements may not look like you thought when AOL members view them—yet another argument for sticking with text as much as possible, which looks the same regardless.

Using cascading style sheets, you can precisely control a surprising number of characteristics for text links, such as color, font face, exact size in points or even pixels, position on the page, and so forth. Placing text in a colored table or over a graphical background can create all but the most complex menu bars. The Microsoft Web site, for example, has an extremely sophisticated look, yet all of its fancy drop-down menus are nothing more than text links placed in colored tables. Judicious use of small graphics allows them to dress up the menus by placing company and product logos around them, thereby giving the menus a rounded edge, and so forth. A clever Web designer can create a navigation menu that uses text links and then dress it up with some very small graphic elements to create a very professional-looking site.

How do text and graphics compare on the scorecard?

✦ **Visual** — Although HTML gives you an amazing amount of control over how text links look, it's undeniable that graphics present literally infinite possibilities for designing navigation elements that look just like you want them to. Remember that the primary drawback to graphics is their *size*.

✦ **Feedback** — Although you have similar options for providing feedback for text or graphic elements, text effects like color changes are easier to implement because they require no programming. Feedback effects on graphics require programming, but because they're graphics, they offer infinite possibilities.

✦ **Accessibility** — Text links are more accessible to the visually impaired because even the oldest browsers that are designed for their special needs are capable of recognizing text links and providing verbal cues to the user. Graphics can range from "okay," if they have ALT properties defined, to "horrible" if they don't.

✦ **Overhead** — Graphics are twenty times (or more) larger than text.

✦ **Scalability** — Text menus accommodate additions better than graphical menus because adding a line of text is generally easier than fitting a tenth graphical element into a scheme designed for nine.

✦ **Real estate** — The amount of screen space occupied by text or graphic links is really more of a design issue. You can create designs using tiny text, large graphics, or vice-versa.

✦ **Compatibility** — With the exception noted in the sidebar "Text versus Graphics: A Browser Question," text and graphics tend to be equally compatible with any browser that your customers are likely to be using.

What do the sample companies choose? Their decision, like yours, depends primarily on the look that they are trying to achieve, the overhead that they're willing to saddle their pages with, and the amount of time that they're willing to spend fussing with details in order to get the look they want.

Retailer.com has a lot of navigation information to present, so they'll use graphics for the navigation elements to which they want to call attention. An animated GIF can be very effective, proven by the millions of banner ads on the Internet, but Retailer.com's main menu bar will be built with simple text links. They'll enhance the design of the menu bar with some small graphical elements like lines and borders, but they will try to accomplish as much as possible using non-graphical techniques like colored table cell backgrounds and so forth.

Services.com wants a flashier site. Because their primary navigation technology will be Java applets, they won't be able to use any graphics that the applet doesn't support. They plan to dress the site up by bordering the applet in fancy graphics, thus creating a complex look for their Web site. Because they're not particularly concerned about bandwidth, and because their frame-based navigation design means that the major navigation elements only have to be loaded once, they'll use graphics more heavily than text.

Great World, Inc. plans to use a mix of text and graphics. Because they're not especially concerned about bandwidth, and because they want to make the site as attractive and inviting as possible, they'll use graphics for major navigational elements like department headings. Small elements like product categories will be implemented as text links on DHTML pop-up menus, but those links will be enhanced with small graphical icons that help users quickly identify the specific categories and items that they need.

Most Web designers prefer to start with the look of the site — even going so far as to mock up entire pages in a graphic design application like PhotoShop or CorelDraw. After they know exactly what the site is supposed to look like, they try to implement as many of the elements as possible by using text links. Web designers then turn to graphics for the elements that require them, or use graphics to enhance the appearance and presentation of the text links.

The decision to use text or graphical navigation elements does *not* affect your ability to draw navigation information out of a database in a dynamic-generation scheme. For text links, the actual text of the link, such as the names of categories, can be stored in the database. If you've chosen to use graphical links, then the database can just as easily contain the URLs of the graphic elements, allowing your dynamic-generation technique to dynamically generate graphic navigation elements along with — or instead of — text elements.

Dynamic effects for navigation

Earlier in the chapter, I talk about DHTML as the enabling technology for dynamic feedback effects. However, I didn't specifically mention the different *types* of feedback effects that you can choose to implement.

As you surf the Web today, you find sites implementing a huge array of navigation-feedback effects. These can range from the simple effects that I use on my own Web site, such as changing the color of a text link when the mouse moves over it, to complex Java-based effects, such as adding a "halo" to a graphical button when the mouse moves over it and playing a sound when the user clicks the button.

The primary advantage of *consistently* using feedback effects throughout your site is that your customers become accustomed to them, and the effects help your customers identify navigation elements making your site easier to use. If moving your mouse over a link changes the link's appearance in some way, you get an inconspicuous invitation to click the link. Feedback effects are an intuitive way of calling attention to a navigation element that may otherwise just appear to be another piece of text on the page.

If your target audience includes individuals with impaired motor skills or poor vision, then visual feedback effects, such as changing an element's appearance when the mouse moves over it (and changing the image in a different way when the element is actually clicked), can facilitate navigation through your site for those users.

You can implement dynamic effects using one of two main techniques: Cascading Style Sheets and DHTML.

Cross-Reference

I discuss exactly how to implement Cascading Style Sheets and DHTML techniques for dynamic effects in Chapter 10.

Cascading Style Sheets

Cascading Style Sheets (CSS) provide a way to implement a limited set of dynamic effects for text links without programming. Essentially, you can define a *style* for normal text links, and separate *metastyles* that define how a link should appear when it is clicked or when the user's mouse pointer is moved over it. These link styles can define any of the text attributes supported by CSS, such as font face, size, color, boldfacing, underlining, or other "decorations." You can create text links that become boldfaced when the mouse rolls over them, and then change color when they are clicked. You can create links that are not underlined, change color and become underlined when pointed at, and change color and lose the underline when finally clicked.

DHTML

You can use DHTML to create a wider range of rollover and click effects for text elements. Because DHTML offers control over nearly every element on the page, including the properties defined by CSS, your navigation effects can extend beyond the navigation element to include the entire page. For example, many Windows applications allow you to point the mouse at a button for a brief explanation of what the button does in the application's status bar. DHTML allows you to trap the mouse's movement and change *other* elements on the page, such as the text in a certain area of the screen, thus allowing you to duplicate this common application behavior. You can also use DHTML to display "pop-up balloons" or "callouts" that explain a particular navigation element whenever the user points the mouse at that element.

Some sites make extensive use of DHTML, changing the entire contents of the page whenever the user points at a particular navigation element. Although the initial download of the page takes longer, the page reacts instantly to the user's actions by displaying information. Using DHTML to change page content is kind of an extension to the pop-up menu idea.

How do the dynamic effect techniques compare on the scorecard?

✦ **Visual** — DHTML provides a much wider range of possibilities for dynamic effects, but also requires programming. CSS, on the other hand, doesn't require any programming and delivers a more limited range of effects — mainly formatting effects — for text links only.

✦ **Feedback** — Because both DHTML and CSS can be used to create feedback effects, they both score about equally. Recall that CSS is limited to text links only.

✦ **Accessibility** — Interestingly, DHTML can actually play havoc with browsers that are equipped to assist the visually impaired because those browsers don't usually do well when the content of the page changes suddenly. CSS, on the other hand, simply applies formatting changes, which these browsers ignore anyway.

✦ **Overhead** — CSS imposes considerably less overhead (figure a couple of extra kilobytes or so) than DHTML. Because DHTML requires all of the dynamic content to be downloaded at once, the size of your effects and the programming code required to implement those effects will play heavily into the extra overhead imposed by DHTML.

✦ **Scalability** — Neither DHTML nor CSS provide any particular advantages or disadvantages in scalability.

✦ **Real estate** — Because most feedback effects are limited to affecting only the navigation element involved, no additional screen space is consumed by either technique.

✦ **Compatibility** — Simpler DHTML effects can be implemented on version 3.0 and higher browsers. Netscape didn't fully expose the complete DHTML object model until later versions of their version 4.x browser, meaning that more complex effects involving content elsewhere on the page may not be possible. Most CSS-based effects are supported on version 4.0 and higher browsers.

What dynamic effects will the sample companies select?

Because Retailer.com is making extensive use of text links, they will use CSS effects to make those links change the color or other properties when customers point at them. This offers a simple, no-programming way of providing navigation feedback, and the technique is common enough on Internet retail sites that customers are likely to immediately recognize the effect as a navigational cue. For their few graphical navigation elements, Retailer.com will define ALT tags on the images, which allows most Web browsers to pop up a text "hint" to the element's purpose.

Services.com will primarily be using Java applets, which limits their feedback capabilities to those provided by the applet. This is not necessarily a restriction because most applets provide excellent special effects for navigation feedback by highlighting links when they are pointed at, animating menus, and so forth. They can achieve any desired effect by writing a custom applet instead of purchasing one.

Great World, Inc. will choose not to implement any navigation feedback effects at all. Site planners have the luxury of being very familiar with their customers (who are employees of the company) and know that they're accustomed to working with intranet sites. Great World, Inc. will carefully design their pages so that the navigation elements are obvious, and will let their employees' experience take care of the rest.

Your choices will be driven by similar considerations. If you are catering to an audience that is not familiar with the Web, then you should go to great lengths to help them use your Web site, so pop-up tips, changing colors, and wailing sirens may be in order. If you're catering to an experienced audience of technical professionals, they may not appreciate glitzy gimmicks, and the right answer for you may be simple understated effects, such as moderate color changes on text links.

Design practices — the "human factor"

One of the nicest things about computers is that you can reliably predict what they will do in any given situation. After all, computers are machines, taught to "think" in specific, logical ways. Unfortunately, the main users of e-commerce sites are people, who are much less predictable and much more fickle.

Because of this fact, millions of dollars have been spent studying exactly how people respond to the material presented on a Web site. The benefit of these studies is that today's Web designers have a better idea than ever before about how their audience will react to their design, so they can utilize certain design practices to achieve the reaction that they want or need.

In the next section, I share design practices for the following four major elements of a site:

- ✦ **Visual techniques,** which you can use to drive attention to desired portions of your site.

- ✦ **Ways people learn to navigate a Web site,** and what's considered intuitive for most people.

- ✦ **Importance of language in a site design,** particularly when the site will deal with an international or non-technical audience.

- ✦ **Impact of graphics on a site's reception,** especially for sites serving an international audience or an audience with a wide range of ages.

Human visual techniques

Most people approach a Web site the same way they approach the page of a book. In English-speaking countries, this means that you start at the upper-left corner and gradually work your way down toward the lower-right corner. Ever notice that most Web sites place their menu bars along the left side of the screen? That's because people naturally gravitate toward content on the left, so placing navigation elements on the left helps to draw attention to those elements.

Take a look at just about any major commercial site. Whether the designers knew what they were doing or whether they were copying from someone else, most Web sites have a startling number of features in common for good reason. Check out the following items:

✦ **Navigation menus.** These are usually along the top or left of the screen, or both, but rarely the right and almost never the bottom.

✦ **Navigation elements.** Most navigation elements automatically appear on the screen — you don't have to scroll down or to the right. This is known as placing the information "before the crease," and ensures that customers can immediately spot the important information. Note that this requires you to design your page for a specific minimum screen resolution (what will fit on an 800 x 600 pixel screen won't fit on a 640 x 480 pixel screen). Current industry standards focus on 800 x 600 as the minimum size, and if you're catering to a technical crowd, you can safely design for 1024 x 768.

✦ **Advertising.** The advertisements often pay for the site, so they are usually located on the top of the page, and are often one of the first things displayed.

As with any other medium, certain design techniques are guaranteed to catch attention:

✦ Larger font sizes

✦ Contrasting colors — especially bright, primary colors like red, green, and yellow

✦ Flashing or otherwise dynamic displays — which explains the overwhelming popularity of animated GIF graphics for advertising banners

✦ Frequently repeated elements

✦ Elements that are surrounded by empty space — also referred to as "white space"

Using this information, you should begin to see your Web site's overall design coming together. Important navigation information should appear on the left, near the top of the page. Your logo should appear at the very top-left if you're interested in calling attention to your brand identity. Advertising should be in bright contrasting colors, and should preferably include an animated display of some kind.

If these suggestions sound like they belong in a department store, newspaper ad, or television commercial, then you're catching on. Human visual techniques are *medium-independent*, meaning that the same rules that apply to television ad and department store sales also apply to your Web site.

Misusing these techniques can backfire. A Web page with six blinking banner ads, bright yellow navigation links on a red background, and flashing text in every paragraph will simply overwhelm the user, and prevent them from paying attention to anything on the page. Use attention-getting techniques sparingly, and only when necessary. For example, if you plan to place an advertising banner in the upper-left corner of the page, don't make it brightly colored and animated; customers will see the banner because it's located in the "sweet spot" to which their eyes are naturally drawn.

If you're catering to an international audience, remember that not everybody reads like English-speakers do. Many Asian and Middle Eastern languages read from bottom to top, or right to left, or both. Even though many people in these cultures also speak and read English, their natural tendencies are governed by their native reading patterns. If you need to cater to a varying international audience, try to keep important information centered near the top of the screen. Place a menu bar there, if possible, to help draw attention to your site's navigation.

Careful use of graphic elements can help govern the way people view your site. An eye-catching graphic that sweeps down and toward the right can naturally draw the eye toward the content on that side of the page. For example, you may choose to place your navigation menu on the right, to be different from the majority of Web sites (which place it on the left), and use a graphical technique like this to draw customers' eyes toward the menu's location.

Tip   After designing your site, show the designs to members of your target audience. Ask them what their eyes are drawn to, and see if these elements are the ones that you intended to catch their attention.

Human navigation techniques

Many software companies have invested millions of dollars investigating how people "want" to use computers, and trying to design their software products to work in that fashion. Microsoft in particular has devoted incredible resources into graphical user interface design, and has developed several human navigation theories that you can greatly benefit from when designing the navigation for your Web site.

For example, one theory of navigation is called *discoverability*. The theory goes like this: As long as all of a user's options are on the screen or on a menu somewhere, he or she will *discover* those options. For example, if I want to print a file, I will click on menus until I see the word *Print*, and suddenly I've learned how to print without ever picking up the manual. The limiting factor on discoverability is called *saturation*. At some point, users have been presented with so many options that they just stop looking and give up. This is particularly true of older users with less computer experience. A rule of thumb to follow: Present your users with no more than ten options at once, and don't bury any important options deeper than three levels.

Another rule of thumb to remember regarding older, less experienced users is that they are often afraid to experiment. Although younger users will merrily click on anything that looks promising, older users may fear causing damaging or irreversible effects.

Take all of these things into consideration when designing your site's navigation. Do your menus contain too many items? Consider creating nested menus, or designing your site to use DHTML menus, which can cascade much like the Windows menus to which users are accustomed. Make sure that the choices are clearly labeled. For example, don't use the word *commit* to link to your checkout, use the word *checkout*. "Checkout" is a familiar term and users will understand its function.

Ease trepidation of the interface by keeping users informed. For example, as customers move through your checkout, provide some indication of how many screens they have left to fill out. Use a phrase like, "Your order still has not been placed. This won't happen until the next screen," to reassure users who may be afraid that they're about to do something irreversible. Amazon.com provides an excellent example of this tactic. Their "Add to Cart" button, shown on every product page, is accompanied by the tagline "You can always take it out later," which reassures less experienced users that adding the item to their cart isn't a final, irreversible step.

 Tip   Test your navigation design on people in your target audience. Are they able to find their way around without trouble?

The importance of language

Language is your most powerful tool for communicating with your customers. Many site designers forget this, or don't specifically plan for it. For example, I worked on a site that required customers to provide a user name and password when they registered on the site. If the customer selected a user name that someone else had already selected, they received an error message, which stated "That user name is already in use." Panicked, one customer called his Internet Service Provider to find out why someone was using his user name. The error message was then changed to state, "Someone else has already selected that user name. Please choose another to use on our site," which was clearer and prevented future panic.

Everyone using your site may not have your technical knowledge. Certainly, you can't reasonably expect the average e-commerce consumer to understand the databases and other technologies that make your site work. To these consumers, the site is just like a store and should be just as easy for them to use. Whatever you do, don't let your development staff word any of the important information—even if *you* are your development staff. Find a writer or editor who is familiar with your audience to write the error messages and warnings, so your customers can understand them.

Another company that I worked with took the step of creating custom error pages, so if customers encountered a bad link on the site, they wouldn't be presented with the standard "401" error message indicating that a page requested by their Web browser was not found. Unfortunately, the software programmer who built the new error page got to choose the wording, so the message stated "A system error occurred. Please click your Back button." When the company's customer support representatives began taking calls from panicked customers who were rebooting their computers to fix the system problem, they had one of their content writers create a friendlier message.

Never forget that the Web is an international communications network. If your site caters to an international audience, be careful to use a more formal, structured style of English on your site because international visitors may be unfamiliar with "Americanisms." Even if your site will only cater to an American clientele, avoid using regional terms or slang that may be confusing for people living on the other side of the country.

Tip   If your site will be based in English but will cater to an international clientele, consider hiring a language consultant. A professional language consultant can analyze your site and point out any text that may be ambiguous to foreign speakers of English.

Usability Testing

One of the most important things you can do with your site design is to put it through some usability testing. The most basic form of usability testing is to simply set the site up on a computer or two, and let various members of your target audience play with it *while you watch.*

Make sure that you choose guinea pigs that have had nothing to do with the site because they'll approach it with a fresh perspective. Take good notes, and ask your testers to talk aloud as they play with the site. Make a note of what they seem to be trying to accomplish, and what they actually do. Have your testers run through some standard tasks. Tell them to "try to find a size B blue widget and buy it," or "see if you can check the status of the order that you just placed." You'll quickly find out if your site and navigation designs are good enough to let them easily accomplish these tasks. If they can't, try to get them to tell you what they would *expect* to do, and consider the possibility that your site isn't implementing the feature the way the tester expected it.

Usability testing should be a formal part of your design process. Prepare a list of the tasks that you want testers to run through. Make some notes about any trouble areas that you want to watch for. Have several testers, with different levels of experience and from different age groups, run through the list of tasks to be tested. You may even consider pointing a video camera at the screen as they test, so you can capture their movements and choices and listen to their comments as they move through the site.

Above all, make sure that the language on your entire site — and particularly in your critical navigational elements — is clear and unambiguous.

The importance of graphics

A good graphic has the amazing ability to communicate ideas and concepts to any user — regardless of the native language, ethnic background, or native region of a country. However, don't let your concept of a good graphic be skewed by *your* native region, ethnic background, or language.

A classic example of a graphic gone wrong is an e-commerce site that used an image of a particular hand gesture. The image was of a person's hand, with the first two fingers held up and apart in the shape of a "V." The symbol was used on a button next to the word *Finish*. The button signified the end of the site's checkout process. Because Americans interpret this symbol as "victory," "peace," or even just "great," the pairing was appropriate. The site's entire graphical theme was hip and modern, and viewers (in America) thought it looked great. When the site began marketing to a European audience, however, all hell broke loose. In much of Europe, the same hand gesture is equivalent to an American raising his middle finger.

Think about Localizing

Several major e-commerce sites have struggled with the problem of creating a site that has international appeal. Many of them have solved this problem by creating *localized sites.*

In a localized site, you ask the user what country they're shopping from (you can save their selection in a cookie so that future visits will automatically carry them to the right country site). Each international site has its own set of graphics, icons, navigation links, and other visual content. All of the sites can pull information from the same product database. In fact, you can even modify your Commerce Server database to include separate product prices for each country, allowing you to display prices in the local currency that correspond not just to the currency conversion factor, but also to local market conditions and competitive pressures.

Creating localized sites requires more than an incremental effort. You have to be willing to generate the extra content, and willing to support the extra maintenance effort that the additional sites will require. On the other hand, if you want to capitalize on the international market, investing in a localized site will show your international customers that you care enough to cater to their specific needs and interests.

For an example of a major Internet retailer making the investment in localized sites, check out www.buy.com. Their "country selection screen" is shown in the following figure. Choosing a country customizes the site to display prices in the local currency, products that are of specific interest to that country's citizens, shipping information specific to destinations in that country, and so forth. By checking the checkbox, you permit Buy.com to place a cookie on your computer that automatically directs you to the proper country's page on your next visit.

Buy.com country selection screen

If you'll be catering to an international audience, make sure that your graphics, particularly the icons, are internationally neutral. Adhering to the following standards can help:

✦ Red is always associated with danger, warnings, or "do not" icons.

✦ Green is almost universally associated with "good," "go" or "do this" icons.

✦ Graphics with a 3-D beveled edge will almost always be interpreted as buttons to be pushed.

✦ Most of the icons used in the base Windows graphical user interface were selected for their internationally-neutral meaning. Notice, for example, that the newest versions of Windows no longer use a red "X" for a critical error. Instead, they use a red "no access" icon, which is more universally understood as being bad when it pops up on the computer screen.

✦ Almost any icon depicting a hand or other body gesture will go wrong for you in at least one major country. Even the "hand" icon that most Web browsers use when pointing to a hyperlink is misunderstood in some countries; browser vendors provide a different cursor icon in these countries.

✦ "Smiley" icons (as well as frowning faces) are almost universally understood.

✦ Arrows representing a direction (back, next, etc.) are universally understood.

✦ The "VCR" icons — an arrow for play, a square for stop, and double arrows for fast forward and rewind — are understood in most technological countries.

✦ None of the icons that are typically associated with the e-commerce functions of a site (a shopping basket icon, dollar signs, etc.) are universally understood. Try to use navigation elements with text on them, rather than icons.

✦ Question marks are universally understood in English-speaking and European countries; most Asian and Middle East countries have enough exposure to English to recognize a question mark as a query.

If these guidelines seem like a lot to remember — they are. If you expect international visitors, you may be better off avoiding the whole situation by simply using words, rather than icons, in your links. Words have the benefit of being all-or-nothing — if the readers understand the language, they will generally assign the intended meaning to the word. If they don't understand the language, they won't mistakenly assign some alternate meaning to it.

Advertising and Promotion

If you're wondering why a section on advertising and promotion is included in a chapter about designing the look and feel for your site, then you may well be the victim of the myth that advertising is the great enemy of e-commerce technologies. In fact, quite the opposite is true. Advertising is the reason that e-commerce came into existence, and advertising plays a vital role in the long-term survival of any e-commerce site.

As a result, you can't possibly finalize your site's design and technologies until you determine how your site will integrate advertising — whether it be your company's own internal advertising or advertising from outside companies and business partners.

When people browse your site, advertising helps drive them to purchase particular products and services. Advertising should also suggest additional products and services that may interest them. Advertising can utilize your company's business partners' advertising dollars to help subsidize the site, and even generate additional profit.

You should be aware of the following common Web-based advertising best practices:

✦ **Predict how frequently an ad will be shown to site visitors.** Combined with data on how many hits a day your site receives, you should be able to predict the number of *impressions* an ad will receive, or, in layman's terms, how many times the ad will be displayed per day.

✦ **Acquire a technology that will allow you to *control* the number of impressions an ad receives.** Many external advertisers will prefer to pay per impression, and you need to make sure they get what they pay for, and not any more than that. You also need to be able to report to them on the number of impressions that their ad has received. Even if your ads are strictly internal, you should know the number of times it is shown per day.

✦ **Track *click through* from ads.** Some advertisers may pay an extra fee every time their ad is clicked on. For internal ads, this number combined with the number of impressions provides useful information. For example, your company needs to know that one ad receives two clicks per thousand impressions, while another receives ten per thousand. This helps drive ad design and placement decisions.

✦ **For internal advertising, track click through all the way to a purchase.** In other words, you need to know how many customers clicked on an ad for a product, how many subsequently placed that product in their shopping cart, and how many of those actually bought that product. This ultimately tells you if an ad is successful or not.

Site Server and Commerce Server provide tools to help you manage this information. For example, Site Server includes an Ad Rotator component that helps manage banner ad rotation. Commerce Server includes an entire set of components dedicated to marketing and advertising. The default product configurations don't provide some of the information that you need, however, so you have to "roll your own" techniques for tracking click through and other factors.

Cross-Reference I show you how to implement advertising techniques in Chapter 10.

For now, start thinking about what type of advertising your site will feature, where the advertising will appear, and exactly how you will present it to your customers.

Who will be advertising?

Your company will have to make a business decision on whether or not to restrict your site advertising to products and services offered by your company (internal advertising), or to open up advertising to selected outside companies and business partners (external advertising).

Internal advertising

If your site plan doesn't include some form of advertising to promote your company's own products and services, you should take a close look at the company's business plan again and make sure you didn't miss that part. Internal advertising is the primary method that companies use to turn single-item sales into double-item sales, or sell higher-priced services to users who came looking for lower-priced (or free) services.

Sure, your entire site is a sales vehicle, but that's no reason not to include some specific, targeted advertising. Consider the following techniques:

✦ Showing banner ads for product accessories to customers who have purchased the main product.

✦ Showing pop-ups that advertise free shipping, special discounts, or some other offer.

✦ Showing interstitials for related merchandise as a customer browses a site.

✦ Showing banner ads for new services and products to help stimulate initial customer interest.

Internal advertising demands meticulous marketing data collection from the ads. Your company's marketing folks will want to know how successful an ad was. They'll ask for a host of data, including:

✦ How many people saw the ad?

✦ What times of day was the ad shown most?

✦ How many people clicked on the ad?

✦ How many people bought something as a result of clicking on the ad?

External advertising

External advertising generally carries less administrative and technical overhead than internal advertising. Outside advertisers are generally content with knowing the number of impressions and clicks their ad has received; it's on them to make their ad perform when the customer lands on *their* site.

An exception to this laid-back attitude is *cooperative advertising*. This occurs primarily on business-to-consumer, product-oriented sites, and is a good marketing tactic for *vendors* (those who supply the products that you sell) who give you money or a substantial discount on your inventory items in exchange for your site displaying ads for that vendor's products. This type of advertising should really be considered internal, and the vendors will not only want to know basic things like how much the sales of their product increased during the period that the ad ran, but also more difficult-to-obtain information like the answers to the questions listed in the previous section.

External advertisers of any kind expect prompt reports for their advertising campaign, and in many cases may not actually be required to pay until you deliver evidence of the ad's performance. If you plan to implement this type of external advertising on your site, make sure that your site is prepared to deliver the necessary information to support the effort.

Many e-commerce companies prefer to save their advertising for themselves, so unless you're running a portal site that doesn't actually sell anything, this is a perfectly sound business decision. After all, how often do you walk into a department store and see ads for other department stores?

Advertising techniques

After you decide who will be placing ads on your site, you need to make business and design decisions about how the ads will be physically presented to your customers. You can choose from the three common layout forms for Web-based advertising: Banner ads, interstitials, and pop-ups. These types of advertising can be compared on a five-point scorecard:

- ✦ **Interference** — how much does the ad detract from the main site or distract (or even annoy) customers?
- ✦ **Attraction** — how likely is the ad to receive the customer's attention?
- ✦ **Flexibility** — how easy is it to use the same advertising technique for a variety of situations?
- ✦ **Frequency** — how often can you safely use the technique without upsetting the customer?
- ✦ **Hijacking** — can a determined customer prevent ads that are using the technique from being shown?

I explain how each of these techniques works, how they compare on the scorecard, and what the sample e-commerce companies would choose to do.

Banner ads

Banner ads are everywhere on the Internet. They come in all shapes and sizes, some are animated and some are static, and some are even mini-forms that customers can fill in and submit. They're ubiquitous, and this may be a problem for you. Customers are so used to looking at banners that they often ignore them.

Banner ads are easy to implement, though, and they're flexible enough that you can include several different shapes and sizes of them on a single Web page and still have a good effect. Remember the human visual techniques that I discuss previously in this chapter, though:

- ✦ Banner ads placed near the top and left of the screen get more attention than those placed to the right or near the bottom.
- ✦ Animated banner ads attract attention when placed on a static page.
- ✦ Contrasting colors get an ad more attention than muted colors, or colors that blend with the other colors on the page.
- ✦ A block of smaller ads can sometimes be more effective than a single large ad.

How do banner ads compare on the advertising scorecard?

✦ **Interference** — For better or for worse, banner ads are typically not distracting. The upside of this is that customers won't stop using a site because it contains a reasonable number of banner ads. On the other hand, many customers rarely notice the ads, having become so accustomed to seeing them.

✦ **Attraction** — Because banner ads are rarely "in your face," getting customers to notice them takes special effort. Animated GIF banners, or even banners created with more robust media like Macromedia Flash, can help draw attention to banner ads.

✦ **Flexibility** — Banner ads are possibly the most flexible form of advertising because they can be made to fit into almost any location, and can be designed to suit a variety of needs.

✦ **Frequency** — Banner ads can also handle the most use — putting several on a page won't necessarily distract from the page if you're careful and if the ads aren't huge.

✦ **Hijacking** — The primary defense to banner advertising is to simply tune it out, which you can combat with careful designs.

How will the sample companies use banner ads?

Retailer.com will use banners for promoting specials and products that are sold on the site. They will most likely enter into cooperative advertising agreements with their vendors after the necessary reporting technologies are in place. Banner ads will form the bulk of the on-site advertising, and will be placed in several shapes and sizes throughout each page.

Services.com prefers not to use banner ads because they can detract from their carefully designed site appearance. They may use a few small banner ads (or *button ads* as they're sometimes called) for special promotions or cooperative advertising, but they'll be kept to a minimum.

Great World, Inc. will use banner ads to promote company events and other internal news, rather than advertising specific products. Because the online store is intended to help employees stay at their desks instead of running all over town, the site will also use banner ads to point out merchandise brought in for special holidays, such as Valentine's Day candy packages or Mother's Day flowers.

Interstitials

Interstitials are also referred to as *in-between ads*, which is literally how they work. When a customer innocently clicks on a link to go to a particular section of the site, a full-page advertisement appears instead. After a few moments, or when customers click a "Continue" link, they are taken to their intended destination.

Used wisely, interstitials can be an effective means of promoting a significant product or service, a big discount, etc. Interstitials are rarely used wisely, however. One e-commerce site that pioneered the use of interstitials had them coming up every five or six clicks. The result, of course, was annoyed customers who vowed never to return.

Since then, a few other sites have made better use of this technique. I worked on a site that often featured site-wide specials that they wanted customers to take advantage of. Upon clicking their "checkout" button, customers were taken to an interstitial reminding them to use a particular coupon code to get 10 percent off their entire order. The ad would then offer to take them on to the checkout, or let them continue shopping to take advantage of the savings. Used in this limited scope, the interstitials were hugely successful. More than half the customers who saw them decided to continue shopping and nearly all of them added additional items to their carts.

Similar interstitial campaigns with internal logic have been used to improve sales. For example, a customer adding a six-month service agreement to her basket may see an interstitial offering a full year agreement for just a few dollars more. The ad still allows customers to continue with the original item, but gives them the option to add the upgraded item instead.

So with the understanding that interstitials should be used sparingly, how do they stack up on the scorecard?

✦ **Interference** — Interstitials represent a total interference with the customer's experience. They effectively stop the customers in their tracks to show them an ad or suggestion, so interstitials should be used knowing the impact that they can have on customers' moods.

✦ **Attraction** — Because interstitials pop up in front of you, full-screen and with no warning, they're the most attention-getting type of ad that you can use.

✦ **Flexibility** — Interstitials can be displayed in response to specific conditions, such as a customer adding a specific product to his basket or browsing a particular area of your Web site, which makes them extremely flexible. On the other hand, because they overtake the entire browser window, you have no way to make them less annoying to customers other than to use them cautiously.

✦ **Frequency** — Interstitials should be used infrequently, so that they maintain their impact while not alienating your customers. They should be the least employed type of ad.

✦ **Hijacking** — Customers have almost no way to avoid interstitial ads.

How will the sample companies choose to use interstitials?

Retailer.com has decided to restrict the use of interstitials to specific areas, and to use them infrequently. They'll only be used for special promotions and at the start of a procedure, such as adding an item to a cart or beginning the checkout process.

Services.com plans to use interstitials in their shopping cart to attempt to talk customers into longer-term agreements and more profitable service offerings. Because the typical customer order for utility services contains only one "item" per order, interstitials will be used anytime anything is placed in the customer's shopping cart to try to upgrade the sale.

Since only internal employees will use their Web site, and since they prefer to use less intrusive marketing techniques, Great World, Inc. has no plans to use interstitials.

Pop-ups

For many e-commerce sites, pop-ups represent a happy middle ground between banner ads and interstitials. They're harder to ignore than banner ads, but they're not as jarring as an interstitial taking over your browser window.

Many e-commerce companies use pop-ups to present their customers with information that is tangential to the main site pages — for example, discounts on shipping or upcoming promotions.

In order to keep pop-ups from becoming annoying to your customers, follow these some basic guidelines:

✦ Keep the pop-up window small, usually less than @bf1/4 the size of your main window, assuming that the main window is full-screen at the optimum resolution for which you designed it.

✦ If you're going to have multiple pop-ups appear as the customer browses the site, make sure that they all open in the same, original pop-up window. Opening twenty additional browser windows will not only annoy your customers, it may well slow old computers to a crawl.

✦ Some browsers support the ability to open pop-up windows that remain on top of all other windows on the user's desktop. This generally irritates users, so avoid doing it.

How do pop-ups compare on the advertising scorecard?

✦ **Interference** — Moderately more annoying to most customers than banner ads, but much less annoying that interstitials, pop-ups offer a middle ground between the two techniques.

✦ **Attraction** — More attention getting than banner ads, and less so than interstitials. Rely on catchy designs and animated graphics to make your pop-ups more eye-catching.

✦ **Flexibility** — Pop-ups can be used anywhere on your site to recommend items that the customer may like, to call attention to shipping discounts or other special offers, and so forth.

✦ **Frequency** — Because pop-ups are parallel to the customer's main experience (unlike interstitials, which interrupt the experience), you can use them more frequently than interstitials. However, the small window size of a pop-up that keeps it less intrusive may present less advertising space overall than a banner ad offers.

✦ **Hijacking** — Careful pop-up design will ensure that subsequent pop-up material always appears in the initial window that your site popped up. If customers close this window, new pop-ups will open it again. Clever customers can choose to minimize the window, though, keeping it out of sight and out of mind.

How will the sample companies implement pop-ups?

Retailer.com plans to use pop-ups to create hour-long sales. During a particular hour, pop-ups will inform customers of items that have been drastically discounted. Several items will be featured each hour, and they will cycle through the pop-up window while the customer browses through the site.

Services.com plans to use pop-ups to remind customers of all the services that their site offers. Customers shopping for electricity providers, for example, will see pop-ups urging them to investigate the site's natural gas suppliers, and so forth.

Great World, Inc. plans to use pop-ups to augment their banner ads, reminding employees of merchandise pick-up hours, special holiday merchandise selections, and so forth.

Planning for Growth

After you put together the formal documentation for your site's design, go over the plan with a focus on where the site will be in six months or a year. How does your navigation scheme hold up if five new departments are added? How much extra work will be required to begin accepting cooperative advertising?

Understanding the direction that your site will be taking is important to coming up with a plan that allows the site to grow with as little pain and effort as possible. Spend time with your company's executives, and explain that if *you* achieve a better understanding of the overall business plan, the result will be a site compliant with that business plan.

In particular, be highly suspicious of any number that anyone tells you. "We will have several more departments in the next six months" is safe, but anyone who says "We will have five additional product categories" will probably be proved a liar sooner or later. The same holds true for marketing and advertising. If you're asked to add one banner ad to every page on the site, chances are it will be two banner ads before long. Make sure that the technologies, techniques, and designs that you settle on are capable of supporting more than your site needs today. Granted, no plan can accommodate an infinite amount of growth — and you shouldn't attempt this — but you can accommodate *some* growth in a good plan, and avoid having to redesign the site every time a minor growth spurt comes along.

Make sure that your project documentation specifies how you've planned for growth. For example, consider this excerpt from Retailer.com's documentation:

> Our navigation scheme will include a vertical menu bar on the left side of each page. The entire menu will be contained in a table cell that spans the entire length of the page, and the actual contents of the menu will be contained in a separate HTML file. This file will be dynamically recreated every evening by a utility written in Visual Basic, so the menu will always contain the latest product categories. We currently have six categories defined, and anticipate that the existing design will accommodate about a dozen more. If we grow beyond 18-20 categories, the left menu will become too long to fit before the "crease" of the page and we will need to consider some kind of hierarchical menu structure to accommodate all of the categories.

This documentation clearly shows that Retailer.com has planned for growth in their site design. If any potential investors conduct a due-diligence investigation, they'll find that the company expects growth and is prepared for growth, which is always a good sign. The documentation also enables the company's technical staff to maintain consistency if the site's original designers leave or take other positions because all of their decisions and intentions are documented for their successors.

Be sure that your plan states your assumptions on the company's growth. This way your plan can be viewed in light of those assumptions. If a successor has to deal with site growth beyond your original expectations, he or she will understand that your original plans may not be suitable and can immediately begin looking at alternatives.

How do the sample companies expect to grow?

Retailer.com expects to add several more product categories each quarter, and will eventually have at least two dozen categories in two years' time. They expect the number of products in those categories to quickly grow until they offer over 60,000 products. They expect their original design to accommodate their growth for about a year, at which time they will have to look at designs that can accommodate more navigational information.

Services.com expects to add more utility suppliers, but because their site has been designed to accommodate all of the basic utilities, they don't expect to have to make any major navigational changes in the foreseeable future.

Great World, Inc. admits that their online employee convenience store is an experiment, and will be adding more products and services, such as oil changes and babysitting, as their employees respond to the online store. They believe that their navigation design, which consists primarily of text links on DHTML pop-up menus, can be easily rearranged to accommodate a much wider variety of goods and services than they currently offer. Like Services.com, Great World, Inc. sees their current designs lasting into the foreseeable future.

Summary

Designing the look and feel of your site is one of the most important steps toward actualizing your site. Involve everyone in your company in the site's design process. Be communicative, be careful to include future growth in your plan, and document everything that you do.

The next chapter takes many of the decisions explored in this chapter to a more detailed level, and discusses how to design the experience that you want your customers to have on your site.

✦　　✦　　✦

Designing the Customer Experience

As you surf the Web browsing different sites and buying merchandise or services online, have you ever wondered what the designers of those sites were thinking when they set up their various processes?

Many times, the technologies employed to actually build an e-commerce site are difficult to work with and understand, especially when many different products and technologies are used together. As a result, designers often build a site to behave in whatever way the technology works by default. Sometimes, this method results in a good customer experience, and sometimes not; it rarely results in an *excellent* customer experience.

Customer Care Is Key

Designers have a tendency to make sites "task oriented" from a technology point of view. Sites include a search function, a shopping cart, a checkout, and other elements. Sometimes, site designers will integrate these elements so that customers can search for products from the shopping cart page, for example. How often will your customers actually want or need to do that? Site designers rarely take into account the tasks that customers will *want* to perform, and so don't design the customer's *experience* on their site. Instead, designers tend to create a site that *they* would like to use, or to create sites that allow them to most easily implement the features they need.

The experience that a customer has on your site should not be a random collection of events, but rather a planned, organized process that customers will enjoy following because the setup meets their needs.

Designing a process that your customers will enjoy requires you to carefully consider your customers' needs. For example, I worked with a company that sold arts and crafts products over the Internet. Their customers were accustomed to shopping for these supplies in traditional "brick-and-mortar" stores, and were divided into two basic groups. The first group went to the store knowing what supplies they needed for a particular project. They wanted to be able to quickly find the products, purchase them, and be finished. The second group didn't have any specific craft projects in mind, so they preferred to browse the aisles of the store looking at the products for sale to see if any ideas popped into their minds. Accommodating the first group on a Web site was an easy task. A clearly defined merchandise taxonomy and well laid-out navigation elements combined with a very accessible search function would lead customers right to the products that they wanted. Accommodating the second group was more difficult because a Web site carrying more than 60,000 products — far more than any physical store — makes "browsing the aisles" difficult. The company responded by creating projects that customers could browse for ideas. If customers found a project that they liked, a single click put all the necessary supplies into their shopping cart, and the project instructions and patterns were e-mailed to them after they checked out.

However, the company failed to design a checkout process around their customers' needs. Again, the majority of the customers were accustomed to retail stores — not Internet e-commerce sites. Although the browsing experience closely approximated and, in some ways, surpassed the brick-and-mortar experience, the checkout process failed to do so. Customers were required to log in or create an account if they were first-time customers. Shipping and billing information was collected, but error messages were ambiguous to many customers (a 72-year-old grandmother may not be able to decipher "Address1 is required"). The checkbox where customers could opt out of the company's e-mail newsletter was buried, so many customers overlooked it and subsequently complained when they received twice-weekly e-mails. The checkout process was problematic because it did not approximate the checkout experience to which the customers were accustomed.

Changes were made, of course. The problem with making changes to a major process like browsing or checkout, however, is that the changes often require extensive reprogramming. Start-up e-commerce companies, and even e-commerce divisions of established companies, rarely have the time to reprogram a major process on their site. Thus, the changes to the arts and crafts site were mere "patches" that adversely affected almost every other part of the company. For example, the marketing division had become accustomed to tracking customers' purchases in order to determine how frequently a customer ordered. The changes to the checkout process allowed customers to check out without logging in or creating an account, so they were effectively anonymous, thus hampering the marketing department's efforts to perform targeted advertising to repeat customers.

The moral of the story is that almost no amount of time or money can apologize for a design that causes a poor customer experience. Before a single byte of code is committed to disk, your developers should have a complete, written plan of exactly how customers will use the site. Concentrate on the tasks that your customers will perform, and remember that the tasks your customers *want* to perform will differ depending on your market and demographic. Consider the following tasks that your customers may want to perform on your site:

✦ Search for a particular product or service

✦ Browse through products or services just to "see what's available"

✦ Check out

✦ Add products to their shopping cart and work within the cart

✦ Sign up for newsletters and other information

✦ Check the status of past orders

✦ Interact with customer service

✦ Search for items that are on sale or have special pricing, or search for some other class of product not based on your product taxonomy

Designing the customer experience is about making your site work the way your customers *expect* it to, not the way the technology makes easiest or the way *you're* accustomed to. Think about how customers are accustomed to performing tasks in a traditional purchasing experience and approximate those experiences as closely as possible.

 Tip　If your audience includes customers with a wide range of Internet experience, then you should include optional shortcuts for more experienced shoppers.

After you work out how customers will use your site, document the customer experience. The best form of documentation is a flowchart that starts with the customer arriving at your home page. Create a different flowchart for each type of customer, and indicate on the flowchart where customers can "hook" into different shopping tasks (such as looking for clearance items) from the task that they started with (such as browsing through a particular product category). This customer experience design will play heavily into your site's navigation design, so be prepared to revisit your navigation concepts and designs, as well.

The primary goal of the customer experience is to get customers from any particular starting point to their desired result in as few clicks as possible. The Internet is all about immediate gratification, and your site has to deliver on that expectation. Take the time to visit e-commerce sites that are similar to yours to see how they've designed their site to accommodate their customers. Make a note of features and processes that you like, and note those you don't like so you can be sure to avoid them.

In the following sections, I discuss some specific points to consider when designing the most effective customer experiences. I also talk about designing the most important customer experience of all—that of making your site as reliable and responsive as possible.

The Browsing Experience

Browsing comprises a major part of the customer experience on any Web site. In this context, *browsing* refers to any activity that customers undertake in order to find products or services on your site. Customers may be looking for a particular product, searching for a class of products so they can compare the individual products that you carry, or just looking through your catalog for ideas on what to buy. The browsing experience that you design must accommodate these shopping tasks, and must also provide "hooks" into any non-shopping tasks your site may offer, such as value-added content (buyer's guides, project ideas, or other non-product information), opt-in programs, and so forth.

Designing a satisfying browsing experience requires you to know a little bit about your customers. Are they likely to know what they want when they arrive on your home page, or are they more likely to browse through your catalog first? Do they need to compare products before making a purchase decision? Are they shopping for themselves, or are they shopping for someone else? If you don't know the answers to these questions, then market research is in order (see the sidebar, "Market Research"). Most importantly, *don't guess.* Guessing about the goals and intentions of your customers will only lead to a customer experience that may not meet their actual needs and desires.

Remember that the ultimate goal of any customer experience is to get customers to the products that they want, get those products into their shopping cart, and then get them through the checkout as quickly as possible. Consider some of the following e-commerce industry statistics:

✦ Customers should have to click no more than three navigation elements to be presented with a complete list of products in a particular category, and that category should be as narrowly defined as possible.

✦ Customers who know the product name or model number of the desired product should be able to type that information on almost any page of your site, and click no more than twice to add the item to their shopping cart.

✦ Customers generally try searching for something by name or number only twice. On the second attempt, they will try less-common names or fill out an "advanced search" screen if presented with one. After two attempts, however, they will generally give up and try a different site.

✦ Customers frequently add items to their shopping cart and then abandon the cart (never actually completing the purchase). An estimated 80 percent of online shopping carts are abandoned. Shoppers do this for various reasons, including to determine what the shipping and tax charges would be on their order, or because they realize that a site doesn't accept the form of payment they want to use.

✦ Customers who are presented with search results that exceed 10 pages are likely to give up on the results, or look at the first two to three pages (at most).

Take these statistics into consideration, and try to design a browsing experience that reduces the number of steps customers have to take to get to the products they want, even if they don't know exactly what products they want. Find out what your customers will consider intuitive, and design your site to work that way.

You can take some specific steps, including:

1. Identify information associated with the browsing process, including the information that you *must* gather from the customer, and the information that you *want* to gather from the customer. (I talk about this process in the next section.)

2. Design a browsing process that specifically reduces the clicks or steps that a customer has to take. (I also talk about this in the next section.)

3. Consider the technologies that you have available to make the browsing experience more accommodating for your customers.

Market Research

Hopefully, your company did some market research before deciding to jump into the e-commerce world, so you should have access to some basic demographic information on your customers. Although a small part of this demographic information (such as how familiar your customers are likely to be with online shopping and the Internet in general) is helpful in designing the customer experience, most of the demographic information serves to point the way for further market research into how your customer demographic expects to use your site. For example, you can expect tech-savvy computer professionals to visit a site that sells computer accessories and start searching for a particular product that they want to buy. They will probably look for some kind of search box to type in a product name, or look for some navigation element that leads the way into the product category that they need to buy from. This customer demographic also wants the ability to browse through the catalog, looking for accessories to solve a particular need — even if they don't know a specific product or manufacturer name. You have to make sure that your site provides a path for both experienced and inexperienced shoppers, so that they both have an enjoyable, efficient customer experience.

Conducting additional market research into your demographic will help you determine how your customers expect your site to work. You can take two different approaches for this kind of research, and you should consider using both of them in order to get the best results. The first approach is to form a *focus group* of customers in your demographic — from outside your company. Have them sign non-disclosure agreements, and then explain the overall vision of your site and what you will sell. Ask them how they expect your site to work, and what different types of shopping approaches they may use on your site. The second approach is to observe your customer demographic as they shop for the same types of products and services that you will sell — both at retail stores and on any popular e-commerce sites selling the same things. Figure out what seems to be working and what's not, and make appropriate notes for designing the customer experience on your site.

Start by drawing a flowchart of how you think the customer browsing experience should work. Remember to draw flowcharts for every possible task that your customers may want to perform on your site.

Consider the customer experience flowcharts that the folks at Retailer.com may draw. Retailer.com's managers expect the company's customers to shop using one of four paths:

✦ A path for customers who know the brand name or model number that they want.

✦ A path for customers who know the type of product that they want, but who also want to see the specific products that Retailer.com carries.

✦ A path for customers who want to browse through a particular category of products to get gift ideas, or just to see what's new.

✦ A path for customers looking for a specific group of products that don't share an actual product category (new products, sale products, and so forth).

Figure 3-1 shows the path for customers who know a brand name or model number that they want. In this path, customers begin by clicking a search button, which is located in the top-left corner of every page on the site. By typing the known information, the customer can get a list of matching products. In the event that only one product matches, the customer is taken straight to that product's detail page. If more than one product matches, the customer is shown a list of matching products, which they can sort by product name, manufacturer, stock number, or price. If more than two pages of results are returned, the customer is given the option to narrow down the results by specifying additional keywords. This same flowchart also accommodates the second customer path, if the search engine is programmed to match keywords across the products' description field. At any time, customers can click an advanced search function that allows them to search for specific values in various product fields, such as price, the date that the product was added to the site, etc.

Figure 3-2 shows the path for the customer who wants to browse the catalog. This path is basically accomplished by the site's navigation design, which allows customers to "drill down" through departments and categories. At each level, the customer is shown the next level's set of catalog links, along with a page of featured products from the particular department or category of interest. This feature also helps customers who are just browsing for ideas by automatically giving them product pictures and brief descriptions. The customer can click any of the featured products in order to access their detail page. After the customer drills down to the bottom-level category, clicking a link displays all of the products in that category. This link actually submits a hard coded search query to the search engine, which displays the products in the category as a set of search results. At this point, customers are back in the flowchart shown in Figure 3-1, where they can refine the search with additional keywords, browse through the results, or re-sort the results by price or another column.

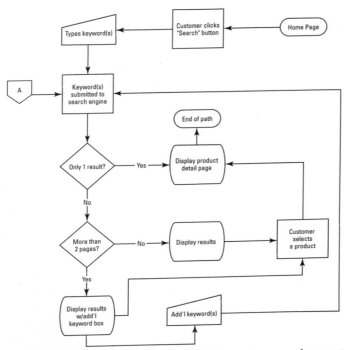

Figure 3-1: Customer experience path for customers who want to search

Figure 3-3 shows the final path for customers who are looking for a group of products, such as new products, products on sale, etc. This flowchart is simple because Retailer.com plans to implement these search functions as banner ads ("Click here to see our clearance products," for example) throughout the site. These banner ads will submit a hard coded search query to the search engine, which will then display the matching products as search results, thus taking the customer back into the path shown in Figure 3-1.

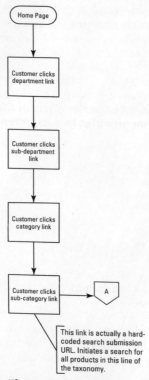

Figure 3-2: Customer experience path for
customers who want to browse the catalog

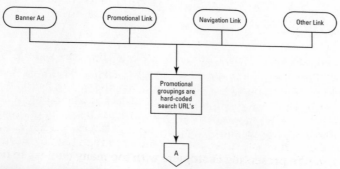

Figure 3-3: Customer experience path for customers looking
for a group of products

Tip Microsoft Visio makes a great tool for drawing flowcharts and is a requirement if you intend to use BizTalk Orchestration to help automate your business processes.

By directing the three paths toward the same basic result (such as a product detail page), customers will quickly become familiar with how the site looks and operates. They only need to learn one graphical interface, and as a result, they will have the flexibility to move between "shopping tasks" as they please because this single interface actually provides all of the functionality required to perform any of these tasks. By building separate paths, however, Retailer.com provides less-experienced customers with "shortcuts" to particular tasks.

Building a "one size fits all" customer experience is perfectly logical, but you have to make sure that this approach is broken down into segments so that beginning customers won't be confronted with the same horde of options that a more experienced customer may prefer.

Identifying required and desirable information

The primary method for making a site easy for customers to use is to minimize the information that a customer has to provide and, wherever possible, allow the customer to choose from lists rather than type information.

In the browsing experience, using this method means providing a clear enough navigation design so that customers don't need to guess the names of your product departments. Present your departments in a list that customers can choose from.

For example, suppose that customers visit your site looking for a blue number four widget. They will need to know certain information in order to find one. If you carry fifty thousand widgets, then typing the word *widget* isn't going to be terribly helpful. If customers don't know that the size they want is referred to as "number four," then that isn't useful information either. Perhaps the customers merely know that they want a six-inch widget.

Customers may take one of two paths to find their widget. They may search for it using a search box on your site. This search box should require the minimum amount of information possible — ideally, a short text box and a submit button. Customers should be able to type "blue six-inch widget" to see what comes up. The wrong way to implement a basic search function is to provide a search button that takes the customer to a search page with three or four text boxes. Even if all of the information is optional and you only mean for customers to type the key words that they're searching for, you're presenting customers with too many choices to perform a simple search. Just ask them to provide some keywords, and then program your search engine to locate products with those words in any of the products' fields. Customers that *want* a more advanced search function, and who are basically volunteering to provide you with more precise search information, should be able to access an advanced search form that breaks things down more clearly and may provide more accurate search results.

Rather than searching, customers may prefer to browse for their six-inch blue widget. In that case, they'll be using your navigation design, which means you have to create a design that anticipates how your customers are likely to want to search. For example, customers will probably do the following:

1. Search for a "Widgets" department link to click.

2. Within the "Widgets" department, search for a "six-inch" category.

3. Within the "six-inch" category, search for the exact shade of blue desired.

By creating a hierarchical browse path like this — whether you use separate screens, a Java applet, or a DHTML cascading menu for implementation — you are allowing your customers to provide one small piece of information at a time. The *wrong* way to introduce a browse path is to provide a giant list of all the departments and categories that you offer, thus making the customer scroll down to the "six-inch" section of the "Widgets" page. Customers generally prefer to locate products on a Web site the same way they would in a store — first by going to the Widgets department, and then to the shelf of six-inch widgets. On the other hand, you may have more experienced customers who *don't* want to drill down through your product taxonomy, especially if it's more than three or four layers deep in sub-departments and sub-categories. These customers may appreciate a site map link that provides a huge list of the entire catalog hierarchy that they can scroll down to arrive at the pertinent section.

If your site provides separate paths for experienced and less experienced customers, you can use cookies or other personalization technologies to help customers get quickly to the path that they prefer. For example, customers who click the advanced search link may get the advanced search screen by default from then on, until they click a basic search link to return to the single-text box form. If you've already determined your customers' preferences, don't make them state those preferences again by making them click an advanced search function. Remember their preferences and present them with the version of your site that they prefer without asking.

Of course, the concept of asking for as little information as possible means that customers performing a complex shopping task have to take more steps to drill down to the information that they need. In the next section, I talk about the need to reduce clicks as much as possible to keep customers interested, and to get them to the result of their shopping task as quickly as possible.

Reducing clicks

The goal of any e-commerce Web site is to get customers to the products that they want and help them check out as quickly as possible. This is the goal of commerce everywhere. Supermarkets have "express" checkout lanes, fast-food stores have drive-thru lanes, and so forth.

The drive-through, in fact, is the perfect example of a customer experience designed to reduce clicks. In a normal fast-food experience, customers must find a parking space, park, go inside, make their selections, pay, find a table, sit down, eat, throw away their trash, and leave. The drive-through reduced this experience to the bare minimum number of steps necessary to complete a transaction: The customer makes their selection, pays, and drives away.

The industry rule of thumb is that four to five clicks should place a product in a customer's basket. Customers may opt for a longer path, but it shouldn't be forced upon them. For example:

✦ Anywhere you list a product, you should include enough information for an informed customer to recognize that product as the one they want, including price, short description, model number, etc.

✦ Any product listing should include a "buy" button as well as a "more info" button that takes the customer to the product detail page (which should also have a "buy" button).

✦ If you showcase "featured products" on your site, whether in banner ads or elsewhere, you should include a "buy" button that immediately adds the item to the customer's cart.

Design techniques like these will help reduce the number of clicks that customers *must* complete in order to add an item to their cart. You should examine your entire site to see if you can reduce the number of clicks that customers have to take to get to products. For example, I worked with a company that had a very complex product taxonomy. Customers wanting to browse to a product had to select a department on the home page, a sub-department on the next page, a category on the page after that, and then they were presented with a list of products in the category maybe four to five pages long. They had to click a product in the listing to get to its detail page, which finally presented a buy button (which totaled at least five clicks to get the product into the cart).

The navigation was redesigned to make the departments narrower, so that clicking on one department resulted in a more focused set of sub-departments, which led directly to product listings. For sub-departments with more than two or three pages of products, the sub-department link displayed the first page of products *and* links for further categories, allowing the customer to get to product listings quicker, but still allowing categories to be used within sub-departments.

Keep in mind that you also have to weigh the concern of overwhelming your customers with too many choices at once. Asking them to select from a list of fifty departments is probably going too far in the name of reducing clicks, and you need to break things down into some kind of hierarchy. However, remember to provide that complete list for customers who are willing to use it, because it will help them complete their shopping tasks faster.

Some on-screen options may simply take the customer to another screen, where they make another navigational selection. These options should be implemented right on the main screen, rather than taking the customer to a second screen, so customers don't have to make the extra click to get there. For example, take a look at Figure 3-4. In this figure, the number of clicks has been reduced by removing the search button from the pages and including a full search box. This type of optimization gets customers to their products faster.

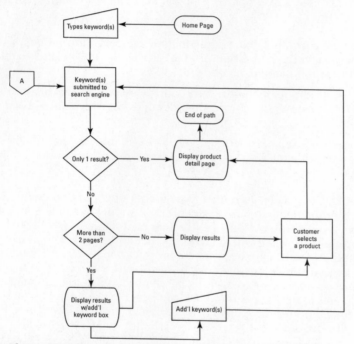

Figure 3-4: Customer experience path for customers who want to search, revised

Similar techniques should be used to drive customers to all the major functions of your site. Depending on the available screen space, you may want to display a small version of the customers' shopping cart with a checkout button, so they can move right into the purchase process without having to review their cart. You should *always* display a "checkout now" button on every page if customers have items in their cart, to facilitate and simplify the checkout process. Marketing opt-in programs should work similarly. Rather than asking customers to "click here to sign up," provide a small text box with the message "type your e-mail address and click sign up," thus removing one step in the process.

The following sections examine specific design techniques that can reduce clicks in the major areas of e-commerce: Catalog browsing, marketing opt-in and opt-out programs, and searching.

Catalog browsing

Here are some general tips for reducing clicks while not overwhelming customers with too many choices when building a catalog hierarchy:

✦ If a parent element has fewer than four children, include the children at the parent's level. For example, if you have a "Cars" department, which is then divided into "SUVs," "Sedans" and "Vans," eliminate the "Cars" department and include the three children on that menu instead.

✦ If you have a block of four or more similarly named menu items, consider combining them into one. For example, categories like "Computer mice," "Computer mouse pads," "Computer trackballs," and "Computer touchpads" can be combined into "Mice and other pointing devices." If necessary, you can include the four types of point devices as categories under the main heading.

✦ If you are using a dynamic menu that expands categories into sub-categories without moving to a new Web page, you're safe including a deeper hierarchy. Customers can navigate up and down the hierarchy without waiting for new Web pages to load. On the other hand, if each click of a menu option loads a new Web page, reduce the number of options to reduce page load time. This restriction is yet another reason to consider Java and DHTML for your navigation design, because they allow more deeply-nested options without additional page loads.

✦ If your top-level category contains a product list *and* subcategories, customers will get to products faster. For example, most computer users prefer a mouse as their pointing device. Therefore, you should have a category named "Mice and other pointing devices" that results in a list of computer mice, with category links to the less-popular trackballs, touchpads, and accessories. This way, you have a good chance of presenting most customers with the product that they want on the first screen, and other customers can still make an extra click to get to their desired category.

In a customer's "perfect world," your home page should magically display pertinent products or services. Any extra clicking or typing of information is just a barrier to the purchase, and your job as site designer is to remove these barriers as often as possible. In the next section, I talk about some of the technologies that you can use to remove these barriers.

Marketing opt-in and opt-out programs

The overwhelming success that most e-commerce companies have with marketing opt-in programs like e-mail newsletters is proof that they work. The trick is to get your site visitors to actually sign up for these programs. Marketing opt-in programs are laced with conflicting goals in this regard. Ideally, you want shoppers to provide you with as much information as possible, allowing you to better target advertising to their specific interests. On the other hand, the more information that you ask for, the more likely shoppers are to shy away from the whole thing.

Your initial opt-in signup should only require shoppers to provide a couple basic pieces of information, such as their e-mail address and name. Your first e-mail to them can then be an offer to visit the site and fill out a short, five-question survey on their interests. You may even reward them with a coupon or special discount for completing the survey. After a few weeks go by, invite them back for a slightly longer survey, with another commensurate reward upon completion. By asking for their information in small doses, you are more likely to get that information.

If you do intend to offer your customers some kind of e-mail newsletter, build your site from the start to support multiple newsletters. The customer's initial signup, for example, may be for a basic, general interest newsletter. As your site matures, you can offer your customers additional newsletters. By building your site to handle this functionality up front, you'll save considerable time and effort in the future.

An opt-out program (which allows customers to remove themselves from your mailing list) *must* accompany marketing opt-in programs. Again, keep the initial opt-out simple. Provide a text box where customers can type their e-mail address to be removed from all of your newsletters and other marketing communications. After they submit their e-mail address, display a brief screen explaining that they're about to be unsubscribed from all the following list of newsletters and communications. Allow customers the opportunity to only remove themselves from one list, if they prefer. Provide some indication of how frequently each type of communication is sent out, such as weekly, monthly, etc., so customers can decide to stay on less-frequent lists. Also offer your customers the opportunity to be removed from all of the lists with one click, because you'll at least retain their goodwill toward your company. On the other hand, don't let them off the hook without offering them the opportunity to stay committed at a smaller level.

Tip   Make sure that any e-mails you send out contain clear instructions on how recipients can remove themselves from the list. Also, make sure your home page includes a clear indication of where visitors can go to unsubscribe.

If a customer does ask to be removed from all e-mail communications, don't just delete them from your existing lists. Make sure that you add their e-mail address to a "negative" list, and run that list against all future e-mails. It is imperative, from a customer goodwill standpoint as well as a legal standpoint, that you not send any marketing or advertising e-mails to those customers again. Doing so will almost certainly rob you of any possible future sales to those customers.

Searching

As with many other click-reducing techniques, the customer should be able to approach your search functionality incrementally. A basic, single text box search form should appear on every major page of your site, giving customers easy access to a basic search. An advanced search link, located on the main search form as well as any search results pages, should link to a complete, comprehensive search form allowing customers to perform more specific, complex queries.

Search results pages should also offer a single-click way to narrow the search results, to perform the same search again with additional criteria.

 Tip   Commerce Server 2000 facilitates building basic and advanced search forms, and has several pre-written searches that you can modify to meet your site's exact needs.

Available technologies

You can improve the customer's browsing experience with a variety of available technologies. In this section, I talk about the pros and cons of the six major technologies, and I describe how they can be used in specific situations to improve the browsing experience.

Cookies

Cookies are small pieces of information stored on the user's computer. The information in the cookie is sent from your Web server to the user's browser, which accepts the cookie (or not — keep reading) and stores it on the user's hard drive. The browser remembers which Web site each cookie came from. Whenever the user accesses a page on that Web site in the future, the browser automatically sends the contents of the cookie with the page request; the server doesn't need to specifically ask for the cookie.

Cookies can be incredibly useful. Because Web sites are inherently "stateless," meaning that you have no way to track a user between page clicks, cookies provide a much-needed workaround. By placing a unique number into a user's cookie, you can program your Web site to identify the user between page clicks. You can also store information on users' preferences in cookies, allowing your site to personalize itself to your customers' needs and preferences.

Unfortunately, many users are suspicious of cookies. Many marketing companies place cookies on users' computers to track the sites that they visit, allowing them to build market statistics and even offer targeted banner ads to those users. Although the great majority of these companies can't actually attach any personal information (not even an e-mail address) to the user's path across the Web, a great deal of bad press has been attached to cookies, as well as a great deal of confusion.

As a result, many users prevent their browsers from accepting cookies, and if your site depends on them, customers may not be able to use your site at all. Commerce Server can be particularly vulnerable to this if it's not correctly configured. I worked on a site that was so dependent on cookies that their checkout simply would not function without them, and sadly, their "no cookies" page (the page that users were automatically directed to if their browser refused a cookie) was their third-most visited page.

Here's my advice: Use cookies to store user preferences to customize the site in ways that won't matter if the cookie isn't accepted. For data that is important to your site's functionality, you'll have to take other steps, which are generally *much* more complicated and discussed at length elsewhere in this book (for a brief discussion, see the sidebar, "The Alternative to Cookies"). The only safe time to use cookies to store critical data is when you're building an intranet site where you can be assured that users will accept cookies from the server.

The Alternative to Cookies

If you've made the decision to use cookies sparingly on your site — a decision that I heartily endorse given the reluctance of many shoppers to accept cookies — then you may be wondering how you can program your Web site to recognize users as they move through your site.

First, you need to understand that Microsoft's Active Server Pages provides a session-tracking capability in its Session and Application objects. Unfortunately, this technology relies on cookies that are automatically handled by Internet Information Server, so it's useless if your goal is to remain cookie-free.

The alternative to cookies works in a very similar fashion to cookies. Essentially, you have to make up a unique ID number for every visitor to your site. Rather than storing this number in a cookie, you encode it into every URL and form that your site uses, ensuring that the number will always be passed to the Web server when pages are requested. In later chapters, I discuss how to create a semi-automated way of doing this.

This alternative misses one significant piece of functionality that cookies provide — the ability to persist information across several days' time by storing it on the user's computer. Any personalization that you want to do can't be applied unless users identify themselves by logging in.

Many Web sites adopt a mixed approach. They use a cookie to store the customer's user name or ID number on their local computer. When the customer visits the site the next time, the cookie is retrieved and their personalized settings are restored. If customers don't accept the cookie, they see the standard, non-personalized site until they identify themselves by logging in. After they are identified by the cookie or log in, customers are identified for the remainder of their visit by URL encoding, eliminating the need to store further cookies. Several major portal sites, including Yahoo.com and Excite.com, utilize this mixed technique for their personalized sites.

If you're going to use cookies to customize your site, make sure that you have a page that clearly explains what you're using the cookie for, and what information it stores. This will help allay any fears that your customers may have about accepting the cookie.

Because the alternatives to cookies are so much more complex, you may simply lack the time to implement a fully cookie-free Web site. If you need to use cookies, make sure that your site is capable of testing whether or not cookies are being accepted by the user's browser. If they aren't, your site should redirect users to a page that clearly explains why and how you're using cookies, and gently pushes them to enable cookies for your Web site.

If your company is partnering with some of the marketing companies that place special cookies on users' systems, make sure to mention this to your users so they don't feel "blindsided" when additional cookies show up on their computer. Be aware that newer browsers, such as Internet Explorer 5.5 SP1 and higher, give users the option to accept cookies from *your* Web site while refusing the "third party" cookies that marketing companies utilize. This can allow users to choose to accept cookies used by your site, but to refuse any cookies passed to their browser by external marketing companies with whom you've partnered.

Forms

Forms, of course, provide your primary means for collecting information from your users. A variety of techniques make forms more engaging, less imposing, and more conducive to a pleasant customer browsing experience. Many of these are simply good graphic design and layout, making the forms easy to read and understand. Some others are unique to good Web design:

✦ Don't make any forms that can't be displayed in one or two screens. Customers generally won't scroll through several pages of form fields and actually fill them all out. Break longer forms into more than one screen, or consider eliminating some information.

✦ Clearly indicate which information on the form is required. Clearly communicate to shoppers that information requested in boldface, red, or whatever technique you choose, is required.

✦ Use DHTML to validate as much of the form's information as possible before submitting it to the server. DHTML provides instant feedback to shoppers, allowing them to provide missing information or correct errors without waiting for a new page to load.

✦ When errors are made, clearly indicate where they are by coloring the appropriate sections of the form, or highlighting them in some other obvious fashion. Use error messages that can be easily understood by the least-experienced customers in your demographic.

✦ Whenever possible, allow customers to choose from a list rather than typing information. When customers must type information, try to fill in a default value for them, if possible.

✦ Use DHTML to hide portions of the form that aren't necessary. For example, if a customer checks a checkbox indicating that their shipping address is the same as the billing address they already typed, hide the shipping address portion of the form. Or, at the very least, use DHTML to copy the information from the billing address fields to the shipping address fields.

✦ Try to name your form fields with standard, common-sense names. For example, use "City" for a form field where a user would logically type the city portion of their shipping address. Many browsers, such as Internet Explorer, feature *auto complete* technology that enables the browser to help the user fill in form fields. Because many Web sites use a form field named "City," the browser will recognize the form field name on your site and allow the user to choose the city that they have typed on other Web sites, thus reducing the time the user has to spend filling in information. Other add-on technologies, such as the various HTML-based "wallet" packages, like American Express Wallet, use form field names similarly.

Multi-form navigation

When forms must span more than one screen in order to collect the necessary information, such as in a marketing server or customer signup process, make sure that the forms are easy to use. Whenever possible, include the following elements in the form set:

✦ Indicate how many screens are involved in the process, and give the customer an indication of where they are in the process. This can be as simple as displaying "Step 2 of 3" along the top of the form, although you should design this element to fit into the rest of your site's design whenever possible.

✦ Use a "wizard-like" interface to allow customers to navigate the form. Many multi-form processes can "break" if the user clicks the forward or back buttons in the browser; discourage this by providing clearly labeled "Previous" and "Next" buttons of your own at the top *and* bottom of every form page.

✦ *Assume* that users will click the back and forward buttons in their browser while moving through a multi-form set. Test your form pages to see what effect this has on them, and make the necessary design and programming modifications to properly cope with this event.

Java applets

Java applets can provide a dynamic browsing experience for your customers. If you're comfortable with using Java, you can use it as the centerpiece of your browsing experience. However, remember that many users either turn off their browsers' Java Virtual Machine (JVM), never bother to enable it, or have it disabled by their corporate security policies.

For example, you can develop a custom Java application that acts as your catalog. By utilizing Java Database Connectivity (JDBC), the application can connect directly to a database server for product information, thus providing a robust, custom-designed catalog experience for your customers.

In practice, this type of development effort is extremely time-consuming, particularly with the current shortage of skilled Java programmers. Java applets that must perform heavy-duty display and database connectivity often run into the limitations of the JVM implementation in many Web browsers, which often simply can't keep up with the demands of the application, resulting in slow performance, "garbage" on the application's display, and so forth. As a result, most e-commerce sites limit themselves to Java applets that assist the user with navigation tasks or display specialized text, including scrolling "marquees," stock ticker-like displays, and so forth.

If you do decide to utilize Java as a central piece of your customer browsing experience, be sure to thoroughly test your Java applets over several connection speeds and on a wide range of browsers and computer platforms.

Dynamic HTML

DHTML can be cleverly combined with other technologies to offer a superior browsing experience. For example, start out with a minimal form any time you have to collect information about the customer. Provide check boxes that entice customers to fill out additional information, and have those checkboxes reveal additional form fields.

For example, a newsletter sign-up page can start by asking for the customer's name and e-mail address. A checkbox may be present that allows the customer to "specify preferences for receiving specific newsletters." Checking the box causes a DHTML script to expand the form to include additional fields that allow customers to check off their five favorite hobbies.

A search page provides another example of using DHTML to enhance forms. Though the basic search form may only contain a couple of text boxes and a "Submit" button, a "More" button can expand the form to include additional fields. An advantage of this approach is that you only have to create a single search page. Customers who want to perform an advanced search have the additional optional fields "revealed" when they click the "More" button.

As I discuss in the previous chapter, DHTML can also be used to improve the navigation involved in the browsing experience. By using drop-down or cascading menus, DHTML allows customers to drill down into a complex hierarchy without leaving the current page. This type of immediate gratification makes customers much more willing to navigate a complex product taxonomy than if they had to wait for an entire page to load every time they clicked a new category.

DHTML can be used to enhance search results, too. Your initial search results may only display a couple of products from various categories, but the page may contain many more search "hits." Customers can click a "+" button to have additional products from a category instantly displayed in the results. Again, DHTML provides immediate gratification to a request for more information, which encourages customers to continue using the site.

If you're trying to present your customers with all the necessary options, but are running short of screen space, use DHTML. I've mentioned the importance of having a single text box search function on every page of your site. You may also want a one-line newsletter subscribe/unsubscribe box. Both of these boxes have to fit on the page with your branding logos, navigation elements, and content. DHTML can be used to conserve screen space by providing a search button that, when clicked, immediately expands into a search box. A single "Newsletter signup" button that instantly expands into a box where shoppers can type an e-mail address also conserves screen space.

The only drawback to DHTML is that it requires a 4.0 or higher browser to reliably perform its tricks. If you can restrict yourself to an audience with that browser capability (which is becoming less of a restriction every day), then you should make elaborate use of DHTML to improve the browsing experience.

Tip   Remember that the client-side code that makes DHTML work can be written in JavaScript or VBScript, but that only Internet Explorer understands VBScript. Unless you're catering to an internal audience, plan to program your DHTML in JavaScript.

Index Server and Site Server Search

Index Server and Site Server Search are part of Microsoft's Search Services products. Each has slightly different features, but they are both designed to allow keyword searches to quickly return results from a large body of material. They work by *crawling* the material, a process in which they read the entire body of material and generate an index of key words that can be searched more quickly than the material itself (much like the index in this book).

Properly leveraging Microsoft's search services means anticipating how your customers will search your site.

✦ If customers will be searching for information contained in a database, make sure that you identify the fields they will be searching against. The fewer fields the search engine has to index, the faster it will perform when searching and when integrating new information into the index.

✦ If customers will be regularly searching for information that only exists in a database, ask yourself if you can find a way to dynamically generate static content from the database, and have the search engine index those static pages. If customers are searching against database fields, then the results of those searches must be queried from the database, meaning higher overhead on the database server. The index crawl will also place a significant load on the database when the search engine creates the search index.

Cross-Reference I talk about ways to dynamically generate "static" content for the purpose of reducing database server overhead in Chapter 17.

The important thing to remember with multi-page form sets is that customers often feel as if the process will never end. Use all the techniques for building good forms, and clearly indicate to the customer where they are in the process and how far they have yet to go.

The Buying Experience

The *buying experience*, which is the culmination of the browsing experience and the way your e-commerce site will earn the money it needs to survive and grow, consists of your shopping cart and actual checkout process. A lot can go wrong in the checkout process. A recent industry survey indicated that more than half of e-commerce shoppers regularly "abandoned" their purchases because of difficulties with their shopping cart or, more frequently, the checkout process.

Fortunately, the buying experience is actually more straightforward to design than the browsing experience. Although the browsing experience can take many paths and involve many different shopping tasks, the buying experience consists of only one path, that of collecting the merchandise or services in a shopping basket and checking out. Customers typically begin the process by clicking a "checkout" button.

However, the buying experience must also accommodate more of *your* needs than the browsing experience. Consider the "perfect checkout" from a customer's point of view, as shown in the flowchart in Figure 3-5. This process more closely resembles a typical "brick-and-mortar" retail checkout. The customer begins by verifying the items in her basket and selecting a shipping method, then she provides billing and shipping addresses. The customer finishes by providing her payment information, and the order is completed.

Many e-commerce sites implement a checkout process just like this because it's quick, straightforward, and easy for even inexperienced customers to understand. This process does not, however, accommodate the information that most e-commerce companies want, nor does it offer any kind of value-add for repeat customers by saving them steps.

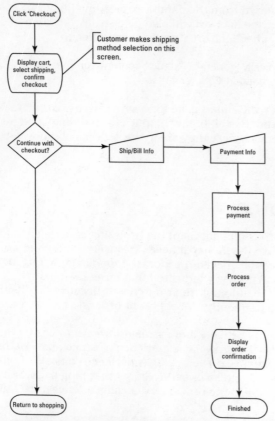

Figure 3-5: A customer's "perfect checkout"

Figure 3-6 shows the checkout process for an e-commerce company that I worked with. This checkout experience was deliberately not designed from the customer's point of view, and has several flaws. To begin with, new customers are required to go through a registration process before they can even begin the actual checkout process, creating a delay in the customer's mind. The registration process does serve to collect marketing information for the company, and to create a profile of the customer. This approach does have advantages for customers. The next time they purchase something, much of their information can be filled in automatically because they are able to identify themselves to the database by logging in. The path for a returning customer is much shorter, and fills in as much of their information as possible.

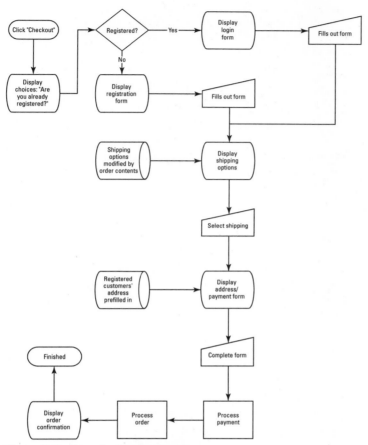

Figure 3-6: Sample checkout process

Unfortunately, new customers don't always perceive this value, and are annoyed by the signup processes. These customers are less likely to become repeat customers, or even to complete their first purchase. This was such a problem for the company, in fact, that they quickly rewrote their checkout process, as shown in Figure 3-7. In this revised process, customers are able to check out without registering or without logging in if they already have registered for an account. This revised process is potentially worse than the original, because at the beginning of the process customers must make a choice to log in (if they are returning), register (if they are new), or do neither and proceed directly to the checkout. Because the language on the Web page makes no attempt to explain the value-add of logging in or registering, almost all of the customers choose to check out "anonymously," thus preventing the company from easily tracking repeat customers or providing any kind of assistance in the process to returning customers.

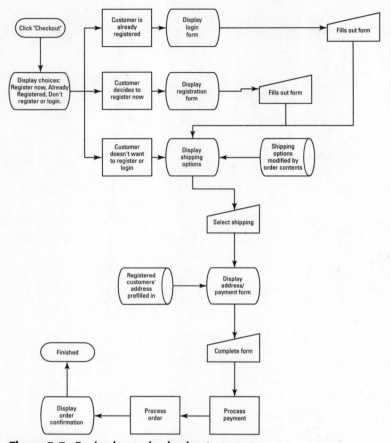

Figure 3-7: Revised sample checkout process

Figure 3-8 shows how I recommended they *redesign*, rather than just *rewrite*, their checkout process. This new process incorporates fewer screens. It starts by asking the customer for their shipping and billing information, and offers returning customers the opportunity to log in to fill in this information automatically.

New customers are not given the opportunity to create an account at the beginning of the checkout process, so they must deal with a minimum number of distractions from the checkout process.

After the checkout is complete, new customers are given the opportunity to have the Web site remember their information for future visits by creating an account. Because the actual checkout is over by then, the company doesn't lose anything significant if customers decline this opportunity to create an account. Language on the site makes it clear that creating an account will provide value to the customer, and encourages them to do so.

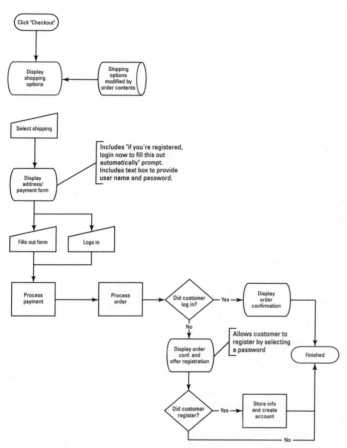

Figure 3-8: Second revision of sample checkout process

The new checkout process removes as many obstacles to the company's selling goal as possible while still providing customers with shortcuts and advantages to help them personalize the experience and make future checkouts even faster. More so than in the browsing experience, the buying experience must take care to reduce the amount of information that a shopper *must* provide, and to reduce the number of clicks necessary to complete their purchase.

Identifying required and desirable information

To begin designing your site's buying experience, make a list of the information that you absolutely must have, at a minimum, in order to complete the transaction. This information may include:

✦ Shipping address

✦ Billing address, if different from the shipping address

✦ An e-mail address to which you can send order status e-mails

✦ Payment information

✦ Shipping method

This bare bones information can typically be completed in two or three well-designed screens. If you offer services like gift-wrapping or the ability to send different parts of an order to different shipping addresses, then your process will be necessarily longer. Even this basic information can be reduced to a single screen through the use of clever design tactics and business partnerships. For example, by offering new customers the ability to create a user ID and password on your site after they check out, you can remember their address and payment information. In the future, simply typing that user name and password allows the site to fill in the information and complete the checkout in a single screen.

Many customers take advantage of "quick checkout" and "wallet" programs designed by service providers like America Online and Yahoo. With these programs, customers click a separate "checkout" button in your shopping cart. Typically, this button is a graphic provided by the service provider that includes specific language and graphics that their members will recognize. After customers click the special checkout button, they log into the service provider using their regular user name and password. The service provider then transmits the customer's address and payment information to you, allowing you to essentially complete the checkout process in zero screens. Supporting these service providers' checkout programs requires additional development work on your part, and requires a contractual business relationship to be established between your company and the service provider, but the extra work is worthwhile because it provides instantaneous gratification to your customers.

Tip   You may want to wait until your site is live to choose which "wallet" or "quick checkout" programs to participate in. This way, you can tell which services the bulk of your customers are coming from, and partner with those services first.

Always try to design your checkout process so that customers have the opportunity to create a user ID that will allow your site to identify them when they log in during future visits. By attaching a user ID to customers' purchases, you create the possibility for tracking the number of purchases that the customer has made, the frequency with which they place orders, and so forth. Ideally, this registration process should also be as short as possible for new customers, perhaps as simple as selecting a password to go with their e-mail address. Future visits can identify the repeat customer and ask them additional demographic and marketing questions in phases.

During a second checkout, customers may be asked basic demographic information, such as their gender and age group. This information is optional and takes up only part of a screen. During subsequent visits, customers have the opportunity to provide additional demographic information but are never asked more than one or two questions at a time. Collecting information in this incremental fashion provides the following two benefits:

✦ Allows you to gather important marketing information without annoying your customers.

✦ Ensures that your most valued customers, or those with multiple repeat purchases, have the opportunity to provide more information about themselves. You want to know as much about repeat customers as possible to better cater to their needs and preferences. Figure 3-9 shows an example of an incremental checkout process.

Reducing clicks

After you've facilitated users in finding products and services on your site and placing them into their shopping cart, you need to follow through on your ease-of-use and click-reducing strategy to make sure that the checkout process provides a similar environment. In this section, I focus on four basic areas for reducing clicks: Shopping carts, suggested selling techniques, the checkout process, and marketing opt-in programs that are a part of the checkout process.

Shopping carts

Shopping carts are generally straightforward, and present an opportunity to reduce clicks in the actual checkout process. For example, consider the sample shopping cart shown in Figure 3-10.

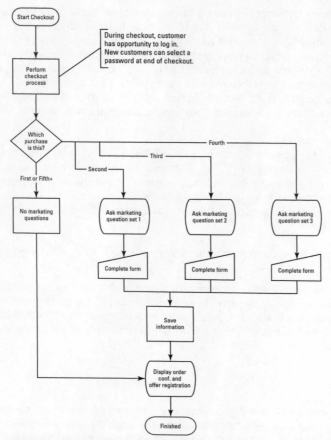

Figure 3-9: Incremental checkout process

This shopping cart offers the shopper a great deal of functionality in a very small amount of screen space:

✦ The ability to see a product's detail page by clicking on the product description

✦ The ability to remove an item from the cart with a single click

✦ The ability to change quantities of items in the cart

✦ The ability to indicate a gift-wrapping preference

✦ The ability to see the cost of shipping with a single click

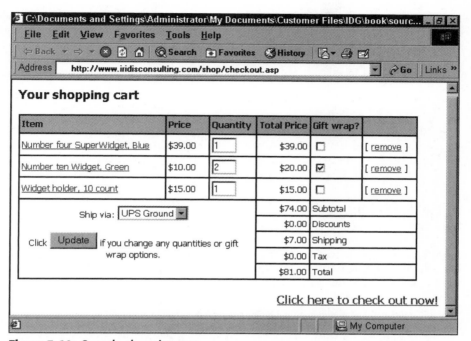

Figure 3-10: Sample shopping cart

Many e-commerce sites offer gift wrapping on customers' purchases, but the majority of them incorporate this choice into their checkout process, adding time and steps to the checkout process that can be avoided. By including this choice in the shopping cart instead, you allow your customers to play with the gift wrapping option in a "safer" environment. Many customers feel uncomfortable "experimenting" after they begin the checkout process because they're afraid of accidentally altering their final purchase. If your site will offer a choice of wrapping papers, you can even incorporate a pop-up window using DHTML. When the customer checks the "Gift Wrap" checkbox for an item, a pop-up window allows them to select their paper preference. This information is then tagged to the shopping cart. You can even design the cart to display a small "swatch" bitmap next to the Gift Wrap checkbox, indicating the paper that the customer has selected.

Most e-commerce sites leave customers in the dark on shipping charges until they decide to check out. The cart in Figure 3-10 displays the shipping cost, and even allows the customer to select a different shipping method. When this page is built server-side, all of the shipping costs for all of the possible shipping methods are built into the page; selecting a new method from the drop-down list box causes a DHTML script to update the cart display *without* submitting the page to the server to be rebuilt. This "instant gratification" is easy to achieve and provides the customer with a better experience.

Take advantage of the simplicity already present in a typical shopping cart to add functionality that will reduce clicks in the all-important checkout process. You can also reduce clicks in the cart by following these tips:

✦ Make sure that customers can remove items from the cart with a single click.

✦ Make sure that customers can get to a product's detail page from their cart with a single click.

✦ Consider using DHTML to eliminate the need for an "Update" button. When customers click a check box or change a quantity, trap that event in DHTML and submit the cart page to the server for updating without requiring a separate button to be clicked.

Suggested selling

"Would you like fries with that?"

American commerce thrives on the art of suggested selling, and e-commerce is no exception, despite the fact that fewer than one quarter of the most popular e-commerce destinations don't have any suggested selling program in place.

The key to a successful suggested selling program is to implement it in small pieces *everywhere* on your site, rather than implementing one huge add-on sales display at one point in your checkout process. Here are some ideas for implementing a constant effort to generate add-on sales:

✦ After an item is added to the shopping cart, display a list of three to four similar items, or a short list of items that other shoppers purchased along with the original item added to the cart. Aggressive suggested selling programs may want to add one or two suggested items directly to the customer's cart. This is acceptable with the right demographic, especially if you take pains to make the items easily removable. This works best with add-ons like extended service agreements, which many customers purchase with expensive products like home electronics.

✦ On every product detail page, include a short list of similar items for the customer's consideration.

✦ If you have a class of items that do extraordinarily well as add-on items, consider dedicating a page in your checkout to these items. For example, a site that sells portable electronics may include a "Don't forget the batteries" page in the checkout process that offers the appropriate batteries for the customer. This can help increase sales, as well as provide a useful service to customers. Make sure that your product detail pages indicate that the customer doesn't need to search your site for the correct batteries because you'll offer them for sale automatically during checkout.

✦ If a customer is placing an order for out-of-stock merchandise, modify your cart to display alternate in-stock choices under the out-of-stock item. A single click should remove the out-of-stock item and insert the selected alternative. Figure 3-11 shows an example.

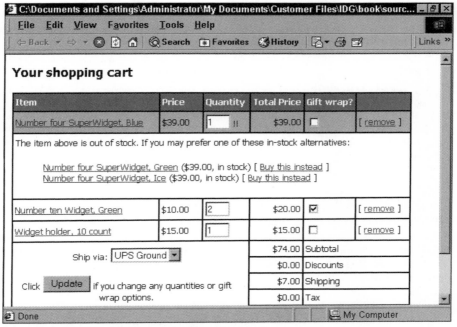

Figure 3-11: Suggesting in-stock alternatives in the cart

Tip

Suggested selling requires your catalog database to know which products "go" with other products. Commerce Server 2000 makes this somewhat easier than in prior versions by specifically supporting product profiles for targeted sales techniques like suggested selling.

In all circumstances, make sure that the suggested selling technique is easy for shoppers to use:

✦ A click on the product description should go right to the product's detail page.

✦ Next to every product should be a "Buy" button that immediately adds the product to the customer's cart.

✦ If you present add-on items in a pop-up window rather than in the main browser window, don't redirect the main window to the shopping cart after adding the add-on item to the cart. Instead, allow the main browser window to stay where it is, giving the shopper an uninterrupted shopping experience.

Most e-commerce sites should have no reason *not* to use suggested selling, provided that you design the process to involve as few clicks and interruptions as possible.

Checkout

Reducing clicks in the checkout process is primarily a function of a well-thought-out process. More so than anywhere else on your site, the real task is to balance "too much information at once" against "too many clicks." After all, you could complete the entire checkout process on a single screen if you didn't mind using a somewhat lengthy page to collect the necessary information.

Flowchart your checkout process to spot redundancies. Rearrange the process on paper to come up with the most streamlined flowchart possible. Remember that "reducing clicks" also means "reducing keystrokes." Spend some time shopping on the Web to experience the different types of checkout processes that other designers have thought of, note the parts that you like and don't like, and pay attention to the processes that may resemble your own.

Opt-in programs in the checkout process

Many e-commerce sites choose to use the checkout as a means of enrolling customers in various marketing programs, typically e-mail newsletters or similar programs. Enough e-commerce sites use this practice that customers will generally accept it as a standard business practice, provided that you follow some general guidelines:

✦ I advise against dedicating a separate page to your opt-in programs in the checkout process, because doing so distracts buyers from the main task of checking out. Instead, place checkboxes on one of the main checkout pages, such as the page requesting the customer's e-mail address.

✦ Don't try to enroll customers in more than two programs at once. Doing so creates the need for the customer to click too many times. This is especially true if the checkboxes for enrollment are checked by default.

✦ Avoid negative actions, such as requiring a customer to "click here if you do not wish to receive a suggested item." You can provide a checkbox stating "Check here to receive our e-mail newsletter" and have the checkbox checked by default. If customers un-check the checkbox, however, you must not only refrain from enrolling them, you must also note their preference. Future checkouts should un-check the box by default, thus saving the customer the additional click.

Opt-ins in the checkout are an inevitable result of the way people use Web sites. Because the opt-in programs generally benefit the e-commerce company more than the shopper, the opt-in winds up in the only place where the site has a somewhat captive audience. Never forget, though, how tenuous the checkout can be, and never let the opt-in programs interfere with the customers' task of completing their order.

One technique for enrolling customers in programs during the checkout without interfering is to use pop-up windows. Customers have the option to ignore the window until they've finished checking out. Another technique is [...] enrollment information on the order confirmation page after the act[...] complete. In both cases, customers have the opportunity to ignore t[...]

Perhaps the ultimate method for successfully incorporating opt-in progr[...] the checkout is to include two radio buttons near the form for the custo[...] billing information. The first radio button should be labeled "Sign me up [...] e-mail newsletters," or something appropriate to your site. The second b[...] should be labeled "Let me choose which newsletters to receive after I fini[...] ing out." Customers have the option to enroll in all of your programs, or [...] sented with a list of available programs after they've finished checking ou[...] approach prevents any major distractions in the checkout process and — [...] tomer selects the second option — creates a sense of obligation that will h[...] have them enrolling in a couple of your marketing programs after their ord[...] complete. Be aware, though, that some customers may be upset at not bein[...] a definite negative option like "Don't enroll me in any programs."

Available technologies

A variety of technologies can help your checkout process. Select the technologies that fit your target audience while helping implement the checkout process you've designed.

Cookies

Many Web sites that forgo the use of cookies still require shoppers to accept them in order to check out. Many sites built in Site Server 3.0 Commerce Edition (SSCE) have little choice; SSCE is extremely "cookie friendly" and makes building a check-out process, including the shopping cart, difficult without the use of cookies. The information I give previously in this chapter on cookies still applies, however, and you should seriously consider taking the time to develop a site that doesn't need them, if possible. I show you exactly how to do this in Part II of this book.

Forms

Forms are the primary component of the checkout process. You can employ a variety of methods to make forms more engaging, less daunting, and more conducive to a pleasant buying experience. As stated in my previous discussion on forms for the browsing experience, many of these tips are merely good graphic design and layout practices, such as making the forms easy to read and understand. Others are unique to good Web design:

✦ Ensure that each form of the checkout process can be completely displayed on a single screen, without scrolling, at your target resolution. Customers often miss information that requires them to scroll, so they spend more time figuring out what they did wrong and correcting errors.

indicate which information on the form is required by boldfacing field names, coloring them red, or employing a technique of your choice. State the technique to your customers for clarity. This is especially important in the checkout, where correct information is critical if you are to successfully process the customer's order.

✦ Use DHTML to validate as much of the form's information as possible before submitting it to the server. DHTML provides instant feedback to the shopper, allowing them to provide missing information or correct errors without waiting for a new page to load. Make sure that all of the required information is present, and validate information to the greatest degree possible. For example, if you don't accept orders that will be shipped to APO or FPO addresses or PO boxes, check for that before submitting the page. Likewise, perform a MOD-10 check on credit card numbers to be sure they were properly typed before submitting a payment information page to the server.

✦ When errors are made, clearly indicate where they are by coloring the appropriate sections of the form, or by highlighting them in some other obvious fashion. Use error messages that can be easily understood by the least-experienced customers in your demographic. Style tags can be used in DHTML to color the offending form fields in an easily-noticeable color, such as light red, thus immediately drawing the shopper's attention to the correct location.

✦ Whenever possible, allow customers to choose from a list rather than type information. When customers must type information, try to fill in a default value for them if possible. Again, this is especially important when collecting address and payment information. Use drop-down boxes for credit card expiration dates and state names, rather than making customers type this information.

✦ Use DHTML to hide portions of the form that aren't necessary. For example, if a customer checks a checkbox indicating that their shipping address is the same as the billing address that they already typed, hide the shipping address portion of the form. At the very least, use DHTML to copy the information from the billing address fields to the shipping address fields.

✦ Name your form fields with standard, common sense names. For example, use "City" for a form field where users would logically type the city portion of their shipping address. Many browsers, such as Internet Explorer, feature *auto complete* technology that enables the browser to help the user fill in form fields. Because many Web sites use a form field named "City," the browser will recognize the form field name on your site and allow the user to choose the city that they've typed on other Web sites, thus reducing the time that the user has to spend filling in information. Other add-on technologies, such as the various HTML-based "wallet" packages, use form field names similarly. Use graphic logos to indicate which wallet packages have been tested and found compatible. Encouraging your customers to use these packages will result in faster, more accurate checkouts and happier customers.

Multi-form navigation

The use of multi-form navigation in the checkout process is basically identical to the use of this technology in designing the shopping experience.

Java applets

Several Java-based shopping cart/checkout applets are available, ranging in price from several hundred dollars to free. Check out www.scriptsearch.com for a long list of applets, or search on your favorite Internet search engine for "Java shopping cart" to get a bevy of results.

The limitation of these applets is their inability to be easily customized to meet your exact needs. If you're trying to put a site together in a hurry, these tools can provide ready-made and near-ready-made solutions. A quick tour of the major e-commerce destinations on the Web, however, turns up very few Java-based sites. Unfortunately, the Java Virtual Machines (JVMs) built into even the most recent browsers still suffer from performance problems, and have the major disadvantage that many users disable them or never enable them at all.

Note　　If you've settled on Commerce Server 2000 as your primary commerce development platform, then you should plan to use the non-Java checkout process that it uses. It's more robust, more flexible, and intended for large-volume sites.

Dynamic HTML

DHTML can be cleverly combined with other technologies to considerably enhance the buying experience. Earlier in this chapter, I discuss how DHTML can allow customers to modify their shopping cart contents with a minimum of additional page loads, and how DHTML can be used to improve how you handle forms by providing instant feedback for simple validation errors. I also talk about how DHTML can be used to speed up the form-filling process by copying information from one set of form fields to another.

DHTML can also be used to present additional information on the checkout screens that customers may not need. For example, if you've chosen to make gift-wrapping selection part of your checkout process, you can display a single checkbox labeled "None of these items will be gift wrapped." This box is checked by default, and unchecking it causes a DHTML script to display a whole new form that allows customers to make wrapping selections. Similar techniques can be used to include discount information ("I have no discounts or coupons") or multiple shipping items ("All of these items will ship to the same address").

A clever programmer can even make the entire checkout process fit on a single page, and use DHTML to make different sections of the page "appear" as the customer clicks "Next" and "Previous" buttons. After all of the form fields are filled out, more DHTML code can be used to perform an initial validation of the information that the customer has provided, and then submit the single mega-form to the server for processing. Even though this is more complex to build and debug, this type of form means that the customer only has to wait for two page loads (the checkout form and the order confirmation form), helping to ensure that customers follow through on their orders, rather than abandoning them.

Tip   You can use IIS' browser capabilities detection component to determine whether or not your customer's browser supports DHTML, and direct them to a less-rich page if it doesn't.

Generating stickiness

Stickiness is an e-commerce term that has come into heavy use with the proliferation of e-commerce sites. Like a "sticky note" that stays attached to your computer monitor, a "sticky" Web site keeps customers coming back, over and over. Because reliable repeat sales are the cornerstone of any business, finding ways to bring your customers back is critical to your site's success and long life.

Generating stickiness is generally the task of a dedicated marketing department or contracted marketing firm. Creating a sticky Web site, however, requires attention to every detail on the site, and many marketing programs integrate tightly with the many features and functions on a site. Make sure that you as the site's designer are closely involved in any discussions about how your site will be designed for stickiness. You should also be thinking about how the various methods of generating stickiness will affect the overall design of your site.

You can employ three basic, non-commercial tactics to get people to come back to a business. These methods are the same for any business, whether it's an online retailer, a utility company, an online portal site, or a "brick-and-mortar" retailer. Ideally, your business will use a combination of these three methods to create a more effective "stickiness campaign." The methods are:

- ✦ Making your business pleasant to deal with by catering to the customer's individual needs.
- ✦ Giving the customer a financial or tangible reward for coming back.
- ✦ Asking your customer to come back.

The traditional, "brick-and-mortar" retail industry has found these methods to be most effective in the order that I've listed them, although many e-commerce sites implement them in reverse order, beginning with sending out e-mails to encourage customers to return.

Take department store retailer Nordstrom, for example. They are famous for their personal shopper service, which is available for free to all of their customers. A polite Nordstrom employee literally shops the store for you, asking you for your preferences, giving advice on what clothes go well together, providing their opinion as to what looks best on you, and so forth. Although Nordstrom certainly uses media advertising like print and television to bring customers into their stores (the last method), it's the personal shopper service that caters to the individual customer (the first method) for which the store is famous.

Whenever an e-commerce site is being designed, everyone involved in the process recognizes that certain compromises must be made. After all, only a certain amount of development time is available, and resources like personnel and money are limited, so no site can possibly accommodate every feature that the management team may want to implement in the first phase. Too often, a compromise is made for less effective stickiness techniques, such as sending out e-mail newsletters, rather than spending the time to develop a site that caters to individual customers' wants and needs.

Unfortunately, creating a site that's personalized for your shoppers is also far more difficult to retrofit into a site that's already up and running. As a result, many e-commerce companies never bother to implement that kind of functionality, and as a result, they miss out on the most lucrative form of stickiness. As you design your e-commerce site, keep in mind that personalization may be difficult to develop, but it will be far more difficult to add in later, and properly done, it remains the most effective means of bringing customers back to your site.

In the event that personalization will require more time and resources than you have available, don't automatically jump down to the "ask your customers to come back" category and start sending out e-mails. Talk to your marketing group about creating incentives, called *loyalty programs*, to get customers to return to your site. This is especially important if you are competing for business with other e-commerce sites. Loyalty programs can make the difference between a customer going to your site, or to one of the competitors.

If all else fails, make sure to develop some kind of stickiness program by using e-mail and other forms of communications to invite customers back to your site on a regular basis. Don't forget that the way to generate stickiness is to use a combination of these methods in a carefully planned overall program of customer loyalty.

In the next three sections, I discuss how each of the stickiness methods can be implemented on an e-commerce site through personalization, loyalty programs, and communications. I tell you what Microsoft tools can be used to help implement them, and most importantly, I tell you how they can each impact your site's overall design. I also show you how to actually implement these methods in Part II of this book.

Personalization

Even though it's the most technically complex sticky tactic, personalization is easily the most effective. By taking the time to learn your customers' interests, needs, and preferences, you can have your site customize itself for them. Customers not only appreciate the effort, they also appreciate a shopping experience that typically requires less time and effort on their part to locate and purchase the products and services that they want. Examples of effective personalization include:

✦ Reordering navigation menus so that a customer's favorite departments appear first.

✦ Suggesting additional products similar to those that the customer has shown interest in on past visits.

✦ Featuring products that are similar to those the customer has purchased in the past.

✦ Selecting content, such as project ideas or site-related news, that targets to the customer's interests.

✦ Customizing the site behavior based on the customer's preferences, such as allowing customers to create their own home page for the site, with "modules" of information, such as featured products or content, that the customer selects.

Site Server Commerce Edition and Commerce Server both feature extensive capabilities for personalization. In fact, Commerce Server 2000 features a complete Targeting system design to match profiles for products and Web site pages with customer profiles, creating a personalized, targeted shopping experience for your customers.

Recognize that a personalized shopping experience is not only more complex and time-consuming to create, it also places a much heavier demand on your server hardware. For example, if you plan to create a navigation system that personalizes itself to your customers' shopping patterns, then you can't take advantage of statically created navigation pages, which load more quickly. Instead, the navigation elements must be dynamically generated to meet the current customer's needs, meaning more overhead on your Web servers and particularly on your database servers. If you will be running a large personalized site, plan to build a significantly more robust back-end data tier involving multiple database clusters that replicate information to each other.

Seriously assess the impact of personalization before you implement it. Personalization is key to the most successful e-commerce sites because customers seek to differentiate between the huge array of online companies offering goods and services. Personalization is not a free advantage, however — it requires a significant investment in design, money, time, hardware, and personnel to work properly. If you can't afford to implement personalization in the first phase of your site's development, then you should plan for the eventual personalization that you desire. This way, the first phase of your site can be built with that personalization in mind, thus reducing the cost of implementing it later.

Loyalty programs

Loyalty programs can take many forms. In "brick-and-mortar" retail stores, for example, such programs often involve "frequent shopper" cards. Traditional retailers, both of products and services, use some of the following loyalty programs:

✦ Programs that award dollars-off certificates after a certain dollar amount has been purchased.

✦ Programs that offer a percentage discount off of every purchase.

✦ One-time coupons sent out to frequent shoppers for special events, such as birthdays or Christmas.

✦ Point-accumulation programs that award points for every dollar purchased, and provide awards for which those points can be redeemed.

✦ Affiliate programs that pay a commission to individuals who advertise your Web site on their own Web sites. The commission is based on sales made by customers who click through to your site from the affiliate's site.

Some programs combine two or more of the above loyalty programs to form their own unique programs. Understanding which programs your company will utilize can drastically affect your site design plans, because every one of them requires additional programming and planning on your part.

What's more, almost all of these programs can be implemented internally — specific to your Web site and company — or they can be implemented as a partnership with companies that specialize in loyalty programs. For example, Commission Junction (CJ) sets up and maintains affiliate programs for several leading Web sites. Every month, CJ provides reports that indicate which affiliates have referred customers to your site, and with a list of the order numbers that those customers placed. You are responsible for interfacing those reports with your systems to obtain additional reporting information on those orders.

Other loyalty companies help build more traditional loyalty programs for you. ClickMiles allows shoppers to earn points for every dollar that they spend on your site. These points can then be exchanged for merchandise and services, or transferred to shoppers' airline frequent flier accounts as miles. Although programs like this will cost you a percentage of every sale, they provide a reason for shoppers to shop at your site rather than the competition, even if that competition is a "brick-and-mortar" store.

You can also take advantage of programs with most major credit card banks that create "affinity" credit cards. These credit cards allow shoppers to accumulate discounts and free merchandise from your site simply by charging purchases on the credit card. Typically, they earn additional bonus credits for charging purchases to the card at your site. These programs often cost little or nothing to start, and the discounts are often paid for by the credit card bank out of their profit on the card's interest fees. Affinity cards also function as free advertising because your site's logo and color scheme are often used in the card's design.

With Commerce Server 2000, you can also implement certain types of loyalty programs, such as providing discounts to shoppers based on their shopping history, and so forth. I get into more detail about how to use these features in Part II.

Tip

Working with a third party like ClickMiles or Commission Junction is often easier than managing your own private loyalty program. You get more visibility because they are larger programs, and you can take advantage of their advertising to drive people to your site.

Communications

Communication is one of the easiest forms of stickiness to implement. Customers will frequently sign up for e-mail on your Web site, but you still need to address a few questions before you can begin incorporating customer communications into your site:

✦ **Where will customers sign up?** From anywhere on your site, from the checkout process, or from some other place? Will you be buying or renting e-mail addresses from other companies?

✦ **How will you track where your e-mail addresses came from?** If you're collecting names from different places, you should know where they came from so that you can monitor the response.

✦ **How will you track the results of your e-mails?** Whether you're issuing a discount code or tracking the number of people who click on links in the e-mail, you need to have some way of judging the response and success of the e-mail. Ultimately, the success is measured in increased sales, but you need a way to associate increased sales with specific e-mails to help you decide what works and what doesn't work in future e-mails.

✦ **How will customers remove themselves from the lists?** Any "opt-out" process should be easy for customers to find and complete. Ideally, customers should be able to send an "unsubscribe me" e-mail to a particular address, or click a link in the e-mail to be automatically removed from the list.

✦ **Who will be pulling the lists together when it's time to send e-mails?** You probably don't want to send e-mail to your entire list every time, so you'll need a tool that can be used to specify which e-mail addresses are desired recipients for a particular e-mail. Ideally, this tool should be designed so that the group responsible for writing the e-mail — often the marketing department — can also pull up the list, thus reducing overhead on the technology department. The complexity of the queries will determine the complexity of the tool. For example, do you anticipate sending e-mails to buyers? Or will you be sending e-mails to buyers who have purchased specific merchandise during a specific time frame?

✦ **How will the e-mails be sent?** If you're planning to send ten thousand e-mails over your company's T1 line from your Exchange Server through your ISP's mail relay server — think again. Most ISPs have strong restrictions on sending bulk e-mail through their systems, and Exchange Server requires specialized knowledge and architecture to be able to directly deliver thousands of e-mails. Many companies use third-party e-mail services like MessageReach to deliver their bulk e-mail, so make sure you've taken into account the cost of such services (which can be as high as $.05 per e-mail).

✦ **How many types of e-mail will you offer?** If your marketing department tells you that they're only going to offer a single e-mail "newsletter," then they're probably not thinking far enough ahead. Any design that you create should allow users to sign up for one or many different newsletters, allow lists to be pulled reflecting the newsletters that users have signed up for, and allow users to remove themselves from all or a certain number of the lists.

✦ **Will your e-mail be sent out as straight text or HTML?** Who will write the e-mail, and what will the approval process be? Can you purchase or build a tool to make the e-mail creation something that a non-technical employee can take care of, or will your HTML programmers also be responsible for designing outgoing HTML marketing newsletters? If a custom tool is required, how complex will it have to be, and how long will it take to write?

✦ **Who will be responsible for handling "bounced" e-mail?** Can you find a way to automate this? A clever Exchange Server script programmer can write scripts to handle incoming "undeliverable" messages and automatically remove those e-mail addresses from future lists. This is especially important if you're paying per e-mail address for your e-mails to be sent.

✦ **Will you rent or sell your e-mail lists to other companies?** If so, make sure that you clearly indicate this possibility to customers when they provide their e-mail address to you. If you acquire e-mail addresses through several methods, ensure that every method provides this warning, or keep track of the e-mail addresses that can be sold and rented (and those that can't) because the customers have been notified of the possibility. If you will sell or rent e-mail lists, how will you generate those lists? What format will they be provided in? What tools will be used to generate those lists?

✦ **How will you keep track of when an e-mail address was acquired?** E-mail addresses can become "stale," and if you are paying per address to send e-mails, you want to be able to track which ones are generating responses — especially sales — and delete e-mail addresses that have not generated a response in a given period of time. In order to do this, you need to know when you acquired the address and when an e-mail last generated a response from that address.

In this age of *spam*, or "junk" e-mail, blocked senders lists, and general e-mail abuse, your company should take care to follow some rules of etiquette with your e-mail communications. Some of these rules require technical support, so be prepared to incorporate the necessary support into your overall site design.

✦ Never send an e-mail to someone who has not asked to receive it. If you're renting or buying addresses from another company, make sure that the people on that list were notified that their e-mail addresses were subject to sale or rental at the time they provided the address to that other company. Do *not* send e-mails to any of your customers who haven't been offered the chance to "opt out" of receiving e-mail from you.

✦ Ensure that all e-mails contain instructions that the recipients can follow to remove themselves from the list. Test these instructions to make sure that they're flawless.

✦ Make sure that you keep a list of people who have asked to be removed from your lists, and make sure you run that "negative" list against any future mailings, so you don't accidentally send them e-mail again.

✦ Keep your e-mails reasonably infrequent. Targeted e-mails that are sent infrequently to a small audience will have more effect than daily e-mails sent to your entire mailing list.

Caution The quickest way to lose the goodwill — and future sales — of a customer is to send them unsolicited e-mail. Don't do it.

The key to successful marketing communications is to make them as targeted as possible. For example, an e-mail describing a great new Widget product has more effect on customers who have purchased Widgets in the past than on customers who only purchase Gadgets. Unfortunately, pulling this type of information out of a database — particularly the default Commerce Server database — can be difficult and time-consuming. Spend time talking with your marketing department and determine how they want to use the data that your database is collecting. Determine what changes can be reasonably made in the first phase of development, and come to an agreement with them on what functionality should be made available to the marketing department for sending e-mails. Make sure that you clearly document these decisions and agreements as part of your formal project documentation for future reference.

Typically, marketing is the second-largest consumer of back-end functionality and reporting, and marketing e-mails play heavily into their requirements. Ideally, you need to expand your Commerce Server database to attach many new attributes to each shopper entry. Your marketing department may conduct online surveys to help better target customer interests and preferences, and the results of these surveys need to be attached to individual shoppers whenever possible. Customers may sign up for many different e-mail newsletters, and these voluntary enrollments should be attached to their shopper entry in the database. Every piece of information regarding a sale must be recorded and traceable to a shopper for marketing purposes. Take the time to fully understand what your marketing department expects to be able to do, and make sure that everyone agrees on the actual functionality to be delivered.

Commerce Server 2000 provides powerful Campaign Manager, List Manager, and Direct Mailer components that greatly assist with the tasks of building and managing lists, performing direct mail pieces that can be tracked through to the sale, and managing specific, targeted marketing campaigns.

E-mail communications can be a powerful tool for generating stickiness. The key to a successful implementation of e-mail communications is to design the functionality as part of the site rather than trying to tack it on afterwards.

Customer self-service

Creating an effective customer self-service system can help your company save money by reducing the number of customer service representatives needed to staff a customer service line, and can greatly improve your customers' overall experience and satisfaction with your site. The vast majority of Internet shoppers prefer to help themselves. That's why they choose to shop over the Internet.

Examine the areas of your site that are good targets for customer self-service. Some examples include:

✦ Checking the status of an order that has been placed.

✦ Making changes to a customer's profile, password, user name, e-mail address, preferred addresses, methods of payment, and so forth.

✦ Providing product-support information, such as how to operate or make adjustments to a product.

✦ Downloading updates, such as new device drivers or product manuals.

✦ Managing participation in e-mail newsletters, "wish lists," and the like.

✦ Accepting customer complaints and comments.

✦ Allowing customers to modify an order that they have placed, or canceling all or part of an order that has not yet been shipped.

Take my advice: Make sure your site implements as many of these self-service features as possible. I worked with a company that didn't implement *any* of these self-service features and customers were forced to make a phone call just to change their password or check the status of an order. This meant a serious amount of incoming phone calls, which resulted in a perpetually overburdened customer support staff. Your "live" support staff should be available to handle the most difficult cases, and can mean the difference between a customer's satisfaction and dissatisfaction. Make sure that these employees aren't tied up with mundane, day-to-day issues like password or e-mail address changes that customers can just as easily perform themselves.

Tip Any information that you collect from a customer is bound to change eventually. If you're going to collect and save any customer information, make sure to provide some way for the customers to update that information on their own.

In an effort to reduce clicks and information overload, a self-service area is a good place to gather more information and offer more options than you may be presenting in other areas of your site. For example, in the interests of simplicity, your checkout process may only allow customers to provide the same address for shipping and billing. In your self-service "customer profile" section, however, you can allow customers to maintain a more complex "address book" and multiple forms of payment. The next time they check out, they can select this information rather than typing it into the checkout, thus saving them time.

Make sure you take the time to design your customers' self-service experience as carefully as you designed your browsing checkout processes. Customers should feel welcomed by the self-service functionality, they should be able to quickly begin the self-service task that they came to complete, and they should feel that additional, "live" help is only a phone call away — particularly for service issues like order information or complaints.

If you create a self-service area to handle complaints, make sure that the customer receives immediate feedback indicating that the information has been accepted, and then provide a definite timeline for a reply, such as 48 hours, 5 days, etc. Repeat this information in an automated follow-up e-mail so the customer will know you're working on their problem. Too often, online complaint-handling systems drop customers' comments into a low-priority queue, saving the customer service department's time for complaints being called in. This process defeats the entire purpose of online self-service, however, which is to *encourage* customers to use the site rather than the phone. Set rules and guidelines about how customer online complaints will be handled, and stick with them.

Your self-service area can also include "live" online support. This method of customer service has become popular on high-volume Web sites, and can result in significant savings on incoming phone charges to a toll-free number. In most implementations, customers submit a question, which is immediately submitted to a live operator's queue. A browser window remains open, and the live operator's response appears in that window as soon as the query has been handled. If necessary, the operator can launch a live chat window to further interact with the customer and gather additional information. CyberRep.com is a good example of a company that offers customer service outsourcing and innovative online service technologies.

No matter what kind of self-service offerings your site provides, make sure that they are effective. Nothing is more frustrating for customers who want to help themselves than to discover that your site won't let them do what they want. Checking their order status, for example, isn't very useful if you don't provide a tracking number so customers can see when their package is due to be delivered. It's good practice to be able to tell a customer that a product is backordered, but it's even better to be able to tell them when you expect to receive more of the product. Make sure that your self-service offering is complete, and that it provides the information and results that customers will expect when they sign on.

Microsoft's e-commerce technologies provide many of the pieces that you need in order to create an effective self-service offering. However, you should never limit yourself to providing only the services that these technologies can support. Determine what services you need to offer, and then locate additional technologies as necessary to provide the customer experience that you've designed.

In this section, I cover some of the most common forms of customer self-service, and talk about the technologies that you can use to implement them.

Note　Make sure that your self-service offerings are in line with your company's customer service philosophy. This philosophy will dictate, for example, how easily customers can get to a live customer support representative.

Downloads

You can provide access to downloads on your Web site. IIS also supports the creation of FTP sites, allowing customers who are comfortable with FTP to download from your site. You can use Commerce Server's membership directory to help secure the download area of your site so that only registered shoppers, or shoppers who have actually purchased a particular product, can access that area.

Order status

Commerce Server's default database schema doesn't provide any specific means for tracking order status. This is largely because every e-commerce company handles order processing differently. For example, some companies maintain their own inventory in their own warehouses, so they can easily track the progress of an order through the fulfillment and shipping process. Because these companies actually ship the product to the customer, the tracking number from the shipping carrier is readily available. Companies in this situation must interface their warehouse and fulfillment systems with the Commerce Server database to attach the appropriate status and tracking information to the order header.

Other e-commerce companies utilize *virtual warehousing*, which means that they don't maintain any inventory at all. Instead, they deliver order information to their distributors several times each day and the distributors are responsible for actually shipping the orders. Depending on the business agreement between the e-commerce company and the distributor, package tracking numbers and order status information may or may not be available at all.

Service-based companies may have a situation with aspects similar to both traditional warehousing and virtual warehousing. Companies providing the services to the final customer can track important information, such as appointment times, personnel dispatch information, and so forth. Companies reselling services from a third party may or may not have access to this information.

Your ability to provide order status information and order tracking depends on the business model that your company has adopted and the agreements that you have with any business partners involved in the order fulfillment process. At a bare minimum, you should be able to let customers know when their order has been sent to the fulfillment channel — whether that channel is internal to your company or handled by outside distributors — and provide tracking information after the package has shipped.

Product support

Often, customers want to return to your site after a purchase to obtain additional product information and support. A common way to provide this support in a self-service format is to use a *knowledge base*. A knowledge base is a database of product information that includes manuals, data sheets, and so forth, which customers can search by using keywords. Microsoft Site Server provides an excellent Knowledge Base system that you can use to build a self-help system for your site. You just need to provide the actual self-help content in a format that Site Server Search can read and index, including text files, Office documents like Word and Excel, and Adobe Acrobat files.

Customers often look to newsgroups for product support, where they can search for information, and ask questions of other customers.

Comment and complaint handling

You have a couple of options for building a robust comment and complaint handling system for your site. Your first option is to use Microsoft SQL Server, which stores customer information in database tables and writes a series of stored procedures and jobs to make sure that these comments are addressed in a timely fashion (perhaps by sending reminder e-mails to customer service managers when comments go unanswered after a specified period of time).

You can also utilize Microsoft Exchange Server. This option allows you to more easily set up workflow rules, create automated initial responses letting customers know that their comment was successfully received, and so forth. Exchange server-side scripting can be used to route messages to customer service representatives upon arrival, and can even be used to create a workflow process that, for example, requires a customer service manager to approve all responses before they are routed to the customer.

The option that you choose depends primarily on your environment, the level of flexibility that you require, and the amount of development that you can deal with. For a basic comment-handling system, using Exchange Server will require less development and integration time than using SQL Server, but using SQL Server does offer the ability to write an entire custom front-end for your customer service representatives to use.

Profile editing

Because Commerce Server exposes all of a customer's information in its SQL Server databases, you can use ASP and COM to write any kind of profile-editing tools that you want to provide to your customers. Make sure that your database schema supports the functionality that you want to deliver to your customers. For example, the default Commerce Server schema doesn't provide for payment information to be attached to a customer profile, so you will need to modify the default schema if you intend to provide this functionality.

Whatever you do, follow the rules for creating a satisfying browsing and buying experience when designing your self-service tools. Make sure that the tools are easy to understand, require a minimum amount of information to be entered, and provide feedback to the customer in the form of easy-to-understand messages — especially in the event of customer mistakes or site errors.

Customer support

Sometimes self-service isn't enough. Customers may need assistance from someone in your company (or at least an agent of your company) to handle their service issue.

Your company's customer service philosophy dictates the different types of customer support that you provide, and the ease with which customers can find your means of support. For example, you may prominently display an e-mail address to which customers can send support requests, but require more digging to locate a phone number they can call. Or, your company may place its customer service phone number on every page of the Web site, thus encouraging customers to call in.

Your company may also opt to use newer forms of live customer support, such as online chat and instant messaging services designed for customer support and service. In this case, you need to provide the necessary integration between the site and your customer support technologies.

Carefully define what tasks your customer service representatives can handle. Provide them with the technological support necessary to enable them to handle these tasks. If your company is outsourcing their customer service line — a common practice in the e-commerce industry — then you need to provide technological support to those representatives, who may not be located at your facility.

Enabling technologies

A variety of technologies are available to connect customers to customer service representatives. If your company chooses to "roll its own" support infrastructure, you will need to look at some of the following technologies to implement effective solutions. Your company may also choose to use third-party technologies to provide online support, such as the variety of "call me now" and "online service" technologies offered by professional customer support firms.

Exchange Server

Exchange Server represents Microsoft's most robust set of technologies for personal interaction. Exchange Server allows you to automate the handling of incoming e-mail through server-side scripting. Exchange Server also supports robust chat technology, including the ability to host moderated chat rooms, which can be a form of online customer service chat. Exchange also offers instant messaging through the MSN Messenger IM client. With the exception of e-mail, none of these technologies are specifically designed to support a customer service environment, so you'll have to make tradeoffs in functionality. However, if you already have Exchange Server in your environment, these technologies can represent a way to interact with your customers until more robust, service-specific technologies can be deployed.

Exchange Server also supports Internet newsgroups. Creating customer support newsgroups and assigning employees to monitor and respond to them can often help several customers at once.

Internet Information Server

IIS supports many of the same technologies as Exchange Server, albeit on a smaller scale. IIS's NNTP service allows you to host newsgroups, although IIS offers less control over the newsgroups and requires more ongoing maintenance than newsgroups that are hosted on an Exchange Server. Likewise, IIS allows you to host an SMTP mail site, but this functionality is primarily intended for outgoing mail (at the time of this writing) rather than for handling incoming mail from customers. Although this is useful for sending automated replies, it isn't useful for allowing customer interaction with customer service representatives.

Supporting the support staff

Commerce Server's base administrative tools may or may not be sufficient to support your customer service organization. The requirements of your support staff should be an important part of your site's functional specification, and should reflect the types of tasks that they will be performing. Consider the following:

✦ **Will support staff need to modify orders?** Will they need to be able to bypass the usual rules for calculating prices, shipping, taxes, and so forth? You may need to develop a separate Commerce Server pipeline for orders submitted by customer service to enable them to sell items at a lower price, to lower or eliminate shipping charges, etc.

✦ **Will the support staff need to search for orders in the system?** The likely answer is yes, and you'll need to find out what information they will have to search with. They may be searching for a customer name, a phone number, an order number, or even just a billing zip code or credit card number. Plan for an interface that offers as much flexibility as possible.

✦ **Your staff may have to help less experienced customers complete tasks that are normally done through your self-service offerings.** Make sure that the support staff can modify customers' address information, credit card numbers, and other stored information.

Find out what other tasks your support staff expects to accomplish on a regular basis, and make sure that your site's functional specification provides them with the necessary tools and interfaces to accomplish these tasks as quickly as possible, so that they can efficiently help as many customers as possible.

Robustness

You want your e-commerce site to be robust, and it's measured in far more than just downtime. Robustness also includes the speed at which your site operates, the speed at which pages download to customers, and the speed at which orders are placed. These factors all require you to identify potential bottlenecks in your site design, and force you to consider factors such as hardware, site operations, software, network connectivity, and more.

Consider the costs involved. Although it's possible to build an e-commerce site that literally never goes down, the cost of doing so is considerably higher than building a site that goes down one or two percent of the year. And although it's possible to build a site that delivers every page with lightning speed, doing so is difficult and will place some restrictions on the actual functionality of your site.

You can improve the robustness of your site using several different methods, which I discuss in detail in Part II. Some of these are intended to help increase the overall reliability of your site, while others are intended to increase the overall responsiveness of your site.

✦ Adding additional Web servers to your server farm can help increase both responsiveness, by taking the load off of the other servers, and reliability, by acting as a backup for any servers that may go down. Windows Network Load Balancing is available to balance incoming traffic between servers, and Application Center 2000 is available to help ease the burden of managing a large farm of Web servers.

✦ Reducing dependence on your database — or alternatively, building an extremely robust data tier — can improve responsiveness by eliminating the data tier as a bottleneck or by providing sufficient throughput that it isn't a bottleneck, and can improve reliability by eliminating a single point of failure in the data tier. Reduce database dependence by not querying unchanging information from the database for every page load. For example, product detail information can be written to static files for faster display by a larger number of Web servers.

✦ Decreasing page size can improve responsiveness by allowing pages to download to customers more quickly. Decrease page size by being careful with your HTML to avoid unnecessary tags (such as using small Cascading Style Sheets instead of a thousand <FONT> tags in your pages), and by avoiding the frequent use of large graphics.

✦ Clustering can be used in your data tier to improve reliability and, with active-active clustering, to improve responsiveness. Clusters allow a "spare" server to take over in the event that the main server fails, and active-active clustering allows each node in a cluster to perform useful work rather than just acting as a "standby" for the main server.

✦ Careful partitioning of your site's functionality can increase both reliability and responsiveness. For example, having each Web server perform general browsing, checkout, search, and other functionality, can place a significant and varied load on each one. By breaking these functions down into a browsing server, a search server, a checkout server, and so forth, you can distribute the type of load across the different servers. Different servers can be specifically configured to handle the type of load that they will incur, and you can add more servers in a specific category to help scale the site in a more targeted fashion.

✦ Simple hardware configuration can increase responsiveness and reliability. Use servers with redundant power supplies and other components, and ensure that your servers have sufficient resources to handle the load you intend to place on them. Windows 2000-based Web servers, for example, will benefit from the fastest disk speeds possible, and the most RAM you can fit into the computer. For simple web browsing, configuring anything more than two processors is probably overkill, and the money would be better spent on RAM or faster drives.

✦ Network connectivity can be configured to provide better reliability and responsiveness. Make sure that your network connectivity is as few hops as possible from a major Internet backbone carrier (referred to as a *first tier* carrier), and that you have sufficient bandwidth to handle the incoming customer demand. If possible, configure redundant connectivity to a different carrier in order to guard against a service outage in your main line, or to load balance between the two. Intelligent switches and routers from companies like Cisco can provide automatic network redundancy and load balancing between multiple network connections.

I talk in depth about implementing all of these technologies in Part II of this book. You can spend an almost unlimited amount of resources, especially money, beefing up servers and configuring network connectivity. To get the most bang for your buck, determine what is important to you and your customers. Also, determine how you will measure your site's responsiveness and reliability by determining *metrics*, the measurements you will use to determine if your site is meeting your company's internal goals for responsiveness and reliability.

I start with a discussion on what your customers will think of your site, and then I talk about how to develop some useful measurements to judge your site's performance.

The customer's perspective

How will your customers feel about the responsiveness and reliability of your Web site? You should consider two main factors from the *customer's* viewpoint (however unreasonable this may seem from a technical perspective):

   ✦ How quickly do pages load?

   ✦ How often do customers get an error message because the server isn't responding?

The first question includes many factors that you have no control over, such as the customer's own connection speed and the speed of their ISP, but if your site is any slower than any other Internet site, the customer will still place the blame squarely on your shoulders. The other question can also include factors outside of your control, including DNS failures, but will most likely indicate overburdened Web servers.

Obviously, you can't just ask your customers what they think of your site's performance. Although their opinions are important, they won't be able to provide objective measurements you can use to determine if performance is poor, or how to improve performance if it is poor. Instead, define some clear forms of measurement, decide what levels of performance are acceptable, and then work to maintain or exceed those performance levels. Those levels are commonly referred to as *metrics*.

Determining metrics

Metrics are points of measurement, and in this context, they measure your site's performance. For each metric, you must define exactly what is being measured, how the measurement will be taken, what measurement is desired, what measurement is adequate, and what measurement indicates that a problem exists

How often should you check your metrics? Daily isn't too often, and weekly should be the longest period of time that goes by without a check. Be sure to record your results, because as your customer base grows, your servers will work harder, and your metrics will be your first indication that it's time to add additional servers or examine your server farm's infrastructure, which should be long before your customers start experiencing delays.

What metrics should you define? In the next few paragraphs, I describe some of the most common metrics used by e-commerce sites. You may want to use these, but make sure to create metrics that measure every facet of your site that's important to your customers.

How fast do pages load?

This should be measured using the slowest computer, browser, and network connection that your customer demographic will be using. For most retail e-commerce sites, this means a 33.6kbps dial-up connection to America Online using the service provider's built-in Web browser software on a Pentium computer running Windows 95 at around 133MHz. In that configuration, an industry "best practice" load time for any single page on your Web site is 10 seconds maximum, with 6 seconds or less being preferred. Any page that requires more than 12 seconds indicates a problem — either with your site's network connectivity or the size of your page. Your home page should load two to three seconds faster than this average because it represents the customer's first contact with your site. Some pages may take longer if you indicate to the customer that the page is graphics-intensive, contains a Flash animation, or is otherwise exceptional.

Note   If you're dealing with a different demographic, create your metrics to measure from a typical customer in *that* demographic.

How often does the server fail to respond?

This is a simple measurement of how often your site can't be reached due to server overload. Regardless of the traffic hitting your site, the desired and acceptable measurement is zero times per hour. Once per hour may be acceptable in rare circumstances, but generally, even this metric should indicate a problem. Usually, adding additional Web servers to the server farm will fix the problem, but if your Web servers are heavy database users, then you may also have a database bottleneck.

How many hits can a single server take?

This metric differs from company to company. Generally, it's a measurement of how many individual *hits*, or requests for information, a single Web server can take during a fixed period of time, such as an hour. This metric can be broken down into the following:

✦ **Burst hits:** Indicate the maximum number of hits that the server can take for a short period of time, such as a few minutes.

✦ **Sustained hits:** Indicate the number of hits that the server can take per hour throughout the day.

For obvious reasons of economy, you want to drive the number of hits a server can take as high as possible while still remaining within the server's ability to handle the requests without errors. The "ultimate" configuration that allows a Web server to handle the maximum amount of hits is a completely static Web site with absolutely no database connectivity and no scripting of any kind. Your site needs both a database and scripting, but the more you can minimize those activities, the more hits each server is able to sustain. If money is no object and you can afford as many servers as necessary, then your site can make more flagrant use of scripting and database connectivity. Generally, you want to fall somewhere in between by using scripting and database connectivity as required, accompanied by an attempt to minimize unnecessary use of both.

Other metrics

You should always measure things that your customers will notice. Depending on the type of site you're creating, you may want to measure some of the following items:

- ✦ How long an order takes to complete.
- ✦ How long a typical shopping basket (containing "x" number of items) takes to display and update if a change is made.
- ✦ How long a search of average complexity takes to display results.
- ✦ How long product detail pages take to display.
- ✦ How long customers wait to receive an order-confirmation e-mail.

Again, determine what your customers feel is important about your site's performance, and develop metrics that measure those aspects of your site. Set strict minimum standards and a cutoff point that indicates a problem, allowing you to remain one step ahead of your customers in noticing performance issues.

Summary

This chapter covers considerable ground, and should give you a good start on the part of your functional specification that describes how your customers will experience your site. Remember the old adage, "measure twice and cut once?" Adapted to the e-commerce industry, it reads "plan twice, and program once." In other words, the time that you spend planning now — particularly if you spend time creating a detailed, comprehensive plan — will be repaid when you don't have to keep reprogramming the site to deal with unforeseen problems and circumstances.

The customer experience must not be allowed to happen by accident; plan, test, and continually monitor your site to make sure that your customers are receiving the experience you intend.

✦　　✦　　✦

Supporting Business Processes

Whether business processes will be established for the first time with your Web site, or whether they are already in place, your Web site has a responsibility beyond just helping customers purchase products and services. It must also support the business professionals who run your company and whose job it is to make the Web site successful. Thus, your Web site design plan must take their needs and requirements into consideration.

Making Business Processes a Priority

Business processes make businesses run, and the employees of a business understand these processes the best. Too often, I have worked with e-commerce companies (and e-commerce divisions of traditional companies) that ignore or downplay this basic fact. The result is a robust Web site that makes customers happy, but requires extensive — and unreasonable — efforts for the employees of the company to do their jobs of actually running the business.

For example, one company was a brick-and-mortar retailer with a reasonably successful mail-order division. The mail-order division had three employees who took orders over the phone and entered them into the company's AS/400. Because the AS/400 was already used for managing the company's distribution center, the system already contained inventory information and other important data. Every day, one of the mail-order employees would go into the distribution center and pack up all of the day's orders (typically, a couple dozen) for shipping.

When the company set up its first Web site and decided to accept online orders, management determined it made sense to have the mail-order division handle online orders as well. Unfortunately, that's where the planning phase stopped. The Web site was hosted off-site, and there was no integration between its database and the AS/400. Instead, the Web site wrote orders to a text file, which was then sent via FTP to the manager of the mail-order division. Each order was manually entered into the AS/400 — just as if it had been called in. When the online order volume rose to several dozen orders per day, an extra staff member was hired to input the online orders into the AS/400. When the volume rose to a couple hundred orders per day, the management team realized that the manual effort wasn't sufficient and that some type of integration was required. Because the Web site continued to amass an overwhelming number of orders each day, the integration had to be performed quickly without taking the Web site offline — precluding the possibility of a thorough integration.

In this situation, the existing business processes were in no condition to handle the volume of orders that the Web site was capable of bringing in. There was almost no automation in the mail-order division, and the burden of the Web site's order volume clearly indicated that the entire process would have to be redesigned.

Note   Don't feel ashamed if you realize that your company needs to redesign its business processes — the real shame comes from not anticipating the problem or planning for it to begin with.

Another company I worked with had a fully-planned marketing program that utilized most of the available advertising channels, such as print media, e-mail, television, and so on. With their "on the ball" methodologies, the marketing department made sure that each marketing piece had some unique information attached to it for tracking purposes. Each television and print ad, for example, included a special coupon code that customers could use to obtain a discount. E-mail pieces contained coded URLs, so that customers could be tracked by the e-mail they had received.

When the marketing department asked for reports on the number of customers who had used the coupon code for a particular television ad, they were surprised to learn that the Web site's database didn't store the information in a way that was easily accessible. In fact, a programmer spent several days pulling the required information out of the database. The marketing department was even more surprised to learn that the special codes embedded in the e-mail URLs were useless, because the site was incapable of tracking that information through to the customer's purchase. They could determine how many people had clicked each link, but not the number of purchases that had been made, let alone *what* had been purchased.

The marketing department's needs had never been part of the Web site's planning process. Because the consulting firm that originally designed the site had not been privy to the management team's marketing plans, they had made almost no provision in the code for the advanced functionality that the marketing department was expecting. This lack of planning potentially cost the company thousands of marketing dollars, because the marketing group was not clear on which marketing tactics were generating actual sales and which were simply bringing traffic to the site.

This company also experienced content-deployment problems, because the original site design didn't call for automated interfaces for content-development professionals (writers and editors). Without an automated interface, the content-development professionals weren't able to place any "free-form" content on the site. They were able to edit product information in the site's database, of course, but when they wanted to have a special promotion or create a non-standard product detail page, the IT department had to commit an HTML programmer to produce the needed pages. Had the site designers understood that the company would be frequently creating free-form Web content, they could have specified interfaces that enabled the content employees to produce and post the information without the need to tie up expensive IT personnel.

Tip It's never too early, or too late, to include your company's business professionals in the design of your site.

You need to understand what the content developers' plans are, and what they require to perform their job functions on the site. Even if your budget or timeline doesn't allow you to accommodate all of their needs in the first phase of development, you'll at least be aware of the long-term requirements and can thus design the site accordingly. You can also enlist the help of your management and other employees in prioritizing the kind of functionality the site and its administrative tools will offer. And, most importantly, by participating in the design process, the other departments will understand what the site will and will not do for them in its first phase, allowing them to adjust their plans and processes accordingly.

Most Web sites need to integrate with three major areas: marketing, content, and fulfillment. Throughout the chapter, I'll be discussing each of these areas, describing typical needs and some of the technologies you can use to support them.

One thing you should keep in the back of your head throughout this discussion is the infrastructure you plan to use for your Web site, because it will affect your technology selections. For example, will your content folks make changes directly to the live site? Or will you have some sort of development-staging-production infrastructure that governs content deployment? Will you edit product and service information in the live database for immediate use on the live site, or will that data be edited on a "staging" data server, and then replicated to the live server on a regular basis?

The more you do on the live database server, the less complex your infrastructure will be. On the other hand, when your employees perform administrative tasks against the live server, they consume processing and network bandwidth that might be better reserved for customer use. Additionally, mistakes made on a live server affect everyone immediately; mistakes made on a staging server can be corrected before they affect the live site. However, a data-staging server requires some complex technologies and compromises, including replication, latency, network connectivity, and more. Part II of this book contains a more detailed discussion of the technical issues involved with creating a staging environment, and the problems that you can run into without one, but you should start thinking now about what your ideal environment will look like from a technical point of view.

Tip Taking the time to think about how you want to set up your infrastructure will help you make better decisions about what technologies you'll choose to implement to support your company's employees.

Marketing

The majority of your marketing department's needs relate to tracking and statistics. Marketing is a "soft" trade, meaning it is sometimes difficult for businesses to directly relate a given marketing expense to a given effect on the bottom line. Marketing professionals overcome this difficulty by creating trackable marketing and advertising campaigns, and by using statistics along with tracking information to closely tie specific efforts to effects on sales.

That said, the majority of Microsoft's e-commerce products lack much of the necessary functionality. For example, Site Server 3.0 Commerce Edition provided no means whatsoever of tracking the necessary type of information. Commerce Server 2000's feature set includes targeted advertising and tracking capabilities, but the product falls short on several marketing fronts, such as detailed management of ad campaigns, powerful mailing-list management features, and tools to help calculate the marketing cost of acquiring a new customer.

In talking to your marketing department to determine exactly what capabilities they want the site to have, you are likely to run into some fairly simple requests. You should plan to implement the necessary functionality for some of these yourself, rather than relying on features built in to the Microsoft platform.

Tracking through URL codes

One common request is the site's ability to have a customer click a URL in an e-mail that contains a marketing code, and then track that code through to the customer's purchase. By attaching the code from the e-mail to the final order, you can easily determine how many of the e-mails resulted in a sale. Similarly, knowing how many customers clicked the link without making a purchase is important — the difference between the two figures is your conversion ratio. A high conversion ratio means most of the people that clicked the link bought something; a low ratio means most did not. Creating a "path" for your customers (in other words, tracking which pages they looked at while on your site) is also useful. This enables your marketing department to determine what parts of the site are engaging and successful in converting shoppers into buyers. This type of tracking can be extremely database-intensive; a common tactic is to randomly select a small portion of your incoming shoppers and track a path for them, rather than attempting to track a path for every shopper who visits the site. Because Microsoft's platform does not provide for this type of functionality, you'll either have to program it yourself or purchase a third-party suite for the task (more on that later).

Tracking customer sales

Another common request is the site's ability to report on statistics for repeat buyers. How many of your buyers make a second purchase? How long do they wait between purchases? What is their average purchase size — both in units purchased and dollars spent? How many of them make a third, or even fourth, purchase? How many make purchases only when lured in with a coupon? Commerce Server's default database schema (even in Site Server 3.0) makes collecting this type of data possible, although the table joins required to do so can be complex.

If your company utilized coupons or other discounts, your marketing department will want to know how effective they were. How many coupons were issued? How many were actually used? What was the average order amount? How many coupon users were first-time buyers? How many were repeat buyers? This type of information will be requested every time a coupon is used, so you would do well to create an interface that enables your marketing department to check the data without having to request IT assistance. The default Commerce Server database schemas generally make this information available, although the queries can be somewhat complex depending on the specific information needed.

Tracking communication flow

Your marketing department also needs a way to manage the communication programs you develop. How many users have signed up for a newsletter? How many of them have provided further demographic information? How many of them enjoy golf as a hobby? How do you create an e-mail list that includes just the golf fanatics who have never purchased from you before? While Commerce Server 2000 is light-years ahead of the previous version in making it easier to track information about your customers, you'll probably need to tweak the "standard" tools to get them just right for your company's requirements.

Much of this marketing functionality (especially data tracking) may require custom programming. You should be aware that the aim of some companies is to provide products for performing data tracking. Some of the products available are complete but also complex and expensive. For example, a company known as Coremetrics (www.coremetrics.com) can modify each page on your site and add a small piece of code that places the necessary tracking information into your site's database. You need to approach this type of solution with the proper caution and respect: any solution that puts information into a database with every page view is going to place an incredible burden on your data tier, and you need to make sure your data tier can handle the load. This may require a separate database server, or even a cluster of active database servers, to handle the necessary traffic.

The Danger of Marketing

Marketing information is necessarily data-intensive. Your marketing department would love to know every link clicked by every shopper, with all of that information related to purchases and available demographic information. However, not only would you need a dedicated server (maybe even a data warehouse), to report all this information, you would probably need an entire, dedicated data tier to collect it. If your company belongs to an industry where the right marketing information can make or break you, then the investment may be worthwhile. If not, get your company's executives to put a reality check on the information that your Marketing department believes needs to be collected and stored — is it all really necessary?

For example, imagine what has to happen before your site can track a user's path. Every single page would have to start with a script that pulls a marketing code out of the HTTP headers and inserts a row into a database indicating that the user with that code visited such-and-such page. Every link on every page would have to contain that code, so that the code would continue to "follow" the user around (unless you're comfortable using cookies to contain the marketing code). Even if you use every possible best practice for designing the data tier — stored procedures to actually insert the data, and so on — a Web server taking a mere 500 hits per minute would be inserting 500 rows per minute. Just three Web servers would generate well over two million database entries every 24 hours. If your site traffic doubled, your database would be adding nearly 5 million rows per day.

Some third-party marketing systems avoid database hits altogether. Instead, they include small, single-pixel graphic files on each Web page. Each file has a unique name, and when the user's browser downloads the graphic, your Web server's log file includes a note of it. Because the graphic is so tiny (just a few bytes), it doesn't impact your site's load time. Rather than inserting information into a database as pages are displayed, these programs scan through your log files and populate a database based on the information they find. Unfortunately, this technique is less precise than generating marketing codes for each user, and it can be difficult to create statistics or paths for a single user. This method is best suited to information that you will aggregate for your entire site.

Properly designed, a process for collecting tracking information and other marketing-related data can be invaluable to marketing professionals — and the data can be collected without bringing your site to its knees.

Content

You'll need to decide who in your company is responsible for putting content on your Web site and how they will do it. Although the initial build of your site may be performed mainly by your technical staff (or by outside technical contractors), and although they may have no problem uploading pages to the site via FTP, your long-term goal should be to remove as much of the burden of content development from your technical staff as possible.

Crafting content

To understand exactly what functionality you will need, determine exactly how the content of your site will be built and rolled out to your production Web servers. Unfortunately, none of the few good solutions for team-based Web development come from Microsoft, and all of them are expensive. You still have several techniques you can use for developing and deploying content, and you can combine these techniques to meet your company's exact needs. The main techniques for creating content are as follows:

✦ Create pages from scratch using a Web development tool like Microsoft FrontPage.

✦ Design a set of page templates. Page content is then entered into an administrative interface and stored in a database; programs are used to create actual pages by combining the content with the templates.

✦ Design a set of page templates. Page content is then entered into the templates using a Web development tool like Microsoft FrontPage.

The main problem with manually creating pages in a tool such as FrontPage is that it generally requires the author to be technically savvy. If your content developers have the expertise, then those methods provide the most freedom and flexibility. Using page templates enables you to maintain a consistent look and feel across your site, and combining templates with a database allows for content creation by non-technical authors.

You may choose to use a combination of these techniques. For example, product information can generally be displayed using a handful of templates, and your product information will usually be entered into a database to begin with. Combining the templates with the database makes the most sense for producing that content. Pages for special promotions and other "free style" pages are better created manually, even if you use a basic template as a starting point. Of course, you will need to employ one or more HTML programmers unless your content authors are sufficiently skilled in HTML manipulation.

Version control

A major concern in most e-commerce companies is version control. What if someone modifies a file by mistake, or worse, deletes one? Version control offers rollback capabilities to prior versions of the file. Although Microsoft offers a fairly robust version-control product named Visual SourceSafe (VSS), this product does not integrate with the content publishing capabilities in Site Server 3.0 or Application Center 2000.

Note Microsoft hasn't really produced a complete document management platform. If you need a robust solution immediately, you need to look outside the Microsoft product line; if your needs can wait a few months, Microsoft may surprise you. See the sidebar in the following section, called "What's the Vision?"

Deploying content

After content is created, you need to deploy it. Site Server 3.0 offered a content deployment and management solution that was unfortunately inadequate for most e-commerce companies' needs. Commerce Server 2000 has no tools for managing content or deployment; instead, that task has been moved to Application Center 2000.

Application Center presents a "best case" scenario of Web content deployment. Your content is moved to one or more "staging" servers, where it can be tested and approved. From there, Application Center handles the task of deploying the content to all of your Web servers, ensuring that each server is identical to the rest. You can create multiple "clusters" of servers that share the same content, enabling you to create servers for content, search, shopping basket code, and so on. Application Center also makes it easier to add new servers to your farm by automating the deployment of content to new machines.

If you choose not to use Application Center, you still have a few Microsoft and do-it-yourself options for deploying content:

✦ The Windows 2000 Distributed File System (DFS) can replicate content between multiple servers. I mention this possibility because I've worked with a couple of companies who tried it; understand that Windows 2000's built-in File Replication System was never designed to handle the number of pages that most Web sites include. Using DFS will likely result in content synchronization issues between servers, because the File Replication System was not designed to replicate large numbers of files across multiple servers.

✦ If you're planning to write your own tool to deploy content, take a look at the RoboCopy utility included in the Windows 2000 Server Resource Kit. It's a robust, over-the-network file copy utility that can be automated and scheduled to run at regular intervals. Also capable of copying only changed files, RoboCopy is an excellent "poor man's" deployment solution.

✦ Leaving the Microsoft arena, you'll find a huge variety of Web content management and deployment solutions. Perforce (`www.perforce.com`) is one of literally dozens of companies that offer solutions for content management and deployment.

Securing content

There is also the matter of content security. Will everyone in your company be able to change any piece of content? Or will content be secured, so that only certain individuals can modify selected documents? In most cases, Windows 2000's NTFS-based file permissions should be sufficient to secure your documents, particularly if you organize your documents into folders based on who needs access to them. When planning your site, consider who needs access to each document and try to organize your directory hierarchy to accommodate this access.

What's the Vision?

Microsoft's server product line and overall e-commerce strategy is a rapidly shifting entity. Prior to the introduction of the .NET server line, Microsoft's e-commerce strategy was sketchy on details like content management and deployment — a key product area the company has overlooked for years.

However, as of this writing, Microsoft is releasing products that will form the backbone of an entirely new e-commerce strategy that addresses content management and deployment in force. Understanding Microsoft's long-term vision may be useful as you plan your site.

In Exchange Server 2000, Microsoft introduced a technology known as the Web Store. Essentially, the Web Store is an enhanced version of the information store present in prior versions of the Exchange Server product that allows you to store any kind of content. All content becomes addressable through Windows Explorer via UNC, through Web browsers via URL, and so forth. The Web Store supports the HTTP extensions for distributed authoring and versioning, known as WebDAV, that provide for team content creation, version control, and content management.

Microsoft's intranet portal server, codenamed "Tahoe," is intended to provide a Web-based content management and workflow system, including functionality for approvals, document check-in and check-out, and so on. The forthcoming version of Office will integrate with Tahoe to form a rich document management solution.

Application Center 2000 will include support for WebDAV and will also enable you to deploy content directly from the Web Store to multiple Web servers in a "cluster."

Ultimately, Microsoft's product line will undoubtedly provide a robust, integrated solution for Web site content management and deployment. If you can afford to wait, these solutions will integrate nicely with the rest of the Microsoft platform, including Windows 2000's Active Directory and SQL Server. If you can't wait, my advice is to look outside Microsoft's product line for a content management and deployment solution that will meet your needs.

Coordinating with content authors

When it comes to content creation, security, and deployment, there are certain issues you should be aware of. Discuss the following questions with your content authors and make sure you incorporate their responses into your Web site's formal documentation and plan.

✦ Will there be a formal content approval process? In other words, will an editor and/or a manager review an author's content before it is deployed? If so, consider how these approvals will be tracked. Microsoft does not currently offer an off-the-shelf document management system, although the upcoming "Tahoe" portal server should provide some solutions in this area. You may need to write your own content-workflow system to support this need.

✦ If your content authors will not be using an off-the-shelf Web development tool such as FrontPage, what will they use? You may need to build an interface that enables them to enter information into templates or into a database for later merging with a template.

✦ How will deployment work? Will newly created pages be deployed immediately, or will you "save up" all changes and deploy them on a regular schedule? Will you have a means for content managers to immediately deploy important pages if necessary?

Take time to understand your content development, management, and deployment processes to be sure the Web site you create meets your company's needs. If these needs include robust content management and deployment, you may need to look outside the Microsoft product line for the immediate future.

Fulfillment

Your company's fulfillment process is possibly one of the most important factors in your continued success. After all, fulfillment is the process responsible for delivering the services and products that customers purchase from your Web site.

Service companies

A service company's fulfillment process will likely involve a great deal of human interaction. Ultimately, it's people who deliver the services that customers purchase. Make sure your Web site integrates with whatever systems you use to deliver those services, including scheduling applications, a dispatch center's database, and so on.

Product companies

Product companies, on the other hand, have the opportunity for significant automation in their fulfillment process. There are three basic types of product-oriented e-commerce companies: the virtual warehouse, the traditional warehouse, and a combination of the two.

The first type of product-oriented e-commerce company uses a "virtual warehouse," which means that the company itself does not maintain any inventory or stock. Instead, orders are passed to one or more distributors, who fulfill the order and ship it directly to the consumer. This is a popular model for smaller e-commerce companies, since they do not have to bear the cost of maintaining and paying taxes on an inventory.

The second type of product-oriented e-commerce company follows a traditional warehousing model and maintains a warehouse or distribution center for its entire inventory. If an item isn't available in inventory, it is back-ordered until more stock arrives. While this model is more expensive, it offers the advantage of better control. For example, a virtual warehouse does not usually enable you to post inventory information on your site, and you may even continue taking orders for products that your distributors have actually sold out of. In a traditional warehousing model, you know exactly what you have in stock and you can update that inventory dynamically as orders are placed against it.

The third product-oriented e-commerce company model is a hybrid, where some portion of the company's inventory is maintained in a traditional warehouse, and some items are virtually warehoused.

Integrating site with fulfillment

You need a thorough understanding of how your company handles fulfillment, both to integrate the Web site with the fulfillment process, and to integrate other product and inventory-related features with the part of the Web site your customers will use. For example, consider the following:

✦ Will you be able to display accurate "in stock" information for your customers? If you use a hybrid model, it may be acceptable to indicate that virtually warehoused items are "special order." If you are based on a full virtual warehouse model, though, you don't want to list "special order" for every item you sell. Some distributors may feed you inventory information that you can integrate into your site, but since other companies will be ordering from that distributor, a product could sell out without your knowledge. How will you handle that situation?

✦ In a virtual warehouse or hybrid model, you need to quickly send order information to your distributors. This is often done through an intermediary such as CommerceHub (www.commercehub.com), but may be done directly with large distributors. Ideally, you want to send orders in batches (since most distributors and hubs charge per transfer), and you want to send batches several times a day to prevent orders from growing "stale" in your system. The Internet is all about immediate gratification. Customers expect orders to be processed instantly, if not faster. How you send that order information depends on your trading partners, but SQL Server's Data Transformation Services and BizTalk Server are key enabling technologies in the transfer of information between companies.

✦ If your virtual warehouse distributors will also be sending information to you, such as inventory levels or price changes, then you need to implement a system to handle that interaction. Data Transformation Services and BizTalk Server are key products in handling that communication.

✦ In a traditional warehouse model, you will have to write some kind of utility or batch process to transfer completed orders into your company's fulfillment system or distribution center system, so that the merchandise can be pulled, packed, and shipped. BizTalk Server and SQL Server Data Transformation Services are your best-bet technologies for this interaction.

✦ In a hybrid model, you will have to interact with a distribution center system, as well as communicate (possibly two-way) with your virtual warehouse distributors. Your product database also requires some indication of how each product should be handled, through your distribution center or through the virtual warehousing channel.

Consider the information that your fulfillment channel can provide to your Web site. Customers are accustomed to e-commerce sites that provide a great deal of information about the status of their order, including whether it has been processed, whether it has been packed in the warehouse (or sent to the distributor), when it will ship, what tracking numbers are associated with the order, and when they can expect to receive it. If you intend to implement these types of features in your site, you need to implement the necessary systems to retrieve that information from your fulfillment channel.

Most distributors who are accustomed to working with an intermediary such as CommerceHub are also accustomed to processing orders and sending back a file containing order status information (for example, which orders have shipped, which items are back ordered, which shipping carrier was used, what the tracking numbers are, and so on). You need to create a system (again, DTS and BizTalk Server will be key players) capable of receiving that file and integrating the information into your live database for customers to utilize. If only some of your distributors can provide this information, then your management team will have to make some careful decisions. Generally, an "all or nothing" approach works better when providing order status information to your customers: if you can't provide the status information for *all* of the orders that will be placed, don't provide it for *any* of them. Your customers may not appreciate the differences in your fulfillment process and will simply wonder why some orders have status information and others don't. Talk to the distributors that aren't providing status information to you and urge them to do so. Your business relationship with them will be greatly improved if they do, because your relationship with *your* customers will be improved.

One word of advice when designing a communications infrastructure with your trading partners: try to create a system that can be expanded easily. Use systems like SQL Server's Data Transformation Services and BizTalk Server, which provide standardized environments for the exchange of data between disparate systems. Avoid a design technique that requires standalone utilities written in Visual Basic or another language to process incoming and outgoing data; as your business grows and the number of partners you share data with increases, the job of keeping up with these various utilities will quickly grow out of hand. Using systems like DTS or BizTalk Server enables you to easily adapt code used with one trading partner to accommodate others, and provide a centralized place to manage and monitor your partner communications. I discuss these systems in great detail in Part II of this book.

If your orders are filled in your own distribution center or warehouse, spend some time investigating how those systems work and how they will interface with the live site's database. Can you create a batch job in DTS that pulls status information out a couple times a day? Will tracking numbers be available once an order has shipped?

 Tip   If all of your orders will be processed internally, then BizTalk Orchestration may offer an excellent solution for automating the process of moving order information into a distribution center system, retrieving order status, and other business processes.

When designing the site's integration with your fulfillment process, make sure you understand how your orders will be shipped out. For example, most e-commerce companies ship from several distribution centers, especially in a virtual warehouse model. That means a customer's order may consist of several packages, each with a different tracking number. Some items may enter the fulfillment process and be back-ordered, while other products are shipped immediately. If you intend to provide order status information to your customers, be prepared to provide this information on a per-*item* basis, not a per-*order* basis. Each item should include status information and a tracking number, if it has shipped. In your customer interface on the site, you can consolidate this information to present a list of orders, and then tracking numbers associated with the order, and so on.

Summary

One of the lengthiest portions of your design process will be determining exactly what functionality the various components of your business require from the site, and what information the site must provide to (and gather from) them. This time is well spent, though, because including support for your business' internal requirements in your site's design plan from the start, even if you don't actually implement all of it in the first phase, is much easier and less expensive than changing your design later because you missed critical internal requirements.

During the planning phase of your design process, be prepared to listen to huge wish lists of feature and functionality. Also be prepared to help your management team understand the costs associated with these wish lists so they can help you make good priority decisions in your Web site's design.

✦   ✦   ✦

Determining Back Office Requirements

Back office is the term used to refer to all the internal systems and processes that your company's management has developed to help run the company. The term comes from the banking industry, where the literal "back office" employees handled everyone's accounts, processed paperwork, and so forth. Today, the term generically refers to the behind-the-scenes processes that run a company. Although back office requirements never directly involve customers, they are necessary for the survival of your company and something your e-commerce site is going to have to deal with. Examples of back office tasks include management reports, accounting, warehousing, payroll, and commissions.

Back office requirements differ from the requirements that I discuss in Chapter 4 relating to marketing, content, and fulfillment. Those requirements relate directly to the day-to-day operation of the site, such as bringing people in, gathering demographics about them, filling their orders, placing content on the site for them to read, and so forth. Technically, you can completely ignore the back office requirements that I discuss in this chapter without affecting the site. After all, if your managers don't get sales reports, the site can continue to run, accept and fill orders, and so on. The reports aren't required for the *site's* operation, but they are required for the *company's* continued good health.

Don't make the mistake of assuming that reports and other back office requirements are easy things to add to your design at a later point. At that "later point," you and your team will be programming additional features, handling unforeseen technical problems, improving and maintaining the site, and so forth. Your company will need reporting information (even simple reports, such as the number of orders taken per day) almost immediately, and so "immediately" is when you should begin planning and implementing back office support in your design.

Identifying Reporting Output

Your primary method of supporting back-end business processes is to provide detailed information in the form of reports. Identifying the necessary reports can be difficult, because many of the people involved with these processes may not yet realize the type of information they need to collect from an e-commerce site.

In order to identify the needed reports, examine existing business processes and learn how they operate. Ask managers which decisions they expect to make on a daily, weekly, and monthly basis, and what information they require to make those decisions. That is your starting point.

I'll start your creative juices flowing by describing some of the most common management reports, what they contain, how they are used, and where the information can be found in your Commerce Server database.

Daily sales

Daily sales reports are critical to the day-to-day management of an e-commerce site. This type of report is best delivered as a Web page, perhaps on a Web server that runs on your reporting database server. This method of delivery allows many people within your organization to quickly view daily sales information and make decisions based upon it.

At a minimum, daily sales information should include these basic statistics:

- ✦ Number of buyers
- ✦ Dollar value of largest and smallest orders
- ✦ Dollar value of the average order
- ✦ Total sales dollars
- ✦ Total profit dollars
- ✦ Average profit margin (a percentage)
- ✦ Number of units (products or services sold)

This type of aggregate information gives managers an immediate view into how the business is performing. This information is also fairly easy to gather from a copy of your Commerce Server database—the orders and order items tables should contain all of the information that you need, including the cost of the goods sold, which is used to calculate your profit margin. Make sure that your database design puts sales information into those tables. Do not, for example, look up the cost of products in the product table, because the cost of products may change over time. The daily sales report needs to reflect a "snapshot" of the costs at the time the order was placed, which is why your database schema should copy that information from the product table into the order items table when orders are placed.

Cross-Reference I talk more about database schema issues in Chapter 7.

Your company may need to expand the daily sales report into a more comprehensive "daily performance report," which may include information such as the number of new newsletter subscribers, the number of addresses removed from newsletter subscriptions, the total number of visitors to the site, and so forth. This information needs to come from other tables and, in the case of site-based statistics like the total number of site visitors, from other reporting systems entirely.

Site performance

Microsoft's product line does not, unfortunately, currently include any robust tools for reporting on site performance, so you need to turn to third party software vendors. Most site performance reporting tools work by analyzing your site's logs and creating reports on the information that they contain. High-end reporting products can analyze the logs from several servers as a set, and create reports that reflect performance for the entire site, rather than for each individual server. If a farm of Web servers is hosting your site — and if users are load-balanced across them — make sure that you acquire a tool with the ability to aggregate the server logs into a single report.

The current reigning champion of Web site reporting tools is WebTrends (www.webtrends.com). Available in several different configurations for different environments, including one designed specifically for intranet environments, WebTrends contains all of the features and functionality that you need to generate a huge variety of reports. Another popular tool is LiveStats (www.mediahouse.com), which has the ability to show certain statistics in real time, rather than requiring you to wait for a batch log analysis job to complete. LiveStats offers a less comprehensive set of reports and information than WebTrends, but WebTrends' suite of reports comes at the expense of a lengthy and time-consuming batch job that is required to process your log files each night. Many companies purchase both tools (they're both very affordable) and use them together to take advantage of their strengths.

Be cautious when using reporting tools like these, however, and make sure you understand how their numbers are being developed. For example, one key statistic that most managers look for is the number of unique visitors that the site receives each day. Combined with the number of daily sales, management can determine the site's *conversion rate*; that is, the number of shoppers or visitors who turn into buyers on the site.

Unfortunately, Web servers by their very nature have difficulty detecting "unique visitors." In the early days of the Internet, this task was easy because each computer on the Internet had a static IP address, which was registered in the Web server's log file. Analysis tools simply had to count the number of different IP addresses in the log to determine how many unique visitors the site had received.

In today's world of rapidly vanishing IP address availability, however, Internet Service Providers (ISPs) and corporate network administrators have had to take some creative approaches to IP address use. As a result, for example, each one of America Online's millions of users is "seen" coming from a handful of IP addresses. Web site analysis tools have to make use of "tricks" to attempt to translate multiple hits from the same IP address into the number of unique visitors actually using that IP address. Most of these translation tasks require the analysis software to make assumptions. For example, WebTrends assumes a new unique visitor when it sees an IP address that has shown no activity in the log for 20 minutes. You can configure this setting, and most of the other settings that guide the software's assumptions, but you and your management team need to be aware of how the software is arriving at its numbers, so that you understand the relative weight to assign those numbers in your decision-making process. Your analysis software's documentation should thoroughly explain how the numbers on the various reports are derived.

Product performance

Another key management report deals with the performance of individual products on your site to determine whether those products are tangible goods or service offerings. This information is necessary for buyers to decide what types of products to bring into the site, for merchandisers to decide how products should be featured and promoted, and so forth. You typically make this type of information available on a daily, weekly, monthly, quarterly, and yearly basis so that the appropriate managers can make necessary decisions regarding your site's product mix.

The information typically needed by these managers includes:

✦ Basic product information—stock numbers, descriptions, etc.

✦ The number of units sold in the period

✦ The average wholesale cost of each unit sold—accounting for any cost changes during the period

✦ The average price of each unit sold—accounting for any changes per transaction, and any discounts that were given to the customer(s)

✦ The average profit margin for the product

✦ The number of units that were returned during the period

You probably need to show this information for any variations of the product. If your site sells shirts, for example, you need to show performance information each size, style, and color combination. Most of this information should be available in your database's orders and order items table, although you may need with the products table in order to retrieve product descriptions.

Other management reports

Your management team members may need other reports, which may or may not be product-related. Give them time to determine what information they require, and then plan a reporting infrastructure that enables you to deliver the necessary information. Depending on the specific information required, you can implement a variety of methods for actually creating these reports (something I discuss in Chapter 13).

Planning a Reporting Infrastructure

Many e-commerce companies get so caught up in the design and development of their site that they forget about the need to gather information from the site in the form of management reports. Most management teams believe that the site's database magically collects all of the necessary data and then produces the necessary reports. Although this might be true for the very smallest e-commerce sites, most sites need to consider implementing a completely dedicated reporting infrastructure in order to regularly obtain the reports that they need.

Consider the following factors:

✦ Do you plan to collocate your live database server with your management team? If not, querying a large amount of data across a WAN connection in order to produce reports will be inefficient and time-consuming.

✦ Does your live database have enough power to handle the minute-to-minute demands of the site in addition to the power required to produce complex management reports?

✦ Is your database design optimized for both the minute-to-minute transactional data of the site as well as the bulk-query data required for reports?

✦ If your site grows to require multiple databases (which it probably will, and faster than you expect), can your reports consolidate all the information from multiple live servers?

The factors that comprise a perfect production database are almost completely at odds with the factors that comprise a perfect reporting database. A reporting database can be located locally, making reports faster and more efficient; a production database must be located close to the Web servers that access it. A reporting database has the power of the entire server dedicated to reports, but a production database's primary task is to support the Web servers. The design of a reporting database is optimized for the task of creating reports; a production database is optimized for fast transactional processing. Finally, a reporting database can easily combine information from multiple production databases to produce company-wide aggregate reports, whereas a production database should generally contain only the data necessary for the production tasks.

Companies that take the time to properly plan their site and their back-end requirements recognize the advantage of designing an infrastructure specifically to handle their reports. If your reporting needs are few and not complex, then your reporting infrastructure should likewise be small and not complex; if your management team requires more complex reporting, then your reporting infrastructure can be scaled to meet those needs — completely separate from the needs of your production Web site.

In the next few sections, I talk about the design differences between the transactional database designs used by your live site and your reporting database. I also talk about the importance of creating a separate reporting infrastructure, and some of your options for doing so, and I talk about some of the Microsoft and third-party technologies available to make a dedicated reporting infrastructure possible. As you read through these sections, keep in mind the types of reports that your company needs, because these help to determine what your initial reporting infrastructure looks like.

Cross-Reference   After you've determined what your needs are, take a look at Chapter 17, where I discuss specific techniques for actually creating a dedicated reporting infrastructure.

Transactional versus reporting databases

Databases aren't generic creations. They are specifically designed for the tasks that they have to support. In an e-commerce environment, databases are designed for *transactional* activity, meaning that they are designed to query small pieces of data about products and services, and to make small updates when orders are placed. These databases are generally very *normalized*, meaning that the data is logically split among several tables following standard rules for database normalization.

A database that's designed for transactional activity rapidly locates some data by using elements like indexes, and enables other data to be easily changed or added to. Unfortunately, the optimizations that make a transactional database well suited for its task can also make it unsuitable for reporting.

Consider several of the optimizations made to the transactional databases that are used by most e-commerce sites (including the default Commerce Server databases):

✦ Indexes are kept to a minimum on frequently updated tables, such as tables used to store order information, because indexes reduce the speed with which the database server can add rows to a table or make changes to existing rows. In a reporting situation, however, the information in order tables is the exact information that you want to report on, and indexes can greatly increase the speed with which information can be read from the database.

✦ Database normalization breaks data into small entities, facilitating the database server's update of the data, and reducing the amount of space the data consumes on disk because repeated or redundant data is eliminated. Unfortunately, because the information needed for most reports is spread across several tables, the database server must deal with complex queries that join the tables back together in order to produce the necessary information. These complex queries create additional overhead on the database server. Large, complex queries, such as those involving many orders and products spread over a great deal of time, can take hours to run.

✦ Transactional databases generally deal with small pieces of information at a time. For example, customers may place an order requiring a few rows to be added to a couple of tables. Customers viewing a product details page may require pricing information for that product, which has to be queried from the database. Transactional database servers have their memory and operating parameters tuned to this expectation. Reports, on the other hand, generally require large amounts of data to be queried from the database server, which can often require a completely different configuration for optimal performance.

These comparisons also describe the difference between a transactional database and a *data warehouse,* or *data mart.* Both the transactional database and the data warehouse employ specialized database designs that are optimized for data reporting and analysis. Although your reporting needs may not be complex enough to warrant a full data warehouse or data mart, you still need to recognize the differences between the database design used for your live site and a database design optimized for your reporting needs.

The importance of a dedicated reporting infrastructure

Knowing the inherent differences between a good transactional database and a good reporting database, you should start to understand the importance of having separate databases dedicated to each task. This is the first step in developing a dedicated reporting infrastructure. The second step, of course, is to recognize that the separate database should be contained on a separate database server entirely.

The database infrastructure that you choose for your live site should not influence your reporting infrastructure. Although the two infrastructures do need to communicate, they also serve entirely different needs. Your e-commerce site may feature multiple database servers, each hosting a portion of your total data store. You may even have multiple database servers hosting the same content, with plans to distribute the load between them. Your reporting infrastructure should most likely consist of one or two servers that can pull data from the live servers.

Regardless of your reporting needs, you should avoid — at all costs — querying the data for those reports from your live database servers. Consider the following reasons:

✦ Your live database servers are intended to support the data needs of your live Web site and, by extension, your customers. Internal processes like reporting should not detract from the server power available to service your customers.

✦ Your live database servers should be located in the same local area network as your Web servers. This may or may not be the same local area network used by the people who need to access reports, which is where your reporting server should be located. This is the biggest point that you must compromise on, which I discuss later on in this chapter.

✦ Your reporting server most likely contains a database specifically designed and optimized for reporting — this is probably a very different database design from your live servers. These design differences probably extend to server-level configuration and optimization, meaning that your reporting database is best hosted on a separate server from your live database.

Should I use a dedicated reporting server?

I've seen many e-commerce companies try to build reports off of their live servers, and all have regretted it. My advice is to assume that some kind of reporting server is required. And, you can make compromises on cost, as well. For example, rather than purchasing an entire server dedicated to reporting, build your live site on a Windows 2000 cluster. You can use the "spare" cluster node for your reporting server, and still have take over for your live site database if the primary cluster node fails. This approach gives you more bang for the buck, although it still places the reporting server on the same LAN as the live site, rather than on your office LAN.

Cross-Reference

For more information on how to build a reporting infrastructure, including building on a Windows 2000 cluster, refer to Chapter 17.

If you can afford it, of course, include a dedicated server entirely for reporting. If your reporting needs are small, it can be a small server, or even a high-powered desktop machine running Windows 2000 Server.

The only other compromise you can make is to have your management team agree that they won't need any reports of any kind — which is not likely to occur. Do *not* make the mistake of agreeing that you'll use the live server for reports "to start with," and then "eventually" purchase a dedicated reporting server. "Eventually" has a funny way of becoming "never" in the fast-moving tech world, and your live site will begin to suffer from the competition for the database server's attention as the site traffic increases.

Where will the reporting server live?

Deciding where your database server should be placed is also an important design decision, and one that usually requires compromise.

✦ If you are going to be hosting your e-commerce site in your own facility, then place the reporting server on a LAN connection with the live site's database server. This is an easy decision, and presents the best possible solution. Unfortunately, it's also an option not often available to smaller e-commerce companies who don't have the resources to build a data center at their headquarters.

✦ If your site is going to be hosted at someone else's facility, placing the reporting server at that site makes it much easier for you to pull the necessary data from the live site's database server. Your actual reporting may be slow, depending on the bandwidth between your location and the hosting facility. You can mitigate this by using Web-based reports and hosting a Web server to display those reports at the hosting facility, or even running the Web site on the reporting server.

Cross-Reference

For further discussion on building Web-based reports, refer to Chapter 17.

✦ The worst option is to have your site hosted by someone else, and your reporting server at your location. This gives you fast reporting, but you will encounter several obstacles, such as problems accessing the server with reporting tools, difficulty managing the server, and poor reporting performance, which you'll need to work around to reliably get data from your live servers. Try to avoid this situation if you must go this route.

Enabling technologies

Given that a dedicated reporting infrastructure is highly desirable — at the very least — you need to know how to actually implement one. Begin by thinking about the available technologies, so you can include them in your site design plan if necessary.

SQL Server provides a lot of the technology that you need to implement your reporting infrastructure. SQL Server 2000, in particular, makes building a reporting server easier by using technologies such as log shipping, backup and restore, replication, and Data Transformation Services.

Log shipping

Log shipping is a technique that enables your live site to send a copy of its transaction log to your reporting server at a predetermined interval. Your reporting server then applies the transactions, and you get a copy of the live database on the reporting server. The reporting server is then "out of sync" with the live server by the interval between shipped logs. Log shipping imposes very little overhead on the live server.

Replication

Replication is similar to log shipping in that it creates a duplicate of your live data on a reporting server. Replication can be more reliable over WAN connections, and you can use transactional replication to keep your reporting server more "real-time synchronized" with the live data. Replication generally imposes a slight additional overhead on the live server, depending on which type of replication you select.

Cross-Reference

I talk about the different replication methods and their pros and cons in Chapter 17.

Backup and restore

The final method for getting a copy of your live data is to use *backup and restore*. The backup process imposes additional overhead on the live server while it is running, but if you're creating the backup file on disk and you have a fast disk subsystem in the computer, this overhead is minimized. The backup file then needs to be moved to the reporting server. This is easy if the reporting server is on the same LAN, but more difficult and time-consuming to automate if the reporting server is across a WAN link — where it can be restored, creating a copy of the live data on the reporting server.

Data Transformation Services

Data Transformation Services (DTS) is SQL Server's primary tool for building a reporting database. After you have a copy of the live data on your reporting server, you can create DTS packages to automatically transform that data into the reporting database schema that you devise.

DTS can also be used to query data directly from your live server and to transform it to your reporting server. This does impose a great deal of additional overhead on the live server, because it must query all of the data for DTS to use, and because DTS doesn't compress data in any way; therefore, performing this task over a WAN link is generally not feasible.

Tip   My recommendation: Use backup and restore or log shipping if the two servers are on the same LAN. Use transactional replication (discussed in Chapter 13) if the two servers are separated by a WAN link.

Integrating with Existing Back-end Systems

If your company has existing back-end systems, such as an ERP, CRM, or other management system, then you probably want to integrate the information in that back-end system with your Web site. Again, you can save time, effort, and money by including the integration as part of your initial site plan, rather than waiting until later in the process.

You need to carefully consider what information available in those back-end systems is beneficial to the site, and what information in your site can be of use in the back-end system. You should also consider the technologies that you use to move data back and forth between the systems. I discuss specific techniques in Chapter 13, but the information in this chapter should help you complete this portion of your design.

Examining back-end systems

Typically, companies with an existing back-end system have made an incredible investment in time and money to load their important business information into that system, and a similar effort to adapt the company's business processes to work with the back-end system. Whether your back-end system is an AS/400, SAP R/3 system, Oracle Financials installation, PeopleSoft, or some other system, you need to examine how those systems integrate with your business and determine what integration they need to have with your Commerce Server database.

For example, does your back-end system already contain inventory information about the products that you carry? Does it contain data on shipping times, or perhaps an address-verification database? Does the back-end system contain customer data that you want to be able to work with on the Web site? If so, you need to consider how you can regularly pull this information out of the back-end system and copy it to your Commerce Server database for use on the site. You need a plan that allows for regular, scheduled updates of the data so that your company's users can continue updating data in the back-end system.

Also consider the information that your Web site generates that can be of use in the back-end system. For example, if the back-end system keeps your company's financial information, then you should devise a way to copy order information from the Commerce Server database into the back-end system on a regular basis. If the back-end system plays a role in your order fulfillment process (as is the case in many established companies who are implementing a new e-commerce arm), then it is useful if your Commerce Server database can "feed" orders to the back-end system, and allow those orders to go through the company's normal process for order fulfillment. Again, you need a plan that allows for regular updates of the back-end system data.

Enabling technologies

Microsoft provides several major technologies to improve integration with back-end systems. The first of these is Microsoft's Host Integration Server 2000 (HIS), which is designed to create a bridge between the Microsoft platform and legacy midrange and mainframe systems like IBM AS/400 computers. HIS allows products like Microsoft SQL Server to treat AS/400 and other mainframe data stores as standard ODBC and OLE DB data sources, which permits greater integration of the host-based data with the SQL Server that supports your production Web site. HIS facilitates access to the data on your host system from SQL Server, which in turn provides a platform for other Microsoft integration technologies to operate from.

SQL Server 2000 includes Data Transformation Services (DTS), which provides robust features for manipulating and transforming data across heterogeneous data platforms. If you're using a host-based system with HIS, or if you're using a system like SAP R/3 running on an Oracle RDBMS, DTS is capable of accessing data on these platforms. This facilitates the transfer of order information from your Commerce Server database into your back-end ERP or fulfillment system, among other things. DTS jobs can consist of complex operations, including Transact-SQL and ActiveX scripts, and they can be saved as packages and scheduled for execution on a regular basis, which helps to automate the interaction between your systems.

Microsoft BizTalk Server is also an incredibly useful platform, and was specifically designed for transferring data between business systems. SQL Server 2000 is capable of natively providing a feed of XML-formatted data to BizTalk Server, which maps your Commerce Server data to a standard intermediate XML schema and then to your back-end systems' preferred format. If your back end systems are already capable of external data communications by using EDI, text files, XML, or other common formats, BizTalk Server presents an efficient, easy-to-use solution. BizTalk Orchestration provides even more functionality, allowing the data in your Commerce Server database to become the starting point for a complete, complex, and fully automated business process that includes interaction with back-end systems such as SAP R/3, Oracle Financials, and others. These processes are handled as complete transactions, which improves the reliability of your back-end interactions.

Note   With a list price (as of this writing) of $25,000 per processor for BizTalk Server's Enterprise Edition, this product limits itself to high-end implementations where BizTalk can be leveraged for a variety of inter- and intra-business communications. BizTalk's standard edition (as of this writing) lists at around $5,000 per processor, but is limited to single-server groups and a small number of connection agreements.

You always have the option of writing custom applications and utilities (perhaps in Visual Basic) to move data between your Commerce Server database and your back-end systems. This type of development tends to be more time-consuming, so make sure it's the right solution to choose over a DTS package or an investment in BizTalk Server's Standard Edition.

Some back-end systems allow you to plug data directly into their databases, and query information directly from them (many AS/400-based applications work this way). Other systems (SAP R/3 being a notable example) require you to interface instead with a set of defined application programming interfaces, such as R/3's BAPI system. One major advantage of BizTalk Orchestration is its bundled components that enable communication with many back-end systems, including R/3; writing your own components to communicate with ERP systems' interfaces can be a big project, too.

Tip   Site Server 3.0, Commerce Edition includes a sample "MS Market" Web site. This is a stripped-down version of the intranet Web site that Microsoft employees use, and provides sample components that are designed to interface with SAP R/3 systems. If you have R/3 in your environment, it may be worth investigating these components to see if you can save time and effort by reusing them in your project.

Summary

In this chapter, I talk about the need to determine the types of reports and information that your company requires from your Web site, and how those reports can support your company's back-end processes.

Make these reporting requirements part of your initial site design, and consider the reporting infrastructure that you can implement to provide these reports. Reporting databases are very different from the transactional databases used to support your live Web site, and you need to consider the technologies and requirements surrounding a reporting infrastructure.

Consider the back-end systems that already exist in your company and how the Web site can provide information to them and extract information from them. Several technologies are available to help you, and by including these technologies in your initial site plan, your site can go live with fewer problems and more robust management capabilities.

✦　　✦　　✦

Developing the Site

Getting your e-commerce site up and running means doing a lot of software development, and understanding exactly how Microsoft's products help get you started. In this part, you'll learn how to start developing your e-commerce site to match your design plans. You'll also learn how to develop real-world site elements that keep your customers coming back over and over again.

Introduction to the Development Phase

◆ ◆ ◆ ◆

In This Chapter

Staffing your project

Selecting technologies

Development documentation

◆ ◆ ◆ ◆

If you have read from the beginning of this book, you may be wondering when I'm going to stop talking about planning your site and get down to the task of actually showing you how to build it. Almost there! The preceding six chapters should serve to illustrate the importance of the design portion of your Web site development. You must determine exactly what you need the site to do, and spend time making decisions about how the site should be built.

Reviewing Your Decisions

Again, if you have read from the beginning of the book, then at this point you should have arrived at some significant decisions:

- ✦ You should have a vision statement that describes the ultimate goal for the site.

- ✦ You should have a project scope that describes exactly what your first phase of development is seeking to accomplish, thus narrowing the vision a bit.

- ✦ You should have a functional specification and a ream of decisions documents, detailing exactly what functionality and features are to be included in this phase of the site's development.

✦ You should have a project plan that outlines which pieces need to be completed on which dates. You may not have enough detail yet to create a complete project plan, but you should have an order or precedence and priority in mind and on paper.

✦ All of the difficult questions should be made and out of the way, including:

- Will we use cookies?

- What will the site look like?

- What forms of advertising will we support?

From this point forward, the big question is "How am I actually going to make all this stuff work?"

The biggest challenge is to keep your project from continually expanding to include additional features. Ideally, take the approach that your functional specification is set in stone, meaning that no additional features or changes will be accepted while the project is underway and anything new will have to wait for the next phase of the project.

In the real world, of course, pressing business concerns and rapidly evolving market conditions may mean almost *daily* changes to your functional specification, even as the project is being written. You simply have to deal with this, so here are some tips for doing so gracefully:

1. Analyze every change according to the project's original scope. Are you being asked to add a feature that would be nice, but isn't really necessary, or a feature that's absolutely required in order for the rest of the site to be useful? The latter type of change should be incorporated into the specification, but the former type of change should be put on a "wish list" for the next revision.

2. Make sure that you formally add changes to your project, fully documenting the reasons for modification. Make sure that the new feature or change is technically documented, and that your functional specification is revised accordingly. Just because you're in the middle of the project doesn't mean you can slack off on your documentation. Maintaining your documentation in the face of changes is an important step toward ensuring that those changes don't pile up and become the reason for the project's failure.

3. Finally, make sure that you and your management team recognize the physical laws of the universe. You can't add features to the project without also adding either resources (generally people) or time, or removing other resources to compensate.

Start thinking about how you want to put your project together, and then begin developing. First, you need to understand what resources are required for your project.

If you're working on the project, but not managing it, you should still pay attention to this type of information — after all, the ability to answer these questions is what makes lead developers out of developers, and project managers out of lead developers.

Understanding the resources that your project requires means understanding the array of technical disciplines that are involved in Web site development; I discuss these later in this chapter. I also give you some insight about the average level of production that you can expect from each of these trades. I also show you what disciplines tend to overlap, and how you can best deploy technical professionals skilled in these disciplines to get your project up and running and completed faster.

If you think it's useless to understand employee productivity and where skills are likely to overlap, think again. Check out these interesting industry statistics:

✦ Approximately 85 percent of all software development projects, including Web site development, go over budget and over time by at least 15 percent.

✦ The average technical employee on a development project is 60 percent utilized. This isn't to say that the employee spends 40 percent of his or her time goofing off. The employee usually spends the extra time trying to get information and support needed to do the job, or trying to perform job tasks outside his or her skill set.

✦ Because of their large scale and faster timeline, Web development projects are three times more likely to fail or go significantly over budget than any other type of development project.

Although the exact figures in these statistics are hotly debated across the industry, there's little question that you need to pay careful attention to things like project planning and technical productivity.

Next, you need to select the technologies that you intend to use in your project. Identify how important they are to the project, where the technologies are in their development process, and what risks are associated with specific technologies. I talk about identifying risks later in this chapter.

Decide which parts of your project you plan to work on first. This decision helps you to establish a set of priorities, and to determine which pieces can be worked on simultaneously.

At the end of this chapter, I give you an overview of a "best practices" development process. Consider using this process, or an adaptation of it, as a model for your development projects. This process is modeled after one that I learned while working for a software development company that created Visual Basic applications for business, and I've found that it works just as well for e-commerce development projects.

Note I don't attempt to define a complete project management methodology; that is beyond the scope of this book. What I want to present is an overall, broad process description to help you fit your e-commerce development into a basic framework for management.

Staffing for Skills

Your technical professionals (the individuals that are doing the actual work) represent one of the most important resources on any project. Consider the various skill sets required to staff an e-commerce project, whether you are going to use your own staff or contractors, and the considerable overlap in skill areas that you can take advantage of in order to make your team more productive.

Skills

What technical skills does your project require? How many people are needed to provide those skills? The various technological disciplines that are required to implement an e-commerce site have become extremely specialized as the individual technologies have become more independently complex. In other words, the days of programmers who knew solid HTML, Visual Basic, database administration, and a little network infrastructure are long gone. These various technologies have become so complex that in many cases, it's all a person can do to keep up with one field.

Understanding the skills that various technical professionals bring to the table is an important part of understanding how an e-commerce team works together. Even if you are not personally in the position of building or managing the team (for example, if you're one of these technical professionals), you still need to understand the skills that the various team members offer. In the following sections, I show you sample job descriptions for each of these positions, which can help you to understand the exact skills each player should have. I also discuss the average output that you can expect each of these positions to produce in a day, so you have some understanding of industry production averages.

Note What's in a name? The titles that I use for the positions that I describe are industry-standard and somewhat generic. Certainly, individual technical professionals may apply these labels to themselves without necessarily meeting the definition that I give here. Use caution when reviewing resumes and interviewing potential team members. Understand their skill set rather than relying on the job title that they assign themselves.

Web developer

Web developers typically have a broad range of technical competencies because Web development represents the convergence of so many important technologies. In some ways, Web developers are "jacks of all trades" because they must understand all of the technologies that contribute to a Web development project. A good

Web developer is very flexible and can fill many roles on a team. However, most Web developers are so hard-pressed to keep up with the various Web technologies that they are often *experts* in none of them. Fortunately, very few Web development projects require experts; solid professionals are sufficient.

Typical job tasks for a Web developer include:

✦ Writing program code in languages like Java or Visual Basic, although few developers are "fluent" in more than one programming language.

✦ Writing script code in languages like VBScript or JavaScript. Some developers are fluent in both of these scripting languages, but most focus on one or the other.

✦ Creating HTML pages, either by using a layout tool like Microsoft FrontPage or "by hand" with a text-based HTML editor or a text editor like Notepad. Many Web developers are comfortable with HTML layout in their development tool, which generally means they don't have the fine-tuned control over the HTML code that you can expect a dedicated HTML programmer to possess.

✦ Creating tables and stored procedures in a database system like Microsoft SQL Server. Most Web developers should not be expected to have a strong understanding of SQL Server optimization topics, such as index creation or index tuning, server operation, and so forth.

✦ Working with Commerce Server component, ActiveX Data Objects, and third-party ActiveX controls. Web developers should be especially strong with these object libraries and a variety of third-party controls, and should be able to quickly write efficient code that employs them.

✦ Working with Active Server Pages objects. Web developers should have a strong understanding of these objects and their functions, including their interaction with client browsers through the use of cookies.

Creating metrics for Web developer productivity is difficult because of the wide variety of tasks that they must undertake to create Web sites. As a baseline, the average Web developer should be able to do the following:

✦ Create an ASP page that includes a basic form for collecting user information.

✦ Lay out the page in HTML in relatively complex configurations.

✦ Add ASP code to accept user input, validate the input, return appropriate error messages, and save the validated information to a database table either as a new record or as an update to an existing record.

This type of task should take about four to six hours.

Web developers are among the most valuable players on an e-commerce development team because their experience and skill set includes many diverse disciplines and allows them to work in the "mixed technology" of a Web project more easily than more "focused" professionals.

Tip

Selecting Web and Visual Basic developers with an industry certification, such as a Microsoft Certified Solutions Developer, helps you to ensure that your team includes developers with an acceptable minimum level of competency in software development. Many other certifications exist specifically for Web developers, including the Certified Internet Webmaster and iNet+ certifications.

Visual Basic developer

Visual Basic (VB) developers work almost exclusively within the Visual Basic Integrated Development Environment (IDE) to do their programming. Although their skill set is not as broad as that of Web developers, they should be expected to have a much deeper understanding and range of experience with Visual Basic than a Web developer. A typical Visual Basic developer's competencies should include:

✦ Working with tables and stored procedures in a database server like SQL Server. VB developers should understand the use of indexes, and the basics of database design, because VB includes tools for working with database objects.

✦ Using VB to produce standalone executables, DLLs, ActiveX controls, and other forms of executables. VB developers should understand the difference between these executable types and the various applications for each.

✦ Using Microsoft Transaction Services (MTS), which are a part of COM+, to write transaction-based components in Visual Basic.

✦ Using COM components, such as ActiveX Data Objects, Collaborative Data Objects and other Microsoft-supplied and third-party COM objects, and ActiveX controls.

✦ Fine-tuning program code in Visual Basic to achieve early-binding of variables, reducing code complexity, using modules and classes to improve program maintainability and modularity, and so forth.

✦ Using strongly-typed variables within Visual Basic applications, correctly selecting variable scope for use within an application, and correctly selecting procedure types when writing functions, subroutines, property control routines, and so forth.

✦ Using Microsoft Message Queuing Services (MSMQ) to support asynchronous communication between applications and components.

✦ Using Visual Basic intrinsic statements to manipulate Registry settings.

✦ Declaring and using Windows API calls from within Visual Basic to accomplish operating system-level tasks.

The average VB developer should be able to produce approximately 1,000 lines of code per day. Many caveats exist around that number, however, because many VB developers find themselves working on poorly-defined projects that require a great deal of time to define a particular piece of the project in sufficient detail in order to code it properly. VB programming is more rigid than script development because VB requires an overall plan to be in place in order for the developer to create the appropriate modules and classes. Script languages, what Web developers tend to work with most, don't offer advanced application architecture features like modules and classes, and are more forgiving to a programmer without a firm plan and design to work from.

In my experience, many VB developers are unfamiliar with the vast majority of the VB language. Many programmers learned the VB language when the third and fourth versions were released, and have had little time to concentrate on updating their skills to the newer, more robust versions of the product that have since been released. Also, many VB developers that are accustomed to working on custom corporate applications lack sufficient breadth of knowledge about the VB product in order to work at maximum efficiency in the more demanding e-commerce development environment.

Database administrator

Database administrators (DBAs) seem to straddle the line that separates developers from network engineers because database administration often encompasses aspects of both positions. Most e-commerce projects require the services of a database administrator — at least at the beginning of the project (to set up the development databases and database servers), and before the project is deployed to production (to create the production database and fine-tune it for use on the live site). Database administrators should be able to perform the following tasks:

✦ Translating a set of business requirements into a database design, and then normalizing that database design to the correct degree for the application.

✦ Analyzing an existing database to determine usage patterns, which in turn can be used to optimize and fine-tune the database's performance. This includes the creation and maintenance of indexes, as well as recognizing when indexes are degrading performance.

✦ General database server maintenance tasks, such as backup and restore, log monitoring, index rebuilding, and so forth.

✦ Creating stored procedures, triggers, views, constraints, rules, custom data types, and other database objects to support the needs of application developers.

✦ Monitoring application interaction with the database to determine what steps can be made to improve application and database performance. This includes determining the appropriate use of database objects, such as stored procedures and views, and determining performance bottlenecks in the database or in the application-database interface.

✦ Strong familiarity with ActiveX Data Objects and how the ADO library interfaces with the database server.

Database administrators generally remain busy in the early stages of the project, and should be involved as much as possible as the project is developed. This allows the DBA to analyze the way other developers are using the database, and constantly make adjustments to the database to optimize its performance. Also, including a DBA in the entire development process can help your developers better understand how the database server works, and how they can write their code to take advantage of the database server's built-in optimizations and avoid performance-degrading operations.

DBA productivity is difficult to quantify because much of their time is spent working with other developers to improve the way their code interacts with the database. However, you should expect a DBA to require a week or two to create your initial development environment, and allot another two or three weeks for the DBA to run simulated traffic through your ready-for-production Web site to fine-tune the database server before moving into a live environment.

Tip   DBAs should carry an industry certification, like Microsoft's Certified Database Administrator, that indicates an acceptable minimum skill set in database administration.

Network/infrastructure administrator

Network administrator is one of the two non-development positions on an e-commerce technical team, but this position is just as important as the development positions. Network administrators are responsible for designing, building, and maintaining the servers that run your product and development Web sites, databases, messaging servers, and more. Make sure your network administrator is proficient with the various technologies that you select for your Web site, including BizTalk Server, Windows 2000, Exchange 2000, SQL Server 2000, Application Center 2000, and so forth. An average network administrator can be expected to:

✦ Install, configure, administer, optimize, and troubleshoot desktop computers and servers running Windows 2000 operating systems.

✦ Install, configure, administer, optimize, and troubleshoot BackOffice and .NET server products, including Exchange Server 2000, BizTalk Server 2000, Internet Security and Acceleration (ISA) Server 2000, Internet Information Services, SQL Server 2000, Application Center 2000, and so on.

✦ Manage connectivity between your office and remotely hosted servers using WAN-based Virtual Private Networks (VPNs) and other technologies.

✦ Design, configure, and administer Local Area Networks (LANs) and Wide Area Networks (WANs) using TCP/IP protocols.

These tasks represent knowledge of a huge array of very different products. Most network administrators have passed individual certification exams for each product that they are competent to support — especially BackOffice or .NET server products. Make sure that you secure a network administrator (or a team of them) capable of supporting the products that your site uses.

Tip   Industry certifications, like Microsoft's Microsoft Certified Systems Engineer, can help you select network engineers who have an acceptable minimum level of competency in the key skills you will need them for perform.

I try to discourage e-commerce companies from outsourcing network administration tasks to contractors. Although outsourcing is definitely possible for the development positions of a technical team, administrators must become intimately familiar with your site and the servers that support it. Ideally, they should be available seven days a week, 24 hours a day in case emergencies arise. This type of familiarity and dedication is difficult to obtain in a contractor, unless you have a very long-term contract that guarantees the contractor or contractors will remain dedicated to your site.

If you are building an especially large e-commerce site, consider hiring more than one administrator. A single entry-level administrator/technician can be expected to support about 150 client workstations. A single mid-level administrator can be expected to support about 15–20 servers after they've been installed and configured, although you may need to hire additional help to initially build that many servers. Web server farms that are managed with Application Center 2000 can increase an administrator's productivity because the product lets administrators treat potentially dozens of Web servers as if they were only a handful.

HTML programmer

Although Web developers should be expected to understand basic HTML programming, most Web developers tend to focus on the code side of Web development and allow their HTML tools to provide them with all the HTML expertise required. These tools are valuable in getting perhaps 90 percent of a Web page completed, but a skilled HTML programmer is needed to manually "tweak" the HTML code to provide the exact layout and look that your company has chosen.

HTML programmers usually display skills in other Web site-related tasks, too. They should be expected to:

+ Use HTML design tools to create Web pages, incorporating elements provided by a graphic designer and Web designer, and work with a Web developer to maintain the integrity of any server-side or client-side program code included in the Web page.

+ Manually edit HTML code to obtain a precise look and feel for a Web page. This may include breaking graphic elements into multiple pieces, formatting complex, nested "invisible" tables, and so forth.

+ Work with Cascading Style Sheets to provide robust formatting with a minimal amount of code.

+ Analyze Web pages to determine how the size of the page can be reduced to provide faster download times to customers.

+ Work with `robots.txt` files to control the behavior "robots" that examine the content in your site for inclusion in various search engines, a process known as *crawling*.

+ Analyze existing Web pages or create new Web pages that meet a certain level of browser compatibility as defined in the site's design plan.

+ Correctly program HTML forms to support back-end server processing.

HTML programmers are often accomplished Web designers, too. The two fields are closely related and many professionals have the time and creative capacity to fulfill both roles on your team.

Tip

Several industry certifications exist for HTML programmers, although most of them are specific to a particular HTML product, such as Macromedia's Dreamweaver or Adobe's Web design products. If you are using these products in your environment, try to find HTML programmers who are certified in them.

Additionally, look for HTML programmers who can provide a portfolio of their work. Review the HTML code for neatness, efficiency, and adherence to a given browser compatibility level.

Most HTML programmers can be expected to produce a handful of complete and unique pages in a day. Obviously, the length and complexity of the page dictates how long the average programmer takes to create it, and you shouldn't underestimate the difficulty of using HTML to achieve specific looks that maintain their appearance across a range of browsers. An especially complex page that must look identical in a variety of browsers may take an HTML programmer an entire day to get "just right."

Web designer

The Web designer *designs* Web sites, rather than actually implementing them. Your technical team should include a Web designer during your design phase and into the early portions of your development phase. After your site development is well underway, you probably don't need a dedicated Web designer unless the need arises for new pages or page elements.

The Web designer also creates the overall "look and feel" of a Web page by using guidelines and specifications provided in your site's design plan. They should have a good sense of space and proportion, and should be able to create attractive pages that appeal to your target demographic. They should understand the restrictions of the HTML languages, and should create designs that HTML programmers can easily implement. Web designers should also be able to "templatize" their designs to the greatest degree possible, allowing you to leverage the design across your site. Templates allow a designer to create a blank, "starter" Web page with all the features (such as buttons, logos, and other elements) that should be included on every page. The templates allow new pages to be created more quickly, and ensure consistency across the site, because all pages start from the same "starter" page. Web designers should be able to maintain a consistent look and branding image across your site, even through different types of pages.

A Web designer should work closely with your HTML programmers to implement their designs in HTML, and should be receptive to feedback from HTML programmers about what is possible to implement and what is not. HTML can be a tricky, finicky language to work with, and its implementation by different browsers makes it difficult to achieve a consistent look and feel. Sometimes, a Web designer's desired look can't be reliably achieved across different browser versions, and the Web designer may need to alter the design in order to accommodate the restrictions of the HTML environment.

Many graphic design firms employ graphic designers who are also skilled Web designers; the disciplines are loosely related and professionals who understand both are in high demand in today's fast-growing Internet economy. Most good HTML programmers have a solid understanding of Web design as well.

Tip Look for Web designers who can provide a portfolio of their work. Look for designers who create professional-looking Web pages that seem to meet the preference of the target audience, and who have a good sense of space and proportion.

Don't underestimate the time necessary for a Web designer to create a good site design. They may often go through a dozen or more prototype pages before finally settling on the one that makes your site look best. Remember that the creative process of Web page design requires lots of "playing" and "tweaking" to arrive at the perfect result.

Graphics designer

Graphic designers are generally considered non-technical employees, but their work is heavily influenced and leveraged by technology. The graphic designer creates graphic elements that meets the needs of your site, and works closely with the Web designer to create the overall look and feel of the site. Because more and more graphic design efforts are being directed at Web sites, it is becoming more common for graphic designers to also be accomplished Web designers.

Many e-commerce companies turn to an outside graphic design firm to provide them with an overall image, including marketing materials, corporate identity materials, such as logos and basic design elements, and so forth. These firms can generally provide the initial design of your Web pages and the associated graphic elements, as well. You may still need (or want) to hire one or more graphic designers for your technical team. Continually going back to a marketing or graphic design firm every time you need a new graphic element can become both expensive and a risk to your project schedule.

A good graphic designer with experience in working with Web sites understands the unique constraints of the Web environment. The graphic elements that they produce need to be as small as possible to facilitate fast download times. The effects that "lossy" compression techniques (which reduce image quality to achieve a smaller file size) like the JPEG format have on a graphic require a graphic designer to be able to create final graphic files that strike a good balance between image quality and small size.

Tip Look for graphic designers who can provide a portfolio of their work. Look for designers who create a wide variety of graphics—you should not recognize a particular personal style across the pieces in their portfolio. Designs should be eye-catching and attractive, and should demonstrate a good sense of space and proportion.

Try not to underestimate the amount of time graphic designers need to accomplish their tasks. Although producing a small GIF file that will be a navigation button on your site seems simple, that first button can be difficult to get exactly right. Graphic designers need adequate time to use their creative abilities in an iterative process to achieve the exact look and feel that makes your site shine.

Overlapping skills

Many technical professionals have some overlap in their skill sets between the positions that I describe in the previous pages. Knowing where this overlap occurs can be useful, because this knowledge helps you better deploy technical professionals for maximum effectiveness and productivity. Table 6-1 shows the various positions that typically overlap. In the table, each row represents the various positions, and the columns represent skill overlap with other positions. A "1" indicates a good familiarity with another skill, a "2" indicates a basic understanding of the other skill, and a blank indicates little or no familiarity with the other skill. A "3" indicates that you can commonly find professionals proficient in both skill sets.

	Web developer	VB developer	DBA	Network admin	HTML progr.	Web designer	Graphic designer
Web developer	n/a	1	2		1	2	
VB developer	2	n/a	1		2		
DBA	2	2	n/a	2			
Network admin			2	n/a			
HTML progr.	2				n/a	1	2
Web designer					1	n/a	3
Graphic designer					2	3	n/a

Table 6-1
Overlapping technical skills

These overlapping skills can help you get the right skills on a relatively small technical team. For example, if your company uses an outside graphics design firm, then you don't need to hire a graphics designer. However, having some graphic design skills on your team is still useful. You should be able to locate an HTML programmer or Web designer with a basic to moderate understanding of graphic design in order to help you fill that role on your team when the outside firm has completed their contract.

Don't make the mistake of thinking that these overlapping skills completely eliminate the need for certain positions. Very few Web designers and even fewer HTML programmers have the artistic ability to completely replace a graphic designer, even though they may have a good eye for basic graphic design and may be able to come up with the basic design elements, such as site icons or banners.

Selecting Technologies

In this section, I help you to determine what technologies to use in order to implement your Web site. In the next chapter, I discuss the various Microsoft and third-party products that you should consider, and I describe how each one meets specific needs. Try to match those needs to the ones in your site plan so you can easily identify the products that you need to pull into play for your project.

Because Microsoft Commerce Server 2000 is almost a given in your project (at least if you're reading this book), I talk about where you should expect to start with Commerce Server — because you have several options. I also talk about the process that you should use in selecting other technologies, and some of the non-technical considerations that you should keep in mind.

Commerce Server's starting point

Out of the box, Commerce Server 2000 does almost nothing in terms of actual functionality. Commerce Server 2000 is less a *product* than a *platform* upon which products, such as your e-commerce site, are built. It provides a robust, flexible architecture, a set of programming components that can save you a lot of time and effort, and a fairly good database schema. Commerce Server 2000 even includes built-in support for a reporting database and provides a default data warehouse schema that uses SQL Server 2000's Analysis Services, making it an awesome platform on which to build your Web site.

Microsoft currently provides two Commerce Server Solution Sites, available for download from the Commerce Server Web site (www.microsoft.com/commerceserver). One of these solution sites is designed to serve as a business-to-consumer retail market, and the other is designed for a business-to-business supplier audience. These Solution Sites provide an excellent example of how you can use Commerce Server's various technologies, which are designed to be almost infinitely customizable. In fact, they are so flexible, so customizable, and work so well "out of the box" that you may be tempted to make a Solution Site the basis for your own production site. Don't do it.

Imagine for a moment that you're an auto manufacturer. You build very expensive, high-end luxury cars. You are concerned about the comfort of the driver seat. After all, nobody is going to plunk down the kind of money that you're asking for unless the driver's seat is *really* comfortable. You can achieve the kind of comfort that your customers expect in two ways. First, you can make a custom-fitted seat for every customer that buys a car, ensuring a quality fit and guaranteeing ultimate comfort. What's more, a custom-fitted seat is easy to maintain because it contains no inner moving parts. Second, you can include a generic, eight-way, power-adjustable seat with inflatable bolster cushions and other fancy pieces that allow the drive to customize the seat to fit almost perfectly. But you can't expect even the most adjustable seat to render as perfect a fit as a custom-fitted seat. After all, you're in the business of making cars, not seats. You decide to provide the generic, super-customizable seat. The downside to this approach, of course, is that every seat has fifty moving parts, any one of which can break down. The driver also has to spend a good deal of time twiddling with the seat controls in order to achieve a custom fit.

This is Microsoft's approach to the Solution Sites — "one size fits all, and make it *really* customizable." The downside to this approach is that every single page in the site requires multiple hits to the database and hundreds, if not thousands, of lines of script code to be processed by the IIS scripting engine. The Solution Sites are a model of how you can use Commerce Server, but they are also a model of inefficiency when it comes to making a robust, scalable, and efficient e-commerce site.

Consider `product.asp`, which is the page that displays product detail information for products from the site's catalog. You won't find any HTML in this page. All of the information on the page is pulled from the Commerce Server database, including various files and COM components that dynamically create the HTML every time the page is viewed. Now compare this `product.asp` page to a static HTML page containing the product information. Perhaps the static page was originally generated from the database, and maybe still queries the product's current price and discounts from the database because that information can change on the fly. This static page requires much less overhead, on both the Web server and the database server, than the `product.asp` page that's included with the Solution Site. To be specific, `product.asp` requires about four times as much processor power, three times as much memory on the Web server, and about four times as much power from the database server.

Can you build an e-commerce site the way Microsoft built their Solution Sites? Absolutely, and it's so flexible that you'll be able to completely change the look and feel of the site on a whim. You'll have an almost infinite amount of flexibility for creating custom catalogs, customized pricing for specific customers, and so forth. You'll also need an almost infinite amount of hardware if your site is expected to support a significant number of users. The Solution Sites don't do *anything* that you can't do with other tools, so you're not giving up functionality by using them.

Tip

My recommendation: Start your Commerce Server development using the Blank Web site provided with the product, and build your site from scratch. Borrow code and ideas from the Solution Sites when appropriate in order to save time, but don't use those sites as a basis for your development.

If you're planning to run a small Web site (maybe a couple of Web servers against a single database), then the Solution Sites may be perfect for your needs. I've done some load-testing, and I would estimate that the Retail Solution Site can support about 800 users per server on a dual-processor Pentium III 633MHz box with 2GB of RAM. A single database server running quad Pentium III Xeon 533MHz with 3GB of RAM can probably support three to four of these servers before things start getting a little hairy. For a fairly significant hardware investment (about $180,000) you can probably support about 3200 users. Remember that these are fairly rough numbers based on load testing that I've done in a lab environment.

Selecting other technologies

Although Commerce Server should be a "given" for use in your project, any other technologies (other than the underlying Windows 2000 platform) should be reviewed for their appropriateness. Although each product brings certain technical advantages (and sometimes disadvantages) to your project, you should also consider the business impact of each product.

All products, for example, have licensing costs. For some products, such as third-party ActiveX controls, these costs are typically in the range of a few hundred dollars, making them easily affordable. Other products, especially the major Microsoft server products, can be much more expensive. Microsoft now licenses most of their .NET server products per-processor, requiring that you purchase a processor license for each processor on which the product is running. BizTalk Server 2000 is currently the most expensive product in the lineup with a list price of $25,000 per processor for the Enterprise Edition. Two dual processor servers running BizTalk runs you up to $100,000 in licensing fees! SQL Server 2000 is also licensed per processor, and Application Center 2000 (which has not been released as of this writing) will likely be licensed for the number of server processors in each "cluster" managed by Application Center. Regardless of the power, efficiency, and desirability of these products, price may sometimes be the determining factor in whether or not you select them for inclusion in your project. Remember that the price does buy you something, though, and in the long run the cost of developing the same functionality yourself, or doing without, may be higher than just paying the price up front.

Support is another critical business factor, especially with the newest .NET server products. You need to feel comfortable with your technical team's ability to implement and support these products, and finding professionals with any familiarity in newer products can sometimes be difficult. As you examine these products, be sure to consider what additional training or outside help your technical team needs in order to use the products that you have selected.

Overall reliability of a product represents another significant factor. Although Microsoft's products are generally as reliable as you can expect these types of technologies to be, third-party products, especially ones from smaller companies, may not be reliable enough to operate in a production e-commerce environment. ActiveX controls are an excellent example of a reliability risk. Contact the authors of the controls and determine what language the control was written in. Is it a multi-threaded DLL capable of working in a robust environment, or was the control designed primarily for use in client-server applications? Try to steer clear of controls written for anything but the most robust, scalable environments, as they will likely prove to be a weak link in your site's technology chain.

Tip   Microsoft has established a logo program for independent software vendors (ISVs) who produce software and software components for use with Microsoft's BackOffice and .NET platforms. Products carrying the "Designed for use with BackOffice" logo have passed a set of strict guidelines and Microsoft-designed tests that are meant to assure a level of compatibility and scalability when the product is used with the BackOffice and .NET platforms.

Establishing Development Priorities

You need to know what you and your development team will start working on first, what will be second, what pieces can be worked on by different developers at the same time, and so forth. Your design documentation should give you a good idea of what your priorities are, but developing a complete project plan is easier if you make a simple priority list. For example, an online retailer may have a priority list similar to the following:

1a. Set up basic infrastructure.

1b. Set up a basic navigational framework to use during development.

1c. Begin programming item detail pages for items with no color or size variations.

2a. Begin working on navigation and basic page elements.

2b. Begin programming shopping cart and checkout.

3a. Begin loading item images for top items.

3b. Begin working on item detail pages for items with color or size variations.

4a. (and so forth)

In this list, like-numbered items are all completed in parallel, so item 1a and 1b are being accomplished at the same time by different members of your team.

A priority list gives you some obvious advantages from a project management standpoint, but you may have some purely practical reasons for prioritizing. For example, your company may want to take the site live sooner than originally planned. Competitive pressure, finance situations, and many other factors can drive a decision like this. Establishing a good priority list means that the most important pieces of the site have the greatest likelihood of being completed if the site does go live early.

When constructing your priority list, keep an eye on which technical disciplines can work in parallel and create matching priorities. For example, developers have a difficult time testing their pages if the site has no navigation elements. So have your graphic designers immediately crank out some utilitarian elements that the developers can use, and then move on to creating the final graphics and other page elements. Programmers should initially focus on the minimum tasks required for customers to locate and purchase products, and then move on to portions of the site that enhance the customer's experience or provide other business benefits. Work on the portions that give you the biggest bang for your buck first. If you have three different classes of items that require programming, finish the largest or best-selling group first, and then work on the others.

Always ask yourself, "If the site went live today, what would I wish had been completed by now?" Then place those items on the top of the priority list.

The Development Process

If you created all of the design documents that are covered in the first five chapters of this book, then you've already started the development process.

In this section, I give you an overview of a development process that is familiar to me and that I've been very successful using. This isn't intended to be a complete project management methodology. Instead, I want you to get a basic understanding of the proper life cycle of an e-commerce site. By following this cycle, or something similar, you'll find that your site's development is easier to manage and keep on track.

I also describe some of the documentation that you should be developing throughout your development process. This documentation should make the site more manageable, and facilitate revisions and improvements in future phases of development.

Process overview

The development process should never be regarded as a one-and-done set of tasks. Rather, the development process is a continuing circle, in which the product, in this case, your Web site, is constantly undergoing revision. Consider the diagram in Figure 6-1, which divides the development process into four distinct phases in a continuing cycle.

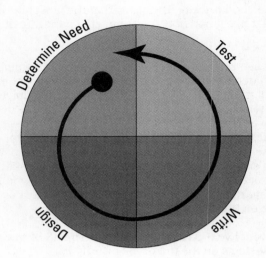

Figure 6-1: The development process

The design phase

This phase consists of the collection of business requirements, development of design documentation, and so forth. Even if you are making revisions to an existing product, you should follow this model and the design process explained in this book. Start with a vision statement. What is the goal of the development that will be done? Define the scope of the development, create a functional specification, and select the technologies you will use. Too many e-commerce companies make the mistake of ignoring the design phase of revisions that occur after the initial site goes live. If you think a set of revisions is too small or inconsequential to bother with a design phase, then why bother to make the revisions at all?

The design phase is also a time to revisit your original project documentation, and to identify areas that were deliberately left out of earlier phases of development. What makes sense to include in this development cycle? How will the new revisions map to the site's original vision statement? How will the new revisions interact with existing functionality on the site? A good design phase answers these questions, and makes the next phase of the cycle easier.

The development phase

In this phase you write the necessary software, design graphics, create HTML pages, and do all the other necessary technical work to bring your design to life. Start by determining what skills and technologies this phase of development requires, and what resources you have available to you. Create a project plan that details how the project should proceed. Set milestones so that you can mark your success, or lack thereof, in quantifiable terms.

The development phase of a project is generally the longest because it requires the most technical work. Keeping a big development phase on track can be difficult without the proper management techniques and documentation (a subject that I discuss in the next section of this chapter).

The result of the development phase is a completed project that is ready to be tested.

The testing phase

This phase is your opportunity to catch any errors that were made during the development phase. Pull out your design documentation and make sure that the completed project matches the original specifications. Make sure all the components work exactly as they should.

I've found that allowing the project's developer to test his/her own work is almost useless. A developer knows his/her own code too well, and will naturally do what the code "expects," thereby bypassing any errors that may result when a real, inexperienced customer tries to use the site. Having another developer test is a little better, but developers' high skill level with code often means they won't detect the bugs that real customers will turn up while using the site.

Instead, consider hiring someone specifically to test the work. Your testers should have two important qualities. They should be as much like your target demographic as possible. If your demographic consists mainly of senior citizens in the Midwest, recruit a couple of them to test your site before releasing it. Testers should also possess good note-taking skills. Testers must document every button they click, every link they follow, and every letter they type. That way, they'll be able to accurately recreate any errors or anomalous conditions. Make sure that your testers understand the site's expected behaviors, but don't give them much more information than your average customer starts with.

The deployment phase

This phase involves more than simply turning on your Web servers and waiting for your customers to show up. This is the time to begin your monitoring and management processes, and to establish baselines for your site's performance. What kind of processor and memory utilization does your site require? How many users can a single Web server support? Use the deployment phase to answer these questions, and to verify that everything continues to work smoothly as real customers begin using the site.

Repeat

Having completed one full cycle of the development process, it's time to start over. By the time you finish deploying this phase, your managers, coworkers, and customers will be demanding new features and functionality, so pull out your design documents and jump right back into a new cycle of your site's next phase of development.

After you establish your site, you may want to break it down into major functional areas and conduct a separate development process for each of them. For example, you may want a separate processes for the shopping cart code, for your data exchanges with business partners, for strictly internal tools like reports and administrative interfaces, and so forth. This allows multiple projects, each with their own development process, to be running in parallel.

Development documentation

Much of your development documentation will be updated to your original site design plan. As business priorities change throughout your project, make changes to the site's original design plan, as I discuss at the beginning of this chapter. Also, completely document your project plan, and continually update that plan to indicate progress, changes to the plan, and so forth.

Your development documentation should additionally include *risk assessment* documentation and a set of descriptions for each piece of your site (ideally, down to the page level), detailing what each piece does, how it is built, and so forth.

Risk assessment

No project should begin without a clear understanding of the project's risk factors. What can go wrong? How likely is it to go wrong? What can you do if it does go wrong? Your risk assessment document takes your entire site design into consideration, along with the skill set of your technological team and the products and technologies you have selected for use in the project.

Walk through your design and make a note of anything you think may go wrong. Assign a likelihood of occurrence to each risk: "likely to go wrong," "may go wrong," "not likely to go wrong." Also assign a priority to each risk based on how devastating the risk will be if it becomes real: "High priority," "Medium priority," and "Low priority." Then, write a brief statement about what can be done to mitigate the risk, or prevent it from happening (or at least reduce the likelihood of it happening). Table 6-2 shows a sample.

Table 6-2
Sample Risk Assessment

Risk	Selected BizTalk Server 2000. Risk is that none of the technical team is familiar with the product.
Likelihood	Likely to be a problem.
Priority	Medium. We need BizTalk for partner communications, but it isn't critical for main operations.
Mitigation	Locate BizTalk training for developers and administrators as early as possible in the project.
Risk	SuperChart ActiveX control to be used in administrative interface may not be compatible with Commerce Server's analysis database.
Likelihood	Not likely to go wrong; seems to work well with other data warehouses.
Priority	Low.
Mitigation	Can eliminate charts from the administrative interface if this is a problem.
Risk	Compatibility of WidgetX ActiveX control to be used on production Web site. May not be compatible with Application Center's deployment technology.
Likelihood	May be a problem.
Priority	High. The WidgetX control is critical to the way we intend to present Widget product data to customers.
Mitigation	Immediately begin testing WidgetX control with Application Center. Contact vendor for more information and to resolve any problems. If problems can't be resolved, switch to WidgetY control, which is less functional but known to work with Application Center.

As the project continues, revisit the risk assessment document on a regular basis. Add any new risks that you have become aware of, remove any risks that have been successfully dealt with, and update the priority and likelihood of the remaining risks as appropriate. Discuss high-priority risks with your management team in order of their likelihood to make sure your mitigation plans are acceptable and that you never find yourself in a "dead end" if a risk does occur.

Site documentation

Although few e-commerce companies bother to create detailed site documentation as they are developing their sites, every single e-commerce company that I have worked with wishes they had taken the time to do so. The fact is that human beings are creating your site, and like any other person, they may forget, misremember, move to a different job, or do any of a dozen things that can reduce or eliminate the knowledge that they have about your Web site. Eventually, though, *every single writ-ten line of code* must be revisited for modifications or enhancements, so it's critical to permanently capture the developers' knowledge.

I recommend documenting the functionality of *each* page of the Web site, as well as any components, such as DLLs or other executables, that are created. This docu-mentation can be a separate document, or it can be in the form of comment lines in the code itself. I recommend the former, because the latter option means more lines of code that the server must parse through and discard every time the page is accessed by a customer.

For each page, document its general purpose, its function (particularly if it contains a form), and the input that the page expects. Also indicate the major areas to which each page is capable of linking, and what parameters the page provides the pages it links to. For example, consider the following documentation of a newsletter sign-up page in Figure 6-2:

Page: signup.asp

Purpose: Allows customers to sign up for the e-mail newsletter.

Authentication: Customers don't have to authenticate to access this page.

Basic function: Accepts an e-mail address. If the customer is registered, fills in the customer's e-mail address automatically. By default, displays a list of available newsletters (from newsletters table) and allows customer to check the ones they want. If customer is registered, the newsletters they are already subscribed to are pre-checked.

Submits: The form submits to the same page. Upon submission, ASP code analyzes customer choices and makes the appropriate changes to the customer profile. If customer is not already registered, this creates a new registered profile with a blank name.

Includes: This page includes I_EmailVerify.asp, which validates an e-mail address to catch common typing mistakes.

Input: This page accepts one optional input parameter: "NID." If provided, this parameter indicates the newsletter ID (the primary key from the newsletters table) that that customer is subscribing to. If provided, the page doesn't display a list of available newsletters; it simply asks for the customer's e-mail address.

Output: Provides no output and does not redirect or submit to other pages.

Figure 6-2: Newsletter sign-up page

Combined with well-placed comments in the code itself, this short piece of documentation allows future developers to understand exactly how this page works and how it interacts with the rest of the site's pages.

Summary

Understanding the proper flow of a professional Web development project is essential to the project's success. Too many companies try to rush through the development process with little or no controls, documentation, or formal processes to their eventual regret. Hiring the right people and selecting the right technologies are two important first steps in that process. Once the players and their tools are in place, you can begin developing your site.

✦   ✦   ✦

Introducing the Technologies

In the past few years, Microsoft has released a bewildering array of products geared for e-commerce development and administration. In fact, almost every one of their major server and development products has evolved or been rewritten to be more "Internet-centric" than ever before. As a result, many of the products' feature sets have changed drastically, overlapped the functionality of other products, and have become convoluted.

In this chapter, I look at Microsoft's current product lineup, including server and development products that you will be using in almost any e-commerce project.

I also discuss some of the non-Microsoft products and technologies that you need to take a close look at. Many of them fill in the gaps left open by Microsoft's line of products, so they're worth getting to know. Finally, I talk about two upcoming Microsoft technologies designed for use in specific e-commerce situations.

As you read about each product, think about where it fits into your overall e-commerce site's architecture. Keep your functional specification by your side and start making notes about which products you'll be using to meet the various goals in the specification. Windows 2000 Server is obviously the base operating system that your servers run, but where do you need Commerce Server? What needs does BizTalk Server fill for your organization? Should you use Application Center? I talk about using specific features of these products to solve specific needs in later chapters, so this brief introduction sets the stage.

Microsoft E-Commerce Project Tools

Microsoft offers almost every tool you need for a full-fledged, professional
e-commerce project:

✦ Windows 2000 Server (and the Advanced Server and Datacenter Server
variants)

✦ Internet Information Services and Active Server Pages

✦ SQL Server 2000

✦ Site Server 3.0

✦ Site Server 3.0, Commerce Edition (and Commerce Server 2000)

✦ Exchange Server 2000

✦ BizTalk Server 2000

✦ Application Center 2000

✦ Visual Basic

Windows 2000 Server

Windows 2000 Server is the basic edition of Microsoft's server operating system
and the foundation upon which the entire Microsoft e-commerce empire is based.
Therefore, if you're building an e-commerce site using Microsoft's technologies, you
need to become very familiar with Windows 2000 Server.

Windows 2000 Server comes in two higher-end editions, known as Windows 2000
Advanced Server and Windows 2000 Datacenter Server. Both of these products provide all the features and functionality of the basic Server product, and add supple-
mentary capabilities and features for higher-end systems.

Windows 2000 Server

The basic Windows 2000 Server product is suitable for use on a Web server. In this
base edition of Windows 2000 Server, a computer can have up to 4GB of physical
memory installed. 2GB of this memory are always reserved for the operating system, and the other 2GB for applications. In fact, all applications run as if they have
2GB of memory. If the server doesn't have that much installed, Windows 2000 uses
its swap file to make up the difference.

Windows 2000 Advanced Server

Advanced Server adds two-node clustering, which is a very valuable feature when
designing a database infrastructure. Clustering allows two servers to act as a
backup for each other, protecting you from a catastrophic hardware failure in
either. It also changes the way memory is allocated between the operating system
and applications.

In Advanced Server, the computer can still contain up to 4GB of physical memory, but only 1GB of this memory is reserved for the operating system. Plus, applications are initially given 3GB of memory space. With memory-intensive applications, such as SQL Server 2000 or Exchange Server 2000, this can make a big difference in performance. Advanced Server is also capable of working with up to eight processors, which is double the capacity of the basic 2000 Server.

Windows 2000 Datacenter Server

Datacenter Server is the heavy-duty version of Windows 2000. It is capable of four-node clustering, can access up to 64GB of physical memory in the computer, and is capable of working with up to 32 processors. Datacenter is, of course, significantly more expensive than its lower-powered siblings and is much pickier about the hardware that it runs on. In fact, you can't even buy Datacenter Server by itself. You have to buy it as part of a complete hardware-and-operating-system package from approved vendors.

Tip   Stick with Windows 2000 Server for your Web servers; this edition offers everything a Web server needs. Consider Windows 2000 Advanced Server for back-end database servers so that you can take advantage of clustering and the better memory architecture.

One of the most important features included in all three versions of Windows 2000 Server is Internet Information Services.

Internet Information Services and Active Server Pages

Internet Information Services (IIS) was first introduced with Windows NT 3.51. Active Server Pages (ASP) was added to IIS 3.0 and quickly made IIS the most popular commercial Web server software on the market. IIS 4.0 was included with the NT 4.0 Option Pack for Windows NT 4.0, and IIS 5.0 is the version included with Windows 2000.

IIS is also one of the primary building blocks for Microsoft's Internet strategy. Site Server and Commerce Server build on IIS to deliver their features, SQL Server 2000 relies on IIS to provide much of its XML functionality, and Exchange Server 2000 integrates with IIS to provide Web-based messaging.

Although IIS is a robust and very scalable Web server, its most important contribution is the inclusion of ASP. The ASP technology allows IIS to read Web pages that include VBScript or Jscript instructions, to execute those instructions, and to feed the output to a user's Web browser. This powerful technology completely replaces older methods of Web server programming, such as the Common Gateway Interface (CGI) techniques that are common in the UNIX Web server world.

ASP also allows the Web developer to add powerful COM components to Web pages. These components can perform complex operations, interact with middle- and back-tier servers, and much more. This is one of ASP's most powerful features.

In fact, Site Server and Commerce Server provide their most powerful and important features as COM components, which are referenced by VBScript and Jscript in ASP pages.

Microsoft continues to refine and evolve ASP, and has created ASP.NET, which should become available when this book goes to press. ASP.NET, formerly known as ASP+, continues to provide developers with powerful scripting and COM tools for Web pages, but does so with a new, simpler language and object model. In effect, ASP.NET merges the static HTML and dynamic script code into a single, combined language that makes writing dynamic Web pages easier. ASP.NET also compiles the script in ASP pages, so the pages can execute faster than in the current ASP version. ASP.NET should be completely compatible with your existing ASP pages, but provides an easier development platform and more powerful feature set for future development.

Tip   Windows 2000 Professional also provides a version of IIS that supports ASP. This allows you to develop ASP-based Web sites on your workstation, and then deploy the site to a Windows 2000 Server when it's ready to go.

SQL Server 2000

SQL Server 2000 is Microsoft's relational database management system (RDBMS). In addition to the basic features found in most RDBMS platforms, SQL Server 2000 provides a wealth of features to make e-commerce development easier, and to make Web sites faster and more robust.

SQL Server 2000 has built-in support for replication, which allows you to easily create separate reporting servers. It has built-in support for XML, which allows you to receive XML-formatted data as the result of a SQL query. SQL Server 2000 also has a powerful set of built-in data manipulation tools, known as Data Transformation Services (DTS). These tools facilitate pulling data from multiple heterogeneous data sources; manipulating and transforming that data into different formats, and then sending the data to another database, to an FTP site as XML-formatted data, and much more. DTS was originally introduced in SQL Server 7.0 and has become an important tool for developers who need to exchange data with business partners or between departments.

SQL Server 2000 is another fundamental building block in an e-commerce project. Most of Microsoft's other server products, including Site Server, Commerce Server, and BizTalk Server, use SQL Server 2000 as their primary data repository. Having a well-optimized SQL Server is critical to the success of any e-commerce site.

SQL Server 2000 Enterprise Edition adds support for clustering — allowing you to build high-availability database clusters that can be used as the data tier for an e-commerce site. SQL Server 2000 Enterprise Edition runs only on Windows 2000 Advanced Server or Datacenter Server.

Site Server 3.0

Site Server 3.0 provides a variety of tools designed to improve e-commerce Web sites, and to make the development and administration of the sites easier. Site Server consists of several major components, which can be used independently or as a set.

✦ **Site Server Personalization and Membership services** — allow you to create member registration services for your site so users can sign up with a user name and password, for example. After they are signed up, your Web site can identify those users when they visit in the future. This allows you to track their activities and preferences, and customize their browsing experience to meet their specific needs and interests — the "personalization" piece of the system.

✦ **Site Server Search** — is one of the most powerful and robust versions of the Microsoft Search technology released to date. It enables Site Server to examine, or *crawl*, designated portions of your Web site and build an index of the content that it finds. Users can then quickly search the index to find a list of Web pages matching their interests. The Search service integrates well — even with dynamically generated Web pages — effectively allowing users to search the contents of a product's database, for example.

✦ **Site Server's Content Management and Content Deployment services** — allow a site administrator to delegate the process of creating content to other developers or even non-technical employees through a powerful system of permissions. Content Deployment simplifies the task of duplicating new content to many servers in a large Web farm by automating the process.

Note   Content Management has been removed from Site Server 3.0's successor, Commerce Server 2000. Microsoft anticipates delivering more robust content management and collaboration capabilities in its forthcoming "Tahoe" server. Content Deployment has been greatly enhanced and is provided by Application Center rather than being built into Commerce Server 2000.

Although Commerce Server 2000 has replaced Site Server 3.0, you may still prefer to use Site Server 3.0 if your Web site was developed with it. Commerce Server 2000 is not a "plug and play" replacement for Site Server 3.0.

Caution   Site Server 3.0 can only be run on Windows 2000 if you install Site Server 3.0 Service Pack 4 or higher.

Site Server 3.0, Commerce Edition and Commerce Server 2000

Site Server 3.0, Commerce Edition builds upon the features in Site Server 3.0 and provides specific functionality for developing powerful e-commerce Web sites. Some of the most powerful e-commerce sites in the world — including Microsoft's own online store — have been built with the Commerce Edition.

Both Site Server 3.0 and Commerce Edition are being replaced with a single integrated product called Commerce Server 2000. This new server product provides significantly enhanced e-commerce features. These features include a completely new Product Catalog system based on SQL Server 2000, which allows you to more easily create product catalogs. The Product Catalog feature also includes built-in search capabilities, making it easier to deploy a searchable catalog than in the older version.

Personalization and Membership have been greatly enhanced, and they include a complete targeting system for managing advertising campaigns, mailing lists, direct mail campaigns, and dynamic content selection.

If you are working on a site that was built with Site Server 3.0, Commerce Edition, you should expect to continue using that product. Commerce Server 2000 isn't a "plug and play" replacement for Site Server or Commerce Edition. If you're starting a new e-commerce project from scratch, though, you should probably use Commerce Server 2000 to take advantage of its new features.

Caution   Site Server 3.0, Commerce Edition can only run on Windows 2000 if you also install Site Server 3.0 Service Pack 4 or higher.

Commerce Server 2000 is designed to meet many of your organization's business needs. Marketing departments, for example, generally have complex needs from an e-commerce site. They need to build mailing lists, create targeted promotional events, query and sort data on customers' purchase history and buying preferences, and much more. In previous versions, these tasks required a significant amount of programming, but Commerce Server 2000 delivers this information, and much more, right out of the box.

Exchange Server 2000

You may be surprised to see Exchange Server 2000 mentioned in a book about e-commerce. After all, Exchange Server is just an e-mail server, right?

Exchange Server is much more than "just" an e-mail server. And don't underestimate the importance of e-mail to an e-commerce site! You may need the power and flexibility that Exchange Server offers, both as an e-mail server and as a document management platform.

Almost every e-commerce site needs to have some kind of e-mail support. Your site may need to send order confirmations, subscription renewal notices, and other routine e-mail. You also probably want the ability to send mass marketing e-mail. One of the best ways to keep users coming back to your site is to lure them in with timely, targeted e-mail newsletters and offers. Exchange Server provides a great platform for this functionality. You can use Exchange server-side scripting to automate the process of subscribing and unsubscribing users from newsletters. Exchange Server's robust SMTP support makes it the best choice for sending important routine e-mails like order confirmations.

Exchange Server 2000 can be a powerful building block for certain types of e-commerce sites. Does your site need to share any kind of documents with your users? Will your users need to search for those documents? If you're nodding your head "yes," then you should consider storing those documents in Exchange Server 2000's Web Store, and allowing your customers to access documents from there.

The Web Store provides a fault-tolerant database for storing documents of almost any type, including Word files, Excel spreadsheets, text files, scanned copies of paper forms, and much more. The Web Store provides complete indexing of everything stored in it, and is completely accessible by using Internet protocols, such as HTTP. If your company has an abundance of sales brochures or product information sheets, put them in the Web Store. Customers can use your Web site to search that content and pull up the information that they need right out of the Exchange Server.

Note   Exchange Server 2000 only runs on Windows 2000 or later versions.

BizTalk Server 2000

BizTalk Server is one of the most exciting products that Microsoft has released in quite some time. The product serves two main functions: To serve as the world's biggest data translator and to coordinate complex business processes.

As a translator, BizTalk Server is designed to read data from almost any file you can imagine — flat text files, XML-formatted files, Electronic Data Interchange (EDI) messages, and so on. It then uses an XML-based schema to translate the data into a platform-neutral intermediate format, which is represented internally using XML. BizTalk then translates the data into whatever data format you need — EDI, flat files, XML files, and more — and delivers the data.

BizTalk targets non-programmers, but initially setting it up requires quite a bit of technical expertise. In the e-commerce world, BizTalk really shines at helping exchange business data with your organization's trading partners. Consider the following examples:

✦ Your company may send purchase orders and invoices electronically.

✦ You may want to send a copy of your product catalog to a trading partner.

✦ Your site may receive inventory information directly from distributors, and then send those distributors the orders that your customers have placed.

All of this data comes in different formats, with different pieces of information, through different methods. This situation may be problematic; for example, your distributor may want to e-mail you the inventory information, but you may want to receive customer orders via fax.

BizTalk accommodates this variety of needs by defining *agreements*, which specify the incoming data format, the outgoing data format, the delivery methods to be used, and other details. After the agreement is set up and BizTalk understands the data formats being used, the rest of the process is fully automated. Most importantly, setting up the data exchange agreement in BizTalk is *much* easier than the old way of writing custom programs in Visual Basic to handle data exchanges.

BizTalk has another major area of functionality called BizTalk Orchestration. One of the first products to facilitate teamwork between non-technical business analysts and software developers, BizTalk Orchestration is designed to logically separate designing business and designing software to carry out those processes.

For example, your e-commerce site may be totally based on Microsoft technologies, but all of the customer order information has to make it into your company's existing order fulfillment process, which may be based on an IBM AS/400. Your company's business analyst can use BizTalk Orchestration to literally draw a flowchart of how that process should work. Your developers can then tie each step in the process to software components that perform each function, including some powerful cross-platform integration components provided with BizTalk Server. BizTalk ensures that the process runs as a complete transaction. If something in the process fails, BizTalk can "undo" the steps already completed. If the business process is ever changed, your business analyst just needs to modify the flowchart. Additional programming may not even be necessary.

BizTalk Orchestration is also great for streamlining purely internal processes. Imagine the business process that a company may follow for adding new products to its catalog. Certain information has to be placed into a database, specific individuals have to approve product selections and descriptions, pricing has to be set in accordance with various policies, and finally the product information must be added to the company's Commerce Server 2000 product catalog. BizTalk allows that entire process to be automated, documented, and maintained in a single easy-to-use environment.

Although it may seem like extra work to build business processes in BizTalk, think of the time you'll save when—not if—those processes change slightly.

Note   BizTalk 2000 requires SQL Server 7.0 or higher in order to run.

Application Center 2000

As I discuss previously in this chapter, one of the best ways to build a Web site that can handle lots of traffic is to build a *Web farm*. A Web farm consists of multiple Web servers that contain the same information. Incoming requests are distributed among the servers, allowing them to handle more traffic than one server possibly can by itself. If the servers start getting bogged down by traffic, you just throw a couple more into the farm. It's a tried-and-true method of building highly scalable Web sites. This technique, however, presents many challenges for those who have to manage the Web site. Although it sounds easy enough to just "throw another server in there," doing so in actuality can be tricky. You have to make sure that all the right Web content gets copied to the new server, that all the right DLL's are in place, and that any other software required by the Web site is installed and working. Copying a couple of new ASP files to two new Web servers is easy enough, but what if you need to completely update the site and you have sixty servers? That's where Application Center 2000 steps in. Application Center's design enables you to treat your entire Web farm as if it was a single server. Application Center deploys new content, loads content onto new servers, and keeps everything synchronized.

> **Note** Application Center's capabilities replace the less-robust Content Deployment services in Site Server 3.0.

Application Center can also handle load balancing across the servers in your Web farm, automatically distributing user traffic to the servers currently handling the lightest load. It allows you to pull servers out of the farm for maintenance, and automatically redistributes the user load across the remaining servers. Application Center also allows you to perform *rolling upgrades*, or taking one server at a time out of rotation, updating its content, and placing it back into the load balancing pool.

If you've been careful to design your e-commerce site so that your business logic is encapsulated in COM+ objects, then Application Center can help you create a more scalable business tier. Carefully written COM+ objects can be installed on several servers in a *COM+ cluster*. As the servers in your Web farm access the COM+ objects (usually by referring to them in script), Application Center automatically distributes the load across all of the servers in the COM+ cluster, effectively creating a *component farm* that supports your Web farm. Although some extra effort is required to ensure that COM+ components can be used in this fashion, it's well worth that effort when you realize that you can double your business tier's load capacity simply by adding a new server to the COM+ cluster!

Visual Basic

Visual Basic, with its many varieties, is the glue that ties the Microsoft .NET products together. Whether you're using VBScript in an ASP page or writing COM+ components with Visual Basic 6.0 (or the forthcoming Visual Basic .NET), you'll find that Visual Basic is an excellent tool.

All of Microsoft's .NET products can be leveraged in some fashion by using Visual Basic. Consider the following facts:

✦ Site Server and Commerce Server both provide most of their functionality through COM components. These components are made to perform and are tied together by using VBScript in ASP pages.

✦ SQL Server 2000 supports the use of VBScript in Data Transformation Services. Additionally, you can control the operation of the entire SQL Server by writing Visual Basic code that works with SQL Server's Distributed Management Objects (DMO) object model.

✦ Exchange Server 2000 can be automated using server-side VBScript, and can be extended by writing COM components in Visual Basic. For example, you can use a combination of VBScript and Visual Basic components to create a self-service e-mail newsletter subscription system.

✦ BizTalk Server 2000 can be extended and controlled by using Visual Basic.

✦ Application Center 2000 can be completely scripted by using VBScript to further automate maintenance and monitoring tasks.

✦ Windows 2000 can be controlled almost completely through VBScript by using the Windows Scripting Host (WSH).

✦ The primary method of programming IIS is to use VBScript in ASP pages, or to write Internet Services API (ISAPI) components by using Visual Basic.

Non-Microsoft Products and Technologies

Although Microsoft continuously makes great strides to provide complete solutions to technological problems, you can't build a successful e-commerce site without turning to other vendors. In some cases, Microsoft just doesn't provide a product that solves your needs. In other cases, Microsoft offers a product, but it doesn't have all of the features that you need — or sometimes, their product may have *too many* features!

COM components

Because e-commerce sites are, at their heart, put together with VBScript and Active Server Pages, little need exists to perform any kind of complicated task by writing script. Instead, you can find a wide variety of third-party COM components that can do things faster and with less effort on your part.

Maybe your Web site needs to send e-mail, but only short messages a few times a day. In this case, Exchange Server would be overkill. What you need is an SMTP component that can send the e-mail through your Internet Service Provider's mail forwarding host. A variety of SMTP components are on the market — check them out and choose one with the features that you like. The site www.scibit.com publishes one that you should check out.

The site www.scibit.com also publishes a great credit card utility. Although it doesn't post a charge to a customer's credit card account, it does perform the complex mathematical routine that tells you if the card number that a customer enters is valid. Because many credit card processors charge per transaction, you want to use a component like this to check the validity of a card before sending the transaction to the processor.

What if you want users to be able to upload files to your site? Microsoft provides a Posting Acceptor component with Site Server, but it's difficult to set up and can be unreliable in some circumstances. The third-party market, however, provides several alternative ActiveX controls that minimize the task of accepting file uploads into a matter of setting a couple of properties and calling an event. Check out www.aspsoft.com for one such component.

Do you want to display graphical charts on your Web pages? Programming that kind of functionality in VBScript takes forever, but you can do it in a few minutes with a component like the one from www.nevron.com.

These components are a *very* small sampling of the inexpensive and powerful third-party components that are available. You can find more components by searching a site like www.activex.com or visiting a retailer like www.vbxtras.com.

Server software

Although Microsoft doesn't always like to admit it, there are other sources for server software in the world. E-commerce sites often use non-Microsoft server software when they need less powerful, inexpensive alternatives.

Many smaller e-commerce sites don't need the powerful e-mail and groupware capabilities of Exchange, but they do need some kind of mail server. Inexpensive, Windows 2000-compatible SMTP servers fill this need nicely with a minimum of additional administrative overhead.

Some small e-commerce sites also use lower-powered database servers. If your e-commerce site is hosted at a professional hosting facility, your only option may be to use the inexpensive database server that they provide. MySQL is a popular database server used by many hosting facilities.

You can develop ASP Web sites without using any Microsoft products at all. Although you limit yourself to basic ASP functionality without add-on products like Commerce Server 2000 or Application Center, companies like ChiliSoft (www.chilisoft.com) provide an add-on to non-Microsoft Web servers that allows them to execute ASP code.

Commerce Server pipeline components

Both Site Server 3.0, Commerce Edition and Commerce Server 2000 support the concept of a *commerce pipeline*. The pipeline is a fairly simple representation of a business process, such as a retail checkout. The pipeline defines certain actions that must occur in a certain sequence. For example, in a typical checkout, the pipeline may first calculate tax and shipping charges, then validate the customer's credit card, and finally generate an order confirmation number and a receipt.

The pipeline also makes all the steps in the pipeline *atomic*. This means that the entire pipeline is considered to be a single transaction, and if one step in the pipeline fails, all of the steps fail. You can imagine how important atomicity is in a pipeline handling customer checkout.

Some of these pipeline steps, such as a basic tax calculator, are built into Commerce Server. Some steps are not built in, such as calculating shipping based on the weight of the items ordered, but they're simple enough to implement in VBScript. Other steps, such as processing a credit card charge, are neither built-in nor especially straightforward.

Microsoft designed their commerce pipeline to support external components precisely for this reason. These components are simply COM components that have been written to follow the rules of the Microsoft commerce pipeline. They accept specific information as input, such as the credit card number, expiration date, and amount to charge, and return other information as output, such as whether or not the charge was successful, and if so, an authorization number.

Common pipeline components that are available from non-Microsoft vendors include credit card authorization components, mail sending components, more complex tax calculation components, shipping calculation components that interface with shipping vendors' proprietary systems for exact quotes, and more.

Third-party component cautions

Be careful when selecting third-party software for use in your Microsoft e-commerce solution. If possible, obtain an evaluation version of the software and try it for a short period of time to ensure that it integrates well into your overall solution. Make sure that the documentation is complete and correct. Make sure that the component does what you want it to do. You should watch out for some specific issues, which I discuss in the following sections.

COM components

COM components that are referenced by an ASP page are started in the same process and memory space as Internet Information Server (IIS). That means an unstable COM component can take your entire Web server with it if it crashes or hangs. Test third-party COM components carefully, and make sure any stress testing that you perform on your Web site includes the functions provided by these components. As a general rule of thumb, test the components with 50 percent more of a load than you expect them to handle in production.

Make sure that the COM components are written completely in 32-bit code, and that they don't depend on any 16-bit or outdated DLLs or OCXs. IIS doesn't handle 16-bit components very well, and your site will suffer a major performance decrease if they're used. Also make sure that third-party COM components' Setup programs don't overwrite any of your system DLLs or other files with older versions. In general, the Protected File System of Windows 2000 should prevent this from happening, but remember: Better safe than sorry!

Server software

As with third-party COM components, ensure that third-party server software is fully 32-bit, completely Windows 2000 compatible, and capable of handling the load that you intend to place on it. Ideally, try to use software that carries Microsoft's "Designed for Windows 2000 Server" logo, which indicates that the software meets certain minimal requirements for Windows 2000 compatibility.

Any server software that must be clustered for reliability should be specifically written to be *cluster-aware*. Any software carrying the "Designed for Windows 2000 Advanced Server" logo meets this requirement; software carrying a lesser designation may be "clusterable" without being specifically cluster-aware. "Clusterable" applications generally don't perform well in high-load situations when one cluster node fails and the other takes over (a process known as *failover*), and generally don't support advanced clustering features like active-active clustering, in which both cluster nodes perform production tasks at the same time.

Commerce Server pipeline components

Pipeline components have to be written to special guidelines in order to function at all. Make sure that the components you purchase can handle the load that you intend for them to handle. For example, a credit card verification component that takes ten seconds to process a transaction and can only handle a single transaction at a time is going to present a serious obstacle when your site is handling a hundred customers at once.

Talk to the pipeline component vendor and inquire about the background of the component's code. Ask if the component was written from the ground up to be a Commerce Server pipeline component. If so, then it most likely meets all the requirements for running properly in the pipeline. On the other hand, if the component was originally written for another platform, and then "wrapped" in additional code to make it compatible with Commerce Server, you may run into subtle problems. Try to stick with components that were natively written to run with Commerce Server.

Caution Commerce pipeline components are specific to the version of Commerce Server. Components written for Commerce Server 2000 may not work properly with Site Server 3.0, Commerce Edition, and vice-versa.

Upcoming Microsoft Technologies

As this book goes to press, Microsoft is preparing to release two new major .NET server products: Mobile Information Server, and a portal server, which is currently code-named "Tahoe."

Mobile Information Server 2001

Mobile Information Server (MIS) simplifies the task of delivering content to mobile devices like Web-enabled cellular phones and personal digital assistance devices (PDAs). MIS sits on your organization's internal network, providing organization employees and partners access to internal resources. Even though it's not specifically designed for the business-to-consumer e-commerce market, MIS shows potential for simplifying the business-to-business relationships between e-commerce companies. Imagine giving access to Exchange Server-based applications (such as a sales-quoting application) to your company's trading partners' field sales force via cell phone. The possibilities for extending the reach of your corporate information into the mobile space are endless.

SharePoint portal server

One of the newest .NET Servers, SharePoint is billed as an "intranet portal, search and document management server." And even though it's certainly not targeted toward the business-to-consumer market, Tahoe nonetheless promises significant advantages to e-commerce companies. For example, Tahoe's document management and collaboration capabilities, which are based on Exchange Server's Web Store technology, will provide the type of collaborative, controlled development environment that e-commerce companies have been looking for. Rather than employing a horde of HTML designers to build Web pages, SharePoint l lets non-technical content producers edit Web pages in a controlled, team-oriented environment. SharePoint also provides a single source for finding internal company documents, and for helping employees and close business partners manage the huge wealth of information that flows through the typical e-commerce company on a daily basis.

Summary

Microsoft offers a variety of products and technologies that you can use to build your e-commerce site. And, where Microsoft's products don't meet your specific business needs, third-party software is available to fill in the gaps.

✦   ✦   ✦

Architecting
the Site

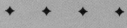

In This Chapter

Exploring the
application tiers

Determining where
code will go

✦ ✦ ✦ ✦

Your site design should already include information on
how your site will be architected. Will it be a 3-tier
design? A 4-tier design? How and where will business logic be
implemented? These are questions you need to answer before
any actual programming can begin. You also need to decide
which tiers will include program code, since the software at
each tier offers the opportunity for some kind of programming
or automation.

In this chapter I'll discuss the four basic tiers of a Web application, and give you some recommendations about how to
implement those tiers. I'll also discuss where code should go
in each tier, and how that code should be implemented for
maximum performance and scalability.

Application Architecture

When designing your application architecture, remember two
basic rules:

1. More application tiers generally result in a more scalable
   architecture.

2. Fewer application tiers generally result in an application
   that is easier to create initially.

Given that application architecture involves an inherent tradeoff between scalability and ease of development, you should
strive to achieve a good balance between the two factors.
Start with a small application architecture, and then ask yourself the following questions:

✦ Will the business rules that run the site change frequently? If so, the rules should be housed in their own
  tier within the application, centralizing them and making
  them easier to change.

✦ Will the site show continuous growth, requiring more and more servers to perform work? If so, a four-tier (or possibly higher) architecture is required. Tiers take on an inverted pyramid shape, as shown in Figure 8-1, so by adding additional tiers closer to the client you can increase the amount of work a single application architecture can handle.

✦ Will the business logic in the application be used by other applications? If so, you should include the shared logic in its own tier, making it more easily accessible to a variety of applications.

✦ Will the business logic change frequently? If so, including the logic its own tier will better isolate it and make it easier to modify in the future.

✦ Will the Web servers be built for specialized tasks, such as a search server, a shopping cart server, and so on? If so, the business logic should be broken into a separate tier, making that logic more easily available to the different types of Web servers.

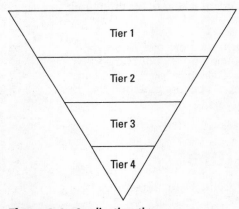

Figure 8-1: Application tiers

Your application's architecture is a key component in its ability to handle increasing traffic, growth, and other factors. Take the time to understand how your application needs fit together and design an application architecture that meets those needs.

Application Tiers

Web applications are by definition at least a three-tier design, and are often a four-tier design, as shown in Figure 8-2.

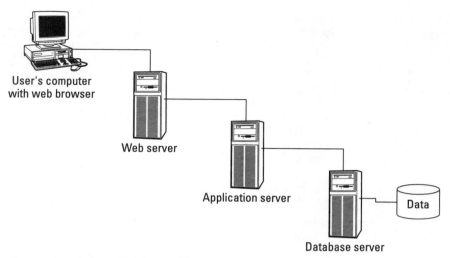

Figure 8-2: Web application architecture

In this architecture, the Web browser itself forms one tier of the application; the Web server forms a second tier; one or more business logic servers, or application servers, form a third tier; and finally, a back-end database server such as SQL Server 2000 forms the fourth tier.

This type of architecture addresses the four basic tiers of an application that must exist.

✦ **The Presentation Tier:** Responsible for displaying information and collecting user input according to predefined instructions.

✦ **The Client Tier:** Responsible for generating the instructions for presenting and collecting data and for actually generating the display a user sees.

✦ **The Business Tier:** Responsible for validating incoming data and properly filtering requested data for the specific task being performed in the client tier.

✦ **The Data Tier:** Responsible for maintaining the data in the application.

Web applications always use the user's Web browser as the presentation tier and the Web server as the client tier, because the Web server is actually responsible for generating the HTML, but the user's Web browser is responsible for rendering that HTML code into a readable display. This contrasts with traditional applications written in C++ or Visual Basic, where the client and presentation tiers are not distinct and always reside on the same computer and within the same set of code.

The business tier in a Web application may also be physically implemented on the Web server, though as you read in the beginning of this chapter, creating a separate physical tier for it is often desirable. The business tier implements the majority of the business logic that drives your site and maintains responsibility for interacting with the data tier. The data tier should contain as few servers as possible, enabling you to keep as few copies of your database as possible. In cases where one database server (or cluster) is unable to keep up with the demand of the lower tiers, you should consider breaking your application into further segments. For example, Yahoo.com is an incredibly large and complex site with a wide variety of user services. While the Yahoo.com site can be considered a single large application, it is broken down into the following sub-architectures that allow for scalability.

✦ The client tier comprises many different Web servers, each serving different tasks — Web searching, e-mail, calendars, auctions, and so on.

✦ A business tier implements business logic specific to each sub-architecture — validating e-mail, handling auctions, and so on.

✦ A shared business tier handles logic shared across the sub-architectures — user authentication and profile maintenance, for example.

✦ Each business tier, including the shared business tier, communicates with a back-end database tier that stores data used by that business tier — user data, auction data, and so on.

As shown in Figure 8-3, your site can be structured with a similar parallel architecture. By breaking the major functional areas of your site into separate, parallel architectures, you can greatly extend the scalability of the site. This specialized architecture requires additional development effort, but pays off with a greatly increased ability to handle growth.

In the next few sections, I'll discuss specific ways to develop each tier of your site and how to make each tier perform the greatest amount of work possible.

Tip

The architecture you select for your site will probably be around for as long as the site is. Redesigning the architecture of a completed site without having to start over from scratch is nearly impossible. So consider your choices carefully, and make decisions that will support your site's needs well into the future.

Presentation tier

The presentation tier of your Web site consists of the customer's Web browser. Unless you are developing an intranet-based e-commerce site, where you will be able to specify a single Web browser for customers to use, the presentation tier of your site will consist of a variety of browsers. The variety of browsers you intend to support may limit the functionality you can place within the presentation tier.

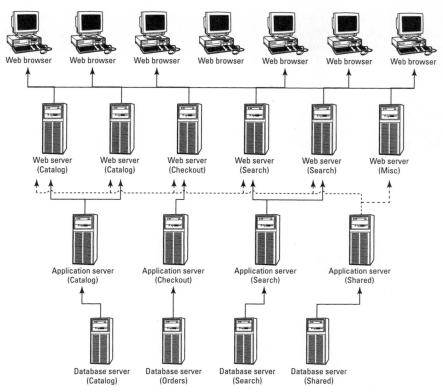

Figure 8-3: Parallel application architecture

At the very least, the presentation tier is responsible for rendering and displaying the HTML and images downloaded from your Web servers. As mentioned in previous chapters, the different browser applications follow slightly different rules for rendering HTML, so you should not expect to achieve a universal appearance in your presentation tier without a significant amount of work by your HTML programmers (who will have to modify their code to make it look the same on every browser you intend to support).

Note Television-based Web browsers, such as WebTV or AOL TV, use radically different methods for rendering HTML to fit on a television screen. If you anticipate that customers using these services will be a major part of your demographic, consider writing code to detect their special Web browsers and redirecting them to a specially designed version of your site that accommodates the restrictions of the television-browsing environment.

If you plan to support only 4.0 or higher browsers — a reasonable choice for many e-commerce sites — you will have the flexibility to include program code in your presentation tier. Implemented as Dynamic HTML (DHTML), this program code could simply extend the client tier into the Web browser by providing dynamic displays of information, or it could partially extend the business tier into the browser by providing basic validation of user input. This approach is becoming more popular as e-commerce architects become smarter about distributing their sites' processing load. After all, every customer's Web browser is running on a computer of some kind. Why not take advantage of the power on that computer to handle some of the site's basic processing needs?

Many experienced multi-tier developers hesitate to place business logic, such as data validation, in their presentation or client tiers because of the difficulty in updating the logic in so many places should it ever change. Ultimately, though, any client-side code you write will still be downloaded from your Web servers, which provides a somewhat centralized location for the code. You can further modularize and centralize by using a content deployment tool such as Application Center 2000, which enables you to maintain a central master image of your code base which it then deploys to your Web servers. This enables you to easily make changes to any presentation-tier logic in a single location and still distribute the processing of that code out to each customer who uses your site. This is an efficient approach to reducing overhead on your servers (since data validation would otherwise require a "round trip" to the Web server), and has the added benefit of providing immediate feedback to your customers when they make a data entry error.

If you do decide to employ client-side code, make sure your client-side code only performs data display manipulation, such as hiding or showing information in response to user interactions, or the most basic data validation logic. Since your presentation-tier code is running on a computer that is not under your control, you risk technically skilled users altering the data validation routines or even bypassing them altogether. Important business logic should be maintained in higher tiers of the application.

If your site will be accessible by "extremely thin" clients such as Wireless Application Protocol (WAP)–enabled cellular phones, provide a separate sub-architecture for customers using those technologies. Not only do WAP devices feature significantly less robust displays, they also do not offer client-side DHTML scripting, meaning all of your application's logic must reside on the client tier or higher. This limitation applies to any device that does not support client-side scripting, including Web browsers on handheld Personal Digital Assistants (PDAs) like Palm or PocketPC devices. Most so-called "Internet appliances" are simply scaled-down computers, and will generally support the robust client-side scripting required to implement presentation-tier logic. Even television-based Web browsers, such as Microsoft's WebTV and America Online's AOL TV, support a rich set of DHTML features.

Client tier

Your Web servers form the client tier of your Web site because they actually control what is displayed for your users in their Web browsers. Your Web servers will always contain a certain amount of program code, even if you implement the majority of your business logic in a dedicated tier. At a minimum, your Web servers will execute enough script code to activate and control the components that actually implement your site's business logic.

I always recommend that large e-commerce sites, or sites that plan on being large e-commerce sites, use a distributed, parallel architecture such as the one shown in Figure 8-3. This architecture enables you to create specialized servers that are fine-tuned for the specific tasks they handle, and makes your site much easier to scale as traffic grows. If your search servers seem a bit overwhelmed, add another. If the checkout process is running too slowly, add another checkout server. The alternative is to use all-purpose servers, each capable of performing every task on your site, and hope that the load balances itself out well enough.

One common objection to building a parallel architecture is the cost of the additional servers. For example, if your site starts small, you may not be able to afford enough servers to implement a dedicated search server, catalog server, checkout server, and so on. However, the lack of physical servers should not stop you from implementing a logically parallel architecture! Go ahead and build dedicated "Web sites" for the major functional areas of your site. For example, Retailer.com might create a set of Web pages to handle searches, a set for catalog browsing, a set for the checkout process, and a set for other site functions such as newsletter subscribing and customer service. Rather than lumping all of these pages on a single "`www.retailer.com`" server, they can be split up into "`search.retailer.com`," "`catalog.retailer.com`," "`checkout.retailer.com`," and "`misc.retailer.com`." Each separate "Web site" can then be physically implemented on a *single server* by configuring separate virtual Web sites in Internet Information Services and configuring them to respond to the appropriate host names and IP addresses.

This "multiple Web sites" technique enables you to begin building a parallel architecture from the start, even if you don't have enough hardware to implement each function on a dedicated machine.

Tip   Building a parallel architecture from the start is *much* easier than trying to retrofit a "monolithic" site that has been up and running for a while. The time to decide on a parallel architecture is *before* you begin building your site.

Your client tier should represent the most generic, most easily duplicated tier in your Web application. Software packages such as Application Center 2000 enable you to manage five or more servers as easily as managing one, and even make the task of adding a new server to the "cluster" virtually as easy as plug-and-play. Building a flexible, scalable client-tier architecture maximizes your ability to quickly grow your site to meet the demands of your customers.

Business tier

The majority of your heavy-duty processing should occur on the business tier, which should run on one or more separate servers and contain COM and COM+ components that do all of the actual work of your site, such as validating data, processing data, interacting with your database tier, and so forth. Your Web servers should instantiate the components on the business tier servers using script, and the components can return the necessary data to the Web servers. Only the business tier should ever communicate with the data tier; Web servers should never attempt to make a direct connection to the data tier. Doing so is a poor design practice and makes it exceptionally difficult to debug your site when problems occur.

With the introduction of Application Center 2000, the business tier has an amazing potential for fault-tolerance and scalability. Combined with a parallel application architecture that dedicates specific business tier servers to specific pieces of site functionality, you can design a business tier capable of supporting the busiest, most processing-intensive Web sites you can imagine. I'll describe these technologies, including Component Load Balancing, in an upcoming section of this chapter.

Data tier

Your data tier consists of one or more Windows 2000 Server computers running SQL Server 2000. In a parallel architecture, you divide your site's database into different "partitions," enabling you to then deploy multiple SQL Servers to create a more scalable data tier.

In general, the Commerce Server database can be divided into three basic partitions:

✦ All the tables that only your company makes changes to, including the product catalog.

✦ All the tables that are changed by customers' actions, other than tables relating to the checkout process. Most important in this set are the tables dealing with customer profiles.

✦ All the tables that hold the results of the checkout process, such as the orders tables.

Properly designed, these sets tables essentially stand on their own enabling you to use, for example, three separate database servers. Each database server contains the entire Commerce Server database (since processes like the checkout require access to the product catalog information, for example), but each server is only "allowed" to modify data in one of the three sets of tables. You can add other servers to handle specific tasks, giving them a read-only copy of the requisite partitions. Table 8-1 shows how you can architect your data tier to take advantage of these partitions.

Table 8-1
Partitioning the Commerce Server database

Server	Owned Partition	Notes
Checkout	Order tables	Replicates customer profile and product catalog data from the other servers, but does not modify that data.
Product browsing	Catalog tables	Replicates other tables from other servers. Your administrative interface makes changes to the product catalog on this server.
Customer profiles	Profile tables	Replicates other tables from other servers. Anything making changes to customer profiles will need to work with this server.
Product search	None	Maintains a read-only replica of the product catalog tables. Since search is such a database-intensive task, it often makes sense to offload it to a server dedicated to the task.

With your data tier architected in this fashion, certain business tier servers may still need to access multiple portions of the data tier. For example, if your checkout process enables customers to modify or add addresses to their "address book" of billing and shipping addresses, then your checkout process will not only need to access its own checkout data tier, but also the customer profile data tier where the address information is stored. (That's fine—having two database servers supporting the checkout process is better than one!)

Once your database has been partitioned, you can use SQL Server replication to keep relatively current data on each of the servers. The type of replication you use depends on how out-of-date the data can be. For example, the product browsing database server, which "owns" the product catalog tables, should publish those tables as articles in a replication publication. Since product data needs to be consistent throughout your site, especially between the product browsing and checkout servers, you should use transactional replication, which offers a low latency between servers. The product search server, on the other hand, primarily uses product information that doesn't change much, including product descriptions and categories. That server might use snapshot replication to make a copy of the product catalog once every evening.

Your data tier can also implement business logic, although I recommend you implement as little business logic as possible, since SQL Server only supports scripting for this type of functionality. Also, business logic processing represents a tremendous overhead for a server, and your data tier is the smallest and least scalable tier in your architecture, which means there are few cures for an overburdened database server. Try to keep the database server's task simple (reading and writing data) and maintain your business logic in a dedicated business tier.

Where Code Will Go

After you build your site's architecture, determine how you will implement the program code that will make the site work. Will you primarily use script, COM and COM+ components, or a mix of the two? Your choices depend on how robust and scalable you want your site to be.

Script has its place in any Microsoft-based Web site, both in the presentation tier and in the client tier. COM and COM+ components also have a place, and can take advantage of COM+ services such as connection pooling and transaction services. COM+ components can also take advantage of Component Load Balancing (CLB) in COM+ clusters, which can greatly increase the scalability and fault-tolerance of your site.

In the next few sections, I'll discuss the proper role for scripts and components in your site and introduce you to CLB and other technologies you can deploy to make your site more efficient and scalable.

Scripts

Scripts represent the easiest form of coding available in a Web application. They are faster to write than traditional compiled code, can be updated on-the-fly, do not require complicated registration or installation tasks, and are, in general, a programmer's delight. Scripts are supported in all tiers of your application, whether they be DHTML scripts written in JavaScript on your presentation tier, VBScript Active Server Pages in your client tier, more VBScript in your business tier, or VBScript and T-SQL scripts running in your data tier.

Unfortunately, scripts also represent the slowest possible form of code execution and the highest level of overhead at every level of your application, as script is interpreted, not compiled. While simple DHTML data-validation scripts meant to run in your customers' Web browsers are fine, complex business logic implemented as scripts in any of the higher tiers are the most "expensive" and least efficient means available to implement that logic. The server must read and interpret each line of script one line at a time, maintain a variety of counters and pointers in memory, and perform much more work than is required when the server runs compiled code created by Visual Basic, C++, or another traditional language.

ASP.NET can help relieve this performance problem, because it enables the Web server to automatically compile each script into a pseudo-DLL the first time the script is run, and again whenever the script is changed. This compilation process is not as efficient or effective as a traditionally compiled DLL or executable, but it does make scripts more attractive for writing server-side code.

A certain amount of scripting is inevitable, especially in the client and data tiers. For example, even if you implement your business logic completely within compiled COM components, ASP still requires you to use script to instantiate and control those components.

SQL Server 2000 has very little support for compiled programming, relying almost exclusively on ActiveX scripting languages and its native T-SQL script for accomplishing most tasks. You can extend SQL Server's functionality using external stored procedures — compiled components that are specially registered with SQL Server — but these components generally provide only a limited set of functionality, and SQL Server's internal architecture is not efficient in dealing with the memory or processing requirements of these components. Any SQL Server scripts written in an ActiveX programming language like VBScript can instantiate COM objects the way ASP pages can, but you must still use a certain amount of script to call and control those objects.

Note The Commerce Server Solution Sites are almost completely scripted, which makes them extremely inefficient compared to other possible solutions. They require an immense amount of server overhead, meaning each server is capable of supporting dramatically fewer users than it should.

I recommend that you use as little script as possible in the higher tiers of your application. While it is perfectly acceptable — and required, for that matter — to use script to call and control COM objects, any significant processing should be accomplished from within those COM objects as opposed to script. Microsoft furnishes COM components, such as ActiveX Data Objects and Collaboration Data Objects, that provide your scripts with the major functionality your site requires; Commerce Server adds an array of components to accomplish specific page-building and commerce-related tasks; and you should plan to build your own COM components in Visual Basic, C++, or another multithreaded language to implement any business logic your Web site needs.

Components

Much of the actual functionality of your site, including messaging integration, database access, and so on, will be handled by components such as ActiveX Data Objects and the various components that come with Commerce Server 2000. So it makes sense for most of your site's business logic to be encapsulated in components, as well, whether those components are written in C++, Visual Basic, or another language.

The key is to make sure the components are written in a language that supports multithreaded operation. No matter where your component is running (on a Web server or on a dedicated business tier server), it will actually be "running" several times at once as multiple users access your site. However, a single-threaded component is only capable of running once, which means it can only work with a single user at a time.

C++ obviously supports multithreading — the entire Windows operating system is written in it! Visual Basic 6.0 supports *apartment model* threading, as does Visual FoxPro 6.0 service pack 3 and higher. This threading model makes both languages suitable for creating business components for your site. Visual Basic .NET supports fully multithreaded operation, giving the component developer a great deal of control over how the component operates on a multiprocessor system and how the component interacts with other COM components.

Another advantage of using components is Windows 2000's COM+ Services' ability to support connection pooling and transactions. *Connection pooling* enables a single component to maintain several open connections to the back-end database server. When scripts call the component, the component simply uses one of the connections it has already made, rather than incurring the overhead of setting up a whole new connection to the server. In contrast, every time a script instantiates an ADO Connection object, a new connection has to be set up. Since SQL Server requires processor and memory overhead to manage open connections, connection pooling is a more efficient way of connecting several scripts to a database.

COM+ Services also includes Microsoft Transaction Server (MTS), which was introduced in Windows NT 4.0. By writing your component to take advantage of transaction services, you can create components that carry out several distinct tasks guaranteed to either succeed or fail as a set. Commerce Server's own pipelines use this technology to ensure, for example, that the entire order processing pipeline, including inventory updates, confirmations, credit card billing, and so on, succeeds. If a single task in the pipeline fails, all the tasks in the pipeline are "rolled back" so that none of them have any net effect. Transaction services are easy to incorporate into components written in Visual Basic or C++ and will make your Web site more robust.

Keeping as much business logic inside components as possible enables you to take advantage of COM+ clusters through Application Center 2000's Component Load Balancing (CLB) technology, which I'll describe in the next section.

COM+ clusters

Application Center 2000 enables you to easily deploy Network Load Balancing (NLB) across your Web servers. This technology enables servers with identical Web content to automatically distribute the load of incoming users across themselves. NLB allows a "cluster" of Web servers to direct new connections to the servers with the lowest current level of activity, remove servers from the cluster when they are down, and so on. This technology was first introduced with Windows NT 4.0, and is commonly used in Web farms with multiple servers performing the same functions.

Application Center 2000 also includes technology designed to perform the same type of load balancing in the business tier — Component Load Balancing (CLB). Essentially, this technology enables multiple servers running the same COM+ components to act as a "COM+ cluster." Access to these components by the client-tier

Web servers is automatically load balanced across the available servers, ensuring that all business-tier servers are put to equal use.

Note that normal COM components cannot be used in conjunction with CLB; the technology is restricted to components written to the COM+ standard, as COM+ (among other things) specifies that components expose configuration information about themselves to the operating system. Visual Basic 6.0 and, of course, Visual C++ 6.0 are capable of writing components that conform to the COM+ specification; Visual Studio .NET is also capable of creating COM+ components.

Functionally, the CLB services run on your Web servers and maintain a routing list of available COM+ servers. Whenever a Web server script needs to instantiate a COM+ object, it does so using the normal VBScript `CreateObject` method. CLB intercepts this method at the operating system level, consults its routing list, and passes the request on to one of the available COM+ servers in the business tier. The COM+ server instantiates the object and returns an interface to the Web server. At that point, CLB is no longer involved; the Web server will maintain its relationship with that particular COM+ server until the component goes out of scope or is destroyed in the script.

CLB works by "pinging" the available list of COM+ servers every 200 milliseconds and tracking the servers' response time. The server with the fastest response will have the least amount of current work, and is placed at the top of the routing list. Servers with a heavy workload will have a slower response time and are placed at the bottom of the list. Servers with no response are assumed to be down and are not placed on the list at all. When new COM+ objects are instantiated, the servers near the top of the list are given the request. Note that each Web server maintains its own list. Web servers do not communicate and attempt to share response time lists, as the communication itself would be too slow to keep up with the rapidly changing load on the COM+ servers.

However, if the script creates a second object, CLB will step in again and load-balance the call to a COM+ server, which could easily be a different server than the one handling the first object. You need to be aware of this possibility and write components that do not need to directly communicate with one another except through some outside agency, such as a back-end database. COM+ components designed for CLB should not be written to maintain any kind of state information. A server that instantiates a component in one script and then instantiates it again in another script may work with two different COM+ servers each time, which means retaining any kind of information in the components is useless. Any information that needs to last beyond the lifetime of the component should be stored in your data tier.

Application Center 2000 includes a deployment wizard that eases the task of deploying new or updated components to multiple servers in a COM+ cluster.

Summary

When you build your Web site's architecture, allow for the kind of robustness and scalability you believe it will need for its entire lifetime. While you don't have to deploy a dozen servers to achieve this type of robustness and scalability, you do need to make some careful choices as you begin developing the site to make sure your work *can* be divided across dozens of servers, if necessary.

Include business logic in a dedicated tier, if possible, making use of transaction services, connection pooling, and Component Load Balancing to make your site as scalable, fault-tolerant, and robust as possible. Use script only when necessary — ideally, only to "glue" components together in your client tier and to offload basic display and data validation processing on your customer's Web browsers.

✦　　✦　　✦

Developing the Database

In This Chapter

Identifying database entities

Commerce Server's default database

Designing for optimization

Before you can program your Web site to do anything useful with a database, you must first develop the database(s). If you're reading this book, it's a given that you plan to use Microsoft Commerce Server 2000 as the base platform for your site, so you need to be aware of the "starting point" provided by the default Commerce Server database schema.

Commerce Server 2000 versus Site Server 3.0

Microsoft Site Server 3.0, Commerce Edition (SSCE) is the predecessor to Commerce Server 2000. If you're currently using SSCE in an existing e-commerce site, you may be forced to stick with it for a while because migrating to Commerce Server is a complex and difficult process. If you're beginning a new site, I advise against using SSCE. The SSCE database schema probably requires significant modification to suit the needs of a major, robust e-commerce site. Commerce Server's default database schema is much more data-driven, allowing you to customize it within the product — saving a great deal of time and effort.

Analyze every piece of information that you expect to gather from your site, and every piece of information that you expect the site to store, and make sure that the database schema contains a place for this data. You need to understand how the default Commerce Server database is built, and how it can be extended to include the exact data that you need to collect.

Rather than attempting to create a database schema that met the needs of every e-commerce business in the world, Microsoft created a database that is capable of extending itself through a simple administrative interface, the Commerce Server Business Desk. You can make significant changes and customizations to Commerce Server's database without really changing the way Commerce Server works. The advantage of this method is the ability to continue using the powerful and flexible administrative tools that are provided by Commerce Server. In earlier editions of Commerce Server, changes made to the database schema — which were common — required that matching changes be made to the administrative tools.

This flexibility comes with a downside, however. Because all of the Commerce Server tools and components are designed to work with a malleable database schema, these tools and components incur overhead by "looking up" the database schema every time they need to access data. Simple queries become more complex when components must first determine the schema that they are working with before the components can actually query the data from the database. My recommendation is to go ahead and use the Commerce Server database schema as much as possible, because doing so saves you a tremendous amount of development time and makes future revisions much easier to implement. From an architectural point of view, though, understand that your database tier must absolutely be as powerful as you can make it.

How powerful is powerful?

One thing you must determine in your development and testing phases is how many users you can expect a single Web server to support, and how many Web servers you can expect a single database server to support.

The Windows 2000 Server Resource Kit provides some stress-testing and user-simulation tools that you can run against your Web servers to determine the load that they can handle. You should *always* use the numbers that you derive from these tests as your benchmark rather than using numbers provided by a third party. The way your Web site works plays a large part in determining how many users it can support.

The default Commerce Server design as implemented, for example, in the Retail Solution Site is extremely dynamic in nature. Every product detail page is created when the user requests it from the browser, rather than ahead of time, requiring several hits to the database and a great deal of VBScript code and COM component processing. If you intend to use this approach in your live site, you'll need a monster database server in order to support a large number of shoppers. For that matter, your Web servers must also be pretty beefy machines in order to chug through all that code every time a product is displayed. On the other hand, your design may take the approach that I recommend, which is to reduce the reliance on the database whenever possible, and produce as much static content as possible, meaning that your database server can work less in order to support the daily shopping experience.

So what are the morals of this story? First, if you plan to use Commerce Server exactly as Microsoft intended, plan on a relatively small site or plan to use significantly large hardware. Second, just because Microsoft intended the product to be used in a certain way doesn't mean that's necessarily the best way for you to use it in your situation. Don't be afraid of taking a different approach if it fits.

Depending on the size of your environment, modifications to the Commerce Server database may be inevitable. For example, Commerce Server is built to assume a single, monolithic database that contains all of the information pertaining to the site. This approach works fine for Web sites where each server performs every possible function in the site, including searching, product browsing, checkout, and so forth. In larger sites where these tasks are divided between servers, you have two choices. Either point all the servers at the same back-end database, which leaves a significant bottleneck in your design, or modify the Commerce Server database and infrastructure to partition the database across several servers, one for search, one for product browsing, and so forth.

In the next few sections of this chapter, I help you to identify the data that your site needs to track. I point out the ways that the default Commerce Server database schema enables you to store this data, and make some recommendations about how you can use or modify that schema. I also describe how the Commerce Server database is designed for optimization, and give you some tips for maintaining and improving that optimization as you develop your Web pages.

Identifying Entities

Carefully review your design documentation and determine which pieces of data you need to track. I cover some of the most common pieces of data that you may be interested in, and you can compare this to your specific needs and make changes as necessary. In the next section, I talk about how Commerce Server's basic database handles this information, and I look at any changes or customization you may need to make.

Product information

What information does your database need to contain to accurately represent your products and services? If your site is like most, the information is quite considerable.

Start by defining your *product taxonomy.* This is the basic hierarchy that you use to organize your products, and may consist of departments, sub-departments, classes, sub-classes, and so forth. Your initial design documentation should already contain a fairly fleshed-out taxonomy plan. This development phase should include finalizing that taxonomy. Make sure that it allows for sufficient growth, if necessary, and lends itself to a flat, easy-to-use navigation system for customers browsing your site.

After defining the taxonomy, determine what product *types* your site will sell. Products within a "type" have similar properties. For example, a "pants" type may have properties such as waist and inseam size, color, material, the gender that the pants were made for, and so forth. For every product type, define the different properties that describe the products in that type.

Make sure that each type includes a property that uniquely identifies individual products. Typically, this is a number like a Stock Keeping Unit (SKU) or product ID, but you may use any identifier you like.

Each product can also have *variant* properties. For example, your catalog may assign a single SKU to a particular style of blue jeans, which may come in fifteen different size combinations. The size combination is referred to as the product's *variant*. Some products may have multiple variant values, and some products, such as a video, may not have any variant values.

In most cases, you probably want your site's catalog to closely mimic your existing print or electronic catalogs, if you have them. Take a look at the structures of those catalogs and use them as your starting point.

Be aware that Commerce Server supports multiple catalogs on a site. For example, a clothing company may have a catalog for general clothing, one for sports clothing, one for men's suits, and so forth. Each catalog may be presented on a Web site specially designed for that catalog, or the catalog may be the "top level" in your product hierarchy. Gap.com, for example, has a "sub site" for Baby Gap, Gap Body, Gap, and Gap Kids. These "sub sites" may be represented as separate catalogs (which is likely, because they are also separate brick-and-mortar stores within the Gap company).

Customer information

What information do you want to track about your customers? Some pieces of information, such as name, mailing address, etc., are a given; other pieces may not be so obvious. For example, do you plan to offer some kind of user survey that asks demographic questions about household income, number of children, hobbies, and such? This may be valuable information that you want to track about your customers, as it can help you create targeted advertising campaigns and other personalized features on your site.

Make a complete list of customer information that your company is interested in tracking. Refer to your design documents. You should have already made some decisions regarding this information and documented them in your site design plan. Some examples of desirable information include:

✦ Basic identifying information, such as name and birth date.

✦ Address information, possibly for multiple addresses. You may want to allow customers to store several shipping and billing addresses, allowing them to select addresses from lists when they check out, rather than typing that information every time.

✦ Payment information, including credit card numbers and expiration dates. Protect sensitive stored information like this with encryption just in case your database is compromised.

✦ Demographic information, such as the customer's age range, salary range, favorite hobbies, number of children, and so forth.

✦ Customization information, allowing you insight into your customers' preferences, such as departments the customer frequently shops from.

✦ Particular dates that are important to your customers, such as family birthdays or anniversaries, special holidays, and so forth.

✦ Subscription information, such as e-mail newsletters the customers have subscribed to or newsletters for which they have discontinued subscriptions.

Although much of this information may be used for marketing purposes, it is not strictly considered marketing information; the information is directly related to, and "owned by," individual customers who visit your site.

Tip

When planning the information you will collect, try to plan for *all* of the information you might ever want. You don't necessarily have to plan to collect all of this information immediately; Commerce Server will be happy to let the information fields remain blank until you decide to start using them. But by defining them up front, you will create a structure for future information collection that will be very valuable. While you can always add more fields later for additional information, Commerce Server will provide better reporting and performance with as many fields as you can possibly define up front.

Marketing information

What sort of marketing information do you want your site to collect, and where in your database do you plan to store it?

In this context, the term *marketing information* does not refer to demographic information associated with a particular user — in most cases, that information should be stored in the user's profile, which I describe later in this chapter. The type of marketing information that you should be thinking about now is statistical in nature:

✦ How many customers are repeat shoppers?

✦ How long do customers wait before making a repeat purchase?

✦ How many customers purchase out of a particular department, and how can you market to them directly to promote that department?

✦ How many customers respond to your advertising campaigns?

✦ How many customers are brought to the site by an advertisement and purchase something on that visit?

✦ How many customers are brought to the site by an advertisement and purchase something on a subsequent visit?

✦ How frequently do customers visit the site without purchasing something?

✦ Which areas of the site do customers visit the most? Which on-site ads entice the most customers to make a purchase?

All of this information is about individual customers, but it is most useful when all of your customers' data is combined to form statistical information. Marketing is about creating effective campaigns targeted at groups of shoppers rather than individuals.

Your site's design documentation should have a considerable body of information that your company's marketing team wants to be able to gather and analyze. In the next section, I discuss how Commerce Server stores some of that information, and what pieces of information you may need to gather on your own.

Order information

Order information presents an interesting challenge in database design. Creators with a good amount of experience in database design have an instinct to normalize their designs, thus reducing repetitive and redundant information. Orders, however, must represent a "snapshot" of data because the order was placed at a specific point in time and should not reflect any changes that occur after the order is recorded. For that reason, your order information tables are fairly de-normalized, and should stand relatively independent of the rest of the database. Independent order information tables allow you to develop a site that uses specialized servers for the checkout process because finalized orders exist "as is" and don't necessarily need to remain related with the product and customer information that was originally used to create the order.

For example, suppose a customer places an order and has it shipped to her home address. The order contains two blue widgets, which sell for $10 each. Because the customer lives out of state, you don't charge her sales tax. A couple of months later, the customer moves into your state. A week later, the price of blue widgets falls to $9each. Assuming that the customer updated her address information on your site, and assuming your buyers updated the price of blue widgets, then the customer's old address and the old price of widgets is lost. If you were to then recall the order that the customer placed over two months ago, what information is displayed?

The information that *should* be displayed is the customer's old address and widgets at $10 each, because this is the information that was placed with the order. Order information *can't* link to your product or profiles tables because the information in these tables can change over time and orders must represent a fixed snapshot of the data as it existed when the order was placed.

So with this in mind, what information do your order tables need to contain? Pretty much everything that your profile and product tables contain, which is:

✦ Customer information, including name, address, e-mail address, phone number, and other contact information. Also, any billing information, such as credit card numbers (which can be encrypted for security), authorization numbers, etc.

✦ Product information for each item ordered, including its stock number (or other appropriate identifier), your cost, the retail price, the price that the customer actually paid (which may be different from the retail price), the tax that was applied, any shipping charges applied, and so forth.

Essentially, your order tables need to contain all of the information that you require to completely re-create the order from scratch and arrive at the original totals. You also need to think about how your site will handle discounts, because these can create some havoc in your bookkeeping processes if you're not careful.

Some discounts are product-based—such as a 10 percent discount off of large widgets—and the discount should be applied to the individual products. This can result in a difference between the retail price and the price paid by a customer, and you should include the dollar amount of the discount in the order table as well, so that all the numbers add up. Some discounts, however, may be applied to an entire order—like a coupon for $10 off any purchase of $50 or more. In these cases, you need to decide if the discount should be divided up evenly across each of the items ordered, or if the discount should be applied to the order as a whole. Your accounting team needs to help you make this decision, and you need to make sure that the data is placed in the appropriate order header or order items tables.

Shipping and tax charges present a similar problem. I generally advise that tax be calculated on the total order, excluding any items that are nontaxable. Most states prefer this method. If you follow this method, make sure that you store the total tax in the order header, and don't try to split it up and store it with each item on the order—or you'll get rounding errors that keep your numbers from ever adding up correctly. Shipping information should be stored where it is calculated; for example, if you figure a shipping amount for each item in an order, store the shipping charge in the same table with the order items. If you calculate a shipping charge based on the entire order (which is more common), store that charge in the order header.

The Default Commerce Server Database

In this section, I describe how Commerce Server handles each of the information groups that I discuss in the previous section. I also make some recommendations for changing the database, as appropriate, or at least point out the database's weak spots so that you can decide if modifications are necessary in your implementation.

 Caution Changing the Commerce Server database schema prevents you from using any of the default Commerce Server tools until they are updated to reflect your schema changes. This is something you need to be aware of from a planning perspective, because every database change will have an impact on keeping the tools updated.

Product information

Commerce Server uses an incredibly flexible system for representing your product catalogs in its database. The actual product databases not only contain your product information—they also contain the catalogs' organization information. This "data-driven" schema essentially means that you can completely customize the product database, and the Commerce Server software—Business Desk, the pipeline components, and the various components used to build pages—can understand your customized schema.

This flexibility does mean an additional layer of complexity when you are building your catalogs. Commerce Server's product database has five basic areas that you need to customize.

1. Begin by deciding what catalogs you will use. The purpose of a catalog is to group related items together in a single module. Commerce Server supports *catalog groups*, which are groups of catalogs to which specific customers have access. For example:

   • You may create a catalog for general videos. This is the only catalog in a catalog group intended for the general public.

   • You may create a second catalog of specialized videos intended for corporate training. This catalog is the only catalog in a catalog group intended for corporate shoppers.

   • Some customers may be corporate shoppers who also shop your site for their personal videos. To accommodate them, you can create a third catalog group containing both catalogs, granting access to these "dual-purpose" shoppers.

   • Some of your customers may be other retailers purchasing from you at wholesale prices. You can accommodate these customers by creating a fourth catalog group that overrides the default product pricing and applies a fixed wholesale discount. Access to this catalog can be restricted to users who are identified as wholesale customers in their profiles.

2. After you have grouped your products by catalog, you need to determine how each catalog should be structured. You do this by defining product categories, which you can name anything you want — "Department," "Sub-Department," "Meta," "Category," "Class," or whatever. You can define categories as being "children" of other categories, creating a product hierarchy, or *taxonomy*.

3. Your next step is to define product types. Remember that each product type defines a set of properties that describe the products of that type. Then define the properties that describe each product type.

4. Finally, you enter your products. For each product, determine what category or categories that it belongs to, what values are allowed for each of its properties, what its default pricing is, and so forth. Products can also be associated with vendors and other business information, allowing you to use the Commerce Server database to completely manage your product mix.

Commerce Server's flexible, "data-driven" product catalog schema provides a major benefit over prior versions in that you can tailor the product catalog or catalogs that your company needs. Pricing is flexible, because it can be overridden at various levels, allowing you to create flexible pricing structures for different customers.

Essentially, you should not have to make any changes to the underlying Commerce Server database because it's designed to incorporate just about anything you can think of.

A major benefit to *not* modifying the basic database schema is that Commerce Server natively interfaces with Microsoft BizTalk Server 2000, and includes schema mappings that tell BizTalk how to map Commerce Server's default database schema to the BizTalk intermediate XML format. Using BizTalk, you can import and export your catalogs to your business partners by simply telling BizTalk how your partners format *their* data files. This type of data interaction, which is increasingly common in the e-commerce industry, used to require weeks of programming in some cases, and can now be done in a day or two with BizTalk's help.

Tip   I have yet to run across a situation where modifying Commerce Server's product catalog schema was absolutely necessary, so try not to make any modifications to it unless you absolutely have to. See the sidebar, "Impact of Schema Changes" later in this chapter for more information.

If your catalog data already exists in electronic format, then your product information can be imported into Commerce Server. Several fairly robust options are available for this, and Commerce Server makes good use of SQL Server features, such as bulk import and Data Transformation Services (DTS), to pull data from almost any source (including back-end systems like SAP R/3 or an AS/400, text files with comma-separated values, or fixed-length fields). Commerce Server is capable of reading existing taxonomy information in those files to properly categorize the products placed into the Commerce Server product catalog.

Tip   If you're planning to import catalog data into Commerce Server, make a couple of trial runs to perfect the import process and weed out any troublesome data to be handled manually.

Customer information

Unlike its predecessors, Commerce Server 2000 gives you an amazing amount of flexibility to store information about your customers with its Profiler service. In order to take advantage of the Profiler, you need to design customer *profiles*, which are essentially templates that you can use to create and populate profiles for your customers.

Creating customer profiles

Commerce Server profiles consist of multiple *properties*. Each property defines a single piece of information that you want to collect, such as names, addresses, and so forth. Each property can have one or more *attributes*. An attribute can determine the type of data that the property contains, such as numbers, 50-character strings, and so forth. Attributes can determine which properties are single-instance (such as names) and which properties may have multiple instances (such as addresses). Attributes also determine which properties are required in a profile, and which properties are mandatory. You can create different profiles for different *types* of customers, but no customer should have more than one profile. Try to stick to one type of customer profile whenever possible so that you can use it for all of your customers.

You can create *terms* for your profiles, which you can use across your entire site. For example, if you create the term *shirt size* with values of S, M, L, and XL, you can use that term both on your user preferences page and on product detail pages that display products available in multiple sizes. Commerce Server automatically generates a drop-down list box with the appropriate choices whenever necessary. Terms help ensure consistency across your site.

Caution   *Overuse* of terms can be a bad thing. If you intend to use Commerce Server's components to generate drop-down list boxes based on terms, then every drop-down box requires a hit to the database to determine the term's possible values. Used judiciously, this is not a problem; overused, the process reduces the scalability of your site by creating a bottleneck at your database.

Commerce Server's profile structure effectively allows you to create a custom database schema, but that schema is contained in a fixed database schema that Commerce Server understands. Like product data, Commerce Server's profile schema is intended to be customized for your specific needs, meaning you can get everything you need without having to make any modifications to the Commerce Server tools, such as Business Desk and the pipeline components.

You may be tempted to keep some information about your customers in separate tables — outside the Profiler system. Try not to — you'll be amazed at the way Commerce Server is able to use information contained in the Profiles. For example, in earlier versions of Commerce Server (such as Site Server 3.0, Commerce Edition), many e-commerce companies used separate tables to keep track of the newsletters to which customers had subscribed. In Commerce Server 2000, you may have to create additional tables, such as a table listing the different newsletters that users can sign up for, but those tables should link to the Profiler tables whenever possible — keeping the primary key of a newsletter in the user's profile when they subscribe. This technique allows Commerce Server's Direct Mail component to easily create mailing lists for selected users when you need to send newsletters out.

Using profiles in analysis reports

Commerce Server's Analysis service, which uses SQL Server 2000's Analysis Services to create a data warehouse based on your site's production database, is capable of using your users' profile information in analysis reports. For example, your management or marketing groups may find it useful to determine how many repeat customers also subscribe to specific newsletters, and shop in particular departments related to their personal hobbies. Although Analysis can use data outside the users' profiles to discover this kind of information, doing so requires modifications to the default data warehouse schema — a complex task that requires significant planning by a database architect trained in building data warehouses.

On the other hand, *every* customer is associated with a *full profile*. Even though empty profiles take up less space in your database than a fully populated profile, they take up room nonetheless. On a high-volume site, this may generate considerable database traffic. Either keep your profiles trim or make sure that your database server can handle the load. One way to keep profiles smaller is to decide if a significant percentage of your users (40 percent or more) will provide the information under consideration. If not, you may want to consider keeping the information in a table outside the profiles.

Tip If 40 percent or more of your users provide you with a desired piece of information, create a place for that information in your users' profiles. If the number of users providing the information is less than 40 percent, consider storing the information elsewhere — unless it is heavily used in analysis reports that you intend to run.

When designing your user profile, remember that nothing is permanent. Properties can be deleted from profiles if you no longer need them (remember to make a backup of the database first, just in case) and properties can be added to profiles if the need arises. When you add a property, it is automatically added to all existing users' profiles with a blank value. You'll then have to provide your users with a means of filling in the new information, perhaps through a demographics survey.

Commerce Server automatically attempts to match users with their profiles; see the sidebar "Tracking Customers" for specifics on how Commerce Server accomplishes this, and what you can do to improve its chances of matching customers to their database profiles.

Marketing information

Commerce Server captures most pertinent marketing information; order information, click histories, and other information is collected as part of standard processes. Commerce Server does not provide real-time reports based on this data. I discuss in previous chapters that this type of reporting is inappropriate when run against a production database. Commerce Server does allow you to export that data, including information from your Web servers' log files, into its analysis database, which is capable of producing robust reports using SQL Server's Analysis Services component.

One piece of information that Commerce Server does not necessarily capture automatically is referral codes embedded in URLs. For example, your promotional e-mails may contain links to various portions of your site; by embedding a parameter in the URL that contains a code, you can determine how many people linked to that location using the link in the e-mail. Properly managed, you can also determine how many people bought something as a result of the visit. Commerce Server offers you a basic ability to pull referral URLs out of your Web server logs in its Analysis module, but this is often insufficient for tracking code through to the order. If you want to employ this type of customer-tracking functionality, you need to implement it on your own.

Tracking Customers

Commerce Server has built-in mechanisms to track your customers and associate them with their profiles in the site's database. When a new customer visits your site, Commerce Server creates a new *Globally Unique Identifier* (GUID), a long alphanumeric string that is unique to each customer. Commerce Server attempts to pass this GUID to the customer as a cookie; if the customer's browser accepts the cookie, Commerce Server is able to identify this customer on future visits by querying the cookie.

If the customer's browser is not configured to accept cookies, Commerce Server places the GUID in the URL and tracks the customer that way. For this to work, every URL on your site—each and every one—must be generated with a special Commerce Server component that embeds the GUID in the URLs. This way, every click that your customer makes will contain their GUID. Commerce Server is not able to identify these customers on future visits until they log in; customers that don't log in are assigned an "anonymous" GUID instead. If they do log in, the information generated on that visit is transferred to their "registered user" GUID for retention.

After a customer *registers* on your site, thus creating their profile, Commerce Server automatically assigns the GUID as part of the profile. This enables you to retain the information generated by the customer while he or she was still "anonymous."

Commerce Server accomplishes tasks such as creating customer click histories by analyzing your Web server's log. The log contains the contents of each cookie passed between the server and the user's browser, and the contents of each URL requested by the user. Because one of these two contains a GUID, Commerce Server is able to assign a GUID and, thus, a user to each request, or click. This method of tracking users is preferred over other methods, because the "tracking" occurs offline during the analysis of the Web server log, without placing any additional burden on your database.

The special component used to generate the GUID-containing URLs (which I discuss in Chapter 17) imposes a minimal amount of overhead on the Web server and does not create additional database traffic.

 Cross-Reference I show you how to implement URL-tracking features in Chapter 10.

Any marketing information that you obtain that is directly related to a user should generally be stored in profiles. This includes demographic information, such as hobbies, salary range, age range, and so forth. (I discuss using profiles for this purpose earlier in the chapter.)

In any event, you should have to do very little custom database development to contain marketing information after you understand that Commerce Server basically stores the information that you need already. Just be ready to export that information into Commerce Server's Analysis component to generate the necessary statistical reports.

 I give you an overview of using Analysis Services to create reports in Chapter 10.

Order information

Commerce Server does a marginal job of de-normalizing the order information into its order tables. Commerce Server uses four main tables to track order information, as shown in Figure 9-1.

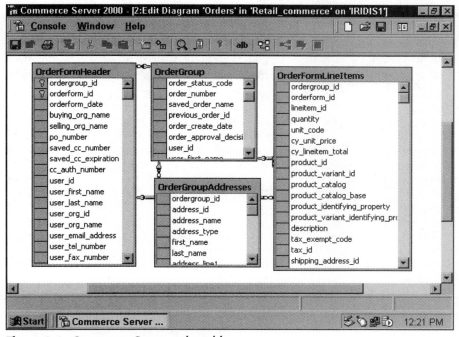

Figure 9-1: Commerce Server order tables

The tables do a good job of storing the information about the products that were ordered, as well as the customer information that applies to the order. In fact, each line item in the order (stored in the OrderFormLineItems table) can be shipped to a different address, which is stored in the OrderGroupAddresses table.

Impacts of Schema Changes

What happens if you try to change the default Commerce Server schema? If you're using one of the Solution Sites, it will probably stop functioning correctly. If you're taking my advice and using the Blank Commerce Site, then you will feel the impact of your changes in the administrative tools, such as the Business Desk application for the site.

The impact of your changes may be subtle. For example, if you add a couple of columns to the OrderFormHeader table to track the total shipping charges that were applied to the order, the main portion of the Commerce Server Business Desk continues to function correctly. Of course, you need to program your order-processing pages and the order-processing pipeline components to correctly populate your new column with data, but by and large the Business Desk doesn't care.

The Business Desk doesn't automatically begin displaying the new information on its Orders screen, however, because that would require modification. If you decided to take advantage of Commerce Server's analysis tools, the predefined jobs that export the Commerce Server data into the Commerce Server data warehouse database won't pick up your new column. You have to modify the data warehouse's schema to support this new column. Performing an analysis of shipping costs in the data warehouse may require significant schema changes (data warehouses use a very specialized and complex schema to accomplish rapid analysis tasks).

Another, possibly major, impact of changing the schema is that you alter Commerce Server's native integration with BizTalk Server 2000. If your site accepts orders from other companies, or feeds your orders to other companies, BizTalk can be a major time-saver because Commerce Server provides mappings from its default database format to BizTalk's intermediate XML format. If you alter the orders tables and intend to use BizTalk, make sure that you update those XML mappings to reflect the changes you made. In some cases, your business partners may not have all of the necessary information. For example, companies sending you electronic orders probably don't know your products' costs. If you add a field to the order items table to store item costs, your database should allow for the field to be blank on new orders that come in from business partners. You can write a SQL Server job that runs regularly to "fill in the blanks" where necessary. You can also program BizTalk Server to look this information up in your database when orders come in, and fill in the information automatically.

Should these considerations stop you from modifying the default database schema? Absolutely not! They should simply be kept in mind when planning the time necessary to modify the other portions of Commerce Server that use this schema.

Some information, however, is not denormalized to the degree I feel is required in a good e-commerce site, including:

✦ *Shipping information* for each line item is stored by indicating which shipping method was used. You can define various shipping methods in Commerce Server, including methods based on total order cost or on the total order weight. Unfortunately, the pricing information remains in the shipping method definition tables; it is not denormalized and stored with the order information.

✦ *Product information* is denormalized into the order table, with the exception of the product's cost. If you intend to perform margin analysis of past orders, you need to include your cost in the order information, because product costs change over time.

✦ *Discount information* is not included in the default order tables. This information is included in the basket, which is included in binary form in a marshaled column of the order and of each line item, but the discount information is not explicitly broken out in the table. Depending on the type of discounts that you plan to offer, this may be a problem. Be aware that Commerce Server, by default, only offers a shipping discount that can be applied to an entire order. All other discounts are applied to single items ($x off $y, Buy x get y for $z, and so forth). The pricing reflected in the OrderFormLineItems table is the final sale price of the item after discounts.

Other than these points, Commerce Server's order tables do a good job of tracking order information for future use. And, if you intend to regularly export information from your Commerce Server databases into some other back-end system for accounting and record keeping purposes, these three points may not be particularly important to you. On the other hand, if Commerce Server is your primary data store, then you should think about modifying the schema and the associated order processing pages to include this additional historical data.

Designing for Optimization

One of the most important things that you can do for your database server is to optimize your database design. This includes optimizing your use of indexes, stored procedures, triggers, and views.

Indexes

Commerce Server implements a sensible set of indexes on the tables that it creates. While those indexes are a good start toward optimizing your database, nothing beats actually *using* the database to determine what optimizations are best. As you program your site, run your queries through Query Analyzer and the Index Tuning Wizard and determine if different indexes can help improve queries, or if you can remove other indexes to speed up write operations. SQL Server's Index Tuning Wizard can be very useful in determining which indexes should be removed, and where indexes should be added. Be sure to re-optimize your indexes periodically as the underlying tables grow. Include a regular rebuild of the indexes on tables that change regularly; old indexes quickly become filled with page splits, making them "defragmented" and less efficient than newly-built indexes.

Tip   SQL Server 2000's DBCC INDEXDEFRAG command allows you to rebuild indexes "on the fly" while the underlying tables are in use. Take advantage of this feature to keep your indexes tuned without significantly affecting your site's performance.

Stored procedures

Commerce Server heavily uses stored procedures, and with good reason. Every time you fire off a query at SQL Server, the server's Query Optimizer must examine the query to determine which indexes may be useful, in what order the various portions of the query should be executed, what table joins have to be made, and so forth. This process doesn't take a long time per query, but the time does add up quickly with multiple queries.

The advantage of a stored procedure is that the Optimizer only looks at the stored procedure when it first runs, and again only if the procedure is changed. Whatever decisions the Optimizer makes (called the *execution plan*) are stored along with the procedure for future use. Subsequent calls to the procedure take less time and processor power because all of the decisions have been made.

Commerce Server uses stored procedures to query, to update, and to delete data. As you add functionality to your site, I advise you take advantage of the stored procedures provided with Commerce Server wherever possible, and write your own if necessary. Your goal should be to *never* submit an ad-hoc SELECT, INSERT, UPDATE or DELETE query to your SQL Server.

Triggers

Triggers are special stored procedures that are "attached" to a table and automatically run whenever the table is changed in some specified fashion. Triggers have incited two schools of thought among users. The first school of thought states that triggers are an excellent way to maintain referential integrity, and that they help centralize business logic on the data tier of your site.

Stored Procedures in ADO

Many programmers use the Execute method of the ADO Connection object to fire off a stored procedure:

```
objConnection.Execute "sp_DoSomething"
```

Or, for stored procedures that return query results:

```
objRecordSet = objConnection.Execute("sp_GetSomeData")
```

This is *not* the right way to have ADO execute a stored procedure. Visual Basic or VBScript have to do a considerable amount of extra work in order to work with ADO to execute this stored procedure, and much of SQL Server's optimizations for stored procedures are bypassed. Instead, use the ADO Command object:

```
objCommand.CmdText = "sp_DoSomething"
objCommand.Execute
```

Personally, I follow the second school of thought, which states that triggers place an undue burden on the database server and are unnecessary if you've been using stored procedures properly. Rather than implementing triggers, which can also lend all kinds of interesting twists to otherwise straightforward replication scenarios, make all of your data changes by calling a stored procedure and passing it the appropriate parameters. The stored procedure can then perform any business logic actions that need to go along with the data change.

Caution　Be careful of writing stored procedures that take a long time to run because they do so many tasks. These cause your Web site to "hang" from the customer's point of view, which is undesirable. If a stored procedure takes more than a few seconds to execute, break it into multiple stored procedures. The Web site page can then call them in turn, perhaps displaying a status bar for customers so they don't get impatient and start clicking Stop and Back buttons in their browser.

Views

Views don't provide the level of optimization that stored procedures do, and Commerce Server doesn't add any views in the product database that it creates. As you create new functionality on your site, I recommend using stored procedures to select small portions of data rather than using views. I *absolutely* recommend selecting data via stored procedures rather than firing off ad-hoc queries against the SQL Server, because ad-hoc queries receive very few optimization benefits.

Summary

Your design phase should give you a solid understanding of the data that your company needs to collect. By understanding what data the default Commerce Server database is intended to store, and where you may need to modify or add tables to store additional information, you can create your final database design.

Although I'm not a big advocate of using the Commerce Server Solution Sites (which I discuss at length in Chapter 6), I am a fan of using the default Commerce Server *database* whenever possible. A lot of perfectly good code, including the Business Desk and the various pipeline components, is designed to use the default database schema. Modifying the schema means modifying that other code, which adds time to your task. Preferences aside, it is sometimes necessary to modify the Commerce Server database, particularly in the case of the orders tables. Even though this requires changes to both the Business Desk and the pipeline components, the changes are not only worthwhile, but required for any e-commerce site set up to use its production site database as its primary source of historical data.

✦　　✦　　✦

Developing the Look and Feel

The time has arrived to dig out your design documents, roll up your sleeves, and start typing. In this chapter, I discuss how to implement specific technologies to enable the navigation, advertising and promotion, and compatibility goals that you have set for yourself in your design document.

For navigation programming, I show you the most common means of building navigation components by using DHTML scripting, HTML code, and basic graphics. I focus on the site design chosen by Retailer.com, one of the sample e-commerce companies you read about in Part 1 of this book.

I discuss some of the built-in technologies and techniques of the Commerce Server 2000 platform that allow you to implement certain advertising and promotion capabilities. I show you how to use them, what they can do for you, and when, why, and how you may want to build your own advertising and promotion technologies.

I also show you all the details about browser compatibility and Java Virtual Machine (JVM) compatibility. I discuss the techniques for building a Web site that will work to some degree — no matter what browser your customers are using.

Navigation

In the first part of this book, I talk about the various techniques and technologies that you can use to implement your site's navigation. In this section, I talk about how to actually implement the techniques and technologies that you are most likely to use on your site.

To briefly review some of my recommendations for the design phase:

✦ Frames-based and no-frames navigation both offer distinct advantages and disadvantages. If your site will be linked to external Web sites, concentrate on an approach of no-frames navigation.

✦ Java applets can be used as visually exciting, flexible navigation elements, but they have the disadvantage of long download times and they require a fixed amount of screen space in a rectangular shape.

✦ DHTML can be used to achieve interesting visual effects, especially when combined with Cascading Style Sheets. DHTML is generally best delivered in JavaScript/Jscript, but if you have an audience that is standardized on VBScript, you can use that language as well.

With these pointers in mind, I show you how to design Retailer.com's home page, and how to set up the navigation infrastructure. The goal is to produce a fairly simple-looking Web page that offers a great deal of functionality. The completed prototype page is shown in Figure 10-1.

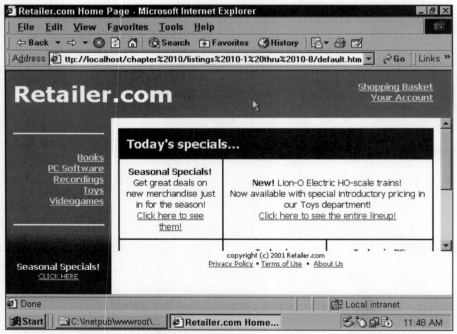

Figure 10-1: Retailer.com prototype home page

Retailer.com has chosen to use a basic, no-frames approach for their site. They've decided to use Jscript-based DHTML to create their primary navigation elements —

pop-up menus of some kind — and they have settled on version 4.0 and higher browsers as their standard. They've also chosen to use dynamically-updated Web pages for their navigation, so they will be making heavy use of server-side include files.

Frames-based navigation

Even though Retailer.com has decided not to use frames-based navigation, they still want a page layout reminiscent of a frames-based page, complete with a menu bar, a title bar, a footer bar, and so forth. They will ultimately implement their design as HTML tables rather than frames, but creating the initial layout by using frames is often easier. Retailer.com will be using server-side includes for the menu bar and other elements, which means that they will basically be treating the HTML tables as a rudimentary kind of frame set — yet another reason to begin the development process by using frames.

 Tip   HTML tables — especially the multi-nested tables necessary to create complex layouts — can require significant development time. Starting with a frames-based layout and converting to tables can save considerable time.

Retailer.com must determine exactly how many frames the page requires, and how they should be broken up. Construction of the frame set page can begin once you've determined how the frames will be laid out.

This layout will accommodate the prototype page design in the following ways:

✦ The left portion of the title bar will contain the store logo, and the right portion will contain the links for the shopping cart and customer account functionality.

✦ The top of the menu bar will contain the majority of the shopping links.

✦ The middle of the menu bar will contain a small graphic that blends the color of the top menu bar into the bottom.

✦ The bottom of the menu bar will contain advertising links.

✦ The main frame will contain the actual page content.

✦ The footer will contain copyright information and global links.

By using invisible frames, the page appears to be a single entity. Compare this layout to Figure 10-1 to see if you can determine where the lines are drawn on the page.

The HTML code for these pages is shown in Listing 10-1 through Listing 10-8. Note that the actual HTML hyperlinks point to dummy URLs at this point in the design and will be corrected later in the process.

Listing 10-1 shows the basic frame set page, which is the first page the user's browser will load.

Listing 10-1: **Retailer.com frame set page (default.htm)**

```
<html>
<head>
<title>Retailer.com Home Page</title>
</head>
<frameset framespacing="0" border="0" rows="70,*,64"
frameborder="0">
  <frameset cols="*,50%">
    <frame name="title-left" scrolling="no" noresize
target="contents" src="title_left.htm">
    <frame name="title-right" src="title_right.htm"
scrolling="auto">
  </frameset>
  <frameset cols="150,*">
    <frameset rows="*,25">
      <frame name="menu-top" target="main" src="menu_top.htm"
scrolling="no" noresize>
      <frame name="menu-mid" src="menu_middle.htm"
marginwidth="0" marginheight="0" scrolling="auto">
    </frameset>
    <frame name="main" src="main.htm" scrolling="auto"
noresize>
  </frameset>
  <frameset cols="150,84%">
    <frame name="menu-bottom" scrolling="no" noresize
target="contents" src="menu_bottom.htm">
    <frame name="footer" src="footer.htm" marginwidth="0"
marginheight="0" scrolling="auto">
  </frameset>
  <noframes>
  <body>
  <p>This page uses frames, but your browser doesn't support
them.</p>
  </body>
  </noframes>
</frameset>
</html>
```

Note the phrase, "This page uses frames, but your browser doesn't support them" in Listing 10-1. This text will be displayed to browsers that don't support frames, and should either link to a no-frames version of your site or advise the user to obtain a newer Web browser. This text, which appears between the <BODY> and </BODY> tags, is also usually read by search engine "robots" that "crawl" your site for inclusion in search engines. Because of this, the text should contain a brief description of your site so the search engine picks up the appropriate keywords.

Listing 10-2 defines the left half of the page's title bar. By defining the title bar as two separate frames, its proportions can be more precisely controlled in the final layout.

Listing 10-2: **Left title bar HTML (title_left.htm)**

```
<html>
<head>
</head>
<body bgcolor="#008080" text="#FFFFFF">
<h1><font face="Verdana">Retailer.com</font></h1>
</body>
</html>
```

Listing 10-3 defines the right half of the title bar, which will be the largest portion of the title bar in the final layout.

Listing 10-3: **Right title bar HTML (title_right.htm)**

```
<html>
<head>
</head>
<body bgcolor="#008080" text="#FFFFFF" link="#FFFF00"
vlink="#FFFF00">
<p align="right"><font face="Tahoma" size="2"><b><a
href="http://link9">Shopping
Basket</a><br>
<a href="http://link10">Your Account</a></b></font></p>
</body>
</html>
```

Listing 10-4 defines the top portion of the menu bar. As with the title bar, the different elements of the menu bar will require precise layout control, which can be easily achieved by defining each in a separate frame.

Listing 10-4: **Top menu bar HTML (menu_top.htm)**

```
<html>
<head>
<base target="main">
</head>
<body bgcolor="#008080" text="#FFFFFF" link="#FFFF00"
vlink="#FFFF00" alink="#FF0000">
<hr color="#FFFFFF">
<p align="right"><b><font face="Tahoma" size="2"><a
href="http://link1">Books</a><br>
```

Continued

Listing 10-4 *(continued)*

```
<a href="http://link2">PC Software</a><br>
<a href="http://link3">Recordings</a><br>
<a href="http://link4">Toys</a><br>
<a href="http://link5">Videogames</a></font></b></p>
<hr color="#FFFFFF">
<p align="right"><b><font face="Tahoma" size="2"><a
href="http://link6">Sign up
for our e-mail newsletter</a></font></b></p>
<hr color="#FFFFFF">
<p align="right"><b><font face="Tahoma" size="2"><a
href="http://link7">Customer
Care</a><br>
<a href="http://link8">Special Orders</a></font></b></p>
<hr color="#FFFFFF">
</body>
</html>
```

Note the `<base target="main">` HTML tag in the `<head>` section of this page. This tag sets the default frame for all hyperlinks to be the "main" frame, which contains the main content of the site. This means that any links in this frame will change the contents of the other frame, which is the exact effect you should expect the menu bar to have.

Listing 10-5 defines the middle portion of the menu bar, which will contain a graphic to transition from the color scheme of the menu bar's top half to its bottom half.

Listing 10-5: **Middle menu bar HTML (menu_middle.htm)**

```
<html>
<head>
</head>
<body background="gradiant.jpg">
</body>
</html>
```

Note that this page contains no actual text, just a background graphic. This background graphic is a simple JPEG file that is exactly as high and as wide as the frame itself (150 x 25 pixels, according to Listing 10-1).

Listing 10-6 defines the bottom of the menu bar, which will be used as advertising space in the final layout.

Listing 10-6: **Bottom menu bar HTML (menu_bottom.htm)**

```html
<html>
<head>
<base target="contents">
</head>
<body bgcolor="#000080" text="#FFFFFF" link="#FFFF00"
vlink="#FFFF00">
<p align="center"><b><font face="Tahoma" size="2">Seasonal
Specials!<br>
</font></b><font face="Tahoma" size="1"><a
href="http://link11">CLICK HERE</a></font></p>
</body>
</html>
```

The page's footer, which will contain copyright notices, is defined in Listing 10-7.

Listing 10-7: **Footer HTML (footer.htm)**

```html
<html>
<head>
</head>
<body>
<p align="center"><font face="Tahoma" size="1">copyright (c)
2001 Retailer.com<br>
<a href="http://ff">Privacy Policy</a> • <a
href="http://ff">Terms of Use</a> 
•  <a href="http://gg">About Us</a></font></p>
</body>
</html>
```

Listing 10-8 defines the main body of the page, which will occupy the largest frame in the final layout.

Listing 10-8: **Main frame HTML (main.htm)**

```html
<html>
<head>
</head>
<body>
<table border="1" width="100%" cellpadding="10" cellspacing="0"
bordercolor="#000000" bordercolorlight="#000000"
```

Continued

Listing 10-8 *(continued)*

```
bordercolordark="#000000">
  <tr>
    <td width="100%" align="center" colspan="3"
bgcolor="#000000">
      <p align="left"><b><font face="Tahoma" size="4"
color="#FFFFFF">Today's
      specials...</font></b></td>
  </tr>
  <tr>
    <td width="33%" align="center"><b><font face="Tahoma"
size="2" color="#000000">Seasonal
      Specials!<br>
      </font></b><font face="Tahoma" size="2"
color="#000000">Get great deals on
      new merchandise just in for the season!<br>
      <a href="http://link15">Click here to see
them!</a></font></td>
    <td width="67%" colspan="2" align="center"><font
face="Tahoma" size="2"><b>New!
      </b>Lion-O Electric HO-scale trains!<br>
      Now available with special introductory pricing in our
Toys department!<br>
      <a href="http://link13">Click here to see the entire
lineup!</a></font></td>
  </tr>
  <tr>
    <td width="33%" rowspan="2" align="center"><font
face="Tahoma" size="2"><b>Did
      You Win a Free<br>
      Trip to Bermuda?<br>
      </b>Maybe it's because you didn't enter our grand prize
giveaway! <a href="http://link12">Click
      here to put your name in the hat!</a></font></td>
    <td width="33%" align="center"><font face="Tahoma"
size="2"><b>Today in
      Recordings:<br>
      </b>Baja Boys' latest album.<br>
      <a href="http://link16">Click here to
preview!</a></font></td>
    <td width="34%" align="center"><font face="Tahoma"
size="2"><b>Today in PC
      Software:<br>
      </b>Robot Warriors on DVD.<br>
      <a href="http://link17">Click here to
preview!</a></font></td>
  </tr>
  <tr>
    <td width="67%" colspan="2" align="center"><font
face="Tahoma" size="2"><b>Deadly
      Kombat</b> for the Super Game System!<br>
```

```
        <a href="http://link14">Pre-order your copy
today!</a></font></td>
    </tr>
</table>
</body>
</html>
```

If your site will use frames-based navigation like Utilities.com (another of the sample companies from Part 1), this should give you an excellent idea of how to develop a flexible frames-based site.

Retailer.com has decided that they like the *look* of a frames-based site, but don't want the actual frames. Creating this initial frame set is useful, however, because it becomes the basis for the non-frames version, which is more difficult and complex to develop.

No-frames navigation

Developing a segmented site that has the appearance of frames without actually using them requires the use of invisible HTML tables. Any frame layout that you can think of can be duplicated with a table, although tweaking the table to the exact size and proportions that you need can be difficult.

Listing 10-9 shows the HTML code necessary to build Retailer.com's basic table layout.

Listing 10-9: **Basic table HTML**

```
<table border="0" width="100%" cellspacing="0" cellpadding="0">
  <tr>
    <td colspan="2" align="center">Title bar left</td>
    <td align="center">Title bar right</td>
  </tr>
  <tr>
    <td align="center">Menu bar top</td>
    <td colspan="2" align="center" rowspan="2">Main</td>
  </tr>
  <tr>
    <td align="center">Menu bar middle</td>
  </tr>
  <tr>
    <td align="center">Menu bar bottom</td>
    <td colspan="2" align="center">Footer</td>
  </tr>
</table>
```

I've filled in each cell with a description of what it should contain—Footer, Main, and so forth—so you can see how the table is constructed.

The next step is to fill in the table cells. Most of the cells contain a fixed type of information. For example, the title bar looks the same on every page of the site. Rather than including the actual HTML in the cells, Retailer.com will use server-side include files. The actual contents of the cell remain in a separate file, which allows you to make changes in one place and have them immediately take effect throughout the site. One of the benefits of creating the initial layout using frames is that the content is already included in separate files. You just need to edit those files to make them compatible with the server-side include method used to build a table-based layout.

Tip   Make sure that your HTML layout tool—whether it's FrontPage or another package—allows you to work directly with the HTML code that defines your page's layout. Multi-nested tables can often require "hand tweaking" to achieve the exact look that you want.

Listing 10-10 shows the complete HTML for Retailer.com's basic page, including the server-side include directives. This effectively replaces the "frame set" from Listing 10-1.

Listing 10-10: Basic table-based page (default.asp)

```
<html>
<head>
<title>Retailer.com Home Page</title>
</head>
<body>
<table border="0" width="100%" cellspacing="0" cellpadding="0">
  <tr>
    <td colspan="2" align="center"><!--#include
file="title_left.htm"--></td>
    <td align="center"><!--#include file="title_right.htm"-
-></td>
  </tr>
  <tr>
    <td align="center"><!--#include file="menu_top.htm"--></td>
    <td colspan="2" align="center" rowspan="2">Main</td>
  </tr>
  <tr>
    <td align="center"><!--#include file="menu_middle.htm"--
></td>
  </tr>
  <tr>
    <td align="center"><!--#include file="menu_bottom.htm"--
```

```
></td>
    <td colspan="2" align="center"><!--#include
file="footer.htm"--></td>
  </tr>
</table>
</body>
</html>
```

 Note The `<!--#include file="xx"-->` directives will only work if the page is saved with an ASP file extension and served from a Web server, as opposed to viewing the file directly from disk with a Web browser.

The remaining listings contain the actual content for everything but the main frame. The main text is included directly in the page. This allows the body of each page to be different, while including the same supporting header, menu bar, and footer. The primary difference between these listings and the earlier frames-based versions is the lack of any HTML header codes. Because these pages will be included in an HTML page, they must not contain any HTML header tags of their own.

Listing 10-11 shows the replacement HTML for the left portion of the title bar.

Listing 10-11: **Left title bar HTML (title_left.htm)**

```
<h1><font face="Verdana">Retailer.com</font></h1>
```

Listing 10-12 shows the new HTML page for the right portion of the title bar.

Listing 10-12: **Right title bar HTML (title_right.htm)**

```
<p align="right"><font face="Tahoma" size="2"><b><a
href="http://link9">Shopping
Basket</a><br>
<a href="http://link10">Your Account</a></b></font></p>
```

Listing 10-13 shows the top portion of the menu bar, recoded for a table-based layout.

Listing 10-13: **Top menu bar HTML (menu_top.htm)**

```
<hr color="#FFFFFF">
<p align="right"><b><font face="Tahoma" size="2"><a
href="http://link1">Books</a><br>
<a href="http://link2">PC Software</a><br>
<a href="http://link3">Recordings</a><br>
<a href="http://link4">Toys</a><br>
<a href="http://link5">Videogames</a></font></b></p>
<hr color="#FFFFFF">
<p align="right"><b><font face="Tahoma" size="2"><a
href="http://link6">Sign up
for our e-mail newsletter</a></font></b></p>
<hr color="#FFFFFF">
<p align="right"><b><font face="Tahoma" size="2"><a
href="http://link7">Customer
Care</a><br>
<a href="http://link8">Special Orders</a></font></b></p>
<hr color="#FFFFFF">
```

Listing 10-14 shows the replacement HTML code for the middle of the menu bar, a simple image tag to place the gradient graphic.

Listing 10-14: **Middle menu bar HTML (menu_middle.htm)**

```
<img src="gradiant.jpg">
```

Listing 10-15 shows the new HTML code for the bottom of the menu bar.

Listing 10-15: **Bottom menu bar HTML (menu_bottom.htm)**

```
<p align="center"><b><font face="Tahoma" size="2">Seasonal
Specials!<br>
</font></b><font face="Tahoma" size="1"><a
href="http://link11">CLICK HERE</a></font></p>
```

Listing 10-16 is the replacement for the footer portion of the page.

Listing 10-16: Footer HTML (footer.htm)

```
<p align="center"><font face="Tahoma" size="1">copyright (c)
2001 Retailer.com<br>
<a href="http://ff">Privacy Policy</a> • <a
href="http://ff">Terms of Use</a> 
•  <a href="http://gg">About Us</a></font></p>
```

Thus far, the Retailer.com page looks like Figure 10-2. As you can see, it still needs some work. The sizing of the table rows and columns from the frames-based layout has not yet been duplicated. Also, because the frames-based layout used separate pages, the `<body>` tag set a background color for each individual frame. To duplicate this in a table-based setup, you have to specify a `bgcolor` property for each table cell that shouldn't use the default color.

Figure 10-2: Table-based page layout

The revised default.htm file, which includes the sizing and color information for the table cells, is shown in Listing 10-17.

Listing 10-17: **Revised table-based default.asp (default_revised.asp)**

```html
<html>
<head>
<title>Retailer.com Home Page</title>
</head>
<body vlink="#FFFF00" link="#FFFF00">
<table border="0" width="100%" cellspacing="0" cellpadding="0">
  <tr bgcolor="#008080">
    <td colspan="2" align="left" valign="middle">
<!--#include file="title_left.htm"--></td>
    <td align="right" valign="middle">
<!--#include file="title_right.htm"--></td>
  </tr>
  <tr>
    <td bgcolor="#008080" width="150" align="center">
<!--#include file="menu_top.htm"--></td>
    <td colspan="2" align="center" rowspan="2">Main</td>
  </tr>
  <tr>
    <td width="150" height="25" align="center">
<!--#include file="menu_middle.htm"--></td>
  </tr>
  <tr>
    <td bgcolor="#000080" width="150" align="center">
<!--#include file="menu_bottom.htm"--></td>
    <td colspan="2" align="center">
<!--#include file="footer.htm"--></td>
  </tr>
</table>
</body>
</html>
```

The addition of color is shown in Figure 10-3.

You will probably need to spend additional time tweaking the sizing and color settings on the table to achieve the exact effect that you want. When you are finished, you will have a basic "template" page that has the look you want every page on your site to share. This can then become the basis for every page that your site includes.

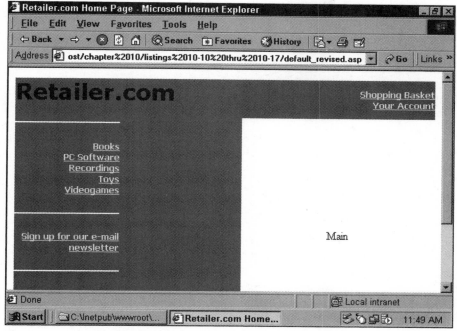

Figure 10-3: Revised table-based page layout

Navigation effects

Basic navigation effects, such as having links change their color when the user moves their mouse over them, can be easily achieved by using Cascading Style Sheets (CSS). In fact, you should plan on using CSS to achieve a consistent look and feel throughout your site because CSS lets you specify *classes* for everything — including tables, different types of text, hyperlinks, and so forth — and then apply those classes to your HTML. For example, if you want to change the color scheme of your site to accommodate a Christmas theme in December, you just have to replace the main CSS file. You can find out more about CSS in any good HTML book, or in Microsoft's online MSDN Library (`http://msdn.Microsoft.com/library`). In this section, I concentrate on using CSS to achieve navigation special effects.

Start by creating a style sheet like the one shown in Listing 10-18. This style sheet defines three different styles for hyperlinks.

- ✦ The first style (a1) allows you to use normal hyperlinks that don't do anything when the user points to them.

- ✦ The second style (a2) removes the link's normal underline and makes it change colors when the user points to it.

- ✦ The third style (a3) is similar to the second but adds an underline.

Using a style sheet like this allows you to create different types of links for different purposes on your pages.

Listing 10-18: Sample style sheet

```
<style>
<!--

a1 { font-weight="bold"; text-decoration:"underline";
font-family: Tahoma; color:"#3A6EA5" }

a2 { font-weight="bold";
font-family: Tahoma; color:"#3A6EA5" }

a2:hover { color:"#009900"}

a3 { font-weight="bold"; text-decoration:"underline";
font-family: Tahoma; color:"#3A6EA5" }

a3:hover { color:"#009900"}

-->
</style>
```

This style sheet can be included in the <HEAD> section of an HTML page by using a server-side include:

```
<HEAD>
<!--#include file="stylesheet.txt"-->
</HEAD>
```

By including the style sheet in every page, you can use the styles throughout your site for consistency and still have a central place to make changes that will immediately take place across the entire site.

Using the styles is also straightforward. Instead of coding your hyperlinks using a normal <A> tag:<A HREF="http://someplace.com">Click here</A>You add a tag indicating the class to which the link should belong:

```
<A CLASS="A1" HREF="http://someplace.com">Click here</A>
```

You can also use the style sheet to define a default style for all links that don't have a class. To do so, just define a style named "A." Any <A> tags that don't specify a class will adopt the look and behavior of the default "A" class.

Dynamic generation of static pages

Retailer.com has also decided to use dynamically generated, static HTML pages for their navigation. This allows their navigation scheme to be based upon their database contents, but doesn't require each page to query the database to retrieve the navigation hierarchy. Instead, a single job will run every night, querying the navigation information and then building a static HTML page.

As developed so far, the layout already contains the perfect place for this dynamically generated page, the menu_top.htm file. By replacing this file, each page on the site will inherit the updated menu.

You can automate the creation of static HTML pages in a couple of ways. For one, you can write a SQL Server Agent job that uses ActiveX script tasks to create the page. Or, you can write a Visual Basic application that can be scheduled to run via the Windows Task Scheduler. For complex tasks that will generate many pages, I prefer to use a Visual Basic application because VB offers better file performance. For tasks like this one, where only a single page needs to be generated, you can use an ActiveX task within a SQL Server job. Either way, the code you write is much the same.

Tip The biggest bottleneck in dynamically generating HTML pages is disk throughput. If you're generating a large number of pages, you'll find that compiled applications that are written in Visual Basic — or better, Visual C++ — provide much faster throughput than scripted languages.

You start this technique by creating a template file. This file contains all of the HTML code that doesn't change, and contains a placeholder where the updated menu information will go. Start by adapting the existing menu_top.htm file, as shown in Listing 10-19.

Listing 10-19: **Menu bar template**

```
<hr color="#FFFFFF">
<p align="right"><b><font face="Tahoma" size="2">
xxMenuHerexx
<hr color="#FFFFFF">
<p align="right"><b><font face="Tahoma" size="2"><a
href="http://link6">Sign up
for our e-mail newsletter</a></font></b></p>
<hr color="#FFFFFF">
<p align="right"><b><font face="Tahoma" size="2"><a
href="http://link7">Customer
Care</a><br>
<a href="http://link8">Special Orders</a></font></b></p>
<hr color="#FFFFFF">
```

This listing includes the original menu, but removes the actual department links and replaces them with "xxMenuHerexx." This is the placeholder that the code will use to determine where the updated menu should be placed. The remainder of the file is unchanged because the remaining menu links are intended to remain unchanged.

The next step is to create a VB or VBScript program that queries the appropriate navigation information from the database. Exactly how you do this depends primarily on how your Commerce Server catalog is structured; in the code below, I call a function named `GetMenus` that returns an ActiveX Data Objects recordset with all of the department names. If you choose to use this code, you will need to provide a `GetMenus` function that provides the appropriate information. In the sample code, I assume that the recordset returned by `GetMenus` has a column named "Description" and a column named "Link," which contains the URL that should be called when the menu link is clicked.

This code, shown in Listing 10-20, can either be the text of a VBScript ActiveX job step in a SQL Server Agent job, or the body of a `Sub Main()` subroutine in a Visual Basic application.

 Note   If you use this code in VBScript, be sure to remove the variable type declarations. VBScript is a weakly typed language and doesn't support declared variable types.

Listing 10-20: **Generating the HTML menu page**

```
'Create variables
Dim sTemplate As String
Dim sMenu As String
Set rsMenus = CreateObject("ADODB.Recordset")

'Get menus
Set rsMenus = GetMenus()

'Walk through menus and
'build the links
Do Until rsMenus.EOF
  sMenu = sMenu & "<a class='a2' href='"
  smenu = sMenu & rsMenus("Link")
  sMenu = sMenu & "'>" & rsMenus("Description")
  sMenu = sMenu & "</a><br>"
  rsMenus.MoveNext
Loop
Set rsMenus = Nothing

'Read the template file into
' a variable
Set FSO = CreateObject("FileSystemObject")
Set TS = FSO.OpenTextFile("c:\template.txt",ForReading)
sTemplate = TS.ReadAll
```

```
TS.Close
Set TS = Nothing

'write out the completed file
Set TS = FSO.OpenTextFile("c:\output.htm",ForWriting)
RS.WriteLine Replace(sTemplate,"xxMenusHerexx",sMenu)
TS.Close
Set TS = Nothing
Set FSO = Nothing
```

The Do...Loop construct spins through the recordset of menus, adding each one — along with the appropriate HTML tags to make it a link — to a variable. Note that each menu is added with a class to allow a cascading style sheet to specify navigation effects for the links.

The next block of code reads the entire template file into a single variable. This code assumes that the file is c:\template.txt; modify this as necessary for your environment. The last block of code writes out the actual output HTML file (again, modify the file location as appropriate). Note the use of the Replace() function to replace the menu placeholder in the template with the actual set of menu links contained in the sMenu variable.

You can also use this technique to generate any static HTML files by pulling information from a database. You can even use multiple placeholders, if necessary. For example, a dynamically generated product detail page may include a placeholder for the description, price, available colors, and so forth. Multiple Replace() functions can be used to fill in each placeholder from an ADO recordset, facilitating the quick generation of static pages based on the information in the database.

Dynamic navigation

Retailer.com has also decided to use Dynamic HTML (DHTML) to create a more flexible menu system. Each major department will be represented by a link on the menu bar, and the categories available in that department will appear in a pop-up menu when the department name is clicked. Any sub-departments that you have will pop up in a new menu, similar to the way Windows menus (including the Start menu) work.

Creating this type of dynamic effect can be difficult and time-consuming. Doing so requires a precise knowledge of the Document Object Model that browsers use to make the HTML elements of a page available to a script. Creating these effects also requires the programmer to fully understand Cascading Style Sheets Positioning, which is a complex subset of HTML that allows pop-up menus to be correctly positioned when they are displayed.

Fortunately, you don't have to reinvent the wheel when it comes to pop-up menus. Several pre-written sets of DHTML scripts are available, which you can customize to your precise needs. One is available from OpenCube (www.opencube.com), which has long been a provider of Java applets suited for navigation, and has recently branched out to include DHTML scripts for navigation. You can find another comprehensive, freely available script at http://www.webreference.com/dhtml. One of the most popular aftermarket pop-up menu packages — implemented completely in DHTML with a very friendly menu-builder interface — is available at popup. jscentral.com. The very powerful and flexible Pop-Up Menu uses a single standardized script, which is then customized by a second script. You can use the evaluation version of the Pop-Up Menu — included on the CD-ROM accompanying this book — to generate a DHTML menu and examine the resulting scripts.

Tip   Given the *significant* amount of time required to develop robust pop-up menus in DHTML, I strongly recommend that you use a preprogrammed menu solution if at all possible.

After you've created the customized menu, place the menu's script files on your site and insert a short block of DHTML code into your page to enable the menu, as shown in Listing 10-21.

Listing 10-21: **Pop-Up Menu implementation script**

```
<HTML>
<HEAD>
<TITLE>Pop-Up menu Sample HTML file</TITLE>
</HEAD>
<BODY>
<!-- Begin of Pop Up Code -->
<Script Language="JavaScript">
<!--
mpx=10;
mpy=140;
if (navigator.appName == "Netscape" &&
navigator.appVersion.indexOf("4") == 0){
document.write('<Scr' + 'ipt Language="JavaScript"
Src="popupnn.js"></Scr' + 'ipt>');
document.write('<Scr' + 'ipt Language="JavaScript"
Src="mypopnn.js"></Scr' + 'ipt>');
}
if (document.all){
document.write('<Scr' + 'ipt Language="JavaScript"
Src="popupie.js"></Scr' + 'ipt>');
document.write('<Scr' + 'ipt Language="JavaScript"
Src="mypopie.js"></Scr' + 'ipt>');
}

window.onload=onloevha;
```

```
function onloevha(){;
if (document.all || document.layers)
popmcreate();
}
////-->
</Script>
<!-- End of Pop Up Code -->
</BODY>
</HTML>
```

Pop-Up Menu creates two scripts — one optimized for Internet Explorer and one optimized for Netscape Communicator. This approach allows your menus to look their best on either of the major browsers, as shown in Figure 10-4. Pop-Up Menu is one of my favorite tools for creating DHTML menus because it's inexpensive, incredibly flexible, and includes a complete graphical user interface (GUI) for creating menus, with no programming required. The user can drag the resulting menus around the screen, dock them, and then include special effects, such as fading and animation.

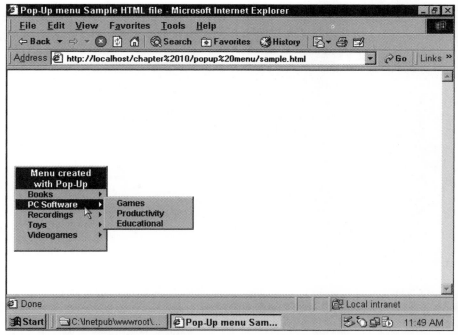

Figure 10-4: Sample Pop-Up Menu

Preprogrammed DHTML or your own?

Until recently, most e-commerce sites tended to use DHTML pop-up menus created by their own developers or contractors. More and more preprogrammed DHTML menus have become available in recent months, however, and these menus allow an ever-increasing number of features and options for customization.

Deciding to program your own pop-up menus is a big decision. Pop-up menus combine the most complex aspects of Cascading Style Sheets (CSS) as well as the most complex aspects of DHTML. Significant development time can be invested in developing even a simple pop-up menu.

On the other hand, preprogrammed menus are easy to implement, can generally be customized to blend in with the look and feel of your site, and require virtually no development time. They are almost always inexpensive — usually from $20 to $50 — and are *always* less expensive than developing your own menu from scratch. As a result, you should seriously consider using a preprogrammed solution.

Most pop-up menus also include separate scripts customized for Internet Explorer and Communicator, facilitating the development of a Web site with wide browser support.

The most common objection to using a preprogrammed menu is that your site will "look just like everyone else's," because many sites tend to use the same menus. The variety of available pop-up menus and the significant degree to which they can be customized renders this objection almost completely meaningless — especially in light of the significantly reduced development and testing time.

Most DHTML pop-up menus are compatible with version 4.0 and higher browsers, particularly if you use a preprogrammed menu that includes separate scripts for Internet Explorer and Communicator (see the sidebar, "What do you mean by 'compatible'?"). Most importantly, these menus are generally easy to adapt to a dynamically generated static HTML situation, where a regularly scheduled utility creates the actual menu structure. Rather than using an HTML file as the template as I did in the previous section, you use the DHTML script file as the template and insert the menu information as necessary. The DHTML script is then included with your site pages, providing a menu on every page. This technique can be somewhat difficult with packaged DHTML menu solutions like the Pop-Up Menu, but careful examination of the mypopie.js and mypopnn.js files reveal where you can use a Visual Basic application to dynamically generate the menu.

Java navigation elements

Even though Retailer.com doesn't plan to use any Java navigation elements, Utilities.com intends to use a Java applet as their primary navigation element. Remember that Utilities.com plans to direct people only to their home page, so they feel comfortable adopting a frames-based navigation system. The frames-based system allows them to place the Java applet in a menu bar, where Java's two primary disadvantages — it requires a dedicated rectangle of space and has some-what slow load times — will be eliminated. They have decided to use a simple site layout with two frames. The left-hand frame will be a narrow menu bar containing the Java applet, and the right-hand frame will contain the actual site content.

What do you mean by "compatible"?

If you examine the browser capabilities charts later in this chapter, you'll see that the Web's two most popular browsers, Microsoft Internet Explorer and Netscape Communicator, both support Dynamic HTML scripts. Although only Internet Explorer support scripts written in VB Script, both browsers support the more common Jscript/JavaScript language. So a JavaScript pop-up menu written for one browser should work with the other, right?

Wrong. Although both browsers' implementations of the JavaScript language are virtually identical, both companies have chosen to implement the Document Object Model (DOM) quite differently. The DOM is the object hierarchy that allows JavaScript to manipulate the appearance and behavior of a Web page, and is the portion of the browser to which both companies add the most proprietary extensions. So even though the *language* of an Internet Explorer script is much the same as a Communicator script, the objects being manipulated can be subtly — often *very* subtly — different, making the scripts incompatible.

Although it's certainly possible to write "browser neutral" scripts that accommodate these differences, achieving precise, complex effects like pop-up menus can often require two separate scripts geared to each browser type.

In fact, the main portion of the Pop-Up Menu script that you insert into your pages is designed to detect the user's browser and include the appropriate version of the Pop-Up Menu code:

```
if (navigator.appName == "Netscape" &&
navigator.appVersion.indexOf("4") == 0){
document.write('<Scr' + 'ipt Language="JavaScript"
Src="popupnn.js"></Scr' + 'ipt>');
document.write('<Scr' + 'ipt Language="JavaScript"
Src="mypopnn.js"></Scr' + 'ipt>');
}
if (document.all){
document.write('<Scr' + 'ipt Language="JavaScript"
Src="popupie.js"></Scr' + 'ipt>');
document.write('<Scr' + 'ipt Language="JavaScript"
Src="mypopie.js"></Scr' + 'ipt>');
}
```

In this case, the script checks to see if the browser returns an `appName` of `Netscape` and a version number of at least 4.0 before including the Netscape Communicator versions of the script. On the other hand, if the `document.all` object (an object unique to Internet Explorer versions with full DHTML support) is present, then the Internet Explorer-specific scripts are included.

This layout dictates the use of a Java applet designed for a vertical orientation. Had they selected a top menu bar with the site content located in a larger bottom frame, a horizontally oriented Java applet would have been more appropriate.

If you prefer to use a prewritten Java applet instead of writing your own, finding the right one can be a time-consuming, but nevertheless interesting, task. OpenCube (www.opencube.com) offers a wide variety of applets designed for navigation, as do many other independent software vendors.

Tip

Given the development time required for custom Java applets, and the difficulty in hiring skilled Java programmers, I advise that you use a preprogrammed applet whenever possible. These generally offer sufficient flexibility and are usually tuned for the fastest possible download.

Most Java applets require you to place the Java files somewhere on your Web site, often in a dedicated folder. You then create HTML code that instructs the user's browser to "call" the Java applet. The HTML code usually contains any parameters that the applet requires or that you want to include in order to customize its appearance and behavior. Some applets allow you to place this configuration information in a separate file, resulting in neater-looking HTML. The applet will actually *execute* on the user's browser, so the applet must have some means of accessing the configuration and customization information that you want to supply.

Because most applets get their configuration information from the HTML page or from an external file, you can use the dynamically generated technique with these navigation elements, as well. Write your Visual Basic utility or VBScript job step to write out the configuration parameters for the applet into the necessary file or files.

For the purpose of demonstration, imagine that Utilities.com has decided to use the Sliding Menu navigation applet written by OpenCube. Their menubar.htm page may look something like Listing 10-22.

Listing 10-22: **Sample Java applet implementation**

```
<HTML>

<applet code="slidem" align="baseline" width="163"
height="315">

<!--General Settings-->
<param name="bgcolor" value="255,255,255">
<param name="delay" value="5">
<param name="jumpsize" value="2">
<param name="Notice" value="Sliding Tree Menu, Copyright (c)
2000, OpenCube Inc.">

<!--Sub Menu Descriptions-->
<param name="desc0-0" value="2|New Applets">
<param name="desc0-0-0" value="1|Tree Menu">
```

```
<param name="desc0-0-1" value="1|Smart Tree">
<param name="desc0-0-2" value="1|Scrolling Window">
<param name="desc0-0-3" value="1|Message Flipper">
<param name="desc0-1" value="2|Implementations">
<param name="desc0-1-0" value="1|3Dfx">
<param name="desc0-1-1" value="1|J &amp; J">
<param name="desc0-1-2" value="1|TV Guide">
<param name="desc0-2" value="1|Composer">
<param name="desc0-3" value="1|Navigation">
<param name="desc0-4" value="1|Presentation">
<param name="desc0-5" value="1|Gold">
<param name="desc1-0" value="1|Composer">
<param name="desc1-1" value="1|Navigation">
<param name="desc1-2" value="1|Presentation">
<param name="desc1-3" value="1|Gold">
<param name="desc2-0" value="1|Customer Service">
<param name="desc2-1" value="1|Tech. Support">
<param name="desc2-2" value="1|Product Sales">

<!--URL Links-->
<param name="loadwhere" value="main">
<param name="desturl0-0-0" value="demo_link.htm">
<param name="desturl0-0-1" value="demo_link.htm">
<param name="desturl0-0-2" value="demo_link.htm">
<param name="desturl0-0-3" value="demo_link.htm">
<param name="desturl0-1-0" value="demo_link.htm">
<param name="desturl0-1-1" value="demo_link.htm">
<param name="desturl0-1-2" value="demo_link.htm">
<param name="desturl0-2" value="demo_link.htm">
<param name="desturl0-3" value="demo_link.htm">
<param name="desturl0-4" value="demo_link.htm">
<param name="desturl0-5" value="demo_link.htm">
<param name="desturl1-0" value="demo_link.htm">
<param name="desturl1-1" value="demo_link.htm">
<param name="desturl1-2" value="demo_link.htm">
<param name="desturl1-3" value="demo_link.htm">
<param name="desturl2-0" value="demo_link.htm">
<param name="desturl2-1" value="demo_link.htm">
<param name="desturl2-2" value="demo_link.htm">
<param name="mdesturl3" value="composer.htm">

<!--Sub Menu Highlight Settings-->
<param name="hlsubtextonly" value="false">

<!--Icon Images-->
<param name="iconfile0" value="micon.gif">
<param name="iconfile1" value="isquare.gif">
<param name="iconfile2" value="idown0.gif">
<param name="iconfile3" value="micon.gif">
<param name="iconswitchfile0" value="micondown.gif">
<param name="iconswitchfile1" value="isquareh.gif">
<param name="iconswitchfile2" value="idownh.gif">
```

Continued

Listing 10-22 *(continued)*

```
<param name="iconswitchfile3" value="mnosub.gif">
<param name="iconupfile0" value="miconup.gif">
<param name="iconupfile2" value="iup.gif">

<!--Main Menu Descriptions-->
<param name="maindesc0" value="0|">
<param name="maindesc1" value="0|">
<param name="maindesc2" value="0|">
<param name="maindesc3" value="3|">

<!--Main Menu Settings-->
<param name="mbgfile" value="mainbg.jpg">
<param name="mbgonmenusonly" value="false">
<param name="mfont" value="Helvetica, bold, 23">
<param name="mheight" value="30">
<param name="mhltextcolor" value="200,0,0">
<param name="miconindent" value="19"><param name="mindent"
value="30">
<param name="mtextcolor" value="175,172,163">
<param name="mtilebg" value="false">
<param name="rfromoff" value="true">
<param name="topoffset" value="19">

<!--Sub Menu Settings-->
<param name="s_bgfile" value="lev1.jpg">
<param name="s_bgfile1" value="level2.gif">
<param name="s_color" value="230,230,215">
<param name="s_hltextcolor" value="153,0,0">
<param name="s_outcolor" value="0,0,0">
<param name="s_textcolor" value="75,75,75">
<param name="s_uhltextcolor" value="153,0,0">
<param name="subfont" value="Dialog, bold, 12">
<param name="subheight" value="14">
<param name="subiconindent" value="0">
<param name="subindent" value="14">
<param name="subindent1" value="15">
</applet>
</HTML>
```

Notice the "LoadWhere" parameter in the section that defines the URL. This applet supports the ability to open selected URLs in a separate frame, which is what enables the applet to work in the framed layout that Utilities.com has chosen. The initial APPLET tag tells the browser where to find the actual Java applet file; in this example, the Java applet should be located in the same directory as the HTML file that calls it. This results in a menu bar that looks something like the one shown in Figure 10-5.

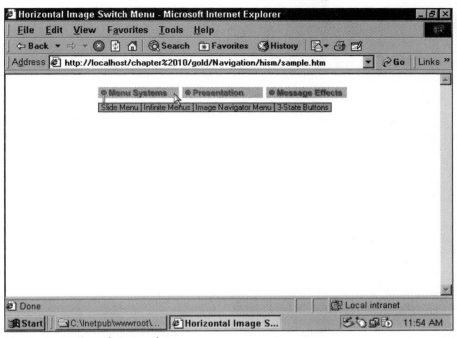

Figure 10-5: Sample menu bar

Most Java applets are used in this fashion, so after you get used to coding the HTML for one, you'll be able to easily use other Java applets elsewhere on your site. Other popular uses for Java applets include scrolling information displays, "news of the day" displays, and so forth. Remember, though, that the fancy effects provided by Java applets can come at the price of a lengthy download. Try to minimize the time it takes your pages to download to your users. For example, if you include a Java applet on several pages, many browsers will cache the applet code so that second and subsequent downloads are almost instantaneous. However, Utilities.com's decision to use a single frame to host their Java applet *ensures* that it only downloads once.

Keep in mind that users have the option to turn off Java support in their browsers. Corporations employing proxy servers and firewalls also have the ability to filter out Java content, whether or not the users have enabled it in their browsers. Corporations using Microsoft Internet Explorer also have the ability to globally disable Java support in their users' browsers. Take these facts into consideration when choosing to implement Java applets on your site, and be sure to provide an alternate means of navigation for users without Java support in their browsers.

Advertising and Promotion

Advertising and promotion is not only a major part of the look and feel of your site, but is often part of the site's lifeblood. You can use advertising to promote your own products and services, specials and sales, and so forth. You can also use advertising to generate revenue by selling ad space on your site to outside companies.

Commerce Server comes equipped with a robust ad management system, but if your needs are simple, you can probably save your servers a bit of processing overhead by developing your own basic ad rotation tool.

Advertising and promotion also encompasses certain marketing and market-research tasks, such as determining where customers have clicked on your site, who referred them to your site, and so forth.

Your site design documents should specify the type of advertising and click history information that you want to use and report on. In this section, I talk about how to implement these design goals by using Commerce Server's built-in tools and, where necessary, by creating your own tools to replace or supplement Commerce Server's built-in functionality.

Commerce Server's advertising tools

Commerce Server includes a complete Ad Manager as part of its advertising campaign tools. The Ad Manager allows you to define several different types of ads:

✦ Text

✦ Non-clickable images

✦ Clickable images

✦ Complex HTML

✦ *Vignette* — an image adjacent to text

✦ "Buy now" ads that add items to the user's cart

✦ Windows Media Services, to create rich-media ads

For each ad type, you can define specific ad sizes. This allows you to customize the placement of the ad within your overall site design, and to include different sized ads in different locations on each page. Ad types and sizes are defined in the Campaign Manager portion of the Commerce Server Business Desk, as shown in Figure 10-6.

Commerce Server lets you use these ad types as the basis for ad items, which you create as part of an overall ad campaign for an advertising customer.

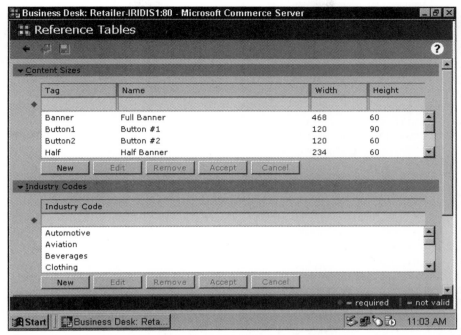

Figure 10-6: Commerce Server's Campaign Manager ad types

Creating an ad campaign

Each campaign that you create must be related to a customer, even if that customer is your own company. Figure 10-7 shows Commerce Server's Campaign Manager being used to create a new customer entry for Retailer.com. Note that the customer type is "Self;" if you were adding an external advertiser, the type would be "Advertiser."

A *campaign* is a complete effort to promote a certain brand, product, service, or other concept, and may consist of multiple ads. Figure 10-8 shows a new campaign being created to promote a Toys department that Retailer.com has recently added.

Figure 10-8 also shows the campaign-wide *goal*, which is set to clicks. This means that each ad item in the campaign must be *clicked* a specified number of times before the campaign will be considered complete. You can also specify a *requests*-based goal, which satisfies the requirements of the campaign after an ad has been *displayed* a specified number of times. Requests-based goals are very useful for taking orders from outside advertisers for a specific number of ads, and allows Commerce Server to automatically help you fulfill the agreement.

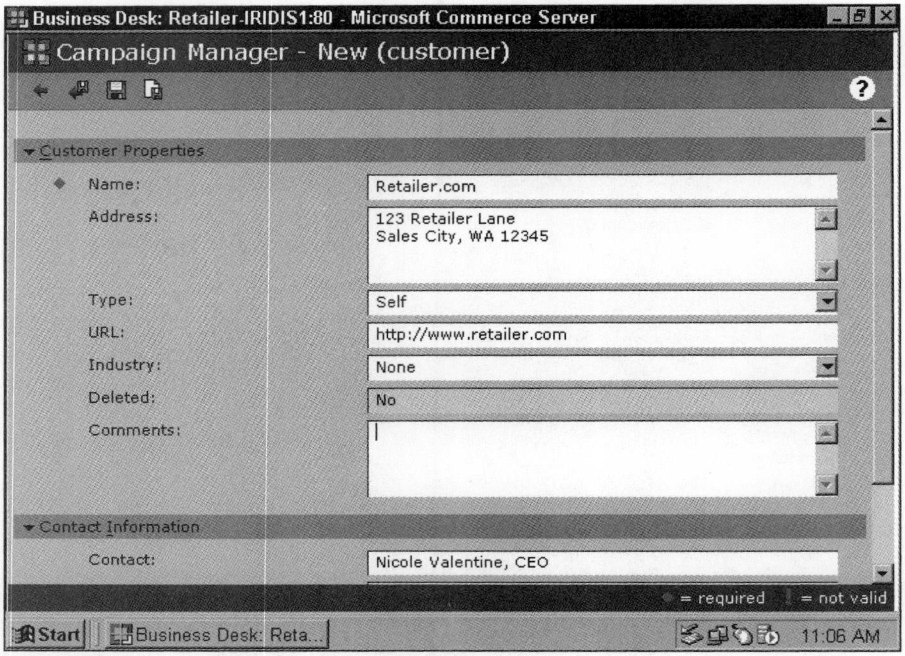

Business Desk: Retailer-IRIDIS1:80 - Microsoft Commerce Server

Campaign Manager - New (customer)

▼ Customer Properties

◆	Name:	Retailer.com
	Address:	123 Retailer Lane Sales City, WA 12345
	Type:	Self
	URL:	http://www.retailer.com
	Industry:	None
	Deleted:	No
	Comments:	

▼ Contact Information

	Contact:	Nicole Valentine, CEO

◆ = required   = not valid

Start   Business Desk: Reta...   11:06 AM

Figure 10-7: Creating a campaign customer

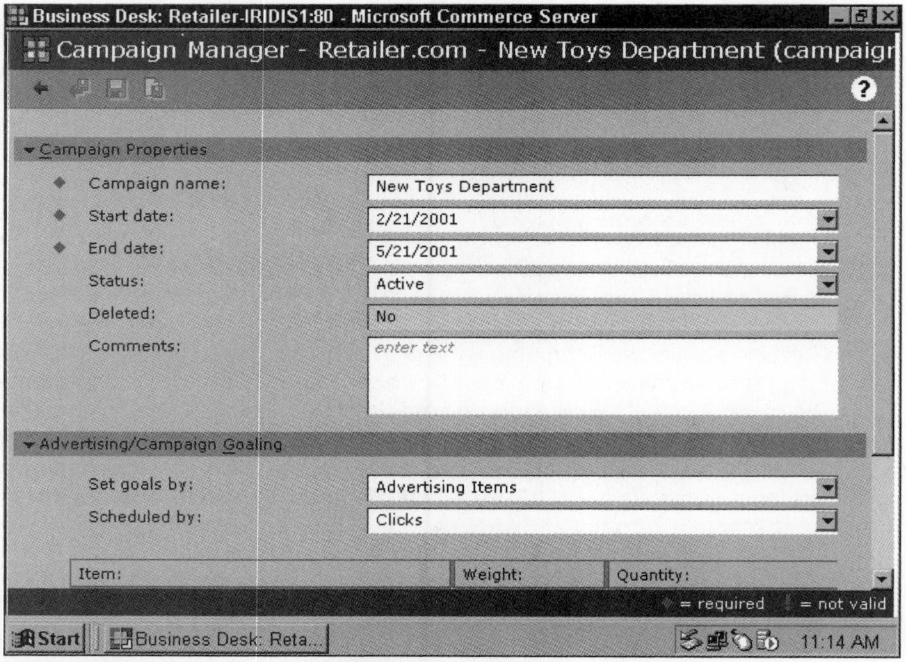

Business Desk: Retailer-IRIDIS1:80 - Microsoft Commerce Server

Campaign Manager - Retailer.com - New Toys Department (campaign

▼ Campaign Properties

◆	Campaign name:	New Toys Department
◆	Start date:	2/21/2001
◆	End date:	5/21/2001
	Status:	Active
	Deleted:	No
	Comments:	enter text

▼ Advertising/Campaign Goaling

	Set goals by:	Advertising Items
	Scheduled by:	Clicks

Item:		Weight:	Quantity:

◆ = required   = not valid

Start   Business Desk: Reta...   11:14 AM

Figure 10-8: Creating a new campaign

Figure 10-9 shows the creation of a new ad for the campaign. The figure shows a house ad being created, although you can also create paid ads from outside advertisers. For each ad, specify a *weight*. The weight determines how frequently the ad will be shown, and how it contributes to the campaign goal. For example, the campaign goal may be 100,000 views, and the campaign may include two ads — the first with a weight of one, and the second with a weight of two. The first ad will be shown half as often as the second ad, thus contributing less to the campaign's overall goal.

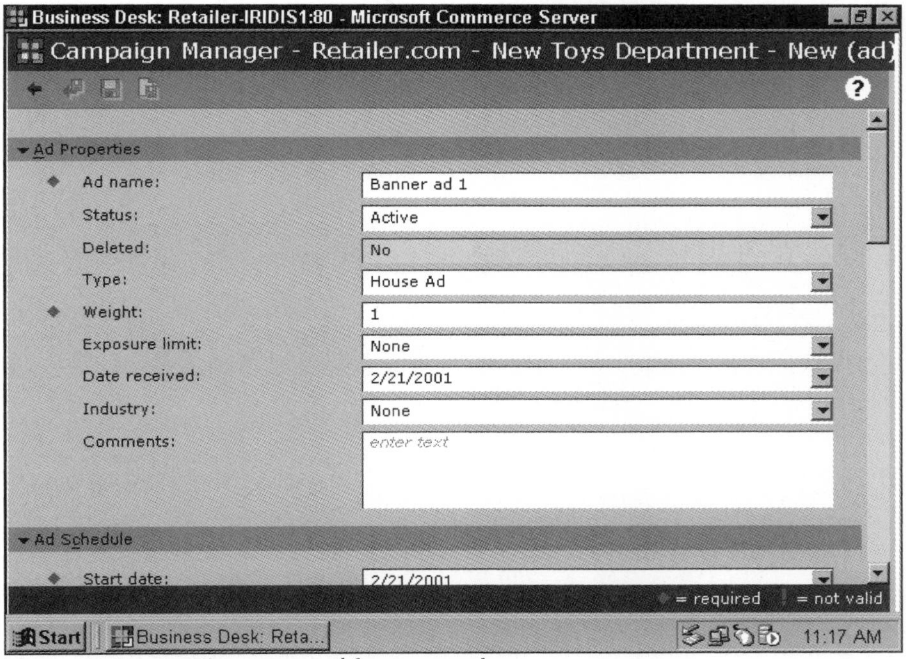

Figure 10-9: Creating a new ad for a campaign

You can *target* each ad in a campaign. Targeting is done based on information in your customers' Commerce Server profiles, and allows you to display the ads to prior customers, for example, or to customers who have never bought anything. Targeting allows you to customize the content and type of the ad to appeal to specific portions of your customer base. For example, if your customer profiles include information on how customers connect to your site — whether by dial-up, DSL, or cable modem — then you can deliver Windows Media audio/video ads to high-bandwidth customers, and traditional static images to low-bandwidth customers.

Commerce Server's analysis tools also provide reports to help you determine how effective a campaign is, keep track of the campaign's progress, and so forth.

Using the ad campaign

An ad campaign is useless unless you implement code to actually display the ads in accordance with the campaign's parameters. This code is built in if you're using the Retail Solution Site. However, you may not be using *any* of the Solution Sites as a basis for your production site because they don't scale well, so I show you how to create your own code to implement Commerce Server's advertising.

Commerce Server provides a COM component called the ContentSelector that allows you to retrieve advertising. The ContentSelector invokes a Content Selection Pipeline, which is a series of components that execute a number of business rules as a single transaction. The result of this transaction is a list of content matching the original input parameters to the pipeline, in this case, one or more ads.

You need to include code in your site's Global.asa file to initialize the content selection framework. If you're creating your own Global.asa, just pull this code out of the Global.asa for one of the Solution Sites, or copy it from Listing 10-23.

Tip   Although I don't encourage you to use a complete Solution Site as the basis for your site, I do recommend that you pilfer code from the Solution Sites' Global.asa files as necessary.

Listing 10-23: Initializing the content selection framework in Global.asa

```
<%
Sub Application_OnStart

' sConnStr must point to a valid Campaigns database.
const sConnStr = "Your connect string here"

Dim oPipe, dCSFAdsContext
Dim oExpEval, oCacheMgr, dCacheCfg

' Set up CacheManager object.
Set dCacheCfg = CreateObject("Commerce.Dictionary")
dCacheCfg.ConnectionString = sConnStr
Set oCacheMgr = CreateObject("Commerce.CacheManager")
oCacheMgr.LoaderProgId("Ads")="Commerce.CSFLoadAdvertisements"
Set oCacheMgr.LoaderConfig("Ads") = dCacheConfig
oCacheMgr.RefreshInterval("Ads") = 15 * 60

' Create the Expression Evaluator and connect it.
Set oExpEval = CreateObject("Commerce.ExpressionEvaluator")
Call oExpEval.Connect(sConnStr)

' Create CSF advertising context, a dictionary.
Set dCSFAdsContext = CreateObject("Commerce.Dictionary")
```

```
' Create an advertising pipeline and add it to the context.
Set oPipe = CreateObject("Commerce.OrderPipeline")
' Load the pipeline configuration
oPipe.LoadPipe(Server.MapPath("Advertising.pcf"))
Set dCSFAdsContext("pipeline") = oPipe

' Other context configuration for CSF ads.
dCSFAdsContext("RedirectUrl") = ".\redir.asp"
Set dCSFAdsContext("Evaluator") = oExpEval
' InitCacheManager, a routine that would
' appear elsewhere in the
' global.asa, returns a reference to a
' CacheManager object.
Set dCSFAdsContext("CacheManager") = oCacheMgr
dCSFAdsContext("CacheName") = "Ads"

' Store a reference to the dCSFAdsContext
' dictionary in the
' Application collection.
Set Application("CSFAdsContext") = dCSFAdsContext
End Sub

%>
```

After you've initialized the framework, using the ContentSelector object to display ads in your pages is simple. Listing 10-24 shows an ASP code snippet that does the job.

Listing 10-24: **Using the ContentSelector object**

```
<%
' Create a ContentSelector object.
Set CSO = Server.CreateObject("Commerce.ContentSelector")

' Use the GetContent method to get some content.
Set Ads = CSO.GetContent(Application("CSFAdsContext"))

' Ads is a SimpleList containing the selected content.
' Write the content to the page, if any.
For Each Ad in Ads
  Response.Write(Ad)
Next
%>
```

The Content Selection Pipeline

All of the functionality in these scripts is actually handled behind the scenes in the Content Selection Pipeline. Figure 10-10 shows a portion of this pipeline opened in Commerce Server's Pipeline Editor.

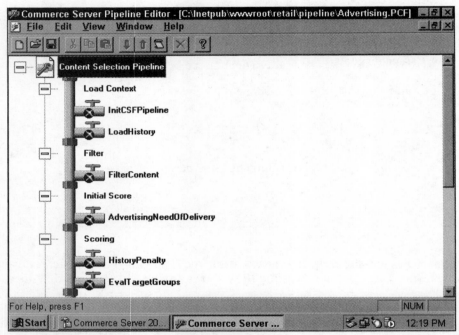

Figure 10-10: Editing the Content Selection Pipeline

The Content Selection Pipeline is one of eight pipelines that come with the Commerce Server Solution Sites. Like Global.asa, these pipelines are part of the Solution Sites that you should probably migrate to your own site. They may require modification, but they'll provide a good basis for the business logic on your site.

The purpose of these pipelines is to execute a series of business logic steps as a single transaction with a single end result. In the case of the Content Selection Pipeline, the business logic includes examining the customer's profile, existing ad campaigns, the ranking of active ad items by their weight, relevance to the customer's profile (if the ads are targeted), and many other factors. Although pipelines can contain a mixture of COM+ components, ActiveX scripts, and built-in components, the Content Selection Pipeline consists almost entirely of COM+ components.

Fortunately, this particular pipeline should require very little customization. The pipeline components are entirely data-driven, and their customization is accomplished through the configuration of your ads, ad campaigns, user profiles, and so forth.

Pros and cons

Commerce Server's ad management tools provide a number of benefits, including the following:

✦ Campaign goals

✦ Multiple ads per campaign

✦ Multiple campaigns per site

✦ View and click tracking

✦ Targeted ads

✦ Automatic handling of multiple media types

Commerce Server campaigns can also include advertising e-mail pieces and other promotional techniques, which allow you to consolidate all of your advertising efforts in a single place, and then report on those efforts as a combined campaign. The Content Selection framework allows you to specify the type of content that you want to select. In Listing 10-24, the code simply selected advertising, but different areas in your site may select other content, such as the text of a direct e-mail.

The downside to this functionality is overhead. Each ad placement requires a run of the Content Selection pipeline and multiple hits to your database server. However, if you need the robustness provided by these tools, then by all means use them because advertising is generally worth the overhead.

Creating your own ad rotation script

Your needs for banner ads may be small enough that you don't want to use Commerce Server's internal advertising capabilities. For example, you may only be using a dozen or so banners for internal advertising (special promotions, new products and services, and so on), and you may not care that the ads are shown in a particular order or with any specific regularity. In cases like this, creating a script to handle the ad rotation can involve less overhead than a dedicated component.

Tip

If you want to do anything more complex with your advertising, such as create weighted campaigns, targeted ads, or multiple campaigns for outside advertisers, I recommend that you use Commerce Server's Campaign Manager.

The simplest type of script selects a random number, and then uses a SELECT...CASE construct to deliver a banner, hyperlink, caption, or other information to the user. Listing 10-25 shows an example of this type of script. Ideally, this script is written in a separate ASP file and included in other Web pages as needed.

Listing 10-25: **Simple ad rotation script**

```
<%
'set the maximum number of banners
Dim MaxBanners
MaxBanners = 5

'choose a random number
Dim RN
Randomize Timer
RN = Int((MaxBanners) * Rnd + 1)

'output the banner with a hyperlink
'and a caption
SELECT CASE RN
  Case 1
    Response.write "<A HREF='/shop/product.asp'>"
    Response.write "<IMG SRC='banner1.gif'"
    Response.write " ALT='Click here!'>"
    Response.write "Click here for savings!</A>"
  Case 2
    Response.write "<A HREF='/shop/special.asp'>"
    Response.write "<IMG SRC='banner2.gif'"
    Response.write " ALT='Click here!'>"
    Response.write "Click here for our sale!</A>"
  Case 3
    Response.write "<A HREF='/ads/november.asp'>"
    Response.write "<IMG SRC='banner3.gif'"
    Response.write " ALT='Click here!'>"
    Response.write "November specials!</A>"
  Case 4
    Response.write "<A HREF='/magazine/nov.asp'>"
    Response.write "<IMG SRC='banner4.gif'"
    Response.write " ALT='Click here!'>"
    Response.write "Check out our savings magazine!</A>"
  Case 5
    Response.write "<A HREF='/shop/service.asp'>"
    Response.write "<IMG SRC='banner5.gif'"
    Response.write " ALT='Click here!'>"
    Response.write "Announcing new services!</A>"
END SELECT
%>
```

If you want your ad rotation script to help you keep track of how many times a particular ad was shown, then you need to switch to a SQL Server-based solution similar to the one that I describe in the previous section.

1. Create a table that will store the ad information, including a column to indicate the number of times an ad was shown and a date indicating the last reset date. The following code shows a SQL Server 2000 Transact-SQL script that will do the job.

```
CREATE TABLE [dbo].[Ads] (
[AD_ID] [int] IDENTITY (1, 1) NOT NULL,
[Banner_URL] [varchar] (500)
    COLLATE SQL_Latin1_General_CP1_CI_AS NOT NULL,
[Caption] [varchar] (500)
    COLLATE SQL_Latin1_General_CP1_CI_AS NOT NULL,
[Target_URL] [varchar] (500)
    COLLATE SQL_Latin1_General_CP1_CI_AS NOT NULL,
[Shown] [int] NOT NULL,
[ResetDate] [datetime] NOT NULL
) ON [PRIMARY]
GO
```

2. Create a SQL Server stored procedure. The stored procedure should accept a number corresponding to a banner's AD_ID value in the table (your script can generate this number randomly). The stored procedure will return the banner's information and increment the banner's Shown value, indicating that it has been shown to a customer. The following code shows the script for the stored procedure.

```
CREATE PROCEDURE sp_GetBannerAd
  @AdId AS Char(10)
AS
  UPDATE Ads SET
    Shown = Shown + 1 WHERE
    AD_ID = @AdId
  SELECT Banner_URL,Target_URL,Caption
    FROM Ads WHERE
    AD_ID = @AdId
GO
```

3. Create a revised banner rotation script that calls the stored procedure. Like the previous script, this should be created as a separate ASP file and included on any Web pages that will display a banner ad. The following code shows the ad script.

```
<%
'set the maximum number of banners
Dim MaxBanners
MaxBanners = 5

'choose a random number
Dim RN
Randomize Timer
RN = Int((MaxBanners) * Rnd + 1)
```

```
'assumes mscs is a valid ADO
'connection object to the database
'with the Ads table
Set objRS=mscs.Execute("sp_GetBannerAd " & RN)

'if the returned recordset is
'not blank, write out the ad:
If objRS.eof and objRS.bof Then
  'no banner was returned
Else
  Response.write "<A HREF='"
  Response.write objRS("Target_URL")
  Response.write "><IMG SRC='"
  Response.write objRS("Banner_URL")
  Response.write ">" & objRS("caption")
  Response.write "</A>"
End If
%>
```

This script will randomly select a banner and retrieve its information from the database. The stored procedure will increment the "shown" counter so that you can determine how many times the banner has been shown. To determine how many times the banner has been clicked, use a URL tracking tool like the one I show you later in this chapter.

How Commerce Server tracks click history

Part of your marketing goals may be to determine where users are visiting on your site. This information can be extremely useful to the folks responsible for designing your site's flow, because it helps them to understand how real customers are actually using the site, and what "paths" through the site most often result in a purchase.

Commerce Server's analysis tools provide complete click history information by importing your Web server's log files into the Commerce Server data warehouse. This is handled by a set of specialized SQL Server Data Transformation Services (DTS) tasks that are installed on SQL Server 7.0 or SQL Server 2000 when Commerce Server is installed.

To create a Data Transformation Services package that imports the Web server's log files:

1. Connect SQL Server Enterprise Manager to the SQL Server computer that hosts the Commerce Server's data warehouse database.

2. Create a new DTS package.

3. Add the "Configuration Synchronization" task to the workspace, and specify the Commerce Server site that you want to synchronize.

4. Add the "Import Web Server Logs" task to the workspace, and specify the Commerce Server site from which you want to import log files.

5. Add the "Prepare Reports" task to the workspace, and specify the Commerce Server site for which you want to prepare reports. If this is the first time this task has been run, specify a "Full load;" otherwise, specify an "Incremental load."

6. Connect the three tasks with "Success" workflow markers. The final DTS workspace is shown in Figure 10-11.

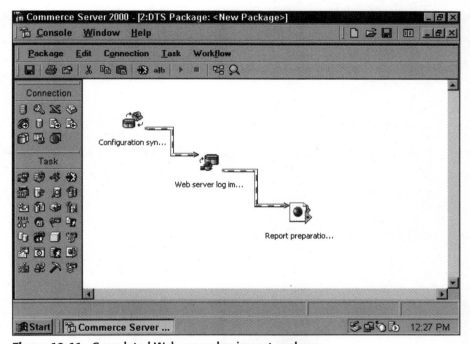

Figure 10-11: Completed Web server log import package

You can then save this package and schedule it for later execution, or execute it immediately. You should schedule this job to run as a part of your site's regular, ongoing maintenance, so that your most recent server logs are always imported into the analysis database.

After the package has executed, Commerce Server will be able to report on click history, number of daily visitors, and other information obtained from the Web server logs and paired with information in the Commerce Server production database. You can view these reports using the Business Desk application, as shown in Figure 10-12.

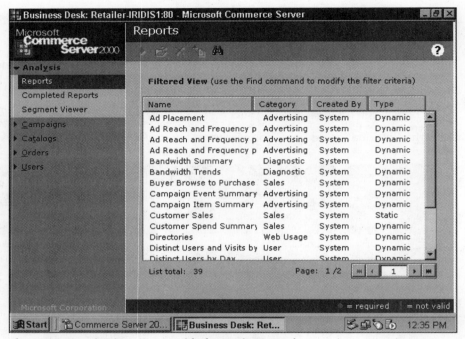

Figure 10-12: Viewing reports with the Business Desk

Creating URL tracking tools

You can use Commerce Server's analysis tools to import your Web server logs, and then run an analysis of shoppers' click history through your site and other statistical reports. You can also generate reports of *referral URLs*, which are URLs that direct shoppers to your site. You may still need to develop your own redirect and tracking tools, however, if you want to easily generate certain types of reports and if you frequently use URLs in promotional e-mails.

The goal and the problems

The promotional e-mails that you send to your customers will usually contain hyperlinks. In fact, you may include many hyperlinks in a single e-mail if you are promoting several products or services. Unfortunately, some e-mail clients—especially America Online and HTML-based clients like Yahoo! and Hotmail—can "break" the hyperlinks in your e-mails when they apply word wrapping to them. This can result in customers being directed to the wrong portion of your site, or receiving an error message because the link that they clicked was incomplete.

Your marketing department will probably want to track the success of those promotional e-mails, as well as the success of hyperlinks (such as banner ads) placed on other Web sites for advertising purposes. Although Commerce Server can generally pick up the URLs of Web sites that refer people to your site, it can't determine if someone linked to your site from a particular e-mail, nor can it necessarily tell you if the e-mail (or ad) resulted in a sale during the shopper's visit.

The solution

By programming your own URL redirection and tracking tool, you can easily keep hyperlinks short enough to survive even the most aggressive e-mail client and you can gather information on how shoppers were referred to your site. The solution involves a three-way approach:

✦ A database table containing marketing codes and destination URLs, as well as click-through information.

✦ An ASP page and SQL Server stored procedure that accepts a marketing code, returns the associated destination URL, and redirects the user to that URL.

✦ Modifications to the Commerce Server shopping cart to attach the marketing codes to the shopper's order for later analysis.

You will also need to produce an administrative interface that allows your marketing department to maintain and analyze the tool and its results.

Follow these steps to build a URL-tracking framework that allows speciallycoded hyperlinks to be tracked in your Commerce Server database:

1. Create a database table that will contain the redirection information. The following code shows a SQL Server 2000 Transact-SQL script that generates a table you can use as a starting point. It includes a column for a marketing code, which your marketing department will determine, and a destination URL that the marketing code represents.

```
CREATE TABLE [dbo].[URL_Tracking] (
 [URL_ID] [int] IDENTITY (1, 1) NOT NULL,
 [URL] [varchar] (500)
    COLLATE SQL_Latin1_General_CP1_CI_AS NOT NULL,
 [MktCode] [char] (10)
    COLLATE SQL_Latin1_General_CP1_CI_AS NOT NULL,
 [Clicks] [int] NOT NULL,
 [ResetDate] [datetime] NOT NULL
) ON [PRIMARY]
GO
```

The code also contains a column for the number of times that marketing code has been clicked, and a date column. The date column allows you to "zero out" the click counter, if you desire. For example, a Transact-SQL script can be used to clear out the click totals on all URLs in the table and reset the date. The date would then indicate when the totals were last cleared. You can modify the script to archive the click totals information in another table, if you desire. Such a script may look like this:

```
UPDATE URL_Tracking
 SET Clicks = 0,
     ResetDate = GETDATE()
```

2. After you've created the URL_Tracking table, populate it with marketing codes and URLs. Consider writing a Web interface to allow your marketing department to populate the table. For every URL that they want to include in an e-mail or place on another Web site, they must add a unique marketing code and that destination URL to the URL_Tracking database.

3. Create an ASP page and stored procedure that accepts a marketing code, looks up the associated URL, and redirects the user to that URL. The following code shows the relevant portion of the ASP page, redirect.asp.

```
<%

'assume input parameter is "redir"
'build query
dim sQuery
sQuery = "sp_GetRedirectURL '"
sQuery = sQuery & Request("redir")
sQuery = sQuery & "'"

' assume mscs is the connection object
dim objRS
set objRS = mscs.execute(sQuery)

'save the code in a cookie
response.cookies("mktcode") = request("redir")

'empty recordset?
If objRS.eof and objRS.bof then
  'redirect to home page
      response.redirect "/default.asp"
Else
  'redirect to requested url
  response.redirect objRS("URL")
End if

%>
```

The following code shows the sp_GetRedirectURL stored procedure.

```
CREATE PROCEDURE sp_GetRedirectURL
  @RedirCode AS Char(10)
AS
  UPDATE URL_Tracking SET
    Clicks = Clicks + 1 WHERE
    MktCode = @RedirCode
  SELECT URL FROM URL_Tracking WHERE
    MktCode = @RedirCode
GO
```

The hyperlinks in your ads and promotional e-mails can now be coded to point to Redirect.asp. By passing a parameter named "redir" with the appropriate marketing code, the customer is automatically redirected to the correct destination URL, and the database is updated to show that someone clicked the link. Because the hyperlink is now shorter — especially if redirect.asp is in the root of your Web site — it is much less likely to be broken by word wrapping. The marketing code is written to a cookie on the user's browser, allowing you to retrieve the code to use on the order form when the user checks out.

For example, suppose that your marketing department wants to send a promotional e-mail that includes a link to a particular product:

```
http://www.retailer.com/shop/products/prod_detail.asp?
prodid=145&customertype=56
```

Instead, add that URL to the URL_Tracking database, along with a unique marketing code. In this case, marketing uses m7584f768a as their code. They then add a generic redirect link to the e-mail, rather than the longer one to the product:

```
http://www.retailer.com/redirect.asp?redir=m7584f768a
```

Customers clicking the link will be immediately redirected to the desired product page, and the database will track how many customers click the link.

If you want to keep track of which clicks result in sales, your last step is to pull the marketing code from the cookie and into the Commerce Server order form. Exactly how you do this depends on how your form is built. You will need to modify the code that saves the form to the database, and also modify the database to add a field to hold the final marketing code.

This technique is easy, performs well, and allows you to quickly report on the number of users that have clicked a link by using a simple query:

```
SELECT Clicks FROM URL_Tracking WHERE
  MktCode = 'm7584f768a'
```

Compatibility

Determining which browsers support which features, and what code will work with which browsers, can be a time-consuming and difficult task. In this section, I try to clarify the issue as much as possible in order to help you make better decisions as you program the look and feel of your Web site.

Be aware that "support" for a feature doesn't necessarily guarantee identical results in the feature's implementation from browser to browser. For example, Netscape Communicator 6 and Microsoft Internet Explorer 5.5 use slightly different rules for rendering tables. Although you may not run into any differences in 90 percent of the tables that you create, it's always that last 10 percent that causes the problems. You need to be able to write a subset of code that will always work, and always provide an "out" that allows users to continue using your site even if their browser doesn't support the features that you expect them to have.

You should also write a robust and detailed cross-browser test plan, so you can quickly identify problems with specific browsers on the list of browsers that you intend to support for your site.

Browser compatibilities comparison

The individual capabilities and implementations of the available Web browsers can — in large part — dictate how your site is designed. Analyze which browsers you expect your customers to be using, and gear your site so that the largest possible percentage of those customers is able to use your site.

The Counter (www.thecounter.com) provides monthly statistics on the most-used browsers on the Web. In January 2001, for example, Internet Explorer 5.x accounted for 72 percent of the Web's browser population; Internet Explorer 4.x, 12 percent; and Netscape Communicator, 10 percent. All other browsers accounted for less than 1 percent of the total traffic on the Web.

A sizeable amount of the Internet Explorer (IE) traffic comes from America Online, which incorporates the IE browser in their client software. Because America Online has special systems for compressing graphics delivered over the Web and caching Web content, you should be aware of the percentage of your customer demographic coming through that company.

From a scripting standpoint, The Counter's January 2001 statistics indicate that 19 percent of the browsers that they served didn't support JavaScript, while the remainder supported JavaScript 1.2 or higher. A figure of 19 percent may represent a significant enough portion of the market for you to provide non-script navigation elements, in addition to any JavaScript DHTML navigation elements that your site uses. Only 1 percent of the browsers served by The Counter supported Java but had it disabled; 78 percent had Java support enabled; and 19 percent — nearly a fifth of the population surveyed — either did not support Java or had it disabled and reported it as unsupported.

These statistics must be used in conjunction with the capabilities of the various browsers on the market. After all, if the majority of your demographic is using Internet Explorer 5.x or higher, then you should focus on the feature set supported by that browser. Tables 10-1 through 10-5 compare the most important capabilities of the most common browsers on the Internet as of February 2001. "X" indicates that the feature is fully supported, "P" indicates partial support, and a blank indicates no support for the feature.

Table 10-1 shows the basic features supported by the most common Windows-based Web browsers.

Table 10-1
Windows browser capabilities comparison

browser	java	frames	tables	font size	font color	java script	style sheets	dhtml	Table color	XML
AOL Browser 3.0		X	X	X	X					
Explorer 5.5	X	X	X	X	X	X	X	X	X	X
Explorer 5.0	X	X	X	X	X	X	X	X	X	P
Explorer 4.0	X	X	X	X	X	X	X	X	X	
Explorer 3.0	X	X	X	X	X	X	X		X	
Netscape 6	X	X	X	X	X	X	X	X	X	X
Communicator 4.7	X	X	X	X	X	X	X	X	X	
Communicator 4.5	X	X	X	X	X	X	X	X	X	
Opera 4.02	X	X	X	X	X	X	X		X	X
Opera 3.60		X	X	X	X	X	X		X	
Opera 3.5		X	X	X	X	X			X	

Table 10-2 shows the basic features supported by the most common Macintosh-based Web browsers.

Table 10-2
Macintosh browser capabilities comparison

browser	java	frames	tables	font size	font color	java script	style sheets	dhtml	Table color	XML
Explorer 5.0	X	X	X	X	X	X	X	X	X	P
Explorer 4.0	X	X	X	X	X	X	X	X	X	
Explorer 3.0	X	X	X	X	X	X	X		X	
Explorer 2.0		X	X	X	X					
Mosaic 3.07		X	X	X	X					
Netscape 6	X	X	X	X	X	X	X	X	X	X

Table 10-3 shows the basic features supported by the most common Linux-based Web browsers.

browser	java	frames	tables	font size	font color	java script	style sheets	dhtml	Table color	XML
Table 10-3 **Linux browser capabilities comparison**										
Netscape 6	X	X	X	X	X	X	X	X	X	X
Mozilla	P	X	X	X	X	X	X		X	X
Communicator 4.7	X	X	X	X	X	X	X	P	X	

Table 10-4 shows the basic features supported by the most common UNIX-based Web browsers.

browser	java	frames	tables	font size	font color	java script	style sheets	dhtml	Table color	XML
Table 10-4 **UNIX browser capabilities comparison**										
Explorer 5.0	X	X	X	X	X	X	X	X	X	X
Explorer 4.01	X	X	X	X	X	X	X	X	X	
Mosaic 2.75			X							
Mosaic 1.0										
Communicator 4.6	X	X	X	X	X	X	X	X	X	X

Table 10-5 shows the basic features supported by the most common television-based Web browsers, WebTV and AOL TV.

browser	java	frames	tables	font size	font color	java script	style sheets	dhtml	Table color	XML
Table 10-5 **Television browser capabilities comparison**										
WebTV		X	X	X	X	X			X	
AOL TV		X	X	X	X	X			X	

Keep in mind that not all browsers implement these features in *exactly* the same way. For example, Internet Explorer 5.5 has a number of extensions to DHTML that haven't been accepted by the Web's standards organizations, and both Internet Explorer and Communicator have always had minor differences in the way they render and display various elements like tables and frames.

If you know that you will be using features such as Java or DHTML, which are unsupported by some of the browsers in your demographic, you can write an Active Server Page script to detect which browser a customer is using. You can then direct them to a backwards-compatible page if their browser is a version that doesn't support the features that your site uses. ASP's Request object exposes a ServerVariables collection that includes a variable named HTTP_USER_AGENT. By querying this variable in an ASP script, you can determine which browser the customer is using to access your site:

```
Dim sUserAgent
sUserAgent = Request.ServerVariables("HTTP_USER_AGENT")
```

You can use the appropriate logic structure, If...Then or Select...Case, to direct users to the portion of your site that supports their browser. Listing 10-26 shows a sample script that redirects all Internet Explorer 3.x users to a special page, but allows all other users to continue viewing the current page. You may want to include this script in your site's home page.

Listing 10-26: **Sample browser version detection script**

```
Dim sUserAgent
sUserAgent = Request.ServerVariables("HTTP_USER_AGENT")
Select Case sUserAgent
    Case "Mozilla/2.0 (Compatible; MSIE 3.02; AOL 3.0;_
    Windows 95)"
        Response.Redirect "ie3.asp"
End Select
```

In order to code for a wider range of browsers, you need to know the User Agent string that each type of browser will send to the Web server. You can determine what User Agent string various browsers will send by using each type of browser to access an ASP script, and printing the HTTP_USER_AGENT value from within the script. Table 10-6 shows the User Agent strings for the most common types of browsers.

Table 10-6
Common user agent strings

Browser	User agent string[1]
Internet Explorer 3.02 (Windows 95)	Mozilla/2.0 (Compatible; MSIE 3.02; Windows 95)
Internet Explorer 4 (Windows 95)	Mozilla/2.0 (Compatible; MSIE 4.0; Windows 95)
Internet Explorer 5 (Windows 98)	Mozilla/4.0 (Compatible; MSIE 5.0; Windows 98)
AOL 3 with IE 3 (Windows 95)	Mozilla/2.0 (Compatible; MSIE 3.02; AOL 3.0; Windows 95)[2]
AOL 4 with IE 4 (Windows 95)	Mozilla/4.0 (Compatible; MSIE 4.01; AOL 4.0; Windows 95)
AOL 5 with IE 5 (Windows 98)	Mozilla/4.0 (Compatible; MSIE 5.0; AOL 5.0; Windows 98)
AOL TV	Mozilla/3.0 NAVIO (11; 13; Philips; PH200; 1; 2.0C36_AOL.0110OPTIK; R2.0.0110_fc9c2)
CompuServe 2000 5 with IE 5 (Windows 98)	Mozilla/4.0 (compatible; MSIE 4.0; CS 2000; Windows 98)
Communicator 4.6 (Windows 98)	Mozilla 4.6 [en] (Win98)
AOL 4 with IE 4 (Macintosh)	Mozilla/4.0 (compatible; MSIE 4.01; AOL 4.0; Mac_PPC)
Internet Explorer 4 (Macintosh)	Mozilla/4.0 (compatible; MSIE 4.01; Mac_PPC)

1 – Note that most User Agent strings also include an indicator for the client operating system. If you don't care about the operating system and simply want to detect the browser, you can generally ignore the information after the last semicolon in the User Agent string.

2 – AOL versions 3.0 and higher will return a customized Internet Explorer User Agent string. However, AOL should still be treated as a separate browser — see the sidebar, "The AOL Difference" for more details.

You should start to see a basic pattern emerging in the User Agent strings that will allow you to anticipate the strings that other browsers will send to the Web server.

Always write your browser-detection script to either detect the minimum version that a particular page will support, or to detect the highest version that the page will *not* support. Never attempt to detect the highest version of the browser supported because new browsers are constantly released. Instead, look for the minimum version for which your page is written and direct all higher version browsers accordingly. For example, Retailer.com has chosen to use a DHTML-based navigation menu. Checking the browser capabilities tables, they see that any browser with a User Agent string of Mozilla/4.0 or higher should have no problems with the DHTML scripts. Any lower version browsers will be redirected to a home page called alternate.asp, which will offer a non-DHTML navigation scheme. Listing 10-27

The AOL Difference

If you look carefully, you'll see that the America Online browser returns a modified Internet Explorer User Agent string. Since version 3.0, the America Online (AOL) client software for the Windows platform hasn't included a browser; rather, it instantiates whatever version of Internet Explorer is installed on the user's computer (if no version is available when AOL is installed, the most recent version of Internet Explorer is installed). AOL's User Agent string indicates that Internet Explorer is being used as a "branded" client; AOL's user interface controls the browser rather than Internet Explorer's normal user interface.

Just because AOL instantiates Internet Explorer does *not* mean you should eliminate AOL as a separate item on your cross-browser test plan (unless AOL users are not a part of your user demographic, which isn't likely). AOL's network systems include special technologies, such as graphics compression and content caching, that can affect the way your pages, especially graphics, display. AOL also sets different defaults for Internet Explorer, including background and text colors, that can affect your pages' appearance. These defaults differ from version to version of the AOL client software, so be sure to include each one in your test plan.

AOL's Webmaster site (www.aol.com/webmaster) includes information on AOL's graphic compression and content caching technologies, as well as information on the most common version of AOL's client software currently in use. This information can help you target your development efforts to where they will have the most effect on maintaining a consistent look and feel within the AOL browser.

shows the code that will go at the beginning of Retailer.com's home page to redirect browsers accordingly.

Listing 10-27: **Redirecting non-DHTML browsers with ASP**

```
Dim sUserAgent, iSlashLocation, sMozillaVersion
sUserAgent = Request.ServerVariables("HTTP_USER_AGENT")
iSlashLocation = InStr(1,sUserAgent,"/")
sMozillaVersion = Mid(sUserAgent,iSlashLocation+1,1)
If CInt(sMozillaVersion) < 4 Then
   Response.Redirect "alternate.asp"
End If
```

This code looks for the first slash in the User Agent string, which separates the browser feature base name (usually "Mozilla," although sometimes "Mosaic") from the base version number. If the version number is 4.0 or higher, the script allows the home page to continue loading; if not, the script redirects the client to alternate.asp and its non-DHTML navigation scheme.

Choosing the lowest common denominator

Your site's design plan should include information on the lowest version Web browser that you intend to support. The capabilities of this lowest version become your "lowest common denominator," and you have to make sure you don't exploit any browser features that aren't supported by that version.

In the early days of browser development, Microsoft and Netscape leapfrogged each other in features and functionality with each new version release. With the version 4 and 5 browsers, the two have stayed fairly compatible from a *feature* standpoint, although the exact implementation of those features varies greatly from one to the other (which I discuss in the next section).

You may choose to implement different levels of support for different browsers. For example, if you feel that the majority of your shoppers will use version 4.0 or higher browsers, you can design the majority of your site to take advantage of the features in those browsers. For the occasional shopper with an older browser, you can program your site to detect their browser version and direct them to a separate section of the site that doesn't use the newer features that their browser doesn't support. This separate section may provide a subset of your site's functionality, such as a basic search and checkout page, rather than a complete set of advanced search and cart manipulation pages.

Java Virtual Machine compatibility

Java applets are a special kind of "executable." Rather than being executed directly by the computer's operating system, as with normal executables, or interpreted by the browser's scripting engine, as with DHTML scripts, Java applets run inside a special "virtual machine." The idea behind the Java Virtual Machine (JVM) is that all properly-written Java applets will run equally well on all properly-written JVMs, no matter what browser or operating system the computer is running. As long as a computer platform or operating system comes with (or can be provided with) a JVM, then it can run Java applets. The JVM takes care of the differences between computers and operating systems.

If you're using preprogrammed Java applets, they will generally work well on the Java Virtual Machines included with the major Web browsers. In fact, part of the price you pay includes the time spent testing those applets on multiple JVMs. If you're writing your own Java applets, however, you may find that Java's "Write Once, Run Anywhere" slogan is more accurately written as "Write Once, Test Everywhere."

Language problems

This problem with compatibility between JVMs has existed almost since Java first became popular in 1997. Microsoft was one of the first major authors of a JVM for the Windows platform, and their JVM differed in many subtle ways from the "reference" JVM developed by Sun Microsystems (creators of the Java language). These

A Brief History of Browsers

You may know that the first Web browser was Mosaic, invented at the CERN laboratory in the 1980s. And you may know that Microsoft's latest browser is Internet Explorer 5.5, and that Netscape recently released Communicator 6, but what happened in between?

✦ Netscape Navigator 2.x introduced JavaScript and Java support, as well as a limited Document Object Model (DOM) that allowed client-side code to manipulate the browser page—the beginnings of Dynamic HTML (DHTML).

✦ Microsoft Internet Explorer 3.0 introduced VBScript and Jscript (Microsoft's implementation of JavaScript), and expanded the DOM to offer more control of the browser. Microsoft also introduced support for tables and frames in this version of IE.

✦ Navigator 3.0 introduced DHTML features to compete with IE's, but implemented almost all of the features in a slightly different way. Support for style sheets was also introduced.

✦ IE 4.0 and Netscape's version 4 browser, now named Communicator, introduced full-fledged DHTML. IE included a DOM that allowed the entire page to be addressed through code, while Communicator relied on a proprietary <LAYER> tag to accomplish many DHTML effects.

✦ IE 5.0 included an expanded DOM, a version of Jscript that was ECMAScript-compliant, and many enhancements to Cascading Style Sheets (CSS). IE complied more closely with the recently released DOM specification from the World Wide Web Consortium (W3C). IE 5.5, an incremental upgrade, offered several user-interface and performance enhancements.

✦ Communicator 6.0 (there was no version 5) discarded Netscape's proprietary DOM, especially the <LAYER> tag, and moved closer to compliance with the W3C DOM specification.

Despite remaining subtle differences, Communicator 6 and IE 5.5 represent the closest that Microsoft and Netscape have come to full compatibility with each other's browsers.

Ironically, the remainder of the browser market, including browsers like Opera, has been complying with the W3C specifications for the DOM and HTML for some time. Unfortunately, these browsers represent less than 1 percent of the total browser market as reported by most surveying firms.

differences have continued to plague the Java community, especially as more JVMs were produced for the Windows and Macintosh operating systems by third-party developers.

For example, the following Java code runs fine on Sun's JVM, but creates odd display problems on some versions of Microsoft's JVM:

```
gbxGrid.setLayout(new BorderLayout(5, 5));
gbxGrid.add(grdDisplay);
```

The problem is a result of Microsoft's JVM not properly handling certain default values. Microsoft's JVM works properly when those values are specified in the code, rather than being assumed:

```
gbxGrid.setLayout(new BorderLayout(5, 5));
gbxGrid.add("Center", grdDisplay);
```

When writing Java code, always be as specific as possible and specify all the parameters that each command accepts — even if some of them should be handled by defaults.

Microsoft made these language compatibility problems worse by introducing proprietary extensions to the Java language in their Visual J++ development product (which is now discontinued). Although the extensions allowed access to the Windows API from within the Java code, the extensions also made any Java applets using them incompatible with any non-Microsoft JVM.

Things to look for

When testing your Java applets, watch for the major areas in which compatibility problems seem to occur. Here are some examples:

✦ Menus can often be displayed differently. Some versions of the Microsoft JVM, for example, will respond to keyboard shortcuts that you define for menus, but will not always display the shortcut "hint" in the menu.

✦ Some JVMs will place the cursor in the first field on a form unless the cursor is programmatically placed elsewhere. Some JVMs will not place the cursor anywhere unless you do so through code.

✦ Programmatically setting the cursor to the first form field in some JVMs, notably earlier Microsoft JVMs, can cause display flickering; this presents a problem for programs that place the cursor, so you may want to avoid any reliance on the cursor being in a specific place when forms are displayed.

✦ A large number of controls on a form can cause display problems in many JVMs. This problem is exacerbated on computers with a small amount of main memory (less than 64MB for Windows NT or Windows 2000).

✦ Proprietary language extensions of any kind will cause cross-browser compatibility issues. Stick with "100% Pure Java" as recommended by Sun Microsystems (www.javasoft.com) to ensure cross-browser compatibility.

Tip   If your customer demographic is fairly tech-savvy, offer a troubleshooting page for your Java applets. Include links to known-compatible JVMs, such as the Sun JVM for Windows (http://www.javasoft.com/products). By installing a JVM known to be compatible with your Java code, you can help your users experience your applets correctly. Also include links to the most recent JVMs so that customers with older JVMs installed can upgrade.

Availability problems

Another major problem with JVM compatibility is the availability of a JVM on a user's computer. Some Internet Explorer 5.0 and higher installations, for example, don't include a JVM by default. In some versions, a JVM may be included but are disabled by users or corporate network administrators. Some installations may have a JVM from a third party, rather than Microsoft's own JVM, which may present a whole new set of compatibility and availability problems.

Making pages that will always work

The key to a successful Internet-based e-commerce site is to produce pages with HTML and DHTML code that will work on all the browsers that your customers use. That's a tall order, even if you limit yourself to the three browsers that command 99 percent of the market. Microsoft and Netscape, who make the top three browsers on the Web, have always been slightly at odds with each other over standards, making the task of creating compatible Web pages difficult.

In this section, I talk about the major areas of compatibility and how you can address them. You should also turn to the Web for more reference material on the latest browser versions and compatibility issues. Sites like Web Monkey (`www.webmonkey.com`) and Web Reference (`www.webreference.com`) contain comprehensive information on the latest subtleties of cross-browser programming.

Cross-browser scripting languages

When writing server-side script, you have the luxury of choosing from a variety of languages, including VBScript, JavaScript, Perl, and so forth. Your client-side DHTML code, however, has to be written in a language that your users' browsers will understand. If your user base will exclusively run Internet Explorer, you can choose between VBScript and Jscript; if your users will run any other browsers, then you need to write your script in Jscript/JavaScript.

Choose your Java

Although most browsers include a Java Virtual Machine (JVM), it is not usually a part of the browser itself, but rather a part of the operating system on which the browser runs. The browser simply installs the component.

JVMs are available from a number of software development firms. Until recently, Microsoft included their JVM with the default installation of Internet Explorer. Some installations of IE 5.0 and 5.5, however, lack a JVM. After initiating their now-famous lawsuit with Microsoft, Sun Microsystems' JavaSoft business unit released a JVM for the Windows platform to compete with the Microsoft JVM and provide a "100% Pure Java" JVM that lacks Microsoft's proprietary Java extensions.

As Microsoft's interest in Java wanes, you should expect more and more of your customers to have JVMs from vendors other than Microsoft, and you should program and test accordingly.

Note *JavaScript Bible,* published by Hungry Minds, Inc., is an excellent resource for the JavaScript language and provides a detailed reference of its implementation in the popular browsers.

Unless you are developing for an intranet environment where you can be guaranteed that *all* of your users will run Internet Explorer, I recommend that you stick with JavaScript for your client-side code. A number of good books and Web-based resources are available for learning JavaScript if you don't know it, and a number of Web sites offer sample code and solutions. The majority of the preprogrammed DHTML solutions available for purchase are written in JavaScript. That said, you should be aware of some advantages to the VBScript language if you're in an all-Internet Explorer environment.

Note Plug-ins allow Netscape browsers to execute VBScript code. However, unless you're comfortable making your users download a plug-in before they can use your site, you should stick with JavaScript whenever possible.

Visual Basic Script

VBScript is closely related to the traditional Visual Basic language and the VBA language subset included in many applications (such as Microsoft Office). With few exceptions, they all share a common language, the same means of creating and working with objects, and nearly identical capabilities. VBScript only supports variables of the *Variant* data type, whereas traditional Visual Basic supports strongly typed variables such as integers, strings, date/time values, and so forth. The close relationship between the Visual Basic variants facilitates learning one if you know the others. In fact, traditional VB programmers can begin writing VBScript for Web browsers as soon as they master the Document Object Model, which is the interface between the language and the actual page.

Microsoft continues to revise the VBScript language, along with the traditional Visual Basic language, to add additional features and functions. You can download the latest version of the VBScript language engine from `www.Microsoft.com/ scripting`. Be advised, however, that your users must run the same (or higher) version of the scripting engine in order to run your scripts correctly. If you plan to use a newer version of the VBScript engine, consider adding code to your pages to detect older versions of the script engine and redirect users to a page where they can download a more recent version. Listing 10-28 shows an example.

Listing 10-28: **Detecting the VBScript engine version**

```
Sub CheckVersion()
   V = ScriptEngineMajorVersion
   If CInt(V) < 4 Then
      Window.Navigate "Upgrade.asp"
   End If
End Sub
```

The version of VBScript installed on your development machine will differ depending on how VBScript was installed on the machine. Table 10-7 shows the version of VBScript installed with each version of Internet Explorer, as well as the other products that include the VBScript engine.

Table 10-7 VBScript versions	
Product	**VBScript version**
Internet Explorer 3.x	1.0
Internet Explorer 4.x	3.0
Internet Explorer 5.x	5.0
Internet Information Server 3.0	2.0
Internet Information Server 4.0	3.0
Internet Information Services 5.0	5.0
Visual Studio 6.0	4.0
Outlook 98	3.0
Windows Scripting Host 1.0	3.0

If you are developing for an intranet environment based on Internet Explorer, I strongly recommend VBScript for your client-side code. VBScript is easy to learn, and you can leverage the wide availability of Visual Basic programmers when allocating resources.

JavaScript

If Visual Basic and VBScript are sister languages, Java and JavaScript are nothing more than third cousins. Besides the similarity of their names and the fact that both are loosely based on C++ syntax, they have little in common. In fact, JavaScript bears a striking resemblance to Visual Basic script in its structure and behavior.

JavaScript was adopted by the Internet community as a standardized scripting language, and a complete specification, ECMA 262 or ECMAScript, was developed to describe exactly how the language works. You can find more information about ECMA, the European Computer Manufacturers Association, at `www.ecma.ch`. You can retrieve the complete ECMAScript specification from `www.ecma.ch/ecma1/STAND/ECMA-262.HTM`. ECMAScript Edition 3 is currently available, and equivalent to JavaScript 1.5.

Microsoft developed Jscript as a proprietary version of JavaScript in the late 1990s. When the ECMAScript specification was released, Microsoft worked to update Jscript to make it compliant with the new standard. Currently, Microsoft's Jscript 5.5

language is the only JavaScript language that is fully compliant with ECMAScript Edition 3 (it also provides non-compliant language extensions to provide for backward compatibility with prior versions of Jscript).

JavaScript, particularly in the form of ECMAScript, continues to evolve with new features and functionality. The ECMA committee in charge of the ECMAScript standard works closely with the World Wide Web Consortium (W3C) and other industry standards bodies to align ECMAScript with evolving Internet technologies, such as the Wireless Application Protocol (WAP), new HTML elements, and so forth. This evolution makes writing to a specific version of the scripting language — and ensuring that your users' browsers have a matching version — important. The trick to doing this is in the <SCRIPT> tag:

```
<SCRIPT LANGUAGE="JavaScript1.2">
</SCRIPT>
```

Ideally, only browsers supporting JavaScript 1.2 (or higher) should try to execute the code contained within these tags. Unfortunately, some browsers, such as Navigator 3.0, don't handle this technique properly, so you may want to check the browser version using the User Agent string. Also, ECMAScript-compliant versions of JavaScript support three functions to return the version of the language currently in use; you can write a function like the one shown in Listing 10-29 to return this information by using those functions. If necessary, users with older versions of the scripting engine can be redirected to a page that allows them to download a newer version.

Listing 10-29: **ECMAScript version check**

```
function GetScriptEngineInfo(){
    var s;
    s = ""; // Build string with necessary info.
    s += ScriptEngine() + " Version ";
    s += ScriptEngineMajorVersion() + ".";
    s += ScriptEngineMinorVersion() + ".";
    s += ScriptEngineBuildVersion();
    return(s);
}
```

Implement error-checking in this function if you expect users with older browsers to visit your site; any browser that doesn't support the ScriptEngineMajorVersion function is not ECMAScript-compliant.

Document Object Model issues

The Document Object Model (DOM) is a programmatic object model designed to represent the contents of a page. The DOM was originally created by Netscape for use with their newly-created LiveWire scripting language, which eventually became JavaScript. Originally, the DOM covered only the major portions of the page, including the <BODY> tag, any <FORM> tags, and any <INPUT> elements. The intent of the DOM at that point (in Communicator 2.0) was to provide scripted access to form fields for data validation.

When Microsoft added scripting to Internet Explorer 3.0, they expanded the DOM to include many additional tags, and added several properties to those tags that enabled script code to manipulate the appearance of the page. Netscape made similar extensions to the DOM in Communicator 3.0, and both companies submitted their revisions to the Web's standards bodies for adoption.

Without actually waiting for that adoption to occur, Microsoft and Netscape made more extensions to the DOM for their version 4.0 browsers. Again, both companies made similar changes for similar reasons, but differences between their implementations meant that code written for one browser would often run into problems when run on the other.

The result is that the fifth-generation browsers from each company, Internet Explorer 5.x and Communicator 6.x, are both capable of the same functionality. Combined with their differences in HTML language support, this can often lead to creating two different scripts, one for each browser type, in order to assure proper behavior.

For example, Communicator supports the <LAYER> tag to create dynamic document divisions and adds the <NOLAYER> tag for use when browsers don't support layers. By contrast, Internet Explorer uses the <DIV> tag to create dynamic document divisions and doesn't recognize the <LAYER> or <NOLAYER> tags. Communicator recognizes the <DIV> tag, though it doesn't behave quite the same way as that of Internet Explorer. So, if you want to create an area in your page that responds to mouse events, you have to use a <LAYER> tag in Communicator, and a <DIV> tag in Internet Explorer. The trick is to get both browsers to react correctly in both cases.

Enclosing the <DIV> tags inside <NOLAYER> and </NOLAYER> tags prevents Communicator from seeing them, while Internet Explorer will see the <DIV> tags but won't recognize the <LAYER> tags. You have to do this with the opening and closing <DIV> tags separately, however, so that the content of the layer/division is only included once. Most of the eccentricities of the browsers' HTML support can be overcome by using tricks like this. Handling the browsers' varying support for certain DOM objects and events is a bit more complex.

The World Wide Web Consortium (W3C) publishes several standards documents that describe how the DOM *should* be implemented. You can access these documents at `http://www.oasis-open.org/cover/dom.html`. Netscape has programmed their latest browser, version 6, to be completely compliant with this standard, thus sacrificing backward compatibility with their older model. As this version begins to push out older versions, the compatibility between Netscape and Microsoft browsers' DOMs should increase, eliminating the current trickery required to get code to work properly on both.

Here are some general guidelines for writing DHTML code that will run on both Microsoft and Netscape browsers:

✦ Use Cascading Style Sheets positioning (CSS-P) for positioning elements because this W3C standard is supported by both IE 4.0 and higher and Navigator 4.0 and higher. Avoid the Navigator 4.0-only `<LAYER>` tag.

✦ Use lowercase event handler names for compatibility with Internet Explorer (for example, `onclick` instead of `onClick`). IE can't handle mixed-case event handlers when they're used as an object property (such as `document.forms[0].button1.onclick = function`).

✦ Name each element that you want to manipulate via its ID attribute, and declare it to be absolutely or relatively positioned via CSS-P markup.

✦ Name elements using alphanumeric characters only; Communicator 4.0 occasionally ignores elements with non-alphanumeric characters in their names.

If you plan to write complex scripts, write one for each browser until the manufacturers settle on a common standard as proposed by the W3C. Write code to detect the browser in use and execute the appropriate subroutines or functions that are coded for that browser.

Compensating for color depth

Users with older computers may only support a limited number of colors (256, or even 16, maximum). If your site is designed for systems with a higher color depth (64,000 colors, 16 million colors, or more), then users with a lower color depth may find your site to be unattractive or unusable as their systems dither your site's colors down to the number supported. Even users with new systems may unknowingly have their display settings configured to display a smaller number of colors than the system is actually capable of.

When you design the graphics on your site, assume that most users will have a color depth of at least 16 bits, allowing for 64,000 colors. More than 40 percent of the users on the Internet support a color depth of 24 or 32 bits, allowing for millions of colors and photo-realistic images.

If color is important to your site's presentation, however, you shouldn't make any assumptions. Instead, provide graphics that have been tuned to the color depth that the user's system supports. You can use DHTML scripts, for example, to redirect users to a page designed for their color depth, as shown in Listing 10-30.

Listing 10-30: Redirecting based on client color depth

```
<HEAD>
<SCRIPT LANGUAGE="VBScript">
Sub CheckDepth()
  Select Case Screen.ColorDepth
    Case 8
      Window.Navigate "8bitcolor.asp"
    Case 15
      Window.Navigate "15bitcolor.asp"
    Case 16
      Window.Navigate "16bitcolor.asp"
    Case 24
      Window.Navigate "24bitcolor.asp"
    Case 32
      Window.Navigate "32bitcolor.asp"
    Case Else
      Window.Navigate "unknown.asp"
End Sub
</SCRIPT>
</HEAD>
<BODY LANGUAGE="VBScript" ONLOAD="CheckDepth()">
...
```

Caution   Some versions of Netscape Communicator return a different value for the `ColorDepth` property of the `Screen` object. Instead, write your code to use the `PixelDepth` property when running in Communicator to retrieve compatible values.

Compensating for screen resolution

Making your site's appearance consistent across different screen resolutions can be challenging. As Figures 10-13, 10-14, and 10-15 show, the same page rendered at different screen resolutions can not only look different, but can appear unacceptable. The problem tends to increase as the user's screen resolution increases, as more unintentional white space is added to the page and as page elements become misaligned or less well laid-out. Customers using a lower resolution may not be able to see parts of the page at all.

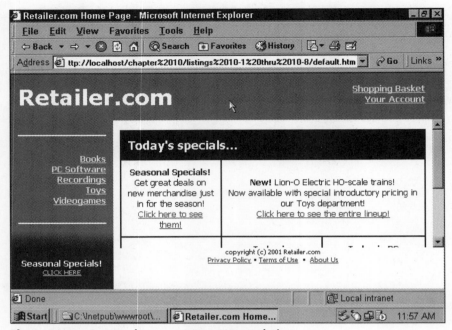

Figure 10-13: Screen shown at 640 x 480 resolution

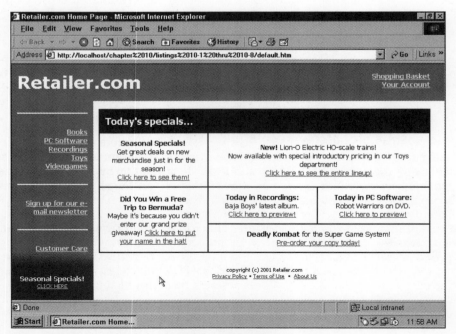

Figure 10-14: Screen shown at 800 x 600 resolution

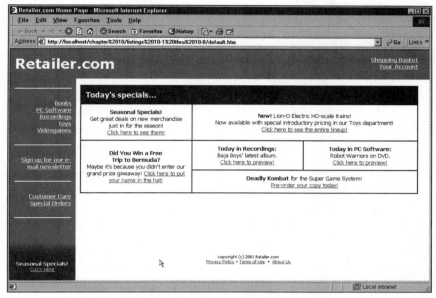

Figure 10-15: Screen shown at 1024 x 768 resolution

In these examples, the target resolution was obviously 800 x 600 pixels. That resolution shows the entire page without excess white space. A resolution of 640 x 480 doesn't allow most of the main page elements to be seen without scrolling, and the 1024 x 768 screen shot shows a large amount of wasted screen space, which ruins the overall balanced look of the page.

Note   Most TV-based browsers use a screen resolution of 640 x 480 pixels. These browsers often include special built-in features to reduce the size of screen elements like text and graphics to make the page fit within the 480-pixel width of the television.

You should either plan your page to look acceptable at the common resolutions, which can be difficult, or design different versions for different resolutions and then direct users to the appropriate page based on the resolution information returned by their browser. Design your site to look its best at your target resolution, generally 800 x 600, and still look acceptable at higher resolutions.

Think about how the page layout can be better arranged to support multiple resolutions. One way to achieve this is to program frame and tables with percentage values whenever possible, and to make sure that the main frame or table cell does *not* have a specified size. This allows that portion of the page to expand to fill the available screen space. Listing 10-31 shows an example of this technique using table cells.

Listing 10-31: Allowing the main table cell to fill the screen

```
<TABLE>
  <TR>
    <TD COLSPAN="2" WIDTH="100%">Title bar</TD>
  </TR>
  <TR>
    <TD WIDTH="150">Menu bar</TD>
    <TD>Main area - no width specified</TD>
  </TR>
</TABLE>
```

Another method is to build your entire site's content inside a table with a single cell (which can contain other nested tables). You can then specify a target resolution for this cell — 750 pixels wide, for example — and specify that the table be centered. Users with a higher screen resolution will still see your site contained in a 750 pixel-wide space centered in their browser, thus assuring a consistent look and feel. Listing 10-32 shows an example of this technique.

Listing 10-32: Constraining the size of the site with a table

```
<TABLE WIDTH="750" VALIGN="CENTER">
  <TR>
    <TD>All site content goes here, even nested tables</TD>
  </TR>
</TABLE>
```

You can design separate pages for users running different resolutions. Although this may be excessive for every page of your site, it may be preferred for your home page, where screen space is especially important. Users with a higher screen resolution can be subjected to additional suggested selling without sacrificing their site experience. Implementing this requires you to create a home page that uses DHTML to detect the user's resolution, and then directs the user to an appropriate resolution-specific page. Listing 10-33 shows an example of this technique.

Listing 10-33: Redirecting based on client resolution

```
<HEAD>
<SCRIPT LANGUAGE="VBScript">
Sub CheckRes()
  Select Case Screen.Width
    Case 640
```

```
        Window.Navigate "small.asp"
      Case 800
        Window.Navigate "medium.asp"
      Case 1024
        Window.Navigate "large.asp"
      Case Else
        Window.Navigate "xlarge.asp"
  End Sub
  </SCRIPT>
  </HEAD>
  <BODY LANGUAGE="VBScript" ONLOAD="CheckRes()">
  ...
```

Writing a cross-browser test plan

Using the browser compatibility tables and your site design plan, develop a comprehensive cross-browser test plan for every portion of your site. Run through your site with each type of browser that you intend to support, and examine the appearance and functionality of each and every part of the site.

Ideally, your test plan should take the form of a chart. This chart should list the major functional areas of your site, and the different browsers and platforms that you expect your customers to use. The plan should include a check of both the functionality and appearance of each item — ensuring that the tested browser correctly interprets and renders visual elements, and that dynamic elements created with DHTML scripts function properly.

You may want to include specific screen resolutions in your chart. This will ensure that your site is examined at various screen resolutions, and that its appearance and behavior are acceptable at those resolutions.

Your developers should contribute to the creation of this test plan as they develop new features and functionality for the site. For example, as the shopping cart code is written, each distinct piece of functionality that includes client-side code or layout should be added as a test item to the chart. Any functionality handled in server-side code should be added as an item on your master site test plan.

Testing the appearance and functionality of your site with different Web browsers is, unfortunately, a completely manual process. Another important part of a cross-browser testing plan is to ensure the validity of your HTML code and Cascading Style Sheets (CSS) code. Validity checking can be accomplished with automated tools, which are available as Web-based services or downloadable testing applications.

Testing tools

Very few tools are designed for automating a cross-browser Web site test. One Web-based resource is NetMechanic (www.netmechanic.com), which is an automated system for testing Web pages. You can configure the system with a number of Web pages to test, and it will create a report that includes information on bad links and, most importantly, browser compatibility issues. Figure 10-16 shows a sample browser compatibility report from NetMechanic.

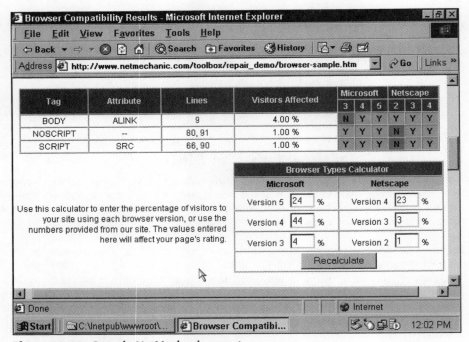

Figure 10-16: Sample NetMechanic report

The report lists each element in your page that is incompatible with a version of Internet Explorer or Communicator. Ideally, you should run this report against each type of page on your site (a product details page, the home page, a department front page, and so forth), and make a note of any compatibility issues. The report also allows you to configure the percentage of customers that use each browser type (information that you can obtain from statistical reports or from your own Web server logs), indicating the percentage of your customers who will have a problem with each incompatible tag.

NetMechanic can be easily confused by embedded style sheets, some kinds of DHTML scripts, and other advanced page elements, so take each report with a grain of salt. However, the reports are more than adequate at pointing out tags and, most importantly, tag attributes that are not compatible across all browsers. If you're creating your initial HTML code in a product like Microsoft FrontPage 2000, expect a surprising number of non-standard tags to creep into your HTML code; NetMechanic can help you find each one and decide what to do about them.

Another HTML validation tool, Site Inspector (www.siteinspector.com), validates that your HTML code is correct. As Figure 10-18 shows, the report from this tool is comprehensive. Your cross-browser test plan should include a full HTML validation report because some browsers, notably Internet Explorer, are very "forgiving" with bad HTML code, and *will* display a page that has poorly written HTML. Other browsers may be less forgiving, so running a validity check will ensure that your HTML code works across all browsers that support the tags you are using.

The Web Design Group (www.htmlhelp.com/tools) offers an HTML validity check tool and a tool designed to validate Cascading Style Sheets. The validity check tool allows you to link directly to a CSS file on a Web site, or cut and paste your style sheet directly into a form. CSS errors are among the most common problems for cross-browser compatibility, so checking your CSS code is a good idea. Similar tools are provided by the World Wide Web Consortium (W3C) at validator.w3.org. Because W3C is the standards organization that approves the official HTML specifications, its validation tools tend to follow a stricter view of HTML than most other tools.

Doctor Watson (watson.addy.com) provides an HTML validation tool that you can configure for various levels of "strictness," and configure to accept Netscape or Microsoft HTML extensions when running its analysis. Figure 10-17 shows a sample report that includes information on which tags are acceptable according to strict W3C standards and which are acceptable according to Microsoft or Netscape's recent extensions to HTML.

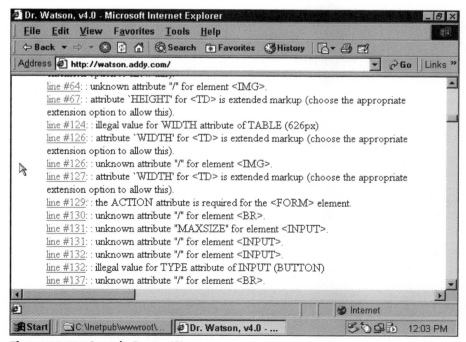

Figure 10-17: Sample Doctor Watson report

Finally, Bobby (www.cast.org/bobby) provides a unique HTML validation tool. Like the other tools I've described, Bobby is available as a Web-based validity checker. Unlike the others, it's also available as a downloadable application that can check batches of pages in a single run. Bobby concerns itself less with the overall validity of your HTML code than with the way your code complies with Web *accessibility* standards for people with physical disabilities. Bobby spots images that are missing ALT attributes, questionable use of color (which may be difficult for color-blind individuals to distinguish), DHTML event handlers that require the use of a mouse (which may not be possible for some physically disabled individuals to use), and so forth. Figure 10-18 shows a sample Bobby report. Unfortunately, some of the techniques used to achieve complex and precise page layouts, such as specifying exact pixel width for tables, are incompatible with some accessibility requirements, so you will need to analyze your custom demographic and determine the correct tradeoff between layout and accessibility.

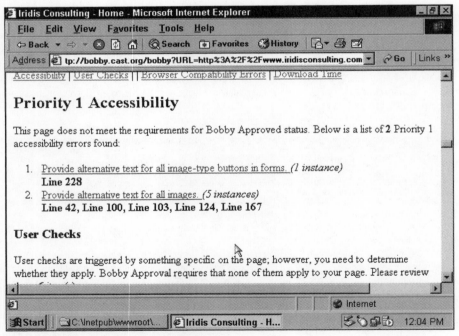

Figure 10-18: Sample Bobby report

Bobby is also useful for finding tags or attributes that are incompatible with specific browsers, and is one of the few validity checkers that includes older browsers like the original America Online embedded browser. Bobby can also impersonate many different browsers when checking your pages, which allows any browser detection scripts you have written to operate properly and direct the validity checker to the appropriate page for that browser version. As one of the few downloadable HTML validity checkers, Bobby is my personal choice for automatically examining cross-browser compatibility. And because Bobby is free, the price is right.

All of these tools can help automate basic HTML syntax checking, and can call many cross-browser issues to your attention. None of them, however, can judge whether a particular browser will correctly render your HTML, and none of them can test your client-side DHTML scripts in multiple browsers. For that, you'll have to try everything manually in the different browsers that you want to support. One technique to reduce debugging time is to immediately test every page that is designed or written for your site in multiple browsers, thus reducing the amount of problems that will be found when the entire site is tested in multiple browsers. Ideally, your developers should have every supported browser installed on their machines, and you should have several dedicated computers with different browsers just for whole-site testing.

Running all those browsers

Unfortunately, few browsers work and play well when installed on a single computer, particularly different versions of the same browser. Microsoft Internet Explorer 5.5, for example, automatically removes all prior versions of IE when it is installed. Many e-commerce companies don't want to commit a half-dozen computers to run various Web browsers for testing purposes. As a result, companies often choose to simply skip a good cross-browser test.

Rather than skipping such an important step in your design and test phase, however, consider a virtual computer product like VMWare (www.vmware.com). For a few hundred dollars, you can configure a reasonably powerful desktop computer to run several operating systems at once by using "virtual" computers. Each "computer" can have a different operating system and Web browser combination installed.

Virtual machine products are much more convenient that using complex multi-boot scenarios, and allow you to quickly and easily conduct cross-browser tests by using a single computer. VMWare Workstation allows you to run the following multiple "computers" on a single desktop machine with Windows NT or Windows 2000 installed:

✦ Windows 95

✦ Windows 98

✦ Windows Me

✦ Windows NT 4.0

✦ Windows 2000

✦ UNIX

✦ Linux

Starting a new "computer" is as simple as clicking an icon, and you can run multiple virtual computers at the same time, thus facilitating testing multiple browsers with your site.

Note At the time of this writing, VMWare Workstation is only $300 directly from the manufacturer, making it an indispensable solution for multi-platform and multi-browser testing.

Accepting deviation

As you begin testing your site on a variety of browsers and versions, you are almost guaranteed to encounter situations where no reasonable amount of coding or design can create the precise look that you want on the browsers you intend to support. HTML is a *guideline* for browsers to render the pages you create, and not an absolute *standard*. Different browser manufacturers implement different aspects of HTML, especially newer features, in subtly different ways. Your customers may modify their browser's default settings to override certain behaviors that you may be relying on to achieve a certain look, such as default background or text colors.

In these instances, you will need to determine an acceptable level of deviation from your design. Don't waste development time trying to achieve *exactly* the same look on every browser, every time, on every possible computer system under every possible set of variables. Make a decision that creates parameters for the look and behavior of the site, and ensure that each browser presents the site within those parameters.

Tip Try to define some acceptable deviation guidelines in your design phase, or even at the beginning of your development phase. Having guidelines during the development process will help save time that may otherwise be spent trying to "tweak" a design that's already within acceptable limits.

Summary

Creating the look and feel for your Web site can be challenging. Many different browsers exist on the Web (fortunately, two major brands cover more than 99 percent of the market), and these browsers run on a staggering variety of computers with different capabilities. The key to successfully implementing your site's design is to carefully consider what technologies and techniques will be used, and try to minimize variations whenever possible. When variations are unavoidable, write code to detect which browser a customer is running and provide a page dedicated to presenting the best look and feel to ensure the consistency of the user's experience.

Many preprogrammed components, including DHTML pop-up menus and Java applets, can be used to drastically reduce development time while still maintaining a consistent, custom look and feel across your site. Hunt around for the best products and prices and you will almost certainly find a preprogrammed solution that you like.

Finally, make sure to have a cross-browser test plan ensuring that your site looks and behaves consistently and within acceptable levels of deviation across the different browsers and computers common on the Web.

✦　　✦　　✦

Developing the Customer Experience — Creating Your Catalog

The user experience is the core of your e-commerce site, and consists primarily of your catalog, shopping cart, and checkout process. The other elements of your site generally exist just to support these core processes, which allow customers to actually purchase the goods and services that you offer.

Commerce Server's primary functionality is designed to implement these functions. Unfortunately, some of Commerce Server's built-in functionality and "way of doing things" doesn't scale well enough to provide a solid foundation for your site. Therefore, you will need to create your own components to implement your site.

In the next three chapters, I explain the "Commerce Server way" of doing things, how you can modify it, the pros and cons of Microsoft's standard approach, and how to — when necessary — completely replace the built-in functionality with your own, beginning with creating your catalog.

The Commerce Server catalog contains all of the services and goods that you sell on your site. Commerce Server actually allows you to create multiple catalogs. For example, Retailer. com may have a standard catalog as well as a special catalog of collectible toys. Catalogs can belong to one or more catalog groups, which can be used to control access to the catalogs.

Catalog groups can also be used to apply catalog-wide pricing to the items in the catalog. For example, Retailer.com may have a default catalog group to which the public has access, and a special "25 percent off" catalog group for other retailers who purchase items at wholesale prices. Access to the wholesale catalog group is restricted to users who signed in and were given permission.

You should carefully consult your site's design documentation when creating your catalogs in Commerce Server. Designing the catalog structure, or *taxonomy*, is the first step. After the taxonomy is in place, you can begin populating the catalog with the goods and services that you will sell. Only then can you actually begin programming your site to allow customers to browse the catalog. You can program your site by using Commerce Server's built-in components or by writing your own.

Designing the Catalog Structure

You create catalogs and their taxonomy in the Commerce Server Business Desk application. Your catalogs' taxonomy should relate closely to how users will browse through the catalogs. For example, if your Books department is divided into different categories, such as Fiction, Biography, and so forth, then you should create categories in your catalog to match this organization.

Commerce Server catalogs are structured as follows:

✦ The *catalog group,* or *set,* is the highest level of organization, and contains one or more catalogs.

✦ A *catalog* is the main unit of organization, and contains a group of products and services that you sell. Most e-commerce sites can use a single catalog for all of their products, but as you will see in some of the upcoming examples, you may find some good reasons to use multiple catalogs if you have complex needs.

Multiple catalogs make sense if your products differ in type, such as clothing and books. Both of these product categories have *very* different attributes, so it may make sense for your site to include them in a "clothing" catalog and a "books" catalog.

This is similar to the way many large department stores, such as Sears, organize their paper catalogs. They offer a main catalog featuring most of their products, and then specialty catalogs for items such as tools, clothing, toys, home interiors, and so forth. Many products may even be included in several different catalogs.

✦ A *category* is a unit of organization within a catalog. Categories can represent a department, class, or any other unit of organization. Categories can have *children* and *parents,* allowing them to be nested to create a product hierarchy, or taxonomy.

✦ A *product* represents a single item or service that you sell. A *property* is a descriptive feature of the product, such as its size, color, or other attribute. Products are essentially a grouping of specific properties.

You can also arrange products into a *product family,* which is a group of products that contain product *variants.* For example, you may carry a brand of blue jeans called Little Miss Jeans. The jeans themselves are a product family, with variants for the waist and inseam sizes. All of the variants within the product family have their own SKU and price, but they all share the same basic description.

Catalogs can also contain *pricing rules.* A *base catalog* contains products, but doesn't contain any pricing rules (although the individual products do have prices associated with them). A *custom catalog* is a derivative of a base catalog. Custom catalogs inherit the products in the base catalog, but can have special pricing rules applied — either to individual products, groups of products, or the entire catalog. This allows you to create a catalog that's accessible only by customers who join a discount club, for example. You can easily apply a discount across the entire catalog.

Catalog sets control access to the catalogs. Commerce Server includes a default Anonymous User catalog set, which makes your catalogs available to unregistered shoppers. A Registered User catalog set is made available to any registered users who sign in.

Because catalog sets can contain only catalogs and not specific products, you should keep in mind which users will have access to your catalogs while you build them. For example, if you will be selling toys that the general public may buy, and if you will also be selling special collectibles that only registered customers may purchase, then you should create two separate base catalogs. The first can be included in the Anonymous User catalog set, and both can be included in the Registered User catalog set. You can also create your own catalog sets to control access by specific groups of customers.

Creating your product taxonomy

Before you begin creating catalogs, you must define your product taxonomy. Specifically, you need to determine:

✦ What product properties will be available?

✦ What types of product categories will be needed?

✦ What types of products will be available?

✦ What product properties will be associated with different product types?

✦ What catalogs will be available?

These settings are configured with the Commerce Server Business Desk's Catalog Designer. By default, the Catalog Designer shows the categories that have been defined in the database. Figure 11-1 shows the creation of a new category named "Sub Department."

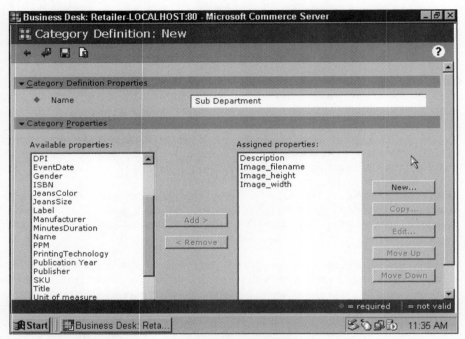

Figure 11-1: Creating a new product category definition

When creating a new category, determine which properties will describe the category. In this example, the category includes a text description as well as an image file. You may want to use this image file on the category's "home page" to illustrate the products that the category contains.

Tip   You can use the New... button to create a new property to associate with your category.

Ideally, all of your categories' definitions should be described by the same properties in order to maintain consistency in your catalogs. At this point, you aren't defining a relationship between the category definitions — just the *types* of categories that will be created later.

You also need to define the types of products that your catalogs will contain. Figure 11-2 shows the product definitions included with the Retail Solution Site.

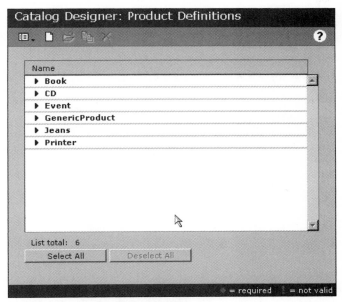

Figure 11-2: Product type definitions

Each product type definition has several properties. For example, the Book product type, shown in Figure 11-3, defines the properties that describe a book sold on your site.

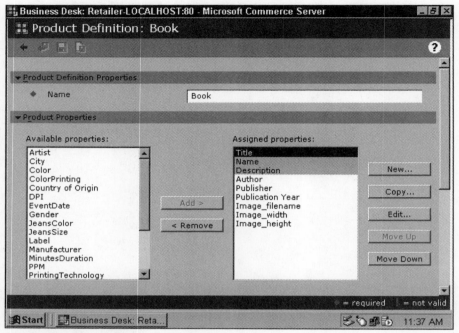

Figure 11-3: The Book product type

Books can also be organized into product families. For example, the same title may be available in either hardcover or paperback. Generally, the ISBN number of the book will be different for each type of binding. The Book product type definition includes these variant definitions, as shown in Figure 11-4.

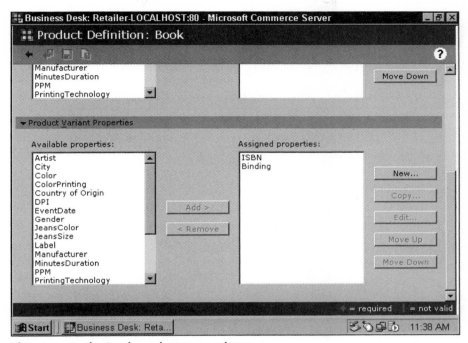

Figure 11-4: The Book product type variants

You must create all of these product properties before you can begin working with them. Figure 11-5 shows the Property definitions included in the Retail Solution Site.

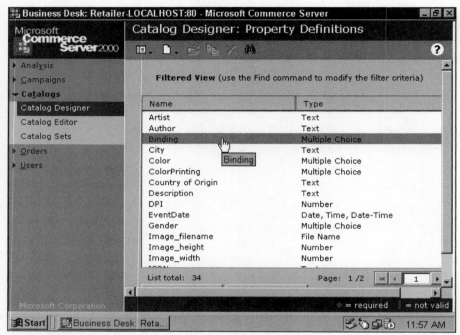

Figure 11-5: Property definitions

Each property definition includes details on how the property may be defined—whether the property is a text string, as in the case of a simple Description property, or whether it must be one of several values, called a multiple-choice property. The Binding property, which is used in the definition of books sold on your site, is a multiple-choice property. The Binding property definition is shown in Figure 11-6.

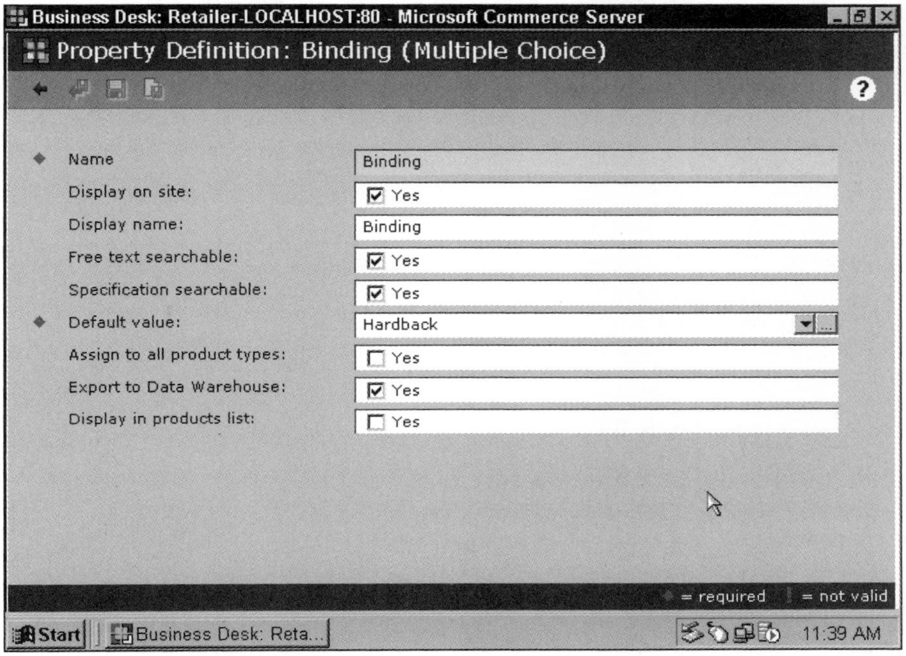

Figure 11-6: The Binding property

The property definition allows you to determine whether or not the property is searchable, whether or not the property is exported to Commerce Server's data warehouse for inclusion in analysis reports, and so forth. You can also define the possible values that the Binding property can contain, as well as the default value, as shown in Figure 11-7.

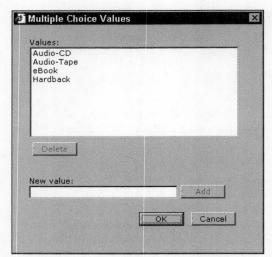

Figure 11-7: Defining the values for a multiple-choice property

After you have created all of the properties, product types, and category types, you're ready to begin creating catalogs.

Creating a base catalog

A base catalog contains your products. You can create multiple base catalogs, as discussed previously in this chapter. Creating a new catalog is done in the Commerce Server Business Desk's Catalog Editor, as shown in Figure 11-8.

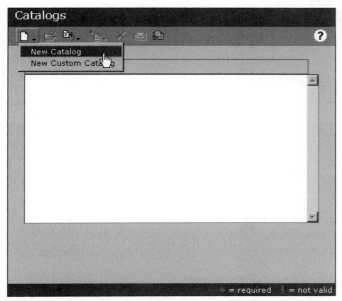

Figure 11-8: Creating a new base catalog

Before beginning a new catalog, make sure that you have defined the properties and categories to be used in the catalog, because part of the catalog's definition includes:

✦ What product property (such as an SKU) will uniquely identify each product in the catalog?

✦ What product property will uniquely identify variants within a product family?

✦ What categories will be included in the catalog?

Figure 11-9 shows the property screen for creating a new base catalog. You must name the catalog, determine what properties will uniquely identify products, and so forth.

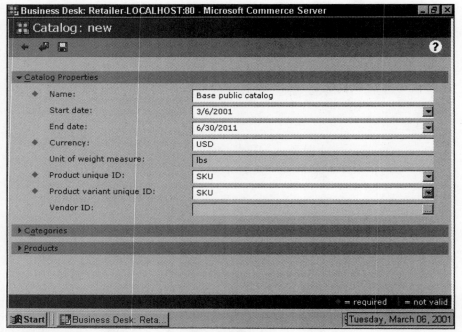

Figure 11-9: Properties for a new base catalog

The properties of a base catalog consist of the categories within the catalog, as well as their relationships to each other. To begin creating categories in a base catalog:

1. Save the catalog definition by clicking the Save icon on the toolbar of the Business Desk application.

2. Open the Categories section of the catalog's properties and click the New button. Figure 11-10 shows the "Create A New Category" dialog box, which allows you to select the *type* of category that you want to create.

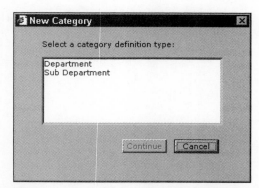

Figure 11-10: Adding a category to a catalog

3. After you select the category type, you are prompted to provide values for the category's properties. Remember that these are the properties you defined as part of the category type in the previous section. Figure 11-11 shows the creation of a new Department type category named "Books."

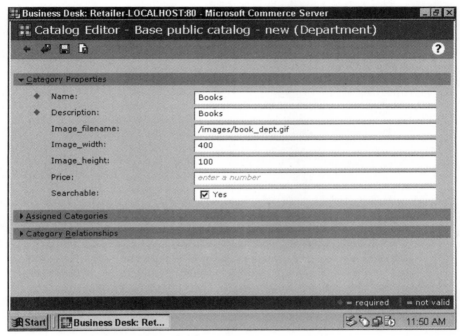

Figure 11-11: Creating the Books department

Figure 11-12 shows the creation of a new sub-department type category named "Fiction."

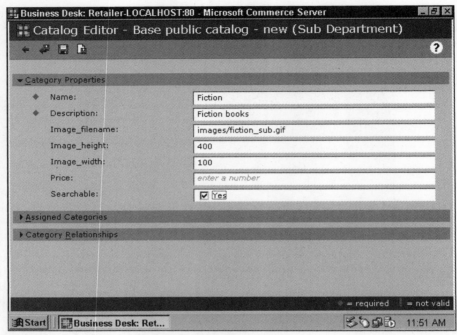

Figure 11-12: Creating the Fiction sub-department

4. Because the Fiction sub-department is intended to be a child of the Books department, you can modify the Assigned Categories section of the Fiction category's definition. As shown in Figure 11-13, selecting Books as the parent category automatically makes Fiction a child of the Books category.

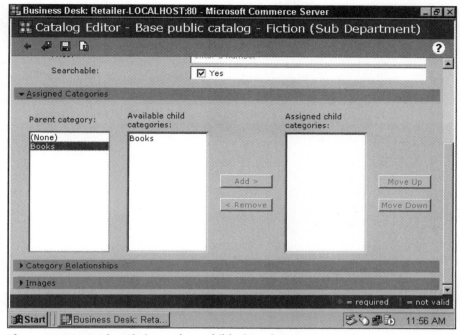

Figure 11-13: Setting Fiction to be a child of Books

You can confirm this by checking the properties of the Books category, which now shows Fiction as one of its children, as shown in Figure 11-14.

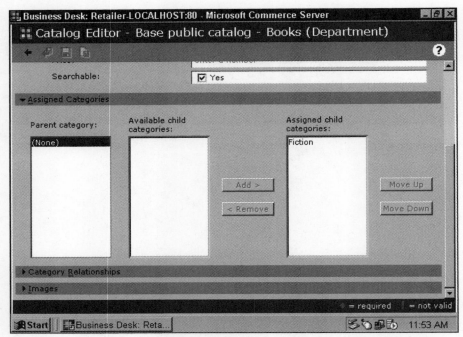

Figure 11-14: Confirming that the Books category is the parent of the Fiction category

After defining your product taxonomy, you can begin populating the catalog with product information. You can also begin creating custom catalogs based on your base catalogs.

Creating a custom catalog

A custom catalog is a special version of a base catalog. Custom catalogs don't contain any products; rather, they inherit all of the products, categories, and other information from their base catalog. The custom catalog exists solely to apply special pricing information to one or more categories within the base catalog.

Custom catalogs are created in the Commerce Server Business Desk application, as shown in Figure 11-15.

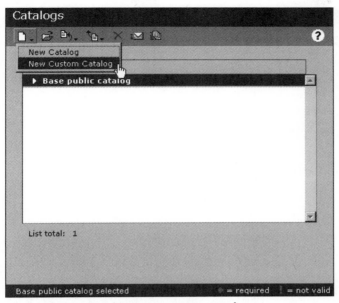

Figure 11-15: Creating a new custom catalog

When you create a new custom catalog, you are prompted to select the base catalog that will serve as its parent, as shown in Figure 11-16.

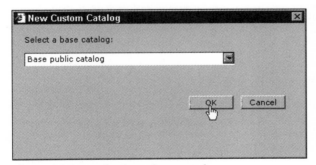

Figure 11-16: Selecting a base catalog

The properties of a custom catalog include its name and any pricing rules that you define. This pricing is on a per-category basis and can include percentage-off pricing applied to an entire category, as shown in Figure 11-17.

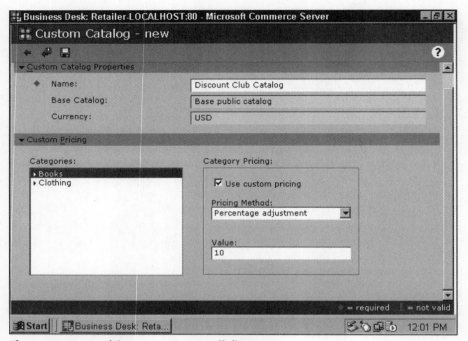

Figure 11-17: Applying a percentage-off discount

Pricing rules can be different for each category in the base catalog. Figure 11-18 shows the same custom catalog being used to apply a dollars-off discount to the clothing category.

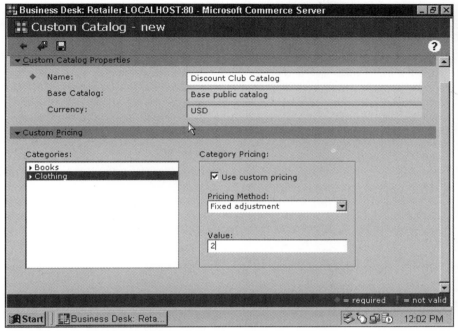

Figure 11-18: Applying a fixed-amount discount

After you save the custom catalog definition, it will appear in the catalog list as a child of its base catalog, as shown in Figure 11-19.

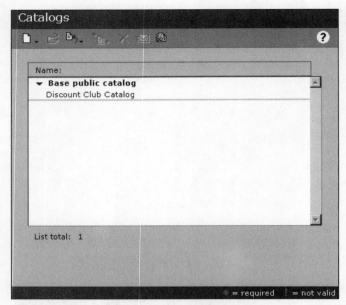

Figure 11-19: Viewing custom catalogs

The custom catalog can't exist without the base catalog; if the base catalog is deleted, the custom catalog is also removed from the system. After being defined, custom catalogs can be treated just like base catalogs when building your catalog sets. The custom catalog shown in Figure 11-19 is being used to apply special discounts to the products in the catalog, and use of the catalog will be restricted to members of the site's Discount Club.

Creating catalog sets

Commerce Server includes two default catalog sets, and both are configured to automatically include all catalogs in the database. The first catalog set is for anonymous users, and the second is for registered users who have signed on to your site. By default, everyone who visits your site will have access to all of your catalogs.

If you want to create a catalog with restricted access, you will need to modify both of the default catalog sets and clear the "Include all catalogs" check box, as shown in Figure 11-20.

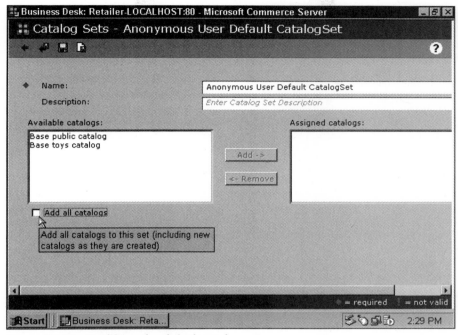

Figure 11-20: Modifying the default catalog sets

After you clear this check box, you will need to specify which catalogs should be included in the set.

You can also create a new catalog set, as shown in Figure 11-21. This gives you the ability to define a group of catalogs, and then restrict access to them. You can also check the "Include all catalogs" check box, which will automatically add all current and future catalogs to the set.

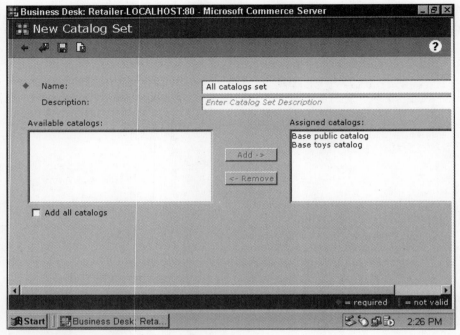

Figure 11-21: Creating a new catalog set

Creating a catalog for non-products

Your site may sell things that aren't tangible products, such as services, service contracts, event tickets, and so forth. Commerce Server's product catalog system is flexible enough to allow you to structure your catalog for these items, as well. The following examples provide a starting point for various types of non-product items, including cellular phone service, musical concerts, and extended product warranties.

Cellular phone service

Generally, a single product type—"cell phone service"—will suffice for the various plans that an online cell phone company may offer. The properties associated with the product define the plan, and may include:

✦ Digital or analog

✦ Length of contract

✦ Monthly price

✦ Early termination fee

✦ Free minutes included in plan

✦ Price per minute of extra minutes

✦ Description of the plan, which may include miscellaneous features

By including the package details as *properties*, rather than in a general description, you facilitate building a side-by-side comparison screen, thus allowing shoppers to compare the properties of various plans.

Musical concerts

An online ticket service may offer several different types of ticketed events. For every event with significantly different properties, a different product type is required. Most musical concerts can probably use a single product type with, perhaps, the following properties attached to it:

✦ Date and time

✦ Artist or group

✦ Music genre (which may be a multiple-choice property with values such as Rock, Opera, Classical, Jazz, and so forth).

✦ Location

✦ Seat type (Balcony, standing room only, etc.)

Properties like the seat type or date and time can define variants within a product family, thus allowing you to create a single product to represent a single concert, and then create variants for seat type, date, and time. By including details like the music genre as a *property,* rather than in a description field, you easily allow music enthusiasts to search for events featuring their favorite type of music.

Extended warranties

A company that sells automobiles or home electronics may also want to offer extended warranties on those products. If so, they need an extended warranty product type, which may include some of the following properties:

✦ Warranty length

✦ Warranty coverage (may be a description type property describing what is covered)

✦ Deductible

✦ Warranty type (walk-in, mail-in, in-house, etc.)

Warranties for a single product, such as a VCR, can be created as a product family, with variants for various lengths of coverage. By creating the warranties as a product, you can associate them with the products that they cover, which allows you to use Commerce Server's suggested selling features.

Best practices for your catalog

With the virtually unlimited flexibility of Commerce Server's product catalog system, it's not hard to make a catalog taxonomy that quickly becomes difficult to maintain. When designing your catalog, try to keep the following best practices in mind:

✦ Start by creating the base catalog to which the general public will have access. Any products that should *not* be accessible should go into separate catalogs. If you have multiple "groups" of product access, you need a different catalog for each.

✦ You probably don't need to duplicate products across catalogs. Instead, break products into multiple catalogs and use catalog sets to give different groups of customers access to them. For example, if anonymous and registered users have access to your Books, but only registered users have access to your Clothing, then both should go into separate catalogs. Create a catalog set for anonymous and registered users and add the appropriate catalogs to each set.

✦ Start defining product properties by defining the properties that *all* of your products share, such as a description. Then create the product properties that are unique to specific categories, such as size or color. Always keep product properties as generic as possible. For example, if you are selling glass beads, create properties such as Color, Size, Shape, and so forth. Avoid creating properties like Bead Shape, which can only be used with a specific product type.

✦ Don't try to wedge a product into an ill-fitting product type. For example, shirts and pants are both clothing items, but have different properties. You can't represent the Waist and Inseam properties of a pair of pants by using the Collar and Sleeve Length properties of a shirt. And casual shirts, which may only come in sizes Small, Medium, and Large, shouldn't be grouped with formal shirts, which have Collar and Sleeve Length properties.

✦ When defining the *terms* for a multiple-choice property, such as Small, Medium, and Large for a Size property, try to make the terms generic, so that the property can be used with other products.

✦ Be careful to define product families and variants wherever necessary. For example, video games should generally belong to a product family, and the various game systems that each title is available for are variants.

✦ Don't try to use a vendor's part number as your own stock number or SKU. Instead, make up your own stock numbers to guarantee uniqueness. You can always include the vendor's part number, such as a book's ISBN number, as a property of the product to help with reordering.

✦ Try to keep as few custom catalogs in a catalog set as possible. For example, imagine that your base catalog includes books and clothing. Members of your

Discount Club get a 10 percent discount on books, and members of your Frequent Shopper club get $1 off discount on clothes. Some customers may be members of both clubs, and should receive both discounts. In this case, make *three* custom catalogs to represent the various pricing scenarios. Doing so will improve performance for Commerce Server when it has to figure out product pricing.

Populating the Catalog

Commerce Server has some fairly powerful options for populating your catalog with products. For example, you can use the Business Desk to manually add products to your catalogs. Commerce Server also provides the ability to import existing catalogs from another platform or from a legacy back-end system in Comma-Separate Value (CSV) or Extensible Markup Language (XML) formats. This XML support also provides the ability to integrate with BizTalk Server, meaning that you can create an automated process for importing catalogs from your own systems or from vendors' systems.

Manually adding products

Anyone with access to the Catalogs module of the Business Desk can manually enter and edit the products in the catalogs. The Catalog Editor provides the interface for product management. Follow these steps to add a new product:

1. Open the catalog to which the product will be added.

2. Under the Products tab, click the New button. A dialog box opens, asking you what type of product you want to add, as shown in Figure 11-22.

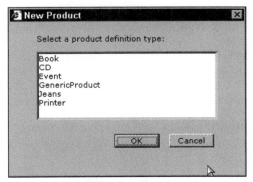

Figure 11-22: Selecting the type of product to add

3. After you select a product type, an Add Product screen opens, allowing you to provide values for the product's properties. The exact properties displayed depend on the product type definition; Figure 11-23 shows a sample Add Product screen for a book.

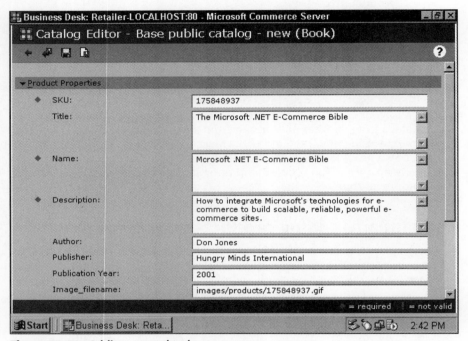

Figure 11-23: Adding a new book

4. To create a product family, such as a book title available in different types of bindings, open the Variants tab of the Add Products page. You can define a separate price for each variant, as shown in Figure 11-24. You must also provide unique values for each of the variant properties, which are defined as part of the product type. Any product with variants is considered to be a product family. In this case, the product type of Book defines two variant properties — the ISBN number and the binding type.

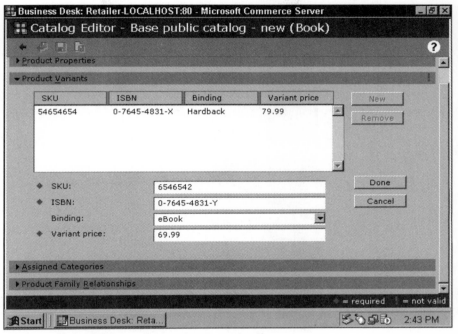

Figure 11-24: Adding product variants to a family

5. Each product can be assigned to one or more categories, which is how you place products within your product taxonomy. By allowing products to appear under different categories, Commerce Server allows a single product definition to become available in multiple places. For example, a garden hose may be appropriate for both a Gardening category as well as an Automotive category, because the hose can be used to wash cars. By including it in both categories, shoppers who are browsing the product catalog will find the product in both places. Figure 11-25 shows the new book being added to the appropriate categories.

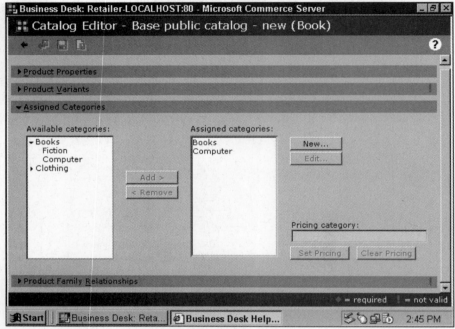

Figure 11-25: Assigning a product to categories

6. Finally, define *product family relationships.* These relationships help Commerce Server understand how different products of different types can be related to each other. Figure 11-26 shows a soundtrack CD available with the book. By defining the relationship between these two products, Commerce Server's suggested selling components can be used to suggest the other product to customers who add one of them to their baskets.

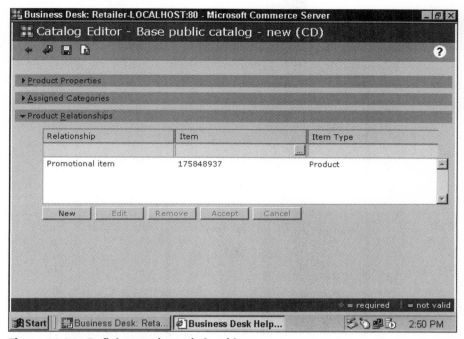

Figure 11-26: Defining product relationships

Importing CSV files

Commerce Server allows you to import products from a CSV file. The file may include any number of columns, provided that the first line contains the column names. However, CSV files cannot contain any provisions for a product taxonomy. As a result, all products in a single file must be mapped to a single product type. In other words, you can import a file of books, a file of clothes, a file of CDs, and so forth.

1. Begin the import process by opening the Business Desk's Catalog Editor.

2. Click the "Import Catalog" icon in the toolbar, and the Import Catalog dialog box displays, as shown in Figure 11-27.

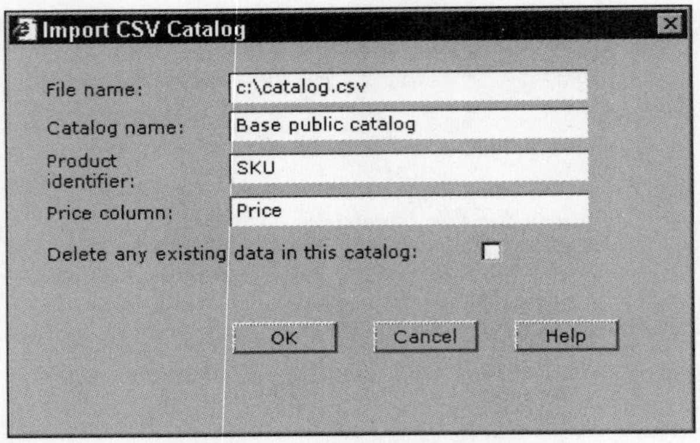

Figure 11-27: Importing a CSV file

3. Specify the name of the CSV file and the name of the catalog to create.

- If you specify the name of an existing catalog, the data will be added to that catalog.

- If you specify the name of a new catalog, Commerce Server will create it and import the data.

- If you check the "Overwrite" check box, any existing catalog of the same name will be deleted before the import.

CSV imports carry some significant restrictions:

✦ A new product type will be created with the same name as the catalog name that you specify. The product's properties will all be string values, and will be based upon the columns contained in the CSV file.

✦ You must indicate which of the columns in the CSV file represent the unique identifier for each product, and which column contains the price.

✦ If you specify a catalog name that matches an existing product type definition, the properties of that product type must exactly match the columns in the CSV file.

✦ CSV imports don't support product variants. Each row in the file will be entered as a distinct product.

Because of these restrictions, CSV imports are extremely limited in their usefulness. Unless you are importing a very small catalog composed of simply defined products, you will find that the CSV import doesn't offer sufficient flexibility for your needs.

Importing XML files

You begin an XML file import the same way that you begin a CSV file import—by selecting the Import File icon on the toolbar in the Business Desk Catalog Editor. As shown in Figure 11-28, the Import File dialog box for an XML import is much simpler than the CSV import. This is because the XML file must contain not only the product data, but also the schema for the catalog.

Figure 11-28: Importing an XML file

The XML file also contains the name of the catalog, and the file is meant to represent the *entire* catalog. If the catalog name shares the name of an existing catalog, the data in the XML file will be added to the existing catalog. If you check the "Overwrite" check box when importing the XML file, any existing catalogs will be emptied before the import begins.

All product definitions must be included in the XML file, and they must match *exactly* any product definitions already in the catalog (if it exists), or the import process will fail.

Note
Commerce Server logs import errors to the Application Event Log. Be sure to check the log for errors after the import process completes.

Listing 11-1 shows a sample XML catalog file, formatted according to Commerce Server's requirements.

Note
This is an abbreviated sample file; a complete catalog contains far more data.

Listing 11-1: **Sample Commerce Server XML catalog**

```xml
<?xml version="1.0"?>
<MSCommerceCatalogCollection>
<CatalogSchema>

 <PropertiesDefinition>

  <Property name="Author" dataType="string"
  IsFreeTextSearchable="1" IncludeInSpecSearch="1"
  MinValue="0" MaxValue="80" DisplayOnSite="1"
  DisplayName="Author" AssignAll="0" ExportToDW="1"
  DisplayInProductsList="0" id="CatalogProperty1" />

  <Property name="Binding" dataType="enumeration"
  DefaultValue="Hardback" IsFreeTextSearchable="1"
  IncludeInSpecSearch="1" MaxValue="128" DisplayOnSite="1"
  DisplayName="Binding" AssignAll="0" ExportToDW="1"
  DisplayInProductsList="0" id="CatalogProperty2" >
   <PropertyValue displayName="Audio-CD" />
   <PropertyValue displayName="Audio-Tape" />
   <PropertyValue displayName="eBook" />
   <PropertyValue displayName="Hardback" />
  </Property>

  <Property name="Description" dataType="string"
  IsFreeTextSearchable="1" IncludeInSpecSearch="0"
  MinValue="1" MaxValue="4000" DisplayOnSite="1"
  AssignAll="1" ExportToDW="0" DisplayInProductsList="1"
  id="CatalogProperty7" />

 </PropertiesDefinition>

 <Definition name="Book" DefinitionType="product"
 properties="CatalogProperty26 CatalogProperty20
 CatalogProperty7 CatalogProperty1 CatalogProperty24
 CatalogProperty23 CatalogProperty11 CatalogProperty13
 CatalogProperty12 "
 variantProperties="CatalogProperty14 CatalogProperty2 " />

</CatalogSchema>

<Catalog name="Base public catalog" startDate="2001-03-06"
 endDate="2011-06-30" productUID="SKU" variantUID="SKU"
 currency="USD" weight_measuring_unit="lbs" >

  <Category name="Books" isSearchable="1"
  Definition="Department" id="Item11" >
```

```
      <Field fieldID="CatalogProperty7"
      fieldValue="Books" />
      <Field fieldID="CatalogProperty11"
      fieldValue="/images/book_dept.gif" />
      <Field fieldID="CatalogProperty12" fieldValue="100" />
      <Field fieldID="CatalogProperty13" fieldValue="400" />
    </Category>

    <Category name="Fiction" isSearchable="1"
    Definition="Sub Department" id="Item12"
    parentCategories=" Item11" >
      <Field fieldID="CatalogProperty7"
      fieldValue="Fiction books" />
      <Field fieldID="CatalogProperty11"
      fieldValue="images/fiction_sub.gif" />
      <Field fieldID="CatalogProperty12" fieldValue="400" />
      <Field fieldID="CatalogProperty13" fieldValue="100" />
    </Category>

<Product Definition="Book" listprice="0" id="Item17"
 parentCategories=" Item11 Item16" >
    <Field fieldID="CatalogProperty25" fieldValue="175848937"/>
    <Field fieldID="CatalogProperty7"
    fieldValue="How to integrate Microsoft's technologies
    for e-commerce to build scalable, reliable, powerful
    e-commerce sites." />
    <Field fieldID="CatalogProperty11"
    fieldValue="images/products/175848937.gif" />
    <Field fieldID="CatalogProperty1" fieldValue="Don Jones" />
    <Field fieldID="CatalogProperty20" fieldValue="Mcrosoft
    .NET E-Commerce Bible" />
    <Field fieldID="CatalogProperty23" fieldValue="2001" />
    <Field fieldID="CatalogProperty24" fieldValue="Hungry Minds
    International" />
    <Field fieldID="CatalogProperty26" fieldValue="The
    Microsoft .NET E-Commerce Bible" />

    <ProductVariant listprice="79.99" >
     <Field fieldID="CatalogProperty2" fieldValue="Hardback" />
     <Field fieldID="CatalogProperty14"
     fieldValue="0-7645-4831-X" />
     <Field fieldID="CatalogProperty25" fieldValue="54654654" />
    </ProductVariant
</Product>

</Catalog>
</MSCommerceCatalogCollection>
```

This XML file contains several distinct sections:

✦ The first section, `<PropertiesDefinition>`, contains the definitions for the properties used in the catalog, such as Size, Binding, Color, and so forth. Within each `<Property>` definition, multiple `<PropertyValue>` tags can be included for multiple-choice properties like Binding.

✦ `<Definition>` tags are used to define each product type. Each tag includes the ID strings of each property associated with the product type. In this sample, the Book product type is defined, and the Binding property ("CatalogProperty2") is included in the list of properties associated with the product type. The properties and products make up the `<CatalogSchema>` section of the file.

✦ The next section of the file opens with the `<Catalog>` tag, which defines the catalog. Although the file format allows multiple catalogs to be included in a single file (by including multiple `<Catalog>` sections), this is not recommended because they would share the `<CatalogSchema>` section.

✦ Within the `<Catalog>` section are multiple `<Product>` tags, each of which references a specific product type definition and defines a single product. The `<Product>` tags can also enclose multiple `<Field>` tags, each defining a value for the properties associated with the product type, and multiple `<ProductVariant>` tags, which define product variants. The `<ProductVariant>` tags also include `<Field>` tags that provide values for the variant properties of the product.

So how do you generate compatible XML files for importing into Commerce Server? You can write a SQL Server Data Transformation Services (DTS) package. Such a package requires a tremendous amount of script because DTS doesn't inherently provide XML output. Another method is to use SQL Server 2000's native XML querying capabilities, although this requires a fairly complicated XML template in order to provide the correct structure.

If you do choose to generate your XML files by using one of these methods, you can perform a quick check to make sure that the final XML is properly formatted. Note that this check *won't* verify the validity of the product definitions, but it will ensure that the XML code conforms to the schema required by Commerce Server. To perform the test, simply add the following line to the XML file:

```
<MSCommerceCatalogCollection xmlns="x-schema:C:\Program
 Files\Microsoft Commerce Server\CatalogXMLSchema.xml">
```

Make sure that the path to the CatalogXMLSchema.xml file is correct. Then, open the XML file in Internet Explorer 5.5. IE will verify the contents of the file and detail any discrepancies that it finds between the file and the Commerce Server required schema.

The easiest way to convert your existing data into a Commerce Server-compatible XML format is to use BizTalk Server.

Integration with BizTalk Server

BizTalk Server 2000 is Microsoft's .NET server for data translation and transportation. BizTalk Server and Commerce Server are designed to work together, allowing Commerce Server orders and catalogs to be imported to and exported from any data source that BizTalk has been programmed to understand.

Configuring Commerce Server for integration

Before you can begin taking advantage of BizTalk, you need to configure Commerce Server to work with it. Start with the Commerce Server Manager snap-in to the Microsoft Management Console (MMC), and open the Site Resources tree. Right-click the `App Default Config` item and open its properties, and then modify the `Properties` tab as follows:

1. For BizTalk Catalog Doc Type, provide the document definition name that is required by BizTalk Server for catalogs — CatalogTransferDoc.

2. For BizTalk Options, type **1** to enable integration. The default value is zero, which disables integration.

3. For BizTalk PO Doc Type, type the document definition name that BizTalk will use for purchase orders — PurchaseOrder.

4. For BizTalk Source Org Qualifier, type the alias qualifier for your e-commerce site — MyCompany.

5. For BizTalk Source Org Qualifier Value, type the alias value for your site in BizTalk — Sender.

6. For BizTalk Submit Type, type a **1** to submit documents to BizTalk Server asynchronously. This allows multiple documents to be submitted in parallel.

7. If BizTalk Server is installed on a different computer, use the Connection Strings tab to modify the Data Link Properties with a connection string to the BizTalk Server.

You will need to either restart the Commerce Server computer or unload the Web application in order for these settings to take effect.

Importing the Commerce Server catalog schema into BizTalk

BizTalk is designed to accept data in any format for which it has a schema. The schema tells BizTalk how to translate the data into its own intermediate XML format. Then, a separate schema is required to translate the data from the intermediate format into the destination format. Commerce Server provides a schema file — CatalogXMLSchema.xml — that describes its required catalog schema. To import these schema into BizTalk:

1. Open the BizTalk Editor.

2. Click Import on the Tools menu.

3. Select XDR Schema.

4. Provide the complete path to the CatalogXMLSchema.xml file provided with Commerce Server and click Open.

5. On the File menu, select Store to WebDAV.

6. Type **CatalogXMLSchema.xml** for the file name and click Save.

7. Close BizTalk Editor.

Creating the BizTalk Document Definition

BizTalk uses Document Definitions to define business document types and associate them with a schema. Your catalog, for example, is a type of business document. When you configured Commerce Server for BizTalk integration, you specified a document type name for your catalogs, such as CatalogTransferDoc. The following steps walk you through configuring this Document Definition in BizTalk:

1. Open the BizTalk Messaging Manager.

2. Select New Document Definition from the File menu.

3. Type the name for the Document Definition — **CatalogTransferDoc**.

4. Select the Document Specification check box, and click Browse.

5. Double-click the Microsoft folder in the browse dialog box, select the CatalogXMLSchema.xml file (which you imported in the last set of steps) and click Open.

6. Click OK.

BizTalk now associates the CatalogTransferDoc name with the XML schema required by Commerce Server. This means that you can begin setting up your server to receive catalog files.

Creating messaging ports and channels

After you've defined the necessary Document Definition, you need to configure BizTalk to accept incoming connections (called *connection agreements*) from the vendors who will be providing you with catalogs. You also need an XML schema file that tells BizTalk how to translate the vendor's catalog file into BizTalk's intermediate format. Your vendor must either provide this file, or you must create it manually.

The next step is to create a messaging port that represents the data's destination and a channel that represents its source, in order to define how the incoming data will be processed. Configuring message ports and channels can be complex, and is beyond the scope of this book.

Tip

For more information on configuring BizTalk Server, see the BizTalk Server documentation or the *BizTalk Server 2000 Bible* from Hungry Minds, Inc.

Creating your own import method

If you need to import catalogs from various sources and *don't* want to use BizTalk Server, then you need to create your own import functionality. Although this can be time-consuming, it gives you the benefit of being able to import from any format that you care to accommodate, without worrying about configuring BizTalk Server.

Note   If you plan on repeatedly importing from a particular source, and you want to be able to manage the reliability of the import process, take the time to use BizTalk Server because it provides data tracking and automation tools that make the job much easier. Writing your own import routines for one-time imports to initially populate your catalog may be easier and more cost-effective.

Importing directly into the database

Assuming you know the format you will import catalog data *from,* the big challenge becomes understanding the format your data will be imported *to.* Unfortunately, the Commerce Server documentation glosses over the SQL Server database schema that is used for products. Fortunately, I cover it in some detail in this section.

Commerce Server's SQL Server database contains several tables that comprise the product catalog system. After you understand what these tables do and how they're related, you can write import routines in Data Transformation Services, Visual Basic, or whatever you're comfortable with, in order to place data directly into these tables. The tables are as follows:

✦ **CatalogAttributes.** This table contains your product property definitions. Generally, you set these properties up by using the Business Desk, rather than importing them. You should know the PropertyName value for each property, because this acts as the primary key for the property.

✦ **CatalogDefinitions.** This table contains all of your category *and* product type definitions. Again, you should plan on using the Business Desk to set up this portion of your catalog rather than importing data.

✦ **CatalogDefinitionProperties.** This table relates the CatalogAttributes and CatalogDefinitions tables to associate properties with product types. If you plan on importing this information from a file, you'll also need to import the information necessary to set up the appropriate relationships in the table.

✦ **CatalogGlobal.** This table contains a row for each product catalog. Most important is the CatalogID column, which contains the unique identifier for each catalog.

✦ **CatalogUsedDefinitions.** This table tracks the product types and category definitions that are being used by one or more catalogs, and helps the Business Desk to prevent deletion of definitions that are being used. If you will be importing definition information, this table must be updated as well.

✦ **CatalogEnumValues.** This table defines the available values for multiple choice properties. If you use the Business Desk to set up your properties and product type definitions, you don't need to worry about this table. However, when you begin importing product information, make sure that any property values associated with the product are already present in this table.

✦ **CatalogCustomCatalogs.** This table contains information about custom catalogs, including the catalog on which they are based.

✦ **CatalogCustomPrices.** This table contains the pricing rules applied to categories in custom catalogs.

✦ *catalogname*_**CatalogProducts.** This table contains all of the products, variants, and categories for the catalog named in the table. This table contains a column for *every property* that a product in the catalog can contain. When you use the Business Desk, this table's schema is actually modified when new product types are added to the catalog — adding the columns necessary to hold the properties of the new product type. Because not all products will use all of the properties, these columns are all set to allow Null values.

Although this may seem like an incredibly inefficient way to store data, remember that Null values occupy very little space in the database (at least for the data types used by Commerce Server). Because Commerce Server is designed to query all product information from the database every time it's needed, this schema allows the information to be pulled from a single table rather than from several tables that must be joined. This is an example of deliberate denormalization to increase performance.

Note that the "oid" column is the unique identifier for each product or category in the table and is only used internally. Within the catalog, the ProductID column contains the unique identifier for the product, and the VariantID column contains the unique identifier for each variant.

✦ *catalogname*_**Relationships.** This table defines product and category relationships. It includes the oid column for the product or category, the oid for the related product or category, and a name and description field for the relationship.

✦ *catalogname*_**Heirarchy.** This table tracks the parent-child relationships between the categories in your catalog. It contains only two columns — the oid for the parent category and the oid for the child category.

Although most of your data should be imported into the *catalogname_CatalogProducts* table, you can make the process easier by following a few best practices:

✦ Determine which product types, categories, and properties will be imported and create these manually by using the Business Desk.

✦ Create a catalog by using the Business Desk rather than importing the catalog definition.

✦ Manually create one product of each product type in the catalog in order to properly define the *catalogname_CatalogProducts* table's schema.

✦ Make sure that your input file contains the appropriate property information for the products that you are importing.

You may want to take Commerce Server's approach and include a single product type in each file that you import. Doing so lets you be more careful when you want to make sure that all the necessary product properties are present in the file. The advantages of manually doing the import instead of using Commerce Server's built-in CSV import functionality include the following:

✦ You can define the catalog name that you want to import to.

✦ You can define the product type that you are importing from those available in the database.

✦ You can more easily import data to an existing catalog without disrupting its schema.

Importing by using programming objects

Unless you're planning to bulk import fairly simple data, importing directly into the database can be a little scary. One wrong move and your database is toast! Fortunately, Commerce Server includes a CatalogManager COM object that you can use from within scripts and Visual Basic programs. This object allows you to programmatically manipulate the catalog, and makes sure that all the necessary schema and relationship changes are made as data is added.

If Commerce Server has been installed, then you can use Visual Basic to create a new instance of the CatalogManager by using the CreateObject statement:

```
Set objCatMan = CreateObject("Commerce.CatalogManager")
```

The Catalog Manager is implemented in the Catalog.dll file. It is a C++ component that supports both threading models, and may be used from within Visual Basic or Visual C++ programs, or from within VBScript or JavaScript scripts. The CatalogManager object is well documented in the Commerce Server documentation. Briefly, it includes the following properties:

✦ **Catalogs_ property Recordset.** This property returns a recordset containing a record for each catalog contained in the product catalog system, including their properties.

✦ **CategoryDefinitions_Recordset.** This property returns a recordset containing the names of all of the category definitions that currently exist in the product catalog system.

✦ **CustomCatalogs_Recordset.** This property returns a recordset containing a record for each custom catalog. These records include the custom catalog names and the names of the catalogs on which they are based.

✦ **ProductDefinitions_Recordset.** This property returns a recordset containing the names of all the product definitions that currently exist in the product catalog system.

✦ **Properties_Recordset.** This property returns a recordset containing the name of each property that currently exists in the product catalog system.

CatalogManager also includes the following methods, which allow you to manipulate the product catalog system.

✦ AddDefinitionProperty

✦ AddDefinitionVariantProperty

✦ AddPropertyValue

✦ CreateCatalog

✦ CreateCategoryDefinition

✦ CreateProductDefinition

✦ CreateProperty

✦ Initialize

✦ SetDefinitionProperties

✦ SetPropertyAttributes

After you've used the CatalogManager to define your catalogs, use the ProductCatalog object to manipulate actual products, which includes the following methods for adding products to the catalog:

✦ CreateCategory

✦ CreateProduct

Tip   For complete details on using these methods and properties, refer to the Commerce Server 2000 documentation's Programmers Reference. Also, see the next section for information on Commerce Server's other catalog objects.

Commerce Server's Catalog Components

When you begin programming your site to display catalog information, you will need to become familiar with the COM object that Commerce Server uses to work with the catalogs. These components will generally provide faster access and more efficient utilization of server resources (like memory). If these objects are run from an Application Center COM+ cluster, you will also be able to take advantage of the cluster's load-balancing and redundancy features.

Note

The Commerce Server documentation includes a complete list of available objects, including a C++ and Visual Basic reference. In this book, I focus on the most common objects for working with the catalog.

The catalog system objects include:

✦ **CatalogManager,** the main object for working with the entire product catalog system. Various properties and methods of the CatalogManager object return the other catalog objects described here.

✦ **CatalogSets,** an object that lets you work with catalog sets. This object includes a `GetCatalogsForUser` method, which returns a list of catalogs associated with a specific user. This method facilitates building a list of catalogs to which a specific customer should have access.

✦ The **Category** object lets you work with categories and their relationships. For example, a specific category's object includes a `ChildCategories` property, which returns a list of all child categories. This is useful for building a list of available sub-departments or for building your catalog navigation hierarchy.

✦ The **ProductCatalog** object allows you to work with entire catalogs. Especially helpful is the `RootCategories` property, which returns a list of top-level categories for the catalog. This can be useful when displaying your catalog's navigation hierarchy.

✦ The **Product** object allows you to work with individual products. Its properties return various recordsets, such as the `GetProductProperties` property and the `Variants` property.

These components provide a great deal of flexibility in creating your catalog pages. One especially difficult task for creating product detail pages is dealing with product variants. Using the Product object's `Variants` property makes this much easier. Listing 11-2 shows a sample ASP page that queries the product information and generates a list of any variants and their price.

Listing 11-2: **Listing variants**

```
<%

'assumes Pc is a valid ProductCatalog object
'assumes pID contains the desired Product ID
Dim p
Set p = Pc.GetProduct(pID)

'output several properties
Set Rs = p.GetProductProperties
Response.Write Rs("Description")
Response.Write Rs("MfgrName")
```

Continued

Listing 11-2 *(continued)*

```
'check for variants and output
'list if present
Set V = p.Variants
If V.EOF And V.BOF Then
 'no variants
Else
 'variants - output table header
  Response.Write "<TABLE><TR>"

  'output variant property names
  For x = 3 To V.Fields.Count - 1
   Response.Write "<TD>"
   Response.Write V.Fields(x).Name
   Response.Write </TD>"
  Next
  Response.Write "<TD>Price</TD>"
  Response.Write "</TR>"

  'walk through recordset
  Do Until V.EOF
   'table row
   Response.Write "<TR>"

   'output property values
   For x = 3 To V.Fields.Count - 1
    Response.Write "<TD>"
    Response.Write V(x)
    Response.Write "</TD>"
   Next

   'write price for this variant
   Response.Write "<TD>"
   Response.Write V("cy_list_price")
   Response.Write "</TD>"

   'Next variant
   V.MoveNext
   Response.Write "</TR>"
  Loop
End If

%>
```

You may adapt this technique to generate drop-down list boxes for each variant property, thus allowing customers to select the exact combination of variant properties that they want. You can use DHTML code to automatically update the price displayed, depending on the combination of variant properties selected. Remember that each row in the Variants table represents a complete product; in a minimalist implementation you can have a drop-down list box that lists each combination of variant properties on a single line, thus allowing the customer to select the one that they want. Listing 11-3 shows an example of this technique.

Listing 11-3: **Listing variants in a list box**

```
<%

'assumes Pc is a valid ProductCatalog object
'assumes pID contains the desired Product ID
Dim p
Set p = Pc.GetProduct(pID)

'output several properties
Set Rs = p.GetProductProperties
Response.Write Rs("Description")
Response.Write Rs("MfgrName")

'check for variants and output
'list if present
Set V = p.Variants
If V.EOF And V.BOF Then
 'no variants
Else
  'write tag
  Response.Write "<SELECT SIZE=1 NAME='Vars'>"

  'walk through recordset
  Do Until V.EOF
   'table row
   Response.Write "<OPTION VALUE='whatever'>"

   'output property values
   For x = 3 To V.Fields.Count - 1
    Response.Write V(x) & ", "
   Next

   'write price for this variant
   Response.Write "Price: $"
   Response.Write V("cy_list_price")
   Response.Write "</OPTION>"

   'Next variant
   V.MoveNext
  Loop

  Response.Write "</SELECT>"
End If

%>
```

Note that the above code listing should be used as an example only; production product detail pages should be generated in advance as static pages whenever possible. The technique demonstrated here can be incorporated into the utility or application that generated the static pages — a technique that I discuss next.

Building Your Own Catalog

As previously discussed, Commerce Server is designed to generate the vast majority of your pages directly from the database. This is how Microsoft's Solution Sites are designed, and is the primary reason I recommend *against* using the Solution Sites as the basis for your Web site. Requiring multiple database hits to view what is primarily static information is unnecessary because it creates the potential for a bottleneck in your data tier, and results in a significantly less scalable Web site.

On the other hand, creating static HTML pages for your product detail pages is no way to build a catalog, either. The information in your catalog *does* change, and it's important from a manageability standpoint to spare yourself the task of manually updating the HTML files every time a piece of information changes.

My proposed solution is to use the database to dynamically generate static HTML files. This gives you the best of both worlds — largely static files that your Web servers can deliver quickly with very little database interaction, as well as automatic updates when information in the database changes.

Preparing the database

You can take one of two approaches to dynamically generate static pages. The first way is to simply regenerate all of your product detail pages on a regular basis. The advantage of this technique is that it requires no modification of the Commerce Server databases. The disadvantage is that if you have a large number of products, regenerating pages for all of them will take forever.

The other approach is to add a column to the *catalogname_CatalogProducts* tables that can change. This column will be used to indicate which rows in the table have changed, thus allowing you to regenerate only the pages that have been altered.

1. Add a column named "Changed" to the *catalogname_CatalogProducts* table for each catalog in your database. The new column should be of the bit data type, with a default value of zero. If your catalog already contains data, you will need the new column to allow Null values.

2. Execute the following query to set it to zero for all existing products and categories:

   ```
   UPDATE catalogname_CatalogProducts SET Changed = 0
   ```

3. Make sure the "Changed" column is always set to 1 whenever another column in the table is changed. You *could* do this by hunting down every piece of code that changes the table, but it's easier to write a trigger. The trigger can be set to fire whenever any other columns are updated, and can take care of flipping the value in the Changed column for you.

Listing 11-4 shows the code necessary to create the trigger. Be sure to provide the correct table name for your database.

Listing 11-4: **Trigger to update the Changed column**

```
CREATE TRIGGER tr_UpdateChanged
  ON catalogname_CatalogProducts
  FOR AFTER Update, Insert
AS
  UPDATE catalogname_CatalogProducts
  SET Changed = 1 WHERE oid =
  (SELECT oid FROM Inserted)
```

Creating a product detail template

The next step is to create an HTML or ASP file that will serve as the "template" for the product detail pages in your catalog. The easiest way to do this is to create a normal-looking product detail page as a starting point. Figure 11-29 shows a sample detail page.

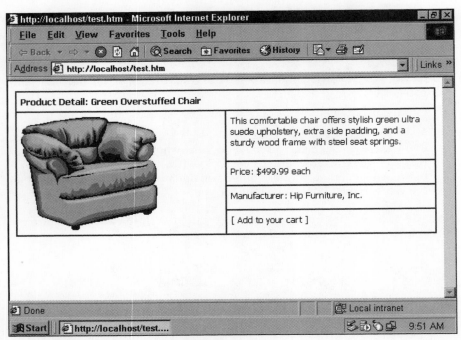

Figure 11-29: Sample product detail page

Listing 11-5 shows the HTML code that created the displayed sample detail page.

Listing 11-5: **Sample product detail page**

```
<table border="1" width="100%" bordercolor="#000080"
 cellspacing="0" cellpadding="6" bordercolorlight="#000080"
 bordercolordark="#000080">
  <tr>
    <td width="100%" colspan="2" valign="top"
align="left"><font face="Tahoma" size="2"><b>Product
      Detail: Green Overstuffed Chair</b></font></td>
  </tr>
  <tr>
    <td width="50%" valign="top" align="left"
rowspan="4"><b><font size="2" face="Tahoma"><img border="0"
src="HH01669_.wmf" width="195" height="169"></font></b></td>
    <td width="50%" valign="top" align="left<font size="2"
face="Tahoma">This
      comfortable chair offers stylish green ultra suede
upholstery, extra side
      padding, and a sturdy wood frame with steel seat
springs. ></font></td>
  </tr>
```

```
<tr>
   <td width="50%" valign="top" align="left"><font
 face="Tahoma" size="2">Price:
      <%

Set rs = cn.execute("sp_GetPrice xOidx")
Response.write rs("price")

%> font></td>
   </tr>
   <tr>
   <td width="50%" valign="top" align="left"><font
 face="Tahoma" size="2">Manufacturer:
      Hip Furniture, Inc.</font></td>
   </tr>
   <tr>
   <td width="50%" valign="top" align="left"><font
 face="Tahoma" size="2">[ Add
      to your cart ]</font></td>
   </tr>
</table>
```

Notice that the price is being pulled directly from the database by using a stored procedure and ASP code. Pricing is the one piece of information that I recommend leaving dynamic, rather than statically generating it, if your prices change more often than once a day, or if price changes *must* go online the instant that they are changed in the database. Also, because so many other pieces of Commerce Server will pull the price from the database, if there is any chance of the price in the database being different from the static file, you should make sure that the price always comes straight from the database.

After you've created your prototype detail page, modify the file to make a template out of it. Do this by removing the actual product values and replacing them with placeholders. The placeholders that I use *exactly* match the associated product property names, and begin and end with a lowercase "x" to make them stand out. Check the *catalogname_CatalogProducts* table to make sure that your placeholders match the column names in the table. Listing 11-6 shows the same product detail page, with the appropriate information replaced with placeholders.

Listing 11-6: **Sample product detail page with placeholders**

```
<table border="1" width="100%" bordercolor="#000080"
 cellspacing="0" cellpadding="6" bordercolorlight="#000080"
 bordercolordark="#000080">
   <tr>
```

Continued

Listing 11-6 *(continued)*

```
   <td width="100%" colspan="2" valign="top"
align="left"><font face="Tahoma" size="2"><b>Product
    Detail: xNamex</b></font></td>
  </tr>
  <tr>
   <td width="50%" valign="top" align="left"
rowspan="4"><b><font size="2" face="Tahoma"><img border="0"
src="xImage_Filex" width="195" height="169"></font></b></td>
   <td width="50%" valign="top" align="left<font size="2"
face="Tahoma">
xDescriptionx</font></td>
  </tr>
  <tr>
   <td width="50%" valign="top" align="left"><font
 face="Tahoma" size="2">Price:
    <%

Set rs = cn.execute("sp_GetPrice xOidx")
Response.write rs("price")

%> xUnitsx</font></td>
  </tr>
  <tr>
   <td width="50%" valign="top" align="left"><font
 face="Tahoma" size="2">Manufacturer:
    xMfgNamex</font></td>
  </tr>
  <tr>
   <td width="50%" valign="top" align="left"><font
 face="Tahoma" size="2">[ Add
    to your cart ]</font></td>
  </tr>
</table>
```

The products in your catalog will probably require multiple templates. For example, clothing generally requires a more complex template than other products, because the customer must be able to select from the available sizes, colors, and so forth. CDs, which include information about the artist and label, will have a different product page than books, which include an author and publisher. In this case, you have two options:

✦ If the products are grouped into categories, and all products in a single category use the same template, you can use the category to determine what template to use when building the catalog pages.

✦ A more direct method is to add a property named "DetailTemplate" (or something similar) to *every product type* in your catalog. When you create new products, this property can then be populated with the filename of the template to use for that product. When you create the property, you can specify a default template filename that will serve for the majority of your products, thus simplifying data entry. This is the method that I recommend using, because it offers the most flexibility.

Generating the pages

The final step is to create a Visual Basic utility (or script) that creates the static pages. This utility can be scheduled to run automatically during a low-traffic period. The basic workflow for the utility is as follows:

1. Query all changed products from the *catalogname_CatalogProducts* table. You do this by executing a query much like the following:

```
SELECT * FROM catalogname_CatalogProducts WHERE Changed = 1
AND
CategoryName IS NULL ORDER BY DetailTemplate
```

This query ensures that only products, not categories, that have changed are selected. This does assume that you have created a DetailTemplate property, assigned it to each product type, and populated it with the filename of the template to use for each product.

Note

Although I normally recommend against using SELECT *, in this case it is usually preferred. Although SQL Server performs somewhat faster if you provide an explicit list of column names, the *catalogname_CatalogProducts* table contains varying columns, depending on the product properties that it must contain. SELECT * becomes the most efficient way to make sure that you get them all.

2. After the preceding query has returned a recordset, reset the Changed column. This ensures that any changes that occur while the utility is running will be caught in the next pass. This reset requires a simple query:

```
UPDATE catalogname_CatalogProducts SET Changed = 0 WHERE
Changed = 1
```

3. Begin working through the recordset. For each row in the recordset:

   a. Use the DetailTemplate column (or whatever you named the column) to determine which template file to load.

   b. Determine if that template file is already loaded. If it isn't, load it into a variable. By specifying an ORDER BY DetailTemplate clause in the original query, you can avoid constantly loading template files, saving a great deal of time.

   c. After the template file is in a variable, start inserting the appropriate information for the current product. Only insert values that are not Null, because not all products will share all of the properties that the table provides.

> **d.** Save the modified variable as a product detail file, and move on to the next product.

You may choose to implement this utility as a VBScript that runs on your SQL Server. Your output files are written to your Application Center staging server, which takes care of deploying the pages to each Web server in your server farm. Listing 11-7 shows a sample script, which you will need to modify with the appropriate table, server, and file names.

Listing 11-7: **Script to generate static detail pages**

```
'assumes oCn is a valid connection object
'get products
Dim Rs
Set Rs = Cn.Execute("sp_GetChangedProducts")

'reset product changes
Cn.Execute("sp_ResetProductChanges")

'create a filesystemobject
Dim FSO
Set FSO = CreateObject("Scripting.FileSystemObject")

'create variable for template file
Dim sTemplate, sTemplateName, Ts, sCopy

'create working variables
Dim sCol, sVal, sFile

'Walk thru products
Do Until Rs.Eof
 'If the template for this product
 'is different from the one loaded,
 'then load it.
 If Rs("DetailTemplate") <> sTemplateName Then
  sTemplateName = Rs("DetailTemplate")
  Set Ts = FSO.OpenTextFile(sTemplateName)
  STemplate = Ts.ReadAll
  Ts.Close
 End If

 'Make a copy of the template
 sCopy = sTemplate

 'Insert non-null values from product
 'into the template - modify these to
```

```
'match your properties
Dim x
For x = 13 To Rs.Fields.Count - 1
 If Not IsNull(Rs(x)) Then
  'get column name and value
  sCol = Rs(x).Name
  sVal = Rs(sCol)

  'replace value in template
  sCopy = Replace(sCopy,"x" & sCol & "x",sVal)
 End If
Next

'save the file - modify the path
'as appropriate to point to your
'staging server
sFile = "\\Staging\ProdPages\" & Rs("oid") & ".asp"
Set Ts = FSO.CreateTextFile(sFile,True)
Ts.Write sCopy
Ts.Close

'next product
Rs.MoveNext
Loop
```

You can also use this code as the basis for a Visual Basic DLL or executable, which can be scheduled by using the Windows Task Scheduler.

 Tip   A compiled Visual Basic utility executes faster than a VBScript.

Note that the script attempts to insert values for every product property contained in the table, unless the property's value in the current product is Null. Column 13 of the *catalogname_CatalogProducts* table begins the property values, and the script simply tries all of them. This makes the script very flexible, so you shouldn't need to update it when new product types with different properties are added to the catalog.

If your product catalog contains product families with variants—and you want those variants to be represented as drop-down list boxes in your templates (for example, a main detail page for a book with a drop-down list box to select a binding type)—then you'll need to modify the script to accommodate those products. As is, this script treats each variant as an individual product and creates a page for it.

Also note that the script uses stored procedures to execute its queries; the stored procedures are shown in Listings 11-8 and 11-9, below. Implementing these queries as stored procedures allows SQL Server to execute them more efficiently.

Listing 11-8: Stored procedure sp_ResetProductChanges

```
CREATE PROCEDURE sp_ResetProductChanges
 AS
 UPDATE catalogname_CatalogProducts SET Changed = 0 WHERE
 Changed = 1
GO
```

Listing 11-9: Stored procedure sp_GetChangedProducts

```
CREATE PROCEDURE sp_GetChangedProducts
 AS
 SELECT * FROM catalogname_CatalogProducts
 WHERE Changed = 1
 AND CategoryName IS NULL
 ORDER BY DetailTemplate
GO
```

Customizing and improving

The scripts and stored procedures provided here will need to be customized to match your environment. You can also improve the functionality and reliability of the scripts by adding error-handling code; I've deliberately left the error-handling code out to make the scripts' primary functionality clear. In particular, the operations dealing with file input and output should include error-handling, in case the template file doesn't exist, in case the script is unable to lock the output file for writing, and so forth. You can even include code to write Event Log messages when errors occur, making monitoring this utility as part of your daily maintenance routine easier.

You can make other improvements, including:

✦ Modify the script to support product families and variants, as described previously.

✦ Modify the script to include suggested-sell items. You can generate a recordset of related products by querying the *catalogname*_Relationships table, and providing the oid of the product for the from_oid column. The resulting list of to_oid columns will contain product IDs for related products.

✦ Modify the template to include the correct code to add products to the customer's shopping cart (which is described in more detail in the next chapter).

Some of these improvements are easier to make if you work with the product information by using Commerce Server's objects, rather than by querying the database directly. The price that you pay for the ease of use is increased server overhead that's required to manage the COM objects; for complex catalogs the flexibility is more than worth the cost, especially if the COM components are implemented on a COM+ cluster by using Application Center.

Listing 11-10 is a VBScript that combines the two techniques for accessing product data. It uses a query (executed in a stored procedure) to retrieve the product IDs of the products that have changed, sorted by template (assuming that the column names are still Changed and DetailTemplate). It then uses Commerce Server's COM objects to access the product data and create the final output pages. In this example, the price is inserted statically into the file, which is a technique that you can use if your pricing doesn't change frequently. This script detects variants and creates a drop-down list box instead of the price. The drop-down box lists all of the variant combinations and their prices.

Note If you prefer to use Visual Basic to create a compiled executable, the code below can be used as the basis for a Visual Basic Sub Main() routine.

Listing 11-10: Improved script to generate static pages

```
<%
'assumes cn is a valid connection object
'get a recordset of changed products
Dim Rs
Set Rs = Cn.Execute("sp_GetChangedProducts")

'reset product changes
Cn.Execute("sp_ResetProductChanges")

'create a filesystemobject
Dim FSO
Set FSO = CreateObject("Scripting.FileSystemObject")

'create variable for template file
Dim sTemplate, sTemplateName, Ts, sCopy

'create working variables
Dim sCol, sVal, sFile, sVars
Dim Pcat, CM, Prod, Vrs, ProdProps

'get the catalog manager
'assumes sCMConfig is a valid config string
Set CM = CreateObject("Commerce.CatalogManager")
CM.Initialize sCMConfig, True

'Get the product catalog
Set Pcat = CM.GetCatalog("catalogname")
```

Continued

Listing 11-10 *(continued)*

```
'Walk thru products
Do Until Rs.Eof
 'If the template for this product
 'is different from the one loaded,
 'then load it.
 If Rs("DetailTemplate") <> sTemplateName Then
  sTemplateName = Rs("DetailTemplate")
  Set Ts = FSO.OpenTextFile(sTemplateName)
  STemplate = Ts.ReadAll
  Ts.Close
 End If

 'Make a copy of the template
 sCopy = sTemplate

 'Get the product & its properties
 Set Prod = Pcat.GetProduct(rs("productid"))
 Set ProdProps = Prod.GetProductProperties

 'Variants?
 Set Vrs = Prod.Variants
 If Vrs.EOF And Vrs.BOF Then

  'no variants - get price
  sVars = "Price: $" & ProdProps("cy_list_price")

 Else

  'variants - instead of a price,
  'build a list box
  sVars = "<SELECT NAME='Variant' SIZE=1>"
  Do Until Vrs.EOF
   sVars = sVars & "<OPTION VALUE='"

   'get the unique ID for this variant
   SVars = sVars & Vrs(3)

   'add the variants
   For x = 4 to Vrs.Fields.Count - 1
    If Not IsNull(Vrs(x)) Then
     SVars = sVars & Vrs(x) & " / "
    End If
   Next x

   'finish list tag
   sVars = sVars & "'>"
   sVars = sVars & "$" & Vrs("cy_list_price")
   sVars = sVars & "</OPTION>" & vbCrLf
   Vrs.MoveNext
  Loop
  SVars = sVars & "</SELECT>" & vbCrLf
```

```
  End If

  'Replace the price placeholder
  'with either the price or the
  'variant drop-down
  sCopy = Replace(sCopy, "xPricex", sVars)

  'replace other common fields
  sCopy = Replace(sCopy,"xProductIDx",Rs("productID"))

  'replace non-null properties
  For x = 13 to Rs.Fields.Count - 1
   If Not IsNull(Rs(x)) Then
    sCopy = Replace(sCopy,Rs(x).name,Rs(x))
   End If
  Next

  'save the file - modify the path
  'as appropriate to point to your
  'staging server
  sFile = "\\Staging\ProdPages\" & Rs("oid") & ".asp"
  Set Ts = FSO.CreateTextFile(sFile,True)
  Ts.Write sCopy
  Ts.Close

  'next product
  Rs.MoveNext
Loop

%>
```

This listing used a revised sp_GetChangedProducts stored procedure, which is shown in Listing 11-11. Rather than retrieving all of the information, this stored procedure just retrieves the product ID in order of DetailTemplate. The sp_ResetProductChanges stored procedure, also used in the above script, is unchanged from the prior example.

Listing 11-11: **Revised sp_GetChangesProducts**

```
CREATE PROCEDURE sp_GetChangedProducts
 AS
 SELECT DISTINCT productid,DetailTemplate FROM
catalogname_CatalogProducts
 WHERE Changed = 1
 AND CategoryName IS NULL ORDER BY DetailTemplate
GO
```

Note the use of SELECT DISTINCT in the query. This assures that only one row will be returned for each product. For non-variant products, this presents no difference. For variant products, only one of the variants will be returned.

This revised script uses Commerce Server's product management object for improved performance and easier code maintenance. The script uses a straight Transact-SQL query to retrieve the updated products from the database. It also uses a flexible placeholder fill-in system that allows it to be used with a variety of templates, and it writes out products to completely static HTML files (assuming that your template contains no ASP code), for maximum Web server performance.

Summary

Creating your product catalog requires a lot of planning. You have to make sure your catalog will include the basic information you need for every product, as well as information specific to different types of products you may carry. Commerce Server's data-driven catalog system gives you the amount of flexibility you will need to create catalogs that suit your business' needs.

Once your catalogs have been created, you'll need to populate them. While importing data from another source may seem straightforward, the inability of common file formats (such as CSV files) to represent a hierarchical product taxonomy can make your data import more difficult than necessary. Consider importing catalog data from an XML-formatted source, such as the data provided by BizTalk Server, to import large quantities of data with relatively little fuss.

✦   ✦   ✦

Developing the Customer Experience – Creating the Shopping Cart

◆ ◆ ◆ ◆

In This Chapter

The built-in shopping cart

Optimizing your cart design

Best practices carts

Handling discount campaigns

◆ ◆ ◆ ◆

The shopping cart is one of the most important sections of your site. In addition to your checkout process, the cart is what enables customers to purchase things from you, and is what makes your entire online business work. Keep in mind that your shopping cart can do a lot more than just enable customers to buy from you — it can also suggest new items for them to buy, enable strategic incentive programs such as discounts, and much more.

The Commerce Server Cart

Although I don't necessarily recommend that you use the shopping cart code that comes with the Retail Solution Site, it is important to understand how this pipeline is built and what it does, because it represents "the Microsoft way" to construct a shopping cart.

The main body of the cart code in the Retail Solution Site is included in two ASP pages, _additem.asp and basket.asp (and the bevy of include files that each of them reference). These pages work together to form the basic Commerce Server shopping cart. Product pages (or any other page that needs to add something to the cart) pass parameters to _additem.asp, which kicks off the shopping cart process:

1. The _additem.asp page builds a dictionary object with the item ID and quantity of the item to add to the basket.

2. The dictionary object is then added to the OrderForm object that is maintained for the shopper, and contains all of the items that the customer has ordered.

3. The page then redirects to basket.asp, which runs the basket.pcf pipeline and renders the basket to the screen.

Basket.asp is responsible for displaying the basket. The vast majority of the page's work is handled by basket.pcf, a transacted Commerce Server pipeline. Basket.pcf is one of the more complicated pipelines, containing the following ten stages:

1. Product Info Stage

   a. QueryCatalogInfo component: This component is responsible for querying the product catalog and retrieving the product information for each item in the order form. It flags any items that can't be found in the database.

   b. RequiredProdInfo component: This component removes any items that were flagged by the QueryCatalogInfo component.

2. Merchant Info Stage (this stage contains no components in the Retail Solution Site; it is intended to look up information about the merchant for future use.)

3. Shopper Info Stage (this stage contains no components in the Retail Solution Site; it is intended to look up information about the shopper for future use.)

4. Order Initialization Stage

   a. RequiredOrderInitCy: This component initializes each of the items' pricing information to zero or Null, as appropriate.

5. Order Check Stage

6. Item Price Stage

   a. DefaultItemPriceCy: This component copies the regular item price, as retrieved by QueryCatalogInfo, to the regular pricing section of the order form.

   b. RequiredItemPriceCy: This component verifies that each item in the order form now has a regular price assigned. If an item is missing a price, the pipeline terminates with an error.

7. Item Adjust Price Stage

   a. RequiredItemAdjustPriceCy: This component verifies that each item has an adjusted price. If an item doesn't have an adjusted price, the regular price is copied into the adjusted price. The component also verifies that the price of the item, as copied from the database, matches the price that the item carried when it was placed into the order form. If the price doesn't match, an error is raised.

8. Order Adjust Price Stage

    a. OrderDiscount: This component selects the discounts that apply to each item of the order form and populates the order form with discount information.

    b. RequiredOrderAdjustPriceCy: This component calculates the total price for each line item (regular price times quantity purchased), the adjusted price (the total price less discounts added by the OrderDiscount component), and the total discount (total regular price less adjusted price).

9. Order Subtotal Stage

    a. DefaultOrderSubTotalCy: This component adds the adjusted prices of all items and creates a subtotal for the order form.

    b. RequiredOrderSubTotalCy: This component verifies that the subtotal has been populated. If the subtotal hasn't been populated, an error is raised.

10. Inventory Stage (this stage contains no components in the Retail Solution Site; it is intended to query and update inventory information in the database.)

From a functionality standpoint, this pipeline is fairly complete. From an operational standpoint, however, basket.pcf has two major problems:

✦ Every time the basket is displayed, each item's information is queried from the database. This creates a tremendous amount of database traffic that isn't really necessary. For example, although verifying the current price of an item is important—because technically savvy shoppers could conceivably write code to insert items into their basket at a discounted price—it doesn't need to be done each time the basket is displayed.

✦ Every time the basket is displayed, the pipeline has to run through a complete selection of applicable discounts. If your site has hundreds of discount campaigns in effect (not unusual for a busy site), and a customer's basket has a couple dozen items in it, then this discount selection process can take a noticeable amount of time, which causes your baskets to display slowly.

Here are some suggestions for modifying the way that this pipeline works to reduce overhead:

✦ When a customer adds a product to his or her cart, place *all* of the necessary product information into the cart. This allows the pipeline to run without querying the database for the information. The "add to cart" button can be linked to a form that has hidden form fields with the necessary product information.

✦ To guard against sneaky customers, write a component that verifies all of the information in the cart, especially pricing, before the order is placed. However, don't place this component in a pipeline that runs every time the basket is displayed, because that would create unnecessary overhead on your servers.

Discounts are a little harder to work with because Commerce Server offers so much flexibility. For basic product discounts, such as a straight 10 percent off everything in a certain category, your product detail pages can include the discount information in hidden form fields. This allows the "add to basket" code to add the necessary discount information without a database hit (assuming that your product pages are static pages generated by a utility application).

For more complex discounts, such as "buy two of 'x' and receive one of 'y' at 10 percent off," you have almost no way to keep the basket display updated without hitting the database each time the basket is displayed. A customer can add one of "y" to their basket, add two of "z," and then add two of "x." Only after the two "x" products are added does the discount suddenly apply, so you need to check that every time. The only way to eliminate the overhead involved in constant discount calculations, or at least reduce the overhead, is to leave the OrderAdjustPrice stage out of the pipeline. In your basket display, include a message stating that "these prices do not reflect discounts which may be available." Offer a button that shoppers can click to see the pricing updated with discounts, and link that button to the full pipeline.

Improving the performance of the cart takes one of two forms:

✦ Use a bare-bones pipeline for cart display, thus reducing overhead by placing information statically into the order form and then checking it before checkout.

✦ Make sure that your pipeline components are running on fast machines and that you have enough of them to handle the traffic generated by your customers.

A Cart Full of Compromises

Building a shopping cart presents an enormous number of decisions and compromises in Commerce Server.

Build versus buy

Should you build your own shopping cart from scratch, or use Commerce Server's shopping cart components, such as the basket pipeline included with the Solution Sites?

The disadvantage of the pipelines, of course, is increased overhead and database traffic that can potentially be avoided. However, because Commerce Server doesn't offer much flexibility in the way baskets work, choosing to not use portions of the basket pipeline means that you can't use any of it (with some exceptions that I discuss in a bit).

The advantage of Commerce Server's basket pipeline is its robust feature set, which calculates discounts by using Commerce Server's complex campaign system, verifies prices, applies discounts, and calculates a subtotal. The feature set can be expanded with your own components to look up inventory levels to offer customers information on when the products that they are ordering will probably ship. Commerce Server's basket pipeline also has the benefit of being well tested by Microsoft, so it basically works "out of the box."

You do have the option of building your own pipeline, but you can't really use components created in Visual Basic. So unless you're planning to write pipeline components in Visual C++ — a lengthy task that most e-commerce companies simply don't have the resources for — you're stuck with using slower-to-execute Scriptor components.

You do have the option of a middle road, where you build your own lightweight pipeline for primary basket use, and use Commerce Server's basket pipeline as a "final check" of customers' baskets prior to checking out. Carefully done, this can represent a "best of both worlds" approach.

Persisting the cart

A problem inherent to Web-based applications is the lack of persistence between user connections. Each Web page is essentially a complete customer experience; no data is natively carried over between pages. Technologies such as cookies and the ASP Session and Application objects (which are built on cookies) allow the illusion of data persistence by identifying the customer on each return "hit" and retrieving their data from a cookie or from a back-end database.

Natively, Commerce Server relies on cookies to identify customers on successive hits to your site. Commerce Server can also be used, albeit more painstakingly, to pass the customers' unique identifiers in URLs, thus reducing the need for cookies.

The customer's shopping cart is perhaps one of the most important sets of data that must be carried throughout the customer's session on your site. Commerce Server builds the cart in an OrderForm object, which can be saved to the database as a *basket*. When the order is completed, the OrderForm object is saved again as an *order*. The OrderForm object provides methods for saving the object to the database, and for loading a previously created basket from the database. This allows the cart to be reloaded from the database whenever necessary.

Working with the cart

The Commerce Server OrderGroup object stores shopping cart data. Each OrderGroup can have one or more OrderForm objects that actually store the items in the cart. Typically, an OrderGroup has only one OrderForm. However, OrderForms are catalog-specific. If a customer is ordering from multiple catalogs, there will be one OrderForm per catalog in the OrderGroup.

The OrderForm object consists of a specially structured set of Dictionary and SimpleList objects that store information about the cart, as well as information about the items in the cart.

Cart maintenance

You can persist information in a Web application in three ways. The first way is to store the information in a cookie. This is suitable for small pieces of data, but not for a shopping cart, which can be quite large. The second way is to store the information in an ASP Session object. Shopping carts are often too large to be reliably stored in a Session object, and Session objects present problems in a large Web farm. The final way is to store the information in a database, and use a cookie to store a unique identifier. The unique ID can then be used to match a customer to the cart information stored in the database.

This last method is the way Commerce Server works. The downside to this approach is that the shopping cart data eventually builds up in the database because Commerce Server never deletes it. You need to make sure that you develop a means of removing old, unused shopping carts. You may choose to delete them after a few hours, after a few days, or some other period of time; whatever you choose, make sure that you implement automated maintenance routines to prevent your shopping carts from filling up your database server. These routines can be implemented as a SQL Server Agent job, a Visual Basic utility, or whatever is convenient in your environment.

The OrderForm object has only three methods:

✦ The `ClearItems` method removes all items in the cart.

✦ The `ClearOrderForm` method clears the order form completely.

✦ The `AddItem` method is used to add an item to the cart by product ID.

The OrderGroup object has a much larger number of properties and methods that allow you to work with the items and information in each OrderForm. The OrderGroup object also stores global information, such as customer billing information for the order.

If you do things "the Microsoft way," you follow these steps:

1. Use the `AddItem` method of an OrderForm object to add product IDs to the cart. This *only* adds the product ID; pricing information is not filled in.

2. Run the basket pipeline (also called the *plan*) to update all of the fields in the OrderForm object, such as price and discount information, to reflect the changes.

3. Display the basket to the customer and allow them to check out or continue shopping.

One way to avoid running the pipeline (and its overhead and database hits) every time an item is added to the basket is to manually add all of a product's information to the OrderForm object. This allows you to immediately display the basket without running the pipeline, although certain pieces of information, such as certain types of discounts, won't be updated.

The Retailer.com Cart

Your site's design plan should include details on how your site's shopping cart should behave, and what features it should provide. This book's sample business-to-consumer company, Retailer.com, has the following specifications for its shopping cart:

✦ Adding an item to the cart should display the updated basket as quickly as possible. Ideally, adding items won't result in additional database access.

✦ Items added to the cart don't need to reflect any discount campaigns that apply. However, each item that *can* be in a discount campaign should be flagged in the basket. For example, if this site features a campaign that provides a 10 percent discount when a customer purchases three widgets, a flag should appear whenever a customer adds any number of widgets to their cart.

Customers should be able to click on this flag to pull up details about the available discount. This may encourage customers to take advantage of promotions that they didn't know about, and purchase the additional products necessary to obtain the discount.

✦ A notice in the checkout will inform customers that the cart may not reflect all available discounts. Discounts will be calculated and updated when the customer checks out.

✦ Anytime an item is added to the cart, it should be reviewed for related items. Up to three related items should be displayed for each item in the cart, along with "buy now" buttons, to encourage customers to add more products to their cart.

✦ When a customer checks out, all cart information should be verified against the database, and discounts calculated and applied. The customer has the opportunity to review the updated cart and continue with the checkout or continue shopping.

✦ Although many different catalogs will be available for different types of customers, they will all be custom catalogs based on a single product catalog. Therefore, no customer will be shopping from more than one catalog, meaning that each customer's basket (and OrderGroup) will contain only one OrderForm.

Building the cart for Retailer.com

Because Retailer.com has goals that conflict with the default pipelines provided by Microsoft, they will need a custom pipeline to process the items placed into their basket. They'll also need to place a great deal of additional data onto their product detail pages. Remember that their detail pages are being built during the off-hours by a utility application; the detail pages are basically static after that point.

Also, because of the way the company wants to handle discounts, they will need to modify the utility that produces these static pages to check for discounts that may apply to products. This will allow the static detail page to include a flag that indicates whether or not discounts are available for a particular product, enabling the "click here for discount information" link that the company wants included in the basket.

Retailer.com will still implement the full pipeline provided by Microsoft in a "confirm your basket" phase that comprises the beginning of the checkout. This will ensure that everything in the basket has the correct pricing and discounts before the checkout begins.

Retailer.com has created a new prototype shopping cart page, which is shown in Figure 12-1.

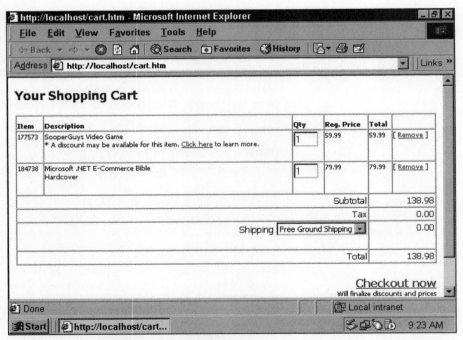

Figure 12-1: Prototype shopping cart page

Providing information on product detail pages

The first step in making this shopping cart work is to provide a great deal of information on the static detail pages, which can be passed to the ASP page that adds items to the cart. The technique that you use for adding this information is the same technique that I discussed previously, when I showed you how to build a static product detail page. You simply need to have the utility (that is building the pages) query more information and write it as hidden form fields on the product detail page. The "add to cart" button on each page then acts as an HTML submit button, submitting the detail page to the ASP page that adds the item to the cart. All of the hidden form fields are then passed to the ASP page, allowing it to construct the cart without hitting the database.

The information needed on the product detail page includes the following:

✦ Unique product ID

✦ A flag indicating whether or not this product is participating in any discounts

✦ Product's regular price

✦ Product's short description, as well as any variants that are selected when the "buy now" button is clicked

Some of this information is readily available. For example, the description of any variants, as well as the variant's unique identifier, is already built into the static page in the form of a drop-down box by the utility that builds the static pages. The product's short description, or *name*, is also readily available and can be inserted into a hidden form field by using a placeholder. The product's regular price is also easily obtained by using the Product object when you are building the static pages.

The most difficult piece of information to obtain is whether or not the product is participating in any discounts. Commerce Server doesn't provide a flag anywhere in its database to indicate that a product is discounted. Commerce Server is designed to run a pipeline component to select the available promotions, filter for the promotions that a particular product is involved in, score the promotions based on relevance, and finally select a promotion. This process will provide the promotions and promotional pricing for a product, but at this stage you don't need that much information.

The key lies in understanding how Commerce Server handles discounts—it supports complex discount expressions, such as "Buy three of product X, get two of product Y at 10 percent off," or "Buy one of product X, get any additional product X at 20 percent off." Discounts must be part of a *campaign*, and must be assigned to a customer. Figure 12-2 shows the Commerce Server Business Desk's Campaign Manager module, with a single customer representing your company ("Internal"), a single ad campaign, and a single discount as part of that campaign.

Figure 12-3 shows the properties of the campaign's discount. In this case, any customer purchasing one of the designated products will receive a 10 percent discount on any additional quantity of that same product. They will also receive a 10 percent discount on the first unit that they purchase, indicated by the "Apply offer on both Get and Buy products" radio button.

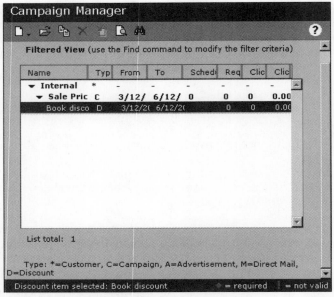

Figure 12-2: The Campaign Manager

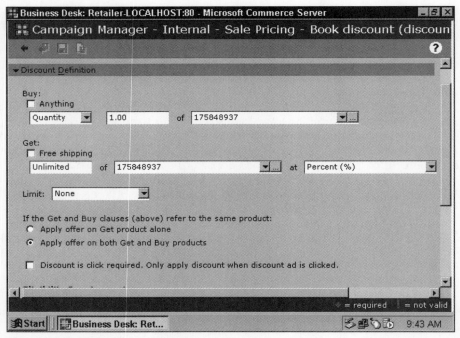

Figure 12-3: Discount properties

The Campaign System

Commerce Server's Campaign System is one of the most complex components of the product. Because it's responsible not only for discounts, but also for direct mail and advertising functions, you should have a basic understanding of how its database tables are structured.

The Campaign System consists of about two dozen tables, which are heavily cross-referenced with foreign key constraints. They include:

✦ Ad_item: Stores scheduled advertising content, describing when ads run. Also stores codes linking the ad to the products that it represents.

✦ Campaign: Defines a single campaign, including who the campaign is for (the "customer") and when it runs.

✦ Campaign_item: Describes the content of a campaign. Campaigns can include different types of content, including ads and discounts.

✦ Campaign_item_types: Lookup table describing the various types of content that a campaign can include.

✦ Campaign_version: Specifies the version of the campaign information. The campaign system is extensible, and extensions are registered in this table along with their versions.

✦ Creative: Contains template information on how an advertisement or discount should be displayed on a Web page.

✦ Creative_property: A lookup table listing the various properties that describe an entry in the Creative table.

✦ Creative_property_value: A join table between the Creative and Creative_property tables; contains the values for various properties associated with a campaign item.

✦ Creative_size: Describes the physical proportions required by a given creative.

✦ Creative_type: Contains formatting information for displaying creatives.

✦ Creative_type_xref: Determines which creative templates are available for each type of campaign item.

✦ Dm_item: Contains information on scheduled direct mail items, such as addresses and formatting instructions.

✦ Event_type: Categorizes marketing events.

✦ Industry_code: A lookup table of industry codes. By assigning campaign items like ads to one or more industry codes, the content selection system can avoid showing multiple items for the same industry (from different customers) on the same page, thus reducing "content conflicts."

Continued

Continued

✦ Order_discount: Defines discounted sale items, including data on how the discount is achieved and what the conditions of the sale are.

✦ Order_discount_expression: Identifies the eligibility requirement expressions for complex discounts.

✦ Page_group: Represents a group of content items used in a marketing campaign.

✦ Page_group_xref: Cross-references page groups with Web pages or sets of Web pages that contain the content.

✦ Performance_total: Stores total counts for events, such as clicks and requests for campaign items.

✦ Target: Defines a target audience for custom content and direct marketing, such as a particular type of user.

✦ Target_group: Defines a group of targets for delivering custom content and marketing materials.

✦ Target_group_xref: Determines which content is delivered to which target groups.

As you can see, the campaign system includes a great deal of complex, interrelated data. Although Commerce Server provides objects to make working with this data easier, understanding the underlying schema can help you make better design decisions when programming your site.

The actual discount is defined in the order_discount table of the Commerce Server database. The actual *conditions* of the discount — what must be purchased and what the award is — are defined in this table as well, although in a somewhat roundabout fashion. Order_discount includes a column named "I_disc_cond_expr," which contains the identifier for the *expression* that specifies the requirements of the discount — "Buy X," "Buy Y," and so forth. A second column, named "I_disc_award_expr," contains the expression for the award — "Get W" or "Get Z." These columns do *not* contain product IDs; instead, they contain expression IDs. The expressions are defined in a table named "ES_ExprInfo." The ExprName column of this table includes the product identifier. Unfortunately, you can't just query ES_ExprInfo because it also contains expressions for products that are part of expired discounts. Additionally, you have to refer to the Campaign_Items table to determine which campaign items are marked as active, and which are within their lifespan.

To determine if a product is part of an *active* discount, you need a somewhat complex query. It's best to implement this query as a stored procedure, as shown in Listing 12-1.

Listing 12-1: **Stored procedure sp_IsProductInDiscount**

```
CREATE PROCEDURE sp_IsProductInDiscount
 @productID nvarchar(30),
 @YesNo bit OUTPUT
AS

/* Default to "not in discount" */
SELECT @YesNo = 0

DECLARE @c1 int
DECLARE @c2 int

/* Find out how many this is
   the BUY for */
SET @c1 = (SELECT COUNT(i_disc_id)
 FROM order_discount o
 INNER JOIN
ES_ExprInfo i
 ON o.i_disc_cond_expr =
 i.ExprID
 INNER JOIN ES_ExprProfDeps p
 ON p.ExprID = i.ExprID
 INNER JOIN
Campaign_Items c
 ON c.i_campitem_id =
 o.i_campitem_id
 WHERE i.ExprName = @productid
 AND
 p.ProfDep = 'Product'
 AND
 c.campitem_active = 1
 AND GETDATE()
BETWEEN c.campitem_start
 AND
 c.campitem_end)

/* Find out how many this is
   the GET for */
SET @c2 = (SELECT COUNT(i_disc_id)
 FROM order_discount o
 INNER JOIN
ES_ExprInfo i
 ON o.i_disc_award_expr =
i.ExprID
 INNER JOIN ES_ExprProfDeps p
 ON p.ExprID = i.ExprID
 INNER JOIN
 Campaign_Items c
 ON c.i_campitem_id =
 o.i_campitem_id
```

Continued

Listing 12-1 *(continued)*

```
 WHERE i.ExprName = @productid
 AND
p.ProfDep = 'Product'
 AND
 p.ProfDep = 'Product'
 AND
 c.campitem_active = 1
 AND GETDATE()
BETWEEN c.campitem_start
 AND
c.campitem_end)

/* Set YesNo */
IF @c1 > 0 OR @c2 > 0
  SET @YesNo = 1
SELECT @YesNo
```

Sp_IsProductInDiscount accepts a product ID, and returns a 1 if the product is found to be part of an active discount. This stored procedure returns a 1 if the product specified is in the "buy" or "get" part of the discount. Note that the product in the "buy" portion of the discount, or the requirement to receive the discount, doesn't necessarily have a discount applied to it. This is fine for Retailer.com's purposes, because they want the customers to be alerted to the fact that by purchasing one product, they are qualified for a discount on a completely different product.

You can use this stored procedure in your utility that creates the static product detail pages. Listing 12-2 shows a code sample for using the stored procedure to write out a hidden form field indicating whether or not discounts are present.

Listing 12-2: Writing a discount flag

```
<INPUT TYPE="HIDDEN" NAME="DISCOUNTS" VALUE="
<%

' assumes cn is a connection
' assumes Pid has product ID
Set Rs = Cn.Execute("sp_IsProductInDiscount '" & Pid & "'")
Response.Write Rs(0)

%>
">
```

Build Your Own Discounts?

I've worked with a couple of companies who decided to ignore Commerce Server's complex campaign system in favor of a simpler system that met their needs. For example, one business-to-consumer e-commerce company already had a very powerful direct e-mail software package that enabled them to perform much more targeted and personalized bulk mailings with less overhead than Commerce Server. Their site didn't use advertising of any kind, so that portion of the Commerce Server campaign system wasn't necessary. Finally, their discount needs were very different from the discount system provided by Commerce Server.

Because the other two major pieces of the campaign system — advertising and direct mail — weren't needed, the company decided to scrap Commerce Server's campaign system entirely and build their own replacement discount system. The system was much simpler, and allowed them to create time-sensitive per-item discounts and "Buy one, Get one" type discounts in just a couple of tables.

The benefit was a much simpler, easier-to-understand discount system that precisely met their needs. The disadvantage was the additional development required. The Business Desk's Campaign Manager was removed and replaced with a custom discount management module, and several pipeline components had to be rewritten in Visual C++ to accommodate their revised discount architecture.

The moral of this story is simple: If Commerce Server doesn't meet your needs out of the box, then consider doing your own thing.

By including this code in your static detail page creation utility, you can have each product detail page include enough information to add products to the customer's shopping cart without having to run a complex pipeline and without having to hit the database.

Note   As with the other information generated by your static page creation utility, the discount information can be out of date. If you are relying on a field in your CatalogProducts table to trigger the regeneration of a product detail page, you will need to apply the same trigger to the order_discounts table to ensure that discount changes trigger the regeneration of the product's detail page.

Adding items to the cart

After your product detail pages have been created and include all the necessary information, you're ready to start actually building a shopping cart for your customers. Each product detail page should essentially be constructed as a big HTML form, with the "add to cart" button acting as the submit button for the form. The form should contain sufficient hidden input fields to carry the necessary product data to the "add to cart" ASP page.

The purpose of the "add to cart" ASP page, which I named "cart.asp," is to accept the input from a product detail page and add the intended product to the shopping cart. It should then display the cart for the customer. The page should also include basic functionality to change cart quantities or remove items from the cart, continue shopping, or proceed to the checkout.

As I discussed in Chapter 3, the cart page can use DHTML to provide instant feedback for certain changes, such as changing the shipping method of an order and immediately recalculating the order total. However, in order to keep the examples in this section as clear as possible, I won't use this method. Instead, each change to the cart will resubmit the page to the server for changes to be calculated. If you prefer to implement some functions in DHTML, you can replace the necessary sections of code with client-side scripts.

Listing 12-3 shows the first part of cart.asp.

Listing 12-3: **Cart.asp**

```
<%

'------------------------------------
' PART I - OBJECTS
'------------------------------------
'declare & create objects
Set oOrderGroup = CreateObject("Commerce.OrderGroup)


'------------------------------------
' PART II - INIT ORDER GROUP
'------------------------------------
'get user's GUID from cookie
'and initialize order group
'assumes we're using cookies; if cookie
'is empty need to add code to create an
'anonymous profile to use
'also assumes dsn is a valid database
'connection string
If Request.Cookies("GUID") = ""
  'take action for anonymous user; need
  'a GUID for a user profile
Else
  oOrderGroup.Initialize dsn, Request.Cookies("GUID")
End If


'------------------------------------
' PART III - LOAD CART
'------------------------------------
'load current cart from database
'or create a new one if not found
oOrderGroup.LoadBasket
```

```
'--------------------------------
' PART IV - TAKE ACTION
'--------------------------------
'determine what action is being taken
'based on ACTION parameter
Select Case Request("action")
 Case "add"
  'adding an item to the cart
  AddItem
  Recalc

 Case "remove"
  'removing an item
  RemoveItem
  Recalc

 Case "recalc"
  'changed qty, shipping, etc.
  'need to recalc basket
  Recalc

 Case Else
  'just displaying the cart
  'no subroutine needed

End Select

'--------------------------------
' PART V - SAVE CART
'--------------------------------
'save cart to database
oOrderGroupID = OrderGroup.SaveAsBasket


'--------------------------------
' PART VI - SUBROUTINES
'--------------------------------
Sub AddItem()
 'build dictionary object with
 'line item to add
 Set oDict = CreateObject("Commerce.Dictionary")

 'note that the product detail page must
 'pass in these parameters
 oDict.product_catalog = Request("product_catalog")
 oDict.product_id = Request("product_id")
 oDict.product_variant = Request("product_variant")
 oDict.quantity = Request("quantity")
 oDict.cy_unit_price = Request("cy_unit_price")
 oDict.description = Request("Description")
 oDict._discountsapply = Request("Discounts")
```

Continued

Listing 12-3 *(continued)*

```
'calculate line item total
Dim LineTotal
LineTotal=Request("cy_unit_price")*Request("quantity")
oDict.cy_liuneitem_total = LineTotal

'add it
oOrderGroup.AddItem oDict
End Sub

Sub RemoveItem()
 'any remove item links pass a RemoveIndex
 'parameter including the index of the item
 'to remove.
 oOrderGroup.RemoveItem Request("RemoveIndex")
End Sub

Sub Recalc()
 'either run a custom pipeline to calculate
 'new total & shipping charges, or calculate
 'these values in script and modify the order
 'group's data appropriately.

 'The OrderGroup's total_lineitems key is
 'auto-updated by the AddItem/RemoveItem
 'methods; the subtotal, shipping, and total
 'must be calculated.
End Sub


'-----------------------------------
'End of code - ready to display cart
'using HTML
%>
```

Note   Because carts can be complex, and because they require interaction with so many Commerce Server components, I've tried to simplify this sample to show the pieces specific to the cart. You shouldn't take this example as a "cut and paste" example, but rather as a guide to how your cart can be built.

I've included comment lines to help break this script down into parts for discussion.

✦ **Part I** declares the objects and variables that the script will be using.

✦ **Part II** initializes the OrderGroup object. As I discussed previously, the OrderGroup object represents the customer's shopping cart. The Initialize method requires a valid Commerce Server user ID, which is a Globally Unique Identifier (GUID). You can save this value to a cookie when a user logs in, or when a new user profile object is created. In any event, you need the GUID to initialize the shopping cart.

✦ **Part III** instructs the OrderGroup object to load any previously created basket (shopping cart) associated with that user. If none are found, a new basket/cart is created in memory.

✦ **Part IV** examines the value of the "action" parameter. In the product detail page, this is included as a hidden field with the value "add." This Select...Case structure allows this single ASP page to be used for adding and removing items from the cart, as well as for updating the cart's quantities. The construct calls an appropriate subroutine. Note that the Recalc subroutine, which is intended to calculate order totals, tax, shipping, and so forth, is also called after items are added or removed.

✦ **Part V** saves the cart back to the database after it has been modified appropriately and the Recalc subroutine has run. This allows the cart to persist, so that the user can continue adding items to it. Until this step is taken, all changes to the cart are strictly in memory and will be lost after the ASP page finishes executing.

✦ **Part VI** contains the subroutines that perform the bulk of the work.

   1. The AddItem subroutine creates a new Dictionary object, and appends the values passed by the product detail page to the Dictionary.

   2. The Dictionary is then added as a line item to the current order.

   3. The RemoveItem subroutine removes an item, based on its item index, from the cart.

   4. Finally, the Recalc subroutine recalculates the order.

This sample cart can basically run a stripped-down version of the Commerce Server plan.pct pipeline template (implemented as basket.pcf in the Solution Site). You can also write a custom pipeline, or you can manually modify the OrderGroup object in memory by using script. Whatever you choose to do, you must recalculate any aggregates or totals displayed on your cart page, such as a subtotal, tax, shipping, and so forth. If your cart page doesn't contain any of this information and simply lists the items in the cart with their list prices, then no recalculation is necessary.

After this portion of the cart is complete, you can begin displaying the cart by using a mix of HTML and ASP code.

Checking for related items

One thing you may want to do when displaying your cart — especially if items were just added — is to display items that are related to products already in the cart, or related to the item just added. This encourages shoppers to consider purchasing additional items.

Note   Product relationships don't occur by themselves; you have to manually create these relationships by using the Business Desk's Catalog module, or write a completely separate utility that creates product relationships based on other customers' past shopping habits.

Assuming that you want to use related items like Retailer.com — displaying up to three related items whenever an item is added to the cart — you have two options for retrieving this information.

The first, most straightforward method is to issue a database query when the cart is displaying. The database query needs the internal product identifier of the item that was just added. You can restrict the results to three by specifying the TOP clause. Listing 12-4 shows the stored procedure sp_GetRelatedProducts that returns a recordset with the product information for related products, given an internal ID number for a product.

Listing 12-4: **Stored procedure sp_GetRelatedProducts**

```
CREATE PROCEDURE sp_GetRelatedProducts
 @oid int
AS
 SELECT TOP 3 *
 FROM catalogname_CatalogProducts c
 INNER JOIN catalogname_CatalogRelationships r
 ON c.oid = r.To_oid
 WHERE r.To_oid = @oid
GO
```

A variation of this technique is to create a reference to a Product object and use the first three rows in the recordset returned by its RelatedProducts property.

Although this method works fine, it does require an additional query against your database. The query is small, and the result set is small, but it's a hit nonetheless. The second way to retrieve related products may interest you if you're trying to eliminate as many database hits as possible.

Assuming that you're already using a utility to generate static product detail pages, why not include three related products as hidden form fields on each product detail page? The related products are known at the time the page is being built, and that allows the detail page to pass the information in three hidden form fields named "RelatedProduct" to the shopping cart. The cart then just needs to display the information, including a link to the related products' detail pages. Listing 12-5 shows the additional HTML that your product detail pages need to include.

Listing 12-5: **HTML for related products**

```
<INPUT TYPE="HIDDEN" NAME="RelatedProduct" VALUE="17430928">
<INPUT TYPE="HIDDEN" NAME="RelatedProduct" VALUE="67484">
<INPUT TYPE="HIDDEN" NAME="RelatedProduct" VALUE="9028659">
<INPUT TYPE="HIDDEN" NAME="RelatedDesc" VALUE="Blue widget">
<INPUT TYPE="HIDDEN" NAME="RelatedDesc" VALUE="Green widget">
<INPUT TYPE="HIDDEN" NAME="RelatedDesc" VALUE="Red widget">
```

Naming these fields the same name causes ASP to handle them as a collection in cart.asp when the form is submitted. Listing 12-6 shows a sample ASP subroutine to display the related products.

Listing 12-6: **Displaying related products**

```
<%
Sub DisplayRelated()

Response.Write "You might also enjoy...<BR>"
For Each x In Request("RelatedProduct")
 Response.Write "<A HREF='/productdetail/"
 Response.Write Request("RelatedProduct")(x)
 Response.Write ".asp'>"
 Response.Write Request("RelatedDesc")(x)
 Response.Write "</A><BR>"
Next

End Sub
%>
```

Either method provides a good way to retrieve lists of related products and create a compelling add-on sales technique for your site.

Displaying the basket

After you use the above methods to manipulate the items in the basket, you need to format and display the basket's contents for your customers. The primary Commerce Server object is still the OrderGroup object. I find the easiest way to work with this information is to write several ASP subroutines that can be called from within the appropriate places in the shopping cart page's HTML. Listing 12-7 shows the section of the cart.asp page containing these subroutines:

Automating Relationships

Commerce Server doesn't contain any "out of the box" methods for automatically creating product relationships, which means that you must use the Business Desk application to manually create relationships between products.

This doesn't mean that you can't create your own automated relationship routines. The table schema is easy to understand — the *catalogname*_CatalogRelationships table includes the internal ID ("oid" field) of two products. Creating this relationship facilitates retrieving related products. You can either query the table directly, or you can use the RelatedProducts property of a Product object to retrieve the recordset.

How you create a routine to automatically create product relationships depends entirely on what you want those relationships to represent. For example, suppose that you want to create a relationship between two products whenever a large number of customers purchase both products in a single order. In this case, your best bet is to write queries that run against your site's data warehouse to produce the list of related products, and then to create the necessary table entries in the production database. If you want to manually bulk-create certain relationships, such as relating batteries to any electronic toys from a certain vendor, you can use simple Transact-SQL queries and SQL Query Analyzer to create the necessary table entries.

Listing 12-7: **Subroutines for displaying the cart**

```
<%

Sub DisplayRelated()
 'displays related items
 'that have been passed in on an
 'add-to-cart
 If Request("action") = "add" Then
  Response.Write "You might also enjoy...<BR>"
  For Each x In Request("RelatedProduct")
   Response.Write "<A HREF='/productdetail/"
   Response.Write Request("RelatedProduct")(x)
   Response.Write ".asp'>"
   Response.Write Request("RelatedDesc")(x)
   Response.Write "</A><BR>"
  Next
 End If
End Sub

Sub DisplayLineItem(vItem,vDesc,vPrice,vQty,vIndex,vDisc)
 'writes out a line item from the cart
 'as a table row
 Response.Write "<TR>"

 'item number
```

```
Response.Write "<TD>"
Response.Write vItem
Response.Write "</TD>" & vbCrLf

'description
Response.Write "<TD>"
Response.Write vDesc
If vDisc = 1 Then
 Response.Write "<BR>"
 Response.Write "Discounts may apply to this item. "
 Response.Write "<A HREF='show-disc.asp?prodid="
 Response.Write vItem & "'>Click here for details.</A>"
End If
Response.Write "</TD>" & vbCrLf

'price each
Response.Write "<TD>$"
Response.Write FormatCurrency(vPrice,2,True,False,True)
Response.Write "</TD>" & vbCrLf

'quantity - with form field
Response.Write "<TD><INPUT TYPE='TEXT' SIZE='2' NAME='qty"
Response.Write vItem & "' VALUE='" & vQty & "'>"
Response.Write "</TD>" & vbCrLf

'total price
Response.Write "<TD>$"
Response.Write FormatCurrency(vQty * vPrice,2,True,False,True)
Response.Write "</TD>" & vbCrLf

'remove link
Response.Write "<TD>"
Response.Write "<A HREF='cart.asp?action=remove"
Response.Write "&removeindex=" & vIndex
Response.Write "</TD>" & vbCrLf

Response.Write "</TR>"
End Sub

Sub DisplayLineItems(oOF)
 'displays all line items in a table
 'oOG is the OrderForm object with
 'the order
 Response.Write "<TABLE>"
 Response.Write "<TR>"
 Response.Write "<TD>Item#</TD>" & vbCrLf
 Response.Write "<TD>Description</TD>" & vbCrLf
 Response.Write "<TD>Price</TD>" & vbCrLf
 Response.Write "<TD>Qty</TD>" & vbCrLf
 Response.Write "<TD>Total</TD>" & vbCrLf
 Response.Write "<TD> </TD>" & vbCrLf
 Response.Write "</TR>"
```

Continued

Listing 12-7 *(continued)*

```
For Each x In oOF.Items
  'call the sub to display a single
  'line item - note this is formatted
  'to make it easier to read
  DisplayLineItem(oOF.Items(x).product_id, _
                  oOF.Items(x).description, _
                  oOF.Items(x).cy_unit_price, _
                  oOF.Items(x).quantity, _
                  x,
                  oOF.Items(x).discountsapply

Next

Response.Write "</TABLE>"
End Sub

%>
```

Note As with prior code examples, this example is intended to show you how the pieces of data in the cart can be accessed and displayed. You will need to customize these subroutines to meet the needs of your site.

This code requires that an OrderForm object be provided to the ShowLineItems() subroutine; the subroutine will handle the creation of an HTML table and will display each line item as a row in that table. You can modify this code to display whatever cart data your site requires.

If this code is included in cart.asp, then the page should already have a reference to the OrderGroup object containing the current user's shopping cart data. Getting a reference to the OrderForm object, which is contained within the OrderGroup that contains the actual line-item data for the order, requires a reference to the correct property of the OrderGroup object. Similarly, the OrderGroup object contains methods to completely clear the order if the user decides to delete their shopping cart.

Displaying discount details

Retailer.com has decided to alert customers to discounts in the shopping cart, but to not calculate those discounts until the customers decide to check out. The "click here for discount details" link, which is included in the basket, links to a page called "show-disc.asp." The link also passes the product ID, so the show-disc.asp page knows which product's discount it should be looking up.

As previously discussed, Commerce Server's discount infrastructure is complex. Although Microsoft provides a pipeline template that calculates and applies discounts to a customer's basket (plan.pct), it doesn't provide any built-in functionality to look up which discounts apply to a certain product.

Making things easier

You *can* write code that selects the appropriate lines from the order_discount table and interpret the structure of the discount, such as what products are required, what the discount is, what the limits are, and so forth. Doing so, however, will require a great deal of code to deal with the various circumstances that Commerce Server's discounts can present.

I recommend that you provide a detailed description of the discount when you create it. Part of the discount's definition is a required field name — "basket display," as shown in Figure 12-4. Provide a detailed description in this field, which is saved in the order_discount table in the u_disc_description column.

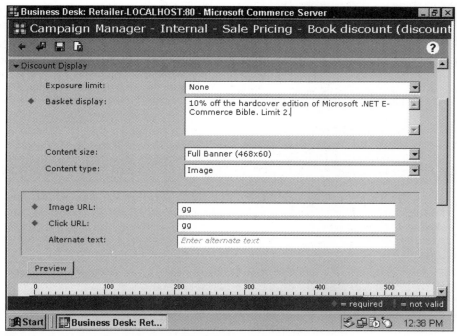

Figure 12-4: Creating a meaningful discount description

Getting the details

You can then use a stored procedure to accept a product ID and return the descriptions of any active discounts that the product is participating in, either as a "buy" requirement, or as the "get" portion of the discount. Listing 12-8 shows a sample stored procedure, sp_GetDiscountDescriptions.

Structure of an OrderForm

Each OrderGroup object can contain one or more OrderForm objects. Every OrderGroup method that deals with OrderForm properties accepts the name of an order form as a parameter; if you omit this parameter, the "default" order form is used (which is useful if your order groups will only *ever* contain one order form — just let them use the default).

The OrderForm object is structured as a Dictionary object, and contains a variety of keys for order form header data. For example, it includes a key for every column in the OrderFormHeaders table. It also contains an Items key, which is a SimpleList object. This object contains a Dictionary object for each line item in the order representing the rows in the OrderFormLineItems table, with a key for each column in that table. For example, to access the quantity of the second line item in an order:

```
oOrderForm.Items(2).Quantity
```

Several keys in the order form begin with an underscore ("_") character. These keys are *not* saved directly to columns in the OrderForm tables; instead, they are maintained in the marshaled_data column, where the complete data from an order form is stored in the tables. Both the OrderFormHeaders and OrderFormLineItems tables have marshaled_data columns for storing the raw cart data.

Listing 12-8: **Stored procedure sp_GetDiscountDescriptions**

```
CREATE PROCEDURE sp_GetDiscountDescriptions
@productID nvarchar(30)
AS

    /* Declare table variable to
       hold results */
    DECLARE @res table(
     u_disc_description nvarchar(255)
     )

/* Get descriptions this is a
   BUY product for */
INSERT INTO @res (u_disc_description)
(SELECT u_disc_description
 FROM order_discount o
 INNER JOIN
 ES_ExprInfo i
 ON o.i_disc_cond_expr =
i.ExprID
 INNER JOIN ES_ExprProfDeps p
 ON p.ExprID = i.ExprID
 INNER JOIN
```

```
Campaign_Items c
 ON c.i_campitem_id =
o.i_campitem_id
 WHERE i.ExprName = @productid
 AND
p.ProfDep = 'Product'
 AND
c.campitem_active = 1
 AND GETDATE()
BETWEEN c.campitem_start
 AND
c.campitem_end)

/* Find out how many this is
   the GET for */
INSERT INTO @res (u_disc_description)
(SELECT u_disc_description
 FROM order_discount o
 INNER JOIN
ES_ExprInfo I
 ON o.i_disc_award_expr =
i.ExprID
 INNER JOIN ES_ExprProfDeps p
 ON p.ExprID = i.ExprID
 INNER JOIN
Campaign_Items c
 ON c.i_campitem_id =
o.i_campitem_id
 WHERE i.ExprName = @productid
 AND
 p.ProfDep = 'Product'
 AND
c.campitem_active = 1
 AND GETDATE()
BETWEEN c.campitem_start AND
c.campitem_end)

/* Return results */
SELECT * FROM @res
```

Using the above stored procedure in an ASP page couldn't be simpler. Listing 12-9 shows a sample ASP page that uses this stored procedure to list the discounts associated with a product. It assumes that the product ID is being passed as `prodid` from the calling page.

Listing 12-9: Displaying discount details

```
<HTML><BODY>
This product is featured in the following
discount offers on our site:
<UL>
<%

'assumes cn is a valid connection object
vSql = "sp_GetDiscountDescriptions "
vSql = vSql & "'" & Request("prodid") & "'"
Set Rs = Cn.Execute vSql

Do Until Rs.EOF
  Response.Write "<LI>"
  Response.Write Rs("u_disc_description")
  Response.Write "</LI>" & vbCrLf
  Rs.MoveNext
Loop

%>
</UL>
</BODY></HTML>
```

Improving the details

You can modify the page to offer a link back to the customer's shopping cart. You can also modify this page and its stored procedure to provide links to the other products involved in the description, or you can even include a "buy the necessary products" button that automatically adds all the products required to receive the discount to the customer's cart. Anything you do to make the process easier for customers to purchase products and services will reward you on the bottom line.

Proceeding to the checkout

Before collecting the customer's payment and address information, you should display a finalized version of their shopping cart with all discounts, taxes, and shipping charges applied. This allows the customer to verify what you are about to charge them, confirm that the order contains the products that they want, and then proceed to the actual checkout.

Because this is where you have the opportunity to "finalize" the order, I recommend that you use the plan.pct pipeline template provided by Commerce Server, and implemented as basket.pcf in the Retail Solution Site. This pipeline will verify all of the information in the basket — including pricing levels — and will select, score, and apply any discounts for which the customer is eligible.

If you want to, you can improve the basic pipeline provided by Commerce Server in a few ways. For example, you can modify the Inventory stage of the pipeline to provide information on when the products can ship. Out of stock items, for example, can be flagged as "backordered."

You can also offer the customer the ability to save this cart for future use. Make certain that you offer the customer the ability to make changes to the cart at this point, such as changing quantities or removing items completely. You should also offer the opportunity to "back out" of the checkout process and continue shopping for more products.

Summary

Shopping carts represent some of the most complicated code in any e-commerce site, and bear a lot of responsibility. They have to be an order management tool, a suggested selling tool, a data validity checker, and much more. The shopping cart included with Commerce Server's Solution Sites accomplishes these functions, but at a somewhat high cost of server overhead and processing time. Writing your own cart may be time-consuming, but you'll be rewarded with a more robust, scalable cart that better suits your company's specific needs.

✦　　✦　　✦

Developing the Customer Experience — Creating the Checkout

The checkout process is one of the most important customer experiences. After all, without an easy-to-use checkout, customers can't pay you. Commerce Server includes a robust set of tools for developing a checkout, and the Solution Sites each offer a sample checkout to get you started. Customizing your checkout, and designing it for ease of use, is a critical step for any e-commerce site.

The Commerce Server Checkout

Before a customer can check out, you must finalize the customer's order, calculate shipping and tax charges, and so forth. Commerce Server provides a pipeline template for this purpose, which is implemented in the Retail Solution Site as total.pcf. The pipeline works as follows:

1. Shipping stage

   a. Splitter: This component is used to split an order into different parts. For example, you may want to split an order based on the catalog that each item came from, or based on the ship-to addresses. In this case, the Splitter is used to split the order by shipment method, so that shipping can be calculated differently for each method.

    b. ShippingMethodRouter: This component is a "wrapper" around several other components, which should never be used directly in a pipeline. This component handles orders that have multiple shipping methods, and calls the necessary components to calculate the shipping charges for each. It also calculates the shipping charge for the entire order.

    c. ShippingDiscountAdjust: The OrderDiscount object, which runs in a previous pipeline, sets the value of the `_shipping_discount_type` key in the order. If that value is blank or Null, the ShippingDiscountAdjust component does nothing. If it contains a 1 or a 2, this component calculates the order-wide shipping discount and applies that amount to the order. Note that shipping discounts are the only order-wide discounts natively supported by Commerce Server.

2. Handling stage

    a. DefaultHandlingCy: This component sets the handling charge for the order to zero. If you charge handling fees, you will need to replace this component with a component such as a Scriptor component, that calculates and applies your fees to the order.

    b. RequiredHandlingCy: This component verifies that the order has a handling charge (even if it's zero). If the order doesn't have a handling charge, a pipeline error is raised.

3. Tax stage

    a. SampleRegionalTax: This component supports the multiple-shipping capabilities of Commerce Server. It retrieves the applicable tax rate from the database and applies tax to each item in the order. It also calculates the total tax for each shipped order and for the entire order. Microsoft provides this component as a sample and they strongly recommend (as do I) that you obtain a third-party tax calculation component with greater flexibility.

    Note the importance of supporting Commerce Server's multiple-ship capabilities. Companies are generally required to collect tax when shipping to any state they have an physical office in, and they must calculate the tax at that state's (or region's) legal rate. Populating the database with the states or regions where you must collect tax enables this component to calculate the correct rate for each portion of the order.

    Card Service International (www.cardservice.com) is a company that provides Commerce Server-compatible tax and payment processing components.

    b. RequiredTaxCy: This component verifies that tax values have been calculated and applied to the order. If they have not, a pipeline error is raised.

4. OrderTotal stage

    a. DefaultTotalCy: This component calculates a total for the order, including item prices, shipping, handling, and tax.

      b. RequiredTotalCy: This component verifies that a total has been calculated for the order. If it has not, a pipeline error is raised.

  5. CopyFields stage

      a. CopyFields: This is a Scriptor component that uses VBScript to copy several pieces of information into the order form so that it will be persisted with the order. This information includes the name of the customer placing the order, information about the items in the order, and so forth. By persisting this information with the order, you maintain the order as a "snapshot" rather than relying on the information in the database, which may change in the future. This Scriptor component can be easily modified by using VBScript.

The checkout process provided by Commerce Server is a pipeline template named "purchase.pct." A good example of the implementation of this pipeline is provided by the Retail Solution Site, and is named "checkout.pcf." Here's how the checkout.pcf pipeline works:

  1. Purchase Check stage

      a. Commerce.Splitter: This component splits an order into different parts. For example, you may want to split an order based on the catalog that each item came from, or based on the ship-to addresses. In this case, the Splitter is used to split the order by item vendor.

  2. Payment stage

      a. Scriptor — PaymentInfo: The VBScript in this component sets the billing currency and billing amount fields — a step required by most third-party payment processing components. The billing amount is set to the order total, and the billing currency is set to U.S. dollars. You can edit this component as necessary to change these properties, or to set other values required by the payment components that you use.

      b. ValidateCreditCard: This component is set to run only when the payment method is equal to `credit_card` in the order. When it runs, it verifies that the payment type is "MasterCard," "Visa," "MC," "AMEX," "American Express," or "Discover." It also verifies that the credit card expiration date, as entered, is a future date. Finally, it runs a checksum to verify that the credit card number was entered properly. If any of these checks fail, a pipeline error is raised.

      This component *does not* perform a credit card authorization with a merchant bank. You will need to supply a pipeline component that handles authorizations. However, this component is an important first line of defense in your pipeline. Many merchant banks charge a fee for authorizations, even if they are declined, so at least this component verifies that you have a correctly entered credit card number. Also, this component can help the customer avoid waiting for a merchant bank to decline a transaction because the credit card number was typed wrong — because the Validate component will catch the error before the authorization process begins.

c. DefaultPayment: This component sets a payment authorization code. In production, you remove this component and replace it with a third-party pipeline component that performs your payment authorization.

d. RequiredPayment: This component verifies that a payment authorization code is present. If the code is absent, this component raises a pipeline error.

3. Accept stage

a. RecordEvent: This component records information in the database regarding the transaction. Specifically, it writes information about items that were sold — information that is then used in the Content Selection Framework for future content selection scoring. For example, a customer who purchases a particular item may be less likely to see ads for that item in the future.

b. IISAppendToLog: This component records information similar to the RecordEvent component, but the information is written to the IIS log instead of the database. This permits Commerce Server's data warehouse and analysis system to work with the data in the context of a user, purchase history, and so forth.

Tip   Notice that both of the pipelines discussed in the Accept stage use separate components to verify that certain information has been populated in the order. This is a good practice because it covers a complete failure of the preceding components and catches empty values before they are permanently written to the database.

You will probably notice that between running pipelines to finalize the customers' discounts, calculating their order totals, and processing their payments, a few processes have been missed. These are the processes that Commerce Server requires you to build into your checkout and populate into the customer's order.

Building the Checkout

After you make your final calculations for tax, shipping, and handling on the customer's shopping cart and allow them to review the items in the cart and your calculated totals, your checkout needs to perform the following basic steps:

1. Determine how and where the customer wants the order shipped.

2. Run the total.pcf pipeline (or a similar pipeline) to calculate the total charges for the order.

3. Collect billing information, including the customer's billing address and payment information.

4. Run a checkout.pcf pipeline to authorize payment and finalize the order.

Each of these steps requires custom programming. Be sure to review your site's design documentation before beginning this programming. These are the steps needed by *Commerce Server* in order to complete an order, but they may not necessarily be the steps that you want your *customers* to have to follow. To build the checkout, you must collect the necessary information while presenting the same customer experience that you originally designed for.

Shipping information

Commerce Server has a built-in flexible shipping system. The system starts in the Business Desk, where you configure shipping types based on total order cost, number of items purchased, or order weight. Note that order weight generally provides the most accurate shipping information, but to use this measurement, you must include weight information for each item in your catalog, which is rarely feasible.

Setting up shipping

You use the Business Desk's Orders module to set up shipping methods, as shown in Figure 13-1. You can add a new method based on weight, order subtotal, or number of items.

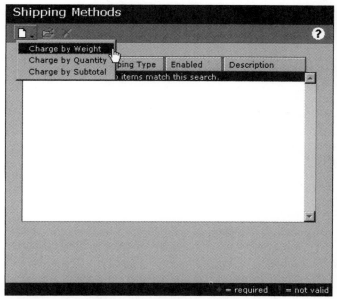

Figure 13-1: Setting up a new shipping method

Third-Party Shipping Components

You can also elect to replace Commerce Server's built-in shipping pipeline components with third-party components. For example, some carriers such as United Parcel Service or FedEx provide Commerce Server-compatible pipeline components. These components examine weight information included with your items, the shipping addresses provided by your customers, and the desired delivery timeframe to provide accurate shipping costs. Generally, the carrier maintains the price tables, thus removing a layer of management from your staff. These components often integrate with the carrier's systems, making obtaining tracking numbers and other information for your customers easier, as well.

For each method, provide both a short and long description, and set up the charges. In the case of a "charge by order subtotal" shipping method, set up price ranges that represent order subtotals, and assign a shipping fee to each range. You must provide a shipping fee for the final "over x" amount, which covers any order subtotal over the highest range that you specify. Figure 13-2 shows the setup of a new shipping method.

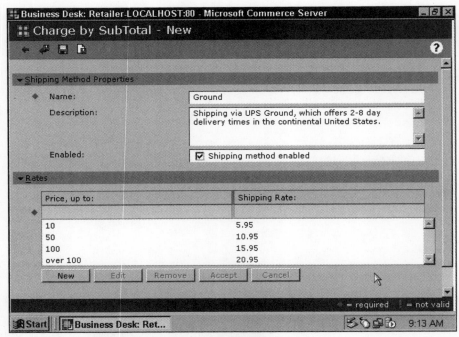

Figure 13-2: Creating a subtotal shipping method

You can set up as many different shipping methods as you want. Each method usually represents a particular mode of delivery, such as ground, overnight, and so forth. Each method can be calculated differently (by weight, quantity, or subtotal) to reflect the different pricing structures that the shipping carriers have in place. Figure 13-3 shows several shipping methods that have been made available to the customers of this site.

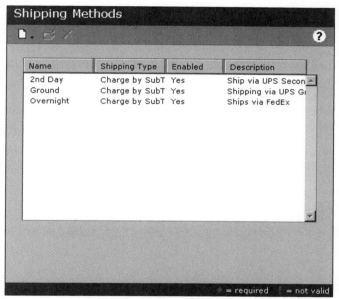

Figure 13-3: Creating multiple shipping methods

Getting shipping addresses

Commerce Server allows each item in an order to be delivered to a different address. You do this by tagging each line item with a `shipping_address_id` and `shipping_method_name` key. Whether or not you implement this level of functionality is up to you, and you will encounter both pros and cons either way.

By allowing each item to go to a different address via a different shipping method, you offer customers a great deal of flexibility. However, the user interface that's necessary to provide that level of flexibility is quite complicated. Most e-commerce companies prefer to limit an entire order to a single shipping address and shipping method. Customers who want to ship different items by using more than one shipping method must place separate orders to do so. If your checkout process "remembers" billing information, it's probably less cumbersome to have customers place many different orders than to have them choose a different shipping address and method for each item that they order.

Pricing Standards for E-Commerce Shipping

Very few e-commerce companies charge for shipping based on weight, despite the fact that weight is the most accurate method of charging for shipping. After all, most shipping carriers charge the company based on weight, so why not pass that cost directly along to the customer?

Most companies simply don't have the time to obtain and enter weight information, or even estimates, for all of the products in their catalogs. Larger e-commerce companies may have enough "weight" with their vendors to demand weight information in the catalog feeds that they receive, but smaller companies have to make do with what they're given.

The industry's solution has been to estimate shipping prices based on order subtotal. Heavy items tend to be expensive. Expensive orders tend to contain either a few heavy items or many lighter items that add up to a similar weight. So, although a pricing structure based on order subtotal may be inaccurate on a per-order basis, it tends to even out over all the orders that a company processes. Some orders wind up being overcharged for shipping, and others wind up being undercharged.

If you decide to build your company's shipping fees on a subtotal basis, be sure to keep an eye on your shipping fees versus the fees that you actually pay. If you find yourself consistently making a profit on your shipping fees, you should consider lowering the fees that you charge your customers across the board. Conversely, if you find yourself losing money on shipping, it's time to raise your prices a bit.

If you decide to limit each order to a single address, then populate the `shipping_address_id` key in each item with the same value. The value in the key must correspond to a value in the `g_shipping_id` column of the Addresses table in Commerce Server's database. Therefore, your customers' desired ship-to addresses must wind up as entries in the Addresses table before they can be used in an order.

Addresses are managed as part of profiles. The Addresses structure is a portion of the Profile System provided by Commerce Server; you can use the Business Desk's Profiles module to modify and extend this structure as necessary.

Normally, you use an HTML form to collect new address information. Then you add that address information to the user's profile by using the following steps:

1. Create an instance of the ProfileService object and initialize it.

2. Retrieve the current customer's profile, or if they don't have one, create a new one. This results in a ProfileObject object of the UserObject type, which represents the current customer's profile.

3. Create a new ProfileObject of the Address type and attach it to the UserObject ProfileObject that you just created.

4. Add the new address information to the Address ProfileObject.

5. Call the ProfileObject objects' Update method to store the changes in the database.

After adding the new address and updating the ProfileObject, you will have the address_id property of the new address. This is the value that you'll need to place into the order form's line items. Listing 13-1 shows a code sample that creates a new UserObject and an Address for that user.

Listing 13-1: **Creating a new user and address**

```
'declare variables
Dim oUser1, oAddress1

'assumes oProfileService is an instance
'of the ProfileService object

'create user
Set oUser1 =
oProfileService.CreateProfile("JoeUser@microsoft.com", _
 "UserObject")
If err.number <> 0 Then
   oProfileService.DeleteProfile "JoeUser@microsoft.com", _
 "UserObject"
EndIf

'create a GUID for a new address
Dim oGenID, sGUID
Set oGenID = Server.CreateObject("Commerce.GenID")
sGUID = oGenID.GenGUIDString

'create new address
Set oAddress1 = oProfileService.CreateProfile(sGUID, "Address")

'add properties to the user
oUser1.GeneralInfo.first_name = "Joe"
oUser1.GeneralInfo.last_name = "User"

'add properties to the address
oAddress1.GeneralInfo.region_code = "WA"
oAddress1.GeneralInfo.country_code = "US"

'update both objects in the database
oUser1.Update
oAddress1.Update

'release both object
Set oUser1 = Nothing
Set oAddress1 = Nothing
```

In this code sample, sGUID is the ID of the address. Note that addresses can contain a great deal of information. By default, Commerce Server includes the following properties for addresses:

✦ address_line1 and address_line2 contain street address information.

✦ address_name contains a "friendly name" for the address, such as "home" or "work."

✦ address_type may be 0 for a regular address, 1 for a ship-to address, or 2 for a bill-to address. This allows you to track how addresses were used, thus allowing your checkout to intelligently help the customer select addresses from their "address book" on future orders.

✦ city, country_code and country_name contain city and country information for the address.

✦ id is the GUID of the UserObject profile to which this address belongs.

✦ first_name and last_name are the names associated with the address.

✦ postal_code, region_code, and region_name represent the postal (ZIP) code and region (or state) for the address.

✦ tel_number and tel_extension allow you to associate a phone number with the address.

You should generally collect as much of this information as possible from your customers when creating new addresses, and you should perform basic data validation on the data that you collect before storing it in an Address-type ProfileObject.

Displaying shipping choices

Provide your customers with a way to select a shipping method. Commerce Server provides a Shipping object with a PreviewShipments method that returns a list of shipping methods and their costs, based on the shipping methods and cost ranges that you have set up in the Business Desk.

Before the method can be successfully used, the customer's order must be updated with the shipping address information. This allows the PreviewShipments method to split up the order by destination, allowing the customer to select a different shipping method for each destination. You may also want to provide a means for customers to indicate items that they want to ship separately to the same destination, and split the order that way. For example, this allows your customers to select an overnight shipping method for part of their order and a ground method for the rest.

You may also employ the option that I discussed previously, which is to require that all items in an order go to a single destination address by using a single shipping method. If your checkout process is programmed to "remember" billing information, then this technique can represent the easiest way to handle shipping, both from a programming standpoint and from a customer experience perspective.

Listing 13-2 shows sample code to use the PreviewShipments method to create a list of available shipping methods and prices.

Listing 13-2: **Previewing shipping methods**

```
' assumes oOrder is an order, and oContext is
' a valid context dictionary object
Set oShip = Server.CreateObject("Commerce.Shipping")
ADistinguishers = Array("shipping_method_id", _
 "shipping_address_id")
slShipments = oShip.PreviewShipments(oOrder, oContext, _
ADistinguishers)
For Each dShipment In slShipments
 For Each dPreview In dShipment.Previews

   ' returns the following information:
   ' dPreview("shipment_error")
   ' dPreview("shipping_method_id")
   ' dPreview("shipping_method_name")
   ' dPreview("description")
   ' dPreview("_cy_shipping_total")

 Next
Next
```

This sample splits the order based on the shipping method and shipping address, thus creating a separate list of shipping prices for each unique address/method combination. If all of the items in the order have the same shipping address and method, then this routine will return a single list of shipping methods.

The For...Each constructs in the sample loop through the available shipping method lists and the individual shipping methods in each list. You can replace the comment lines in the loop with code to produce, for example, an HTML drop-down list box with the available shipping methods and their prices. Listing 13-3 shows the same procedure, but revised to produce a drop-down list box.

Listing 13-3: **Selecting a shipping method**

```
' assumes oOrder is an order, and oContext is
' a valid context dictionary object
Set oShip = Server.CreateObject("Commerce.Shipping")
ADistinguishers = Array("shipping_method_id", _
 "shipping_address_id")
slShipments = oShip.PreviewShipments(oOrder, oContext, _
ADistinguishers)
```

Continued

Listing 13-3 *(continued)*

```
For Each dShipment In slShipments
 Response.Write "<SELECT NAME='Shipping'>"
 For Each dPreview In dShipment.Previews
    Response.Write "<OPTION VALUE=''>"
    Response.Write dPreview("shipping_method_id")
    Response.Write ">"
    Response.Write dPreview("shipping_method_name")
    Response.Write " - $"
    Response.Write dPreview("_cy_shipping_total")
    Response.Write "</OPTION>" & vbCrLf
 Next
 Response.Write "</SELECT>"
Next
```

After your customer has selected a shipping method, you will need to update each line item in the order with the `shipping_method_id` value that the customer selected.

Billing information

Collecting billing information is one of the last steps in a checkout. It's also a sensitive area, because you're asking customers to provide you with their private information. Take steps to ensure the privacy of that information as it is transmitted across the Internet.

Ensuring security

The page that you use to collect your customer's billing information should always be delivered via HTTPS rather than HTTP to ensure a secure, encrypted connection. This requires your servers to have a valid server encryption certificate from a commercial signing authority, such as Verisign (www.verisign.com). A secure, encrypted connection also requires that the customers' browser specify the HTTPS:// protocol when making the connection. You should test the connection to ensure that it is encrypted; but if it isn't encrypted, you need to redirect the customer to an encrypted page by using HTTPS. Listing 13-4 shows an example ASP script that checks the encrypted status and redirects the customer if necessary:

Listing 13-4: Ensuring an encrypted connection

```
<%

If Request.ServerVariables("HTTPS") = "off" Then
 Response.Redirect "https://www.retailer.com/checkout_bill.asp"
End If

%>
```

 Tip
Make sure that your server certificates are valid. Set a reminder in your personal information manager for a month before the certificate expires, so you'll be reminded to renew the certificate. Otherwise, customers will see an error message in their browser indicating that your certificate has expired and the browser may refuse to make an HTTPS connection.

Offering a non-secure checkout path for customers whose browsers didn't support HTTPS, or for customers accessing the site through a firewall that blocked port 443 (the port used for HTTPS traffic) used to be common practice. I recommend against using this practice. If your customers can't use HTTPS, advise them to call you and provide their credit card number, or fax their credit card number directly to you. The risk of passing an unencrypted credit card number across the Internet is not worth the convenience of providing it online.

Collecting information

After you've established an encrypted connection with your customer, you can begin collecting their billing information. Commerce Server first requires the billing name, address, and phone number. This information is all part of an Address profile object, and can be added in the same way as a shipping address. The ID of the address must be added to the order because the billing information is carried at the order level rather than at the item level (like shipping addresses).

You also need to collect the customer's payment information (a credit card number and expiration date).

 Note
Commerce Server assumes—and most credit card banks require—that the name on the billing address is the same as the name on the credit card. You should encourage customers to provide a billing name and address that match their credit card statement. Most payment components will verify the billing address when authorizing the credit card.

Streamlining the process

A well-designed checkout will usually offer a "quick checkout" method for repeat customers.

1. Offer customers the ability to create a user name (often their e-mail address) and password.

2. Store their information, including shipping and billing addresses and payment information, in your database.

3. When customers return to your site, their user name and password authorizes the site to retrieve the stored information and to complete the checkout with little, if any, further input from the customer.

Providing this type of functionality requires careful planning, involves an interaction between Commerce Server's Profile Service and your shoppers, and requires you to understand exactly how Commerce Server handles shoppers and profiles.

Anonymous shoppers

Every shopper on your site must have a profile. Unless you want to require users to create a profile and sign in before shopping, shoppers will be assigned *anonymous* profiles. The anonymous profile allows Commerce Server to track the shopper's click history and other actions, even though you don't know the shopper's name or other personal information.

Tip   Profiling of anonymous shoppers can be costly in terms of performance. Unless this data is important to you, turn the feature off.

Registered shoppers

A registered shopper is a shopper who has provided personal information to you, and who usually uses a password to sign in to the site. If an anonymous shopper signs up for a user account (*registers*), Commerce Server will "convert" their anonymous profile to a registered profile, thus maintaining their click history and other information (assuming you have enabled anonymous profiling to begin with).

Commerce Server also attempts to save information when an anonymous shopper logs into their account. A certain amount of data will carry over so that their actions, although anonymous, won't be lost (assuming that you have enabled anonymous profiling).

Allowing anonymous buyers

Anonymous shoppers are one thing, but anonymous *buyers* are quite another. From a customer experience perspective, anonymous buyers offer some obvious advantages, the most important of which is that customers don't have to go through a registration process in order to buy something. A registration process is generally considered an obstacle, and you want to avoid placing obstacles in the customer's path when they're ready to spend money.

From a site management perspective, however, anonymous buyers are a nightmare for the following reasons:

✦ Shipping and billing addresses are attached to user profiles—even anonymous ones. This means that your anonymous buyers will create essentially useless UserObject and Address profiles *every time they buy something*.

✦ Anonymous buyers are untraceable, so you won't be able to develop a buying history or other valuable demographic and marketing information for anonymous buyers.

✦ Because the buyers are anonymous, Commerce Server won't be able to "match" them with a profile when they visit your site again. This means that Commerce Server will create *another* anonymous profile for the same user, thus filling up your resources more quickly.

One solution is to allow returning buyers the opportunity to log in before checking out. This gives them the advantage of having their information on file with you, making their checkout process easier. In general, new buyers should *not* be given the opportunity to register at this point, because the registration process may go poorly and you will lose the sale.

Instead, wait until their purchase is complete. At that point, you have their information in an anonymous user profile; give them the opportunity to create a user name and password. This allows you to convert the anonymous profile into a registered profile, maintain the address and payment information that you just collected in the checkout, and allow the customer the convenience of a simpler checkout on their next visit. On the other hand, if the registration process goes poorly, at least you still got the sale.

Make sure that you *strongly* encourage customers to register after checking out. Spell out the benefits of registering, such as faster future checkouts. If you offer discounts or special offers to your registered customers, you should make them aware of that fact.

Incorporating Marketing Features into the Checkout

E-commerce sites have taken advantage of their checkout process to plug marketing features that improve sales. In this section, I discuss a couple of the more common tactics, and give you some pointers on how to implement them in your own checkout.

Opt-in e-mail

If you offer an opt-in e-mail program, such as an e-mail newsletter, you can use the checkout as a way to encourage customers to sign up. For example, on the page where you collect the customer's billing information, including their e-mail address, offer check boxes that allow them to subscribe to your mailings with a single click. Depending on your company's philosophy, the check boxes may start off already checked, meaning that the customer has to take action to *not* be subscribed.

Handle these subscriptions in whatever way your opt-in program requires. Be sure that the check boxes are *obvious* to your customers, especially if "sign me up" is the default action. Don't bury them in text or at the bottom of the screen.

Demographic information

If you've modified your Commerce Server user profiles to include demographic information on your customers, such as annual household income, number of household residents, favorite hobbies, and so forth, then the checkout is an excellent place to collect some of that information.

Don't be greedy. Customers are interested in getting through the checkout as quickly as possible and won't enjoy having to fill out a lengthy questionnaire. You don't want to take the risk of having them abandon their order. However, most customers won't mind an extra question or two.

One approach is to retrieve the customer's profile and loop through its properties looking for Null values. When you find one, add a question to the checkout page that asks for the desired information. Each time the customer checks out, a new piece of demographic information will be collected, and eventually you'll have a complete customer profile.

Advertising

If your site accepts advertising from outside companies, particularly the manufacturers of products that you sell, you can include additional advertising in your checkout process. The *best* place to include advertising is on the last page of the checkout, after the process has been completed. The last page can display an order confirmation number, information about where the customer can check their order status, and several advertising banners. A strategically placed banner is a perfect opportunity to grab the attention of customers looking for their next destination on the Web.

Use Commerce Server's built-in ad campaign system to manage these ads.

I discuss building an advertising infrastructure in Chapter 10.

Express Checkouts

In an effort to make online shopping easier and to help build consumers' trust, several major online portals have started offering "express checkout" services to their members. These services include the Yahoo! Wallet (wallet.yahoo.com), Microsoft's Passport (www.passport.com) and America Online's Quick Checkout (www.aol.com).

In all of these services, members use the service's site to enter their address and credit card information, which is securely stored on the services' servers. Express checkout then proceeds as follows:

1. A customer purchases something from your site and selects a branded "express checkout" method rather than your normal "check out now" button.

2. The express button takes the customer to a sign-in page hosted by the express checkout service. The button also passes information, such as your merchant number, to the login page.

3. The customer signs in to the service, and the service securely transmits the customer's address and payment information directly to your servers.

4. You continue processing the information as you would in a normal transaction.

The benefit to these services is that they allow customers to almost completely bypass your normal checkout process, because their information is provided to you by the express checkout service. Customers often feel more secure because they can presumably trust the express checkout service to store their information more securely than you can (obviously, this is more a matter of appearances and brand loyalty than reality).

In order to implement these services on your site, you have to enter into a contractual agreement with the service provider, and you have to modify your checkout process to accommodate the service. This involves adding a special checkout button to your site along with your normal checkout button. You must also provide a special portal page (and sometimes a special COM component) that allows the service's servers to securely communicate with yours. Some services, such as America Online, will work with you to implement their service, even going so far as to provide free consultants to make the necessary modifications to your site. Your contract will determine exactly what needs to be done, and who will be responsible for implementation.

These services are becoming increasingly popular. Microsoft has a significant marketing push behind their Passport, and even includes Express Checkout integration information in the Commerce Server documentation. The Yahoo! Wallet is gaining acceptance because Yahoo! requires their members to maintain a Wallet for any recurring services that they purchase on Yahoo!, such as auctions. America Online puts a tremendous push behind their Quick Checkout, especially during the holiday season, and encourages their members to look for sites that feature the Quick Checkout.

Split Decision

Split payments occur when a customer uses two or more types of tender to pay for an order. In a retail store, this may include a check and a credit card. On an e-commerce site, this may include two different credit cards, or a credit card and some form of "New Economy" money, such as Flooz or CyberCash, or a gift certificate. Although the majority of your customers will pay for their order with a single credit card, split payments are not uncommon when gift certificates or other forms of tender are available.

Unfortunately, Commerce Server doesn't include support for split payment orders. The transaction system built into Commerce Server, including the pipeline components and default database schema, is designed only for credit card transactions. The credit card information is stored in the OrderFormHeader table.

In order to implement split payment support, you need to normalize the payment information into a separate table, thus allowing multiple payment entries to be associated with an order form. You also need to modify the pipelines, and possibly replace some pipeline components—particularly those components that save final order information to the database—because the database schema will be different.

Demonstrating a change of this size is beyond the scope of this book. Although these changes involve complex programming, it may be worth the effort to offer your customers as many options for payment as possible. Many shoppers are still uncomfortable with the idea of using credit cards on the Internet, so payment systems like CyberCash and Flooz offer a degree of additional comfort to those customers. Offering split payment allows your customers to use all of their available options.

If you want to see some of these services in action, check out these sites:

✦ www.blockbuster.com, which uses the AOL Quick Checkout.

✦ www.officemax.com, which uses the Passport Express Checkout.

✦ www.gap.com, which uses the Yahoo! Wallet.

Accepting Payment

Commerce Server doesn't include any built-in payment system. Instead, it offers a credit card validation component that verifies the checksum of a credit card number and its expiration date; the component doesn't verify that the card number is valid or acceptable. Commerce Server also includes a "placeholder" component that provides a bogus payment-approval number; this component will be replaced later by an actual payment verification component.

Whatever forms of payment you choose to accept (credit cards being the primary form), you need to obtain a third-party payment verification component. The component must not only be compatible with Commerce Server (generally, it should be implemented as a pipeline component), but must also be compatible with the payment vendor (such as a credit card merchant bank) that you have selected. Most credit card merchant banks can provide you with a compatible pipeline component; VeriSign (www.verisign.com) offers a component called "PayFlow Pro" that works with most major merchant banks and supports both credit cards and electronic check processing.

Summary

Creating an easy-to-use, secure checkout that also collects all of the information your business needs is relatively easy when you use Commerce Server's built-in tools. Payment is the most difficult part of the checkout to program, as Commerce Server doesn't include any payment-processing components. However, most third-party payment processing organizations do provide Commerce Server-compatible pipeline components, allowing you to quickly create an integrated, robust checkout.

✦　　✦　　✦

Customer and Company Support

Your e-commerce site has to do more than just take orders. It also has to provide your customers and your internal business processes with different kinds of support. Developing this support will keep your business (and your income) running smoothly. In this part, you'll learn how to leverage Microsoft's .NET Enterprise Servers to integrate your e-commerce site with your existing business processes, and how to create the site elements necessary to keep your customers happy.

Supporting the Customer Experience through Personalization

◆   ◆   ◆   ◆

In This Chapter

The pros and cons of personalization

What personalization can do for you

Designing and implementing personalization

◆   ◆   ◆   ◆

*P*ersonalization is the process of making your site "unique" for each customer that visits, and tailoring that uniqueness to the personal tastes and preferences of that customer. Commerce Server 2000 improves on its predecessor by offering powerful and complex personalization features—all at a cost, of course.

Pros and Cons

Personalization gives two primary benefits to your site. Customizing your site for each customer can make the site easier to navigate and use, which makes your customers happier and provides them with a better shopping experience. Judicious customization can improve sales, because it brings customers in closer contact with products and services that they are more likely to buy. For example, a customer interested in blue widgets is more likely to make a purchase if the advertising and other elements of the site feature blue widgets than if the site featured a variety of other products that may not be of interest to that customer.

On the downside, personalization is very expensive in terms of server overhead. Every page featuring personalization requires multiple hits to your database server in order to query the personalized content, and additional processing overhead on your middle-tier or Web servers to process the query results and construct the personalized portions of each page. Also, personalization generally involves dynamically generated HTML, which places an additional burden on your Web servers.

As a result, personalization requires additional planning and architecture. Not only must you plan and create the actual personalization components in the site, you must also plan and design for the additional server power that personalization requires.

What Personalization Can Do

Commerce Server 2000 features two types of built-in personalization: *Expression-based targeting* and *prediction*.

You use expression-based targeting, also known as *explicit targeting*, when you know the profile properties of the users to whom you are delivering content, and you know what content is to be delivered. You use prediction, or *implicit targeting*, when you don't know all the necessary profile properties to target the user, or when you don't have specific content to deliver. You use the Commerce Server Predictor to extrapolate user preferences from existing user data so you can deliver content of interest to each user.

An example of explicit targeting is the use of direct-mail messages, promoting a new release to customers who purchased a previous version of the product. You know the specific customers that you want to target, and you know exactly what you want to deliver to them. An example of implicit targeting is the use of personalized banner ads. Commerce Server examines a user's existing information, and makes reasonable guesses as to what advertisements that user may like to see.

The key to either type of personalization is the profile. You can target personalized information to any entity with a profile — anonymous users, registered users, business partners, and so forth.

Here are more examples of how Commerce Server 2000 supports personalization:

✦ Creates a direct mail campaign that delivers personalized messages to customers.

✦ Delivers content advertisements to customers based on certain user profile properties. For example, you can advertise books to users who have their Favorite Hobby property set to "Reading." This requires that you collect the necessary demographic information from your customers and store it in their profiles.

✦ Identifies groups of Web pages, and then target content to be displayed only on those pages or only when users with specific properties access those pages.

✦ Displays content on a page that's based on the properties of other content on the page. For example, if your site sells vacation packages, you can assign profiles to the content specifying whether a Season_Type property is "Summer" or "Winter." This allows you to display the appropriate content for summer or winter vacations during the appropriate season.

✦ Applies discounts to certain products in your catalog, based on characteristics of the product or based on the user profile. For example, products falling into a "new product" category may receive a 10-percent "introductory" discount, or customers who are members of a special "discount club" may receive a standard discount on all products.

You can use the other available types of personalization, but they don't strictly fall within Commerce Server's definition of the term. Providing a product catalog with products and pricing tailored to specific customers is a form of personalization that Commerce Server doesn't handle through its personalization modules. Instead, you create a custom catalog, and then give specific customers permission to use it. You can customize pages for customers so that personal information — for example, displaying "Welcome back, Don!" at the top of each page — falls within the broad industry definition of personalization, but this isn't handled by Commerce Server. For those "minor" types of personalization, you need to create your own components to deliver and render the appropriate information into the pages delivered to your customers.

Designing for Personalization

You can control the impact that personalization has on your site in two ways: First, by preventing personalization overhead from affecting your primary Web servers and database servers; second, by making sure that you can temporarily "turn off" personalization, so periods of high incoming traffic can be accommodated by eliminating or sharply reducing the overhead of personalization on the site.

Preventing personalization overhead from affecting your primary servers requires that you use dedicated servers to handle personalization; these servers also provide a convenient way to "turn off" personalization if necessary.

Dedicated database

Personalization requires a great deal of database interaction, primarily between the Commerce Server profiles and product tables. Although your primary Commerce Server database is capable of providing this information, replicating that data to a second database server provides a read-only copy for personalization purposes. Personalization data doesn't tend to change rapidly, so your replication schedule can be relatively infrequent — once per day during a low-traffic period, or even once per week, depending on the nature of your personalization implementation.

When you create a dedicated database server for personalization, you are also creating a scalable model; if your personalization grows more complex than one database server can handle, you can add another one, and then split your Web servers between the two database servers to distribute the load.

Dedicated Web servers

The distributed nature of the Web and HTML pages makes it easy to dedicate specific Web servers to the task of personalization. Your site's ASP and HTML pages remain on your "primary" Web servers, which actually receive the requests from your customers. Portions of these pages, though, reference content located on dedicated personalization servers. For example, if you implement personalized banner ads, these ads are generated by code on the personalization servers. The following code sample shows a personalized ad being added to the page by using an INCLUDE statement that pulls from another Web server:

```
<BODY>
<!-Insert ad -->
<!--#INCLUDE URL="http://pers.retailer.com/ad/banner.asp"-->
<!-End ad insert-->
```

In this technique, the Web server communicates with the personalization server, so that the end customer is never aware of more than one server being involved. The Web server and personalization server can be connected using high-bandwidth network connections — making communication between them as fast as possible. In fact, in this scenario, the personalization servers don't need to be accessible from the Internet at all; they can be located on a back-end network that's accessible by a second network card installed in the Web servers.

Because the page referenced is an ASP page accessed through the #INCLUDE URL method, the personalization Web server has the opportunity to process the ASP page. This means that the personalization server will deliver a static page to the primary Web server, which can easily deliver that static content to the customer's browser with little additional overhead.

If you use multiple Web servers to deliver the personalized content to your customers, your site's architecture may start to look like the diagram shown in Figure 14-1.

Temporarily removing personalization

Implementing a distributed architecture for personalization, with the actual work being done by separate Web servers accessing a separate database, allows you to easily disable personalization for a period of time, if necessary. For example, if your company purchases advertising time during halftime of the Super Bowl, you may want to make sure that your site is ready to handle the maximum amount of traffic possible. Disabling dynamic content — which includes personalization — is a good way to maximize your site's traffic throughput. By including the personalization code in separate include files, you can temporarily replace those include files with files that include generic, non-personalized content instead. This will immediately reduce the overhead that the site needs to process a single Web page for a customer, and can be easily reverted back to personalized content when the site's traffic falls to normal levels.

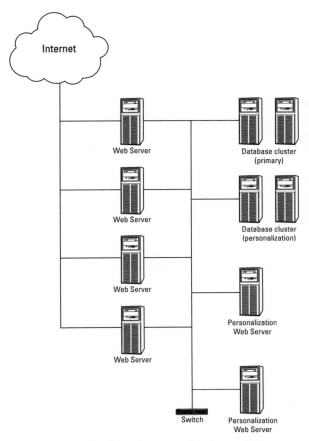

Figure 14-1: Distributed personalization architecture

Implementing Personalization

Commerce Server uses a complex system to implement personalization, thus allowing you considerable flexibility in how you deliver personalized content. This system is primarily based on expressions, which tell Commerce Server what content should be shown to which customers.

Expressions

Expressions are logical statements that evaluate to a "true" or "false" result. These expressions determine whether specific, customized content is displayed for users. For example, if you have an ad that should only be shown to users who have visited your site at least fifty times, then the expression `user.totalvisit > 50` is applied to the content. If the expression evaluates to "true" for a specific customer, that individual is shown the personalized content. You use the Campaigns module in the Commerce Server Business Desk to create expressions, and to create the action that will be taken when the expression is evaluated. You can create two types of expressions:

✦ **Target expressions** — allow you to identify where, when, and to whom content should be displayed. For example, you can target content to users who have specific profile properties. You can also target content to specific sections of a Web site, called *page groups*. For example, you can create a target expression that will display certain ads only on pages containing a certain type of content.

✦ **Catalog expressions** — specify the products in a catalog to which a discount can be applied. For example, you may have a `Product.price = 50.00` catalog expression. If this expression evaluates to "true" for a particular product, then a discount may be applied to the price of that product when purchased by a customer.

After you have created the necessary expressions, you combine them into *target groups*, which consist of one or more expressions and associated actions. For example, you can create a target group to display advertisements to avid readers who frequently visit your site. If the customer has visited the site 50 times, *and* has indicated that Reading is a major hobby, then display an ad for the new collection of Classic Reader books at 10 percent off.

Target groups allow you to tag each expression with a multiplier. You can add a multiplier that takes effect if the expression is true, or you can add a multiplier that takes effect if the expression is false. These multipliers add together to form a score for the target group's expressions. These multipliers can be combined with require/exclude conditions that allow you to precisely control the delivery of the content:

✦ **Target** — If the expression is true, increase the score for the content, which increases the probability that it will be shown. If the expression is false, no change is made to the score.

✦ **Require** — If the expression is true, the content may be delivered. If the expression is false, the content may not be delivered.

✦ **Exclude** — If the expression is true, the content may not be delivered. If the expression is false, the content may be delivered.

✦ **Sponsor**—If the expression is true, then the content provided by a sponsor is eligible for delivery, and no content without a Sponsor setting is eligible for delivery. The idea is that sponsored ads will take precedence over non-sponsored content.

In the event that multiple target groups are eligible for delivery to a customer, the one with the highest score will be delivered. This decision is made by the Content Selection Framework (CSF), which also contains factors to reduce a target group's score when that group has already been shown to the customer, thus giving other content a chance in the cycle.

Coding for personalization

Commerce Server's ContentSelector object is used to invoke the CFS, which is implemented as a Commerce Server pipeline. The ContentSelector object is essentially a Dictionary object with an additional method named `GetContent`. The object returns a SimpleList object, which contains the content to be displayed. The SimpleList object's strings can be written with a simple `Response.Write` command to cause the Web server to render them to the outgoing HTML stream.

The ContentSelector object requires supporting code in your site's Global.asa file. Listing 14-1 shows the code that is included with the Commerce Server Solution Sites. Simply add this code to the Application_OnStart event in your Global.asa file, or copy the Global.asa file from the Solution Sites.

Listing 14-1: **ContentSelector support in Global.asa**

```
' Modify sConnStr to point to a valid Campaigns database.
' Create directory.
const sConnStr = "provider=SQLOLEDB;Data Source=(local);Initial
Catalog=Retail_commerce;User ID=sa;Password=;"

Dim oPipe, dCSFAdsContext
Dim oExpressionEval, oCacheManager, dCacheConfig

' Set up CacheManager object.
Set dCacheConfig = CreateObject("Commerce.Dictionary")
dCacheConfig.ConnectionString = sConnStr
Set oCacheManager = CreateObject("Commerce.CacheManager")
oCacheManager.LoaderProgId("Ads") _
   ="Commerce.CSFLoadAdvertisements"
Set oCacheManager.LoaderConfig("Ads") = dCacheConfig
oCacheManager.RefreshInterval("Ads") = 15 * 60 ' 15 minutes

' Create the Expression Evaluator and connect it.
Set oExpressionEval = _
CreateObject("Commerce.ExpressionEvaluator")
```

Continued

Listing 14-1 *(continued)*

```
Call oExpressionEval.Connect(sConnStr)

' Create CSF advertising context, a dictionary.
Set dCSFAdsContext = CreateObject("Commerce.Dictionary")

' Create an advertising pipeline and add it to the context.
Set oPipe = CreateObject("Commerce.OrderPipeline")
' Load the pipeline configuration
oPipe.LoadPipe(Server.MapPath("Advertising.pcf"))
' Store a reference to the pipeline object in the Context
' dictionary.
Set dCSFAdsContext("pipeline") = oPipe

' Other context configuration for CSF ads.
dCSFAdsContext("RedirectUrl") = ".\redir.asp"
' Add a reference to an expression evaluator to the Context
Set dCSFAdsContext("Evaluator") = oExpressionEval
' InitCacheManager, a routine that would appear
' elsewhere in the
' global.asa, returns a reference to a CacheManager object.
Set dCSFAdsContext("CacheManager") = oCacheManager
dCSFAdsContext("CacheName") = "Ads"

' Store a reference to the dCSFAdsContext dictionary in the
' Application collection.
Set Application("CSFAdsContext") = dCSFAdsContext
```

After this support code is in place, it's easy to make a call to the CSF for a list of content to display. Listing 14-2 shows an example.

Listing 14-2: **Sample call to the ContentSelector**

```
<%
' Create a ContentSelector object.
Set CSO = Server.CreateObject("Commerce.ContentSelector")

' Use the GetContent method to get some content.
Set Ads = CSO.GetContent(Application("CSFAdsContext"))

' Write the content to the page, if any.
For Each Ad in Ads
    Response.Write(Ad)
Next
%>
```

Of course, you need to take the time to set up your expressions and target groups in the Campaigns module of the Business Desk before any of this will work properly.

How Personalization Works

Understanding the exact process that Commerce Server uses to select personalized content can help you develop expressions that perform better, deliver better end results, and improve the performance of the Content Selection Framework.

Sample content selection

The following steps illustrate how the Content Selection Framework (CSF) initializes and selects content based on the expressions that you have created. These steps start when a customer requests an ASP page that activates the CSF pipeline and requests personalized content:

1. The code in the ASP page creates the ContentSelector object (CSO), as described previously. The code in the ASP page sets the CSO page context properties and calls the CSO's GetContent method. This causes the CSO to invoke the Advertising pipeline.

2. The InitCSFPipeline component calls the GetCache method of the CacheManager object. The first time that the GetCache method is called, the CacheManager invokes the CSFLoadAdvertisements component to load the available content from the Commerce Server database.

3. The InitCSFPipeline component creates filters for the Size and PageGroups properties, which will be used to filter out content that is inappropriate (ads of the wrong size, for example) for the situation.

4. The LoadHistory component loads the user-specific history string. This allows Commerce Server to determine what content this user has already seen, which will affect the scoring process.

5. The FilterContent component applies the filters loaded by InitCSFPipeline. This can eliminate a great deal of content from the selection process, which reduces overhead.

6. The AdvertisingNeedOfDelivery component assigns each ad an initial score based on the start date and end date of the ad, the duration of the ad run, and how many events have been served to date.

7. The HistoryPenalty component applies penalties for ads that have already been shown to the current user and enforces exposure limits. These penalties take the form of lowered scores for ads that have already been displayed.

8. The EvalTargetGroups component evaluates target groups and adjusts the scores for the ads under consideration.

9. The SelectWinners component selects the winning advertisements, prevents "industry collision" by removing ads provided by other advertisers from the same industry, and uses the PageHistory string to avoid showing the same ad multiple times on the same page. (Keep in mind that the ContentSelector object can be used to retrieve multiple pieces of content per page. The purpose of this component is to make sure that all of the content shown on a page is "compatible.")

10. The SaveHistory component saves the user-specific history string, updating it with the ads that have just been selected.

11. The FormatTemplate component formats the selected advertisements by using a template that brings together ad properties, page context, and global context, and puts the resulting strings into a SimpleList object.

12. The CSO returns a SimpleList object of formatted advertisements, and the content is rendered onto the ASP page.

Improving performance

Because one of the major downfalls of a heavily personalized site can be the slow server response times that result from poor performance of the Content Selection Framework (CSF) pipeline, you should carefully design your personalization scheme to take advantage of the CSF's internal optimizations:

✦ Although you can create your own pipeline components to extend the capabilities of the CSF, you should write these components in Microsoft Visual C++, and *never* Visual Basic 6. Visual Basic 6 is an apartment-threaded language, which requires the pipeline to create a new instance of the object for every content request. This creates a tremendous amount of overhead for the server running the pipeline. Ideally, use Microsoft's Active Threading Template (ATL) when writing pipeline components in Visual C++ to achieve maximum performance.

✦ Avoid making the CSF access the database every time content is requested. By default, the CSF attempts to cache all content information in memory, refreshing it as necessary (and during slow periods) to keep the content up to date. For example, if more than 1,000 content items are available for consideration, the CSF may not be able to fit them all into memory cache. Try to keep the number of personalized content items as small as possible, or provide the CSF with a dedicated server architecture, as discussed previously, to minimize the impact of the content load and consideration.

Implementing Loyalty Programs

One way to engender customer loyalty is to offer great prices, service, and support. Another way is to offer incentives, such as frequent-buyer programs and discounts that entice customers to return for future purchases. Smart e-commerce companies use both methods. Pricing, service, and support are functions of your business model — not your technology. Incentives, on the other hand, are implemented by the technology of your site.

Unfortunately, Commerce Server offers practically no incentive capabilities out of the box. Commerce Server's built-in discount capabilities apply only to the product level — "Buy 2 widgets, get the third at 50 percent off," and so forth.

In this section, I discuss some common types of incentive programs, and how you can implement them in your site. Refer to your design documentation to see exactly what types of programs your site needs to have. Keep an open mind, too, because many different incentive programs can often be implemented as variations on a theme.

Types of incentives

You can take advantage of a variety of programs to encourage shoppers to give you repeat business. Some common examples include:

✦ Giving out dollars-off coupons to past customers. These coupons generally offer a set dollar amount or percentage off of a purchase with some minimum total value.

✦ Giving customers "points" for every purchase, and allowing them to exchange those points for rewards, such as dollars-off coupons. For example, each dollar spent at your site may equal one point, and a thousand points ($1,000 in purchases) can be exchanged for a coupon worth $50 off their next purchase.

✦ Selling a membership in a discount club, which gives the customer a fixed discount percentage off of their purchases.

Of these examples, Commerce Server offers only the last method by default. To implement this method, develop a special catalog with the same products as your normal catalog, but with blanket "10 percent off" pricing, for example. Access to the catalog is restricted to customers who purchase a membership in your discount club. You can automate this process by writing code that modifies their profile to permit access to the discount catalog when they purchase the membership. Customers will be required to log in to access their lower pricing. You can also achieve this type of loyalty program by using personalization, as discussed in the previous section of this chapter. You can create a discount that is applied to all products (or certain products) whenever the customer's profile contains specific information, such as membership in your discount club.

A fourth type of incentive encourages customers by giving them rewards not associated with your site. For example, you can give away frequent flier miles to customers for every dollar that they spend on your site. This type of reward program is generally best established through a partnership with a company like ClickMiles (www.clickmiles.com), which allows you to periodically feed them your order information. They take this information and then assign rewards as appropriate.

You will be charged a fee to participate in their programs, but you also benefit from advertising on their site.

The other common types of incentive programs almost universally offer some kind of discount on the total price of a customer's order. Unfortunately, Commerce Server doesn't offer this type of discount "out of the box," so you need to build your own. Ideally, you should build a system that's flexible enough to handle many different discount situations, so you can use the same system for a variety of different incentives.

Implementing incentives

Essentially, the common types of incentives can be boiled down to a small number of options that you can implement with a single system:

✦ The ability to offer coupons that specific shoppers can use, or coupons that any shopper who knows a "coupon code" can use.

✦ The ability to specify a dollar- or percent-off amount of the coupon.

✦ The ability to specify a minimum purchase amount for the coupon to apply.

✦ The ability to specify whether the coupon can be used multiple times or not.

✦ The ability to specify starting and ending dates for the coupon's validity.

When you can issue coupons with these characteristics, you can implement the actual issuing methods. This may include a weekly job that scans for customers who have exceeded certain purchase levels, and then automatically assigns those customers a coupon, and so forth. The first step, though, is to give your site the ability to handle the coupons. Implementing this functionality will require several new tables, a coupon workflow process, and quite a bit of code.

Creating the tables

The first table provides a place to define the actual coupons and their characteristics. Listing 14-3 shows a Transact-SQL script to create a coupons definition table.

Listing 14-3: **Creating the Coupons table**

```
CREATE TABLE [dbo].[Coupons] (
[cpn_ID] [int] IDENTITY (1, 1) NOT NULL ,
[cpn_Desc] [varchar] (100) NOT NULL ,
[cpn_ShortDesc] [varchar] (25) NOT NULL ,
[cpn_StartDate] [datetime] NOT NULL ,
[cpn_EndDate] [datetime] NOT NULL ,
[cpn_AllowAnon] [bit] NOT NULL ,
[cpn_AllowUses] [int] NOT NULL ,
```

```
[cpn_DiscType] [bit] NOT NULL ,
[cpn_DiscAmount] [float] NOT NULL ,
[cpn_Code] [varchar] (15)
NOT NULL ,
[cpn_MinPurchase] [float] NOT NULL
) ON [PRIMARY]
GO
```

This table provides all of the features that most discount programs require:

✦ The cpn_Desc and cpn_ShortDesc provide description fields for the coupon.

✦ The cpn_StartDate and cpn_EndDate allow you to specify a start and end date for the coupon.

✦ The cpn_AllowAnon column determines if the coupon can be used by anyone who knows the code, or if the coupon must be specifically assigned to a customer's account before they can use it.

✦ The cpn_AllowUses field allows you to specify how many times the customer can use the coupon, and allows you to specify a "1" for single-use coupons.

✦ Cpn_DiscType and cpn_DiscAmount let you specify a discount type — percentage or dollar — and a discount amount.

✦ The cpn_Code field allows you to create a memorable code that customers can type to receive the coupon in their purchase.

✦ Cpn_MinPurchase allows you to specify a minimum purchase requirement for the coupon to be used.

After you define the coupons, you need to be able to assign them to customers. As previously mentioned, you can create coupons that anyone can use simply by typing a code, so you can send out "coupon codes" to the general public in promotional e-mails or other advertising. However, most of your incentive coupons will be given to specific customers, so a CouponAssign table is needed to track these assignments. Listing 14-4 shows a Transact-SQL script that creates the table.

Listing 14-4: **Creating the CouponAssign table**

```
CREATE TABLE [dbo].[CouponAssign] (
[assign_id] [int] IDENTITY (1, 1) NOT NULL ,
[cpn_id] [int] NOT NULL ,
[user_id] [int] NOT NULL ,
[DateAssigned] [datetime] NOT NULL ,
) ON [PRIMARY]
GO
```

This table acts as a simple join table, allowing you to specify a coupon ID and a user ID to which the coupon should be assigned. This table also allows you to track the date on which the assignment was made.

You need to be able to match the coupon usage to an order, however, and because your system offers the ability to use coupons more than once, you can't do this in the CouponAssign table. Instead, you need to create a third table, CouponRedeem, to match the redemption of coupons to an order form. Listing 14-5 shows the T-SQL script to create this table.

Listing 14-5: **Creating the CouponRedeem table**

```
CREATE TABLE [dbo].[CouponRedeem] (
 [orderform_id] [int] NOT NULL ,
 [cpn_id] [int] NOT NULL ,
 [user_id] [int] NOT NULL
) ON [PRIMARY]
GO
```

This table links the OrderFormHeader table, via orderform_id. The table provides the coupon ID number that was used. You can't link directly to the CouponAssign table, because the customer may use coupons that, rather than being directly assigned, are available to all shoppers. The CouponRedeem table also denormalizes the user ID value from the OrderFormHeader table to facilitate determining what customer has redeemed the coupon.

Coupon workflow

Develop a new workflow for the coupon system. The workflow is shown in Figure 14-2.

This workflow implements all of your desired features. Customers must enter a coupon code to begin the process, typically during checkout. Before continuing, the checkout process verifies the customer's ability to use the coupon. This is accomplished through a series of decisions:

✦ Is the customer permitted to use the coupon? The coupon must either be marked as usable by anyone (cpn_AllowAnon in the Coupons table), or it must have been assigned to the customer's user ID in the CouponAssign table. Note that this requires the customer to sign in, so you can determine their user ID number and check for the existence of the coupon assignment.

✦ Does the customer's order meet the coupon's minimum purchase requirement?

✦ Is the coupon being used within its valid date range?

✦ Has the customer already used this coupon (as indicated in the CouponRedeem table) the maximum number of times allowed, as defined in the Coupons table?

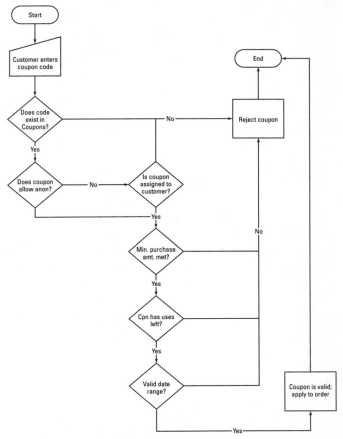

Figure 14-2: Coupon acceptance workflow

If the coupon meets the required criteria, then it is accepted and applied to the order. If the coupon is not accepted, the site should display some meaningful rejection notice that clearly indicates why the coupon was not accepted. Here are some sample rejection messages:

✦ "Sorry, your coupon has expired," or "Sorry, your coupon will not be effective until [startdate]."

✦ "Sorry, your coupon requires a minimum purchase amount of $50.00, not including taxes, shipping, or handling."

✦ "Sorry, that coupon code is not available for your use. Please make sure that you entered it correctly."

✦ "Sorry, you have already used that coupon the maximum number of times permitted."

Writing the SQL Server code

The first step in creating your coupon-handling code is to fashion several stored procedures that will allow you to work with the coupons. The first stored procedure, which I call sp_GetCouponList, should accept two optional parameters — the user ID of the current customer, and the dollar amount of the order in that customer's shopping cart. The stored procedure will return a list of applicable coupons based on the input:

✦ If no parameters are provided, the stored procedure will return a list of coupons that may be used by all shoppers, and whether they may be used on this order.

✦ If the user ID is provided, the list will also contain any coupons specifically assigned to the current user.

✦ If the order total is provided, the list will include coupons available to any shopper that can be used on the current order, given the minimum purchase requirements of the various coupons.

✦ If the order includes both parameters, the list will include all coupons that may be used on the current order, based on the coupons available to those users who have a suitable minimum purchase requirement.

This stored procedure can be used to retrieve a list of coupons to display to the shopper, or to retrieve a list of coupons to automatically apply to the order. The code for this stored procedure is shown in Listing 14-6.

 Note   Because this stored procedure returns an output parameter of the *table* data type, it can only be used with SQL Server 2000.

Listing 14-6: The sp_GetCouponList stored procedure

```
CREATE PROCEDURE [sp_GetCouponList]
 @userid int, @order_total float,
 @list table (
 [cpn_ID] [int] IDENTITY (1, 1) NOT NULL ,
 [cpn_Desc] [varchar] (100) COLLATE
SQL_Latin1_General_CP1_CI_AS NOT NULL ,
 [cpn_ShortDesc] [varchar] (25) COLLATE
SQL_Latin1_General_CP1_CI_AS NOT NULL ,
 [cpn_StartDate] [datetime] NOT NULL ,
 [cpn_EndDate] [datetime] NOT NULL ,
 [cpn_AllowAnon] [bit] NOT NULL ,
 [cpn_AllowUses] [int] NOT NULL ,
 [cpn_DiscType] [bit] NOT NULL ,
 [cpn_DiscAmount] [float] NOT NULL ,
 [cpn_Code] [varchar] (15)
 COLLATE SQL_Latin1_General_CP1_CI_AS NOT NULL ,
 [cpn_MinPurchase] [float] NOT NULL
) OUTPUT
```

```
AS

/*                        */
/* only order total provided */
/*                        */
IF @userid IS NULL AND @order_total IS NOT NULL
BEGIN

 /* get anon coupons */
 INSERT INTO @list
  SELECT * FROM Coupons WHERE cpn_MinPurchase
  <= @order_total AND cpn_AllowAnon = 1

END

/*                     */
/* only userid provided */
/*                     */
IF @userid IS NOT NULL AND @order_total IS NULL
BEGIN

 /* get anon coupons */
 INSERT INTO @list
  SELECT * FROM Coupons WHERE cpn_AllowAnon = 1

 /* get user-specific coupons */
 INSERT INTO @list
  SELECT c.* FROM Coupons C INNER JOIN
  CouponAssign A ON C.cpn_ID = A.cpn_id
  WHERE A.user_id = @userid

 /* update coupon usage */
 UPDATE @list SET cpn_AllowUses =
 cpn_AllowUses -
 (SELECT COUNT(cpn_id) AS uses FROM CouponRedeem
 R WHERE r.cpn_id = cpn_id AND r.user_id = @userid)

 /* remove overused coupons */
 DELETE FROM @list WHERE cpn_AllowUses <= 0

END

/*                */
/* both provided */
/*                */
IF @userid IS NOT NULL AND @order_total IS NOT NULL
BEGIN
/* get anon coupons */
 INSERT INTO @list
  SELECT * FROM Coupons WHERE cpn_AllowAnon = 1

 /* get user-specific coupons */
```

Continued

Listing 14-6 *(continued)*

```
INSERT INTO @list
 SELECT c.* FROM Coupons C INNER JOIN
 CouponAssign A ON C.cpn_ID = A.cpn_id
 WHERE A.user_id = @userid

/* update coupon usage */
UPDATE @list SET cpn_AllowUses =
cpn_AllowUses -
(SELECT COUNT(cpn_id) AS uses FROM CouponRedeem
R WHERE r.cpn_id = cpn_id AND r.user_id = @userid)

/* remove overused coupons */
DELETE FROM @list WHERE cpn_AllowUses <= 0

/* remove coupons not meeting purchase */
DELETE FROM @list WHERE cpn_MinPurchase >
@order_total

END
```

A stored procedure that updates the appropriate information when a customer uses a coupon is also useful. This stored procedure, sp_RedeemCoupon, is shown in Listing 14-7. It requires two input parameters — the order ID number that the coupon was used in, and the coupon ID that was used.

Listing 14-7: The sp_RedeemCoupon stored procedure

```
CREATE PROCEDURE [sp_RedeemCoupon]
 @orderid [int],
 @couponid [int]
AS

 /* Get user ID */
 DECLARE @userid [int]
 SELECT @userid = (SELECT user_id FROM
 OrderFormHeaders WHERE orderform_id = @orderid)

 /* Insert row in CouponRedeem */
 INSERT INTO CouponRedeem (orderform_id,
 User_id, cpn_id) VALUES(@orderid,
 @userid, @couponid)
```

To remind or not?

A crucial decision that you and your management team will have to make is whether to remind customers that they have coupons to use. On one hand, doing so is a good customer service policy. You can simply add code to your shopping cart display to remind customers of their available coupons. This technique also encourages customers to buy more because they'll be saving money on their purchase anyway. On the other hand, customers who were going to make a purchase anyway shouldn't be reminded of any profit-cutting coupons.

Another decision that you and your team must make is whether to have the system automatically use any coupons that the customer has waiting. Again, you will have arguments for both sides of the issue. One compelling argument to *not* automatically apply the coupon is for percent-off discounts—customers may prefer to save these coupons for future, larger purchases.

You can split the difference by adding two additional fields to the Coupons table, or even to the CouponAssign table. These fields will allow you to specify whether the coupon should be listed for the customer as a reminder, and whether the system should automatically apply the coupon to any purchases that qualify. This allows you to control the coupons that are shown and automatically applied, thus giving you the ability to treat different types of coupons differently.

Modifying the checkout

Once the sp_GetCouponList and sp_RedeemCoupon stored procedures are in place, the checkout process will need to be revised. You must provide your customer with a means of entering coupon codes. You should already have decided whether the system will list a customer's available coupons for them, and whether the system will automatically apply any coupons that the customer has available. You must also decide whether customers will be able to use multiple discounts on a single order. These business decisions will dictate the design of your coupon code entry form in your checkout process.

Include code that adds the applicable coupons to the customer's order, and modify the order-processing pipeline to calculate the total discount and charge the customer accordingly. If you want the total discount value to be stored as part of the customer's receipt in the database (which is advisable), you will have to modify the receipt schema (the OrderFormHeaders table) and the checkout pipeline to write this information to the database.

Another approach, which may be more acceptable to your company's accountants, is to never apply an order-wide discount. Instead, calculate the total percentage that each item in the order contributes to the order total, and then divide the order discount coupons across each item independently.

For example, imagine that a customer places an order containing five items. Each item is priced at $2.00 for an order total of $10.00. The customer also has a $1.00-off coupon to apply to the order. Because each item's cost represents one-fifth of the order, one-fifth of the coupon, or twenty cents, is applied to each item. The adjusted price for each item is then $1.80 for an order total of $9.00. Because this is the method that most accountants generally prefer, this is the method that I focus on implementing. As it happens, this method also works better with Commerce Server's built-in functionality, which only recognizes item-level discounts. This means that you won't necessarily have to modify any of the OrderFormHeaders schema because the discount information will be maintained in OrderFormItems instead.

To implement this method, modify the checkout by adding a field to the customer's order form containing the total order-wide discount that should be applied. You can't calculate the per-item discount in the checkout because Commerce Server will recalculate discounts on each item later, when the pipeline is run. Any per-item changes that you make in the checkout are likely to be overwritten.

Fortunately, the Commerce Server OrderForm object is fairly flexible (it's basically just a modified Dictionary object) and allows you to add keys to it. You need to add a key that contains the total order-wide discount; you also need to write a pipeline component to calculate the per-item discount and apply it to each item in the order. You can do this with a single line of code, assuming that you have a valid reference to the OrderForm object:

```
ObjOrderForm._coupon_disc = iTotalCouponAmount
```

Note   Prefixing the new field name with an underscore automatically prevents Commerce Server from trying to save the field to a column in the database. The data will still be saved in the marshaled basket data for future reference.

Modifying the pipeline

After the OrderForm object contains the total discount amount that is to be applied to the order, you need to modify one of the Order Processing Pipelines (OPPs) to perform the calculation that distributes the discount across the items in the order. You do this by using Commerce Server's Pipeline Editor, as shown in Figure 14-3.

If you are using the pipelines included with the Solution Sites, consider modifying the Basket pipeline (basket.pcf) to contain your order-wide discount code. If you are creating your own pipelines, place the additional order-wide discount component wherever it is most appropriate.

The exact modifications that you make to the pipeline depend on how you have created the pipelines and how they are using the Commerce Server OrderForm object. You basically need to modify the adjusted price of each item in the order to reflect the order-wide discount. *Which* pipeline that you modify depends, again, on how your site is constructed. Chapter 11 contains a more detailed discussion on how some of the various Solution Site pipelines are used; if you are creating your own pipelines, examine them to determine which one is best suited to contain order-wide discount processing.

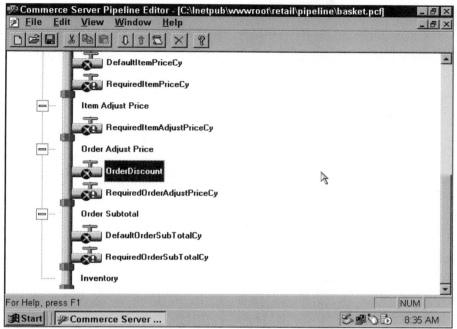

Figure 14-3: Commerce Server Pipeline Editor

Caution   Modifying the Commerce Server pipelines is a complex task. The pipelines represent a major piece of critical functionality within the Commerce Server product,
and you should make sure that you understand all of the implications of your
changes, and that you thoroughly test any modified pipelines.

Modifying Commerce Server Pipelines

You have two options for adding components to a pipeline: You can provide a COM+ control
in the form of a DLL, or you can write VBScript or JavaScript in a *Scriptor* component. The
advantage of writing script, of course, is that it's easy to do. However, Scriptor components
require more processing overhead because the script must be interpreted at run-time.

You can achieve the best pipeline performance by adding compiled components in the
form of a DLL. Unfortunately, Visual Basic 6 is not the best candidate for writing these components. Although it can be done, Visual Basic 6 only supports an *apartment-threading
model*, which means that Commerce Server must create a new instance of the component
in memory *every time the component is called.* This can potentially create even more overhead than a simple script would.

Pipeline components are best written in Visual C++, by using the Microsoft Active
Threading Template. The components should be marked as *poolable,* and they should be
compiled to support *both* available threading models.

Final steps

You may want to take these additional steps to complete your coupon system:

✦ Create some form of administrative interface by adding to the Commerce Server Business Desk. This will allow the appropriate users to create, assign, and administer coupons. For example, you may want to give your customer service staff the ability to assign dollars-off coupons to help with customer-satisfaction issues.

✦ Modify your shopping cart code to display available coupons, if desired.

✦ If you want your order-processing pipeline to automatically apply any coupons that are appropriate for the customer's purchase, then you should also create that code. This code will need to include logic to determine which coupon or coupons to use if multiple coupons qualify. Typically, you don't want a huge number of coupons applying to an order, but if multiple coupons *can* be used, your logic will need to determine which *one* is used.

✦ Create a reporting system to keep management informed about the use of coupons. Discounts of this type can be the biggest reason for declining profit margins in e-commerce companies, so you shouldn't begin using coupons without adequate reporting mechanisms in place to track their usage.

✦ Modify the OrderFormHeader table, and the related data warehousing schema in the Commerce Server data warehouse database to hold the total dollar amount of any order-wide discounts that were applied to an order. This will allow you to more easily generate statistics for order-wide discounts and maintain your company's profit margins.

Summary

Personalization makes your site easier to use and more engaging for your customers, providing them with a better experience, and Commerce Server's built-in functionality makes it relatively easy to take advantage of the information that you have on your customers. Although you may need to "roll your own" technology for specific features, personalization is usually worth the time and effort for increased repeat traffic and sales.

✦   ✦   ✦

Supporting the Customer Experience with Sound Customer Communication

Customer communication in the e-commerce world takes
the form of e-mail. Your site will employ two types of
e-mail communications: Ad-hoc e-mail to communicate specific information to a single customer, such as the status of an
order; and bulk e-mail to communicate with large groups of
customers at the same time.

Ad-hoc Communications

Ad-hoc e-mails are sent to update a customer on order status,
confirm that an order has been placed, and so forth. These
e-mails are automatically generated in response to a certain
event, such as an order being completed or shipped. You can
take advantage of several different techniques for processing
and sending these e-mails, and you may want to choose a variety of techniques for different situations.

How Commerce Server does it

Commerce Server's built-in method for sending ad-hoc e-mails
is limited to a pipeline component that processes and sends
the e-mail at the time the order is completed. The benefit of
using a pipeline component is that the e-mail only gets sent if
the entire order processing pipeline (and thus, the order)
completes successfully (assuming that you place the e-mail
components at the end of the pipeline). The down side is that

the Web server processing the order is stuck with the task of delivering the e-mail message, unless you configure the Web server to forward all messages to a central e-mail server for final delivery.

To configure the order-processing pipeline to support this functionality, take the following four steps:

Step one

Update your Global.asa file with the text of the order confirmation e-mail, as shown in Listing 15-1. This code should be added after the call to Main, at the end of the MessageManager strings.

Listing 15-1: Message text to be added to Global.asaDim objMM

```
Set  objMM = Server.CreateObject("Commerce.MessageManager")
Call objMM.AddLanguage("usa", &H0409)
objMM.defaultLanguage = "usa"
Call objMM.AddMessage("email_subject", "Confirmation")
Call objMM.AddMessage("email_body", "Order completed!")
Call oMessageManager.AddMessage("email_total", "Total:")
```

Step two

Create a VBScript file. This file should be saved in the Pipeline directory of your site, and will serve to format the message. The script will actually be called by a Scriptor pipeline component, which you add in the next step. Listing 15-2 shows a sample script. Essentially, the script needs to use the field values that the pipeline will provide.

Listing 15-2: Formatting the messageFunction mscsexecute(config, orderform, context, flags)

```
Dim objMM, objDF
Set objMM = context.MessageManager
Set objDF = context.DataFunctions

orderform.[_email_subject] = _
         objMM.GetMessage("email_subject")
orderform.[_email_body] = _
         objMM.GetMessage("email_body") _
         & chr(10) & chr(13) _
         & orderform.[order_id] _
         & chr(10) & chr(13) _
         & objMM.GetMessage("email_total") _
         & objDF.Money(CLng(orderform.[_total_total]))
mscsexecute = 1
End Function
```

Step three

Modify the order-processing pipeline to include a Scriptor component that will call the script that you just wrote. The pipeline files are generally stored in the pipeline directory of your site; if you've used the Solution Site's order processing pipeline as a starting point, it will be named Purchase.pcf.

1. Open the pipeline file by using the Commerce Server Pipeline Editor.

2. Open the Accept stage, and right-click the last component in the pipeline.

3. Select Insert Component from the pop-up menu, and click After.

4. Select the Scriptor component type.

5. Double-click the new Scriptor component to edit its properties.

6. Select VBScript as the scripting engine, specify an external source, and specify the filename of the script that you created. Click OK.

7. Save the modified pipeline.

This component will take care of creating the e-mail.

Step four

Send the e-mail. To do this, add another component to the pipeline, just after the Scriptor component that you've created. This time, add a SendSMTP component, configured to send e-mail to your SMTP server.

Note that most Internet Information Services (IIS) installations include a basic SMTP server, so that each Web server can, in theory, send its own e-mail. I discourage this approach, because it puts a burden on the Web server that can be placed elsewhere (namely, on a dedicated SMTP or Exchange 2000 server). Be sure that the mail server allows the Web servers to log in and relay mail, or the delivery won't work correctly.

Immediately sending to the recipient

You may not want to build your ad-hoc e-mails into the order-processing pipeline. In fact, you gain several advantages by *not* doing it this way. E-mails sent from the pipeline are *not* treated as a transaction, which is why the SendSMTP component must be located at the *end* of the pipeline, when any other steps in the pipeline have already succeeded. This means that you may as well wait until the pipeline completes without errors to send the e-mail from the ASP page that calls the order-processing pipeline. If the pipeline *does* encounter errors, you can send a "non-confirmation" e-mail, letting the customer know that his or her order was *not* processed and that he or she won't be charged.

I recommend that you implement your own ad-hoc e-mails. You'll be able to use a wider variety of technologies than just the Commerce Server SendSMTP pipeline component. The first method that you can use to send e-mails is the *immediate method,* which means having the Web server send the e-mail as soon as the event that triggered the e-mail, such as an order completing, has finished processing.

You should be aware of how SMTP e-mail is delivered across the Internet. The server that originally generates the e-mail is responsible for delivering it, either to the final recipient, or to a "middle man" e-mail server known as a *relay server.* Your Web servers will generally deliver the e-mail that is to go out immediately, and I do *not* recommend that you burden your Web servers with the task of delivering the e-mail to its final recipient. Doing so will require the Web server to make *at least* three DNS queries to locate the recipient's e-mail server, and then establish a connection with that server to deliver the e-mail. Instead, program all of your Web servers to deliver their e-mail to a *smart host,* or *mail relay.* This should be a robust messaging server like Microsoft Exchange Server 2000, but you can use a less expensive SMTP-only server if necessary. That server can then be configured to perform the final delivery of the e-mail.

Tip   Using Exchange advantageously provides fault-tolerant message delivery, message tracking, and better troubleshooting if something goes wrong. It's also a transaction-based system and is less likely to "lose" e-mails if an error or hardware failure occurs.

Unless you absolutely *have* to, I do not recommend dumping your outgoing e-mail onto your Internet Service Provider's relay server. Your customer communications — especially ad-hoc e-mails, which often include important information — are too important to entrust to someone else.

After you've established a messaging infrastructure to deliver ad-hoc e-mails, you can begin configuring your Web servers to create and send the e-mails. Internet Information Services (IIS) 5.0 contains all the necessary pieces to make this an easy task. Just make sure that you've installed the SMTP Server component of IIS on each Web server that will need to send mail.

Configure the properties for the IIS SMTP virtual server. On the Delivery tab, click the Advanced button and configure the name of your mail relay server, as shown in Figure 15-1.

By providing the name of a "smart host" and configuring the virtual server to *never* attempt direct delivery, you ensure that the Web server will immediately deliver all outgoing e-mail to your mail relay server rather than attempting to deliver the e-mail itself. Be sure that your mail relay server permits the Web servers to connect and relay e-mail (you can generally do this by specifying the IP addresses of your Web servers in the mail server's configuration).

Next, write VBScript code in the appropriate ASP pages to create and send the e-mail. You'll be using the Collaborative Data Objects (CDO) object library, which is a messaging library included with Windows 2000. Listing 15-3 shows a sample for sending e-mail from script.

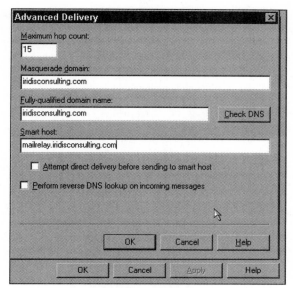

Figure 15-1: Configuring delivery properties of the SMTP server

Listing 15-3: **Sending e-mail using CDO-NTS**

```
Dim objMsg
Set objMsg = Server.CreateObject("CDO.Message")
objMsg.To = "recipient@someplace.com"
objMsg.Subject = "Order confirmation"
objMsg.From = "service@retailer.com"
objMsg.TextBody = "Thank you for your order!"
objMsg.Send
```

Some programmers prefer to use a third party SMTP mailer component, such as Server Objects' ASPQmail (www.serverobjects.com). My experience has been that IIS' built-in SMTP service is more than sufficient for delivering the message to a mail relay server located on the same LAN without imposing significant additional overhead on the Web server.

Of course, having ad-hoc e-mail sent immediately does impose a small burden on the Web servers, a burden which grows as the traffic on your Web site grows. Other approaches to sending e-mail may be more appropriate in a high-volume environment, and can help keep your Web servers focused on the task of serving Web pages.

Another problem with using the SMTP service is the possibility of your mail relay server being unavailable, or being too busy with other tasks, such as sending out 100,000 direct e-mails for an advertising campaign, to accept a connection from the Web servers quickly enough. In these circumstances, the Web servers' SMTP service will encounter delays and expend additional processing cycles trying to connect to the mail relay server.

Sending to a mail queue

Using Windows 2000's message queuing services (Microsoft Message Queue Server, or MSMQ) allows your Web servers to place their outgoing ad-hoc e-mails into a fault-tolerant queue. You can write a standalone utility application that periodically polls its queue for new e-mail messages to be sent, pulls those message from the queue, composes the outgoing SMTP e-mail, and delivers it to the mail relay server. Because you control the operation of the utility application, you can ensure that it runs frequently enough to provide timely delivery of the e-mail messages, but does not try to run against major outgoing e-mail batches like a direct mail promotion.

The first step is to configure a central message queue server, perhaps on your mail relay server. Then install and configure message queuing services on each of your Web servers that will need to send e-mail, and create a queue for your utility application.

Next, program your ASP pages to place a message on the queue for each ad-hoc e-mail that you need to send. Listing 15-4 shows an example of how to do this.

Listing 15-4: **Placing a message on a queue from ASP**

```
<%
Dim MsgBody
MsgBody = "/recipient@someplace.com"
MsgBody = MsgBody & "/Order Confirmation"
MsgBody = MsgBody & "Thanks for your order!"

'Open Queue
Set objInfo = CreateObject ("MSMQ.MSMQQueueInfo")
objInfo.PathName = "MachineName\QueueName"
Set objQ = objInfo.Open (2, 0)
set objInfo = Nothing

'Send message
Set objMsg = CreateObject ("MSMQ.MSMQMessage")
if Not msg Is Nothing Then

   objMsg.Label = "Outgoing e-mail"
   objMsg.body = MsgBody
   objMsg.Send objQ, false
```

```
End If
Set objQ = Nothing
Set objMsg = Nothing
%>
```

You can use MSMQ's administrative tools to verify that your ASP code is placing messages on the queue properly. In this example, I've used the slash character ("/") to separate the fields of the message; you can use any character that you feel is appropriate.

The final step is to write an application to retrieve messages from this queue, format them as SMTP messages, and send them to your mail relay server. You can write this either as a Visual Basic compiled executable that you schedule with the Windows Task Scheduler, or as an ActiveX script (say, as a SQL Server Agent job). The syntax is pretty much identical. Listing 15-5 shows two VBScript subroutines that retrieve the messages and send them as e-mail; this can also be used as the source for VB subroutines. The second subroutine assumes that the computer running the script has been configured to deliver e-mail messages to your mail relay server.

Listing 15-5: **Sending messages from the queue in VBScript**

```
Sub ReadMessage()

 'Open Queue
 Set objInfo = CreateObject ("MSMQ.MSMQQueueInfo")
 objInfo.PathName = "MachineName\QueueName"
 Set objQ = objInfo.Open (1, 0)
 Set objInfo = Nothing

 'Read first message from queue
 Set objMsg=objQ.Receive (0, true, true, 100)
 If objMsg is Nothing Then
   Exit Sub
 Else
   Do Until objMsg is Nothing
     ProcessMail objMsg.Body
     Set objMsg = objQ.Receive (0, true, true, 100)
   Loop
 End If

End Sub

Sub ProcessMail(Body As String)
```

Continued

Listing 15-5 *(continued)*

```
'locate slashes
p1 = InStr(1,Body,"/")
p2 = Instr(p1,Body,"/")

'parse to,subj,body
sTo = Left(Body,p1-1)
sSubj = Mid(Body,p1+1,p2-1)
sBody = Right(Len(Body)-p2+1)

'send e-mail
Set objMsg = Server.CreateObject("CDO.Message")
objMsg.To = "recipient@someplace.com"
objMsg.Subject = "Order confirmation"
objMsg.From = "service@retailer.com"
objMsg.TextBody = "Thank you for your order!"
objMsg.Send

End Sub
```

This may seem like a complicated way just to send an e-mail or two, but MSMQ provides a great deal of fault tolerance and gives you considerable control over the overhead imposed by sending e-mail messages.

Processing e-mail in a batch

Another approach to ad-hoc e-mail is to send the e-mail in a batch, rather than send it immediately. For example, you can write a script or utility application that sends order confirmation e-mails every couple of hours, programming the script or utility to scan through recently received orders to send confirmations as necessary.

I recommend that you modify the order head table in Commerce Server's database to include a "send e-mail" column with a `bit` data type. The default value for the column should be zero, indicating that no e-mail has been sent. The utility application must simply query the database for all of the orders with a zero value in this field, send an appropriate e-mail, and then set the value of that field to one, indicating that an e-mail has been sent.

This technique also allows you to process order update e-mails by setting the value of the field to zero again. The next time that the utility application runs, it will re-select the record and send a new order confirmation e-mail. If you want the utility to send an e-mail that's worded differently for initial order confirmations than for subsequent order updates, change the field type to `int` and set it to zero when a confirmation needs to be sent, set it to one when an update needs to be sent, or set it to two if no e-mail needs to be sent. The utility application can then select the appropriate records for confirmation e-mails or update e-mails, and set the "send e-mail" column to two when it has sent the appropriate messages.

You can use the same techniques described earlier in this section to send the e-mail by using a mail relay server, or to place the messages on a message queue for a second utility application to retrieve and send. Again, the MSMQ method offers fault tolerance and provides a way of centralizing all of your ad-hoc messaging. For example, the utility application that's responsible for reading new messages from the queue and sending the e-mail messages can be programmed to look for a "message type" indicator, which may instruct the application to format the message differently for outgoing order confirmations, order updates, newsletter subscription confirmations, opt-out confirmations, and other types of ad-hoc e-mail.

Bulk Communications

Bulk e-mail is mainly used for marketing and advertising purposes. You may choose to send an e-mail as part of an overall advertising campaign for a new product or service, or you may have an ongoing campaign, such as an e-mail "newsletter," to which customers subscribe. In either event, you have the option of using Commerce Server's own built-in direct mail management capabilities, or building your own mail manager.

Build it or buy it?

Commerce Server 2000 comes with an incredibly flexible and robust Direct Mail component that allows you to completely manage multiple e-mail campaigns. It includes built-in support for opt-out lists, and seems to be the perfect solution. It is — if you can afford some serious server hardware — but be aware that its flexibility and power come at the price of incredible overhead. It's all in the way the Direct Mailer operates.

Commerce Server Direct Mail

Commerce Server's Direct Mail component works on a campaign basis. In other words, a direct mail piece must be associated with an advertising campaign. You can use a campaign that already has advertising items attached to it — after all, direct mail is simply another form of advertising — or you can create a new campaign.

The first step to using the Direct Mailer is to create a mailing list. In general, you provide this as a comma-separated text file, although the Direct Mailer supports other means (such as a SQL Server query) of creating the list. The list must contain specific fields, and the fields must appear in a certain order, as detailed in the Commerce Server documentation. You can generate these lists from analysis reports, but those reports must be saved as text files in the proper format and then imported into the List Manager.

Next, you have to create the actual mail piece. In order to allow the pieces to be completely customized, you must create them as ASP pages. Then schedule a direct mail job to merge the content with a designated mailing list. Commerce Server's Direct Mail component launches into action. For each name on the mailing list, the Direct Mail component will "hit" the ASP page to generate the actual mail content. It will also directly deliver the e-mail to the recipients, acting as an SMTP sender. This entire process is orchestrated by the Direct Mail pipeline, which is responsible for configuring the process to remain within certain processing or bandwidth constraints, filtering out users who have asked to be removed from lists, and so forth.

Direct Mail is also capable of handling opt-out information generated by users who ask to be removed from a mailing list. The Solution Sites come with a sample opt-out ASP page, which you can link to directly from your e-mail body. This page makes a nice starting point for your own opt-out pages and will, by default, remove a recipient from the *campaign's* mailing list, but not from other mailing lists used by your site.

Do it yourself

If you don't want to use Commerce Server's built-in direct mail functionality — because the hardware or the connectivity requirements are too high, or for other reasons — you can build you own system without much hassle. However, you need to duplicate the basic components of Commerce Server's functionality:

✦ If you intend to have opt-in newsletters, create a way for customers to sign up, so you can track their names and e-mail addresses.

✦ Create some kind of opt-out list so customers can ask to be removed from the mailings.

✦ Create a list-generation tool that constructs your mailing lists and removes customers who have opted out.

✦ Establish a relationship with a bulk e-mailing firm, or create a bulk-mailing infrastructure of your own, such as a dedicated Exchange server.

All of these tasks are relatively straightforward, and I discuss exactly how to build them later in this chapter.

Weighing the pros and cons

Exactly how you implement your customer communications depends mainly on whether or not you feel you can support Direct Mailer's requirements. With the close integration to Commerce Server, the ability to manage multiple direct mail campaigns and lists, and the preprogrammed opt-out functionality, Direct Mailer gives you everything you could ask for — even personalized direct mail pieces. Unfortunately, your direct mail server has to be a pretty serious computer, capable of running SQL Server, the Direct Mailer components, and a Web server all at once. If you will be sending 100,000 e-mails a day, a small number for even start-up e-commerce companies, then the direct mail server will likely need multiple processors, fast hard drives in a RAID 5 array, and lots of RAM, in addition to good DNS and Internet connectivity. And the requirements will grow with your direct mail volume. The goal is to have hardware that is capable of pumping out the number of e-mails you need to send in a timely fashion.

If you can afford this kind of hardware, and if you have sufficient bandwidth to DNS servers and the Internet, you should use Direct Mailer. If you *can't* afford this kind of hardware, or don't have sufficient connectivity, then you should consider designing your own direct mail solution, but understand that you're not going to get all the features that Direct Mailer provides. A do-it-yourself direct mail solution may even include having an outside firm actually send your mail for you, which will all but eliminate overhead on your own servers.

Tip

If you *must* have the great features provided by Direct Mailer, then you simply *must* come up with the hardware and connectivity to run it all.

If you decide to go with a do-it-yourself direct mail solution, consider using an outside firm to send your bulk e-mail for you (a topic I discuss next). These services can often return some of the features that you lose by not using the Direct Mailer component, such as content customization.

Mail it yourself . . . or not?

Launching a customer communications program means that you need to have a way to send thousands, if not hundreds of thousands, of e-mail messages in a short period of time, a process referred to as *bulk e-mailing*. Many e-commerce companies do *not* handle their own bulk e-mail simply because of the tremendous amount of required resources. Companies like MessageReach (www.messagereach.com) exist primarily to handle this type of bulk e-mail work on your behalf, for fees from 1 to 5 cents per message sent. Many e-commerce companies *do* send their own bulk e-mail, though, and you *can* too, if you understand the technical requirements for doing so.

Sending bulk e-mail is not like sending a single message with a few thousand "cc:" addresses. Bulk e-mail is usually individually addressed, to make it seem more personal and to ensure that it doesn't contain the names of every other recipient. Also, the SMTP mail protocol has limitations on how big the "cc:" field can be, so one-message-per-recipient is also a practical requirement.

For a mail server to send a single e-mail message, it must follow these steps:

1. Contact a DNS server to resolve the domain name of the e-mail's recipient.

2. Contact a DNS server *in* that domain to find the address of a mail server.

3. Establish an SMTP communications session with that mail server.

4. Pass on the e-mail message and sign off of the mail server.

Most mail servers will *cache* the DNS information for a short time, so that subsequent messages to the same domain require less work.

For example, sending an e-mail to Microsoft.com requires your mail server to first contact a ".com" DNS server, referred to as a *root* server, to get the address of a "Microsoft.com" DNS server. The mail server then contacts that DNS server to get a list of Microsoft.com "MX" records, which list the servers capable of receiving mail for Microsoft.com recipients. The server then establishes a connection with a mail server via the SMTP protocol and delivers the message. For bulk e-mail, multiply that process, which may take a couple of seconds, by the number of e-mails that you need to send. Exchange Server is actually capable of carrying this task out with several messages in parallel, so the whole process doesn't take as long, but the cost is more server overhead.

One way to relieve some of the overhead is to configure your mail server to forward all mail to a mail server maintained by your Internet Service Provider (ISP). This simply transfers the burden to *that* server, however, and most ISPs won't allow this type of activity without a significant extra fee. You *can* build an e-mail system capable of handling the load. Key requirements include:

✦ Make sure that your bulk e-mail server is dedicated to the task. It will be able to process outgoing messages and the inevitable incoming "undeliverable" messages much more quickly if it doesn't have to deal with other e-mail tasks.

✦ Make sure that the server is not configured to save copies of outgoing messages in its database. This results in vastly increased disk throughput and additional strain on the server.

✦ Provide the mail server with a high-speed connection to a fast DNS server. This DNS server should be configured with *root hints* that allow it to directly contact root DNS servers. Do *not* use a DNS server that relies upon *another* DNS server to resolve root name queries.

✦ Provide the mail server with a high-speed connection to the Internet. The more bandwidth available to it, the more messages it can deliver at once, and the faster they will be delivered.

✦ Try to avoid using Exchange Server 5.5 or earlier. That version used X.400 as its internal mail protocol, which means its performance with SMTP mail is somewhat lacking in bulk e-mail situations. Exchange Server 2000 uses SMTP as its native protocol, and was written specifically to handle SMTP messages — including those in a bulk e-mail — faster than the older versions.

✦ Try to group your outgoing e-mail addresses by domain name. This allows Exchange to connect to the destination mail server and transfer all messages for that domain, rather than continuously connecting and reconnecting. Exchange has optimizations to help it group messages by domain name internally, but it will take better advantage of these optimizations if your messages are sent in order of domain name.

If you're planning to use Commerce Server's built-in Direct Mailer component, it will benefit from most of the same configuration optimizations. Also, Microsoft (and I) *strongly* recommended that the Direct Mailer be run on a server dedicated to the task — *not* on one of your Web servers. Direct Mailer must be installed on the same computer as the Direct Mailer database, which means that the server must also have sufficient horsepower to run SQL Server 7.0 or SQL Server 2000. The Direct Mailer also has the additional overhead of having to access and render an ASP page for each and every e-mail sent, which means that it should be run on a fairly robust server, or a couple of servers working together.

Whether or not you will mail your bulk mail yourself is a pretty easy question to answer:

✦ Will you be using Commerce Server's Direct Mailer component? If so, you have no choice but to send the e-mails yourself.

✦ Will you be writing your own direct mail solution because you want to simplify the hardware requirements, but you have plenty of bandwidth? You can mail it yourself.

✦ Will you be writing your own direct mail solution and don't have sufficient bandwidth or connectivity to send the intended volume of e-mail from your own network? Write your solution to use an external mail firm.

If you do elect to go with an outside firm to handle your bulk e-mail, select one with a good per-message rate that offers customization ability. For example, MessageReach allows you to create "mail merge" fields in your e-mail body. Each field corresponds to a field in the mailing list file that you send them, and their server merges the information as the e-mails are sent, much like the mail merge feature found in most word processors. A good bulk e-mail partner can provide features like this that help achieve the same functionality delivered by Commerce Server's built-in component.

Reviewing your direct mail goals

Before you begin implementing your direct mail features, review your design documentation and your direct mail goals. Make sure that you understand the functionality that your direct mail features must provide, and remember that Commerce Server's Direct Mail component, while heavy on the hardware requirements, provides just about every conceivable goal.

Using Commerce Server Direct Mail

Commerce Server's Direct Mail component is a flexible, robust solution that is completely integrated with Commerce Server's ad campaign system and Analysis services. The Direct Mail component allows you to plan, monitor, and manage your direct mail campaigns along with your other advertising. For customer opt-in communications like newsletters, you can create a dedicated, ongoing ad campaign that contains only the direct mail component responsible for sending the newsletter.

Direct Mail is a complex system and requires a carefully planned messaging infrastructure for best performance. It provides complete opt-out support, allows you to use mailing lists from a variety of sources, and allows you to create dynamic content for each outgoing message in a campaign. Direct Mail also allows you to automate the e-mail process so that it can occur during off-hours, thus reducing the impact of the campaign's overhead on your servers.

Building the direct mail infrastructure

Commerce Server has some fairly stiff requirements for the Direct Mail component, including:

✦ Windows 2000 (or higher), which must be running a compatible version of ActiveX Data Objects (ADO) and Collaborative Data Objects (CDO).

✦ SQL Server 7.0 or 2000 must be running on the same machine as the Direct Mailer, and must provide access to the Direct Mail database.

✦ The computer running Direct Mailer must have the best possible connection to a DNS server capable of resolving domain names on the Internet.

✦ The computer running Direct Mailer must have a high-speed connection to the Internet in order to deliver messages in a timely fashion.

Direct Mailer does not require Exchange Server; it uses Windows 2000 and its own built-in SMTP capabilities to send e-mail. And, if you intend to use generic content in your messages, you have no other requirements. However, if you intend to customize the outgoing messages, the Direct Mailer computer must also have high-speed access to a Web server that's capable of running Active Server Pages. The ASP page must provide the customized content to the Direct Mailer, and may require access to one or more databases in order to provide this information. I recommend that you run the Web server on a separate machine for optimum performance.

Creating opt-in mailings

Commerce Server doesn't feature built-in support that allows customers to sign up for specific mailings, such as an e-mail newsletter. However, Commerce Server *is* capable of using a mailing list that you create to send a newsletter, so you may want to implement your own opt-in program. See "Creating your own direct mail solution," later in this chapter for more information.

Commerce Server is also capable of sending e-mail to a *segment list*, which is a group of user profiles that share similar characteristics. If you design your user profiles to include your various e-mail newsletters as profile options, and if you provide customers with the means to edit these profile settings, you can create an opt-in program. I talk about creating segment lists in the next section.

Creating the opt-out page

Commerce Server features built-in support for opt-out lists, and the Commerce Server Solution Sites ship with a sample opt-out ASP page. This page is designed to be accessed from a URL in a campaign e-mail, and will "unsubscribe" the user's e-mail address from that campaign. Commerce Server's Direct Mail pipeline automatically removes opt-out e-mail addresses from the campaign's mailing list before beginning the mail process. Commerce Server also maintains a global opt-out list, which is run against every outgoing direct mail job. If you intend to use the Direct Mailer's opt-out support — and you should — use the opt-out.asp page provided by one of the Solution Sites as a starter for your own opt-out.asp page. Be sure that your e-mail content provides a hyperlink to this page, with the appropriate parameters, so that users can remove themselves from the list with a single click (note that this will require customized, ASP-based e-mail content rather than a static text-based content file).

Creating mailing lists

Direct Mailer accepts four types of mailing lists:

✦ Text files, such as a comma-separate values (CSV) file

✦ SQL queries

✦ Analysis reports, which may include a list of all customers who purchased a certain type of product within a certain timeframe

✦ Segment lists, which are a group of user profiles with similar characteristics

Commerce Server has a mandatory file format for text file mailing lists, and for the results of a SQL Query. This format includes several fields or columns as follows:

✦ **E-mail address.** This field is required, and must be formatted as a standard SMTP address.

✦ **GUID.** This is optional, and must be left blank if not provided. When sending customized message content, Direct Mailer will provide this value to the ASP page that is building the content. The ASP page can use this GUID to identify the user (rather than using their e-mail address, which is less accurate) and customize the e-mail content accordingly. You can use the user's Commerce Server customer number, for example.

✦ **Message format.** Another optional field, which instructs Collaborative Data Objects (CDO) how to encode the outgoing message. Possible choices include Text, MIME, or MHTML. This value also tells the recipient's e-mail client how to handle and render the message.

✦ **Language.** Again, optional. When provided, this field specifies the code page value that the e-mail uses. Useful for international companies who need to send messages in different languages.

✦ **URL.** Optional. Provides the ability to pass an individual URL on a per-user basis to CDO.

Although most of these fields are optional, the field must still be present in the mailing list (even if it's blank) in order for Direct Mailer to process the list correctly.

Segment lists are created by Commerce Server's Analysis module, and represent groups of users who share similar behaviors. You must first export data to the Commerce Server data warehouse and update the analysis data before segments will become available. After you have defined a segment and it has been populated with matching users, you can export the segment list to the Commerce Server List Manager, which makes it available to Direct Mailer for use as a mailing list.

> **Note** Building new segments requires you to build a complete analysis model, which is a complicated and involved task beyond the scope of this book. Refer to the Commerce Server documentation for more information on building analysis models.

Creating content

If you intend to create a non-personalized campaign, you can simply include your message content in a text file.

> **Note** Text files are cached in RAM by the Direct Mailer pipeline, and must be smaller than two million characters. Any content beyond this length is discarded.

If you want to create a personalized campaign, you need to create an ASP page to provide the content. Listing 15-6 shows a sample ASP page designed to create personalized content.

Listing 15-6: **Personalized content ASP**

```
<%
Option Explicit
Response.AddHeader "pragma", "no-cache"
Response.Expires = 0
%>

<html>
<head>
</head>
<div class=Section1>
<%
'create objects
Dim objAuthManager
Dim objUPM
Dim objProfile
Dim strUserID
Dim sCookieData

On Error goto 0
' Get User ID from AuthManager object.
' this comes from the mailing list itself
' via the direct mail pipeline
SET objAuthManager =
Server.CreateObject("Commerce.AuthManager")
objAuthManager.Initialize(Application("MSCSCommerceSiteName"))
if( Err.number <> 0 ) Then
  Response.Write "<P>AuthManager Failed to initialize</P>"
```

```
End If

' part of a campaign?
strUserID = objAuthManager.GetUserID(1)
if( Err.number <> 0 ) Then
 Response.Write "<P>Failed to get UserID</P>"
End If

' Create an instance of the profile service
Set objUPM = Application("MSCSProfileService")
If (Err.Number <> 0) Then
 Response.Write "<P>Failed to create
 Commerce.ProfileService</P>"
End If

' Get UserObject from profile Service
Set objProfile = objUPM.GetProfileByKey("User_ID", strUserID,_
 "UserObject")
If (Err.Number <> 0) Then
 strErrMsg = "<P>User profile not found: " & strUserID & "</P>"
 Response.Write strErrMsg
End If

%>

<table>
 <tr>
  <td>
  <p>From: E-mail Notifier</p>
  <p>Sent: <% = Date() %></p>
  <p>To: <% = objProfile.GeneralInfo.First_Nam %> 
  <% = objProfile.GeneralInfo.Last_Name %></p>
  <p>Subject: E-Mail News</p>
  </td>
 </tr>
</table>

<p>Dear <% = objProfile.GeneralInfo.First_Name
    %>,</p>
<p>We have added some exciting
    new products to our Web site.
    <A HREF="<%
=objAuthManager.GetUrl("default.asp", False, False)
    %>">Come see us today!</A>.</p>

<p>_____</p>
<p>TO UNSUBSCRIBE: You
    have received this e-mail notifier as a result of your
personal
    registration.<BR>To unsubscribe from this e-mail notifier,
click
    the link below.</p>
```

Continued

Listing 15-6 *(continued)*

```
<p><A HREF="<%
    On Error Goto 0
    Response.Write objAuthManager.GetUrl
    ("opt-out.asp", False, False, _
    Array("rcp_email", "campitem_id", "campitem_name"), _
    Array(CStr(objProfile.GeneralInfo.email_address),
    CStr(Request.Cookies("CampaignItemId")),
    CStr(Request.Cookies("CampaignItemName"))) _
    ) %>">Click here to opt-out of future
    mailings.</A></p>
</div>
</body>
</html>
```

This personalized e-mail is relatively simple, because it uses the UserID to pull the customers' names out of their Commerce Server profile. You can also construct an e-mail that lists customers' "frequent shopper" points or other information from a database by writing the appropriate code.

Sending the e-mail

To send an e-mail, you need to create a complete Direct Mail campaign. You do this by using the Commerce Server Business Desk interface. Open an existing campaign, as shown in Figure 15-2, and add a Direct Mail campaign.

You can specify the following in a Direct Mail campaign:

✦ You can specify the type of mail that you want to send.

✦ You can specify whether or not the mail should be personalized.

✦ You can specify the path to the mail content.

✦ You can schedule the campaign to automatically run at preset intervals, allowing you to "click and forget."

If you specify a text file in a non-personalized campaign, then the text file must be smaller than two million characters, because the Direct Mail pipeline caches this file in memory to improve performance. Any extra characters are discarded.

Note   Direct mail schedules depend on the SQL Server Agent service on the local machine. This must be configured to start automatically or the direct mail scheduled events may not occur.

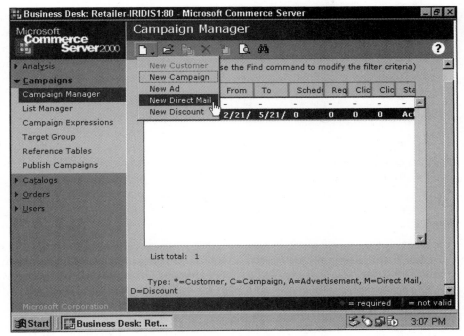

Figure 15-2: Adding a Direct Mail campaign item

Creating your own direct mail solution

If you don't have the hardware necessary to support Commerce Server's built-in Direct Mail capabilities, then you need to build your own solution. Remember that this solution will *not* have the rich functionality that Commerce Server's component provides; if you *must* have that functionality, you need to get the right hardware and use that component.

You should be able to quickly build a direct mail infrastructure to handle basic needs, including opt-in e-mail newsletters and promotional e-mails associated with a marketing campaign. Start by doing the following tasks:

1. Develop the database to run the mail system.

2. Build a signup page for opt-in mail.

3. Create a page that allows customers to opt out of a particular program (or globally opt out of all e-mail).

4. Develop the content of your e-mails.

5. Look at ways to create mailing lists from your Commerce Server database.

6. Design a mail server to send the e-mail, unless you plan on having a third party company handle the actual mailing for you.

Building the database

The database design for your direct mail infrastructure doesn't need to be incredibly complicated. I do recommend that you create a separate database, rather than create additional tables in the Commerce Server database. This allows you to more easily maintain both, and also allows you to more easily separate them onto different database servers if you want to.

At a minimum, you need four tables:

✦ The first table will track the mailing lists that you create. Each mailing list should represent a particular mail program, such as a newsletter or a promotion.

✦ The second table will hold all of the e-mail addresses, and should contain columns for the customers' first and last names — if you have them — to allow for personalized e-mail.

✦ The third table will join the first two, matching e-mail addresses with different lists. It will also contain a status indicator showing how the customer was added to the list — whether you added them or if they added themselves to the list via a sign-up page — or if they have asked to be removed from the list.

✦ A fourth table will include e-mail addresses that have asked to never receive certain types of e-mail from you. This *negative list* can be used to filter future mailing lists to exclude customers.

Listing 15-7 shows the Transact-SQL script used to create all four tables.

Listing 15-7: **Direct mail table creation script**

```
CREATE TABLE [dbo].[Addresses] (
[emailID] [int] IDENTITY (1, 1) NOT NULL ,
[dateAdded] [datetime] NOT NULL ,
[emailAddress] [varchar] (250) NOT NULL ,
[firstName] [varchar] (50) NULL ,
[lastName] [varchar] (50) NULL ,
[source] [varchar] (50) NOT NULL
) ON [PRIMARY]
GO

CREATE TABLE [dbo].[ListAddresses] (
[listID] [int] NOT NULL ,
[emailID] [int] NOT NULL ,
[dateAdded] [datetime] NOT NULL ,
[status] [int] NOT NULL
) ON [PRIMARY]
GO

CREATE TABLE [dbo].[Lists] (
[listID] [int] IDENTITY (1, 1) NOT NULL ,
```

```
[listName] [varchar] (50) NOT NULL ,
[listType] int (1, 1) NOT NULL
) ON [PRIMARY]
GO

CREATE TABLE [dbo].[OptOut] (
[listID] [int] NOT NULL ,
[dateAdded] [datetime] NOT NULL ,
[status] [int] NOT NULL
) ON [PRIMARY]
GO
```

Figure 15-3 shows the three main tables in a diagram illustrating their relationships.

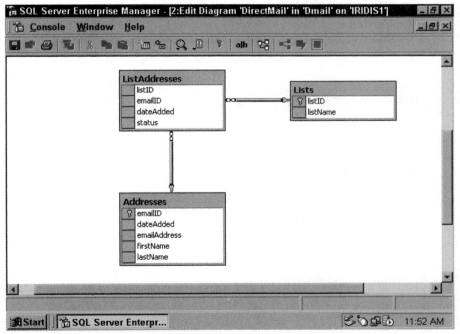

Figure 15-3: Direct Mail database diagram

Adding customers to lists

Although you may have some direct mail programs (such as e-mail newsletters) that customers sign up for, you will want to create other lists that *you* populate with customer names, based on their purchase history, demographic information, or other data. You may also want to add e-mail addresses that were purchased from business partners or marketing firms.

The Addresses table contains a source column that allows you to keep track of where the e-mail address came from. For example, you can specify a source of "internal" for e-mail addresses gleaned from your Commerce Server's customer profiles, or use the name of the marketing firm that provided the e-mail address to you.

Remember that adding e-mail addresses to the database does *not* mean that e-mails will be sent to them. Your next step is to create lists in the Lists table, which will be used as the mailing lists for newsletters and other promotional mailings. Ideally, you should create lists that represent classes of customers. For example, you could probably use a list containing the e-mail addresses of customers who have made purchases, and a list of customers who have not purchased anything within the past three months. Lists of this nature will require constant updating — a task that you can accomplish with a SQL Server Data Transformation Services (DTS) package that regularly scans your Commerce Server orders tables for new e-mail addresses. Listing 15-8 shows a Transact-SQL script that creates a stored procedure named sp_AddNewBuyersAddress. This stored procedure accepts a starting date for its scan, which should be the day after you *last* ran the stored procedure. It then inserts any new buyers' e-mail addresses into the Addresses table with a source of "buyer," so they can be easily identified. Any repeat buyers in the time frame won't be added to the table a second time.

Listing 15-8: **sp_AddNewBuyersAddress**

```
CREATE PROCEDURE sp_AddNewBuyersAddress
 @StartDate datetime
AS
 INSERT INTO Addresses
  (EmailAddress,FirstName,LastName,Source)
 (SELECT user_email_address,user_first_name,
  user_last_name,'buyer' as source
  FROM
  Retail_Commerce..OrderFormHeader
  WHERE
   Orderform_date >= @StartDate
  AND
  User_email_address NOT IN (SELECT
  EmailAddress FROM Addresses))
GO
```

Similar stored procedures can be written to bring in e-mail addresses from other sources, and to subscribe those e-mail addresses to particular mailing lists that you have set up in the Lists table.

Building the signup page

Some customers, of course, will want to sign up for e-mail communications that you offer. You can take a couple of approaches with this sign-up process.

✦ The simplest opt-in form allows customers to provide their name and e-mail address, and to select the marketing pieces to which they want to subscribe.

✦ A more complex form will allow customers to provide a password, which they can use to log in again in the future to unsubscribe from specific mailings, or to review their settings.

The latter scenario is complicated, and requires interfacing with the Commerce Server profile system. If you need that type of functionality, you should really consider using Commerce Server's Direct Mail component, which interfaces nicely with Commerce Server's Profiles component to keep track of which customers want to receive which mailings.

If a simpler signup form is acceptable to you, then take a look at Figure 15-4, which shows the Utilities.com sign up page. This page features a list of available newsletters and allows the user to select which ones they want.

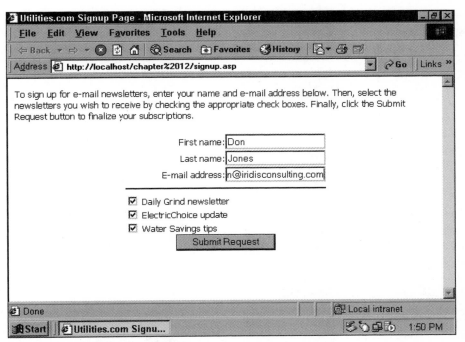

Figure 15-4: Utilities.com's signup.asp page

Listing 15-9 shows the complete source code for this page, including the stored procedure that retrieves the list information. Note that the code only displays those lists with a ListType of 1, indicating a list that customers can sign up for. This allows your Lists table to hold lists that customers shouldn't see by giving them another ListType value.

Listing 15-9: **Signup.asp page**

```asp
<%
'assumes cn is a valid
'connection to the direct mail
'database

'if submitting, e-mail will be populated
if request("email") <> "" then

 'create dictionary for validation
 'errors
 set vErr = createobject("Scripting.Dictionary")

 'These validation routines rough -
 'you can expand these to be more
 'efficient or complete

 'validate e-mail address
 if instr(1,request("email"),"@") = 0 then
  vErr.Add "Email","E-mail address is not valid."
 end if

 'validate first name
 if request("firstname") = "" then
  vErr.Add "FirstName","First name must be provided."
 end if

 'validate last name
 if request("lastname") = "" then
  vErr.Add "LastName","Last name must be provided."
 end if

 'validate checkboxes
 if request("signup") = "" then
  vErr.Add "Signup","You didn't check any boxes."
 end if

 'any validation errors?
 if vErr.Count = 0 then
  'no validation errors - process signup

  'first add the e-mail
  'and get its id
  sCmd = "sp_AddEmail "
  sCmd = sCmd & " '" & request("email") & "',"
  sCmd = sCmd & " '" & request("firstname") & "',"
  sCmd = sCmd & " '" & request("lastname") & "'"
  set rs = cn.execute(sCmd)
  emailID = rs("emailid")

  'subscribe that id to each list
```

```
    for each x in request("signup")
     sCmd = "sp_AddSignup "
     sCmd = emailid & ","
     sCmd = request("signup")(x)
     cn.execute sCmd
    next

     'redirect to thank you
     response.redirect "opt-in-thanks.asp"

   end if

  else

   'get lists into a recordset
   set rs = cn.execute("SELECT ListID,ListName FROM Lists WHERE_
   ListType = 1")
   if rs.eof and rs.bof then
    response.write "Error: No Public Lists"
    response.end
   end if

  end if
%>
<html>
<head>
<title>Utilities.com Signup Page</title>
</head>
<body>
<form method="POST" action="signup.asp">
  <p><font face="Tahoma" size="2">To sign up for e-mail
newsletters, enter your name and e-mail address below.
Then, select the newsletters you wish to receive by
checking the appropriate check boxes. Finally, click
the Submit Request button to finalize your
subscriptions.</font></p>
   <div align="center">
     <center>
     <table border="0" cellspacing="0" cellpadding="0">
       <tr>
         <td width="50%" align="right"><font face="Tahoma"
size="2">First name: </font></td>
         <td width="50%"><font face="Tahoma" size="2">
<input type="text" name="FirstName" size="20"><%
         if vErr.Exists("FirstName") then response.write
vErr.Item("FirstName")
         %></font></td>
       </tr>
       <tr>
         <td width="50%" align="right">
<font face="Tahoma" size="2">Last name: </font></td>
         <td width="50%"><font face="Tahoma" size="2">
```

Continued

Listing 15-9 *(continued)*

```
<input type="text" name="LastName" size="20"><%
        if vErr.Exists("LastName") then_
 response.write vErr.Item("LastName")
        %></font></td>
      </tr>
      <tr>
        <td width="50%" align="right">
<font face="Tahoma" size="2">E-mail
          address: </font></td>
          <td width="50%"><font face="Tahoma" size="2">
<input type="text" name="EMail" size="20"><%
        if vErr.Exists("Email") then_
 response.write vErr.Item("Email")
        %></font></td>
      </tr>
      <tr>
        <td width="100%" align="right" colspan="2">
          <hr color="#000000"><%
        if vErr.Exists("Signup") then_
 response.write vErr.Item("Signup")
        %>
          </td>
      </tr>
    </center>
    <tr>
      <td width="100%" align="right" colspan="2">
        <p align="left"><font face="Tahoma" size="2">
<%
do until rs.eof
 response.write "<input type='checkbox' name='Signup'"
 response.write " value='" & rs("ListID") & "' checked>"
 response.write rs("ListName") & "<br>"
 rs.movenext
loop
%>
</font></td>
    </tr>
    <tr>
      <td width="100%" align="right" colspan="2">
        <p align="center"><font face="Tahoma" size="2">
<input type="submit" value="Submit Request"
 name="cmdSubmit"></font></td>
    </tr>
    </table>
  </div>
</form>
</body>
```

This basic signup page provides a great deal of functionality, including basic input validation and an easy-to-program way of providing feedback to the user in the event that some of their data fails the validation checks. You can also implement these validation checks in a separate script file included in this ASP page; doing so allows you to implement the same validation code elsewhere in your site simply by including the appropriate script files.

 Note Plan on modifying this code to fit your exact database and situation. Although this provides a useful starting point, you should take the time to use more complete data validation routines and customize the page to fit your environment.

Building the opt-out page

The opt-out page provides your customers with an opportunity to remove themselves from one or more mailing lists. You can provide a simple opt-out page that allows customers to type their e-mail address to be removed from all of your lists, but taking a more granular and automated approach allows you to retain *some* customers on *some* lists, rather than losing them completely. Automating the process also helps reduce errors, such as typos, that can prevent a customer from being completely removed from your list when they request it. For example, without automation, a customer might have to type his e-mail address in order to be removed from your lists. If he mistypes his e-mail address, your system won't remove his actual e-mail address from your list. This can often confuse customers, who don't usually realize that they've mistyped their address.

Utilities.com plans on using e-mail marketing as a major portion of their marketing strategy, and needs to implement a fairly robust opt-out program. They do this by providing an "unsubscribe" link in every marketing e-mail that looks something like this:

```
http://www.utilities.com/opt-out.asp?id=6338565&pgm=17
```

The two parameters in the URL allow the opt-out.asp page to identify both the customer and the e-mail that they receive. Properly written, this allows you to identify which mailing list the customer's e-mail address came from and offer to remove them only from that list. The parameters also allow the page to identify the customer and fill in their e-mail address for them. Figure 15-5 shows the opt-out.asp page.

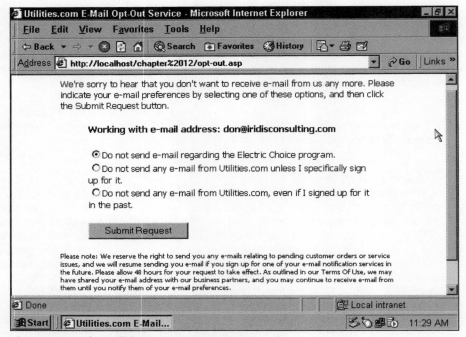

Figure 15-5: The Utilities.com opt-out page

Listing 15-10 shows the ASP and HTML code that makes it work.

Listing 15-10: **The Utilities.com opt-out page**

```
<%

' all codes assumes
' that cn represents a
' valid connection to the
' direct mail database.

'see if the form was submitted
if request("submit") = 1 then

'get user ID and list ID
 userID = request("user")
 listID = request("list")

 'choose action
 select case request("optOptOut")
  case "program"
   'just remove from this list
   sCmd = "sp_RemoveEmailFromList "
```

```
    sCmd = sCmd & request("user") & ","
    sCmd = sCmd & request("list")
    cn.execute sCmd

  case "marketing"
   'remove from all except opt-in
   sCmd = "sp_RemoveEmailFromNonOptIn "
   sCmd = sCmd & request("user")
   cn.execute sCmd

  case "all"
   'remove from all
   sCmd = "sp_RemoveEmailFromAll "
   sCmd = sCmd & request("user")
   cn.execute sCmd

 end select

'redirect to thank you page
response.redirect "opt-out-thanks.asp"

else

 'not submitting; retrieve values
 'to display
 set rs = cn.execute("sp_GetMailInfo " & request("user"))
 sEmail = rs("EmailAddress")
 set rs = cn.execute("sp_GetListInfo " & request("list"))
 sList = rs("ListName")

end if

%>
<html>
<head>
<title>Utilities.com E-Mail Opt-Out Service</title>
</head>
<body>
<div align="center">
<center>
<table border="0" width="80%" cellspacing="0" cellpadding="0">
<tr>
<td width="100%">
<form method="POST" action="opt-out.asp">
<input type="hidden" name="user" value="56478">
<input type="hidden" name="list" value="17">
<input type="hidden" name="submit" value="1">
<p><font face="Tahoma" size="2">We're sorry to hear that
you don't want to receive e-mail from us any more. Please
indicate your e-mail references by selecting one of these
options, and then click the Submit Request button.</font></p>
<blockquote>
```

Continued

Listing 15-10 *(continued)*

```
<p><font face="Tahoma" size="2"><b>Working with e-mail address:
<% =sEmail %></b></font></p>
<p><font face="Tahoma" size="2"><input type="radio"
value="program" checked name="optOptOut">Do
not send e-mail regarding <% =sList %><br>
<input type="radio" name="optOptOut" value="marketing">
Do not send
any e-mail from Utilities.com unless I specifically sign up
for it.<br>
<input type="radio" name="optOptOut" value="all">Do not send
any
-mail from Utilities.com, even if I signed up for it in the
 past.</font></p>
p><font face="Tahoma" size="2"><input type="submit"
value="Submit Request" name="cmdSubmit"></font></p>
</blockquote>
<p><font size="1" face="Tahoma">Please note: We reserve the
 right to send you any e-mails relating to pending customer
 orders or service issues, and we will resume sending you
 e-mail if you sign up for one
of your e-mail notification services in the future. Please
 allow 48 hours for your request to take effect. As outlined
 in our Terms Of Use, we may have shared your e-mail address
 with our business partners, and you may continue to receive
 e-mail from them until you notify them of your e-mail
 preferences. </font></p>
</form>
<p> </td>
</tr>
</table>
</center>
</div>
</body>
</html>
```

Using an opt-out method like this requires your company to practice some restraint. If the customer elects to be removed from some of your lists, you have to be very careful not to add them back in again accidentally. For this reason, the code (as written) maintains a *negative list* for every mailing list, which includes people who *must not* receive any e-mail sent to that list. When generating mailing lists, you should remove the addresses on the negative list before using the final list to send an e-mail.

The opt-out.asp page uses several stored procedures to accomplish its work, because stored procedures allow SQL Server to process requests more quickly. These stored procedures include:

✦ sp_RemoveEmailFromList accepts an e-mail address ID number and a list ID number. This stored procedure marks that e-mail address with an "opt-out" status in the list.

```
CREATE PROCEDURE sp_RemoveEmailFromList
 @EmailID int,
 @ListID int
AS
 UPDATE ListAddresses SET Status = 2
  WHERE ListID = @ListID AND
  EmailID = @EmailID
GO
```

✦ sp_RemoveEmailFromNonOptIn accepts only an e-mail address ID number. This stored procedure marks the address with an "opt-out" status on any list where it was added by the company, rather than by the customer. This also adds the customer to the global OptOut list indicating that they should never receive any e-mail that they didn't sign up for.

```
CREATE PROCEDURE sp_RemoveEmailFromNonOptIn
 @EmailID int
AS
 UPDATE ListAddresses SET Status = 2
  WHERE Status = 1 AND EmailID = @EmailID
 DELETE FROM OptOut WHERE EmailID = @EmailID
 INSERT INTO OptOut (EmailID, Status)
  VALUES(@EmailID,0)
```

✦ sp_RemoveEmailFromAll accepts an e-mail address ID number. This stored procedure marks the address with an "opt-out" status wherever it appears, and adds it to the global OptOut list indicating that it should never receive any e-mail again.

```
CREATE PROCEDURE sp_RemoveEmailFromAll
@EmailID int
AS
 UPDATE ListAddresses SET Status = 2
  WHERE EmailID = @EmailID
 DELETE FROM OptOut WHERE EmailID = @EmailID
 INSERT INTO OptOut (EmailID, Status)
  VALUES(@EmailID,1)
GO
```

✦ sp_GetEmailInfo accepts an e-mail address ID number and returns a single-row Recordset with the full information on that e-mail address from the Addresses table. This is used to look up the current e-mail address when a customer goes to the opt-out page.

```
CREATE PROCEDURE sp_GetEmailInfo
@EmailID int
AS
 SELECT EmailAddress,DateAdded,FirstName,
  LastName,Source FROM Addresses WHERE
  EmailID = @EmailID
GO
```

✦ sp_GetListInfo accepts a list ID number and returns a single-row Recordset with the full information on that list from the Lists table. This is used to look up the name of the list for use on the opt-out page.

```
CREATE PROCEDURE sp_GetListInfo
@ListID int
AS
 SELECT ListName, ListType FROM Lists WHERE
  ListID = @ListID
GO
```

Notice how these stored procedures maintain integrity with the opt-in stored procedures in the previous section. If a customer signs up for a future e-mail offering, they remove themselves from the "opt-out" list at the same time, allowing you to once again send e-mail to them.

Creating content

Creating content is a completely manual task. You can create plain text messages, HTML-formatted messages, or a mixture of the two. You should be aware that different e-mail clients — notably America Online — provide varying levels of support for HTML formatting messages. Always send test messages to be read by several different mail clients in order to be sure that your message will come across consistently to all of your subscribers.

Creating mailing lists

Creating mailing lists is simply a matter of querying your SQL Server database for the appropriate information. I recommend that you write some kind of Web-based administrative interface that allows non-technical users, such as your marketing department, to select the list that they want to pull and receive the results in a comma-separated values file. This file can then be transferred into a bulk mailer program or sent to a third-party e-mail service for use as the master file.

Be sure that all lists remove your "negative list" e-mail addresses. Listing 15-11 shows a stored procedure named sp_MakeMailList. This stored procedure creates a new table (dropping it first, if necessary) to hold a mailing list. It requires two input parameters — the list ID of the list that you want to use as the base and the type of e-mail this is (0 for a marketing e-mail, 1 for another type of e-mail). This value is used to exclude the appropriate customers.

Listing 15-11: **sp_MakeMailList**

```
CREATE PROCEDURE sp_MakeMailList
 @ListID int,
 @ListType int
AS
 DROP TABLE MailList
 GO
 CREATE TABLE [dbo].[MailList] (
 [Email] [varchar] (50) NOT NULL,
 [FirstName] [varchar] (50) NULL,
 [LastName] [varchar] (50) NULL
 ) ON [PRIMARY]
 GO
 INSERT INTO MailList
  (Email,FirstName,LastName)
  (SELECT EmailAddress,FirstName,
   LastName FROM Addresses A
   INNER JOIN ListAddresses L
   ON L.EmailID = A.EmailID
   WHERE ListID = @ListID AND
   A.EmailID NOT IN (SELECT
   EmailID FROM OptOut WHERE
   Status = @ListType))
 GO
```

After running the stored procedure, you can use Data Transformation Services (DTS) or another utility to export the MailList table into a CSV file or other format appropriate for your mail server.

Sending the e-mail

If you're building your own direct mail infrastructure, I strongly recommend that you work with an outside firm to actually send your e-mail messages. These companies will generally accept the text of your e-mail and an uploaded CSV file of e-mail addresses, will often support customization of the outgoing messages through a mail-merge feature, and will allow you to offload the significant overhead that direct e-mail can involve, especially when large lists are being targeted.

If you intend to use your own mail server, I recommend that you use a third-party bulk e-mail application rather than Exchange Server 2000. These e-mail programs will usually accept a CSV file for the outgoing mail list and allow you to work with any mail format that you prefer.

If you intend to use Exchange Server, you need to write a Visual Basic application that uses Collaborative Data Objects (CDO) to create and send each e-mail message, one at a time, to each recipient in your list. The VB program can be written to pull the list from your SQL Server, and it can (and should) be run on the same machine as Exchange Server.

Providing Customers with Information

Your customers deserve—and will demand—access to certain information from your Web site. Most e-commerce customers will expect much of this information to be available on your site in a self-service format, including information on the status of their orders and self-service support. Other information may only be available through a live support staff, and many customer complaints will have to be handled by a live staff.

Providing this information in an easy-to-access, scalable fashion is key to supporting your customers and *keeping* them as customers.

On-line self-service

Most e-commerce customers are accustomed to self-service; after all, they buy things online without help from you, so they usually expect to be able to help themselves without your assistance, provided that you make the necessary information available. The most common forms of online self-service involve checking the status of orders and obtaining support information about your products and services.

Order information

Customers expect to be able to retrieve order information from your site, and expect that order information to include some indication of the order's status. Unfortunately, because Commerce Server has no idea how your company actually fulfills your orders, it doesn't provide any built-in means of tracking order status. So providing status information to your customer will require some customization. I suggest that you consider the following alterations to Commerce Server and your site to provide the information that customers expect:

✦ Modify the OrderFormHeader table in the Commerce Server database to include a column for each of the following:

  • Order status

  • Shipping carrier

  • Ship date

  • Shipping origin

  • Tracking number

  If you allow items in an order to be shipped at different times or from different locations, add these fields to the OrderFormLineItems table instead.

✦ Provide an Order Status screen that lists all of a customer's orders. Make sure that customers have to sign in by using a password before providing this information. The OrderFormHeader table contains a user_id column that contains the Commerce Server user ID of the buyer.

✦ Use BizTalk, or other methods, to obtain shipping information from your shipping systems or your business partners' systems. Ideally, these systems should link the order number to one or more tracking numbers so that you can import the tracking information into the correct orders in your Commerce Server database.

✦ Establish a list of order status codes, and store these codes in the database. For example, you may include codes for the following order statuses:

  • Order placed

  • Order processed and sent to fulfillment channel

  • Backordered and waiting for product

  • Order shipped

  • Order held pending customer contact

  • Order cancelled

Similar codes can be established if you will track order status on a per-item basis rather than for the entire order.

Exactly how you obtain this status information, especially tracking information, depends on how your items are shipped. If you ship items from your own warehouse, it will be relatively easy to use BizTalk or SQL Server Data Transformation Services (DTS) to import the necessary information into the Commerce Server database. If you send orders to outside distributors for fulfillment (referred to as *virtual warehousing*), your business agreements with those distributors will determine how you get tracking information.

Self-help knowledge bases

Knowledge bases are an important way for customers to help themselves, especially if you are selling products or services that tend to be support-heavy. For example, Microsoft maintains an extensive searchable knowledge base on their site, filling it with articles on how to solve specific problems and work around specific situations with their products. Customers use this knowledge base to look up support information on their own, rather than spending time on the phone with a support representative. Knowledge bases not only provide customers with a convenient "first line of defense," but also help reduce your support costs by reducing the need for live staff.

Site Server 3.0 contained a Knowledge Base component that made creating knowledge bases relatively easy. Commerce Server 2000, however, does not contain any knowledge base functionality, nor should it; a knowledge base isn't really a function of an e-commerce platform. Fortunately, Microsoft's base technologies, particularly Internet Information Server, provide a splendid way to create a knowledge base on your site.

The Key to Communications is the Relationship

Obtaining order status information from outside distributors can be complicated—everyone has a different system with different capabilities. Products like BizTalk Server help make the task easier because they support many different communications methods and practically unlimited data translation capabilities, but even that may require more time and effort than you have available.

Enter the hub. Usually run by a third party like Commerce One (www.commerceone.com), hubs provide a central information interchange between trading partners on the Internet, effectively making themselves a giant "BizTalk Server." If you select a popular hub company, the odds are good that your trading partners are already dealing with them, or will be able to with very little effort. You simply have to program your systems to talk to the hub's systems, and the hub will translate for your trading partners. This allows everyone to trade information—orders, inventory status, tracking information, and so forth—more easily than if you dealt with each other directly.

The cost of hubs' services varies, and may be too expensive to fit your business model in the long term. But they can provide an important jumpstart even if you don't plan on sticking with them, thus allowing you to take your time to develop an infrastructure to directly communicate with your business partners.

The first step is to actually create content for the site. Generally, content should be in the form of static HTML pages that describe a problem or frequently asked question, and then describe the solution or answer. Gather these pages into a single directory on a Web server, or — if you expect a great deal of traffic — on multiple Web servers. Use the Internet Services Manager on the Web server to add this folder as a virtual directory in the Web site, as shown in Figure 15-6.

As shown in the figure, make sure that the "Index this resource" checkbox is selected. This will cause IIS' built-in content indexing service to treat the contents of the virtual directory as a *corpus,* or body of work to be indexed. The indexing service can then create *catalogs,* which contain quickly searchable keywords pulled from the pages.

You can use the Indexing Service's Microsoft Management Console (MMC) snap-in to control the properties of the Indexing Service, and to perform test queries. You need to build a search page for your site that allows users to search the appropriate catalog for your knowledge base content. Microsoft provides a sample query form in the Winnt\Help folder of Windows 2000 Server computers.

You can also use other methods to create a knowledge base, but they tend to be more complex and don't scale as well if you need multiple servers to support it. For example, SQL Server 2000 features full-text indexing of text columns in databases; you can store each knowledge base entry as a database record and enable full-text searching on a column containing an article's text. Because the text of an article will rarely change, however, it is more efficient to place the information in a static file and allow the Indexing Service to provide the search capabilities.

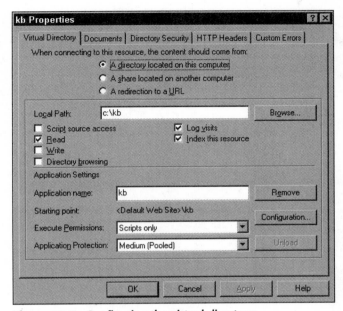

Figure 15-6: Configuring the virtual directory

Live customer service

Sometimes, the most robust Web-based self-service techniques just aren't enough. Your customers will eventually want to talk to a live person. Your live customer support staff, assuming that you're implementing one, needs to be able to provide customers with all of their order information, and have a great deal of flexibility in dealing with your customers' orders.

Providing information

The Commerce Server Business Desk application provides all of the information that your service staff should require in order to help your customers. Unfortunately, the Business Desk also provides a great deal of functionality that your service staff *doesn't* need, and in many cases shouldn't have access to.

Fortunately, the Business Desk has built-in modules, and those modules are separated into different physical folders. By placing NTFS file permissions on the folders, you can prevent unauthorized users from accessing the different modules of the Business Desk. For example, your service staff may only need access to the `orders` folder, which contains the Business Desk module that provides access to information on customer orders.

As shown in Figure 15-7, the Business Desk allows your service staff to search for customer orders based on a variety of criteria, or to look at all of the orders in the system.

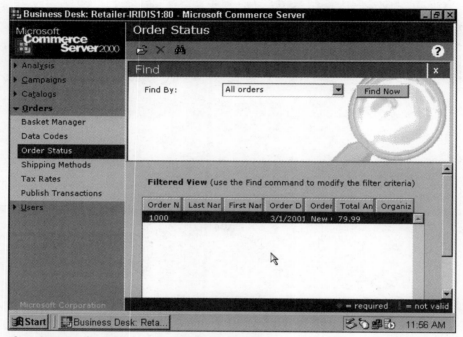

Figure 15-7: The Business Desk orders module

Figure 15-8 shows the order detail screen, which allows your service staff to view the details of an order. The order search screen can also be used to delete orders, just in case a customer wants to cancel an order that they recently placed. Unfortunately, the Business Desk has no information on whether or not orders have been sent to your distribution channel for fulfillment, nor does the Business Desk allow your service staff to *change* any orders, such as changing the quantity of an item in an order. This type of functionality requires customization of the Business Desk's orders module.

If you find that the Business Desk doesn't provide the access or all of the information that your service staff needs, you can write a Web-based administrative interface to provide the necessary access and information.

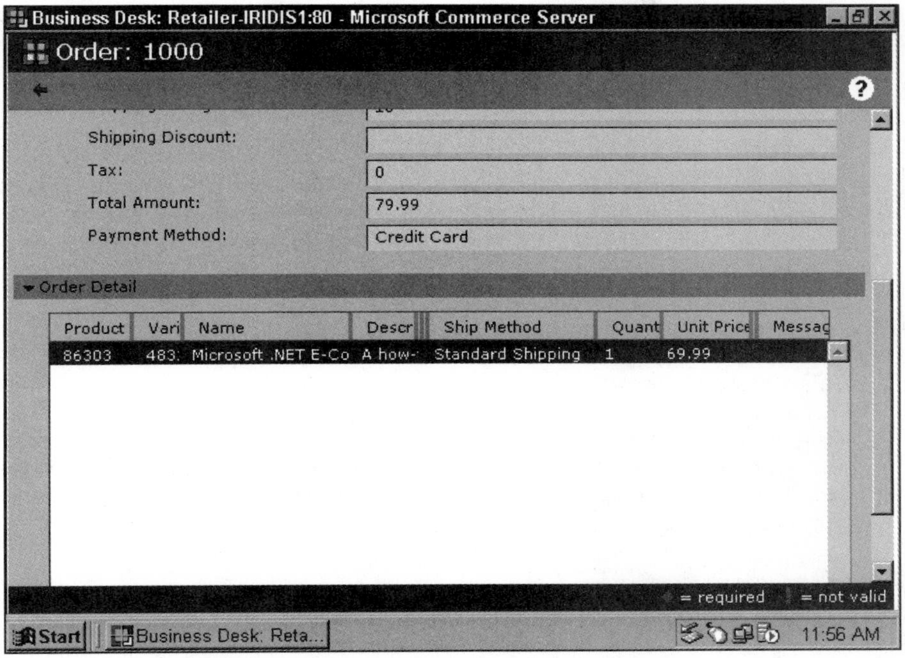

Figure 15-8: The Business Desk order detail screen

Providing flexibility

Although the Business Desk provides a great deal of information to your service staff, it doesn't provide them with a great deal of flexibility; they're unable to make any changes to orders to help customers. For example, many customers will want to cancel a single line item of their order, or increase or reduce the quantity of a particular item.

Your service staff may also need the ability to place orders with modified parameters, such as free or reduced shipping costs, or even reduced product prices. In customer service situations, offerings like a minor discount or free shipping can often turn an upset customer into a happy one. Once again, however, the Business Desk doesn't provide an interface for this type of action.

One solution is to create an entire administrative interface geared to giving your staff the flexibility that they need. An easier solution is to make a special version of your Web site that your service staff can use to place non-standard orders.

This site should be a duplicate of your normal site, with the same catalogs and everything else. However, only members of your service staff should have access to it. You may, for example, place the site on your intranet instead of the Internet, or configure security on the duplicate site so that only your service staff can access it. This site needs to have only minor modifications:

✦ Add a new set of shipping options that range from free to various levels of discount, as appropriate for your business. Service staff members can use these options if necessary to reduce the shipping costs of an order.

✦ Modify the site to allow prices of items in the basket to be modified. This allows your staff to reduce prices, if necessary.

✦ Modify the order-processing pipeline to eliminate the price-check component. This permits modified prices to pass through the pipeline in the special site. You can also implement a different price verification component that allows reduced prices, but not prices that are below the items' cost.

When the service staff needs to modify an order with one of these options, they simply delete the original order and place it again on the special site, which allows them to customize it as necessary.

Note   Orders placed by service staff members won't be "attached" to the actual ordering user's profile in your system, because the actual user didn't place the order. Make sure that you and your management team understand the implications of this in your reports.

Summary

Customer support continues with robust customer communications, whether they are ad-hoc status or informational messages or promotional e-mails. You can use Commerce Server's powerful Direct Mail features with your own methods for sending ad-hoc e-mails to create a reliable, efficient customer communications infrastructure that will keep your customers coming back.

✦   ✦   ✦

Supporting the Customer Experience with a Robust Site

Building a robust site is a matter of careful architecture and use of Microsoft's availability and load-balancing technologies. These technologies were introduced with Windows NT 4.0 Enterprise Edition, and have been significantly expanded and enhanced both in Windows 2000 and in the .NET Server product line. Microsoft's technologies, combined with hardware-based high-availability features such as hot-plug devices and redundant components, make creating a Web site that can serve your customers every hour of every day easier than ever.

The Ideal Web Site Architecture

The "ideal" Web site architecture looks something like the one shown in Figure 16-1.

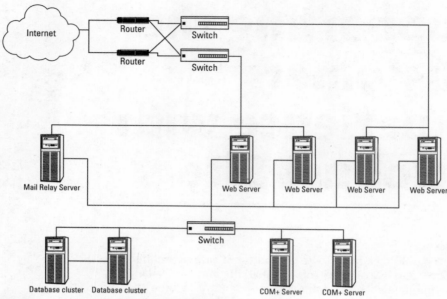

Figure 16-1: The ideal Web site architecture

In this architecture, the Web farm is connected to the Internet by redundant routers (ideally, the connection to the Internet backbone also uses redundant WAN links). These routers each connect to two switches, and each switch connects to about half of the site's servers. This provides fault-tolerance at the network level: If a router fails, both switches can continue to access the Internet. If a switch fails, half of the site still has access to the Internet.

Only the Web servers and the mail relay servers — the computers that actually require Internet connectivity — are connected to the Internet. These servers contain two network interfaces, and are also connected to a high-speed back-end network, which they share with the COM+ servers and database servers. The database servers are configured in a cluster, and the COM+ servers are configured in a COM+ cluster. The Web servers themselves are configured in a network load-balancing cluster. Thus, the entire architecture provides reliable load balancing for almost all servers, and can survive the failure of one or more servers in each portion of the architecture (with the exception of the mail relay server; for full fault tolerance you need to provide a redundant mail server, perhaps an Exchange Server cluster).

Microsoft provides the technologies that you need to implement this architecture with the Windows 2000 or Windows XP platform, and with Application Center 2000.

Clustering

Two-node clustering is available in Windows 2000 (and later versions) Advanced Server, and four-node clustering is supported in the Datacenter Server edition. Each server in a Windows cluster can use different hardware, but for optimal performance, I recommend that the servers be as close to identical as possible. All of the servers in a cluster are physically connected to the same external drive storage. Generally, this is a RAID array using SCSI or Fibre Channel (FC). The external storage must connect to an identical hardware SCSI controller in each server (in the case of SCSI storage) or to the same FC hub. Each node must also share a network connection with the other nodes. Ideally, this should be a dedicated network connection used for no other purpose because it will carry the *heartbeat* signal indicating the status of each cluster node.

How it works

The simplest cluster configuration is a two-node, active-passive cluster. In this configuration, both servers are connected to a single external drive array. Both share a dedicated network connection, and both are connected to the main network. Also, both servers are configured with their own server name and IP address.

The external drive array represents a *resource*, which can be *owned* by only one of the servers at a time. Generally, whichever server is powered on first will "seize" the drive array and become its owner.

The servers share other resources, including a third "server name" and IP address that represents the cluster. The node that owns the external drive array is also said to own the entire cluster, meaning that it will respond to the cluster "server name" and IP address, as well as its own server name and IP address. Client computers, such as Web servers or COM+ servers, should only access the cluster server name and IP address, and never the individual servers' names or IP addresses. Doing so ensures that the client computers will always receive a response from the cluster, no matter which individual servers are up and running at the time.

The network connection that is shared by the two servers is "pulsed" every second by the server that owns the cluster — the "active" node. The "passive" node monitors this "heartbeat" signal. If the heartbeat signal fails for more than three seconds, the passive node performs a SCSI reset sequence on the drive controller that's connected to the external array. This has the effect of resetting the drive array and making it "pay attention" to the passive node. The passive node then waits a couple of seconds to see if the active node attempts to perform its own SCSI reset to "recover" the external drive array. If the active node doesn't do this, the passive node assumes that the active node has failed, and begins seizing control of the cluster in a *hostile takeover,* also known as *failing over.*

Note   A *non-hostile* takeover occurs when an administrator instructs the active node to relinquish control to the passive node. This is often done when maintenance is required on the active node, and is a less disruptive way of transferring control of the cluster.

The formerly passive node modifies a portion of the external drive array to indicate that it has become the active node. The node begins responding to the cluster server name and IP address, and begins starting up any services, such as SQL Server or Exchange Server, that are required. A complete node takeover generally requires about 30 seconds to complete.

Clustered resources

Other resources can be shared between the two clusters, including printers and file shares. Special configuration techniques set up these clustered shared resources, including a technique to ensure that both servers have access to the necessary printer drivers and that any shared files are stored on the external drive array to which the two nodes are connected.

Network applications that support clustering, such as SQL Server 2000 Enterprise Edition or Exchange Server 2000 Enterprise Edition, install themselves on *both* nodes during their normal setup (which requires basic clustering to be set up in advance). These products create their own virtual server name and other resources that are "owned" by the cluster's active node. Both nodes have all of the application's services and executable files installed locally; all data files reside on the shared external drive array. The services on the passive node are stopped, and only start when that node gains control of the external drive array. Clients access the application only by using the clustered virtual server name — meaning that they will receive a response from whichever server currently "owns" the cluster.

Active-Active clustering

The scenarios described previously are known as active-passive clustering, because one node passively waits for the other to fail. In an active-active cluster, both nodes perform productive work. In a two-node cluster, this requires an additional external drive array to be connected to both nodes. One node owns one external array, and the other owns the remaining external array. Both nodes send a heartbeat signal over their shared network connection. Essentially, two virtual clusters are created, and each node is active in one cluster and passive in the other, capable of becoming the active node for both clusters, and owning both external drive arrays and all other shared resources if one node fails. Performance will generally be degraded because the remaining node is trying to handle the load of two servers, but reduced performance is generally better than no performance at all.

Four-way clustering is similar, with each node owning an external drive array and a variety of shared resources. Any of the nodes in the cluster is capable of "picking up" for a failed node, all the way down to — in a worst-case scenario — one server handling the load of all four.

Hardware requirements

All of the hardware used in a cluster must be on Microsoft's Cluster Hardware Compatibility List (Cluster HCL), which is a very small subset of the overall Windows 2000 HCL. Most server vendors offer pre-configured cluster packages that will remove much of the configuration work from your shoulders. If you choose not to purchase a pre-configured cluster, be aware that the initial cluster configuration is extremely hardware- and vendor-specific, and you must obtain and closely follow cluster configuration instructions from the hardware vendor — not from Microsoft. The major vendors offering cluster-compatible hardware and pre-configured cluster packages include Dell, IBM, Compaq, and Hewlett-Packard.

Other cluster benefits

A major benefit of a cluster is the ability to perform *rolling upgrades*, where one cluster node is taken offline for maintenance, such as a service pack installation, and then brought back online. The newly upgraded node is instructed to take control of the cluster, thus allowing the formerly active node to be taken offline while the same upgrades are completed.

Be *very* careful when performing this type of upgrade, especially when installing service packs for clustered applications. If the service pack makes any changes to the structure of the data files, then a rolling upgrade may not be possible. Carefully review the documentation that comes with the service pack, or contact the application's vendor (Microsoft Product Support in the case of Exchange Server or SQL Server) to determine if a rolling upgrade is possible and, if so, what the supported procedure is.

Configuration recommendations

As you become more experienced with Microsoft clustering, you'll develop a set of best practices to help avoid most of the major problem areas that you can run into with clustering. To save you some time, here are the best practices I've learned from my experience:

✦ Always use a private, dedicated connection for cluster communications (the "heartbeat" signal). Using a network card that also handles client traffic can result in long enough signal latencies to trigger an undesired cluster takeover by the passive node.

✦ Don't use a crossover cable for the private cluster communications. Although this is a supported solution, Windows 2000's Media Sense feature can't detect a crossover cable and will disable the NIC; you can disable Media Sense, but this feature can be useful in clustering. You're better off using a hub or switch for the cluster connection.

✦ Although you can't install Terminal Services in Application Mode on a cluster, you can install it in Remote Administration Mode, which allows you to remotely control both nodes for administrative purposes. I recommend that you always install Terminal Services in Remote Administration mode on all servers, including cluster nodes.

✦ *Regularly* review the event logs of the cluster nodes and investigate any warning or error messages that you find. Misconfigured cluster nodes can be prone to unexplained failover, network connectivity issues, domain authentication issues, and more.

✦ You can configure cluster nodes to attempt a *fail back*, where the originally active node attempts to regain control of the cluster after a failover occurs (assuming that the original node is brought back online). You can configure specific hours, such as low-traffic times, for fail back to occur. I recommend against using automated fail back because you need to monitor your clusters closely enough to know when a failover has occurred, and you should be responsible for determining if and when the original node will be made the active node again.

✦ Carefully document which virtual server names and IP addresses are in use, which nodes should own each name or address under normal circumstances, and so forth. You will need this information to get your cluster back to a normal operating condition after a failover occurs and repairs to the failed node have been completed.

Application Center 2000

Application Center 2000 is one of the newest .NET server products, and is designed to make Web farms easier to manage and deploy. It includes several technologies that build upon COM+ and IIS to make Web sites more scalable and fault-tolerant, and is a must for any company with a Web site that includes more than a couple of Web servers. The major features that you need to implement include:

✦ Application imaging, which allows you to create a single "image" for all of the components and ASP files in your site. Application Center allows you to create new Web servers by deploying the image to them.

✦ Application Center features a Microsoft Management Console (MMC) snap-in that consolidates the event logs, performance information, and other data for *all* of your Web servers in a single view — making management easier.

✦ Content synchronization allows you to deploy content to a staging server, and allows Application Center to replicate that content to all of your Web servers.

✦ Component Load Balancing allows you to create clusters of COM+ servers to create a scalable and fault-tolerant middle tier for your Web site.

✦ Network Load Balancing integrates with Application Center to provide clusters of fault-tolerant Web servers.

✦ Request forwarding allows ASP Session variables to be used by identifying incoming clients and passing their connection to the server that contains their Session variables.

Application imaging and content synchronization

Application Center allows you to define *applications,* which are collections of ASP pages, components, certificates, and other resources that make a Web application work. You define your applications on a *cluster controller,* which acts as the master server for a cluster, and then deploys applications to cluster members (the Web servers in your Web farm). Application Center can control multiple applications, thus allowing you to deploy different types of servers, such as a search server, catalog server, etc.

Application Center allows an application to include a variety of resources, including:

✦ ASP pages, virtual Web sites, and virtual directories

✦ COM+ applications

✦ Global ISAPI filters

✦ Folder and files

✦ Exportable certificates

✦ Certificate Trust Lists

✦ Data Source Names (DSNs)

✦ Windows Management Instrumentation (WMI) settings

✦ Registry keys

✦ IIS 5.0 settings and metadata

Essentially, Application Center allows you to make changes to the cluster controller and have all of those changes replicated across the members of the cluster. This ability makes it more feasible for you to deploy a large Web server farm, which in turn means that your Web site will be more robust for your customers.

Synchronization models

Application Center supports two types of automatic synchronization. In *change-based synchronization*, Application Center detects changes to files and settings and replicates them as necessary. In *internal-based synchronization*, Application Center completely refreshes cluster members' content from the cluster controller on a periodic basis. However, Application Center doesn't automatically replicate any changes to security ACLs on files and folders. Application Center will replicate the ACL information if the file itself changes, but a change to the ACL is insufficient to trigger synchronization.

Tip　Stick with changed-based replication whenever possible. Interval-based replication is not generally appropriate in an e-commerce site and can occupy significant bandwidth when active.

Caution　COM+ component and ISAPI filters must be manually deployed because they require the Web service to be restarted.

Application Center also supports on-demand synchronization, thus allowing you to manually synchronize a member cluster or a particular application across the cluster.

Caution   Changing a large number of files may escape detection in a change-based replication model. Whenever you make a large number of changes, perform a manual synchronization to ensure complete deployment.

Synchronization requirements

Application Center synchronization requires all participating servers to have closely synchronized system clocks. Servers that are members of a Windows 2000 domain are automatically time-synched to support Windows 2000's Kerberos authentication protocol; this automatic time-synch is sufficient for Application Center's purposes. If you have Windows NT 4.0 Web servers, you need to manually synchronize their clocks or use third-party tools to do so automatically.

Application Center works best when all servers involved are members of the same domain, and when security principles on ACLs are for domain accounts only. This allows the ACLs to be replicated properly without losing information. If you assign permissions to a security principle that is *not* available to all member servers, such as a local account, then Application Center will be unable to properly replicate the complete ACL.

Consolidated management

Application Center allows you to centrally configure and monitor your Web servers, add new servers to clusters, remove servers, or temporarily take servers offline for maintenance. After you have added a Web server to an Application Center cluster, the Application Center management console allows you to work with that server's event logs, performance settings, and other settings in a centralized location.

Component Load Balancing

Component Load Balancing (CLB) is a new technology introduced with Application Center 2000. The basic idea behind CLB is that your Web servers don't actually contain copies of the COM+ components that they instantiate. Instead, these components remain on a "cluster" of COM+ servers, which accepts requests for components and instantiates them on behalf of the Web server. CLB servers in your site communicate with each other to evenly distribute component requests across the servers in the cluster — making your middle tier scalable simply by adding COM+ servers to the cluster. You can create multiple clusters for different uses, thus breaking your middle tier into functional groups.

How it works

The actual CLB software runs on your *Web* servers, and allows them to communicate with the COM+ servers and make CLB load-balancing decisions. The COM+ components run on COM+ servers, which don't require any special software to be installed. Each COM+ server must, however, be configured with the same COM+ components. The CLB software is configured with the list of available COM+ servers.

CLB intercepts all COM+ calls made on the Web server by intercepting object instantiation calls (like the Visual Basic `CreateObject` command). CLB suspends the object creation request and transfers it to a COM+ server. Although the object is actually instantiated and executed on the COM+ server, CLB abstracts the object's programming interface and presents it on the calling Web server, which "thinks" that the object has been created locally.

Each of the Web servers with the CLB software installed creates a *routing list* of available COM+ servers and their response times. The response times are obtained by "pinging" each server and measuring the time — in milliseconds — that it takes to respond. This routing list is refreshed every 200 milliseconds to maintain accuracy. When CLB intercepts an object creation request, the server with the fastest response time — which it achieves by having the smallest processing load — is used to complete the request. The next COM+ request is routed to the next-fastest server, and so forth, in a round-robin fashion until the routing list is refreshed. The CLB software on a Web server doesn't attempt to communicate with other Web servers, because any attempt at replication would be slower than the 200ms refresh time for the routing list.

CLB can also be deployed in a "cluster master" mode, in which a single server with no Web functionality acts as a COM+ router. The CLB software on each Web server obtains a routing list from the router server rather than polling each COM+ server. In a large deployment, this can reduce traffic and overhead because only one server (the router) needs to maintain the routing list and constantly poll the COM+ servers.

COM+ requirements

For components to operate properly in a cluster, they must be written to the COM+ standard. The components must also meet other basic requirements for operating in a COM+ cluster:

✦ Components must not attempt to maintain state in memory. A Web server may be directed to many different COM+ servers, instantiating the same component on each. Components that need to maintain state information between calls must do so in the back-end data tier, where the state information will be available to all of the COM+ servers and the components that they execute.

✦ Components must not assume anything about the local server that they are running on, because they may be instantiated on any server in the cluster. Components must always use process-wide storage, such as a back-end data tier or common file server, for data storage and retrieval.

✦ Components using transactions must begin and complete transactions in a single call. They should not attempt to persist the transaction across multiple calls because subsequent calls to the component may take place on a server other than the one that handled the initial call, thus rendering the transaction invalid.

Deploying CLB

Application Center 2000 includes a Deployment Wizard to help create and deploy COM+ clusters. In general, you must follow these steps:

1. Set up the clusters. To do so, one cluster must hold the routing lists (which are generally on the Web servers, although you can create a separate routing server or routing cluster as described previously). The COM+ servers act as the second cluster.

2. Use the Deployment Wizard to deploy Application Center Applications, which are groups of COM+ components, to the COM+ servers. Application Center allows you to use a staging server that has the COM+ components manually installed and "packaged" into an Application Center Application for easier deployment.

3. Install the COM+ components on the Web servers. This is required so that the necessary Registry information and object references are available on the servers. Remember that installing these components generally requires IIS, and possibly the entire server, to be restarted.

4. Use Application Center to mark the COM+ components on the Web servers as supporting CLB.

When CLB is appropriate

CLB imposes a new dynamic factor into your Web application, and shouldn't be recklessly used for every COM+ component in your site. Observe the following guidelines:

✦ Creating an object with CLB is somewhat slower than creating an object locally, because CLB requires network traffic to communicate with the COM+ server and set up the object. Small, one-time objects with limited functionality will probably be better performers if left local on each Web server. Local calls can be three to five times faster than a CLB object call.

✦ If the components in your site are security-sensitive or if they perform complex operations, then CLB is appropriate. CLB allows you to better manage component security (for example, you can place the COM+ cluster behind a firewall). CLB also allows you to centralize component management and more easily balance the components' processing load across several servers.

✦ If your Web servers *won't* be single tasked, CLB can help break some processing load off of the Web servers, thus allowing them to handle additional client connections more easily.

Network Load Balancing

Network Load Balancing (NLB) was first introduced in Windows NT 4.0 Enterprise Edition (as *Windows* Load Balancing), and is available with the Advanced Server edition of Windows 2000 and Windows XP. Application Center 2000 integrates with Network Load Balancing to create self-balancing Web farms.

Note   Application Center can also integrate with third-party load balancing tools that have been written to work with it. The Application Center 2000 Resource Kit includes information on integrating third-party load balancing tools with Application Center; I recommend that you use NLB unless you have a specific reason not to.

NLB allows you to create "clusters" of Web servers. This type of cluster is different from the one that I talked about earlier; these servers don't technically provide any failover for each other. Instead, an NLB cluster, which can consist of up to 32 servers, is comprised of servers providing identical TCP/IP services, so that it doesn't matter to which server a user is directed. The servers don't share any hardware or other resources and are, in every regard, treated as separate machines.

NLB functions very similarly to the load balancing features found in high-end hardware switches (like Foundry switches) and products like LocalDirector. The basis of an NLB cluster is a single virtual IP address that represents all of the servers in the cluster (each server is also configured with its own dedicated IP address).

Each server in the cluster is assigned a *host priority*; the server with the highest priority will respond to all requests made to the cluster's virtual IP address for traffic types *not* intended to be load balanced. Should this server become unavailable, the next-highest priority server will begin handling non-load-balanced traffic for the cluster.

Load balancing is configured on a port-by-port basis, which allows you to balance different types of traffic, such as HTTP or HTTPS, according to different rules. For each load-balancing port that you define, you can specify whether the port will be handled by a single server without load balancing, or whether incoming requests on that port should be balanced across multiple servers. If you select multiple servers, you can also specify what percentage of the overall load each server should handle, which allows you to accommodate different levels of server hardware within a single server farm.

Client affinity

Load balancing also supports three *client affinity* modes.

✦ In *no affinity* mode, each request from a different source IP port is load-balanced, meaning that a client can connect to one server for HTTP traffic and another for HTTPS traffic. This is the best scenario for load balancing because it allows the servers to evenly distribute their overall traffic. However, this may cause problems for your Web application if you are using state information like ASP Session variables to maintain user information, because users may connect to several different servers in a single session.

✦ *Single-client* affinity causes *all* traffic from a single source IP address to be directed to a single server, thus ensuring that a single client will receive services from one server. However, because most Internet Service Providers use Network Address Translation (NAT) services, many clients will appear to be using a single IP address, which reduces the effectiveness of your load-balancing scheme. Also, because of the way NAT works, some clients may appear to be using multiple IP addresses during a single session, which defeats this affinity mode.

✦ *Class C affinity* attempts to solve the problem of some clients appearing to use multiple IP addresses by directing all traffic from a single Class C network to a single server in your server farm. This helps ensure that all clients connecting from a single ISP will connect to the same server, further reducing the effectiveness of your load balancing, but helping to maintain connections required for state information that is server-based.

How NLB works

When NLB is installed, configured, and running on a server, that server will examine *all* traffic destined to the NLB cluster's virtual IP address. Because the server has been configured to handle only a portion of the cluster's traffic, it will select and respond only to a portion of the traffic that it actually sees. Servers within an NLB cluster transmit a heartbeat signal to each other with status information, and communicate to redistribute the total cluster load if a server stops sending a heartbeat. This is a distributed means of managing the cluster load and status, rather than the centralized cluster management employed by Windows clustering.

Caveats

If you intend to employ NLB in a server farm, I recommend that you connect all of the servers in a cluster to a *hub* rather than to a switch. In order for NLB to work, every server has to "see" all traffic directed to the cluster's virtual IP; if you use a switch, this means that the switch must be told to broadcast incoming traffic across all of its ports. The NLB service is capable of telling the switch to do this, but many switches will suffer degraded performance when they are put in the position of acting as a hub.

I also recommend that you provide a dedicated network interface card and high-speed network to carry the inter-cluster heartbeat and communications traffic. This way, you will avoid any contention between the client and cluster traffic, and the cluster will be allowed to maintain its state more efficiently.

Request forwarding

Request forwarding is a service that Application Center adds to the base Network Load Balancing (NLB) technology. Rather than attempting to maintain client affinity based on IP address, request forwarding uses the session-state cookie that IIS automatically creates and passes to the customer's Web browser when the Session object is used. When a Web server accepts a load-balanced connection from a customer, it checks to see if the customer's browser already contains a cookie for a Web server in the farm. If it does, the customer is redirected to the appropriate server.

Request forwarding is implemented as an ISAPI filter (RfFilExt.dll.) that intercepts every connection received by the Web servers. Requests for non-ASP files are never forwarded because they can't, by definition, use Session variables. You can also configure the forwarder to never forward requests for certain file types, if you want.

Request forwarding reduces the performance of the Web site as a whole, because load balancing takes place and then a redirect occurs, if necessary. If you must use Session variables, request forwarding is the best way to take advantage of a degree of load balancing while using them. However, I recommend that you avoid the use of Session variables altogether. Instead, store state information in your data tier, where it will be available to any Web server to which the customer connects. This provides maximum load balancing in your Web farm.

Web technologies

You can use a variety of general techniques and technologies to improve the robustness of your site. Many of these include simple tweaks to your ASP code, but some involve outside technologies and services designed to improve the response time of your site.

General techniques

Several "generic" best practices help reduce overhead and improve performance of any Web site. These include:

✦ Make your servers as specialized as possible. This means having more servers, with different ones handling catalog browsing, search, checkout, and other functions. By specializing, you can easily pinpoint the services that require more power, so you can add additional specialized servers for those tasks.

✦ Keep your page content as small as possible. Smaller pages transfer more quickly. This means that you must be careful when using tools like Microsoft FrontPage 2000, which can produce very "heavy" HTML code with a lot of unnecessary tags.

✦ Reuse graphics as much as possible — especially common graphical elements like logos and navigation elements. Customers' browsers will cache these graphics, preventing them from having to download the graphics from your servers every time they see them.

✦ Split large graphics into pieces. Most Web browsers will make up to four connections with your Web server to download content. Large graphics must be downloaded all at once, but by breaking graphics into smaller pieces, you allow the Web browser to download several of the pieces at the same time.

✦ Be careful to exclude any files that aren't necessary. For example, it's common to place a set of DHTML subroutines into an include file and simply include that file with every ASP page, so that the subroutines are always available. Avoid making any blanket decisions about include files; instead, include them only when necessary.

ASP techniques

You can do a number of things to help ASP code execute more quickly and reduce the overhead that your code imposes on your Web servers.

Reduce dots in object references

Whenever you refer to objects, Visual Basic or the scripting engine that is interpreting your script has to be able to reference those objects in memory. For each object that you refer to, a new reference has to be created. Many of the object models used in a commerce site have complex object hierarchies, so your object references can become quite long:

```
Object.Collection.Collection.Collection.Property
```

Every time a period is encountered in an object reference, memory and processing time is required to create a temporary "image" of the object preceding the period. These "images" are destroyed after the line of code has been executed, and are recreated on the next reference. To avoid this overhead, reduce the number of consecutive periods, or dots, in object references.

For example, consider the following code that references a specific folder by using the FileSystemObject in VBScript:

```
Set objFSO = CreateObject("Scripting.FileSystemObject")
A = ObjFSO.RootFolder.Folders(1).Folders(4).Path
ObjFSO.RootFolder.Folders(1).Folders(4).DeleteFolder
```

By assigning the last object to an object variable and working with that, you can reduce the memory and processor overhead of this code:

```
Set objFSO = CreateObject("Scripting.FileSystemObject")
Set objFld = ObjFSO.RootFolder.Folders(1).Folders(4)
A = ObjFld.Path
ObjFld.DeleteFolder
```

This is especially true when the object will be used more than once, because the object variable forces the computer to retain the object "images" that are necessary to work with the object, rather than recreating the object each time in an ad-hoc reference. You can also use the With construct:

```
Set objFSO = CreateObject("Scripting.FileSystemObject")
With objFSO.RootFolder.Folders(1).Folders(4)
  A = .Path
  .DeleteFolder
End With
```

Again, the With construct is best used when the object will be referred to more than once.

Reduce use of Application and Session variables

Application and Session variables are convenient ASP tricks for persisting data across a customer's connections to your site, but they also impose a fairly heavy burden on a Web server, particularly in a high-traffic site.

Reduce database calls

Try not to make calls to the database for information that rarely changes. For example, if you have an address information page that includes a drop-down box for the customers' state or province, don't pull that information out of a database. Instead, hard-code it into the page. State and province information *rarely* changes, so the benefits of pulling the information from a database are far outweighed by the performance hit that you'll pay for doing so.

Similarly, examine any page with more than a few dynamically generated items. If all of those items do, in fact, contain information that changes constantly, you're fine. If some of the information only changes rarely, or even daily, then you should consider creating a static version of the page that doesn't require a database hit to display.

The usual COM tricks

If you intend to write your own COM/COM+ components in Visual Basic for use in your site, be sure to follow basic best practices:

✦ Make sure that your components are written to explicitly declare variables to take advantage of early binding; failure to properly declare variables forces Visual Basic to resolve them at runtime, which reduces performance and increases memory usage.

✦ Test your components thoroughly so they can be safely run inside of IIS' memory process. Forcing them to run out-of-process increases processor and memory overhead when IIS instantiates the components on behalf of your script.

✦ Make sure that your components are using a threading model that allows multiple threads to be used for multiple instances of the object. Visual Basic usually handles this automatically by selecting "apartment model" threading.

Appropriate use of Secure Sockets Layer

The encryption technique used by Secure Sockets Layer (SSL) requires approximately *triple* the processing power of an unencrypted Web page. To minimize the impact this has on your servers, you should consider the following when designing your site:

✦ Only encrypt pages that will contain confidential, private information. In the checkout process, for example, only the page that contains the customer's credit card number usually needs to be encrypted.

✦ Use a dedicated server (or set of servers) for processes requiring encryption, such as checkout. This focuses the encrypted traffic to those servers, thus allowing you to better scale the site by making it easier to determine where bottlenecks are.

✦ Minimize the content on the page. *All* of the content on a secure page must be encrypted — even graphics — so try to keep encrypted pages as small as possible.

Hardware vendors like CacheFlow (`www.cacheflow.com`) make hardware products — ranging from external "black boxes" to special network interface cards — that handle SSL encryption on behalf of your server. Basically, you configure these devices with the list of Web pages that should be encrypted, and then leave the encryption to them. Your server is no longer responsible for encrypting the outgoing content; instead, the hardware device — with a dedicated RISC processor, in most cases — encrypts the file *after* your server has finished transmitting it. This type of device can save an incredible amount of processing overhead on SSL-heavy sites.

A few users out there have browsers that are not SSL-compatible, or may be accessing your site through a firewall that permits HTTP traffic but not encrypted HTTPS traffic. Make sure that your site provides a non-encrypted version of secure processes for these users, and make sure that you remind them of the risk of their private information being intercepted on the Internet.

Tip   Make sure that all HTML links, including image URLs, are *relative* on pages using SSL. Any links starting with HTTP: will try to display in unencrypted mode, causing the customer's browser to display a "mixed security" warning message.

Third-party content delivery

One great way to improve the performance of your Web site is to have someone else deliver your bandwidth-hogging content (graphics, video files, and so forth). This is an increasingly popular way to improve Web site performance, and a company named Akamai (`www.akamai.com`) is at the forefront of the technologies involved.

Akamaized graphics and media use a special URL, similar to the following:

```
http://a232.g.akamai.net/f/232/1338/360m/www.craftopia.com/
shop/assets/images/globalnav/logo/60k.gif
```

The actual URL is generated by a script that Akamai provides when you sign up for their service. This URL directs your customers' Web browser to retrieve the graphic from one of Akamai's servers, which are strategically positioned around the world at key Internet backbone points, thus providing fast connections to most of the world. Akamai retrieves the graphic from your site, and caches it on their servers, which allows customers' browsers to retrieve the graphic faster.

Akamai has partnered with many hardware vendors, including CacheFlow (www.cacheflow.com) to provide hardware-based "Akamaization." This on-the-fly capability involves a hardware "black box" that automatically Akamaizes your site's graphics and media content *without* the need for specially-coded URLs. Although the expense of this type of solution is more than the non-hardware-based Akamai service, your site and your customers immediately begin to benefit from faster content delivery, and your Web servers are freed up to concentrate on delivering your site's *content*, rather than the graphic elements surrounding that content.

Summary

Customers rely on your site to give them timely information on their order status and many other topics. Careful architecture can make your site more responsive to your customers, and Microsoft provides plenty of technologies to implement a robust, scalable, highly available architecture, including Network Load Balancing, Windows clustering, Application Center 2000, Component Load Balancing, and more.

✦   ✦   ✦

Supporting Your Business Processes

As you allot time and other resources to develop your site, don't forget about the "behind-the-scenes" activities that are necessary to keep your site running and productive. Many e-commerce development efforts neglect these factors, saving them for the last minute or handling them on a reactionary basis. This approach won't help your site grow and prosper; rather, it will create additional stress and it can deter other employees in your company from doing their jobs.

The two primary back-end processes that you should focus on are *reporting* and *order fulfillment*. Reporting provides your company with the information necessary to make informed business decisions, and reporting will affect every aspect of your site's future growth and development. The order fulfillment process, the most important of back-end processes, allows you to actually fill your customers' orders. Carefully created, your order fulfillment process can also allow you to accept orders for products from business partners, extending your sales reach to other Web sites.

Reports

Commerce Server 2000 offers *major* improvements in reporting over the previous version of the product (Site Server 3.0 Commerce Edition had practically no built-in reporting capabilities). Commerce Server comes equipped with a complete business analysis system based on SQL Server's data warehousing capabilities.

Even so, your company will likely want to create a number of customized reports to meet your specific needs. Commerce Server provides several features to help you build custom reports, and you always have the option of working directly with your Commerce Server database and data warehouse to retrieve important business information.

Chapter 19 includes more information on building reports with Commerce Server, working directly with Commerce Server's databases, and building a reporting infrastructure for your organization.

Keep in mind that Commerce Server's databases can only provide you with information based on the data that they contain. This may sound obvious, but many of the business reports needed by folks in your company will require data *not* normally contained in the Commerce Server database. For example, unless you modify the default database schema, Commerce Server doesn't track cost information, and so can't provide reports on your site's profitability. Nor does Commerce Server track inventory information, so it can't provide you with inventory reports or period-end inventory tax summaries. For these types of reports, you will need to either collect the data in a separate back-end system and run reports from there, or you will need to modify the Commerce Server database schema and create custom reports for the necessary information.

Commerce Server reports

Commerce Server's Business Desk includes 39 business reports that are designed to deliver information on your advertising, site statistics, user information, and more. Some of these reports can be customized to a great degree, offering a starting point for your own custom reports.

Commerce Server's built-in reporting functionality is based almost entirely on the data warehouse that Commerce Server creates on a SQL Server in your organization. Before reports can be run against this data warehouse, you must complete a number of preliminary steps (which are covered later in this chapter). Regular maintenance of the data warehouse is also required to keep your reports up-to-date.

Maintaining the data warehouse is a task for SQL Server's Data Transformation Services, and the necessary DTS tasks are covered in Appendix C.

Types of reports

Commerce Server offers two basic types of reports — *static* and *dynamic*. Static reports are run and stored in the data warehouse, along with the data used to create the report. After they have been run, static reports offer the advantage of instantly displaying when requested because the entire report is statically stored in the data warehouse. The disadvantage to static reports is that they represent a "snapshot" in time, and not the most current data.

Note Keep in mind that a data warehouse, by definition, represents a "snapshot" of your live data and will never contain "real-time" data.

Static reports can be posted as Web pages on your site, and they can serve as the source for mailing lists that are imported into the List Manager. You run static reports from the Business Desk's Analysis module by selecting the Reports screen. Completed static reports can be viewed on the Completed Reports screen, as shown in Figure 17-1.

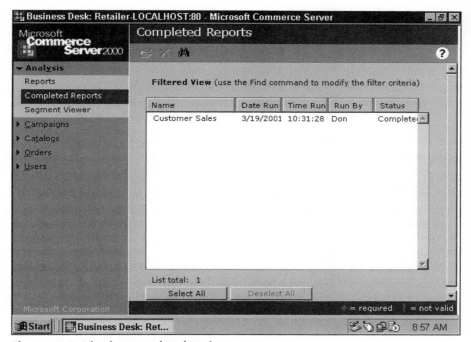

Figure 17-1: Viewing completed static reports

Completed static reports are, by default, stored under the Business Desk's virtual root on your Web server as static HTML files, as shown in Figure 17-2. You can print or easily move these static files to an intranet Web server.

Figure 17-2: Completed static reports are stored as HTML files

Dynamic reports, on the other hand, are not stored in the data warehouse. The data for the report is pulled from the data warehouse, and you have many options for customizing the columns that are shown in the report. You actually view the report in a PivotTable or PivotChart in your browser window. This requires that your computer have a licensed copy of Microsoft Office 2000 installed, because the PivotTable and PivotChart functionality is provided by instantiating Microsoft Excel 2000.

As shown in Figure 17-3, dynamic reports allow you to specify column names, and the necessary data is immediately queried from the data warehouse and added to the PivotTable in your Web browser.

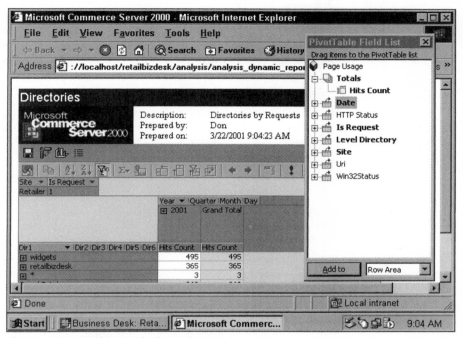

Figure 17-3: Working with dynamic reports

After you have the report configured as desired, you can save it — including columns selected, sort order, values selected, and so forth — as a new dynamic report in the Business Desk for future use.

Available reports

Commerce Server's built-in reports are broken down into nine categories. These categories, and the reports included in each, are as follows:

✦ **Advertising.** The reports in this category are designed to help you manage your ad campaigns. Reports include:

• **Ad placement:** This dynamic report lets you review how effectively ads have been placed on your site. It includes a summary of campaign activity by the different locations on your site that display ads.

• **Ad reach and frequency per day:** This dynamic report shows you the behavior of users in relation to the campaign items on your site, displaying the activity of unique users per day for each campaign item.

• **Ad reach and frequency per campaign item:** This dynamic report shows the activity of unique users per day for each campaign item over a period of time.

- **Ad reach and frequency per campaign:** This dynamic report shows the activity of unique users per day for entire campaigns over a period of time.

- **Campaign item summary:** This dynamic report shows a summary of the activity for each campaign item on your site, including click through, remaining clicks to fulfill a campaign goal, and so forth.

- **Campaign event summary:** This dynamic report shows the effectiveness for entire campaigns on your site, including the total number of events associated with all of the items in a campaign.

✦ **Product sales.** The reports in this category provide details on the performance of specific products on your site. Reports include:

- **Buyer browse to purchase:** This dynamic report identifies first time and repeat buyers, and the average number of visits each buyer made per purchase. This helps you determine, for example, how frequently visitors to your site make a purchase.

- **Customer sales:** This static report shows the details of individual customer purchases, including total sales and total orders. This report can be exported to the List Manager, allowing you to target campaigns, for example, to customers with high dollar value purchases.

- **Customer spend summary:** This dynamic report allows you to review sales volume and income by customer.

- **Order events:** This dynamic report allows you to review order submission events, such as a user clicking a checkout button. The difference between the number of order events and the number of completed orders tells you how many customers abandoned their purchase after deciding to check out. If this ratio is high, you should investigate your checkout process for possible problems.

- **Product sales:** This dynamic report allows you to review product sales, both by volume and by income, for specific date ranges.

- **Shopping basket events:** This dynamic report allows you to review user behavior in your shopping cart modules. The report displays products, the number of times those products have been added to and removed from shopping carts, and so forth.

✦ **Web usage.** The reports in this category allow you to review statistics for page requests from your Web site. Reports include:

- **Directories:** This dynamic report shows you which of the URI (Uniform Resource Indicatory) directory levels on your site are the most visited. This can help you identify popular areas of the site, which can be useful both from a marketing and resources-planning perspective. For example, extremely popular content may be better hosted on standalone servers to provide better response times.

- **Entry path analysis:** This static report shows you the top *entry paths* to your site. An entry path is a URL or URI used by customers to gain access to your site. Generally, your home page is at the top of the list. Note that this is an extremely long-running report.

- **Top referring domains by request:** This static report shows you the top domains that referred users to your site. You can use this to help determine where your most effective advertising is taking place.

- **Top request pages:** This static report shows you the individual pages most requested by users who visit your site. By default, this report displays up to 5,000 of the most active pages in order of popularity. You can change this value, or change the report to show the least active pages, by modifying the CSDW_MakeAggRequestsByUri stored procedure in the Commerce Server data warehouse database.

- **Usage summary by day of week:** This dynamic report shows you your Web traffic broken down by day of the week. Most e-commerce sites notice specific trends in their traffic throughout the week; this report can help you determine the best days, for example, to perform maintenance that requires taking servers offline.

- **Usage summary by hour of day:** This dynamic report breaks down a day's traffic into the hours of the day, helping you determine when your site is busiest each day. You can use this report to determine the best times to run limited time offers (when traffic is high), or when to perform maintenance (when traffic is low).

- **Usage summary by week of year:** This dynamic report shows your site's traffic patterns by week over the course of a year. This can help you determine your busy seasons. Note that this report may not be useful in your first couple of years of operation because your customer base should be continuously growing during this time.

- **Usage trends:** This dynamic report provides a summary of daily page requests, user counts, and visits, and provides a quick snapshot of your site's traffic trends.

- **Visits by browser, version, and OS:** This dynamic report shows you the breakdown of users who visit your site with specific Web browsers, Web browser versions, and client operating systems. This can be important as your site undergoes further development, because you can identify the basic feature set shared by the majority of your users.

✦ **User.** The reports in this category let you work with information regarding your site's users. The static reports in this category are especially useful for generating records that can be imported into the List Manager and used for direct mail campaigns. Reports include:

- **Distinct users and visits by week:** This dynamic report shows your site's traffic broken down by unique users. This allows you to determine how many users are creating the overall traffic on your site, and determine how sales to those users correspond with their traffic. This report shows unique users *per week,* as opposed to per day.

- **Distinct users by day:** This dynamic report shows you how many unique users visited your site on a given day. Use this report to correlate daily traffic with the number of users that generated the traffic.

- **New registered users:** This static report identifies newly registered users on your site, and can be used to create "welcome" ad campaigns.

- **Registered user properties:** This static report allows you to review the information provided by registered users, so you can create List Manager lists for use in promotional campaigns that target specific groups of users based on their properties.

- **Registered users by date registered:** This dynamic report allows you to review the registration behavior of your registered users by showing you the number of users who registered during specific time periods (day, month, quarter, or year).

- **User days to register:** This dynamic report shows you the average number of days a user visits your site anonymously before registering. This report relies on cookies and IP addresses to identify anonymous users between visits, and unfortunately, may have a significant margin of error.

- **User registration rate:** This dynamic report shows the rate at which anonymous users register on your site. As with the previous report, the margin of error on this report can be high depending on how users' computers are set to handle cookies and whether or not users are coming from different IP addresses each time.

- **User trends:** This dynamic report shows you how successfully you attract new and repeat users by showing the number of new and repeat users who visit your site on particular dates or weeks.

✦ **Visit.** The reports in this category help you understand how users are using your site. Reports include:

- **Entry pages:** This dynamic report helps you determine the top 5,000 pages that users see first when they visit your site. Generally, the top page is your home page.

- **Exit pages:** This dynamic report shows you the *last* page that users see before leaving your site. Ideally, this is your order confirmation page, indicating that most users leave your site after making a purchase. If a particular page shows up with a disproportionately high score as an exit page, you should determine why that page is failing to sustain shopper interest in your site.

- **General activity statistics:** This dynamic report helps you review general information about user visits to your site, including the average duration of a visit, the average number of pages seen during a visit, and so forth.

- **User visit trends:** This dynamic report shows you the number of user visits to your site over a period of time, helping you to understand visit trends. The report separates visits by anonymous and registered users.

✦ **Diagnostic.** Reports in this category help you measure diagnostic and technical information about your site. Reports include:

- **Bandwidth summary:** This dynamic report displays a PivotChart of the weekly network bandwidth used by your site. You can use this report as a "double check" of your ISP's bandwidth-based fees, if necessary, and to determine how "heavy" your site is. If you have a relatively low number of visits but high bandwidth usage, then your site may require excessive bandwidth for your customers.

- **Bandwidth trends:** This dynamic report shows bandwidth utilization over a period of time. Overlaid with your site's traffic and visit trends, this report should match your increasing visits fairly closely.

- **Hits by HTTP status:** This dynamic report shows the HTTP status code returned to clients who requested the top 5,000 pages in your site. This can help resolve problems with broken hyperlinks, missing graphics, and so forth.

- **Hits by Win32 status:** This dynamic report reveals any ASP- and Win32-related error messages associated with the top 5,000 pages on your site, which is useful for spotting ASP errors or component-related problems.

✦ **Query string.** The reports in this category allow you to track the information being requested by your customers. Dynamic pages supply information based on the query string passed to the page; these reports summarize the query strings, thus allowing you to notice popular products, for example.

If you use static pages for the majority of your information, then the "Top request pages" report will be more useful for your needs. On the other hand, if you have an ASP page appearing as a top requested page, the query string reports can provide insight on what information that page was actually supplying to your customers.

This category includes two static reports. The first summarizes multi-valued query strings, and the second summarizes single-value query strings.

Note All reports use the time and date information of your SQL Server as their basis. For example, if your SQL Server is configured with a language option that specifies Sunday as the first day in the week, then all of your reports will be built accordingly.

Reporting requirements

Before any reports can be made available on your site, data must be imported from the production database (and your Web server logs) into the data warehouse. Then, the data warehouse's OLAP cubes must be populated with the data dimensions, allowing reports to be run against the cubes.

Unfortunately, none of this data makes its way into the data warehouse automatically. You must import it manually or create a regularly scheduled process to do it for you. Fortunately, Commerce Server provides several SQL Server Data Transformation Services (DTS) tasks to handle the data import for you. These include:

✦ Importing data from your Web server log files.

✦ Importing catalog data.

✦ Importing campaign data.

✦ Importing transaction data.

✦ Importing user profile data.

You may want to create a single DTS package that imports all of your data into the data warehouse on a regular basis. To do so, open SQL Server Enterprise Manager and create a new DTS package. Then follow these steps:

1. Use the Task menu to add a Configuration Synchronization task, and specify the Commerce site from which you will be importing data. This task is required before any data can actually be imported.

2. Use the Task menu to add a Product Catalog Import task.

3. Use the Task menu to add a Campaign Data Import task.

4. Use the Task menu to add a Transaction Data Import task.

5. Use the Task menu to add a User Profile Data Import task.

Note   Each of the import tasks must be configured to perform a "full load" the first time the task is executed. Subsequent imports can be configured for an "incremental load," which will only import new and changed data.

6. Use the Task menu to add a Web Server Log Import task. Specify the Commerce Site and specify the location of the Web logs for your site. You can specify that all new log files be imported, or that only log files containing entries within a certain date range be imported.

7. Use the Task menu to add a Report Preparation task, and specify the Commerce Site that you are working with. This task will populate the OLAP cubes by using the imported data.

8. Add workflow markers. Click the Configuration Synchronization task, and hold down the Ctrl key and click the Product Catalog Import task. Select "On Completion" from the Workflow menu to connect the two tasks. Continue connecting all of the remaining tasks. After you finish, they should indicate a workflow order as follows:

    a. Configuration Synchronization

    b. Product Catalog Import

    c. Campaign Data Import

     d. Transaction Data Import

     e. User Profile Data Import

     f. Web Server Log Import

     g. Report Preparation

9. Click the "Auto Layout" button in the toolbar to neatly arrange the task icons in order of their workflow. *Double check* to make sure that the Configuration Synchronization task is first and the Report Preparation task is last; both of these icons should only have one workflow line attached to them. The completed package should look something like the one shown in Figure 17-4.

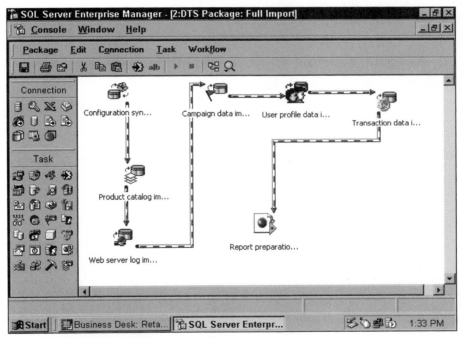

Figure 17-4: Full data import DTS package

10. Save the package to the local SQL Server.

    You may want to execute the package now if you need to run your first full load. Then, you can modify each of the import tasks to specify an incremental load, and re-save the package.

11. Exit the DTS Designer and right-click the package that you just saved. Select "Schedule Package" to schedule the package for regular execution, thus automating your import process.

The package may take anywhere from a few minutes to several hours to run, depending on how much data needs to be imported. The last task in particular can take a long time to run when the data warehouse becomes full, because it must populate the OLAP cubes. You can monitor the package's progress when running it manually, as shown in Figure 17-5.

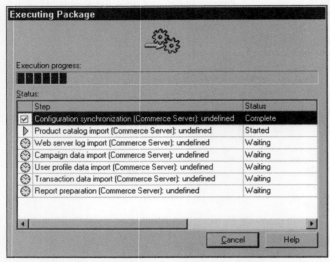

Figure 17-5: Manually running the import DTS package

Tip   Schedule the package for regular execution — once a week or once a day — to keep the amount of data that has to be imported each time as small as possible.

To prevent the import process from negatively affecting your production database server, try to observe the following guidelines:

✦ Create and execute the DTS package on the same server that contains the data warehouse database.

✦ *Do not* place the data warehouse database on the same SQL Server that contains your production database.

✦ Try to maintain high-speed network connectivity between the production database and data warehouse database servers. Use LAN bandwidth connections whenever possible.

Cross-Reference   I discuss how to build a robust reporting infrastructure in Chapter 19.

Making your own reports

Commerce Server's Business Desk allows you to create your own dynamic and static reports. These reports run exactly like the built-in reports, and require the Commerce Server data warehouse to be their data source. Commerce Server allows you to create static reports that execute traditional SQL queries or OLAP-related MDX queries; you can also create dynamic queries that run against the OLAP cubes in the data warehouse. Understanding how Commerce Server uses these reports, and how Commerce Server's data warehouse is built, is pivotal to creating your own useful reports in the Business Desk.

 Cross-Reference You may need to create reports that pull data from a copy of your production database or other places; this is most often required when supporting back office functions like accounting. I discuss methods for building this kind of reporting infrastructure in Chapter 19.

Static SQL reports

Remember that static reports are stored in the data warehouse after they run. So creating a static report is, essentially, simply a process of querying data from one part of the data warehouse, performing your calculations, and storing the result somewhere else in the data warehouse.

Imagine that you want to create a report that displays all users who registered during 2001, had a UserType of 1 (a normal user), and provided an e-mail address during registration. This may be useful, for example, for importing into the List Manager to use in a campaign welcoming all the users who joined you in the past year.

1. To retrieve the desired information, create a SQL query like the following:

```
SELECT
  rcp_guid as UserID, DateCreated, DateRegistered,
  rcp_email, FirstName, LastName, TelephoneNumber,
  UserTitle, UserType
FROM RegisteredUser
WHERE (DateRegistered >= '01/01/2001'
  AND DateRegistered <= '12/31/2001')
  AND UserType = 1
  AND Email is not Null
```

2. Add any appropriate parameters to the query. These will become parameters that can be set by the person running the final report. The following code shows a modified SQL query with parameter information added.

```
SELECT
  rcp_guid as UserID, DateCreated, DateRegistered,
  rcp_email, FirstName, LastName, TelephoneNumber,
  UserTitle, UserType
```

```
INTO [$ResultTable]
FROM RegisteredUser
WHERE [$DateRange]
 AND UserType = 1
 AND Email is not Null
```

This modified query allows the report's user to specify the date range for the report, and provide a parameterized table name to hold the resulting data.

3. Create the basic report definition by using a set of SQL INSERT statements. One field in the report definition is named "Query," and will contain the query that you just created. The following code shows how to create the basic report definition for the preceding query. Note that this simply creates a new entry in the data warehouse's Report table.

```
DECLARE @ReportID int, @ReportStatus int
INSERT INTO Report (
   DisplayName, Description, ReportType,
   Category, Query, DmExport, UpmExport,
   CreatedBy, Protected
)
VALUES (
   'Registered Users by date range',
   'A report of registered users by date range.',
   @Static_SQL,
   'Users',
   'SELECT
 UserId, rcp_guid, DateCreated, DateRegistered,
 rcp_email As Email, FirstName, LastName, TelephoneNumber,
 UserTitle, UserType
INTO [$ResultTable]
FROM RegisteredUser
WHERE [$DateRange]
 AND UserType = 1
 AND Email is not Null',
   1,
   1,
   'Administrator',
   0
)
SELECT @ReportID = @@identity
```

This script will complete with the variable @ReportID containing the unique ID of the report definition that you just created.

4. Create the *dimensions* of the report by inserting information into the ReportDimension table. You'll need the value of the @ReportID variable from the end of the previous script. The following code should be appended to the end of the previous script.

```
INSERT INTO ReportDimension (
 ReportID, DimensionType,
 DisplayName, FieldName, Ordinal
)
```

```
VALUES (
@ReportID, 0, "Email", "rcp_email", 1
)

INSERT INTO ReportDimension (
 ReportID, DimensionType,
 DisplayName, FieldName, Ordinal
)
VALUES (
@ReportID, 0, "UserId", "rcp_guid", 2
)

INSERT INTO ReportDimension (
 ReportID, DimensionType,
 DisplayName, FieldName, Ordinal
)
VALUES (
@ReportID, 0, "FirstName", "FirstName", 3
)

INSERT INTO ReportDimension (
 ReportID, DimensionType,
 DisplayName, FieldName, Ordinal
)
VALUES (
@ReportID, 0, "LastName", "LastName", 4
)

INSERT INTO ReportDimension (
 ReportID, DimensionType,
 DisplayName, FieldName, Ordinal
)
VALUES (
@ReportID, 0, "DateCreated", "DateCreated", 5
)

INSERT INTO ReportDimension (
 ReportID, DimensionType,
 DisplayName, FieldName, Ordinal
)
VALUES (
@ReportID, 0, "DateRegistered", "DateRegistered", 6
)
```

With each INSERT statement, you insert a new report dimension's column, row, or measure. Generally, only fields specified in the original SELECT statement can be specified.

5. Add the report parameters that you specified in the original base query. These are inserted into the ReportParam table, and must correspond with the parameters that you included in the query. The following code shows the additions to the script that will add the parameters.

```
INSERT INTO ReportParam (
 ReportID, ParamName, ParamDescription,
 ParamType, DataType, Opnd1, Val1, Opnd2,
 Val2, FieldName, Ordinal
)
VALUES (
@ReportID, '[$DateRange]', 'User registration date',
ParamType_DateRange, DataType_date,
DateRangeOpnd_From, '1/1/2001', 0,
'12/31/2001', "DateRegistered", 2
)
```

Note that the [$ResultTable] parameter in your query will be filled in automatically by Commerce Server when the report is run. After you complete these steps, the report will be available in the Business Desk and can be run like any other static report.

Static MDX reports

For reports that need to do more than query simple tables, you can use static MDX reports to query the data warehouse's OLAP cubes. The process for creating this report is similar to the process for creating a static SQL report, but requires you to be familiar with writing MDX queries.

Note Learning to write MDX queries is a book in itself; I recommend that you find a good book on programming data warehouses as a starting point if you're interested in creating custom static MDX reports.

For example, to create a report that lists the top 50 domains that refer users to your site, follow these steps:

1. Begin by writing an MDX query like the following.

```
SELECT
 {Measures.Visits, Measures.Requests} ON COLUMNS,
 TopCount({Referrer.Referrer Domain Name.members}, 50,
 Measures.Visits) ON ROWS
FROM [Web Usage]
WHERE (Retail)
```

2. Add parameters to the query, as shown below:

```
SELECT
 {Measures.Visits, Measures.Requests} ON COLUMNS,
 [$TopCount]({Referrer.Referrer Domain Name.members},
 [$TopCount],Measures.Visits) ON ROWS
FROM [Web Usage]
WHERE ([$SiteName])
```

This modified MDX query allows you to parameterize the Commerce Site being queried, as well as the top number of referring domains to return in the report.

3. Create the base report definition. This requires a query similar to the one required for a static SQL report's base report definition.

```
DECLARE @ReportID int
DECLARE @ReportStatusID int
INSERT INTO Report (
 DisplayName, Description, ReportType,
 Category, Query, CreatedBy,
 Protected, Definition
)
VALUES (
 'Visits by Referrer', 'Visits by Referrer',
 @Static_MDX, 'Web Usage',
 'SELECT
 {Measures.Visits, Measures.Requests} ON COLUMNS,
 TopCount({Referrer.Referrer Domain Name.members},
 [$TopCount],Measures.Visits) ON ROWS
 FROM [Web Usage]
 WHERE ([$SiteName])',
 'administrator', 0,
 'Shows top referring domains'
)
SELECT @ReportID = @@identity
```

4. Add the report's parameters to the ReportParam table, as shown in the following code:

```
INSERT INTO ReportParam (
 ReportID, ParamName, ParamDescription,
 ParamType, DataType, Opnd1, Val1, Ordinal
)
VALUES (
 @ReportID, '[$TopCount]', 'Max. referrer domains',
 @ParamType_SelectOrder, @DataType_integer,
 @SelectOrderOpnd_Top, 50, 1
)

INSERT into ReportParam (
 ReportID, ParamName, ParamDescription,
 ParamType, DataType, Opnd1, Val1, Ordinal
)
VALUES (
 @ReportID, '[$SiteName]', 'Site Name',
 @ParamType_SiteName, @DataType_text,
 @SiteNameOpnd_Equals, 'Retail', 2
)
```

The report will now be available in the Business Desk's Reports module for anyone who needs it.

Dynamic reports

You can create new dynamic reports in one of two ways. The first way is the easiest, and involves modifying an existing dynamic report — a task that I described earlier in this chapter. You can also create new dynamic reports from scratch and use them to reference a basic SQL query or an OLAP cube — just like static reports. Follow these three steps to create a new dynamic report:

1. Microsoft provides scripts to create dynamic reports' basic definitions in the Commerce Server SDK. You need to modify one of these scripts with the appropriate SQL query or cube reference and then run it on your SQL Server. This creates the base report definition.

2. Open the newly created report in the Business Desk and modify the report using the pivot controls — adding columns, changing sort orders, and so forth.

3. Save the modified report under a new name.

The complex part of this task is modifying the provided SQL scripts with the desired queries. Listing 17-1 shows one of the scripts provided by Microsoft in the Commerce Server SDK.

Listing 17-1: **SQL script for creating dynamic reports**

```
------------------------
-- Report Constants
------------------------

-- ReportType
Declare @Dynamic_SQL tinyint
Select @Dynamic_SQL = 0


------------------------
-- Report Variables
------------------------

Declare @ReportName [nvarchar] (128)
Select @ReportName = 'New dynamic SQL report name'

Declare @ReportCategory [nvarchar] (128)
Select @ReportCategory = 'Report category'

Declare @ReportCreator [nvarchar] (128)
Select @ReportCreator = 'Your name'

Declare @SQLQuery [nvarchar] (2000)
Select @SQLQuery = 'select * from sysobjects'
```

```
------------------------
-- Report Definition
------------------------

Insert Into [dbo].[Report] ([DisplayName], [ReportType],
 [Category], [CreatedBy], [XMLData])
Values (@ReportName, @Dynamic_SQL, @ReportCategory,
 @ReportCreator,
'<xml xmlns:x=''urn:schemas-microsoft-com:office:excel''>
 <x:PivotTable>
  <x:OWCVersion>9.0.0.3821</x:OWCVersion>
  <x:DisplayFieldList/>
  <x:FieldListTop>357</x:FieldListTop>
  <x:FieldListLeft>837</x:FieldListLeft>
  <x:FieldListBottom>726</x:FieldListBottom>
  <x:FieldListRight>1024</x:FieldListRight>
  <x:CacheDetails/>
  <x:ConnectionString>Provider=SQLOLEDB;Integrated
   Security=SSPI;Initial Catalog=;
   Data Source=</x:ConnectionString>
  <x:CommandText>' + @SQLQuery + '</x:CommandText>
 </x:PivotTable>
</xml>' )
```

By providing the appropriate data in the "Report Variables" section of the script, you can create a new SQL-based dynamic report (a separate script is provided to create OLAP-based dynamic reports). The key variable to change is @SQLQuery, which specifies the SQL query that will be used as the basis of the report (the OLAP script contains a similar variable for the OLAP cube that will provide the report data). You can specify any SQL query that you want—just be sure to reference only the columns that you want to include in the report. (Specifying a "SELECT *" statement to pull all of the columns out of a table is not recommended, because it forces SQL Server to do extra work and determine what columns should be returned.)

How you build these queries depends entirely on the data on which you plan to report. Having a strong understanding of Commerce Server's data warehouse will help you build queries that return the data you need.

Making reports available

After you begin adding reports to Commerce Server's built-in reports, you may find the Business Desk's simple list of reports, shown in Figure 17-6, to be unwieldy.

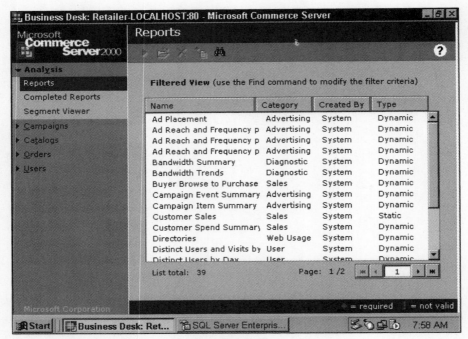

Figure 17-6: The Business Desk's list of available reports

For example, you may want to display reports in categories, or you may want to control which users have access to particular reports. Commerce Server facilitates this by providing all of the basic report information in the Report table of the data warehouse. This table contains the descriptions, categories, and names of all the reports that Commerce Server can make available, as shown in Figure 17-7.

You can easily write your own ASP pages to query specific categories of reports to make a more manageable display. You can also create a table assigning report permissions to specific users, allowing you to restrict the reports that each user has access to.

Commerce Server's data warehouse

Data warehousing is a complex topic. Unless you are comfortable with data warehousing topics like cubes, star schemas, and dimensions, you should simply accept the default data warehouse schema that Commerce Server provides, and work with the OLAP-based reports included with the product.

If you're reasonably comfortable with data warehousing, then this section provides some insight on the default data warehouse schema used by Commerce Server. I also discuss the basic steps involved in extending the schema, although an in-depth discussion of this task is beyond the scope of this book.

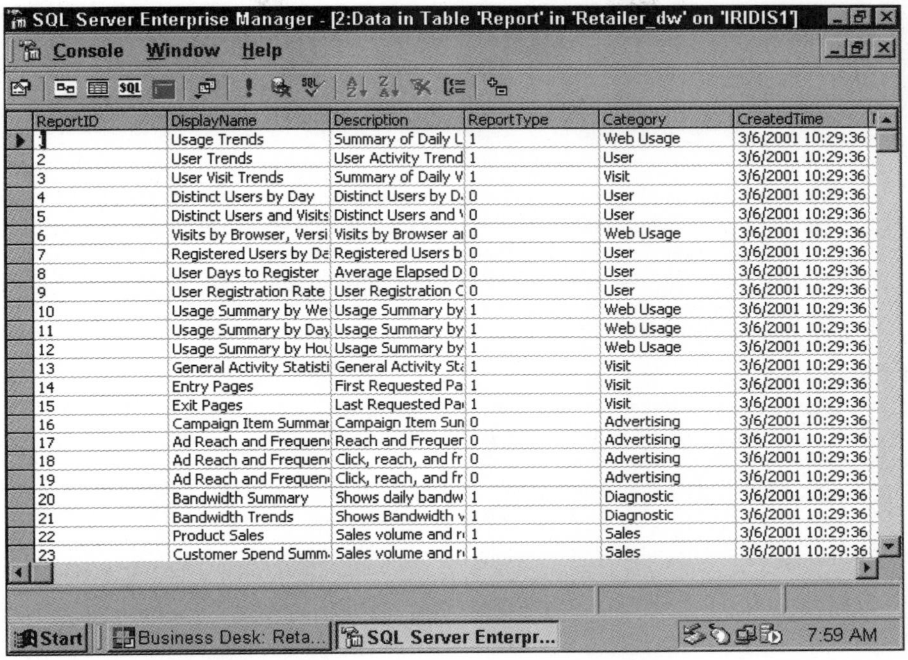

ReportID	DisplayName	Description	ReportType	Category	CreatedTime
1	Usage Trends	Summary of Daily L	1	Web Usage	3/6/2001 10:29:36
2	User Trends	User Activity Trend	1	User	3/6/2001 10:29:36
3	User Visit Trends	Summary of Daily V	1	Visit	3/6/2001 10:29:36
4	Distinct Users by Day	Distinct Users by D	0	User	3/6/2001 10:29:36
5	Distinct Users and Visits	Distinct Users and V	0	User	3/6/2001 10:29:36
6	Visits by Browser, Versi	Visits by Browser ai	0	Web Usage	3/6/2001 10:29:36
7	Registered Users by Da	Registered Users b	0	User	3/6/2001 10:29:36
8	User Days to Register	Average Elapsed D	0	User	3/6/2001 10:29:36
9	User Registration Rate	User Registration C	0	User	3/6/2001 10:29:36
10	Usage Summary by We	Usage Summary by	1	Web Usage	3/6/2001 10:29:36
11	Usage Summary by Day	Usage Summary by	1	Web Usage	3/6/2001 10:29:36
12	Usage Summary by Hou	Usage Summary by	1	Web Usage	3/6/2001 10:29:36
13	General Activity Statisti	General Activity Sta	1	Visit	3/6/2001 10:29:36
14	Entry Pages	First Requested Pa	1	Visit	3/6/2001 10:29:36
15	Exit Pages	Last Requested Pa	1	Visit	3/6/2001 10:29:36
16	Campaign Item Summar	Campaign Item Sun	0	Advertising	3/6/2001 10:29:36
17	Ad Reach and Frequen	Reach and Frequer	0	Advertising	3/6/2001 10:29:36
18	Ad Reach and Frequen	Click, reach, and fr	0	Advertising	3/6/2001 10:29:36
19	Ad Reach and Frequen	Click, reach, and fr	0	Advertising	3/6/2001 10:29:36
20	Bandwidth Summary	Shows daily bandw	1	Diagnostic	3/6/2001 10:29:36
21	Bandwidth Trends	Shows Bandwidth v	1	Diagnostic	3/6/2001 10:29:36
22	Product Sales	Sales volume and r	1	Sales	3/6/2001 10:29:36
23	Customer Spend Summ	Sales volume and r	1	Sales	3/6/2001 10:29:36

Figure 17-7: The Report table

Basic Schema

Commerce Server's logical data warehouse schema includes four basic structures:

- A *class* is the fundamental unit of the schema, and represents a logical collection of data members, such as the transaction data imported into the data warehouse. For example, the OrderFormLineItems class represents the line items imported into the data warehouse and roughly corresponds to the table of the same name in the production database.
- A *data member* is a single piece of data. Classes contain varying numbers of data members that define the class, and new data members may be added to classes to extend their definition. Data members roughly correspond to the columns of a normal database table.
- A *key* is a special data member or set of data members that uniquely identifies the instances of class. This is similar in function to the primary key in a normal database table. For example, in the OrderFormLineItems class, the key is comprised of the OrderForm_id and OrderGroup_id data members, along with the lineitem_id data member. These three members together uniquely identify each line item in the class, and are therefore considered to be the class's key.

✦ A *relation* connects two classes, much like a relationship in a normal database connects two tables. Most relations are one-to-many. For example, the OrderFormHeader class includes one instance for each order form in the system. That instance may have several "child" OrderFormLineItems class instances, which represent the line items of the order. This represents a one-to-many relation between the two classes.

Relations also define data inheritance. The child instances in a relation may inherit any number of data members from the parent in the relation. For example, the OrderFormLineItems class includes data members named OrderForm_id and OrderGroup_id. These data members are inherited from the parent OrderFormHeader class.

Primary classes

Commerce Server's data warehouse includes six major categories of classes that represent business data. Each category includes several classes. Generally, these classes *roughly* correspond to tables in the production database. Note that some of the classes are derived from data *not* obtained from the production database, such as the classes derived from imported Web server log files.

✦ **The Campaigns category.** This category includes classes involved in ad campaigns and marketing operations. The classes include:

- EventType
- CommerceEvent
- Customer
- CreativeSize
- Creative
- Campaign
- CampaignItems
- OrderDiscount
- PageGroup
- CampaignEvent
- PageGroupXref
- CreativeType
- CampaignItemTypes
- CreativeTypeXref
- DmItem
- AdItem

- TargetGroup
- TargetGroupXref
- Target

Note that these classes also have relations with the Web Log Import classes.

✦ **The Catalog category.** This category includes classes that derive from the Product Catalog System. The classes include:

- CatalogGlobal
- Category
- CatHierarchy
- Products

✦ **The Transactions category.** This category includes classes involved in shopping cart and purchase order data, which are used in handling online transactions. The classes include:

- OrderGroup
- OrderGroupAddresses
- OrderFormHeader
- Basket
- Order
- OrderFormLineItems

These entities closely correspond with the tables of the same name in the production database. Note that these classes also have relations with the Profile Management and Web Log Import classes.

✦ **The Profile Management category.** This category includes classes used for managing user profiles and profile-related information. The classes include Address and RegisteredUser. Note that the name "RegisteredUser" is somewhat misleading; this class also includes instances that represent anonymous users on the site.

✦ **The Web Log Import category.** This category includes the classes derived from imported Web server log files. The classes include:

- Task History
- Hostname Ref
- IpRef
- LogUser
- LevelNDir
- URI

- Visit
- UserAgent
- ReferrerDomain
- Visit Info
- OpenUser Visit
- Import Options
- Referrer
- HttpStatus
- Win32Status
- HitsInfo
- UriQuery
- Request

✦ **The Web Topology category.** This category includes the classes that define Web site structure and access. The classes include:

- Site
- Site Summary
- Crawler
- Server Binding
- Server Groups
- Virtual Server
- SiteURL
- SVQStringName
- MVQStringName

Modifying the data warehouse

If you make modifications to the production database — for example, to include cost information or inventory data in the product catalog tables — you may also need to modify the data warehouse schema to support these new attributes. Changing the data warehouse schema can be complex, but the basic steps involved are as follows:

1. Connect to the data warehouse database and instruct your OLE DB provider to enter schema change mode.

2. Create the new classes or modify the existing classes.

3. Add appropriate data members to new classes.

4. Create a key for new classes, and if necessary, data members for the key.

5. Create relations involving the new classes and data members for the relation, if necessary.

6. Commit the schema changes using the CommitSchema command of the OLE DB provider.

7. Turn off schema change mode.

These steps require that you use the OLE DB Provider for Commerce Server, which provides properties, methods, and collections for working with classes, data members, keys, and relations. Although the details on working with this provider are beyond the scope of this book, you can find detailed documentation and examples in the Commerce Server help files.

Caution You can *carefully* add to the default data warehouse schema, but *don't delete anything from it.* Doing so is not supported and will cause unpredictable results.

Modifying the Commerce Server data warehouse schema is a serious proposition. If you modify existing classes, then the DTS tasks provided with Commerce Server will no longer correctly import data into those tasks, which means you'll have to create custom tasks to import data into the data warehouse. If you create entirely new classes, then you must also create custom DTS tasks to populate those classes with data.

Tip If you accidentally alter the data warehouse schema, you can restore it. Delete the database, recreate it with the same name, use SQL Server's Query Analyzer to load the csdwschema.sql script found in the root Commerce Server folder, then execute it to recreate the default schema.

Creating a custom DTS task requires careful planning. You must determine from where you will import the data. Then consider how much of the data is required for the data analysis that you intend to perform. You should *only* import the data that is absolutely necessary for the analysis you intend to perform, because populating a data warehouse is a time-intensive operation that gets longer with every additional data element that is imported.

After you have planned for the data that needs to be imported, create your custom DTS tasks by using the OLE DB Provider for Commerce Server and the OLE DB Provider for SQL Server. The latter is used to access the production data, and the former is used to place that data in the data warehouse. Coding any data transformations necessary for maintaining relationships or rearranging the data for use in the data warehouse is your responsibility.

Reporting *without* the data warehouse

You may need to create basic reports from the tables in the production database. I recommend against running reports against your production database server, but you can certainly make a replica of the production database and write your own reports against it. Reports of this nature are usually intended to support back office functions like accounting, and I discuss them in detail in Chapter 19.

Commerce Server reporting versus third-party reporting

Commerce Server is designed to do all of its reporting from its data warehouse. You may also want to create reports and perform your own business analysis on the data in the data warehouse by using tools that provide more flexibility and power than Commerce Server's own reports.

Because Commerce Server's data warehouse is designed much like any other data warehouse and uses standard SQL Server Analysis Services to provide access to the data, you can use any OLAP tool compatible with SQL Server Analysis Services. This includes tools like Excel's PivotTable service, which you can use directly against the data warehouse, or the more powerful OLAP and analysis tools, such as those made by Cognos (www.cognos.com) or Crystal Decisions (formerly Seagate Software; www.crystaldecisions.com).

Fulfillment

Hopefully, your site will be able to successfully take and process orders after you've put it online. Commerce Server and your Web site, however, can only *take* the order — they can't *fulfill* the order. By itself, Commerce Server isn't even equipped to share your order with other computer systems. Fortunately, Commerce Server integrates well with BizTalk Server, which is great at communicating with partners.

This communication runs both ways: You may also *accept* orders from business partners. You'll still be responsible for fulfilling those orders. For reporting purposes, you want to make sure that the orders enter your Commerce Server system just like orders taken directly on your own site.

Sending order data to partners

If you will be implementing a virtual warehouse and submitting order information to distributors for final fulfillment, you will need to create a robust method for sending that order information. One benefit to using a hub like Commerce One (www.commerceone.com) is that the hub takes on much of the responsibility for data translation and distribution. For example, if your product catalog includes products from four different vendors, the hub may allow you to submit entire orders, dividing them among the final distributors as necessary.

Commerce Server's integration with BizTalk Server also allows you to manage this function on your own, which can save thousands of dollars a year in hub fees. You just need to understand how Commerce Server and BizTalk perform this integration.

A World of Partnerships

Exchanging order information with other companies has become almost unavoidable in the "New Economy," particularly in the fulfillment process. Many e-commerce companies save money by not warehousing the products that they sell. Instead, they use a technique called *virtual warehousing* for some or all of their products. In a virtual warehouse, the e-commerce company acts strictly as an order-taker; orders are transmitted to and ultimately fulfilled by the products' distributors.

Virtual warehousing can be made less complex by using a data-exchange partner, or *hub*, which I discussed in the previous chapter. These hubs allow e-commerce companies and distributors to use a common data format. Products like BizTalk Server also make virtual warehousing easier by performing data translations and supporting a wide variety of destinations, including EDI, fax, and so forth.

E-partnerships come with an added bonus — better customer exposure. Many e-commerce companies gain better customer exposure by participating in sites like Catalog City (www. catalogcity.com). These sites accept periodic catalog "feeds" from multiple e-commerce sites, creating an online "superstore." The superstore site allows customers to shop from a variety of merchants in a single interface, and allows them to place orders from those catalogs in a single shopping cart (in fact, this is the ultimate purpose behind Commerce Server's multiple-catalog capabilities).

These sites accept payment from the customer, and then transmit the order information to you. They generally keep a percentage of the customer's payment, and then pay the rest directly to you on a periodic basis (either weekly or monthly). Giving your site the capability to accept orders from outside sites in this fashion opens up a wide range of promotional and profit-making opportunities.

You can also create the basic data-sharing functionality yourself if you find BizTalk to be too pricey for your company; I discuss how to do this in the next section.

Caution   BizTalk may *seem* expensive, but mimicking even a portion of its functionality will be extremely time consuming. Review the anticipated costs carefully and you may find that BizTalk looks more affordable.

Using BizTalk

Commerce Server includes a built-in understanding of the concepts necessary to implement virtual warehousing. Make sure that each of your product catalogs only contains products for a single final distributor. This partitioning of your products by vendor is the key to helping Commerce Server and BizTalk communicate correctly with the distributors.

How it works

By configuring Commerce Server and BizTalk to send order information to your suppliers, you're actually configuring Commerce Server to feed order information to BizTalk, and configuring BizTalk to send *purchase order* information to your suppliers. After all, you've already received payment for the goods; effectively, you're buying them from the supplier on behalf of your customer, so a purchase order (PO) is the way to go.

Configuring Commerce Server

You must first configure Commerce Server with the correct BizTalk information, and enable BizTalk integration. Use the Commerce Server Manager to modify the App Config properties of your commerce site. You must provide the following key pieces of information:

✦ The name of the BizTalk document definition that represents Commerce Server's catalog schema.

✦ The name of the BizTalk document definition that represents Commerce Server's Purchase Order (PO) schema.

✦ The qualifier that Commerce Server will use to identify your organization to BizTalk.

✦ The connection string for the BizTalk Interchange database.

Finally, you must set the BizTalk option to "1," which enables integration between the two products.

Configuring BizTalk Server

BizTalk also requires several pieces of information in order for data interchange to be possible, including a document definition for Commerce Server's catalog and PO schemas. Create a new document definition and link it to the CatalogXMLSchema.xml and POSchema.xml files provided with Commerce Server. The document definition names should match the names that you configured in Commerce Server. Document definitions are configured in the BizTalk Messaging Manager, as shown in Figure 17-8.

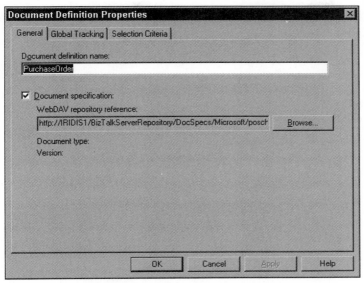

Figure 17-8: Creating a new document definition

You also have to create document definitions that represent your suppliers' catalog and PO schemas. They may provide you with XDR or well-formed XML files that describe their schemas; you can import these into BizTalk's WebDAV store by using the BizTalk Editor, as shown in Figure 17-9. (The WebDAV store is the repository for the schemas that can be linked to a document definition.)

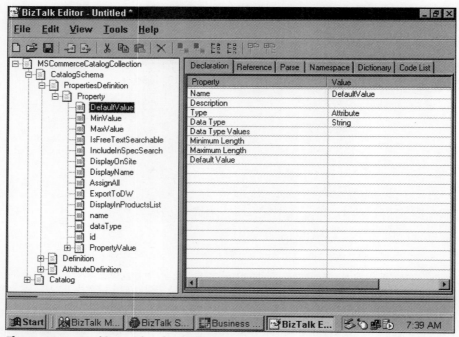

Figure 17-9: Working with schema files

Configure a BizTalk *connection agreement* for your suppliers to send catalog information to you. The first step is to define an *organization* in BizTalk that represents the supplier. Figure 17-10 shows a new organization being created in the BizTalk Messaging Manager.

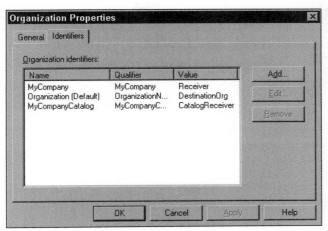

Figure 17-10: Creating a new organization

After the new organization is set up, you can create *messaging ports* and *channels* to represent the connection agreement. A *channel* represents the source of the data, and is linked to the organization and document definition that will provide the data to BizTalk Server. Each channel is linked to a *messaging port*, which represents the data's destination. The messaging port is also linked to a destination organization and a document definition, which describes the format that the data must be in for the destination.

A messaging port also defines the transport method used to send the data, as shown in Figure 17-11. BizTalk supports several methods, including HTTP (where the data is submitted to an ASP file on the destination organization's Web server), HTTPS, EDI, flat files, and SMTP.

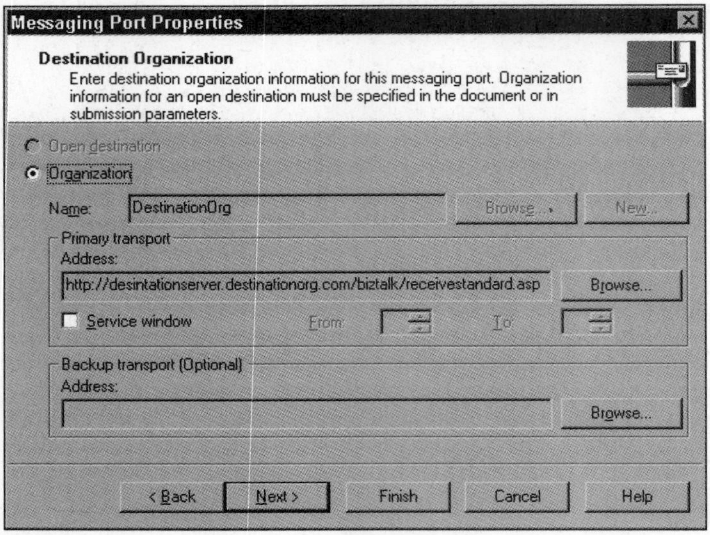

Figure 17-11: Defining a message port

Note that BizTalk Server also allows you to define a *service window* for a messaging port, which represents the hours that the port may be used. This allows you to control your BizTalk traffic to business hours or to low-traffic periods.

After configuring the connection agreement for the catalog data, you need to configure another connection agreement for purchase orders to be sent out.

Catalog Exchange

You may plan to import your catalogs from a flat file, or by using your own process, as discussed in Chapter 11. However, if you plan to use BizTalk to send PO information to your suppliers, you *must* configure a connection agreement in BizTalk for catalog data as well.

In order to send PO information to a vendor, Commerce Server requires that your catalogs be linked to the vendor supplying those products. This link is only possible after the vendor has a connection agreement set up in BizTalk Server. If you want to send PO information to a vendor, Commerce Server assumes that you will also receive catalogs from the vendor.

You don't *have* to receive any catalog data from the vendor through your connection agreement, but you should. If your Commerce Server catalog doesn't precisely match the supplier's catalog, problems will occur when Commerce Server sends PO information. You may end up sending purchase orders for products that don't exist, out-of-date products, and so forth.

If you choose not to use BizTalk to receive catalog information from your suppliers, be sure to have some other mechanism to keep your catalog synchronized with theirs.

Also, configuring the connection agreement for the catalog data will allow Commerce Server to recognize your vendor's organization as capable of exchanging catalog data. This allows you to use the Commerce Server Business Desk's Catalog module, as shown in Figure 17-12, to link your catalogs to the vendors that supply those products.

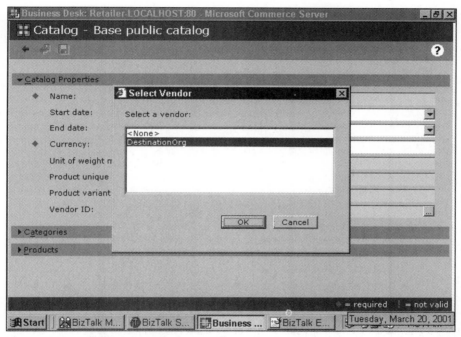

Figure 17-12: Linking a vendor to a catalog

Processing orders

Your site may offer products supplied by dozens of different vendors. Because a catalog can be linked to only one vendor, each catalog is defined as the products from a single vendor. You can use catalog sets to control access to entire groups of catalogs.

Commerce Server is designed to hide your catalog complexity from your customers as much as possible. Customers can shop from any catalog that they have access to (access can be granted to a group of catalogs via a catalog set). All of the products that they order can be placed into a single basket, where Commerce Server will work with them as if they came from a single catalog.

In your final order processing pipeline, however, you must use the Splitter pipeline component to rearrange the order into multiple order forms — one order form per catalog. The default pipeline template, plan.pct, includes the Splitter component and is configured to rearrange the order in this fashion. All of the resulting order forms are processed internally as separate orders, but they remain grouped in an *order group*, thus allowing Commerce Server to apply a single payment to the entire group.

Breaking the order group into multiple forms based on the catalogs that the products came from allows Commerce Server to treat products coming from different vendors as *units*. This serves two purposes:

✦ Commerce Server is able to send a purchase order for an entire order form to each vendor, as necessary. This would be impossible if products from different catalogs were mixed together on an order form. However, because the Splitter component ensures that each order form contains products from a single vendor, sending purchase orders through BizTalk is easy.

✦ Because different vendors will ship the products, shipping should be calculated per order form rather than on the entire order group. This allows you to more accurately charge your customers for shipping based on where the products are actually coming from.

For example, suppose you charge for shipping based on the cost of an order (a common method of calculating shipping costs). You charge $4.95 for orders up to $10.00, and $5.95 for orders up to $20.00. Your suppliers charge you roughly similar fees when they ship products to your customers. If a customer orders two items costing $8.95 each, you calculate $5.95 in shipping. However, if those two items each come from a different supplier, you are charged a total of $9.90 ($4.95 times two) from your suppliers, meaning you lose $3.95. By splitting the order by vendor and calculating shipping on each order form, your customer is charged $9.90, helping you to recoup the shipping fees charged by your suppliers.

The order-processing pipeline is also a good place to submit the purchase order information to BizTalk for processing, although you can also create this functionality in your ASP pages. Microsoft's Solution Sites implement this functionality and provide a useful example of how you can programmatically submit purchase order information to BizTalk. Listing 17-2 shows a function adapted from the Retail Solution Site that processes an order form if BizTalk integration is enabled in the site. Note that this function can also be implemented in a pipeline Scriptor component or in ASP code.

Listing 17-2: **Process orders for BizTalk**

```
Sub InvokeBizTalk(ByVal mscsOrdGrp)
 Dim sOrdName, mscsOrdFrm, oVndr, sXML
 Dim sVndrQualID, sVndrQualVal
```

```
' assume dictConfig is a dictionary set
' with the site configuration options
' and only do this if BizTalk integration
' is enabled.
If dictConfig.i_BizTalkOptions = BIZTALK_PO_XFER_ENABLED Then

  ' For each order form in the order group:
  For Each sOrdName In mscsOrdGrp.Value.OrderForms
  Set mscsOrdFrm = _
  mscsOrdGrp.Value(ORDERFORMS).Value(sOrdName)

   ' Process each vendor in the order form:
   For Each oVndr In mscsOrdFrm.value("_vendors")

    ' Skip the default vendor, which
    ' is the home organization...
    If StrComp(oVndr.vendorID, DEFAULT_ORDERFORM, _
    vbTextCompare) <> 0 Then

     ' retrieve an XML string containing only
     ' items associated with the current vendor
     sXML = GetXMLForVendorItems(mscsOrdFrm, oVndr)

     ' Get the vendor delivery information from
     ' the orderform item:
     sVendorQualID = _
      mscsOrdFrm.items( _
      oVndr.itemindexes(0)).vendor_qual)
     sVndrQualVal = _
      mscsOrdFrm.items( _
      oVndr.itemindexes(0)).vendor_qual_value

     ' submit the single vendor PO to BizTalk Server...
     Call SubmitUsingBizTalk(sXML, oVndr.vendorID, _
      sVndrQualID, sVndrQualVal)
    End If
   Next
  Next
 End If
End Sub
```

This subroutine moves through each order form in the order group, and through each vendor in each order form. It ignores any order forms related to catalogs that are linked to the default vendor (your company) because it assumes you will fulfill those items yourself.

For the other order forms, the subroutine calls a function that returns an XML string for the items in the current order form belonging to the current vendor. The subroutine then uses a second function to submit a purchase order to BizTalk for those items.

The first function, GetXMLForVendorItems, is shown in Listing 17-3. The second, SubmitUsingBizTalk, is shown in Listing 17-4.

Listing 17-3: **GetXMLForVendorItems function**

```
Function GetXMLForVendorItems(ByVal mscsOrdFrm, ByVal oVndr)
 Dim oXMLTforms, oXMLSchema, oOrdFrmXML, oXMLDoc
 Dim oNode, oAttrb
 Dim sFilePath

 ' Create objects:
 Set oXMLTforms = _
  Server.CreateObject("Commerce.DictionaryXMLTransforms")

 sFilePath = Server.MapPath("\" & MSCSAppFrameWork._
  VirtualDirectory) & "\poschema.xml"
 Set oXMLSchema = oXMLTforms.GetXMLFromFile(sFilePath)

 ' Create an XML version of the order form:
 Set oOrdFrmXML = _
  oXMLTforms.GenerateXMLForDictionaryUsingSchema_
  (mscsOrdFrm, oXMLSchema)

 ' Create a copy of the XML version of the order form:
 Set oXMLDoc = Server.CreateObject("MSXML.DOMDOCUMENT")
 oXMLDoc.loadXML oOrdFrmXML.xml

 ' For each item in that copy:
 For Each oNode In oXMLDoc.documentElement.childNodes
  If (oNode.nodeName = "Items") Then

    ' If this vendor ID of this item is not the
    ' same as the passed vendor ID, remove it
    For Each oAttrb In oNode.Attributes
     If (oAttrb.nodeName = "vendorid") Then
      If Not(oAttrb.nodeValue = oVendor.vendorID) Then
       oNode.parentNode.removeChild oNode
      End If
      Exit For
     Else
     End If
    Next

  End If
 Next

 ' Return an XML string containing the remaining items,
 ' all of which correspond to the passed vendor:
 GetXMLForVendorItems = oXMLDoc.xml
End Function
```

This function creates an XML-formatted version of the order form passed to it. It then walks through that order form, removing any items that aren't from a catalog linked to the vendor specified in the function's parameter. The resulting XML-formatted order form — now containing only items corresponding to the specified vendor — is returned.

Listing 17-4: **SubmitUsingBizTalk function**

```
Function SubmitUsingBizTalk(ByVal sXML, ByVal sVendorName, _
  ByVal sDestQualID, ByVal sDestQualValue)

Dim sSubmitType, sDocName
Dim sSourceQualID, sSourceQualValue
Dim oDBConfig, oOrg, sID, sName, sDef, oRes
Dim oInterchange

  ' Retrieve the source BizTalk config values
  ' from the configuration dictionary (assumed
  ' this is set in Global.asa)
  sSubmitType = dictConfig.s_BizTalkSubmittypeQueue
  sDocName = dictConfig.s_BizTalkOrderDocType
  sSourceQualID = dictConfig.s_BizTalkSourceQualifierID
  sSourceQualValue = dictConfig.s_BizTalkSourceQualifierValue

  ' Create a BizTalk Interchange object and
  ' call its Submit routine:
  Set oInterchange = Server.CreateObject("BizTalk.Interchange")
  oRes = oInterchange.Submit(sSubmitType, _
    sXML, sDocName, sSourceQualID, sSourceQualValue, _
    sDestQualID, sDestQualValue)

End Function
```

This function accepts the XML order form created by the previous function, along with the vendor name and qualifier information retrieved from the original order form. The function also retrieves the BizTalk integration parameters for the site (which are configured in the Commerce Server Manager). All of this information is passed to the BizTalk Interchange object's Submit method, which submits the order form to BizTalk. BizTalk then processes the order form according to the channel and messaging port rules already defined for the vendor's organization, and the purchase order is on its way to your business partner.

What BizTalk Gives You That You Can't Do Yourself

At $25,000 per processor, BizTalk is pretty expensive for a glorified data translator. After all, it doesn't seem to do a whole lot that you can't do with Data Transformation Services, and DTS is free with SQL Server. So what's the BizTalk advantage?

From a functionality standpoint, BizTalk's data messaging services may seem to be just an automated version of DTS, but it has a *lot* more under the hood. That's why embarking on your own data interchange components can be so time-consuming — if you're going to provide the features that BizTalk provides, you're going to need considerable programming resources.

To begin with, BizTalk provides almost unlimited capabilities for schema reuse. You only have to provide BizTalk with a single schema describing *your* data; suppliers provide you with schemas describing theirs. By providing a schema for your data, you allow BizTalk to import and export your data from any other source. With DTS and do-it-yourself data interchange schemes, however, you have to start almost from scratch every time you want to import or export from a different data format.

Unlike DTS or most do-it-yourself schemes, BizTalk provides complete transactional capabilities to your data interchange, and ensures "exactly once" delivery of data. This means that either your entire data package or none of it will be delivered, and once delivered, BizTalk will *never* attempt to deliver the same data twice. This requires a great deal of complex code and data tracking to pull off, and it's built right in to BizTalk.

Finally, BizTalk provides complete tracking capabilities. You'll be able to tell exactly where your data is "in the pipeline" at every moment. This is a great troubleshooting tool, and also provides good management data so you can make sure that your processes are functioning smoothly at all times. Building these extensive tracking capabilities into your own DTS packages of Visual Basic apps can prove extremely time-consuming.

So before you decide to skip BizTalk and create your own data interchange infrastructure, take a look at the value-added features that BizTalk offers to your business, and the expensive programming resources that BizTalk lets you do without. You may find that the investment in BizTalk is worthwhile. And remember, if you won't need more than one BizTalk Server and five connection agreements, the Standard Edition is much less expensive (about $5,000). And, remember, you can always start small with the Standard Edition and upgrade later if you need the additional power and features.

Doing it yourself

You may need to provide the functionality for a portion — if not all — of your order-sending features, depending on your specific needs. For example, BizTalk requires a considerable up-front investment ($25,000 per processor for the Enterprise Edition at the time this book goes to press). It also requires that you have a schema compatible with both the incoming and outgoing data, which can be tricky with less technologically advanced suppliers. BizTalk also has some limitations in its current version. For example, BizTalk can't deliver data via FTP, which is the most common form of transport used by e-commerce companies.

Supplementing BizTalk

Allowing BizTalk to use FTP is not complicated. Simply tell BizTalk to use a flat file transport and to save the output file on a computer on your network. Create an FTP script to transfer the file to your supplier, and schedule the FTP script to run on a regular basis using Windows' Task Scheduler.

The downside of this approach is that BizTalk will consider the document as "delivered" after the flat file has been successfully created. The part of the process that can actually run into problems — the FTP transfer — won't fall under BizTalk's document tracking system. If you need an FTP process that is intelligent enough to recover from errors, then you need to write a utility in Visual Basic that uses a third-party FTP control. This allows you to perform the file transfer under program control, and lets you perform logging and error recovery.

You can also use Microsoft's Internet Transfer Controls 6.0, which is included with Visual Studio 6.0 (and updated by the Visual Studio 6.0 Service Pack 4). Just include the control in a Visual Basic project, and write code as shown in Listing 17-5.

Listing 17-5: **Using the Internet Transfer Control**

```
Sub Main()
 Dim sHost As String
 Dim sSrcFile As String
 Dim sDstFile As String

 'set up inet control
 Inet.Protocol = icFTP
 Inet.UserName = "username"
 Inet.Password = "password"
 sHost = "ftp://ftp.partner.com"

 'set up source and destination
 'file names
 sSrcFile = "orders.txt"
 sDstFile = "retailer-orders.txt"

 'put the file
 Inet.Execute sHost, "PUT " & sSrcFile & sDstFile

End Sub

Private Sub Inet_StateChanged(ByVal State As Integer)

 'monitor state of Inet control
 Select Case State
  Case Is = 0
    'no state
```

Continued

Listing 17-5 *(continued)*

```
    Case Is = 1
      'resolving ip address
    Case Is = 2
      'found ip address
    Case Is = 3
      'connecting
    Case Is = 4
      'connected
    Case Is = 5
      'sending request
    Case Is = 6
      'request sent
    Case Is = 7
      'receiving response
    Case Is = 8
      'received response
    Case Is = 9
      'disconnecting
    Case Is = 10
      'disconnected
    Case Is = 11
      'error occured
    Case Is = 12
      'request complete
      '(file sent OK)
  End Select

  End Sub
```

The Internet Transfer Control provides plenty of feedback for your program to determine if the file has been successfully sent. If it hasn't, your program can log an event, send an alert e-mail, or take some other action to let you know that manual intervention is required.

Tip   You can also use the Internet Transfer Control to retrieve files via FTP, if necessary.

Creating your own data interchange

If BizTalk is totally out of the question for your company, but you still need to exchange data with business partners (few e-commerce companies *don't* need to), then you need to write your own data interchange functionality.

1. Begin this process by treating your order data is if you *were* going to use BizTalk. Keep products from different vendors in separate catalogs, and use the Splitter component in your pipelines to generate separate order forms for

each vendor. This allows Commerce Server's shipping components to still calculate shipping on the different order forms, and makes the data easier to retrieve from the database.

2. Make a minor modification to the database schema. Add a column to the OrderFormHeader table to keep track of orders that have already been sent. The column type should be "bit;" the following code shows a Transact-SQL script that adds a column named "Processed" with a default value of zero.

```
BEGIN TRANSACTION
SET QUOTED_IDENTIFIER ON
SET TRANSACTION ISOLATION LEVEL SERIALIZABLE
SET ARITHABORT ON
SET NUMERIC_ROUNDABORT OFF
SET CONCAT_NULL_YIELDS_NULL ON
SET ANSI_NULLS ON
SET ANSI_PADDING ON
SET ANSI_WARNINGS ON
COMMIT
BEGIN TRANSACTION
ALTER TABLE dbo.OrderFormHeader ADD
Processed bit NOT NULL CONSTRAINT
DF_OrderFormHeader_Processed DEFAULT 0
GO
COMMIT
```

3. Write a Visual Basic executable or a Data Transformation Package to pull the new orders out of this table (and from OrderFormLineItems), and reformat the data into whatever your vendors require. The same process should set the Processed value to 1 for any rows that it completes, so they won't be sent twice.

4. Write a stored procedure that returns any unprocessed (new) orders, along with their line item information. The following code shows the Transact-SQL code for a stored procedure named "sp_GetNewOrders."

```
CREATE PROCEDURE sp_GetNewOrders
AS
SELECT ofh.*, ofli.*
 FROM OrderFormHeader ofh
 INNER JOIN OrderFormLineItems ofli
 ON Ofh.orderform_id = ofli.orderform_id
 WHERE ofh.Processed = 0
 ORDER BY ofli.product_catalog_base,
   Ofli.Orderform_id
GO
```

5. The stored procedure returns a complete list of line items and order header information. The result set is ordered by the base catalog that the products were ordered from. This allows you to build a "batch PO" for all the products to be ordered from a single vendor.

6. I recommend that you mark each order as "processed" after your Visual Basic executable or DTS package has actually written the necessary information to an output file. The following code shows a stored procedure called "sp_MarkOrderAsProcessed," which accepts an order form ID number and marks that order as "completed."

```
CREATE PROCEDURE sp_MarkOrderAsProcessed
 @orderform_id int
AS
 UPDATE OrderFormHeader SET Processed = 1
   WHERE orderform_id = @orderform_id
GO
```

7. To complete your order-sending process, write a Visual Basic utility or DTS package that utilizes these stored procedures and writes the necessary data to files for your suppliers. Transfer those files to the suppliers, usually by using FTP. You can use the sample Visual Basic utility from the prior section to do this, or use the FTP DTS task to upload the file.

After you've created the Visual Basic utility or DTS package, you can use the Windows Task Scheduler or SQL Server Agent, respectively, to schedule your order export to run on a regular basis. If your order information will be passing through a hub like Commerce One, you should carefully review your contract with the hub. Most hubs charge you per-transfer, so you want to strike a balance between a minimum number of transfers, to minimize cost, and frequent enough transfers to make sure that your customers' orders are promptly fulfilled.

Receiving orders from partners

Many e-commerce companies need the ability to receive order information from business partners. Perhaps you want your customers to be able to place orders for your products on other sites (such as Catalog City or Yahoo! Shops). Perhaps you are in a business-to-business situation, and are serving one or more business-to-consumer companies who send you their virtual warehouse orders for fulfillment. In any event, having the ability to accept orders and place them into your system for processing is a valuable piece of functionality.

As with the rest of Commerce Server's data interchange capabilities, accepting orders from other sites is a feature provided by BizTalk Server. Even if you decide to skip BizTalk and create this functionality yourself, it's useful to understand how BizTalk provides this functionality because you can leverage the same techniques yourself, if necessary.

Using BizTalk

Ideally, you want received order forms to be processed in the same way as orders that are placed directly on your site. This ensures that the orders will follow the same processing and business logic, and that orders received from off-site will be handled in the same fashion as "native" orders placed directly on the site.

The easiest way to import orders from BizTalk is to create a special ASP page capable of receiving order information from BizTalk. BizTalk is capable of receiving order information in several formats, including text files, EDI documents, and so forth; after it translates the data into your required schema, BizTalk can submit it to an ASP page by using the HTTP protocol. This is essentially the reverse of the process that you use to send purchase orders to *your* suppliers.

These incoming orders can, in fact, be treated as purchase orders. After all, you didn't accept payment for them — the other Web site took the payment and is passing the order information on to you, along with the ship-to information for the final customer. The other Web site is responsible for forwarding payment to you, which they generally do by cutting a periodic check or by direct Automated Clearinghouse (ACH) transfer to your company's bank account.

Note   This process describes exactly how sites like Yahoo! Shops and Catalog City work. They accept orders and payment from customers and forward the information to you, typically in a text file sent via e-mail. They transfer payment to you on a regular basis, withholding a portion of the payment as their fee for handling the transaction. You can regard their submitted orders as purchase orders because effectively, they are purchasing products from you on behalf of their customer.

Caveats

You should make some important considerations when accepting purchase orders from other sites, and you will likely have to set up a special pipeline to process these incoming orders. These considerations include:

✦ Product pricing shouldn't usually be pulled from your catalog, which you would do for an order placed directly on your site. Instead, prices should be taken from the incoming purchase order. This is because no matter what price your catalog has for the product, the end customer has already paid. If they paid the wrong price, it's too late by the time you receive the order. Your job includes making sure that your prices are updated with the other site as necessary, usually by exporting your catalog to them.

✦ Like product prices, shipping shouldn't be calculated on the order. Instead, the order's shipping should be pulled verbatim from the submitted order.

These two facts alone may require you to do some number-juggling in your accounting systems, especially if you will be sending the orders on to other suppliers for final fulfillment. For example, suppose that a customer orders a product from your store on Yahoo! Shops. The customer pays $10.00 for the product plus $4.95 for shipping. Unfortunately, the catalog on the Yahoo site is outdated; your current price on the item is $15.00, and your cost is $9.00. Plus, you don't actually carry the item yourself, but send the order to an outside supplier for fulfillment. That supplier has raised its shipping cost on the item to $5.95 because of its higher price. Your order creates an income of $14.95 (less any fee Yahoo charged for handling the order), and your cost to fulfill the order is $14.95 (your $9.00 cost plus $5.95 for shipping). You'll probably lose money on the order. What's the point?

The point is to make sure that your off-site catalogs contain updated pricing, and that your back-end accounting systems show this transaction properly. If you simply use the data in Commerce Server, which by default doesn't include a *cost* for the product, you won't be able to determine if you're losing money, breaking even, or actually making a profit on transactions like this.

Configuring BizTalk

BizTalk Server's configuration is the reverse of the configuration previously discussed in this chapter.

Create a channel from an organization that represents the external order taker, and a messaging port representing your own site. The messaging port should be configured to use the HTTP transport to submit the incoming data to a specific ASP page.

That ASP page accepts the data, turns it into an order group containing an order form, and runs it through a modified pipeline. This modified pipeline doesn't implement product pricing rules or shipping calculations; it simply accepts whatever is in the order form object.

Creating the ASP page

The Microsoft Solution Sites include a sample ASP page designed to receive PO information from BizTalk Server and process them as orders. The sample page is _recvpo.asp, and can be found in the root of either the Retail or the Supplier Solution Sites. The page's main subroutine is reproduced in Listing 17-6.

Listing 17-6: Main subroutine from _recvpo.asp

```
Sub Main()
 Dim objXMLTransforms, szXML, xmlSchema
 Dim mscsOrderGrp, mscsOrderForm
 Dim sFilePath, sTrackingNumber, sOrderID

 szXML = ParseRequestForm()

 Set objXMLTransforms = _
  Server.CreateObject("Commerce.DictionaryXMLTransforms")

 sFilePath = Server.MapPath("\" & _
  MSCSAppFrameWork.VirtualDirectory) & "\poschema.xml"

 Set xmlSchema = objXMLTransforms.GetXMLFromFile(sFilepath)

 Set mscsOrderForm = _
  objXMLTransforms.ReconstructDictionaryFromXML _
  (szXML, xmlSchema)
```

```
Set mscsOrderGrp = GetOrderGroup(m_userid)
Call mscsOrderGrp.AddOrderForm(mscsOrderForm)
Call RunOrderPipeline(mscsOrderGrp)

sOrderID = mscsOrderGrp.SaveAsOrder(sTrackingNumber)
End Sub
```

The actual workings of this page are fairly straightforward.

1. BizTalk submits purchase orders to the page one at a time in the HTTP headers of the request.

2. The ASP page's main subroutine calls a function (ParseRequestForm) that retrieves this data from the HTTP headers and returns it to the main subroutine. Keep in mind that BizTalk Server translated this HTTP header information into the format that you specified for incoming purchase orders. Usually, you tell BizTalk to use POSchema.xml, which is a schema provided with Commerce Server that just happens to represent Commerce Server's native XML representation of an order form.

3. The main subroutine then uses Commerce Server's XML transforms library to reconstruct an order form from the XML. Because the XML is in Commerce Server's native order format (as defined in POSchema.xml), this reconstruction happens quickly and an OrderForm object is created.

4. The main subroutine retrieves the current user's default OrderGroup object. Because the "current user" is null, a new OrderGroup object is created.

5. The reconstructed OrderForm object is appended to the OrderGroup, and the OrderGroup object is then passed to a subroutine that runs the order-processing pipeline. In this case, the subroutine runs the recvpo.pcf pipeline, which is a good example of an "abbreviated" pipeline suitable for accepting purchase orders.

The pipeline

The recvpo.pcf pipeline consists of the following stages and components:

1. **Product Info stage**

   a. **Scriptor:** Fixup product_variant_id: For products with no variant ID, BizTalk passes an empty string in the product_variant_id field. Commerce Server, however, requires a Null value in this field if the product has no variant ID. This Scriptor component loops through the items in the order form and replaces any blank product_variant_id fields with a Null.

b. **QueryCatalogInfo:** This component populates the catalog information fields for each item in the order form. Any item that can't be matched with catalog information is flagged for deletion.

c. **RequiredProductInfo:** This component ensures that every product in the order form has complete product information, and deletes any items flagged by the previous pipeline component.

2. **Order Initialization stage** (This stage has no components in the Solution Site pipeline, but can be used to initialize any components required by later subsequent pipeline stages, or to prepare the order for processing by custom pipeline components.)

3. **Order Check stage**

a. **RequiredOrderCheck:** This component ensures that at least one item is present in the order, and raises an error in the absence of one.

4. **Item Price stage**

a. **DefaultItemPriceCy:** This component retrieves the current regular price (as opposed to the "put price" that the item sells for) for each item from the catalog.

b. **RequiredItemPriceCy:** This component raises an error if each item in the order doesn't have a regular price assigned.

5. **Item Adjust Price stage**

a. **RequiredItemAdjustPriceCy:** This component ensures that each item in the order has an adjusted price. Errors are raised if any items are found without an adjusted price. A primary difference between this pipeline and the regular order processing pipeline is that this stage doesn't attempt to calculate an adjusted price; it accepts whatever price is in the purchase order submitted by BizTalk Server. This component merely checks to be sure that each item *has* an adjusted price.

6. **Order Adjust Price stage**

a. **Scriptor:** Use Submitted Prices: This Scriptor component uses a VBScript to copy the "put price" submitted in the purchase order into the current price of the order. This component distinguishes this pipeline from the regular order-processing pipeline, which calculates the current price based on prices in the catalog.

b. **RequiredOrderAdjustPriceCy:** This component raises an error if the order doesn't contain complete pricing information.

7. **Order Subtotal stage**

a. **DefaultOrderSubTotalCy:** This component calculates the order subtotal by summing the price of each line item in the order.

b. **RequiredOrderSubTotalCy:** This component raises an error if the order doesn't contain a subtotal.

8. Order Total stage

    a. Scriptor: MyTotal: This Scriptor component uses a VBScript to set the shipping, handling, and tax values of the order to zero, and to copy the order's subtotal into the total field. The assumption in this script is that shipping will not be charged; you need to modify this component in most cases. Generally, the script should copy the shipping, tax, and handling information from the purchase order into the order form.

    b. RequiredOrderTotalCy: This component raises an error if the order doesn't contain a total.

9. Accept stage (This stage contains no components in the Solution Site pipeline; it is intended to contain components that process the order for fulfillment.)

The Accept stage of this pipeline is a great place to add your own wrap-up components. These can be compiled components or Scriptor components, and may include components to accomplish the following tasks:

✦ Updating data in a back-end accounting system to reflect item costs versus item sale prices.

✦ Submitting the completed order to BizTalk Server for transmission to suppliers, who will ultimately fulfill the order.

✦ Transmitting the order to a back-end warehousing system for final fulfillment.

✦ Updating a back-end accounts receivable system to track how much money is owed from the business partner that originally accepted the order.

✦ Sending order confirmation e-mails to customers, indicating that their order has been received into your system and is being processed.

You should plan to create components to handle these tasks because they're important business functions that aren't handled directly by Commerce Server.

Doing it yourself

You can use the same basic tactic that BizTalk and Commerce Server use when working together to create your own order-acceptance functionality. The steps are as follows:

1. Create an application capable of reading the order data provided to you by the site that accepted the order. This may include reading in a text file, picking up a file of orders from an FTP site, and so forth.

2. Have the application read in the data for a single order and construct an OrderForm object from it.

3. Have the application append the OrderForm object to a new OrderGroup object and submit it to an abbreviated pipeline, like the recvpc.pcf pipeline discussed above.

Do-it-yourself pros and cons

The big difference in doing this yourself rather than working with BizTalk is that BizTalk provides you with preformatted XML that Commerce Server's objects can instantly turn into an order form. Without BizTalk, you have to read in raw data as provided by your business partner, and programmatically construct an OrderForm object from it. Exactly how you do this depends on the format of the data supplied by the business partner. At a minimum, you will need the following information:

✦ The product ID for each item sold

✦ A variant ID for any variant items sold

✦ The price of each item sold

✦ The cost of any taxes or shipping charges that the customer paid

✦ The customer's shipping information

With this information in hand, you can programmatically create a new OrderGroup object and start adding items to its default OrderForm objects. After adding an item, you need to update its properties to reflect the sold price and the shipping information. You also need to update the OrderForm's global shipping, tax, and handling charges. After you have a populated OrderGroup object, submit it to your abbreviated pipeline for processing.

The downside to this approach is that you will eventually want to do this information exchange with more than one business partner. Using BizTalk means creating a schema that describes each partner's incoming data. BizTalk takes care of translating that to Commerce Server's native POSchema.xml format, and none of your order processing code has to change. Without BizTalk, you will wind up having to write a new order-import utility for every vendor that uses a different file format (and in my experience, they *all* use different file formats).

Example order import process

Much of the code in any order import application is concerned with reading and parsing the order data from the file supplied by your business partner. Because that code will entirely depend on how the file is formatted, I focus on showing you some sample functions and subroutines that accept the parsed order information and build the necessary Commerce Server objects.

Your Sub Main() procedure needs to declare and create the necessary Commerce Server objects for these sample functions to work with. Listing 17-7 shows an abbreviated Sub Main() that declares these objects before opening the file to be imported.

Note   These samples are intended to run in Visual Basic 6.0, and assume that you have included the appropriate Commerce Server object libraries in the project references.

Listing 17-7: **Abbreviated Sub Main()**

```
Sub Main()

    Dim oOrdMgr As Commerce.OrderGroupManager
    Dim oOrdGrp As Commerce.OrderGroup
    Dim vConnect As Variant
    Dim sUser As String

    'get instance of order manager
    'assume vConnect is a valid connection
    'string to the database
    Set oOrdMgr = CreateObject("Commerce.OrderManager")
    oOrdMgr.Initialize vConnect

    'create order group and assume
    'sUser is the GUID of an administrative
    'user who will "place" the orders
    Set oOrdGrp = CreateObject("Commerce.OrderGroup")
    oOrdGrp.Initialize vConnect, sUser
    oOrdGrp.LoadBasket

    'begin importing order items

End Sub
```

As your import routine reads order items from the file, it will need to add the line items to the order group. Listing 17-8 shows an AddOrderItem function that takes care of this. Note the input parameters required by the function; this information is imported from the order information file provided by your business partner.

Listing 17-8: **AddOrderItem function**

```
Function AddOrderItem( _
    sProductID As String, _
    sProdVarID As String, _
    iQty As Integer, _
    sAddrID As String, _
    sShipMethod As String, _
    nPrice As Single, _
    oOrdGrp As Commerce.OrderGroup, _
    ) As Commerce.OrderGroup

    'create a dictionary object
    Dim dItem As New Commerce.Dictionary
```

Continued

Listing 17-8 (continued)

```
'build the dictionary with the item data
dItem.product_catalog = sProductCatalog
dItem.product_id = sProductID
dItem.product_variant_id = sProdVarID
dItem.quantity = iQty
dItem.shipping_address_id = sAddrID
dItem.shipping_method_name = sShipMethod
dItem.cy_unit_price = nPrice

'add the item to the order
Dim lIndex As Long
lIndex = oOrdGrp.AddItem(dItem)
End Function
```

This function accepts the parameters describing the item, including its price. The function also accepts a reference to the OrderGroup that you want the item added to, and returns a reference to the OrderGroup with the item added.

Note that this function requires you to pass it an address ID. This must be the GUID for an address entry in your Commerce Server profile system. How you obtain the address ID depends on how you want to store these addresses. For example, you may want to read the address information from the import file to see if it already exists in your profile system. If the information is already present in your profile system, you can obtain both the address GUID *and* the customer's profile GUID from the profile system, and use those to create the order. The benefit of this is that the order will show up in your system as having been placed by the customer, which can be beneficial for demographic and marketing purposes.

Another method is to read the address information from the file and create a new address entry, attached to a default "anonymous" user. This provides the benefit of easier implementation, but unfortunately, also causes all the orders placed from another site to show up as having been placed by that single anonymous user, which is less helpful for marketing and demographic purposes.

You also need to provide the name of a shipping method for the item to ship by. You and your business partner should agree on a set of codes to represent the various shipping methods that you offer. This allows you to match shipping codes from the import file with the correct shipping method names.

Submitting the order

After you've completely populated the OrderGroup object with all of the necessary item and shipping information, you're ready to submit the order to your abbreviated order processing pipeline. Listing 17-9 shows an example of how to do this.

Listing 17-9: Submitting an order to the pipeline

```
Dim oPipe As Commerce.PooledTXPipeline
Set oPipe = CreateObject("Commerce.PooledTXPipeline")

'modify this to load the correct file:
oPipe.LoadPipe "\inetpup\wwwroot\pipelines\recvpo.pcf"

'run the pipe
'oOrdGroup is the Order Group to process
'oContext is a valid context object
Dim lResult As Long
lResult = oPipe.Execute(1,oOrdGroup,oContext,0)

'examine lResult for error flags
'raised by the pipeline components
```

Summary

Commerce Server offers a fairly robust set of "canned" reports, and gives you the ability to create your own. For complex custom reports, there is no substitute for working directly with the raw data, and Commerce Server also offers this capability. In the end, even your most critical business processes can be supported with the information provided by your Commerce Server site.

Commerce Server can also support your fulfillment processes. Whether you need to exchange order information with business partners or support a virtual warehousing model, Commerce Server integrated with BizTalk Server provides powerful data exchange capabilities. Even if BizTalk Server is out of your price range, Commerce Server's database schema is easy enough to understand that you can create your own basic data exchange functionality.

✦   ✦   ✦

Managing the Site

In This Chapter

Managing and
deploying content

Day-to-day
maintenance

Business continuity

Content management is the process of determining who has the ability to modify your site's pages and create new pages. Depending on your company's policies, you may be able to adopt a fairly cavalier approach to content management — by making all of the files available on a Windows file share, for example. Most companies, however, prefer to exercise some control over how content is modified and created.

In this context, *content* refers to the main body of your site — the text and images that display your products and services. Content does *not* refer to heavily coded pages like a shopping cart, or to ancillary elements like navigation bars. Content is the "meat" of the site that your customers are primarily interested in.

Microsoft has not traditionally offered robust content management tools. The Web development industry as a whole, in fact, has been fairly casual about content management, producing very few tools or technologies to enable robust content management and delegation. In this section, I explore common content management concerns, and discuss the options you have for addressing them.

Content Security

How you approach content security is very much a factor in how the content on your site *works,* so to speak. A typical e-commerce site contains two basic types of content. The first type of content can be thought of as "free-form" pages, which are usually created by HTML programmers or Web designers and follow no particular structure. The second type of content is referred to as "template" content, such as product detail pages. The actual content, product descriptions, images, and so forth are stored in a database and entered through some form of administrative interface like the Business Desk by non-technical users, such as a buyer or merchandiser. This content is then married to an HTML template, usually by running a utility that inserts the content from the database into the template, thus creating a new page.

Securing the content

Securing template content is simple: You control access to the administrative interface that allows data to be entered and modified. The Business Desk allows you to do this by applying NTFS file permissions to the folder that contains the Catalog module, and you can build in your own security controls, if you want. The actual "look and feel" of the final pages is determined by the HTML template, which can be secured using NTFS file permissions. Generally, only a Web designer or HTML programmer has access to the template.

Free-form content can be more difficult to secure, depending on who needs to work with it. If all of your free-form pages will be created and modified by Web designers and HTML programmers, then security is a matter of applying the correct NTFS permissions. Generally, the pages are created from a static document, such as a Word document or a FrontPage mock-up, which is written by a writer or editor in your company. The Web designer or HTML programmer simply turns that content into a Web page. Unfortunately, this approach usually requires one or more Web designers or HTML programmers who are completely dedicated to creating free-form content — an expensive use of technical resources. You can make the Web pages available to the original writers and editors for altering, but they are usually not hired for their HTML or Web design skills. The resulting Web pages are likely to require a Web designer or HTML programmer to "polish" them, which can be just as time-consuming as starting from scratch.

Note   Keep in mind that even the simplest page on your site will probably have several included files for navigation elements, style sheets, and so forth. This complexity makes easy-to-use tools like Microsoft FrontPage virtually useless for creating new pages or editing existing ones, because the tools can't present a true "what you see is what you get" view of the page. This makes page editing more abstract, and better suited to professionals than non-technical users.

Pros and cons

From a security and resource utilization standpoint, template content is ideal. The users that are responsible for creating the content — writers, editors, and so forth — enter the content body into an administrative interface. A Web designer or HTML programmer creates a single template (or set of templates) that defines how this content will be displayed. From there, no technical resources are required to produce new pages or edit existing ones.

From a design standpoint, however, template content is far from ideal. Although perfectly suitable for product detail pages and other pages that you *want* to look alike, templates are far less suitable for your home page, pages dealing with special promotions, and so forth. Templates lack layout flexibility and unique visual presentation, and can make your site look too "cookie-cutter."

The perfect world

The ideal solution to the cookie-cutter problem is for a Web developer or HTML programmer to create a basic "blank page," complete with your site's headers, navigation elements, style sheets, and other included files already laid out. These elements should somehow be "locked" so that only those users with special permissions could modify them. Regular users can then edit the "body" of the page by using specific elements, such as text styles, colors, and so forth, that have been defined by the original page designer.

This solution is available only in very few products, such as NetObjects' Fusion (www.netobjects.com). Unfortunately, because the HTML language provides no method for defining this kind of "meta template," or for defining acceptable body elements such as text styles and colors, products like Fusion have to use proprietary technologies in order to achieve this functionality. This means that the product is not edited directly in HTML (although it can be exported to HTML for final publishing), may not work as desired with embedded ASP code, and may introduce quirks into the final HTML. (Fusion, for example, makes *extensive* use of invisible HTML tables to achieve its layout effects, which may not be desirable for your site.) Also, because the "source code" for your pages isn't in HTML, you are restricted to using the tool that you selected rather than being able to use a variety of standard HTML tools in different strengths.

Defining your approach

You will likely use a mix of both free-form and template content on your site. The template content is the easier of the two to administer because you can create controls to add to the administrative interface, which allow users to enter data into whatever database that supports the template. Your free-form content will probably be restricted to your technical staff, who are responsible for creating new content and editing existing content according to the instructions provided by your actual content developers (writers, editors, and so forth).

Create templates for as much of your content as possible. Forcing all of the content on your site to fit into templates is needlessly restrictive, but fitting as much content as possible into templates can help maintain a consistent look for different aspects of your site, and is an efficient use of technical resources. You can maximize the flexibility of your site and minimize a "cookie cutter" appearance by using a variety of templates that have been customized to specific situations. For example, you might provide one template for press releases, another for product detail pages, another for featured products, and so forth. This gives your site a dynamic appearance while minimizing the work required to develop new pages. You can reduce the management burden of maintaining these templates by creating a template-based content management system.

Version Control

Version control is a very important feature in any development environment, and e-commerce development is no exception. However, Microsoft's product line only does a marginal job of addressing version control with their Visual SourceSafe product.

Visual SourceSafe (VSS) is a one-tier, file-based system that is somewhat awkward for use in an e-commerce development environment. VSS provides fairly complete source and version control capabilities, but is designed to manage content through a "check in" and "check out" process that doesn't normally leave copies of the files laying around after they are checked in. In a Web development environment, though, you *want* the Web files to be left on the server (perhaps in a read-only state) so that you can test them.

To make VSS better suited to a Web development environment, you and your development team can adopt the following guidelines:

✦ Provide a common Web server that will be used for development.

✦ Share the root folder of your Web site by using Windows file shares.

✦ Create a VSS project that contains all of the site files.

Relief Is on the Horizon

In the past, Microsoft's biggest problem with e-commerce development was their lack of well-thought-out Web-based development support in the company's major development products. Microsoft's original Web development tool, Visual InterDev, was included with Visual Studio but it wasn't well integrated. Visual InterDev did include Visual SourceSafe integration for source and version control, but the environment was in all other ways a standalone product. Even the Visual SourceSafe integration was somewhat unusual and made working with both InterDev and non-Microsoft editors difficult.

With the introduction of Visual Studio .NET, however, Visual InterDev becomes obsolete because Web development will now be accomplished by using the regular Visual Studio .NET languages, including C# (pronounced "C Sharp") and Visual Basic .NET. Visual Studio .NET will also feature a completely integrated, language-independent development environment that provides integrated source and version control.

Because Visual Studio .NET is not expected to provide a robust upgrade path for Visual InterDev 6.0 projects, you should carefully consider your options before selecting Visual InterDev for your current development environment. And, until the new Visual Studio is released, you will either have to choose between the somewhat cumbersome source and version control with Visual SourceSafe or a non-Microsoft source control product that's better suited to Web development.

✦ Have each developer install VSS on their client computers, and post the "working folder" for the project to the file share on the Web server.

✦ Instruct each developer to de-select the "remove local copy" option when checking files into VSS.

Following these guidelines allows you to maintain a single, centralized Web server with read-only copies of the latest files. Developers can edit these files by checking them out of VSS, which marks the files as readable. When they finish editing the file, they can check it back into VSS, leaving a read-only copy on the server for testing and deployment purposes.

Some non-Microsoft version control systems offer a larger array of features and functionality than VSS. Some of them are designed primarily for Web development and offer features and operations designed to complement a Web development environment. Unfortunately, many of the best systems, such as the open-source Concurrent Versioning System (or CVS, located at www.cvshome.org), are designed to run on a UNIX server, not Windows (although Windows client software is available).

An important new technology that will affect next-generation version control systems is Web-based Distributed Authoring and Versioning, or WebDAV. Based on extensions to the ubiquitous HTTP protocol, WebDAV is designed to provide source and version control for a wide variety of documents, including the files that are used in a Web development project. WebDAV-based version control systems promise to fill the gap between modern Web development environments and last-generation version control systems, and Microsoft appears to be on the forefront of the technology. Exchange Server 2000's Web Store has built-in WebDAV support, and allows you to host a Web site right out of the Web Store, thus potentially offering perfect in-place control for Web development projects. Microsoft's SharePoint Portal Server creates an intranet-based, WebDAV-enabled content management system that may be a part of a version control system. Microsoft's Visual SourceSafe .NET is likely to take advantage of these technologies to provide a more Web-centric and robust version control system, but, as of this printing, no information about VSS .NET is available.

Content Deployment

Microsoft included content deployment services in Site Server 3.0 and Site Server 3.0 Commerce Edition. When they set about developing the .NET servers, however, the content deployment functionality was deemed inappropriate for Commerce Server 2000, and was instead incorporated into a new product, Application Center 2000, which also incorporates other site management features from the old Site Server product.

Application Center far surpasses Site Server's content deployment capabilities, allowing administrators to completely control the deployment of multiple Web applications across multiple server clusters. These capabilities make Application Center suitable for managing a large, enterprise-class set of Web servers that use ASP, COM+, and other advanced technologies.

Application Center architecture

Application Center is designed to group servers in *clusters*. This isn't the same type of cluster used by Microsoft Cluster Services, in which two servers share an external data storage device and provide failover services for each other. In an Application Center cluster, each server is completely standalone, but shares a common configuration and content set.

The first member of a cluster is designated as the *cluster controller*, and is responsible for administering the cluster as a whole. Subsequent servers are *cluster members*, although you can promote any member that you want to be the cluster controller. A cluster is designed to be accessed via one or more virtual IP addresses, which represent the cluster as a whole. When using Windows Network Load Balancing (NLB), the cluster members take turns responding to these IP addresses. You can also use Application Center with external third-party load balancing devices.

Cluster members can use different hardware, and Application Center allows you to assign a "server weight" to servers using more powerful hardware, which causes more incoming requests to be directed at your most capable servers. Each cluster member must share an identical software configuration, including Windows version, Application Center version, file system, file structure, and so forth. Their identical configuration is the key to Application Center's content deployment system.

Defining applications

Application Center defines a group of content as an *application*. Applications can include the following items:

✦ Web sites and virtual directories, as well as referenced Internet Services Application Programming Interface (ISAPI) filters

✦ Files

✦ Certificates and certificate trust lists

✦ COM+ applications

✦ Data Source Names (DSNs)

✦ Registry keys

✦ Windows Management Instrumentation (WMI) settings

✦ Exportable Certificate Application Programming Interface (CAPI) certificates

✦ IIS configuration settings

✦ Global ISAPI filters

All of these components can be included in an application, and can be replicated across cluster members or across different clusters.

Application Center creates four applications by default when it is installed on the first member of a cluster (which becomes the cluster controller). These are:

✦ **AllSites:** This application contains all Web sites and virtual directories configured in IIS. You can remove or change this application. Any changes made to IIS (adding or removing Web sites or virtual directories) are automatically detected and applied to this application.

✦ **Administration Web Site:** This application includes the IIS administrative Web site and virtual directories. You can modify or remove this application.

✦ **Application Center 2000 Administrative Web Site:** This application includes the Application Center administrative Web site, which by default is accessible on port 4242 of your Web server (`http://webservername:4242`). You can modify or remove this application.

✦ **Default Web Site:** This application includes your Web server's default Web site. You can modify or remove this application.

You can define your own applications to represent the Web sites used by your servers. You can do this by using Application Center's Microsoft Management Console (MMC) snap-in, as shown in Figure 18-1.

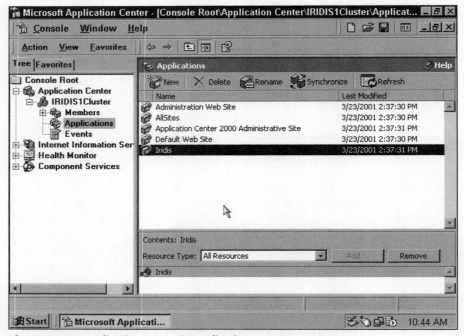

Figure 18-1: Application Center's application management screen

Keep in mind that you can configure multiple applications per cluster, and that an application must be configured on each cluster to which that application will be deployed. This means that you can deploy applications from a single staging server to multiple dedicated Web clusters, as shown in Figure 18-2.

This technique also allows you to define applications to deploy COM+ components, which I discuss in more detail later in this chapter.

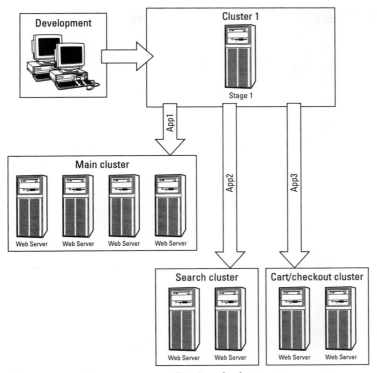

Figure 18-2: One-to-many application deployment

Application Center deployment and synchronization

Deployment is the process of replicating an application (which includes content and configuration settings) from one cluster to another cluster. The application is deployed only to the controller of the destination cluster.

Synchronization is the process of replicating an application from a cluster controller to one or more cluster members. When new members are added to a cluster, they are automatically synchronized, facilitating the increase of a cluster's capacity.

Other than these distinctions, the process and resources involved in replicating content are identical whether you use deployment or synchronization, so I use these terms interchangeably in this section.

Even though you can configure your own deployment/synchronization methods, Application Center automatically synchronizes content in certain circumstances:

✦ When new members are added to a cluster, Application Center automatically synchronizes them with the cluster controller. This allows you to easily add new servers to a cluster and move servers between clusters. Keep in mind that the operating system and Application Center must first be installed on the servers before they can be added to a cluster.

✦ Cluster members that are taken offline for maintenance may miss content changes. Application Center keeps a change log and automatically synchronizes members with the most recent content when they are returned to active service.

✦ Application Center automatically synchronizes cluster configuration settings, network settings, and other system information to all cluster members, regardless of whether you have configured any other automatic content synchronization.

Application Center's MMC snap-in allows you to monitor the synchronization and deployment status of applications, clusters, and cluster members, as shown in Figure 18-3.

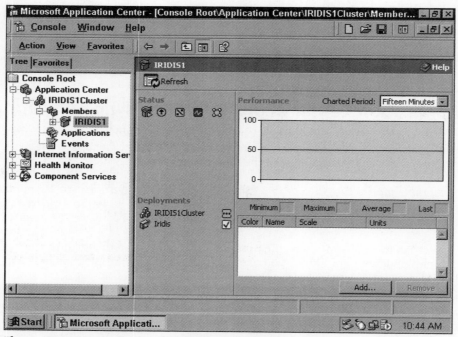

Figure 18-3: Monitoring synchronization and deployment

In this figure, the application "Iridis" has been successfully deployed to the cluster member being monitored.

Synchronization methods

Application Center offers different types of synchronization for different scenarios. The three basic types of synchronization are *automatic, on-demand,* and *advanced.* Deployments that occur *between* clusters are always the result of a manual action by an administrator.

Automatic

Automatic synchronization allows the members of a cluster to remain synchronized with the cluster controller without requiring administrative attention. This is appropriate in a cluster of production Web servers and ensures that each member always has the most recent content. Application Center offers two types of automatic synchronization:

✦ Change-based synchronization allows Application Center to detect changes to synchronized files and folders on the cluster controller. These changes trigger an immediate synchronization of the changed content to the cluster members.

✦ Interval-based synchronization allows Application Center to scan for changed content on a periodic basis (every 60 minutes by default). Changes that are detected during the scan are immediately synchronized on the cluster members.

Automatic change-based synchronization is generally appropriate for production Web clusters that receive a few updates each day. Change-based synchronization can "lose track" of what files to synchronize if a large number of changes occur at once; if you are planning a major deployment of new content, consider changing the cluster to interval-based synchronization to reduce the overhead of the synchronization process. You may also want to consider temporarily disabling automatic synchronization, thus allowing you to manually determine when the new content set is deployed. You can enable both change- and interval-based synchronization; this ensures that any files "missed" by the change-based synchronization are "picked up" during the next interval-based synchronization.

Automatic synchronization does not synchronize COM+ applications. You must specifically deploy these by using the New Deployment Wizard, and the deployment will require a restart of the destination servers' Web services when completed.

On-demand

On-demand or *manual* synchronization allows you to determine when content is replicated within a cluster. Application Center supports three types of manual synchronization:

✦ Cluster synchronization forces all cluster members to synchronize with the cluster controller. All applications configured in the cluster (except COM+ applications) are synchronized.

✦ Member synchronization forces a specific cluster member to synchronize with the cluster controller. All applications configured on the controller (except COM+ applications) are synchronized.

✦ Application synchronization forces a specific application (except a COM+ application) to synchronize on every member in the cluster.

On-demand synchronization is appropriate when you have a great deal of content to synchronize, or when you want to control which applications or cluster members participate in the synchronization. On-demand synchronization can't be used to deploy COM+ applications; you must deploy these by using the New Deployment Wizard.

Advanced

Advanced synchronization offers a finer level of control over the synchronization process, and allows you to synchronize content across clusters (also called *content deployment*). Advanced synchronization is accomplished with the New Deployment Wizard, which offers a variety of advanced options:

✦ **The ability to deploy content without COM+ applications or ISAPI filters.** This type of deployment is sent directly to each destination cluster's controller and does not require a restart. The cluster controller then uses automatic or on-demand synchronization to synchronize the cluster members.

✦ **The ability to deploy COM+ applications.** This deployment communicates with each individual target server, and not just the cluster controller. In addition, the deployment must restart the Web services on each server after the deployment completes. This requires you to take the entire cluster offline while the Web services restart.

✦ **The ability to deploy global ISAPI filters.** You can deploy the ISAPI filters to a cluster's controller, but each cluster member's Web services must be restarted.

✦ **The ability to create phased deployments.** You can deploy content, typically COM+ applications that require a Web services restart, to a portion of a cluster. Because this allows the cluster members to be out of sync with each other, be sure that the phase-deployed content is backwards compatible with the older content on the servers.

Application Center also allows you to specify synchronization *exclusions*. These exclusions are configured on the *target* servers (cluster members) and can therefore be different on each target. The exclusions prevent deployed or synchronized content from affecting that target, and can include files, entire folders, or certain types of files (specified by file extension).

File security

Application Center's synchronization is tightly integrated with Windows 2000 security. You must be aware of how these factors play against each other in the synchronization process in order to avoid security problems.

By default, Application Center replicates Windows 2000 Access Control Lists (ACLs) along with the files it replicates. These ACLs *do not* contain user names; rather, they contain the unique Security Identifiers (SIDs) that identify the security principals on the ACLs. This means that the replicated ACLs are valid only when replicated to computers with the same security context.

For example, imagine that you've created a content deployment environment like the one shown in Figure 18-4.

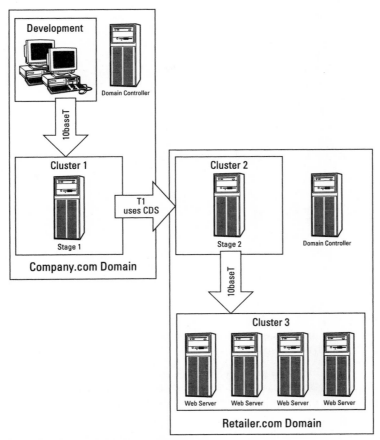

Figure 18-4: Multi-domain staging environment

In this environment, your company's development computers and first staging server are located in the Company.com domain. Your second staging server and your production Web servers are located in a different physical location, and are members of the Retailer.com domain. These domains are both forest roots, and have no trust relationship between them.

Windows 2000 NTFS file permissions are applied to the files on the Stage 1 server. Application Center replicates these ACLs to the Stage 2 server, which replicates them to the Web servers. Because the Stage 2 and Web servers are in a different domain with no trust relationship, however, the SIDs on the replicated ACLs are useless, therefore the ACLs are also useless.

Similar problems occur if you assign permissions to local computer accounts rather than domain accounts, and you then replicate the ACLs. The replicated ACLs have no context outside the local machine and become invalid when replicated. Therefore, you must make sure that the ACLs will remain in context even after replication. All computers involved in the replication must belong to the same domain, or all domains involved must trust each other. You must also take care to only assign permissions to domain user accounts.

You can instruct Application Center to *not* replicate ACLs. In this case, the ACLs on the replicated files will be inherited from their parent folders on the destination computer, following normal Windows 2000 rules for copied files.

Application Center will not detect the changes on an ACL and initiate content synchronization. In order for ACL changes to be replicated, the file must be changed so that Application Center schedules it for synchronization, or you must manually synchronize the file.

Synchronization security

Whenever synchronization occurs, potentially sensitive information is transmitted across network connections. If portions of your synchronization occur across the public Internet or another vulnerable network, you should be aware that Application Center uses three distinct communication protocols during synchronization: DCOM, HTTP, and RPC.

✦ Distributed COM, or DCOM, is used to handle synchronization control communications within a cluster. These communications are encrypted using Windows 2000 RPC packet privacy.

✦ The Remote Procedure Call protocol, or RPC, is used to carry synchronization control information when synchronizing between clusters. This communication is also encrypted using Windows 2000 RPC packet privacy.

✦ HTTP is used to physically transport files and COM+ components for synchronization within a cluster and between clusters. This traffic is *not* encrypted, and may be intercepted if carried over a vulnerable network.

This is important because many ASP developers hardcode database connection strings into ASP pages, and these connection strings often include passwords. If your synchronization will take place across a non-secure network, use IPSec, Virtual Private Network, or some other means to secure the transport layer of the network connection to protect the information in the files being synchronized.

Wide-area synchronization

Application Center's synchronization is designed primarily for use in well-connected local area network (LAN) environments. Application Center doesn't feature compression or any protocols to deal with low-bandwidth connections. However, you may need to deploy content over a wide area network (WAN) connection in your environment. For example, your development computers may be located in a different physical location than your production Web servers.

Microsoft introduced the Content Replication Service in Site Server 3.0. That service has been enhanced and included in Application Center 2000 as the Content Deployment Service, or CDS. The CDS is designed to deploy content, such as Application Center applications, across WAN links. Figure 18-5 shows a sample WAN-base deployment strategy using CDS.

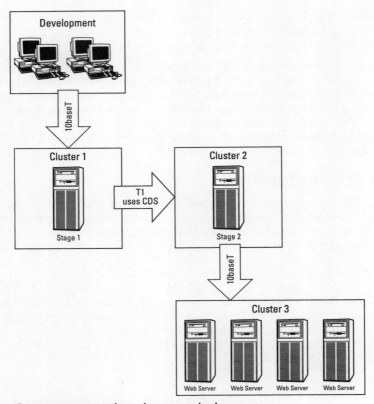

Figure 18-5: WAN-based content deployment

In this scenario, your development workstations and a single-node staging cluster are at one physical location. A second single-node staging cluster and your production cluster are in a different physical location. The Stage 1 server uses the Content Deployment System to deploy content to the Stage 2 server over your WAN link. The Stage 2 server then uses normal content synchronization to deploy content to the production cluster. This scenario takes maximum advantage of the CDS' capabilities because it requires the over-the-WAN portion of the deployment to take place only once.

Tip Always synchronize to a single server across WAN links. Doing this allows the server to then synchronize to multiple clusters that are locally connected to it, thus saving time and bandwidth.

The CDS is not installed with Application Center by default, but is included on the Application Center CD. Locate the `Content Deployment Service` folder on the CD and launch `SetupCRS.exe`.

Deploying COM and COM+

Application Center is also capable of deploying COM+ applications, as well as COM components that are installed into a COM+ application. You can deploy COM+ applications by adding them as a resource to an existing Application Center application. Application Center automatically restarts the Component Load Balancing (CLB) service after deploying COM+ applications, making the process fairly automated.

Note   When you add a COM+ application to an application definition, be sure to also add any registry entries or associated files required by the COM+ application.

Configuring a COM+ deployment

Figure 18-6 shows a sample application configured with a COM+ application and a set of registry keys. You can deploy this application by right-clicking the Applications node and selecting the Deploy Application option.

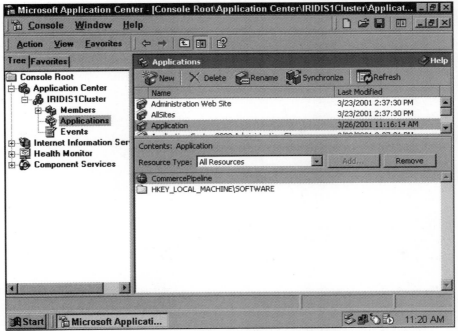

Figure 18-6: Configuring a COM+ application for deployment

This action launches the New Deployment Wizard, which allows you to specify the clusters or cluster members to receive the deployment. When you select the Deploy COM+ applications option in the Wizard, you can specify *draining options* for the deployment. COM+ application deployments require the target servers' Web service to be restarted; draining is the process of allowing existing Web connections to finish up and disconnect, and is set to 20 minutes by default. You can also specify that no draining occur, which causes the Web service to be immediately restarted when the deployment is complete.

Adding COM components to a COM+ deployment

The ability to deploy COM+ applications to remote machines is one of the major new features of COM+, and is not available for older "COM Classic" components. However, COM components *can* be installed as part of a COM+ application, making deployment possible.

Start by using the Component Services MMC snap-in to create a new COM+ application. The New Application Wizard allows you to create an empty COM+ application, as shown in Figure 18-7.

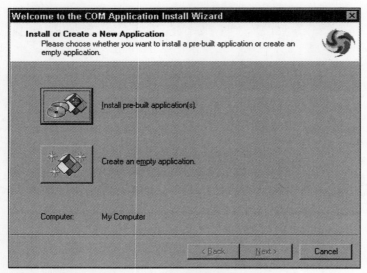

Figure 18-7: Creating a new COM+ application

1. Specify a *server application,* which can take advantage of all COM+ services.

2. On the application identity screen, specify a domain user account that will be used to run the COM+ application (and the installed COM applications).

3. After creating the new COM+ application, use the Component Services MMC to add COM components to it. These components must already be physically installed and registered on the computer where the application is being created.

Daily Maintenance

No e-commerce site is completely self-maintained. Each of the various components of the site require continuous monitoring and maintenance to ensure that they are functioning correctly and will continue to do so. You should adopt a complete, documented program of *daily* maintenance to ensure the proper operation of your site.

Microsoft's products provide many tools for monitoring the health and performance of your site's components. These components also require ongoing periodic maintenance to keep them functioning at their best.

Reviewing logs

The applications on your servers are designed to log a great deal of information to various log files. These log files are a valuable source of information about those applications, and may include informational messages, error messages, and even advice for better using or configuring the applications. All of this information is wasted if you don't regularly review the logs, as tedious as that may seem. In fact, reviewing your servers' logs is the most important part of any daily maintenance routine.

Web server logs

Web server logs can be a valuable way to find errors on your site. For example, Figure 18-8 shows a portion of a Web server log that indicates ASP and bad link errors.

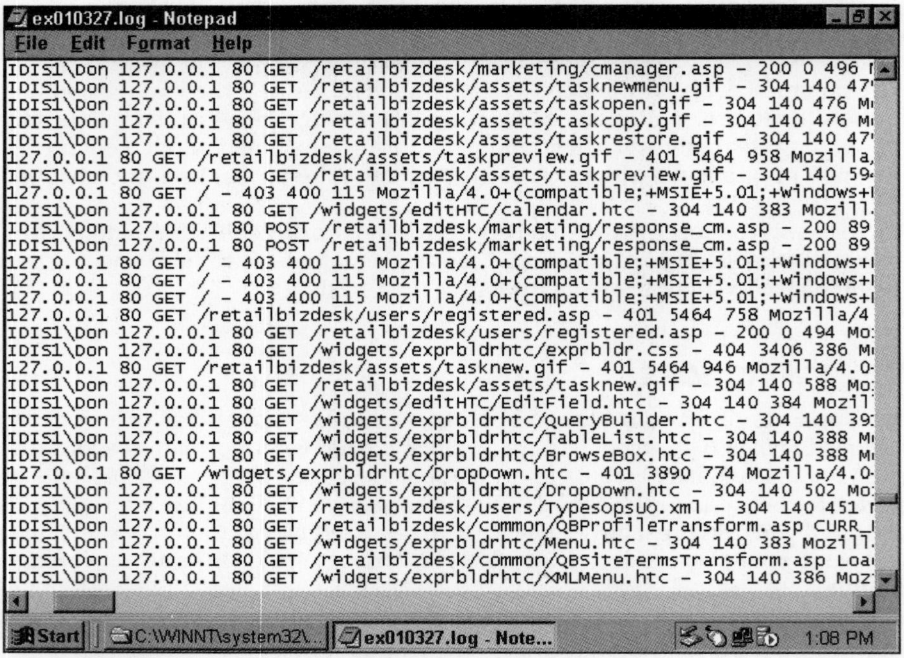

Figure 18-8: Configuring database integrity checks

Monitoring your Web logs manually isn't really practical. Fortunately, Commerce Server's Analysis module helps you review the information in a more straightforward fashion. By importing your Web server log files into Commerce Server's data warehouse, the Analysis module's Hits by HTTP Status report allows you to view the pages delivered from your Web site with a specific HTTP status, as shown in Figure 18-9.

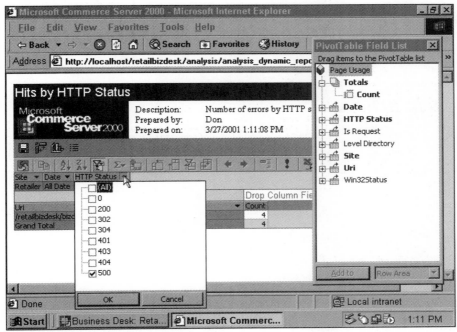

Figure 18-9: Viewing Hits by HTTP Status

HTTP status code 500, for example, indicates a server processing error, which is generally an ASP error. As shown in Figure 18-10, the report can tell you exactly which pages generated a status 500, how many times this occurred, and on what dates. By sorting on these columns, you can locate pages that are frequently returning ASP errors and target them for further testing.

You can also use this report to locate pages that show up as bad links and so forth.

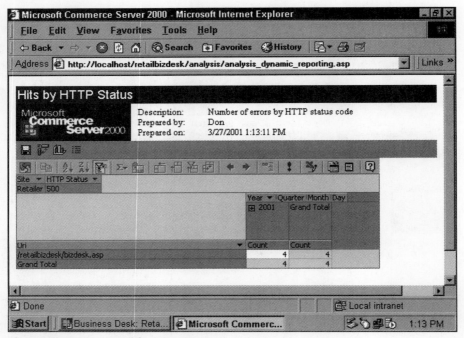

Figure 18-10: Pages with ASP errors

Windows Event Logs

The Windows Event Logs provide a wealth of useful information about the operation of your servers. The System Log provides information directly related to the operating system, and the Application Log contains errors returned by applications that are running on the server. A few applications, such as Internet Explorer and the DNS Server, maintain their own dedicated Event Logs.

Figure 18-11 shows a portion of a server's Application Event Log. Notice that many of the events are informational and don't represent error messages. Actual errors, indicated by a red "X" icon, should be examined and corrected. Warnings, represented by a yellow triangle icon, should be examined because they often contain useful information.

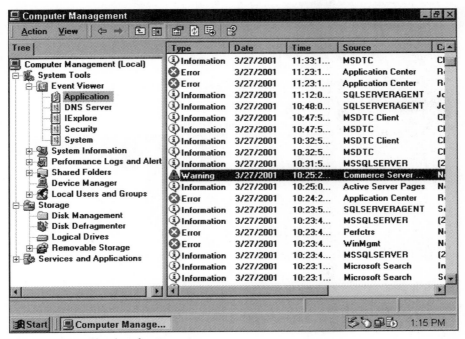

Figure 18-11: Viewing the Event Log

Warnings don't necessarily represent a problem with the server. Rather, they usually represent an unexpected and unavoidable situation that the application software was able to successfully handle. They also often contain tips for eliminating the problem; see the warning shown in Figure 18-12.

This warning indicates that the campaign system was unable to load any advertisements as requested by a Web page. This may mean that no advertisements fit within their campaign dates, and the message advises you to schedule one or more *house*, or internal ads, to prevent blank ads from showing up on your Web site.

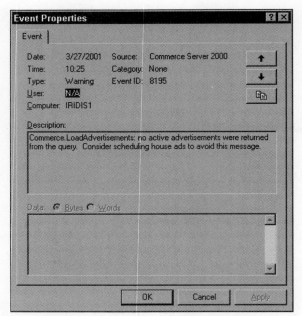

Figure 18-12: A Commerce Server warning event

Database maintenance

E-commerce sites make extensive use of databases, and these databases require continual maintenance to remove old data, maintain performance levels, and minimize data errors and corruption. In addition to the general database maintenance that's suitable for all SQL Server databases, the databases used by specific Microsoft products, such as Commerce Server and BizTalk Server, require their own ongoing maintenance.

Commerce Server database

Certain parts of the Commerce Server database will accumulate data *forever* unless you take steps to remove and archive old data.

Order tables

All of the tables associated with the ordering process, including OrderGroups, OrderFormHeaders, and OrderFormLineItems, maintain all of the orders ever placed on your site, as well as all of the shopping carts used on your site. Old, completed orders should periodically be archived into a separate database for long-term storage to free up room on your database server. Commerce Server has no built-in mechanism for clearing away old, abandoned shopping carts, and because these can rapidly consume space on your database server, they must be manually cleaned up.

Cleaning up abandoned carts can be manually accomplished in the Business Desk by using the Orders module, as shown in Figure 18-13. Select older carts, as shown, and delete them.

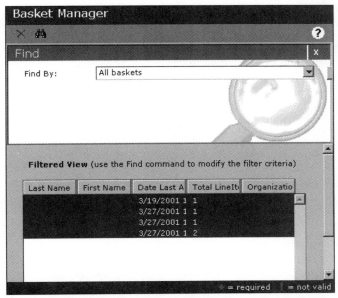

Figure 18-13: Deleting old baskets with the Business Desk

You may also want to automate this process by creating a SQL Server job that automatically deletes any carts older than 24 hours (or some other period of time). Listing 18-1 shows a Transact-SQL script that accomplishes this. Automating the cart cleanup gives you two benefits: You don't have to remember to do it yourself, and the carts are prevented from consuming an excessive amount of space on your database server.

Listing 18-1: **Cleaning up old baskets**

```
DELETE FROM BasketGroup
  WHERE order_status_code = 1 AND
  order_create_date < ( GETDATE() - 1 )
```

You should carefully consider how long you want abandoned carts to remain in the database. Commerce Server tracks carts by the user ID of the user that created them. This same user ID is placed into a cookie on the user's computer. If they return to the site, Commerce Server will "reunite" them with their abandoned shopping cart, allowing them to continue working with it. For this reason, you may want to allow old carts to remain in the database for a few days before removing them.

Product and profile tables

Part of your ongoing maintenance routine should involve removing old products and user profiles from the database. For example, you may want to clean out user profiles that have not been used in more than a year, or remove products that you are no longer carrying.

Determining when a user profile is "old" can be difficult according to Commerce Server's built-in profile definitions, which include a "last changed" date but no "last used" date. You can modify the UserObject table to include a d_last_login column, and modify your login process to update this column with the current date whenever a user logs in. For example, you can set users' accounts to "Inactive" after a year has passed.

Setting the account to be inactive allows a user to contact you if he or she does return to the site. You can then use the Business Desk to reactivate the account without losing any of the customer's information.

After another year passes, you may want to delete all of your inactive accounts. You may also choose to delete any anonymous user accounts older than six months. Listing 18-2 shows a Transact-SQL script that accomplishes these tasks. You can schedule this script to run once a week as part of an automated maintenance routine.

Listing 18-2: **Setting user accounts to inactive**

```
UPDATE UserObject
 SET i_account_status = 0 WHERE
 d_last_login < DATEADD("year",-1,GETDATE())

DELETE FROM UserObject
  WHERE i_account_status = 0
  AND d_last_login = ( GETDATE() - 730)

DELETE FROM UserObject WHERE
  i_user_type = 0 AND
  d_date_created = ( GETDATE() - 120)
```

Cleaning up product tables is more of a manual process because someone in your company will need to determine when a product is no longer needed in the catalog.

Campaign tables

Make a habit of removing campaigns from the database that are no longer active. Doing so will not only reduce the size of the Commerce Server database, but it will also improve the performance of the Content Selection pipeline, the discount calculation pipeline components, and many other portions of Commerce Server.

As with other table maintenance in Commerce Server, you can manually remove old entries by using the Campaigns module in the Business Desk. You can also write a Transact-SQL script as part of a SQL Server job to automatically remove old items. Because of the complexity of the campaign system, however, I recommend only using the Business Desk to remove inactive campaign items.

Figure 18-14 shows the Business Desk's Campaigns module, which you can use to search for old campaigns that haven't been deleted. You can then select the campaign item that you want to remove and delete it.

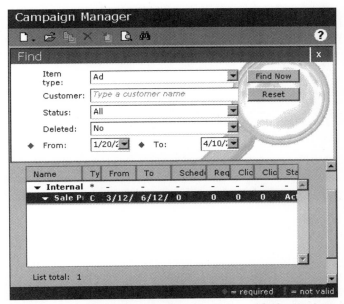

Figure 18-14: Deleting old campaign items with the Business Desk

Commerce Server data warehouse

Like the Commerce Server production database, the Commerce Server data warehouse has no built-in automatic mechanism to remove old data. This is mainly because *you* have to determine when data is "old" and no longer needed for analysis reports.

Your first maintenance action for the data warehouse should be to delete old completed static reports. You do this in the Business Desk's Analysis module by using the Completed Reports tab, as shown in Figure 18-15.

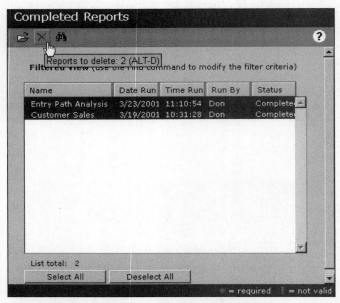

Figure 18-15: Deleting completed reports with the Business Desk

Your next step is to remove old analysis data from the data warehouse. Commerce Server provides a Data Deletion DTS task to help you clean up old analysis data.

Note   Before deleting any data from the data warehouse, run and print (or export) any reports that you may need in order to use that data. That way, you will have a record of the reports derived from the deleted data.

Deleting data requires you to create a DTS package in SQL Server, and add one or more Data Deletion tasks to the package. Each task can be configured to delete specific types of data, as shown in Figure 18-16.

You can choose to delete the detail data from specific Web logs, or all of the data from specific Web logs, which includes summarized data calculated during the import. You can also choose to delete *all* of the data in the data warehouse.

Caution   Deleting all data will empty the data warehouse. You can re-populate the data warehouse by running "full load" import tasks from your production database. You can't run "incremental load" tasks against an empty data warehouse. See Chapter 17 for more details.

Figure 18-16: Deleting data warehouse data by using DTS

After deleting data, you must run the Report Preparation task in order to recalculate the OLAP cubes in the data warehouse.

Note Deleting Web log data requires a certain amount of free space in the data warehouse. A full or nearly full data warehouse database may need to be expanded to successfully remove Web log data from it.

BizTalk Server databases

One important feature of BizTalk Server is that it tracks every document it handles, along with information about each processing step that each document undergoes. This information is stored, by default, in a database named InterchangeDTA.

BizTalk Server doesn't perform any automated maintenance on the InterchangeDTA database to remove old tracking information. Instead, you must manually remove old data or create a SQL Server job to remove old data on a regular basis.

Note The InterchangeDTA database contains several tables that participate in a complex operational relationship. The task of removing old data from these tables should be part of a regular maintenance routine, which is beyond the scope of this book.

SQL Server databases

All of the databases used by your e-commerce site—from the Commerce Server production database to the BizTalk Server messaging database—are hosted by SQL Server, and require the regular maintenance associated with any SQL Server database. SQL Server's own databases—master and msdb—also require periodic maintenance. In general, your regular maintenance plan should include:

✦ **Checking databases for signs of excessive page splits.** In other words, the database's indexes have grown beyond their original projected size. Excessive page splits should be handled by rebuilding the indexes.

✦ **Checking databases for excessive transaction log size.** As long as a database is regularly backed up, its transaction log size should remain relatively constant. If backing up the database doesn't reduce the transaction log size, you may need to perform a database shrink operation to delete old and unused pages from the log. This situation can result when the database regularly receives a large number of updates or inserts.

✦ **Checking databases for consistency using the Database Consistency Checker (DBCC).** This tool verifies the database's physical structure and can correct many problems that would otherwise lead to data corruption.

SQL Server can help you perform many of these tasks on a regular schedule with a *database maintenance plan*. Follow these steps to create a new plan:

1. Use SQL Server Enterprise Manager to open the Management folder.

2. Right-click the Database Maintenance Plans folder.

3. Choose the New Maintenance Plan option to launch the Database Maintenance Plan Wizard.

Each maintenance plan can help maintain several databases. The Wizard allows you to select the databases to which a plan will apply, as shown in Figure 18-17.

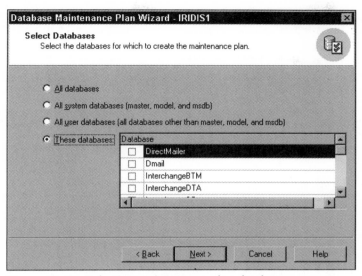

Figure 18-17: Selecting maintenance plan databases

The second screen of the Wizard, shown in Figure 18-18, allows you to configure database optimization options.

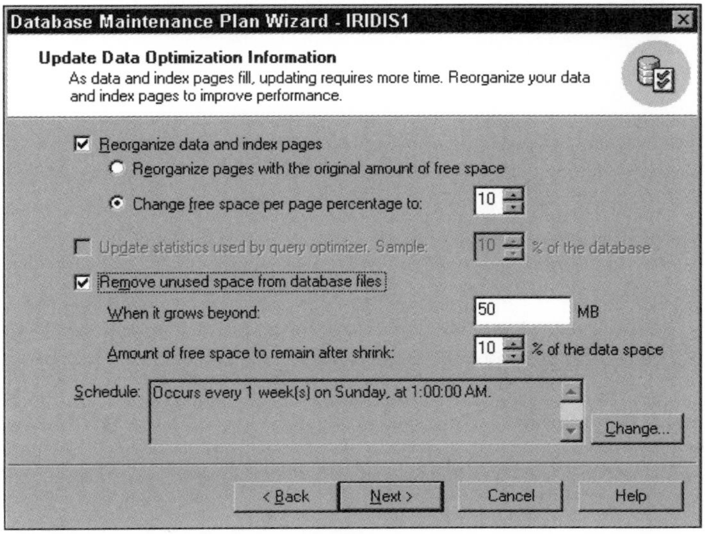

Figure 18-18: Configuring database optimization

Your options include reorganizing data and index pages to allow extra room on each page for growth (which reduces or eliminates page splits), and automatically shrinking database files that have grown beyond a certain size. These options are run as a discrete task, and can be scheduled to occur on a regular basis.

Your plan can also include data integrity checks, as shown in Figure 18-19.

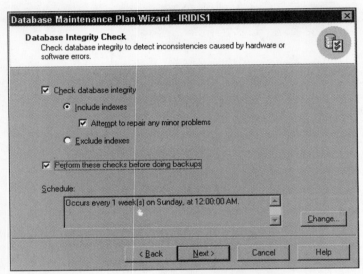

Figure 18-19: Configuring database integrity checks

These checks allow SQL Server to verify the physical structure of data and index pages, and attempt to correct any problems that are discovered. You can have these checks occur before any database backups included in the plan, which helps ensure that your backups are error-free and usable in the event of a more serious failure.

The maintenance plan can also include an automated backup of the database files and their transaction logs — either to disk or a locally attached tape drive — and can be configured to write maintenance history to special tables in the msdb database for reporting purposes.

The maintenance plan creates several SQL Server jobs to carry out the tasks that you select, and you can modify the schedule on these jobs as necessary. Create a plan for each server in your company, because plans are server-specific.

Performance maintenance

Performance monitoring is also an important part of a daily maintenance routine. By the time your users — your customers, especially — notify you that your site seems slow, the problem is usually already out of control. Performance maintenance consists of three basic steps:

1. **Establish a baseline.** This step requires you to determine what level of performance is normal for your site. Without a baseline, you'll be unable to recognize abnormal or unacceptable performance.

2. **Regularly monitor performance.** A regular performance check will let you compare ongoing performance to your baseline. You'll be able to spot performance trends, such as gradually declining performance due to regular growth in site traffic.

3. **Take corrective and preventative action.** When performance becomes unacceptable, or when you detect a declining performance trend, you can take steps to improve performance. This might include upgrading your server hardware, adding more servers, performing database maintenance, and so forth.

Centralized alerting

Your daily maintenance routine should help you identify most errors and problems with your site's various systems, but some problems will happen unexpectedly. Most Microsoft products provide fairly good error reports via the system Event Log and other logs, but by default, don't offer good centralized reporting. Centralized reporting is important in an environment with many servers, and allows you to be actively notified when errors occur on any of your servers.

SQL Server alerts

SQL Server is the only Microsoft product currently capable of actively sending alerts to an operator, rather than just passively logging an error in a log somewhere for you to find. SQL Server alerts work in conjunction with the Windows Application Event Log and SQL Server Agent, and operate as follows:

1. When an error occurs on SQL Server, an event is written to the Windows Application Event Log. The source of the event is SQL Server, and the text of the event contains the SQL error information.

2. SQL Server Agent runs as a service and monitors the Windows Application Event Log. When SQL Server Agent finds events with a SQL Server source, it checks to see if the event text matches a configured alert.

3. Alerts are configured as part of SQL Server Agent, as shown in Figure 18-20.

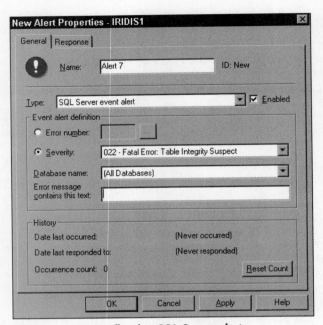

Figure 18-20: Configuring SQL Server alerts

If the event in the log matches a configured alert, SQL Server Agent checks to see what response is configured for the alert.

4. Alert responses can include executing an external program, or notifying a SQL Server operator by e-mail, pager, or NET SEND message, as shown in Figure 18-21.

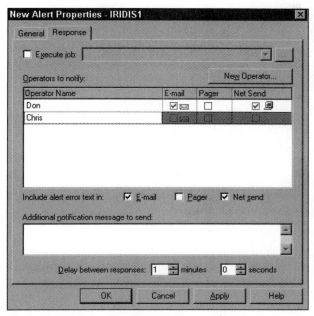

Figure 18-21: Configuring SQL Server alerts

SQL Server's alert handling system can be configured to create sophisticated responses targeted at almost any possible alert condition. If you have multiple SQL Server computers, then you don't need to manually configure alerts on each server. Instead, you can configure all of the servers to forward their alerts to a central alert server. You do this by modifying the properties of each server's SQL Server Agent, as shown in Figure 18-22.

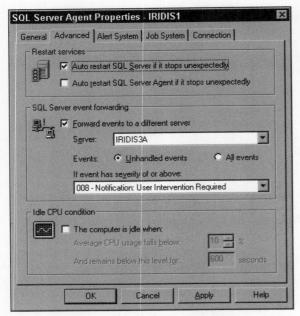

Figure 18-22: Configuring central alerting

All alerts at the specified severity level or higher are forwarded, allowing you to configure all of your alerts on a single centralized server. The central server will track the name of the server that the alert was received from, telling operators who receive notifications to immediately address the problem.

Other alerts

Most other Microsoft products simply write their errors to the Windows Application Event Log, where they rely on your daily monitoring of those logs to discover the error. Some third-party products periodically poll your servers' event logs and notify you of any problems that they find, allowing you to centralize your error reporting and eliminate the need to perform daily log checks of every server. These third-party products include Compaq Insight Manager, IBM's Netfinity Directory, and similar systems management products.

Business Continuity

Business continuity is the process of ensuring that your business is not affected by failures in technology. Even though it's a step beyond "disaster recovery," which simply means preparing to fix things that break, business continuity starts in the same place: making sure you have reliable backups of your important business files and data. In practice, this means having reliable, frequently updated backups of your Web server content and databases, and knowing exactly what to do in the event of a failure.

Backup and restore theory

Although the methods and options for backing up different Microsoft products vary, they do revolve around a standard operational theory. Understanding this theory can help you understand how to best create a business continuity plan that suits the needs of your business.

Backup methods

An important aspect of any backup and restore plan is the *type* of backups that you make. Here are three general types of backups:

✦ **Full backups** are a complete copy of whatever you are backing up. They take the most time to create because the entire source must be copied. They take just as long to restore, if necessary, but offer the benefit of a single-step restore. (Only the full backup needs to be restored.)

✦ **Incremental backups** contain everything that has changed in the source since the last full or incremental backup. These often offer the advantage of being very fast, because they only back up a portion of the source. On the other hand, a restore requires you to first restore the last full backup, and then to restore any incremental backups made since that time. This is more time-consuming and complex than simply restoring a full backup.

✦ **Differential backups** contain everything that has changed since the last full or incremental backup. If you create a full backup once a week and a differential backup each day, then the differential backups will gradually become longer as the week progresses because they include everything that has changed since the full backup. Restoring is less complex with this type than with incremental backups because only the full backup and the most recent differential backup are required.

Any good backup and restore plan will be a compromise in fast backup time and fast restore time, using a mixture of these methods.

How backups work

The basic backup methodology is appropriate for backing up files, but requires special handling for some types of files, such as database files residing on a SQL Server.

Backing up files

If you are backing up files, the backup software asks the server's operating system to open the file. The backup software reads the file, just like any other application would, and copies it to the backup (which may be a special file on disk or a backup tape drive). If the backup software is on a different computer than the file being backed up, the file is accessed through the server's normal file sharing system.

The downside of this approach is open files, because they cannot be easily backed up by a file-level backup system. Typically, the operating system will allow applications to open files as "read only" or "read and write." A Web server, for example, opens ASP pages as read only because it doesn't need to make any changes to the files. The operating system will allow multiple applications to open a single file as read only because they can't change the file. The normal backup process has no problem backing these files up because it also opens them as read only.

Some applications need to open files and modify them. They need to be assured that no other application will attempt to change the file at the same time. They open the file with a *lock*, which usually prevents other applications from opening the files, including backup software. Unfortunately, some of the most important files on your servers, such as the files containing SQL Server databases, are opened in this fashion.

Most backup software packages will ask the operating system to open the file in a read only mode. This gives the backup software access to the file, but because the other application has a lock on the file, its contents may change *as it is being backed up,* resulting in an essentially useless backup.

Backing up databases

Most major third-party software packages offer "agents" that are capable of backing up chronically open files like SQL Server databases. Each agent works in exactly the same way — they use SQL Server's own built-in backup and restore functionality. Rather than attempting to back up the physical database file, they simply "request" the data from SQL Server, which launches its own backup and restore subsystem to perform the backup. So even though third-party backup software packages offer great backup management features, they can't generally improve on the performance of a database backup because they are constrained by SQL Server's own built-in capabilities.

Fortunately, SQL Server's built-in backup capabilities are pretty good. SQL Server is not only capable of backing up a database while in use (although it does come with a fairly stiff performance hit), it is also capable of including in the backup *any data that changes while the backup is in progress.* This means that the backup is completely accurate as of its completion time.

Other agent-based backup schemes for products like Microsoft Exchange Server work in the same way — by using the server's own backup and restore functionality.

Backing up Web servers

Web servers consist mainly of files, which are normally opened by the server process in a read-only mode. This makes the process of backing up Web servers fairly straightforward, because a simple file backup is capable of capturing everything.

In an Application Center environment, you can designate one server to be the "backup source." Because all servers are the same, backing up this one server is just as good as backing up all of them individually. Ideally, this backup source should be the cluster controller, because it also contains the configuration information for the cluster. You may even start your backup by first taking the designated server out of rotation, which prevents customers from connecting to it. This helps to ensure that the server is in as "quiescent" a state as possible, enabling your backup software to capture as much data as possible.

Web servers also contain a great deal of configuration information in the IIS metabase, which can be backed up by using the Windows 2000 Backup utility or most major third-party backup software packages. The servers' registry should also be included in any backup.

Commerce Server throws an interesting twist into the backup situation. Because Commerce Server uses so many COM+ components, some files can remain open when the backup is running, making it difficult to obtain a reliable backup. Although a file-based backup can generally be relied upon for day-to-day backups, you should periodically create a *package* of your entire Commerce Server site. This package, which you can create with the Commerce Server Site Packager, can then be easily deployed to a "blank" Web server in the event of a failure.

Note   Keep in mind that Application Center Web clusters can help eliminate the need for a restore by allowing you to automatically deploy the site from a cluster controller to a freshly installed Web server.

The Site Packager is implemented as a wizard, and is included with Commerce Server 2000. This wizard allows you to create new packages or unpack a previously packaged site, as shown in Figure 18-23.

Figure 18-23: The Commerce Server Site Packager

The Site Packager's first configuration screen, shown in Figure 18-24, prompts you to specify which Commerce Server site to package and for the name of the .pup file to create.

The Site Packager also allows you to create Transact-SQL scripts to recreate your site's profile schema when the site is unpackaged. This is a good step to take, and will supplement your backups of the SQL Server databases. A copy of the final package can be kept on a cluster controller and included in your normal file backups for extra protection.

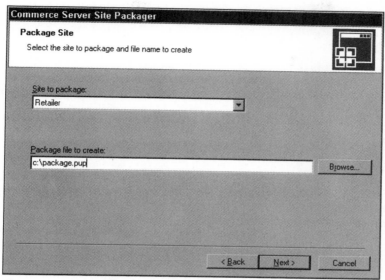

Figure 18-24: Specifying the site to package

Backing up databases

Most of the rest of your site's important data resides in SQL Server databases, allowing you to take advantage of SQL Server's built-in backup capabilities. SQL Server supports full and differential backups of databases, plus a *transaction log* backup.

Transaction log backups

Transaction logs play a key role in both the recoverability and regular operation of SQL Server databases. Whenever data is changed on a SQL Server, the following steps are followed:

1. SQL Server determines which *pages* hold the data that needs to be changed. A page is a single 8-kilobyte block of data, read directly from the server's hard drives.

2. With the necessary pages in memory, SQL Server makes the change. The instructions for the change, such as the original query that resulted in the change, are written to the transaction log.

3. When SQL Server has the opportunity, the changed pages are written back to hard disk, and the entry in the transaction log is "checked," indicating that the change has been committed to hard disk.

This process means that SQL Server may operate for a time with one copy of the data on hard disk and a different copy in memory. The most *recent* copy of the data is the one in memory, and SQL Server always uses pages in memory before loading them from hard disk. This means that any subsequent operations requiring the same data will use the more recent copy stored in the server's memory.

If a failure occurs and SQL Server is restarted, it first checks the transaction log for transactions that have not been checked. These transactions are read from the log in the order that they originally occurred and "replayed," causing the data changes to occur again. As part of this recovery process, SQL Server immediately writes changed pages to hard disk and "checkpoints" the transaction log before it begins accepting new transactions.

The transaction log can be used to restore data by *replaying* changes made to the data, rather than simply restoring a copy of the data. Normally, the transaction log keeps a copy of the "checkpointed" transactions, which causes the transaction log to continually grow in size. When a transaction log or full database backup is performed, SQL Server clears the transaction log, emptying out all checkpointed transactions and starting from scratch. If your server experiences a complete database corruption, you can restore the most recent database backup and any logs backed up since that database backup. By default, SQL Server attempts to "replay" any transactions that have occurred since that backup, making your restore as "up to the minute" as possible and reducing the amount of lost data.

SQL Server backup strategies

A typical SQL Server backup strategy includes all three types of backups supported by the server. A full backup is made on a periodic basis, and differential backups are made at least once a day. Transaction log backups are made more frequently, perhaps every hour. In the event of a total database failure, you will need the last full backup, last differential backup, and any transaction log backups since the last differential backup in order to restore the database. Only data entered since the last transaction log backup will be lost.

Because your SQL Server computers may contain multiple databases, you can "load balance" backup activity for maximum efficiency, minimum overhead, and maximum protection. Table 18-1 shows a sample backup plan.

	Table 18-1	
	Sample SQL Server backup plan	
Database	**Backup type**	**Occurs**
Commerce Server production	Full database	Sunday nights
	Differential database	Monday through Saturday nights
	Transaction log	Hourly
Direct Mailer	Full database	Saturday nights
	Differential database	Sunday through Friday nights
	Transaction log	Every four hours
BizTalk Server (all)	Full database	Monday nights
	Differential database	Tuesday through Saturday nights
	Transaction log	Hourly

Where you store your backups can significantly affect your restore times. One strategy is to save all of your backups to a file, located on a separate hard drive on the SQL Server computer. This file can be backed up to tape by using a normal file backup, but having it located on hard disk makes the backup process *much* faster, and also makes a restore, if necessary, much faster. Many organizations schedule a SQL Server backup job to execute at a given hour, and then a couple of hours later backup the resulting file to tape drive by using their normal backup software. This provides the fastest restore possible, and, with hard drives costing as little as they do, is a worthy investment.

Tip After implementing your backup plan, *check on it.* Make sure that the backups are actually occurring when you set them to and that your plan is working smoothly every day. You have no excuse for waiting until you *need* the backup to find out that it didn't run.

Recovering from failures

Exactly how you recover from a loss of data depends on your backup plan. If you need to perform a restore, you will need to follow the correct procedure for restoring a full backup and any incremental, differential, or other backups that you have. Most backup software packages have wizards or other tools to help make restores less confusing; Windows 2000's own Backup utility offers a wizard that walks you through the restore process. SQL Server Enterprise Manager includes a complete graphical user interface for performing restores. I recommend that you use this graphical interface because it's much less confusing (and harder to forget critical steps) than using Transact-SQL commands.

Tip   After implementing a backup plan, *test it.* Try to restore a completely blank server with your critical data. Remove a critical file, and try to restore it. Waiting until you *need* to restore data to see if your plan works defeats the whole point of business continuity.

Make sure that you clearly document how your backup plan works, and how restores should be performed. Provide sample step-by-step procedures to cover anticipated backup and restore scenarios, so that even a junior member of your technical staff has a good chance of performing the restore successfully.

Continuity without backups

I would never for a minute imply that you shouldn't have a well-thought-out backup plan in place, but you should be aware that you can improve the business continuity of your site in *many* ways besides just using backups and restores. In fact, a backup should be your *last* line of defense, because it generally means making a resource temporarily unavailable, which is the very scenario that business continuity strives to avoid. Microsoft products offer many technologies and features to help reduce the need to resort to a backup tape, including:

✦ Clustering, both Microsoft Cluster Services and Application Center's Web and COM+ clusters, provides a complete hardware alternative to a failed server. With Cluster Services, a failover server stands ready to take over if a cluster node fails. In Application Center, the fact that multiple identical servers exist to handle the load means that the failure of a single node is less than disastrous.

✦ Log shipping, standby servers, and other features of SQL Server supplement the clustering technology in the product and help to maintain a "hot spare" SQL Server, ready to plug in should the primary server fail. The spare server may not be as powerful as the original, but it's better than nothing.

✦ BizTalk Server Enterprise Edition has the capability to load-balance incoming and outgoing document exchanges across multiple independent BizTalk Servers. If a single server fails, the others continue responding to requests while the failed server is repaired or replaced.

In addition, the redundancy features found in many modern servers make your server hardware less vulnerable to failure. These redundancy features include:

✦ Redundant network interface cards

✦ Redundant power supplies

✦ RAID arrays

✦ Redundant processor power supplies

✦ "Chipkill" error correcting memory

Additionally, hot-plug technologies give you the option of replacing a failed component without taking the server offline. Some of these hot-plug technologies include:

✦ Hot-plug PCI cards

✦ Hot-plug drives

✦ Hot-plug power supplies

✦ Hot-plug cooling fans

You should carefully investigate and invest in servers with these capabilities to maximize your company's business continuity capabilities. Remember, a server with these capabilities can mean the difference between no downtime (or only a few minutes), versus hours or days of downtime in servers without these capabilities.

Summary

Managing your site can be a complex experience, but with careful planning and judicious use of third-party products, you can automate much of the administrative drudgery to focus on more important tasks.

Developing a suitable approach to content management, and using tools like Application Center to deploy that content, makes one of the most complex administrative tasks much easier. Application Center's built-in deployment and synchronization capabilities also offer a form of business continuity by spreading the risk of a failure across several servers in a cluster.

Log reviewing, another tiresome task that is often ignored by busy administrators, can be assisted by tools such as Commerce Server's reports, SQL Server's centralized alerting capabilities, and third-party utilities to track your various servers' Event Logs. These tools make a cumbersome task manageable, and help ensure that the very important task of log maintenance isn't ignored.

Finally, having a well-planned and well-documented business continuity plan, including a good backup and restore plan, helps to ensure that even if disaster strikes, your business is unaffected, or is affected as little as possible.

✦　　✦　　✦

Supporting Back Office Requirements

"**B**ack office" refers to all the internal systems and processes that your company's management has developed to help run the company. The term comes from the banking industry, where the literal "back office" employees handled everyone's accounts, processed paperwork, and so forth. Today, the term generically refers to the "behind-the-scenes" processes that run a company. Your company may refer to it as the "back end," the "operations division," or by another term. Although back office requirements never directly involve customers, they are necessary for the survival of your company and something your e-commerce site is going to have to deal with. Examples of back office tasks include management reports, accounting, warehousing, payroll, and commissions.

Another way to look at back office requirements is to think about the terms *data* and *information*. Your e-commerce site will generate plenty of *data* — customer orders, credit card authorizations, and so forth. Although this data is useful for the day-to-day operation of the site, it isn't very useful for helping the company develop long-term plans and strategies. You need to turn this data into *information* that your company's management team can use to plan the company's "big picture." For example, knowing that the average order size is $30.00, and that almost every customer places a second order within two weeks, is very important to your company's overall success.

Very few e-commerce sites plan to meet the needs of these requirements up front. Developers often find themselves scrambling to develop the necessary reports and functionality after the site goes live. Obviously, this is a bad time to start. Your functional specification should include detailed information about the type of information and processes needed by the e-commerce site for support and integration. The purpose of this chapter is to help you figure out exactly how to deliver those features.

You must first figure out where your data is coming from, and what information is required. From there, you'll be able to determine the best tools to create that information and deliver it to the people in your company who need it.

Where Will All the Data Come From?

Where your data comes from depends on the type of e-commerce site that you're running. Table 19-1 shows some different types of e-commerce sites, and lists the various types of data that each site can be expected to collect. I compare a retail site that sells tangible goods and a services site that sells intangibles. I also compare a hybrid of the two — a subscription site that sells recurring deliveries of tangible goods or intangible services.

Table 19-1
Types of Data Collected by E-Commerce Sites

Retail	Services	Subscriptions
Customer information — name, address, etc.	Customer information — name, address, etc.	Customer information — name, address, etc.
Order headers — date ordered, total amount, etc.	Order headers — date ordered, total amount, etc.	Subscriptions — start date, initial length, etc.
Ordered items — quantity, price each, SKU, etc.	Ordered services — price, description, etc.	Renewals — number of consecutive renewals, renewal price, etc.
Discounts — coupon amounts, total discount amount, source of the discount, etc.	Discounts — coupon amounts, total discount amount, source of the discount, etc.	Discounts — coupon amounts, total discount amount, source of the discount, etc.
Path to checkout — products browsed, areas of the site visited, etc.	Path to checkout — products browsed, areas of the site visited, etc.	Path to checkout — products browsed, areas of the site visited, etc.
Referral — where customer came from to get to site	Referral — where customer came from to get to site	Referral — where customer came from to get to site

All of the items in the table are data elements that an e-commerce site can collect. Obviously, the site has to be built in order to gather this data and put it into your SQL Server. Retrieving some of this data, such as order information, is fairly straightforward. Commerce Server collects that for you as part of its standard checkout process. Other pieces of data don't come for free, however. Tracking a customer's movement through your site, and tracking which clicks result in products being placed into the shopping cart, for example, requires some of your own development.

You can find information about building site-tracking tools in Chapter 10.

Think of all the wonderful information that you can produce with this data! With just the data in the above table, you can generate the following information:

✦ Which banner ads are leading to products being placed into shopping carts?

✦ Which of your partner sites are referring the most customers?

✦ Which of your partner sites are referring the most *new* customers?

✦ How much do customers spend per order, on average?

✦ How often do customers place a second, third, or subsequent order?

✦ How closely are discounts tied to getting customers to buy things?

✦ Which products or services are the most popular?

✦ Which products and services are typically bought in multiple quantities?

✦ How much money can you expect to collect in orders in a month?

You can see how this type of information is useful to managers in your marketing department, purchasing group, accountants, and so on.

Your functional specification should also include detailed lists of the types of reports and information that the rest of your company needs to see. Determine exactly which pieces of data are going to be needed to produce that information, and where that data is going to come from. For example, suppose that your Marketing department has told you that it's absolutely critical that they be able to tell how many customers came from such-and-such a place. What if you can't see anyplace in your SQL Server where that data would come from? In a case like this, you need to go back over your functional specification and add a feature to your site to collect that data.

Implementing a Reporting Infrastructure

At this point, your task is to start deciding exactly how you're going to turn your site's data into the required information. In this section, I talk about the various technologies and tools available, and how to leverage each one for the best result.

Chapter 5 includes a detailed discussion of how to determine your company's back office requirements.

In Chapter 5, I talk about the need to implement a reporting infrastructure. You don't want to try to build your reports off of the same database server that your site uses. Unless you're going to be pulling all of your data into an existing back-end system, you need to create a reporting infrastructure.

Exactly how you produce your back office reports depends largely on the type of reporting infrastructure that you develop. Again, Chapter 5 explores your options for building the reporting system. To quickly review the two major options:

✦ You can set up a separate SQL Server to use for reporting. It can either have a recent copy of the live database, or it can have a database designed specifically for reporting.

✦ You can use the "spare" node of a database cluster as a reporting server. It can either have a recent copy of the live database, or it can have a database designed specifically for reporting.

The method that you choose is a matter of what you can afford. Having a dedicated server for reporting is certainly nice, but it definitely carries a higher cost. If you don't have a database cluster, however, then you don't have a "spare" node to use for reporting purposes. Your situation and budget will drive this decision. No matter what your situation, though, you should never try to run your reports from the server that supports your live e-commerce site. The additional overhead of running complex reports will reduce the server's ability to support your income-producing Web site.

Tip   Try to avoid running reports from your live database server "just for now," with the plan of getting a dedicated reporting server later. "Just for now" situations have a way of becoming permanent, and your site performance will eventually suffer from the additional reporting overhead.

If you are able to use a dedicated server for reporting, then you need to decide where you're going to physically place it. Consider the following:

✦ If you are going to be hosting your e-commerce site in your own facility, then place the reporting server on a LAN connection with the live site's database server.

✦ If your site is going to be hosted at someone else's facility, place the database server at that site — this will facilitate pulling the necessary data from the live site's database server. Your actual reporting may be slow, depending on the bandwidth between your location and the hosting facility.

✦ The worst option is to have your site hosted by someone else, and your reporting server placed at your location. To make a situation like this reliable, you must work around several obstacles. I discuss those obstacles and what you need to do, but try to avoid this option if you can.

The primary differences between these three options are the amount of network bandwidth between the reporting server and the live database server, and the amount of bandwidth between the reporting server and you. The amount of network bandwidth you purchase is largely going to be decided by your budget and specific situation, but keep in mind that your company *needs* the information that the reporting server will generate. It may be worth your while to spend a little extra money to have the reporting server located where it will do the most good.

The final decision that you need to make is whether or not your reporting server will contain an exact copy of the live database or a specially-designed reporting database that gets updated with data from the live database. Again, I discuss the pros and cons of these approaches in Chapter 5.

After you decide what basic type of reporting infrastructure you're going to implement, you can start working on actually building it. In the next section, I talk about how to build an infrastructure that uses a standalone reporting server, and then I show you how to build an infrastructure by using the "spare" node of a database cluster.

Standalone reporting server

SQL Server 2000 provides four primary tools for creating a reporting infrastructure based on a standalone reporting server. All of these tools are much easier to use when the reporting server has a LAN connection to the live database server. However, I will also show you how some of them can be made to work over a WAN connection.

Log shipping

Log shipping is an important new feature of SQL Server 2000. Originally designed to facilitate maintaining a "hot spare" server, log shipping is useful for keeping a reporting server updated with a copy of the live database.

Log shipping is useful only when you want the reporting server to maintain an exact replica of the live database. It works by packaging the transaction log on the live database server, and copying that log to the reporting server. The reporting server then executes the transactions in the log, thus bringing its copy of the database up to date.

Note　Log shipping is only available when both servers are running SQL Server 2000 Enterprise Edition.

Before you begin configuring log shipping, you need to complete a few preliminary steps:

1. On the live database server, share the folder containing the live database's transaction log (kept by SQL Server).

2. Make sure that both the live database server and the reporting server are registered in Enterprise Manager and that you can connect from one to the other.

3. Make sure that the reporting server doesn't already contain a copy of the live database—the database will be set up when log shipping is configured.

After you complete these preliminary steps, launch the Database Maintenance Plan Wizard on the live database server. You use this wizard to configure log shipping as follows:

1. In the Select Databases screen of the wizard, select the These databases check box, and then select the live database. Don't select any additional databases; you can only configure log shipping on one database at a time.

2. Select the Ship the transaction logs to other SQL Servers (Log Shipping) check box.

3. Continue through the wizard, specifying the rest of the database maintenance options, until you get to the Specify the Log Shipping Destinations screen.

4. Click Add to add a destination database.

5. In the Add Destination Database screen, select the name of the reporting server.

6. Select the Create New Database check box. You need to specify the file directories for the data and log on the new database.

7. In the Initialize the Destination Databases screen, click Take full database backup now.

8. In the Log Shipping Schedules screen, click Change to modify the log shipping schedule.

9. In the Copy/Load Frequency box, indicate how often, in minutes, that you want the reporting server to back up and restore the transaction logs from the live database server. This allows you to determine how "out of date" the data on the reporting server is. You may want this to occur several times a day, or you may be comfortable with the data being updated less frequently.

Note

Keep in mind that more frequent updates will mean smaller updates, and that very little overhead is placed on the live database server. Less frequent updates will mean larger updates that take longer to copy to the reporting server. If your reporting server is connecting to the live database server over a WAN connection, I recommend that you set this option for fairly frequent updates, such as every 60 minutes.

10. In the Log Shipping Thresholds screen, set the Backup Alert Threshold.

This is the maximum elapsed time since the last transaction log backup was made on the live database server. After the time exceeds this threshold, an alert is generated. You can use this alert to let you know when log shipping isn't working for some reason.

11. Similarly, in the `Out of Sync Alert` box, specify how much time may pass between the last transaction log backup on the live database server and the last transaction log restore on the reporting server. After the time exceeds this threshold, an alert is generated.

12. In the `Specify the Log Shipping Monitor Information` screen, type the name of the server that will monitor log shipping. I usually configure the reporting server to handle this task. If you have a third SQL Server, use it to monitor the log shipping events. Click either `Use Windows Authentication` or `Use SQL Server Authentication` to connect to the monitor server. The `log_shipping_monitor_probe` login name must be used to connect to the monitor server. If this is a new account, choose a new password. If the account already exists on the monitor server, you must specify the existing password.

Log shipping will now be configured between the two servers, and the reporting server will have a copy of the live database. Log shipping is fairly reliable and will generally work without any extra attention from you. You must still regularly review the logs of both servers, and check the monitoring server, to make sure that everything is working properly.

If your reporting server and database server have to talk to each other through a firewall, you need to ensure that the reporting server can access both the SQL Server services and the file shares on the live database server, and vice-versa. If your reporting server is at your location, and the live database server is at a remote location, consider using Windows 2000 Routing and Remote Access (RRAS) to create a Virtual Private Network (VPN) connection between the two servers. This will guarantee that all the necessary communications can pass between the two servers, and will encrypt the communications to prevent outsiders from "listening in" to your company's data. See the sidebar on WAN communications for more information.

Replication

Replication is the most common method of keeping two databases synchronized, and is perhaps the most reliable method to use if your database servers are connected only by a WAN link. Like log shipping, replication is designed to create exact duplicates of a database on other servers.

SQL Server 2000 supports several types of replication, each designed for slightly different circumstances.

✦ *Merge replication* is designed to take data from two or more servers and "merge" it into a single database. Merge replication can be configured with rules to help the servers determine which piece of data "wins" a conflict. For example, you might configure merge replication to always favor changes made by your main office over changes made by a branch office. Merge replication isn't really suitable for your needs, because the data will only be changing in one place — on your production server.

✦ *Transactional replication* is better suited to your needs, because it works somewhat like log shipping in that transactions, rather than raw data, are copied from server to server. The destination server then "replays" these transactions to update its copy of the database. The destination server has to start out with an exact copy of the live database before transactional replication can begin. Transactional replication does place some additional overhead on both servers, but it is perhaps the most reliable form of replication when the two servers share a small-bandwidth network connection, such as a WAN link. A significant benefit of transactional replication is that the destination database, your reporting server, can be almost continually updated with live data, so it's never very far "out of date."

✦ *Snapshot replication* is less suitable for your needs because it basically copies the entire database from one server to another. This type of replication is reasonably fast, but because it must literally take a "snapshot" of the live database, it has to lock the entire database to prevent changes from occurring while the snapshot is being made. This means that no customer orders or other additions to the database can occur while the snapshot is being run. This may be suitable in your environment if your site isn't used 24 hours a day. If so, snapshot replication is certainly the easiest to configure and generally presents the least administrative hassles. Snapshot replication is always more "out of date" than transactional replication, because you usually only run a couple of snapshots a day. SQL Server 2000 does have the capability to compress a snapshot file into a CAB file, which requires significantly less time to transmit than an uncompressed snapshot. If your servers will be connected by a low-bandwidth link, this option may make snapshot replication attractive.

As with log shipping, you need to make sure that both SQL Servers are able to communicate with each other. If they're connected by a WAN link, make sure that any firewalls or proxy servers between them are capable of passing communications on the correct ports. In general, replication only needs to use the port assigned to the SQL Server for general client communications (port 1433 by default).

When you begin to configure replication, identify which severs fill each of three roles: the *Subscriber,* the *Distributor,* and the *Publisher.*

✦ The Subscriber is your reporting server, which will be receiving the replicated data.

✦ The Publisher is the live database server, which will be sending the replicated data.

✦ The Distributor is the server that will be doing the actual work of moving the data from the Publisher to the Subscriber.

I generally recommend that you make the live database server the Distributor as well. You need to make sure that the live database server has enough hard drive space to essentially keep another copy of the database, because the Distributor function will need this space to perform its job.

WAN Communications

When two SQL Servers—or any two servers, for that matter—need to communicate over a WAN link, you need to address several concerns.

If the WAN link is *private*, meaning that it directly connects two facilities owned by your company, then the obstacles will usually be few. In fact, the bandwidth of the WAN link is usually the only concern. You just need to take into account the amount of traffic that the link can handle, the amount of traffic that it's already handling, and the amount of traffic that you intend to add to it with your inter-server communications.

If the WAN link is connected to the public Internet, on the other hand, the obstacles to communication can be many. In addition to bandwidth concerns, your biggest problems are likely to be firewalls and proxy servers.

The best way to mitigate the risk of a firewall or proxy server disrupting communications is to do some testing. Acquire a network monitoring tool (or "sniffer") like Microsoft's Network Monitor (which is included with Windows 2000 Server). Run the tool while you perform all of the inter-server communications that will normally occur in production. Examine the tool's trace file to determine what ports and protocols the two servers are using to communicate with each other.

You can then use this information to configure a firewall or proxy server to allow the necessary communication ports and protocols to flow uninterrupted between the two servers.

The most common port for SQL Servers is the servers' configured client communications port. By default, this is port 1433 for the first instance of SQL Server 2000 running on a given server. You can reconfigure this port by using SQL Server 2000's Server Network Utility, if necessary. Other ports may need to be opened to allow Enterprise Manager to function (which communicates on SQL Server's administrative port), or to allow features like file sharing to function properly.

Another solution for servers that are connecting across the Internet is to create a Virtual Private Network (VPN). Windows 2000's Routing and Remote Access Services (RRAS) supports two types of VPN technologies—Point-to-Point Tunneling Protocol (PPTP) and Layer 2 Tunneling Protocol (L2TP). Your firewall or proxy server may support these or other VPN technologies. By establishing a VPN between the two SQL Servers, or at least between the firewalls protecting those servers, you guarantee a clear line of communication between them. VPN technologies also encrypt the network traffic that passes through the tunnel, so your company's data will be protected from Internet eavesdroppers.

To configure replication, make sure that you have both servers registered in the other's Enterprise Manager. You need to configure replication from the Publisher—in this case, the live database server.

1. Run the Create and Manage Publications Wizard on the live database server.
2. Select the live database and click the `Create Publication...` button. The Create Publication Wizard starts.

3. On the `Select Distributor` page, choose the first option to make the live database server the Distributor.

4. If the `Configure SQL Server Agent` page appears, select the option to start SQL Server Agent automatically. This page won't appear if SQL Server Agent is already configured to start automatically.

5. On the `Specify Snapshot Folder` page, specify the folder that will be used to contain snapshot files. Even transactional replication requires an initial snapshot to get things started. In most situations, you can accept the default folder.

6. On the `Choose Publication Database` page, select the live database.

7. On the `Select Publication Type` page, select the type of replication that you want to use. I recommend that you *not* use merge replication for a situation like this; select either transactional or snapshot replication.

8. On the `Specify Subscriber Types` page, indicate that only SQL Server 2000 servers will subscribe to this publication.

9. *Articles* are individual tables that are replicated from the published database. Generally, you will want to replicate all of the tables in your live database, so select all of the tables as articles. You shouldn't need to select any stored procedures or views.

10. The next page alerts you to any `Article Issues`. The main issue that you may run across is the identity columns of the database. If you need the identity columns to replicate their values to the reporting server — and you usually will — then you need to manually create the subscription tables and specify the "not for replication" option on the identity columns. This allows the Publisher to replicate the same primary key values to the Subscriber.

11. Click `Next` a couple of times to finish the wizard and your publication is created. Now you need to configure your reporting server as a Subscriber of the publication.

12. In the `Create and Manage Publications` dialog box, select the publication that you just created and click the `Push New Subscription...` button to launch the `Create Push Subscription Wizard`.

13. On the `Choose Subscribers` page, select the reporting server.

14. On the `Choose Destination Database` page, type the name of the database on the reporting server that will receive the replicated data. You can use the `Browse or Create...` button to select the database from a list, or to create a new database.

15. On the `Distribution Agent Schedule` page, you can specify when the subscription should be updated. You can also specify that it be continually updated for transactional replication.

16. The `Initialize Subscription` page gives you the option of initializing the database schema and other information necessary for the subscription to run. You should always let SQL Server perform this task when setting up a new subscription.

17. Click `Next` a couple of times to finish the wizard and your subscription is initialized and made active.

A new icon, `Replication Monitor`, is added to the Enterprise Manager on the live database server. You can use these new functions to monitor the status of your replication publication. Don't forget to regularly review the normal SQL Server and Windows 2000 logs to check for any other errors or issues that may arise.

Backup and Restore

Probably the most obvious method for getting a copy of your live database onto a reporting server is to back it up on the live database, and restore it to the reporting server. This method offers the advantage of being straightforward and easy to implement. Unfortunately, it also offers some significant disadvantages:

✦ Even though you can back up the live database while it is up and running, you can't restore the database to the reporting server without taking the database offline. If you can schedule a regular period of down time for the reporting server, this restriction won't present a problem. If your reporting server needs to be available at all times, however, you need to consider another method of bringing data over.

✦ If your servers are connected by a high-speed network, such as a LAN, then this method is probably the fastest and easiest to set up. If, on the other hand, your servers are connected by a WAN link, then this method is going to involve a lot of manual work every time you need to bring the data over.

✦ If your live database is especially large, then your backups are going to be quite large, too. More importantly, if your live database's transaction log gets to be large, then your backups may be so large that restoring them to the backup server will take too long.

As I discuss in the next section, the backup and restore method is ideal when your reporting server is the "spare" node of a cluster. This method is almost as ideal when both the live database server and the reporting server are connected to the same LAN. In any other circumstance, you should consider another option for replicating the live data to the reporting server.

The backup and restore method, like the previous methods I've explained, is good for restoring the entire live database to the reporting server. It is not suitable, however, for moving data into a specially designed reporting database.

Implementing this method is straightforward. Create a SQL Server Agent job on the live database server to back up the live database to a file on disk on a regular schedule. Run the job a couple of times to determine how long it takes to complete the backup operation. Then, create a job on the reporting server that is scheduled to run sometime after the live server's backup job completes. This job should drop the existing reporting database, and then restore the database from the backup file on the live server.

The live server's job needs to contain a single Transact-SQL step, with the following statement:

```
BACKUP DATABASE DatabaseName TO DISK =
'c:\backupfiles\backup.bak'
```

Change the database name and output location to suit your environment. The reporting server's job needs to have two Transact-SQL steps.

1. Drop the existing database:

```
DROP DATABASE 'DatabaseName'
```

Note that this step will fail if any processes or users have the reporting database open at the time. You should configure the job to alert you via e-mail whenever it fails, so you can manually kill any processes by using Enterprise Manager and drop the database.

2. Restore the database:

```
RESTORE DATABASE DatabaseName FROM DISK =
'\\LiveServer\backups\backup.bak'
```

Note that the database files will be restored to the same folder on the reporting server that they were in on the live server. Make sure that this path is valid. If it's not, you can add the WITH MOVE clause to the RESTORE command to move the files to the location that you specify.

Scheduling jobs like this to run late at night or very early in the morning will generally avoid the possibility of a user attempting to access the database while it is being dropped or restored.

If your servers are connected by a WAN link, then this task becomes more difficult. You still need to create a pair of jobs. The first job runs on the live server to back up the database to a file. The second job runs on the reporting server and drops its existing reporting database, and then restores that database from the live server's backup file. The trick is getting the live server's backup file from the live server to the reporting server.

Copying the backup file over the WAN link is almost always going to be out of the question. You're going to have to write the job on the live server to use a utility like PKZIP to compress the backup file, and then either copy the ZIP file to the reporting server or use a scripted FTP session to send it over. The reporting server must then unzip the file before trying to restore it. The additional complexity and potential points of failure makes this task both unreliable and undesirable for regular use.

Comparing the methods

All three of the methods that I've discussed attempt to achieve the same goal: Creating an exact replica of the live database on a reporting server. Which method you choose depends heavily on your circumstances. Table 19-2 compares the primary differences between these three methods.

Table 19-2
Methods of Replicating Data to a Reporting Server

Feature	Log Shipping	Replication	Backup/Restore
Product requirements	Only on Enterprise Edition	No restrictions	No restrictions
Connectivity requirements	Works best on a LAN, tolerable across a WAN especially if a VPN is used	Works best on a LAN, works well across a WAN	Works best on a LAN, very poorly across a WAN
Up-to-date data on reporting server	Reasonably up-to-date; depends on how often you have the logs applied to the reporting server	Can be very up-to-date with transactional; snapshot is usually much more likely to be out of date	Depends on how often you do the backup/restore cycle — typically no more than once or twice a day
Overhead on live server	Very little	Transactional is somewhat higher than log shipping; snapshot is much higher	Fairly low overhead — between log shipping and transactional replication
Managing	Has to be monitored for problems	Has to be monitored for problems	Problems are rare
Troubleshooting	Fairly straightforward to troubleshoot; process is easy to understand and logs give good information	Can be very complex to troubleshoot, especially if connectivity issues arise	Very easy to troubleshoot

Data Transformation Services

The last major method for copying data from the live database into a reporting database is SQL Server's Data Transformation Services, or DTS. Although DTS can easily be used to copy the entire database from one server to another, it is probably the least efficient method for doing so, particularly with regard to the required server overhead and network bandwidth.

DTS shines in its ability to copy data from the live server, transform and rearrange it, and put it into the reporting server. In Chapter 5, I talk about the need to recognize when some reports would run better if they ran against a deliberately denormalized database, rather than against a well-normalized production database. DTS is the tool that you need to copy normalized production data into a denormalized reporting database. In fact, data warehouses and data marts, the primary tools for heavy-duty reporting, are built from heavily denormalized databases, and are often populated from production databases by using DTS.

The simplest interface to DTS is the Import/Export Wizard in SQL Server's Enterprise Manager. DTS' more powerful interface, and the one that I show you how to use, is the DTS Designer. The Designer lets you build packages that pull data from multiple sources, rearrange and transform it, and put it into multiple destination databases. DTS Designer lets you create these packages by using an intuitive graphical interface from within Enterprise Manager.

Suppose that your live database uses a database structure similar to the one shown in Figure 19-1 (which is actually a simplified version of Commerce Server's default database schema).

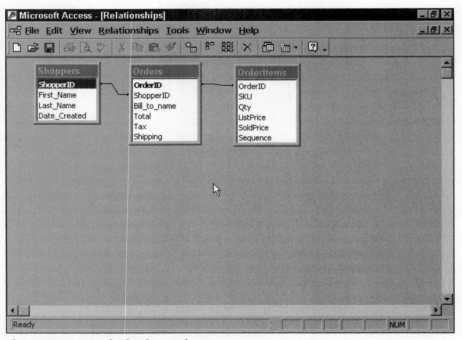

Figure 19-1: Sample database schema

If your management team needs a report showing the name of every customer who purchased a particular product and the total amount that they spent on that order, the database has to join three tables. If several million people purchased the product, the server would need quite some time to produce the necessary information.

Copying all of this information into a single table makes the process much faster. Rather than joining three tables and then filtering for the appropriate rows, the server can simply filter for the desired rows in a single table.

The destination table includes all of the columns from the three original tables. If a customer placed an order for two items, then two rows are copied into the new table, with duplicated information in the columns that came from the Shoppers and Orders tables.

This is a fairly basic example of why you may want to use this technique, and you should be aware that you'll only notice the benefit gained from this technique if you are joining several tables and querying hundreds of thousands — or even millions — of rows from the server. Larger e-commerce sites need to make regular use of this technique, and may benefit from the more complex and far-reaching goals of a dedicated data-warehousing infrastructure.

In any event, DTS is the enabling technology behind this technique. A comprehensive tutorial on DTS is beyond the scope of this book, but I certainly want to take a few pages to introduce you to the DTS Designer and its most important features.

You can launch the DTS Designer by right-clicking `Data Transformation Services` in Enterprise Manager and selecting the `New Package` option from the context menu that pops up. You will start with a completely blank DTS workspace that includes a variety of icons on the left-hand side, as shown in Figure 19-2.

The icons on the left are divided into two categories. The top icons represent the various types of data connections that DTS is capable of making. Icons are available for SQL Server, Oracle, Access databases, Excel spreadsheets, and so on. The bottom icons represent the tasks that DTS is capable of performing. These include data transformations, VBScript or Jscript code, Transact-SQL code, FTP commands, Microsoft Message Queue (MSMQ) tasks, and so on. You can build DTS packages by dragging connection icons to the workspace, and then configuring them to connect to specific data sources. You then connect the data sources with various tasks. The Designer helps you to visualize the data "flowing" from one data connection, through one or more tasks, into another data connection. Next, I show you how to create a simple package to demonstrate what DTS can do.

1. In Enterprise Manager, open the DTS Designer to create a new package.

2. Locate the connection icon for a SQL Server and drag it onto the workspace. The connection's configuration dialog box displays.

3. Give the connection a meaningful name, such as "Source," and configure it to connect to the local SQL Server. Because you're just experimenting, configure it to connect to the sample Northwind database.

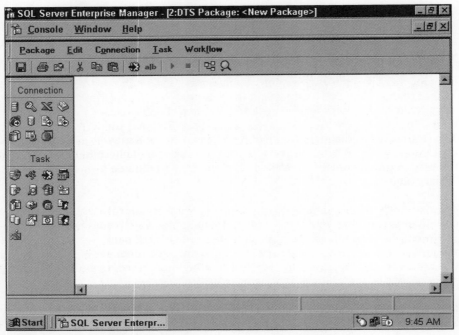

Figure 19-2: The DTS Designer

4. Drag a second SQL Server icon onto the workspace. Name it "Destination" and configure it to connect to a new database on the same server. Name the new database "Reporting" and accept the defaults for the remaining options.

5. Drag the Transform Data icon onto the workspace. Your cursor directs you to click the data source and destination connections; select the Source icon and the Destination icon. An arrow appears, connecting the two SQL Server icons.

6. Double-click the arrow to display the properties of the transformation task. Click the SQLQuery radio button and enter the following SQL query into the box:

```
SELECT Orders.OrderDate, [Order Details].ProductID, [Order
Details].Quantity, Customers.Region
FROM Customers
INNER JOIN Orders
ON Customers.CustomerID = Orders.CustomerID
INNER JOIN [Order Details]
ON Orders.OrderID = [Order Details].OrderID
```

7. Click the Destination tab. You are prompted to create a new table to hold the query results. Name the table "OrderReport."

8. Click the `Transformations` tab to display the default transformation actions. By default, DTS copies every column in your query to a column of the same name in the destination table. You can instruct DTS to copy information to different columns. You can also click the `New...` button to create a new type of transformation, which can be a VBScript or Jscript script, or one of several data-manipulation functions.

9. Click OK to finish editing the transformation task.

10. Click the Execute Package icon on the DTS Designer toolbar to run the package. After it completes, exit the DTS Designer (you may want to save the package first, in case you want to play with it later) and check out the OrderReport table that was created. DTS denormalized the columns from three tables into a single table.

If you find that your live database schema isn't suitable for the types of reports that you need to generate, then DTS is probably the best way to copy your live data into a reporting database schema that suits your needs. DTS packages can be saved for future use, and you can use SQL Server Agent to have them automatically run on a regular schedule. To schedule a DTS package for regular execution, right-click the package and select `Schedule...` from the pop-up menu.

DTS packages can also be easily exchanged between servers. When you save a package in the DTS Designer, you have the option to save it to the local server, to save it to the Repository (which makes it available to all of the servers sharing that Repository), or to save it to a COM-structured file. This file can then be taken to another server on floppy disk, copied to a file share, or even sent via e-mail.

DTS was first introduced in SQL Server 7.0, but SQL Server 2000 made some significant enhancements, such as adding new task capabilities. With SQL Server 2000, the following major tasks are available:

✦ **ActiveX script:** This task allows you to write a complete programming script in any installed ActiveX scripting language. By default, SQL Server 2000 allows you to write scripts in either VBScript or Jscript. Other ActiveX scripting languages are available from third parties, including PerlScript.

✦ **Transform data:** This task is the heart and soul of DTS, and allows you to move data from one connection to another while transforming it. Your transformations can be as simple as mapping columns from the source to columns in the destination, or as complex as writing an ActiveX script to examine the data and make decisions about what data is passed to the destination connection. The transformation task also has several built-in transformations for performing string manipulation and data conversion.

✦ **Execute process:** This task lets you execute operating system commands from within your DTS package.

✦ **Execute SQL:** This task allows your package to execute any Transact-SQL statements that you may need.

✦ **Send mail:** This task gives your packages the ability to send an e-mail by using SQL Server's built-in SQL Mail services. Because DTS packages can be built with success/failure logic and branching, you can use the Send mail task to send an e-mail whenever a particular DTS task fails. This task is new in SQL Server 2000.

✦ **Bulk insert:** This task allows your DTS packages to perform bulk insert operations. The database that you are inserting into must be configured to allow bulk inserts. Keep in mind that bulk insert operations are not logged to the transaction log, so if a failure occurs, SQL Server will be unable to recover the operation. Make sure to back up your database after performing any bulk insert operations. Using the Execute SQL task, you can even have the DTS package perform a backup immediately following the bulk insert.

✦ **Execute package:** This task gives you the ability to create modular DTS packages that perform important, discrete functions, and then reuse those modules from other packages. For example, you may have four trading partners from which you receive inventory information. All of those partners provide you with flat files that are formatted somewhat differently. You can create a single DTS package that imported those flat files into a temporary SQL Server table. That import module can then be executed from the four DTS packages designed to handle each partner's file. This approach, like modular programming in general, saves a lot of time when you're creating complex packages. This task was introduced in SQL Server 2000.

✦ **File Transfer Protocol:** This task gives your DTS package the ability to send and receive files using the FTP protocol. As discussed in Chapter 18, this can make DTS an excellent "poor man's" substitute for a more complex data exchange product like BizTalk Server. Your DTS packages can FTP data from partners, and then transform that data into your own database or vice versa. This task is new in SQL Server 2000.

✦ **Message queue:** This task allows your package to interact with Microsoft Message Queue (MSMQ) services, placing messages on the queues for other applications. This task is new in SQL Server 2000.

✦ **Transfer tasks:** SQL Server 2000 provides several tasks that allow your packages to transfer error messages, logins, jobs, stored procedures, and other SQL objects between servers. These tasks may not seem significant in terms of transforming and translating data, but they can be incredibly useful in creating a development/staging/production environment for your SQL Servers. You can create new objects (stored procedures, logins, and SQL Server Agent jobs) on a development server, and use DTS to automatically deploy those objects to a staging SQL Server, and then to your live SQL Server. Many of these tasks are new in SQL Server 2000.

DTS packages can be programmed with logical "success/failure" branching. If a particular task fails or encounters an excessive number of errors, you can program the package to take corrective or notification actions using a "fail" branch, or to proceed with the next task through a "success" branch.

Finally, DTS supports multi-threaded operations. A single DTS package can have several *starting points*, which are defined as any connection object that doesn't have any incoming tasks. DTS will execute up to four separate "paths" in a package at the same time.

Cross-Reference   Appendix B presents a detailed description of the DTS connections and tasks, along with details about how to use each.

Clustering

If you've decided to deploy a database cluster as the back-end of your e-commerce site, one of the cluster's nodes can be used as a reporting server. Windows 2000 Advanced Server and SQL Server 2000 Enterprise Edition are required to take advantage of clustering, and they support the type of "active-active" clustering that you need, where both nodes are capable of performing independent work *and* covering for the other node should it go down.

A major advantage of using the "spare" node as a reporting server is that, in addition to providing better utilization of expensive server hardware, the server is well-connected to the live database server, making it easy for you to use the most easy-to-configure data replication strategy — backup and restore.

An important disadvantage of using the "spare" node for this purpose is that, should the primary node in the cluster fail, the "spare" node will wind up with the full burden of the live database, and may not have sufficient power to act as a reporting server. In a case like this, your company may be willing to live without timely reports until the primary node can be fixed and the load of the live database transferred back to it. Also, in the configuration that I discuss next, the reporting database will only be installed on the second node, so if that node fails, your company will have no reporting capabilities until it is repaired.

To configure the second node as a reporting server, you should first make sure that the two cluster nodes have fairly similar hardware. Identical hardware is not a requirement of Microsoft's clustering technology, but it's highly desirable in this situation. The second node should also have sufficient local hard drive space to install a second copy of SQL Server 2000 and to hold the reporting database. Remember that the live database is not stored on the local hard drive of either node, but on the external drive array that the two nodes are connected to.

1. Make sure that SQL Server 2000 is running on the first node of the cluster. Use Cluster Administrator to designate that node as the "preferred" owner for the resource group containing the SQL Server 2000 resources. I refer to this server as the *primary node*.

2. Make sure that you can successfully fail SQL Server 2000 over to the second node, which I refer to as the *secondary node*. Make sure that you can then fail back to the primary node.

3. With SQL Server 2000 running on the primary node (meaning that the primary node *owns the cluster*), begin running SQL Server 2000 Setup on the secondary node.

4. When prompted, have Setup create a second instance of SQL Server 2000. Name the instance something useful, such as "Reporting." When you access this second instance, you will do so by referring to it as "Server\Instance." For example, if the secondary server is named "SQL2," and you create an instance named "Reporting," you need to address the new SQL Server installation as "SQL2\Reporting."

5. After Setup completes, you should be able to begin using the new instance on the secondary node.

Every Windows 2000 server has a server name. For example, two servers participating in a cluster may be named "SQL1" and "SQL2." A Windows 2000 cluster has a name all its own, such as "WINCLUSTER." This is called a *virtual server name*, and the cluster node that "owns" the cluster will respond to this virtual server name as if it were its own server name. So, in your theoretical cluster, if SQL1 owned the cluster, it would respond to both names: SQL1 and WINCLUSTER.

When SQL Server 2000 Enterprise Edition is installed on a cluster, it installs its program files on both servers, and stores data files on the drive array that they share. It also creates its own virtual server name—SQLCLUSTER, for example. Like the cluster's virtual server name, the node that owns the cluster will respond to the SQL Server virtual server name. When configuring your Web servers to access the SQL Server, you configure them to access the virtual server name, SQLCLUSTER. This way, no matter which node owns the cluster, your Web servers will get a response.

After you've installed a second instance of SQL Server 2000 on your secondary node, SQL2, that server has the potential to run two instances of SQL Server at the same time.

 New Feature   The ability to run multiple instances of SQL Server is a new feature in SQL Server 2000.

If the primary node, SQL1, suffered a hardware failure, then your Web servers will continue to access the live database by connecting to SQLCLUSTER, but the server named SQL2 will actually be handling those requests. You can continue to connect to SQL2\Reporting to access the *other* instance of SQL Server, which runs the reporting database. Whether SQL2's server hardware performs well under those conditions depends on how powerful the hardware is and what kind of load is being placed upon it by the two instances of SQL Server.

After SQL1 had been repaired, you can fail the cluster back to it. SQL1 will then begin handling requests for SQLCLUSTER, and SQL2 will only handle requests sent to SQL2\Reporting.

If reporting is absolutely essential to your company on a day-to-day basis, and you have some extra money to spend, you can configure the cluster to support a full "active-active" configuration. In this configuration, *either* cluster node can run the live database, the reporting database, or if one node fails, both databases. Make sure that both nodes are running sufficiently powerful hardware to support the load of two databases. You also need to configure the cluster with two external drive arrays instead of one.

Consider the configuration diagram in Figure 19-3. Both cluster nodes are connected to both external drive arrays. In normal operation with both nodes up, each node owns one of the two arrays. SQL Server 2000 Setup is run on both nodes for a clustered installation. Each time, Setup creates a new SQL Server virtual server name — for example, LIVE and REPORTS. Both nodes run a single instance of SQL Server 2000. One node (Node A) responds to the LIVE virtual server name, and the other node (Node B) responds to the REPORTS virtual server name. The LIVE server stores its data on Array 1, for example, and the REPORTS server stores its data on Array 2.

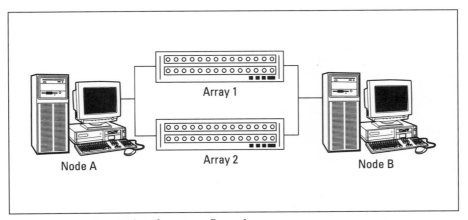

Figure 19-3: Active-Active cluster configuration

If Node A fails, Node B seizes control of both external drive arrays. It also starts a second instance of SQL Server 2000, and begins directing requests to LIVE to that second instance. Node B continues to direct requests for REPORTS to its original instance of SQL Server 2000. When Node A returns to active duty, one of the two SQL Server virtual server names is transferred to it, along with "ownership" of the associated external drive array.

In this configuration, one entire server can suffer a major hardware failure, and both "SQL Servers" continue running on the remaining node, providing live database support and reporting database support to the Web farm and your internal employees. This type of active-active clustering makes the most efficient possible use of the expensive hardware used in a database cluster.

Creating Reports

Now that you know where your report data is coming from, start thinking about how you're going to create the actual reports. Your functional specification should clearly list all of the different reports that you need to create to start with, although you should expect to need additional reports as your e-commerce site grows and matures.

In Chapter 5, I show you some examples of the common reports that your company is probably going to need to start with, and you no doubt came up with even more requirements as you developed your functional specification. As I mention in Chapter 5, you also need to know how those reports are going to be used, how they need to be delivered, and how often they need to be delivered.

For each report that you need to create, answer the following questions. These will help you narrow down the easiest way to create and deliver those reports.

✦ Will the report have to be automatically delivered to a group of individuals by e-mail, or will the people who need the report be creating it on demand?

✦ How often will the report have to be updated? Can you schedule this report to run in the evenings, or is it something that will need to be generated on-demand throughout the day?

✦ How "pretty" does the report need to be? Does it need to be well-formatted and nicely laid out for presentation at a board meeting, or can it be rough-and-ready as long as it contains the necessary information?

✦ How complex is the report? Can the report's data be generated with a simple (or even complex) SQL query, or will you have to write a program or script of some kind to analyze the data first?

✦ How much time do you have to develop the report?

In a Microsoft e-commerce shop, you have four basic options available to you for generating reports:

✦ **Data Transformation Services** can be used to execute queries and return the results via e-mail. DTS can also be used as a preliminary step in more complex reports to create denormalized reporting tables, perform data translation, etc.

✦ **Active Server Pages** can be used to write Web-based reports.

✦ **SQL Server Agent** can be used to execute queries on a schedule and send the results via e-mail.

✦ **Non-Microsoft reporting tools,** such as the all-time champion of reporting tools — Crystal Reports, give you a wide variety of options for creating reports to be delivered via e-mail, Web pages, and more.

The tools that you use may vary from report to report, and will depend primarily on your answers to the questions above. Each of these tools has a different way of producing information, which means that they produce reports that look different, can be delivered in different ways, can be executed at different times, and so forth. Table 19-3 compares these different tools and the report functionality that they provide.

Table 19-3 Comparing Reporting Tools				
Feature	**DTS**	**ASP**	**SQL Server**	**Crystal Reports**
Overview	Execute queries and move data around. Can also be used as a step in other reporting methods	Write ASP pages that query data and generate reports as HTML	Execute queries and return the results as reports, or use automatic Web publishing capabilities	Develop complex reports of almost any kind
Delivery methods	Via e-mail	As HTML within a Web browser	Via e-mail or Web	Printer, screen, e-mail, Web pages, etc.
Good-looking	Minimal formatting available in e-mail reports	Reports are HTML, so formatting and presentation options are unlimited	Almost no formatting — whatever SQL Server returns in the result set. With the Web publishing, almost unlimited formatting but only with simpler queries	Yes, very easy to design great looking reports
Can be scheduled	Easily, using SQL Server Agent	No. However, you can use another reporting method to generate the report information to a standalone table, and write an ASP page that simply formats and displays that information on demand	Easily, using SQL Server Agent	Yes, although it's complicated, and the reports created with Crystal Reports will more likely be suitable for on-demand production

Continued

		Table 19-3 *(continued)*		
Feature	*DTS*	*ASP*	*SQL Server*	*Crystal Reports*
Development time	Generally fast, although complex packages do take longer	Quick, because script code is easy to write, but takes longer than writing straight queries	The fastest of the bunch — just write queries	The slowest of the bunch, especially if you're not familiar with the product. Crystal Reports is a complicated product, but the results can be worth it
Suggestions	Use for reports that need complex information but don't need to look pretty	Use for simpler reports, or reports that can be generated from a pre-loaded table of information	Great for simple reports	If your reports have to be complex and beautiful, this may be your best bet

The rest of this section explores each of these reporting methods, where they're best used, and how to get the best effect out of them in the least development time.

Note You also have the option of creating reports by using the full Visual Basic development environment. These reports can be displayed on-screen, directed to a printer, or even sent via e-mail with the help of a mail-enabling ActiveX control. I don't discuss this option, however, because it's extremely rare to find it in an e-commerce environment. The same capabilities can be more easily achieved through Active Server Pages, even if those ASP pages have to implement server- or client-side ActiveX controls to create special reporting features, such as graphs and charts. ASP development is usually faster than VB development, and the resulting reports can be delivered to anyone with a Web browser. You don't have to deploy a VB-compiled executable.

Data Transformation Services reports

After reading my introduction to DTS earlier in this chapter, it may not have occurred to you to lump DTS in with other reporting tools. In fact, DTS can be a lifesaver when it comes to reporting. Remember that DTS' primary role is to move data from one place to another, while performing transformations on it in the middle. This process is the basis of reporting — looking at data, performing some kind of analysis, aggregation, or other operation on it — and putting it into another place, such as a report. Even if you don't use DTS to create and deliver the final report, you will probably need DTS to help you build the information that other reporting tools will use.

Keep in mind that, when scheduled to run as a SQL Server Agent job, DTS packages execute on the SQL Server itself. This means that the package has the fastest possible connection to the data. If you're writing a report that requires data to be rearranged and aggregated in a complex fashion, it will be faster to have DTS manipulate the data and have another tool report on *those* results, than to have an external tool do the manipulation and the reporting. This is an almost universal rule of reporting: The less data manipulation the final reporting tool has to do, the better.

When you're using DTS as part of a reporting solution, you should follow this fairly straightforward strategy:

1. Make sure that you know what the source data looks like.

2. Make sure that you know what the report information has to look like.

3. Create a single table to hold the information that the report should contain.

4. Use DTS to transform the source data and put it into the reporting table.

5. Use DTS or a more powerful reporting tool to create a report based on the reporting table.

This strategy works best when the reporting information can be generated at infrequent intervals, such as every evening. The DTS package can be run in the evening to create the reporting information, and then external reporting tools can be run against that information whenever necessary. This is actually the case for most business reports. For example, a report summarizing daily sales information can have the report information generated at the end of each day. That information isn't going to change because that day is over. "Snapshot" reports used throughout the day are less suited to this method. A short report tallying up the number of orders taken so far in a day can be run several dozen times throughout the day. If you use DTS to generate the report information, then you must have the reporting tool execute the DTS package and then wait for it to finish. Fortunately, most "throughout the day" reports are very short, and can often be generated with a single, simple query, so DTS isn't necessary.

After DTS has generated the reporting information, you have two options. If the final report doesn't need to be especially attractive, you can have DTS query the information from the reporting table and then e-mail it to the people who need it. This allows you to automate the entire reporting process, and gives the report recipients the convenience of having their reports waiting for them in their Inbox first thing in the morning. DTS can't produce e-mails that are more complicated than simple columnar reports, however. Therefore, if the report needs to have nice formatting, shaded columns, numbered pages and so forth, you need to use an external tool, such as writing an ASP page or using Crystal Reports, to query the reporting information and generate a more attractive report. The downside to this method is that the report then becomes on-demand. You don't have a good, reliable way to automatically "run" an ASP page and have the output "delivered" to someone.

Building a DTS package can be a useful example of how this reporting technique works. Because you may not have installed Commerce Server yet, I use SQL Server 2000's Northwind database in this sample. Northwind's schema for customer and order information is roughly similar to Commerce Server's default schema, so you get a good picture of how DTS' capabilities as a reporting tool work.

Imagine that management has asked for a report that lists every item that was sold on a particular day. The report needs to list the item number, the description, the list price, the number sold, the total amount charged, and the total discounts that were given on the item. The three tables you need to work with are Orders, Order Details, and Products, as shown in Figure 19-4.

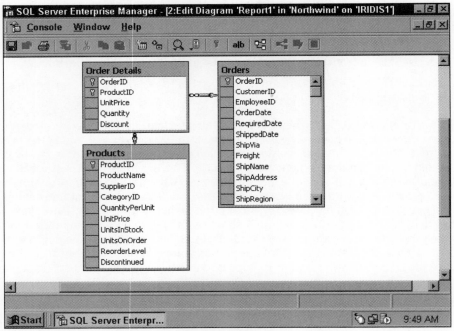

Figure 19-4: Source data tables for report

Referring back to my strategy for using DTS, you see that the first step is "Know thy data." Define the data that is necessary to create this report. Table 19-4 shows the columns that you need to examine.

	Table 19-4	
	Source Data from Northwind Database	
Orders	*Order Details*	*Products*
OrderDate	ProductID	ProductName
	UnitPrice	
	Quantity	
	Discount	

You already know what your report should look like, which is the second step in the strategy. The third step is to create a table to hold the report's information. You can do this with Enterprise Manager's graphical tools, but I prefer to fire off a quick CREATE TABLE query in SQL Query Analyzer. Listing 19-1 contains the statement.

Listing 19-1: CREATE TABLE Statement to Create a Reporting Table

```
CREATE TABLE ProductSalesReport
(
OrderDate datetime NULL,
ProductNumber int NULL,
UnitPrice money NULL,
Quantity smallint NULL,
Discount real NULL,
ProductName nvarchar(40) NULL
)  ON [PRIMARY]
```

Notice that all of the columns are defined as nullable; the DTS package that you create will take several passes to fill in all of the data that you need, so some columns will start out Null and then be filled in by the package as it executes.

The next step in the strategy is to create a DTS package that will change the data in those three source tables into the information needed by the report. Because this is a daily report, you can schedule it to run just after midnight every morning and report on the prior days' sales.

SQL Server 2000's Northwind database was created back in 1996, so all of the order dates are from 1996. I use SQL Server Query Analyzer to execute a statement to change some of those orders to yesterday's date, so this sample DTS package will have some work to do. Executing `UPDATE Orders SET OrderDate = GETDATE()` `- 1 WHERE OrderDate BETWEEN '10/1/1996' AND '10/30/1996'` will give you about 25 orders that were placed yesterday.

1. In SQL Server Enterprise Manager, right-click `Data Transformation` `Packages` and select `New Package` from the pop-up menu.

2. Drag a SQL Server connection object onto the DTS Designer workspace. Name the connection "Source" and configure it to connect to the Northwind database on the local server.

3. Drag a second SQL Server connection object onto the workspace. Name the connection "Destination" and configure it to connect to the Northwind database on the local server.

4. Drag a Transform Data task onto the workspace. Click the Source connection object as the source, and the Destination connection object as the destination.

5. Double-click the Transform Data arrow connecting the two SQL Server connection objects.

6. Change the description of this task to `Get Products`. Specify a SQL Query for the data source, and enter the following query in the box:

```
SELECT DISTINCT o.OrderDate, od.ProductID,
od.UnitPrice, p.ProductName
FROM Orders o
INNER JOIN [Order Details] od
ON o.OrderID = od.OrderID
INNER JOIN Products p
ON od.ProductID = p.ProductID
WHERE o.OrderDate < GETDATE()
AND o.OrderDate > GETDATE() - 2
```

7. On the `Destination` tab, select the ProductSalesReport table as the destination.

8. Click the `Transformations` tab to initialize the default transformations. Because I use a different column name for the ProductID, DTS won't pick up that column automatically. Select `ProductID` in the left column and `ProductNumber` in the right column. Click the `New...` button to create a new transformation. Select the `Copy column` transformation type and click `OK`.

9. Click `OK` to close the property dialog box.

10. Drag an Execute SQL Task onto the workspace. Its property dialog box opens automatically. Change the description of the task to `Update Totals` and select `Destination` from the connection drop-down box. Specify the following SQL statement:

```
UPDATE ProductSalesReport
SET Quantity =
```

```
(SELECT SUM(Quantity)
 FROM [Order Details] od
 INNER JOIN Orders o
 ON o.OrderID = od.OrderID
 WHERE OrderDate < GETDATE()
 AND OrderDate > GETDATE() - 2
 AND od.ProductID = ProductNumber),
Discount =
(SELECT SUM(Discount)
 FROM [Order Details] od
 INNER JOIN Orders o
 ON o.OrderID = od.OrderID
 WHERE OrderDate < GETDATE()
 AND OrderDate > GETDATE() - 2
 AND od.ProductID = ProductNumber)
```

11. Click OK to close the property dialog box.

12. Click the Destination connection object. Hold down the Ctrl key on your keyboard and click the Update Totals task object. With both objects highlighted, select On success from the Workflow menu of the DTS Designer. A green arrow now connects the two objects.

13. Click the diskette icon on the toolbar, or select Save from the Package menu to save the package. Name the package "ProductSalesReport" and save it to the local SQL Server.

14. Click the execute icon on the toolbar, or select Execute from the Package menu to execute the package.

    After running the package, you can open the ProductSalesReport table and see the information that it created. Essentially, this table now contains the complete report. If it doesn't need to be pretty, you can modify the DTS package to e-mail the results directly to the folks who need it.

15. Drag a new SQL Server connection object onto the workspace. Name it "Master" and configure it to connect to the Master database on the local server.

16. Make sure that SQL Mail is properly configured (if it isn't, see the sidebar, "Configuring SQL Mail") and drag an Execute SQL task onto the workspace. Name the task "Send Email" and make sure that it's set to use the Master connection. Configure the task to execute the following SQL statement:

```
xp_sendmail
@recipients = 'name@company.com',
@query = 'SELECT * FROM ProductSalesReport',
@attach_results = True,
@message = 'Here is the daily product sales report',
@subject = 'Product Sales Report',
@dbuse = 'Northwind'
```

    Be sure to change the recipients parameter to meet your needs. Click OK to close the dialog.

17. Select the Update Totals objects, and CTRL-click the Send Email object. Select On Success from the Workflow menu, and save your package again. Execute your package, and the recipient that you specified will quickly receive a report in his or her Inbox.

If the report needs to be more attractive, skip the last three steps. The DTS package will populate the ProductSalesReport table with the information that your report needs, and you can use Crystal Reports or write an ASP page to create a nicely formatted version of the information in that table. By using SQL Server Agent to schedule the package for daily execution, you can rest assured that the report information will be put into the table when you need it.

This quick sample should give you a good idea of what DTS is capable of doing for your reporting needs, both as a complete reporting solution and as an important step in producing complicated reports.

Active Server Page reports

Even if you use DTS to create your reporting information table, ASP is a great way to create good-looking reports that users can run on demand. As an e-commerce shop, you should have a spare Web server sitting around that can run these reports, so make sure that it can connect to your reporting database server to access data.

ASP reports come in two types:

✦ The first report type is an ASP page that pulls information out of a single table. This table may be a single table from your live database schema, or it may be a specially generated reporting table that was created by a DTS package. These "single table" reports are the easiest to write. In fact, I show you how to write a template report that can be changed to report on different tables in a matter of minutes.

✦ The second type of ASP report is more complex, and involves multiple tables, programming logic, special formatting needs, and so on. These reports require that you use your VBScript skills to write server-side ASP code to manipulate data, format it into groups, draw bar charts, and so forth.

I start with the simpler, single-table ASP reports. In fact, I use the ProductSalesReport table that I created in the last section. Suppose that the folks who receive that report want it to be formatted in nice columns on a page that they can scroll through and print out from their Web browser, the perfect setting for an ASP-style report.

Configuring SQL Mail

SQL Server is capable of sending mail to individual mailboxes or distribution lists in your organization. Configuring the SQL Mail service is fairly simple. Just follow these steps:

1. Make sure that the SQL Server service is configured to log on with a domain user account, not the LocalSystem account.

2. On your mail server, create a mailbox that the SQL Server's service account can log on to.

3. Log on to the SQL Server computer by using the same user account that the SQL Server service is configured to log on with.

4. Make sure that a MAPI-compatible mail client, such as Outlook, is installed on the SQL Server computer. You don't have to use Exchange Server as your mail server, but you do need to use a MAPI mail client. Outlook Express is *not* MAPI compatible.

5. Configure the mail client to access the mailbox that you created in Step 2. Open the mail client and make sure that you can send and receive e-mail.

6. Open SQL Server Enterprise Manager. Under `Support Services`, **right-click the** `SQL Mail` **icon and select** `Properties` **from the pop-up menu.**

7. Select the name of the MAPI profile that you created in Step 5. Click the `Test` button to send a test e-mail.

You are now able to use SQL Server's built-in e-mail capabilities, including the `xp_sendmail` extended stored procedure and the DTS Send Mail task. If you run into problems, they're likely to be security-related. Be sure that the logon account that the SQL Server services are using has permission to the necessary files and to the mailbox you configured in SQL Mail.

The entire report can consist of a single ASP page, although to users it will appear to be two pages. Keeping everything in a single page facilitates modifying, cloning for other reports, and moving to a different server if necessary. The page starts with a section of ASP code. This code checks to see if the necessary input has been provided; in this case, the day you want to report on. If it has input, the ASP code runs the report and displays the results. If it doesn't have input, the ASP code skips ahead to some static HTML, which creates a short data-entry page for the user to enter the date that they want to report on. Listing 19-2 is the complete page.

Listing 19-2: **Single-table ASP Report**

```
<%

'see if input has been provided.
'if not, skip to the static HTML.
if request("ReportDate") <> "" then

'create an end-of-table-cell variable
'we will use this later.
VarTD = "</td>" & vbcrlf

'pull the input into variables
'you can modify this section to include
'additional variables for more complex
'reports
dim varReportDate
varReportDate = request("ReportDate")

'create a connection to the database -
'this uses a DSN, but you can use a DSN-less
'connection string as well. In any event, change
'this to suit your environment.
set objConn = server.CreateObject("ADODB.Connection")
objConn.Open "ReportServer"

'create the base SQL query
dim varSQL
varSQL = "SELECT ProductNumber,ProductName,UnitPrice,"
varSQL = varSQL & "Quantity,Discount FROM "
varSQL = varSQL & "ProductSalesReport "

'add the WHERE clause for this report
varSQL = varSQL & "WHERE OrderDate = '"
varSQL = varSQL & varReportDate & "'"

'execute the query and retrieve the records
set objRS = objConn.Execute(varSQL)

'was the report empty?
if objRS.eof and objRS.bof then
'write an error message
response.write "No sales data was found for "
response.write varReportDate & ". Sorry."
response.end
end if

'the report was not empty.
'write out the table header - modify this to suit other
'reports if necessary
%>
<html>
```

```
<body>
<h1>Daily Product Sales Report for
<% response.write varReportDate %></h1>
<table border=1>
<tr>
<td>Product Number</td>
<td>Product Name</td>
<td>Price each</td>
<td>Quantity sold</td>
<td>Total discounts</td>
</tr>
<%

'step through each row in the recordset and write out
'the information into table rows
do until objRS.eof
'keep this good-looking in code and
'it will be easier to modify it for
'other reports in the future.
response.write "<tr>" & vbcrlf
response.write "<td>" & objRS("ProductNumber") & varTD
response.write "<td>" & objRS("ProductName") & varTD
response.write "<td>" & objRS("UnitPrice") & varTD
response.write "<td>" & objRS("Quantity") & varTD
response.write "<td>" & "$" & objRS("Discount") & varTD
response.write "</tr>" & vbcrlf
objRS.movenext
loop

'close the table
%>
</table>
<%

'since we're done with the report, stop processing
 response.end

end if
%>
<!-- This is the static HTML used to create the initial input
form -->
<p align="center">Daily Product Sales Report</p>
<form method="POST" action="list12-2.asp">
<p align="center">What date to you want to report on?</p>
<p align="center">mm/dd/yyyy: <input type="text"
name="ReportDate" size="20"
 value="<% response.write date-1 %>"><br>
 <input type="submit" value="Run Report" name="B1"></p>
</form>
<p align="center"> </p>
</body>
</html>
```

Modifying this single-table ASP report to provide details on other single tables is pretty easy to do:

1. Modify the static HTML portion to get the input that you need for the query.

2. Modify the query to pull the columns that you need.

3. Modify the section that writes the information out to table rows.

The Web browser takes care of keeping everything in nice columns, word wrapping within columns when necessary, etc. For even nicer formatting, you can add alignment tags, such as like `align=right`, to the numeric columns' `<td>` tags. You can also use the `FormatNumber()` function to display the dollar amounts with a fixed number of digits after the decimal, a dollar sign, thousands separators, etc.

Adding logic that analyzes the report information can make the report more useful from a business standpoint, even in simpler single-table reports. Listing 19-3 shows a section of code designed to replace part of Listing 19-2. This new code highlights an item's row whenever the quantity sold for the day is less than 10.

Listing 19-3: **Improving the Look with Logic**

```
'step through each row in the recordset and write out
'the information into table rows
do until objRS.eof
'keep this good-looking in code and
'it will be easier to modify it for
'other reports in the future.
If objRS("Quantity") < 10 then
 varColor = " bgcolor=#FF0000"
Else
 varColor = ""
End If
response.write "<tr" & varColor & ">" & vbcrlf
response.write "<td>" & objRS("ProductNumber") & varTD
response.write "<td>" & objRS("ProductName") & varTD
response.write "<td>" & objRS("UnitPrice") & varTD
response.write "<td>" & objRS("Quantity") & varTD
response.write "<td>" & "$" & objRS("Discount") & varTD
response.write "</tr>" & vbcrlf
objRS.movenext
loop
```

You can also use ASP pages to create more complex reports that implement programming logic. Depending on the amount of raw data that the ASP page has to process, these reports can take longer to run, and even place an unnecessary burden on your database server. Whenever you can, use a DTS package to transform the data as much as possible before programming an ASP page to manipulate the data. Ideally, ASP reports should always be based on one or two tables. Anything more complicated can take a long time to run, and would be more efficiently written as a DTS package. Some basic rules of thumb apply when trying to decide whether a report should be written entirely in ASP, or whether you should prepare the report information with DTS first. Generally, if it's more complicated than a couple of tables, or will take more than a couple of minutes to process, use DTS to prepare a reporting table, and use your reporting tool to pull data from that.

A special circumstance arises when a report is complex and must be run against "real time" data. This presents two challenges.

✦ Reporting tools like ASP or Crystal Reports have difficulty executing a DTS package, waiting for it to complete, and then creating the report from the reporting table that the DTS package populated.

✦ If you've implemented a reporting infrastructure, the copy of the data that you run reports against may not be "real time."

In these circumstances, your management team will have to weigh the factors and determine their priorities. The answer is often a compromise. For example, your management team may want an on-demand snapshot of the orders that have been placed on the site that day. In similar circumstances, I've talked management teams into accepting an hourly report. I've then modified my reporting infrastructure to use log shipping with hourly updates. After each log is applied, a DTS package runs and refreshes a reporting information table. The managers used their Web browser to access an ASP page, which built a great-looking report from that table. They understood that the data was only updated hourly, and everything worked out great.

 Tip No matter what decisions you make regarding your reports, make sure that everyone in your organization understands where the data is coming from, such as a day-old (or hour-old) copy of the data on a reporting server. This way, those using the reports can make accurate business decisions.

Don't forget that ASP pages can take advantage of ActiveX controls. One of the best reasons to use ASP reports is because you can utilize advanced ActiveX controls to create special report features, such as graphs and charts, with very little effort. For example, EM7 (www.em7.com) makes a great ActiveX control that allows you to produce 3-D charts that the user can rotate and interact with. At the VDS Tech Web site (www.vdstech.com), you'll find an ActiveX control that allows ASP pages to produce geographic charts, such as a breakdown of sales figures by state or region. Finally, Release Systems (release-systems.8m.com) makes a special set of ASP components that allow your ASP pages to use almost *any* ActiveX control that creates visual output. Their components convert the ActiveX control's output to an image file, which your ASP page can then send to the user's Web browser. This set of components allows you to use almost any kind of graphing, charting, or other report-output controls from within ASP pages.

The flexibility of VBScript makes writing even complex ASP pages relatively easy, and the power of HTML makes it a snap to create ASP reports that are good enough to show to the chairman of the board. After you understand how your raw data needs to be manipulated into a report, you can combine ASP with a DTS package to make things run fast and on time.

SQL Server reports

SQL Server offers two ways to create reports. The first way is to simply use the xp_sendmail extended stored procedure to execute a query and e-mail the results. This doesn't produce the most attractive-looking reports in the world, but they are quick and easy to create and certainly have their place in the e-commerce world.

The other way is to use SQL Server's built-in Web publishing capabilities to produce output that's formatted in HTML. You can even use HTML templates to insert the data into, making this way almost as good as ASP for generating simpler reports.

I talk about the xp_sendmail method first.

Using xp_sendmail to send reports

If the reports that you need to generate require a simple query of your regular database schema, and if the output doesn't have to be particularly attractive, then you can consider running those reports directly from SQL Server (in relatively the same way I showed you how to have a DTS package produce reports).

The xp_sendmail extended stored procedure can be used within a SQL Server Agent job to execute a query, attach the results to an e-mail, and send that e-mail to anyone that your messaging system has access to, including across the Internet. The xp_sendmail extended stored procedure will only work if SQL Mail has been properly configured. If you need to configure SQL Mail on your SQL Server, see the sidebar, "Configuring SQL Mail," earlier in this chapter.

The complete syntax for the xp_sendmail extended stored procedure is as follows:

```
xp_sendmail
@recipients = 'recipient;recipient;...'
,@message = 'message'
,@query = 'query'
,@attachments = 'attachment'
,@copy_recipients = 'recipient;recipient;...'
,@blind_copy_recipients = 'recipient;recipient;...'
,@subject = 'subject'
,@attach_results = 'True'
,@width = width
,@separator = 'separator'
,@set_user = 'user'
,@dbuse = 'database'
```

The only required parameter is `recipients`, although you will obviously want to specify a query to use as well.

✦ The `recipients` parameter specifies the e-mail addresses that the e-mail should be sent to. These addresses may be any type that your mail server will recognize. For example, Exchange Server will accept Internet e-mail addresses as well as aliases for any local recipients. You can specify multiple addresses by separating them with semicolons.

✦ The `query` parameter allows you to specify any valid SQL Server query. By default, the results of the query will be included in the body of the e-mail. The `message` parameter specifies what the body of the e-mail will contain. This text will precede the query results, so you can use it to include a brief message about what the query results represent.

✦ The `copy_recipients` and `blind_copy_recipients` parameters work just like the `recipients` paramater, including the specified e-mail addresses on the CC: or BCC: lists of the e-mail. The `subject` parameter specifies what the subject of the e-mail message will contain. If you include the `attach_results` parameter and assign it a value of `True`, then the query results will be attached to the e-mail as a text file, rather than being included in the body of the e-mail. This can be much more convenient for longer queries.

✦ The `width` parameter specifies the width of the message, or, if you specify `attach_results`, the width of the attachment. The default is only 80 characters, and the query results will word-wrap if you don't specify a wide enough parameter. Experiment with this value to achieve the results that you want. The `separator` parameter specifies the character that will separate the columns in the query. If the people receiving the e-mail want to be able to import the query results into another application, such as Excel, you should specify a separator character that the application will recognize. I recommend that you use the "pipe" character, because it rarely occurs in the actual query results.

✦ The `set_user` parameter allows you to specify the database user account that will be used to run the query. You won't generally need to use this parameter, but it can be useful if you want the query run as a user other than dbo. Finally, the `usedb` parameter specifies what database the query should be run in. The `xp_sendmail` extended stored procedure can only be executed from within the master database, so you will always need to use the `usedb` parameter to specify which database the query should be executed from.

✦ The `xp_sendmail` extended stored procedure is often the best way to send quick reports that don't need to be specially formatted. For example, suppose that your management team wants an hourly e-mail indicating how many orders have been placed that day. You can set this up to run entirely on SQL Server. Here's how:

1. Use Enterprise Manager to make sure that SQL Server Agent has been started. You will probably want to configure SQL Server Agent to start automatically when SQL Server starts, so the jobs that you configure will always run on time.

2. In Enterprise Manager, open the `Management` folder and select the `SQL Server Agent` icon. In the right-hand pane, right-click the `Jobs` icon and select `New Job...` from the pop-up menu.

3. Give the job a descriptive name, such as "`Hourly Orders Report.`"

4. On the `Schedules` tab, click the `New Schedule` button. Name the schedule "`Hourly`" and click the `Change...` button. Configure the schedule to run every hour of every day and click `OK`. Click `OK` again to return to the job properties.

5. On the `Steps` tab, click the `New...` button to create a new step. Name the step "`Mail report`" and specify a step type of `Transact-SQL Script` using the drop-down list.

6. Set the database to `master` and enter the following T-SQL statement in the `Command` text box:

   xp_sendmail

   @recipients='managers',

   @query='SELECT Count(OrderID) FROM Orders WHERE _

    OrderDate = GETDATE()',

   @subject='Hourly order count for today',

   @message='The number of orders so far today is:',

   @dbuse='Northwind'

   Click `OK` to return to the job properties.

7. Click `OK` to save the job and you're all done.

Of course, this query is set to run from the sample Northwind database. If you change the `dbuse` parameter to point to your Commerce Server database, and change the query to reflect the column and table names that you've chosen, it should work fine from your reporting database.

Because this particular report is only returning a single value, it doesn't make sense to use `attach_results`. Had this query returned several columns of information, `attach_results` may have been included to have the query attached to the e-mail as a text file.

The results returned by this technique aren't the prettiest reports in the world. The one thing that you can do to make them easier to read is to substitute more user-friendly column names for the column names in your database. For example, consider the results of this query:

```
SELECT ordID,prdID,prdName,prdLstPrice,prdCst FROM ProdOrders
```

Those column names may be easy for you to figure out, but management may prefer something less cryptic. You can use SQL's AS clause to create nicer column names. Taking the same query again:

```
SELECT ordID AS [Order ID],
PrdID AS [Product ID],
PrdName AS [Product Name],
PrdLstPrice AS [List Price],
PrdCst AS [Cost]
FROM ProdOrders
```

This query produces the same results, but with nicer-looking column names. In many instances, this step may mean the difference between being able to use an easy-to-configure SQL Server-based report, and having to take the time to write an ASP page instead.

Using SQL Server's Web Assistant

The Web Assistant was introduced in SQL Server 7.0, enhanced for SQL Server 2000, and is probably one of the product's most useful — and overlooked — features. It's designed to execute a query and put the results into an HTML page. At its simplest, the Web Assistant creates an HTML page from scratch and formats the page according to some simple specifications that you supply. It's also capable of inserting data into an HTML template, meaning that you can have reports that are formatted however you want — even to match the "look" of your company intranet.

Because the Web Assistant can only deal with a single query, you're not going to be able to do any data analysis or manipulation with it. I recommend that you create a DTS package to pull in the necessary data, process it into the desired information, and put it into a reporting table. The Web Assistant can then query that table to produce your report.

I use the ProductSalesReport table to show you how the Web Assistant can create Web reports from scratch.

1. In Enterprise Manager, make sure that you're connected to the SQL Server containing the information that you want to put into a Web page. Click the server's icon. From the Tools menu, choose Wizards. Expand the Management section and double-click the Web Assistant Wizard.

2. Select the database that contains your reporting table, in this case, Northwind.

3. Give the report a name, such as "Daily Product Sales." In this case, the report should only include a single day's products, so you need to specify a query. Select the Data from the Transact-SQL statement I specify option. You can also have the Web Assistant execute a stored procedure, which can execute more complex logic operations before returning a result set, or simply pull everything out of a particular table or view.

4. Specify the query that you want the Web Assistant to execute:

```
SELECT *
FROM ProductSalesReport
WHERE OrderDate > GETDATE()-2
AND OrderDate < GETDATE()
```

5. Specify when you want the Web Assistant to produce the HTML page for you. You can set the Web Assistant job up to run on a schedule. You can also set it up to run whenever the data changes, but be careful using this particular option. If the data will be changing frequently, the SQL Server is going to spend considerable time pumping out HTML pages to keep up. In this example, just select the `Only one time when I complete this wizard` option.

6. Tell the Web Assistant where the HTML should go, and what it should be named. You can use a UNC to specify a shared path on your Web server, or write the file to the SQL Server's local hard drive.

7. On the next page, you can specify an HTML template that the data should be placed in. I cover templates a bit later; for now, select the `Yes, help me format the Web page` option.

8. Formatting takes up three pages in the wizard.

   a. On the first page, specify what you want to name the HTML page, as well as the title that you want to appear before the table containing the actual data.

   b. On the next page, you can make formatting selections that will affect the table.

   c. On the last formatting page, you can include additional information at the bottom of the page.

9. After specifying your formatting options, you can tell the Web Assistant how much data you want returned from your query. You can either return the first "x" rows or the entire query. You can also specify that the Web Assistant only show a certain number of rows per page. If you select this option, the Web Assistant will generate however many HTML pages are necessary to hold your data and it will automatically include "Next" and "Previous" links at the bottom of the pages.

10. Click the `Finish` button and check out the HTML page that the Web Assistant produced.

If you followed the steps above, you'll see that the resulting HTML page is rather plain. Templates are definitely the way to go for a more professional-looking appearance. When creating a template, start by creating a normal HTML file that looks however you need it to look. Keep in mind that a table full of data must be inserted somewhere in the template when the Web Assistant runs.

The Web Assistant lets you control where it inserts the query results by using special tags within the HTML template. The primary tag is `<%insert_data_here%>`, which specifies the location where data should be inserted. If you use this tag by itself, the Web Assistant will insert a complete HTML table with the query results.

For more precise control, you can create a complete HTML table yourself by using
<TABLE>, <TR>, <TD>, </TD>, </TR> and </TABLE>. Surround the portion of the
HTML that builds a single table row with <%begindetail%> and <%enddetail%>.
Then use the <%insert_data_here%> tag wherever you want a column of data
inserted. Make sure that you use the tag as many times as the number of columns
in the query results that the Web Assistant will be working with. I show you a couple of examples: Listing 19-4 shows a simple template that uses the
<%insert_data_here%> tag.

Listing 19-4: **Simple Web Assistant Template**

```
<HTML>
<BODY>
<H1>This is the company's report</H1>
<%insert_data_here%>
<H4>Copyright 2001 by the company. Confidential.</H4>
</BODY>
</HTML>
```

Listing 19-5 shows a more complex template that includes complete control over
the line-by-line appearance of the table.

Listing 19-5: **Detailed Web Assistant Template**

```
<HTML><BODY>
<H2>Company Product Report</H2>
<TABLE>
<TR BGCOLOR=#CCCCCC>
 <TD>Product Name</TD>
 <TD>Product Number</TD>
 <TD>Order Date</TD>
 <TD>Quantity</TD>
  <TD>Discounts</TD>
</TR>
<%begindetail%>
<TR>
 <TD BGCOLOR=#CCCCCC><%insert_data_here%></TD>
 <TD><%insert_data_here%></TD>
 <TD><%insert_data_here%></TD>
 <TD><%insert_data_here%></TD>
 <TD><%insert_data_here%></TD>
</TR>
<%enddetail%>
</TABLE>
</BODY></HTML>
```

After you create the template file, re-run the wizard following the steps above. In Step 7, specify your template. This causes the wizard to skip Step 8 completely.

With its ability to automatically produce good-looking HTML pages, you may find that the Web Assistant, combined with DTS for the pre-processing effort, provides for a good portion of your reporting needs.

Third-party Reporting Tools

Microsoft has never really produced an application specifically designed to produce reports from databases. As a result, a competitive third-party market has sprung up offering reporting tools. This market's current king of the hill is Seagate Software's Crystal Reports (www.seagatesoftware.com). In fact, earlier versions of Visual Basic bundled a Crystal Reports ActiveX control, allowing VB developers to produce great-looking reports with their VB applications. Crystal Reports has since evolved into a full-fledged reporting platform with the ability to create printed reports, Web-delivered reports, on-screen reports, and more.

Crystal Reports features several different methods of report delivery to meet different reporting needs. For any of these methods, you first need to use Crystal Reports' designer interface to actually create your report. If Crystal Reports has a downside, it's the time that you must spend learning to use the designer. Crystal Reports has considerable power and flexibility, and with that comes complexity. Seagate offers training classes on the product, and if you have to produce multiple complex reports, it may be worth your time to attend one.

After you've built your report — a process that can be as simple as specifying a few columns and picking a font, or as complex as building custom aggregate functions, specifying data groups, and more — you can start using Crystal Reports' various delivery methods.

✦ Use a client-side ActiveX control to deliver reports via Web pages. The HTML references the Crystal Reports ActiveX control, which is downloaded and installed on the user's computer. The control then loads the report definition that you created and executes it, displaying the results in the Web browser.

✦ If your users have copies of Crystal Reports, you can send them the report definition files, which they can then load into Crystal Reports and execute. The reports display on-screen and can be printed.

✦ Crystal Reports also allows you to "package" reports, effectively combining the report definition with a "run-time" version of the product. This standalone package can be sent to anyone, even if they don't already have Crystal Reports. Users execute the package and the report is displayed or printed.

The caveat to Crystal Reports is that reports are *executed* in all of these scenarios, which means that the Crystal Reports engine must access the database, query data, perform necessary analysis, and so forth. For this reason, Crystal Reports is often best combined with DTS, just like ASP reports. Use DTS to perform all the complicated data analysis and manipulation, and save the results to a specially designed reporting table. Crystal Reports can then pull from that table, which requires less time, less processing, and less overhead on the reporting server.

All in all, Crystal Reports is a fine tool that you will probably have to start using eventually. After you get to know it, it's definitely the fastest way to produce the most complex reports, and if you use it in conjunction with DTS as I previously described, it can be a powerful way to provide access to important business information.

Other third-party reporting tools exist, although many are designed exclusively for use with data warehouses. Companies like Knowsys (www.knowsys.com) produce OLAP (online analytical processing, the type of reporting you run against a data warehouse) reporting packages, and companies like ReportSoft (www.reportsoft.com) produce general-purpose database reporting software. You should investigate these solutions to see if they meet your needs. You may find that OLAP reporting tools are overkill, and that other third-party tools don't provide much flexibility.

Integrating with Existing Back-end Systems

If you work for a large company or organization, chances are you already have some sort of back-end system in place to deal with mundane matters like accounts payable, accounts receivable, and so on. If so, one of the features in your functional specification probably had something to do with getting data out of the e-commerce system and into the back-end system.

For example, imagine that a "bricks-and-mortar" retailer decides to set up a Web site to hawk their wares over the Internet. Because they have already been selling those items in their stores, they undoubtedly have some kind of system for tracking sales, tracking inventory, placing orders for merchandise, and allocating merchandise to stores. Because the Web site will effectively become its own "store," feeding information into the retailer's existing systems, just like the traditional stores do, makes sense. The site should be able to upload sales data to the retailer's back-end system so that merchandise can be shipped to customers, the warehouse can be replenished, and the sales figures can be tallied along with the other stores' figures.

This same retailer may have all of their inventory information in a back-end system already (it's pretty likely). Rather than recreating their product catalog from scratch for Commerce Server, they will probably want to somehow transfer the product information out of their back-end system.

Commerce Server by itself, however, effectively hangs on to its data without sharing it with the rest of the world. Fortunately, Commerce Server keeps that data in SQL Server, and Microsoft provides many technologies for getting data out of SQL Server and into other systems. The best method depends on the information that you want to move into the back-end system, and whether or not the back-end system is already accepting that type of data from some other external source.

If the back-end system is already getting data from other outside sources, your best bet is to do the same thing that they're doing. It may take some investigation to turn up exactly what's involved, but in general you'll find one of the following methods at work:

✦ Companies sending in flat files, such as comma-separated value files. Your company is then translating those files and loading them into the back-end database directly.

✦ Companies communicating with your back-end system via Electronic Data Interchange (EDI).

✦ External data being manually keyed in by employees at your company.

The first situation is a clear call to SQL Server and Data Transformation Services (DTS). If a means for loading external data into the back-end system is already in place, then you can take advantage of this to load data from the e-commerce system the same way. The second situation is a job for BizTalk Server. BizTalk isn't just for communicating between companies — it's also great at communicating within a company. The last situation, although horrible to contemplate, is still something that you can work with. Those employees are manually keying data through some kind of application, and whatever that application is doing, you can probably do too.

Whatever the situation, you generally have two primary technological means of getting data into (or out of) a back-end system. The first is the direct method. Back-end systems all run on some kind of database system — SQL Server, Oracle, Sybase, DB2, or some other standard platform. Database systems are designed to have data taken out and put in, so there's no technological reason why you can't just program DTS to connect directly to the back-end's database and pull data in and out.

Many larger back-end systems, such as SAP R/3, don't appreciate this approach, however, because it allows the system's data to be modified without first passing through the business logic of the system's management software — R/3 itself, for example. Those systems provide their own software interfaces, which allow other computers to access the back-end system like the system's regular users do. SAP, for example, provides an entire software interface called the Business Application Programming Interface (BAPI), specifically for the purpose of allowing R/3 to communicate with other computer software. This type of situation is far more complicated than executing a few SQL queries against the back-end system's database. In some cases, you'll need to write custom software utilities to handle the communication between the e-commerce system and the back-end system, or purchase utilities from someone else who has written them. Other times, you'll be able to take advantage of industry-standard communications supported by the back-end system, such as EDI. If the back-end system supports an open communication protocol like EDI (or some kind of XML support), you can treat the back-end system as a business partner.

Cross-Reference A detailed discussion of exchange data with business partners is included in Chapter 17.

Any detailed discussion of how to write custom software utilities for specific back-end systems is beyond the scope of this book. I will, however, talk about the first method, which is the method of connecting your e-commerce site database directly to the back-end system's database.

Your first task is to understand the schema of the back-end database. If you want to pull data from the back-end to your e-commerce system, you need to understand exactly what data you're going to pull, what tables are involved, what tables are related to those tables, and so on. If you're planning to push data from your e-commerce system into the back-end system, it's even more critical that you know what you're doing, because inserting the wrong bit of data into the wrong table can be devastating to a business system.

The next step is to somehow link your SQL Server to the back-end database so that it can "see" the back-end data. You can do this in one of two ways. One way provides the SQL Server with real-time access to the back-end data, and the other way provides batch access to it.

Real-time access with linked servers

For real-time access, SQL Server provides a feature called *linked servers* that should do the trick nicely. A linked server can be any external data source that SQL Server has an OLE DB or ODBC driver for — Oracle, Access, Sybase, or even Excel. After a server has been linked, SQL Server can treat the data on that server as if it were local, executing queries against it, changing it, copying it, and running DTS packages on it. The primary purpose of the linked server configuration is to create a *security mapping* between the SQL Server's login accounts and the security accounts of the remote database. A security mapping may specify, for example, that anyone using a login name `WebUser` on the SQL Server should be logged into the remote server as `User715`, with an appropriate password. The following steps set up a linked server.

1. In Enterprise Manager, expand the `Security Folder` and right-click `Linked Servers`. Select `New Server...` from the pop-up menu.

2. Specify a name for the linked server. This will be the name that SQL Server uses to refer to the remote server; it doesn't necessarily have to be the name that the remote server uses for itself.

3. If the remote server is a Microsoft SQL Server, choose the `SQL Server` option. If not, select the correct data source from the drop-down list and fill in the necessary connection information in the boxes.

Tip   If you place the cursor in one of the text boxes, the status bar displays tips about what information is required.

4. On the `Security` tab, list any local logins that should be mapped to specific remote logins on the remote server. At the bottom of the page, you can specify how local logins should be treated if they are *not* specifically mapped to a remote login.

    You can choose to have SQL Server deny access, allow access using the remote server's "Guest" or "Anonymous" access (if available), pass through the local login credentials unchanged, or be mapped to a "catch-all" remote login and password.

5. Finally, on the `Server Options` tab, you can specify specific configuration options that will govern how the connection treats certain information and situations. Unless you have a specific reason to change one of these from the default, don't.

Your linked server has been created. Accessing the data on the server simply requires you to use SQL Server's fully qualified object names:

```
Server.database.owner.object
```

You may not realize that SQL Server uses this naming format to refer to every database object that it works with, even local ones. If you don't specify the server name, SQL Server will use the local server name. If you don't specify a database name, SQL Server will use whatever database you're currently attached to. If you don't specify an owner, SQL Server will default to `dbo`, because that user usually owns everything in a database. You can always provide your own values for the different parts of the name, though. For example, to access the Customer table in the Data1 database on a linked server named "RemSvr1," you type this:

```
RemSvr1.Data1..Customer
```

Notice that the owner portion of the name is left out. The remote system will be allowed to default this to whatever it wants — generally its own database owner user, which probably owns the table. You can leave out any portion of the name that you want (except for the object name). Be sure to always use the correct number of periods. Notice in the above example that two periods come between `Data1` and `Customer`.

After you've linked to a server, you can treat the data on that server as if it were stored on the local SQL Server. For example, if you want to copy all of the products beginning with "P" from the remote server into your Commerce Server database, you may write a query that looks something like this:

```
INSERT INTO tct_Product
   SELECT * FROM RemSvr1.Data1..Products AS r
   WHERE r.ProductName LIKE 'P%'
```

Notice that I created an alias, "r," for the linked server. This technique is much easier than typing out the fully qualified name every time you need to refer to a column in that table.

Real-time access through linked servers comes with a few caveats. The most important one is the network bandwidth between the SQL Server and the linked server. If it's not a fast connection, then the SQL Server is going to be slowed down considerably when querying data from the linked server, because it will have to wait while that data transfers over the slow network connection.

Security is another concern. If you are not in control of security on the linked server, there's always the possibility that someone will change a password or login name without notifying you. If this happens, everything that you've set up to work with the linked server will stop working until you correct the problem, either by having the account information changed back, or by changing the properties of the linked server definition on your SQL Server.

Often, real-time access through linked servers is nice, but not strictly necessary. Most business situations do fine with a periodic batch transfer of information between the e-commerce database and the back-end database. This type of batch transfer is best accomplished with Data Transformation Services.

Batch access with Data Transformation Services

SQL Server 2000 excels at connecting heterogeneous data systems together, primarily through the use of Data Transformation Services (DTS) packages. I discussed DTS in some depth earlier in this chapter; but I didn't cover the great breadth of non-SQL data sources to which DTS is capable of connecting. Check out this list:

✦ Microsoft SQL Servers

✦ Microsoft Access

✦ Microsoft Excel

✦ dBase III through 5

✦ HTML data sources

✦ Paradox

✦ Text files

✦ Oracle

✦ FoxPro and Visual FoxPro

✦ LDAP directories, including Active Directory

✦ The Microsoft Web Store and Exchange Server information stores

✦ OLAP Services

✦ ISAM sources

✦ Practically any data source for which you have an ODBC driver

The list is extensive. Combined with DTS' ability to translate and transform data as it moves it between databases, and the ability to schedule DTS packages to run on a regular basis, you should have a fairly powerful means of moving and copying data between a back-end database and your e-commerce system's database.

The ability to transform data when moving it between databases can be especially important, because back-end data can often be in a format that isn't what you want on the e-commerce site. Read the sample situation below, and then read how to build a DTS package to deal with it.

Amazing Chemicals sells bulk chemicals to other businesses across the world. Currently, they take orders primarily by phone, but they want to put up an e-commerce site to allow existing customers to place orders. They offer several thousand chemical products, all of which are fully detailed in their existing back-end system. The back-end system consists of a custom Visual Basic application running against an Oracle database.

Customers are used to ordering chemicals by their "reference number." The reference number is actually a combination of three columns from the Products table in the Oracle database named "AmazChem." The first column is named "ContainerType" and consists of a single letter. The second column is named "ProductNumber" and consists of a sequential number. In the reference number, this must always be eight digits, and should be padded with zeros if necessary. The third column is named "ShippingRestrictions." This column contains three letters, only the last of which is included in the reference number.

For example, the Products entry for a 55-gallon drum of Super Acid consists of a "D" in the ContainerType column, a ProductNumber of 42, and a ShippingRestrictions entry of "XXG." The reference number for this product is D00000042G. The e-commerce site requires two pieces of information in its product catalog: The product number and the reference number.

Amazing Chemicals is constantly updating its product line, adding and removing container types and negotiating new shipping contracts that change the shipping restrictions on products. Also, the e-commerce site will be moving all order data into the back-end system, so the site's database doesn't need to maintain order information after the order has been copied into the Oracle database. For these reasons, you decide to build a DTS package to copy all of the Amazing Chemicals product information into the e-commerce site every night.

The first step is to modify the Commerce Server product catalog's Product table to include a ReferenceNumber column. The second step is to build a DTS package that wipes out the existing Products table on the site and copies in the updated data from the Oracle server. The package can be scheduled to run every night.

1. Use Enterprise Manager to create a new DTS package.

2. Drag an Oracle connection object onto the workspace and configure it to connect to the back-end system's Oracle server.

3. Drag a SQL Server connection object onto the workspace and configure it to connect to the e-commerce site's SQL Server database.

4. Drag a Transform Data task onto the workspace. Select the Oracle connection object as the source, and select the SQL Server connection object as the destination.

5. Double-click the Transform Data task to edit its properties. Specify the source table for the Oracle database and the destination table for the SQL Server database.

6. On the `Transformations` tab, click the `Delete All` button to remove the default transformations.

7. Certain information, such as the product description, on the Oracle table will be copied over without changes,. For these items, select the source and destination columns and click the `New...` button. Select the `Copy column` transformation task and click OK.

8. The remaining transformation, creating the reference number from the three source columns, will be easiest to accomplish in VBScript. Select the three source columns and the destination column, click the `New` button, and select the `ActiveX` transformation task.

9. Name the task "`Create Reference Number`" and click the `Properties` button to edit the script code.

10. Replace the default VBScript with the following:

```
Function Main()
Dim vContainer, vProduct
Dim vShipping, vRef
vContainer = DTSSource("ContainerType")
vProduct = DTSSource("ProductNumber")
If Len(vProduct) < 8 then
 vProduct = String(8-Len(vProduct),"0") & vProduct
End If
vShipping = Right(DTSSource("ShippingRestrictions",1)
vRef = vContainer & vProduct & vShipping
DTSDestination("ReferenceNumber") = vRef
Main = DTSTransformStat_OK
End Function
```

11. Click OK to close the dialog boxes.

12. Drag a Transact-SQL task onto the workspace. Name the task "`Delete Products`" and type the T-SQL statement `DELETE * FROM Products` in the text box. Make sure that the selected Connection is the SQL Server connection object, not the Oracle connection object.

Caution   Selecting the wrong connection object will cause all the product information in the back-end system to be deleted.

Note that you can also use the TRUNCATE TABLE command to delete the data in the table. SQL Server will execute this command faster and produce only a single log entry.

13. Select the Transact-SQL task. Use CTRL-click to select the Oracle connection object. From the `Workflow` menu, select `On Success`.

14. Save the package and do a test run.

If everything is working correctly, the SQL Server's product catalog should be emptied out and populated with fresh, transformed data from the Oracle server. The ReferenceNumber column should be correctly populated for each product.

Now that you know how to build a DTS package that pulls data from a back-end system and transforms it, you should be able to see how the technique applies to your particular situation. You can now decide whether you need to move data from the back-end system into the e-commerce site's database, or vice versa.

Summary

You should know how to select an appropriate technology to implement your reporting infrastructure, and how to leverage the spare node of a database cluster to get a "free" reporting server. This chapter shows you how to create reports using a variety of technologies, each suitable to different specific reporting needs. And this chapter talks about integrating your e-commerce site with your company's existing back-end system. Taken together, you should be ready to program your e-commerce site to meet any back office requirements that your company may have.

✦　　✦　　✦

What's on the CD-ROM

This appendix provides an overview of the software included on the Microsoft .NET E-Commerce Bible CD, and explains how to install the software from the CD.

Microsoft Commerce Server 2000, Trial Version

Commerce Server 2000 is Microsoft's e-commerce development platform, and a member of the .NET Servers family. It runs best on Windows 2000 Server (or a later version), and requires SQL Server 7.0 (or a later version; SQL Server 2000, preferably) to be present in the environment when it is installed.

To install Commerce Server 2000, simply insert the CD into your server computer. The Setup program should start automatically. If it doesn't, use Explorer to locate the Setup program on the CD and double-click it.

Be sure to read the documents located in the root folder of the CD. These documents describe installation prerequisites, including minimum service pack levels and Microsoft hot fix requirements. You must have the correct software installed prior to starting Commerce Server 2000 Setup.

Remember that Commerce Server 2000 doesn't set up an e-commerce site when you install it. If you want to begin developing an e-commerce site from scratch, locate the file named "blank.pup" on your hard drive after Commerce Server Setup is complete. Double-click that file to unpack the blank Commerce Server site. If you want to install one of the Microsoft Solution Sites as a starting point, or to use it as a tutorial, you will need to download the Solution Sites from http://www.Microsoft.com/commerce.

◆   ◆   ◆

Outsourcing Your E-Commerce Project

The rapid pace of technological development in the e-commerce industry, coupled with the almost staggering shortage of qualified technical professionals, often makes the prospect of outsourcing some or all of your e-commerce development not only appealing but *required*. Good consulting firms bring the following advantages to the table: A qualified technical staff with years of experience, a large pre-existing library of code that can be used as a basis for your project, and relationships with vendors like Microsoft to help resolve any problems that crop up faster than you can handle on your own.

The majority of the e-commerce projects that I have worked on were started by outside consultants. In some cases, I *was* the outside consultant, and in other cases I was part of the internal staff hired after the consultants had built much of the site. This mix of experience has given me a good look at both sides of the consultant-customer relationship, and in this appendix, I share some tips and advice that I've picked up over the past few years. In fact, the whole goal of this appendix is to help you understand both sides of the customer-consultant relationship so you can recognize what "the other side" needs in order to do the best possible job. Although this appendix is directed specifically to readers in a technical management position, such as a Chief Technology Officer or a Director of Development, you should keep reading even if you're not in one of those positions. Odds are, you'll pick up some good information about how to work in an out-sourcing situation.

The whole process gets started when you and your management team begin looking at outside consultants to help build your site. Many e-commerce executives have been barraged by "industry studies" insisting that the entire design and development of their site can be safely outsourced. In my experience, this approach succeeds in very few situations, so I strongly recommend that your company dedicate at least one technically competent individual to lead the design process and work with your outside consulting firm if they are to help with the design phase.

Tip   Never leave the design of a site entirely in the hands of the executive management and an outside vendor. Unless the consulting firm is more conscientious than most, the site may be built with shortcuts and shortcomings that you will fight for months, if not years. Always have a technically savvy architect on staff to work with the vendor during the design phase. This architect can ensure that your company's technical interests are being represented in the project.

After you have selected a vendor, you need to carefully manage the relationship. After all, your company is paying for the consulting work, and should get the most out of the deal. This isn't to say that you should turn into a tyrant. Most consulting firms are staffed with incredibly agreeable individuals who want to do a good job, but you can do numerous things to make communication between your two companies flow more smoothly and keep things on track at both ends. For example, you could schedule regular status meetings to keep everyone updated. You could also make sure key players in your company and the consulting firm exchange office and cell phone numbers so they can be reached in emergencies.

Keep in mind that consultants can be expensive. You'll want to eventually end your reliance on them for day-to-day maintenance and possibly even for future development after the site is up and running. Don't wait until it's time to scale back your consulting budget to think about how you'll break the news; make your transition to an internal technical staff part of the original consulting agreement so that everybody is aware of the expectations.

Tip   As with everything else, the key to a successful relationship with a consulting firm is planning, planning, planning.

Selecting Your Vendors

After you decide to use outside consultants to help with your site, you need to begin the sometimes-painful process of selecting a vendor. Just finding vendors to consider can be a monumental task. Examine each vendor's skill set and experience (this also entails learning how to interpret what the vendor's sales force tells you).

How to find vendors

Typing a few key words into an Internet search engine to get a short list of consulting firms is no longer possible. You can find literally *thousands* of qualified consulting firms all over the world. They range in size from the giant consulting practices operated by the "Big Five" accounting firms to small "mom and pop" consulting firms based in major cities across the world.

A good place to start is Microsoft's directory of Microsoft Certified Partners at `http://www.microsoft.com/mcsp`. This directory will help you locate consulting firms in your area with experience in the Microsoft products and platforms. You can specifically look for Partners who are "Gold Certified" in e-commerce, which is a premium-level certification that Microsoft only bestows after examining several successful e-commerce projects that were completed by the firm.

You can also talk to other e-commerce firms to find out who developed their sites. Word-of-mouth recommendations are the best kind because you get insight into exactly how the vendor performs. You can also contact your local Microsoft sales office. They maintain relationships with select Partners in their region and can make recommendations regarding firms' experience with e-commerce development projects — and may even be able to provide references for specific consultants within particular firms. Microsoft even maintains their own worldwide consulting arm, Microsoft Consulting Services (MCS). Even though MCS consultants are among the most expensive on the market, it may be worth your while to solicit their help in selecting a consulting vendor to do the bulk of the work. Not only can they provide references, but they can also conduct reliable technical screens to help you narrow the field in your vendor selection.

Things to look for

So what should you look for when you begin examining potential consulting partners? Obviously, you need to find a vendor with experience in the technologies that you will be using, but a consulting partner can — and should — offer much more than programming talent to make your project move quickly and smoothly. Create a "laundry list" of characteristics that your ideal vendor has, and use this list to compare and contrast the different vendors. You need to consider the following questions:

✦ **What is the vendor's experience with the products you will be working with?** Ideally, the vendor's staff should include consultants who write articles for trade publications, or even books, on at least some of the major technologies that you will be using. Although you won't necessarily require their expertise on your project, the rest of the vendor's technical staff is more likely to know their stuff if these folks are around.

✦ **How does the vendor treat their employees?** Look for a vendor whose employment policies reflect your own. These vendors will be more likely to retain technical professionals long enough to complete your project. Beware of so-called "body shop" consulting firms that experience a high rate of turnover; a rotating consulting team will seriously endanger your project's deadlines and budget.

✦ **How does the vendor create their estimates?** Too many customers accept estimates without knowing how they are created. Some firms base their estimates on a thorough knowledge of your project, while others make an

Getting an Estimate

As a customer, you have every right to expect an accurate, detailed estimate for the work that you need to hand off to a consulting firm. And, whether you realize it or not, that firm has every right to expect to be compensated for the considerable time involved in coming up with an estimate.

You're completely justified in asking for a "ballpark" figure for your project—especially if you've already completed most of the design phase. Your design documents should contain sufficient detail for a rough estimate. However, this estimate may vary by as much as 60 percent or more, even for consulting firms who are experienced in rough estimates and your type of project. It's unfair to you and to the consulting firm to hold them to that estimate, and a good firm will stress the rough nature of the estimate.

If you're willing to expend the resources necessary to build your site, and if you're willing to outsource a major portion of that development, then you should also be willing to invest a small amount up front to get a detailed estimate. An average retail e-commerce site should require one or two talented architects and developers working a week or so to review and create a detailed estimate that you *can* hold the consulting firm to. Pay the consulting firm for that time. Make your expectations clear—you want a written, detailed proposal that breaks down the site's development appropriately. Even if you decide to go with another vendor, having that first detailed estimate should make subsequent ballpark estimates easier and more accurate for other vendors to make, as some work has been done to establish the first estimate, which you can share with subsequent vendors. A detailed first estimate can also provide a reality check against subsequent ballpark estimates, helping you make sure estimates are reasonable.

"educated guess" and add a considerable margin of error (both in time and dollars) to their estimate.

+ **Has the vendor completed a knowledge transfer process in past projects?** Make sure that the vendor is comfortable with the approach that you want to take, and make sure that you get a good feeling that they know what they're talking about.

+ **Will the vendor stop you from doing something stupid?** For example, try indicating that you want to take a particular direction with your site that's obviously a bad idea. Make sure that the vendor is willing to point this out and correct you. You're paying them for their expertise; you should expect them to prevent you from doing something unwise.

How to read vendors' resumes

Like any other resume, a vendor's resume is designed to present the vendor in the best possible light. You won't see any mention of projects that went poorly, and the projects that are mentioned may gloss over the firm's actual role or the customer's level of satisfaction with the project.

Interview your vendors like you would interview any job candidate, and ask tough questions that help you determine how much of their marketing material is real and how much is fluff. Be sure to ask the following questions:

✦ **What projects would you consider total or partial failures, and why?** *No* consulting firm has an unblemished record. They may not be willing to divulge names, but they should be willing to share the circumstances. Look for firms that can admit their mistakes, and explain what they learned from them and what measures they now take to prevent similar situations from occurring.

✦ **How will you understand my expectations for this project?** This is actually a trick question. They shouldn't try to understand your expectations. Instead, they should try to understand your needs and then clearly communicate how they can help, thus setting your expectations for the project and the firm's services to be within their actual capabilities.

✦ **What exact methods will you use to transfer knowledge to my staff?** The answer to this question should be specific. If it isn't, you have reason to suspect that the firm has never been involved in a successful knowledge transfer before. They should be able to describe past projects that involved knowledge transfer, and describe exactly how they accomplished that transition.

✦ **How will you keep the project on time and on budget?** The vendor should be willing to put some responsibility for keeping the project on time and on budget in your hands, and you should see some backbone in their answer indicating that their consultants will carefully discuss changes that come along mid-project in order to resist "scope creep." You should not get the impression that the vendor will do whatever you ask without question. You're hiring them to help you make decisions, and they should be willing to tell you when to back down.

✦ **What is your project management methodology?** Don't settle for fancy names and acronyms. Make them explain exactly how their project management methodology works, and take notes. In a second interview, ask them to bring one of their *mid-level* developers along, and question that person about the project management methodology. If they can't describe it in the same terms, then the methodology is most likely just for show.

✦ **Who will work on my project?** Be cautious of firms who bring their top talent along to sales meetings and interviews. That talent is often taken off your project as soon as another sales opportunity comes along. You shouldn't expect a consulting firm to commit to specific names in a sales meeting, or to promise that every person will remain on your project for the duration, but you can ask them about their policies for leaving people on a project. Make it clear that you consider a small set of dedicated individuals more valuable than a large, rotating pool of consultants. Ask them if they are willing to contractually dedicate specific individuals to the project — especially the high-level talent that will lead the project. Make sure you get an opportunity to interview consultants that the firm considers to be mid-level, rather than settling for meeting their top brass only.

✦ **What was your role in past projects that your company worked on?** Most vendors' marketing materials include descriptions of past projects, and may even include customer names. Request exact descriptions of the vendor's role in each project, and ask for customer references that you can contact to verify the information and the customer's satisfaction. If a vendor can't provide at least two references, you should suspect a lack of experience or customer satisfaction.

✦ **Why would I invest in your company?** Even if the vendor is not publicly traded, ask them to convince you to "invest" in their company. After all, they're asking you to spend money on them. You need to understand why their company has been successful, how they run their day-to-day business, what they do to retain qualified technical employees, and how they keep their staff up to speed on the latest technologies. If they can't convince you to invest in their company, you should seriously consider why you would want to do business with them at all.

✦ **Why am I important to you?** Certainly, the money that you are willing to spend on the project is important, but look for a vendor that wants more than just a check. Perhaps your project offers them an opportunity to enter a new vertical market, or perhaps your project will help them build their resume for future projects. Maybe they have a particular passion for the type of project that you are about to undertake, and if so, make them explain that to you. A vendor who is in it for more than just the money makes for a better working relationship and you'll have common ground to fall back on in the event of a money-based dispute.

Working with Vendors

After you've selected your vendor, start thinking about how you'll work with them. Ask yourself the following questions:

✦ How can you communicate your needs in enough detail?

✦ How can you develop a relationship that will last for the length of the project?

✦ How will the project be managed, and who will be responsible for that management?

✦ How can you and the vendor work together in order to prevent the scope of the Web site from growing out of hand in the middle of the project?

As you and your vendor form a contract, you should discuss these issues and come to mutually agreeable decisions. In the next few sections, I give you some recommendations that have helped make some of my past projects run much smoother for everyone involved.

Communicating the plan

Even if you intend to have your consulting firm complete most of your design phase, you should still begin with the basic vision and scope statements, and you should provide this information to the consulting firm as a starting point. Do *not* think that the consulting firm can complete the design process without following the steps that I outline in the Part I of this book. If your consulting firm insists that they don't need to conduct interviews of your different business units, or analyze your customer demographic, or do any of the other tasks that I talk about in Part I of this book, then you probably need to think about finding a different consulting firm.

Ideally, you should complete the planning phase internally and then turn the resulting documentation over to the consulting firm. Giving the firm a brief period of time to review this plan and ask questions should sufficiently communicate your intentions and desires, and enable them to get the project off to a good start.

Developing rapport

The consulting firm that you choose should be able to provide you with a "single point of contact" for your project — a person on their team who will be *your* representative in *their* company for the duration of the project. You should immediately begin developing a relationship with this person because the two of you will be working closely together to complete your development phase.

Create a regular schedule for communication, and make sure that no more than two or three weeks pass in between personal, face-to-face visits. A phone call can too easily lack the impact of a personal meeting, and issues communicated over the phone can be mishandled simply because the other party didn't understand their full scope. Phone conversations also tend to be rushed, and you can be easily distracted by the rest of the office when you're on the phone. Face-to-face meetings avoid all of these potential problems, and can be supplemented by regular weekly or twice-weekly phone calls to make sure everything is staying on track.

You should also make sure that you have access to the developers who will be working on your project — whether you're managing them directly or not. They should feel free to contact you to resolve questions and clarify issues as they are working. If they are forced to funnel requests through a middleman or the project manager, then the project will only proceed more slowly and you will run a higher likelihood of the project not getting completed to your specifications. Developers will avoid asking a question entirely if they can't ask the person who can give an immediate answer. Make sure that your consulting firm is comfortable with this type of interaction between your company and their developers, and make sure that the project manager feels comfortable not being involved in every interaction that takes place between your two companies.

Managing the project

Although you may be tempted to manage the project yourself and to use the consulting firm's developers as extensions of your own staff, try to resist the urge. Your consultant's estimates and timelines are only valid if *they* are allowed to manage the project to *your* specifications. They should provide a project manager, who will likely be your main point of contact, to be responsible for managing resources and timelines on the project. Having someone on the consultant's team also helps to keep the scope of the project under control.

Managing scope creep

Ideally, you should not add any features or functionality to your project after it has started (I discuss this principle continually throughout the book). Because of the cruel reality of business, however, you will probably change your project specification several times during its course.

Having a project manager on the consulting team is one good way to help manage "scope creep." The project manager should help review what the desired changes will do to your timeline and will revise his or her company's estimates and timelines in light of these changes. *Never* believe a consultant who says that changes can be "fit in" to the original schedule and estimate. If they're right, then the original estimate was flawed. More than likely, they are wrong.

Equipped with a new timeline and estimate, you can decide whether to accept the necessary revisions to the project timeline and budget, or put the change on a wait list to be completed sometime after the current committed project is finished.

Transferring Knowledge

Hopefully, the time will come when you and your company are ready to rely more on your internal technical staff and less on your outside vendor. If you've been honest with your vendor about your long-term plans for their involvement, this time will come as no surprise to them. In fact, if you've been careful in selecting your vendor, they should stand ready to help you make the transition.

The process of transferring knowledge about the site's inner workings is no less important or complex than the original site design. Plan the transition process carefully — sit down with your vendor and your internal technical staff and outline the process, and make sure everyone agrees that the strategy will work. Select a specific, small project to begin the transfer process to get your internal staff and outside vendor to work together. If you're still in the process of hiring your internal staff, ask your vendor to lend their technical expertise to the hiring process.

Deciding when the time is right

You should decide when to begin the knowledge transfer process when the project *begins*, not when it is over. Make the transition part of your basic project timeline, and make sure that your technical staff is ready to begin the transfer process when the time finally rolls around.

Deciding where the transfer fits into the project plan can largely depend on how your company plans to use consulting services. If the consultants are responsible for the major portion of the site's initial development, then I recommend that you let them finish the development before you begin bringing your internal staff into the main stream of the project. If your plan is to somehow divide the work between the consultants and your internal staff, then the knowledge transfer process should occur throughout the project. In the next few sections, I discuss some common project scenarios and give you some recommendations for where to implement knowledge transfer.

Wait for it

Most e-commerce companies that decide to make use of consultants have them complete the vast majority of the sites' initial design and development phases. Internal staff may be used for small, specific pieces of the site, but the consultants are generally the stars of the show.

In these projects, wait until the consultants reach the end of the development process before bringing your own staff into play. Consultants make their estimates and timelines with only their own resources in mind; bringing another developer into the middle of the project would only throw these estimates and timelines off and possibly delay the completion of the initial development phase.

Instead, wait until the project has reached completion and the site goes live. Then bring your internal staff into the *next* phase of development, and have them work side-by-side with the consultants. This allows your staff to learn by working on the actual site's code. Make sure that initial projects in the second phase of development represent a variety of the site's functionality, including search, checkout, catalog, navigation, customer service, and so forth. This way, your developers are exposed to these portions of the site while the consultants are still available to explain how things were done in the *first* phase of development.

After your developers have completed a few projects alongside the consultants, you can begin scaling the consultants back to a few days a week, then to specific major projects, and then eventually (if you want to), you can begin to rely completely on your own internal technical staff.

Side by side

You may have chosen to use consultants not because you lacked internal staff, but because your internal staff lacked sufficient knowledge or experience to complete the site's development on their own. If this is the case, your staff should have been working on projects with the consultants from the start. The consultants should not only develop portions of the site, but also mentor your internal developers during the development process to bring their skills and experience up to the level required by the project.

When you're certain that all the major portions of the site have been completed and deployed to production, scale back on your use of the consultants and begin relying more on your internal developers. You may still need the consultants on an occasional basis to play a developer/mentor role in special projects in order to help immediately bring your own staff up to speed on the technologies.

If you do plan to run your project this way, try to find a consulting partner who is familiar with training and mentoring because their consultants will slip into the role more comfortably than consultants who are accustomed to working strictly as developers.

Piecemeal

You can phase your technical staff into the project while the first phase of development is still underway, although this approach is the riskiest in terms of adding time to the project's timeline.

Identify specific portions of the development phase where additional staff can be added to the project. For example, after the design phase is complete and the consultants have set up the initial development environment, you can phase in an on-staff network/infrastructure administrator to maintain the development environment and to begin building the production servers. The consultants will still be on the project to provide assistance and advice to your new administrator, but you need to carefully consider how much of their time will be needed for this task and how much can be dedicated to ongoing site development.

Phasing in developers can be more difficult, and requires significantly more planning in the design phase when you create your project timeline. For example, you may plan for the consultants to program the major functional pieces in the checkout process, and then phase in your own staff developer to complete the checkout, customize it, and add smaller pieces of functionality.

This approach allows you to involve your internal staff in the development of the site from almost the very beginning, making knowledge transfer an ongoing process. The danger is that, without detailed planning, adding individuals to the project who may not have the skill set or experience to be immediately productive can cause your consultants to spend more time mentoring than actually developing, which can drastically increase the site completion time. Choose this approach only if your consulting firm agrees with the approach and the project timeline, and has experience in working on this type of project.

Outlining the transfer process

How is knowledge transferred, exactly? Most technical professionals learn by doing, rather than by reading about it in project documentation, so the best way to transfer project knowledge is usually to begin working on a particular project — "diving right in." Of course, the danger with diving right in is that developers can run up against techniques, technologies, and situations that they are unfamiliar with, causing them to waste valuable time trying to figure out how to do something. Your consultant mentors, who already possess the necessary knowledge about the site, can supply immediate answers if and when trainees require them.

This is not to say that learning by reading is not helpful. Developers should be familiar with the site's design and development documentation before they begin looking at any code, and they should be required to contribute to that documentation as they make changes and expansions to the site.

I generally like to use a knowledge transfer process that goes something like this:

1. Select a portion of the project for an internal staff member to tackle. This project should represent some key piece of the site's functionality. For example, if your site is a retail e-commerce site, have your staff take on projects involving search, the catalog, the checkout, or some other piece of critical functionality. Don't have them work on ancillary functionality until they've mastered the key pieces of the site.

2. Have the developers review all of the development and design documentation for the portion of the project on which they will be working. They should be familiar with the decisions that have been made, the work that has already been accomplished, how this functionality interfaces with other portions of the site, and so forth.

3. Have the developers begin reviewing the work that they will complete with a consultant. They should all agree on the approach to be taken, and the consultant will have the opportunity to point out particular portions of the existing code of which they need to be aware.

4. As they begin working on the code, make sure that your developers have a contact on the consulting portion of the team who they can speak with immediately should they require assistance or clarification on any portion of the project.

I find that this approach works pretty well in most circumstances because it allows developers to get right in and start programming, armed with a reliable resource to make their learning process faster than if they were on their own.

Selecting the transfer projects

When you do begin to involve your internal developers, select projects that will give them the range of experience that they need to support your site on their own one day. This means selecting the portions of your site that offer key, customer-focused functionality.

Ideally, *everything* on your site is key and customer-focused. But concentrate on the really *fundamental* pieces of your site (checkout, search, catalog, navigation, and so forth). Let your consultants help you identify the major areas of functionality on your site so you can create a priority list for getting your internal staff acquainted with these areas. The priority list should account for your developers' skills and experience and should start them working on pieces of the site that they are *least* experienced with first, so that they learn as much as possible from the consultants while the consultants are still engaged full-time on the project.

Involving the vendor in staff selection

You should have a good enough relationship with your development vendor to ask them to help you hire qualified technical staff members, if necessary. The consultants who worked on your site know *exactly* what mix of skills and technologies that candidates need in order to successfully support and expand your site; take advantage of this expertise by including those consultants in technical interviews for potential new hires. Ask them to evaluate the skills of your existing staff and make recommendations for additional staff members or training to help fill gaps in your staffs' knowledge of the necessary technologies and products.

Staff selection and technical interviews are another area that your consulting firm can help you transition to your internal staff. By having senior members of your technical staff sit in on technical screenings of job candidates, your staff members can learn tips and tricks for conducting a technical interview. This will not only help you grow the staff by using internal resources for tech screenings in the future, but will also provide valuable personal and professional development for your senior staff members.

Summary

Working with outside consultants can be a rewarding, intelligent decision for an e-commerce company. The danger lies in thinking that the consultants have the same level of understanding and dedication to the site that you and the rest of your company have. Plan carefully and communicate to enable the consultants to see the site in the same way that you see it, and develop a relationship that will encourage the consultants to be as dedicated to the site as you are.

Select your consulting partner by asking tough questions — ask them to prove that they can do the work, are excited about doing the work, and are willing to provide every bit of expertise that they have to further your effort.

◆   ◆   ◆

Data Transformation Services Reference

◆ ◆ ◆ ◆

In This Appendix

Data transformation connections

Data transformation tasks

Commerce Server–specific tasks

Working with DTS

◆ ◆ ◆ ◆

Data Transformation Services (DTS) is one of the most useful (and often overlooked) capabilities of Microsoft's data platform. Far more than just simple data copying or column mapping, DTS is a powerful development platform complete with scripting languages, decision logic, and much more.

Learning how to use DTS will allow you to create robust, time-saving utilities and data-handling routines for your e-commerce site. Once you've learned to use DTS to transform data, you'll never write another standalone Visual Basic utility again to handle data manipulation tasks.

About Data Transformation Services

Data Transformation Services was first introduced in SQL Server 7.0, and was significantly enhanced for SQL Server 2000. The basic purpose of DTS is to move data and database objects from one place to another, performing whatever data manipulation or transformation may be required in the process.

DTS packages are generally stored in a SQL Server, although they can be stored in an Enterprise Microsoft Repository or in a COM-structured file (which facilitates sharing them through e-mail). Packages are accessed through SQL Server Enterprise Manager, as shown in Figure C-1.

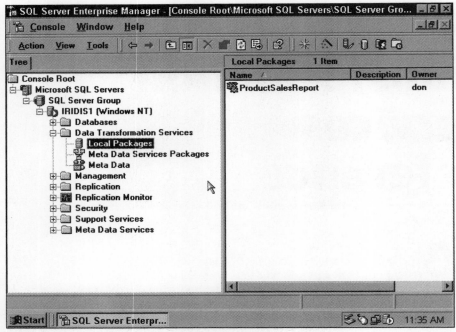

Figure C-1: DTS packages in Enterprise Manager

Enterprise Manager offers two ways of creating a new DTS package. The simpler of the two is the Import/Export Wizard, which allows you to create basic packages in order to move data from one table to another with basic transformation functions. You can build more complex packages by using the DTS Designer.

DTS packages are created from DTS objects, which include *connections* and *tasks*. These objects are joined together with *workflow connectors,* which define the order in which package objects are executed.

DTS Objects

SQL Server 2000 includes nine distinct connection objects, which are used to represent connections to data sources. You can make additional connections to any ODBC data source for which you have an ODBC driver. You can add these connections to the DTS Designer workspace by dragging them from the toolbox, or by selecting them from the Connections menu, as shown in Figure C-2.

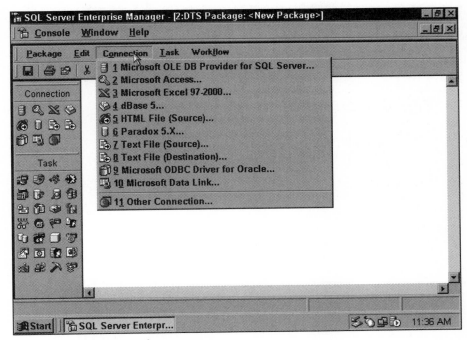

Figure C-2: The Connections menu

SQL Server includes nearly 20 DTS tasks, and Commerce Server 2000 adds another handful of tasks for performing Commerce Server-specific actions. You can add these tasks to the workspace by dragging them from the toolbox, or by selecting them from the Tasks menu, as shown in Figure C-3. I prefer the Tasks menu because the icons for the nearly 30 tasks can be difficult to distinguish.

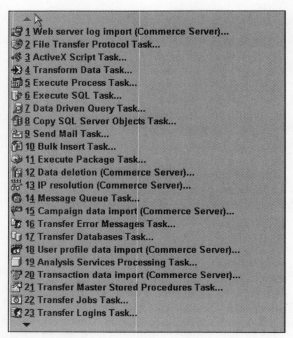

Figure C-3: The Tasks menu

Connections

Each connection represents a specific data source or destination. Connection objects representing database system connections each connect to a specific database. Other connection objects allow you to use Excel, text, and other flat files as data connections, and their connection objects represent a single file.

Each connection type requires that you provide the necessary parameters for DTS to actually open the connection. This may include information like a file name, user name, password, or server name, and differs depending on the connection that you are creating. Each connection object can be configured with a name that will identify it on the DTS Designer workspace and in any tasks to which the object is connected. You must define the name of the connection when you create it, and you won't be able to modify this name after the connection has been added to the workspace. I recommend that you choose a distinctive name for each connection object to make working with them easier.

Microsoft OLE DB Provider for SQL Server

The Microsoft OLE DB Provider for SQL Server allows DTS to connect to any version of Microsoft SQL Server, using a high-performance OLE DB connection. The configuration dialog box is shown in Figure C-4.

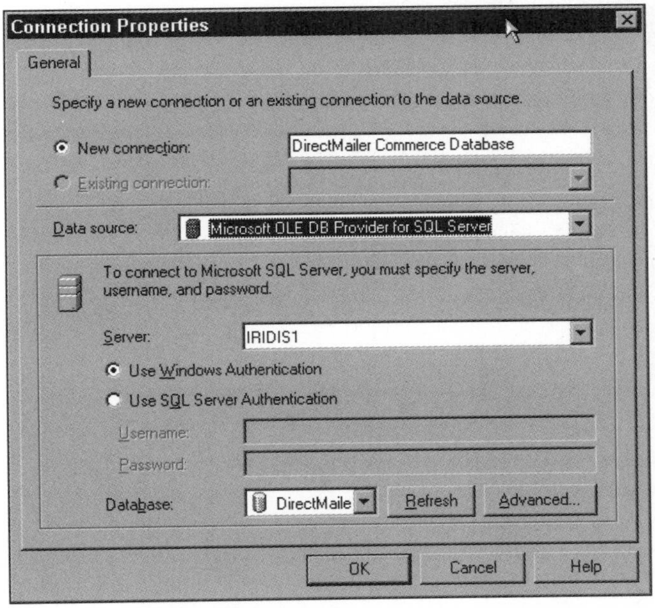

Figure C-4: OLE DB Provider for SQL Server properties

This connection object requires that you specify the name of a SQL Server and provide login credentials. Be wary of using the Windows Authentication method because this forces DTS to use the credentials of the user who executes the package. If the package is scheduled to run at a later time, it is invoked by whatever user account SQL Server Agent is logging in with. If your SQL Server supports SQL Authentication, I recommend creating a login for the DTS package to use and specifying that in this dialog.

After you specify login credentials, you can refresh the list of available databases and select the database that this connection object represents.

Microsoft Access

The Microsoft Access connection also uses an OLE DB provider to open Microsoft Access databases in an MDB file, as shown in Figure C-5. The specific version of the Microsoft Data Access Components (MDAC) installed on the SQL Server computer will determine which versions of Access are supported. Access connections are *file-type* connection objects, because the information resides in a physical file, rather than on a database server.

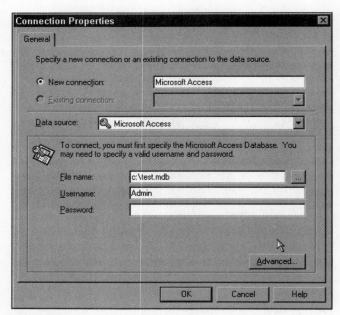

Figure C-5: Access properties

This connection object requires that you specify the file name of the Access database to which you want to connect. If the file is located on another server, it must be accessible by the user account that launches the DTS package. Remember that if the package is scheduled to run at a later time, it is executed under the user account that the SQL Server Agent service uses. Make sure that this user account has access to the file. You can also specify a user name and password if the Access database is protected.

Tip   All of the file-type database connections, including Access, Excel, and many others, must be accessible to the user account being used to run the DTS package.

Microsoft Excel 97/2000

This file-type connection object allows DTS to access data in a Microsoft Excel 97 or Excel 2000 file, as shown in Figure C-6. Each worksheet in the file is treated as a table, with rows and columns in each worksheet representing the rows and columns of the database.

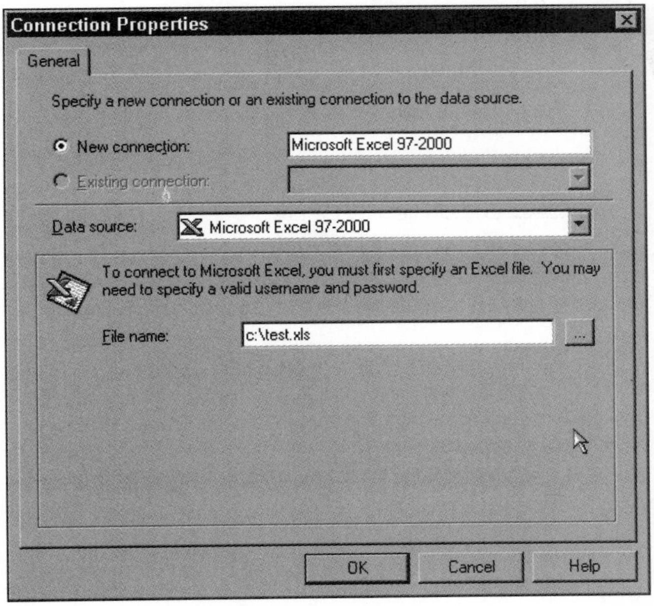

Figure C-6: Excel properties

dBase III, IV, and 5

dBase connection objects are file-type connections to a DBF file, as shown in Figure C-7. They are configured in the same way as an Access or Excel connection. Although dBase and FoxPro both use the DBF file type, you should not use the dBase connection object to connect to a FoxPro database; use the generic ODBC connection object for FoxPro databases.

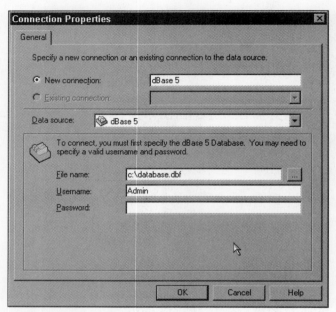

Figure C-7: dBase properties

DTS is capable of working with dBase III, IV, and 5 files; simply choose the appropriate version when configuring the connection object.

HTML File (Source)

This connection object uses an HTML file as a data source. The file can be accessed through the file system by configuring a complete path, as shown in Figure C-8, or configured to use an HTTP connection to access the file.

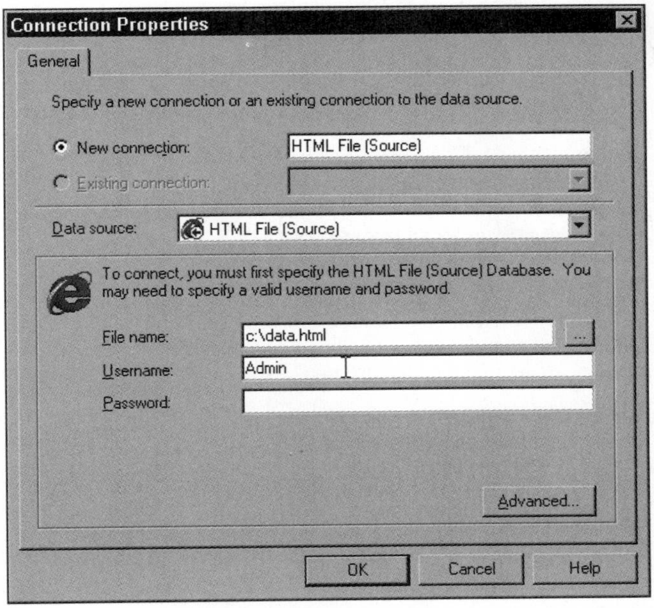

Figure C-8: HTML file (source) properties

The JET database engine, which is the heart of Microsoft Access, is used to access the HTML file. The HTML file must, therefore, be formatted to be compatible with Access. In general, this means that the HTML file must contain the data in an HTML table. Listing C-1 shows a sample HTML file produced from the Categories table of the Northwind sample database that comes with Microsoft Access 2000.

Listing C-1: **Sample HTML data file**

```
<HTML DIR=LTR>
<HEAD>
<META HTTP-EQUIV="Content-Type" CONTENT="text/html;
charset=Windows-1252">
<TITLE>Categories</TITLE>
</HEAD>
<BODY>
<TABLE DIR=LTR BORDER>
<CAPTION>Categories</CAPTION>
<TR>
<TD DIR=LTR ALIGN=RIGHT>1</TD>
<TD DIR=LTR ALIGN=LEFT>Beverages</TD>
<TD DIR=LTR ALIGN=LEFT>Soft drinks, coffees, teas, beers, and
ales</TD>
<TD></TD>
```

Continued

Listing C-1 *(continued)*

```
</TR>
<TR>
<TD DIR=LTR ALIGN=RIGHT>2</TD>
<TD DIR=LTR ALIGN=LEFT>Condiments</TD>
<TD DIR=LTR ALIGN=LEFT>Sweet and savory sauces, relishes,
spreads, and seasonings</TD>
<TD></TD>
</TR>
<TR>
<TD DIR=LTR ALIGN=RIGHT>3</TD>
<TD DIR=LTR ALIGN=LEFT>Confections</TD>
<TD DIR=LTR ALIGN=LEFT>Desserts, candies, and sweet breads</TD>
<TD></TD>
</TR>
<TR>
<TD DIR=LTR ALIGN=RIGHT>4</TD>
<TD DIR=LTR ALIGN=LEFT>Dairy Products</TD>
<TD DIR=LTR ALIGN=LEFT>Cheeses</TD>
<TD></TD>
</TR>
<TR>
<TD DIR=LTR ALIGN=RIGHT>5</TD>
<TD DIR=LTR ALIGN=LEFT>Grains/Cereals</TD>
<TD DIR=LTR ALIGN=LEFT>Breads, crackers, pasta, and cereal</TD>
<TD></TD>
</TR>
<TR>
<TD DIR=LTR ALIGN=RIGHT>6</TD>
<TD DIR=LTR ALIGN=LEFT>Meat/Poultry</TD>
<TD DIR=LTR ALIGN=LEFT>Prepared meats</TD>
<TD></TD>
</TR>
<TR>
<TD DIR=LTR ALIGN=RIGHT>7</TD>
<TD DIR=LTR ALIGN=LEFT>Produce</TD>
<TD DIR=LTR ALIGN=LEFT>Dried fruit and bean curd</TD>
<TD></TD>
</TR>
<TR>
<TD DIR=LTR ALIGN=RIGHT>8</TD>
<TD DIR=LTR ALIGN=LEFT>Seafood</TD>
<TD DIR=LTR ALIGN=LEFT>Seaweed and fish</TD>
<TD></TD>
</TR>
</TABLE>
</BODY>
</HTML>
```

Paradox

You can connect to Paradox databases using the Paradox connection object, as shown in Figure C-9. Paradox connections are file-type connections, and must be configured similarly to Access connections.

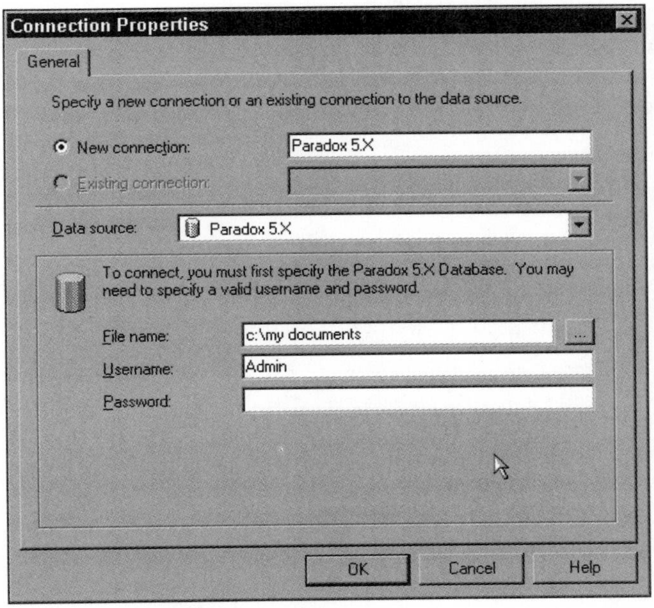

Figure C-9: Paradox properties

DTS is capable of working with Paradox 4 and 5 files; simply choose the appropriate version when configuring the connection object.

Text File (Source)

DTS can import data from a text file using the Text File (Source) connection object, shown in Figure C-10. This is a file-type connection, although as text files cannot contain internal user names or passwords, configuring this connection type is simpler than other file-type connections.

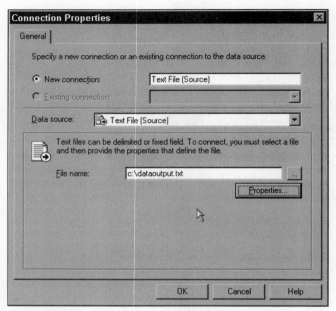

Figure C-10: Text file (source) properties

This connection allows you to specify a text file that is used as a data source. The text file may be formatted as a comma-separated, tab-separated, or fixed-length field file, and represents a single table. Unless you are using disconnected editing (which I discuss later in this appendix), the text file must exist when you attempt to create the connection object. After you have specified a file, you can click on the Properties button in the connection object dialog box to specify the format of the file.

Text File (Destination)

This connection allows you to specify a text file that is used for data output. If the text file doesn't already exist, SQL Server creates it. If the text file does exist, it is overwritten when the package is run. You can click the Properties button to bring up the dialog box shown in Figure C-11, which allows you to specify how the output file should be formatted.

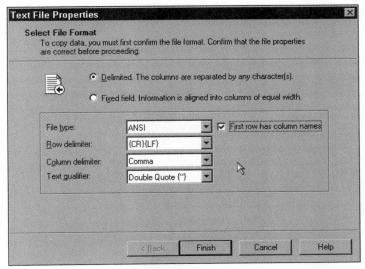

Figure C-11: Text file (destination) properties

Microsoft Data Link

Microsoft Data Links allow you to create connection objects to data sources that may change when the DTS package is actually run. The Data Link configuration dialog is shown in Figure C-12.

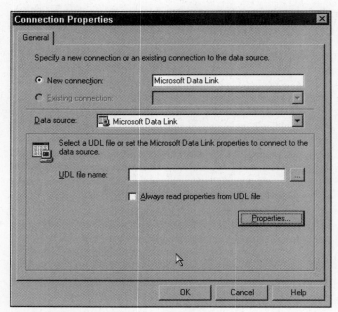

Figure C-12: Data Link properties

The Data Link connection object is used to specify a connection that is configured in a UDL file. This allows you to create a somewhat "generic" connection object that you can reconfigure without opening the DTS package; simply changing the UDL file changes the connection's properties. Be sure to check the "Always read properties from UDL file" if you want this behavior. If you don't, SQL Server reads the UDL file when the connection object is created, but won't read it again when the package is executed.

Other Connections (ODBC)

If you need to connect to a data source, but don't have an OLE DB provider for it, DTS allows you to create a generic Open Database Connectivity (ODBC) connection. The ODBC configuration dialog is shown in Figure C-13. ODBC drivers are available for a wider range of data sources, and are a good last resort for creating data connections to older data sources not supported by OLE DB.

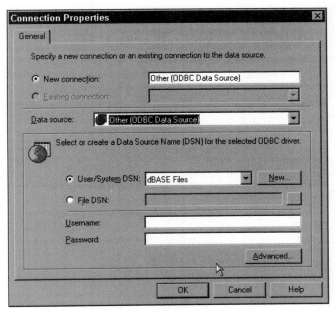

Figure C-13: ODBC Connection properties

Any data source for which you have an ODBC connection can be used with this connection object. The Microsoft Data Access Components (MDAC) library includes multilingual ODBC drivers for dBase, FoxPro, Visual FoxPro, and many other types of data sources. Using an ODBC connection is somewhat slower than using an OLE DB connection because SQL Server only "speaks" OLE DB natively. Using an ODBC connection requires the server to load a generic ODBC to OLE DB "translation" layer, on top of the ODBC layer and the actual ODBC driver.

Other connections (OLE DB)

If you have other OLE DB drivers, such as the OLE DB provider for Oracle or the many OLE DB providers installed along with Commerce Server, you can start with the SQL Server OLE DB provider connection object and select a new connection type in the object's dialog box. As shown in Figure C-14, several other OLE DB providers are available. Selecting a provider changes the appearance of the connection's dialog box to reflect the parameters required by the new provider.

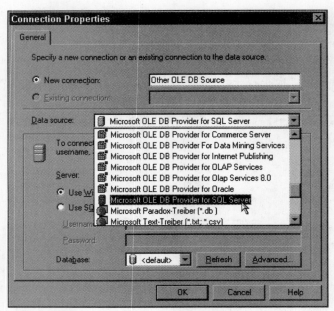

Figure C-14: OLE DB Connection properties

Tasks

Each DTS task performs a specific operation. Some tasks require a connection object in order to perform their operation; others are capable of acting on their own. Each task requires specific configuration parameters to define how it works.

Notice that some of the tasks described below are specific to Commerce Server 2000, and are only available after installing Commerce Server 2000 on the SQL Server 2000 computer. All of the Commerce Server tasks are designed to import data from the production database into the matching data warehouse that Commerce Server configured for the Web site. In all cases, you should execute the Configuration Synchronization DTS task, run any import tasks, and then run the Report Preparation task to ensure that the data warehouse is updated and processed correctly.

Web Server Log import task

The Web Server Log import task, shown in Figure C-15, imports Web server log data into the Commerce Server data warehouse for analysis.

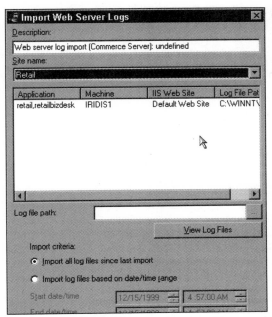

Figure C-15: Web Server Log import task properties

This task is designed to import information from your Internet Information Services (IIS) log files (or any Web server that uses W3C-compliant log files) into the data warehouse. By analyzing your log files, Commerce Server can report on user click histories, most-visited page, and so forth. When configuring this task, you can specify the log file name and the oldest log that you want the import process to capture.

File Transfer Protocol

The FTP task allows you to send and receive files via the File Transfer Protocol (FTP) as part of a DTS task. If you are planning to use DTS to exchange data files with trading partners (as opposed to using BizTalk Server), the FTP task can allow you to easily retrieve files from remote FTP sites for processing.

The first tab in the task properties dialog, shown in Figure C-16, allows you to specify the FTP site and your login credentials.

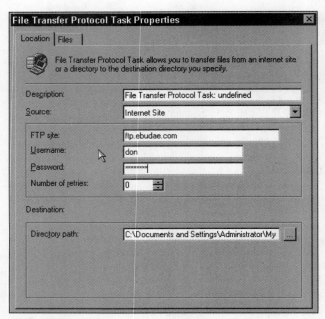

Figure C-16: FTP task main properties

You must provide the information requested in the Location tab before continuing to the Files tab, as shown in Figure C-17.

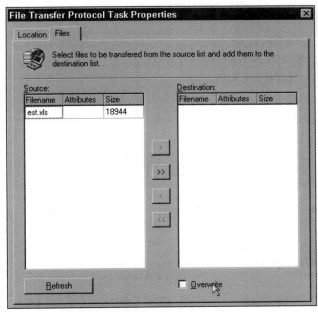

Figure C-17: FTP task file selection

The Files tab reads the files that currently exist at the site and in the destination directory that you specified. You can then indicate which files should be transferred when the task is executed.

ActiveX Script

This task allows you to write a complete program script using an ActiveX scripting language such as VBScript or Jscript. As shown in Figure C-18, the window provides a convenient reference to the selected language's functions and statements, and allows you to quickly build a script. The script can refer to any connection objects already present in the DTS Designer workspace, allowing you to use the task to manipulate data in various connections.

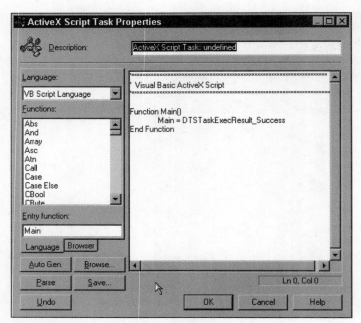

Figure C-18: ActiveX Script task properties

Transform Data

This task is the heart and soul of DTS. It must be connected to two connection objects, a source, and a destination. As shown in Figure C-19, you must specify the source connection object properties — you may specify a table to transform, or you may specify a query — and the results of that query form the source for the transformation.

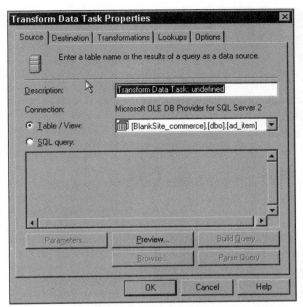

Figure C-19: Transform Data task source properties

Figure C-20 shows the destination connection's properties. You may select either an existing table to receive the transformed data, or have DTS create a new table to your specifications.

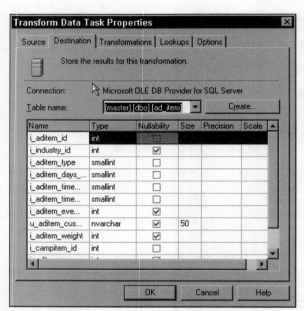

Figure C-20: Transform Data task destination properties

Figure C-21 shows the actual transformation properties. For each column in the source data, you can specify a variety of transformation operations, such as a direct copy, several string-handling functions, numeric formatting functions, and so forth. You can also specify a complete ActiveX script for each column, or for the entire task, that can perform more complex transformation and column-mapping operations.

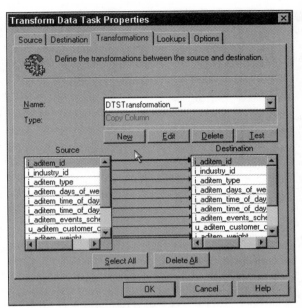

Figure C-21: Transform Data task transformation properties

Execute Process

This task allows you to execute an operating system process. Keep in mind that the process executes under the SQL Server Agent's security credentials, so make sure that the account has the necessary permissions to execute properly. As part of this task's configuration, you can specify a return code that indicates success; if a different return code is received from the process when it completes, DTS looks for a "failed" workflow path to execute. You can also specify a maximum time that the process should run, or specify 0 for an unlimited run time, as shown in Figure C-22. If you specify a timeout value and the process doesn't complete with a return code in that time, DTS terminates the process and looks for a "failed" workflow path.

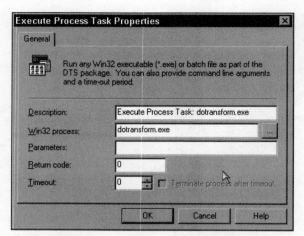

Figure C-22: Execute Process task properties

Execute SQL

This task, shown in Figure C-23, allows you to execute a standalone Transact-SQL task. You must specify an existing connection object to run the T-SQL statement against, and you can specify a maximum time in which the statement should be allowed to execute. If the statement runs longer, SQL Server will terminate the statement and look for a "failed" workflow path to execute.

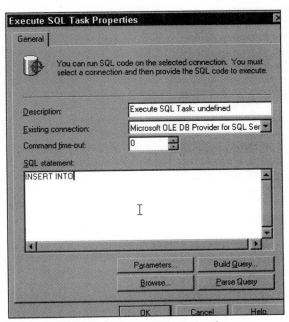

Figure C-23: Execute SQL task properties

Data Driven Query

This task, shown in Figure C-24, allows you to perform Transact-SQL operations on data, including stored procedures and INSERT, UPDATE, or DELETE statements. For each row in the source, which may be a table or query returned from a connection object, the task selects, customizes, and executes one of several SQL statements. You select which statement to execute via a constant return value set in an ActiveX script transformation. Based on the return constant you use in the script, one of four different parameterized SQL statements that you create may be executed for each source row.

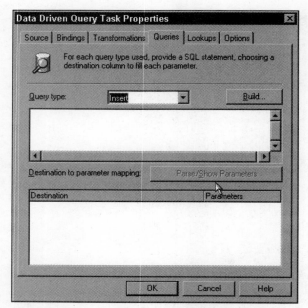

Figure C-24: Data Driven Query task properties

This task allows you to handle data in a very customized and flexible fashion, but be cautious of using it with extremely large result sets. Because each row in the result set is examined and handled individually, large result sets fed to this task can take a very long time to execute and can generate considerable traffic in the destination's transaction log.

Copy SQL Server Objects

This task allows you to copy database objects between SQL Servers or between databases on the same server. As shown in Figure C-25, you have the ability to copy data and objects, and SQL Server can be told to drop any existing objects first (a good idea if you will be copying objects that may already exist at the destination), and copy any dependent objects if necessary (ensuring that the objects you copy will work properly at the destination). This task is useful for creating a reporting database that only contains a subset of the main production database. This task can take some time to execute with large tables, however, and can generate considerable traffic in the destination database's transaction log.

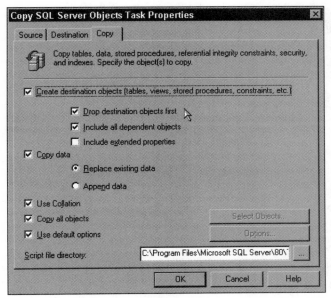

Figure C-25: Copy SQL Server Objects task properties

Send Mail

The Send Mail task allows your DTS packages to send e-mail. Your SQL Server must have SQL Mail configured and running properly in order for this task to work. This task can be used to send e-mail notifications in the event that a particular task in a DTS package fails, or can be used to send the results of the package, such as a report, to recipients via e-mail.

Bulk Insert

This task, shown in Figure C-26, allows you to perform bulk inserts of data from external files into the specified database table (which must be an existing connection in the DTS Designer). The destination database must have Bulk Insert enabled in its properties. Remember that Bulk Insert is a non-logged operation, meaning that the inserts are not recorded in the database's transaction log. This means that a failure is impossible to recover, so you should always back up the database after a Bulk Insert.

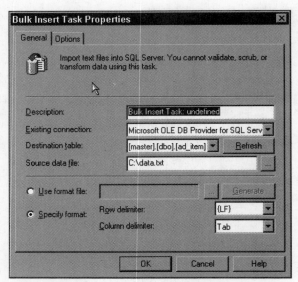

Figure C-26: Bulk Insert task properties

Execute Package

This task allows you to execute another DTS package on the local or a remote SQL Server. The configuration dialog is shown in Figure C-27. You can create modular DTS packages to perform specific tasks, and then link them all together with a single "master" package that can be scheduled for execution or run on demand.

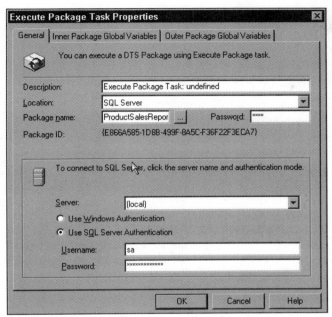

Figure C-27: Execute Package task properties

Data Deletion

This Commerce Server 2000–specific task allows you to clean out your data warehouse. You can select different types of data to delete. Figure C-28 shows the task configured to delete imported Web server log files. After selecting a data type, the task displays all currently loaded data, allowing you to delete data older than a certain date, for example. This lets you remove historical information that is no longer needed in your regular analysis reports.

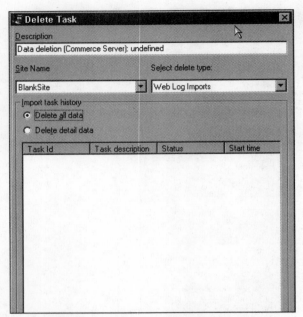

Figure C-28: Data Deletion task properties

IP Address Resolution

When you import your Web server log files, Commerce Server doesn't attempt to resolve the IP addresses in the log to actual domain names. However, domain names can make the report easier to read and more meaningful, so you should consider running an IP Address Resolution task on a regular basis.

As shown in Figure C-29, this task allows you to specify your local domain name, and allows you to configure domain name caching. Domain name resolution can be a time-consuming process; by caching names, Commerce Server is able to run through the complete database much faster. However, the longer you cache the names, the more likely your data will be incorrect. The default setting is 30 days, but because domain name-to-IP address mappings don't typically change that often, I recommend changing this setting to 90 days.

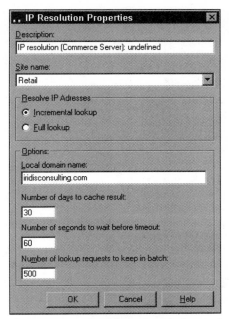

Figure C-29: IP Address Resolution task properties

You can also specify a full or incremental resolution. A full resolution resolves all IP addresses in the data warehouse; incremental resolution only resolves IP addresses that were not resolved in a past run. You need to run a full resolution the first time you use this task; subsequent tasks should be set to use incremental resolution unless you want to re-run all of your resolutions to ensure their accuracy (as names on the Internet do tend to change from time to time).

Message Queue

The Message Queue task, shown in Figure C-30, allows a DTS package to place messages on other applications' message queues, or retrieve messages from a specified queue. This allows DTS to integrate and cooperate with other applications. For example, your site may include a function that allows users to request a copy of a past order via e-mail. Rather than having your site process that request immediately, which would require more overhead through your Web servers and application servers, you can write a component to place the request in a queue.

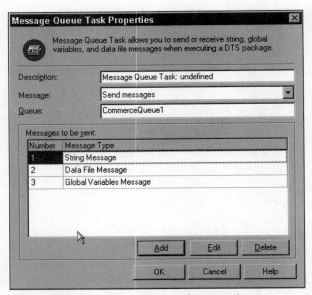

Figure C-30: Message Queue task properties

A regularly scheduled DTS package can run and retrieve the messages from a queue, query the database, and compose outgoing e-mail messages as required. If you have a large number of jobs like this, you can even have them run on a separate SQL Server machine that contains a copy of the Commerce Server database. This offloads the processing onto a separate machine, keeping your main database servers free to support the active Web site.

Campaign Data Import

When you create a discount or other campaign with Commerce Server, your production database builds up a great deal of useful data that can be utilized in your analysis reports. The Campaign Data Import task pulls the appropriate data out of the production database and inserts it into the appropriate locations in the site's data warehouse for later analysis. You can use the configuration dialog, shown in Figure C-31, to specify a full load, which pulls all data from your production database, or an incremental load, which only pulls information created since the last full load. Always specify a full load the first time you run this task.

Transfer Error Messages

If you have defined custom error messages on a SQL Server and want to transfer them to another SQL Server, this task accomplishes the job in a single DTS step. Just specify the source and destination servers and the error messages that you want to transfer, or have the task transfer all encountered error messages. See Figure C-32.

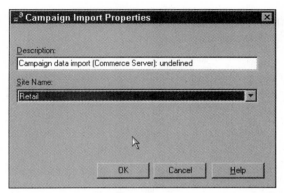

Figure C-31: Campaign Data Import task properties

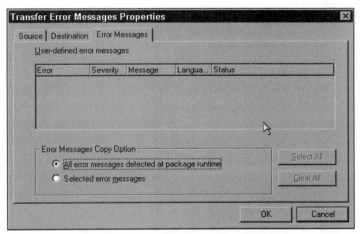

Figure C-32: Transfer Error Messages task properties

Transfer Databases

The Transfer Databases task, shown in Figure C-33, allows you to move or copy a database and all of the objects that the database contains from one SQL Server to another (or make a copy on the same SQL Server). Be aware that this can be an intensive, time-consuming operation for large databases, and use of this task over a slow network connection is not recommended. The primary use of this task is to copy your development database to create your production SQL Server computers when you begin to deploy your site.

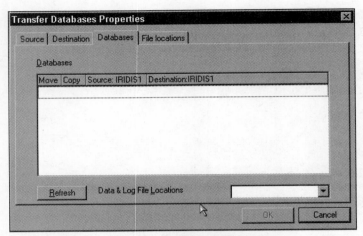

Figure C-33: Transfer Databases task properties

User Profile Data Import

The information stored in the user profiles in Commerce Server can be extremely valuable for analysis purposes. This task, shown in Figure C-34, pulls the appropriate data out of the production database and inserts it into the appropriate locations in the site's data warehouse for later analysis. You can specify a full load, which pulls all data from your production database, or an incremental load, which only pulls information created since the last full load. Specify a full load the first time you run this task.

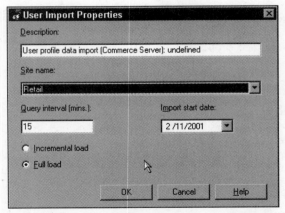

Figure C-34: User Profile Data Import task properties

Analysis Services Processing

This task kicks off the Analysis Services processing for a specified analysis database. The object type that you select may allow you to specify a full processing run, a data refresh, or an incremental processing run, as shown in Figure C-35. This task is designed for use with *any* analysis database. Commerce Server's site data warehouse should generally be processed by using the Report Preparation task described later in this appendix, rather than with this generic processing task.

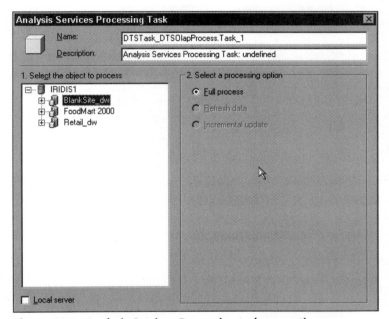

Figure C-35: Analysis Services Processing task properties

Transaction Data Import

As users place orders for your products and services, your production database builds up a great deal of useful data that can be used in your analysis reports. The Data Import task pulls the appropriate data out of the production database and inserts it into the appropriate locations in the site's data warehouse for later analysis. You can specify a full load, which pulls all data from your production database, or an incremental load, which only pulls information created since the last full load. Obviously, you must do a full load the first time you run this task.

Transfer Master Stored Procedures

If you have defined stored procedures on a SQL Server and want to transfer them to another SQL Server, the Transfer Master Store Procedures task accomplishes the job in a single DTS step. Specify the source and destination servers and the procedures that you want to transfer, or have the task transfer all encountered procedures, as shown in Figure C-36.

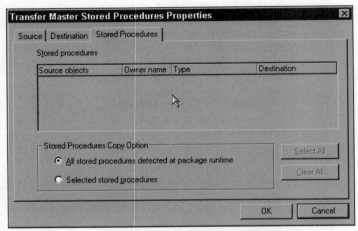

Figure C-36: Transfer Master Stored Procedures task properties

Transfer Jobs

If you have defined SQL Server Agent jobs on a SQL Server and want to transfer them to another SQL Server, the Transfer Jobs task accomplishes this in a single DTS step. As shown in Figure C-37, specify the source and destination servers and the jobs that you want to transfer, or have the task transfer all jobs that it finds.

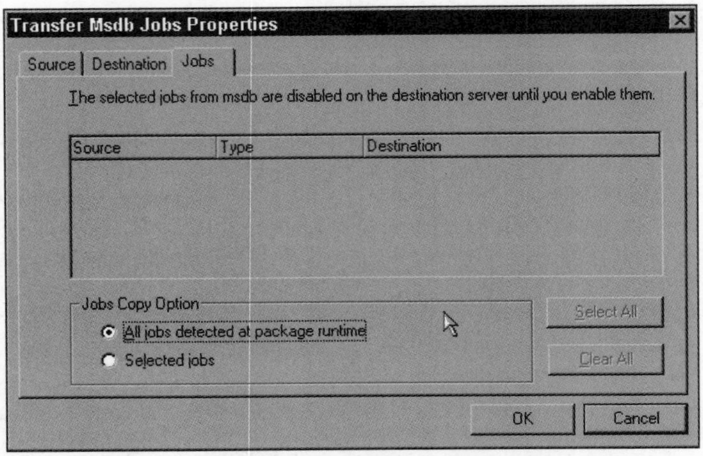

Figure C-37: Transfer Jobs task properties

Transfer Logins

If you have defined custom logins on a SQL Server and want to transfer them to another SQL Server, the Transfer Logins task can accomplish the job. Specify the source and destination servers and the logins that you want to transfer, or have the task transfer all encountered logins, as shown in Figure C-38.

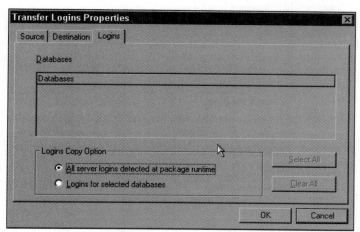

Figure C-38: Transfer Logins task properties

If you are copying logins from a SQL Server in one domain to a SQL Server in another, you must avoid copying any Windows-integrated logins. These logins are domain-specific, and cannot successfully be copied to a server in another domain. SQL Server logins can be safely copied regardless of the servers' domain membership.

Report Preparation

This task, shown in Figure C-39, performs the analysis services processing that is necessary for a Commerce Server data warehouse to provide useful reporting data. You should run this task after loading new data into the data warehouse, and before running any reports against the data warehouse. You must also run this task after using the Delete Data task to remove data from the data warehouse.

The first time you run this task, select the Full option. You can then specify the Incremental option for future runs of the task, unless you delete and then reload data by using an import task's Full option.

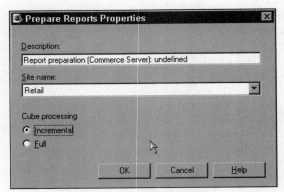

Figure C-39: Report Preparation task properties

Be advised that this task may take a considerable amount of time to process due to the inherent design of a data warehouse. The benefit is that reports run against the fully processed database are much faster than they would be otherwise. Under no circumstances should you run this task on a production database server that is used to support the site — only run this task on a dedicated reporting server.

Configuration Synchronization

This task must be run before running any import or delete tasks on your Commerce Server data warehouse. It synchronizes the configuration between your live site and your data warehouse to ensure that the imported data is handled properly. The configuration for this task, shown in Figure C-40, requires you to indicate which site you want to synchronize.

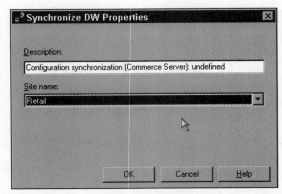

Figure C-40: Configuration Synchronization task properties

Product Catalog Import

Your product catalog contains a great deal of pertinent information for your analysis reports. For example, analyzing what your customer purchased isn't very useful without product stock numbers and descriptions. This task, shown in Figure C-41, allows you to import your product catalog from your live database into your Commerce Server data warehouse. Again, a full load or incremental load may be specified.

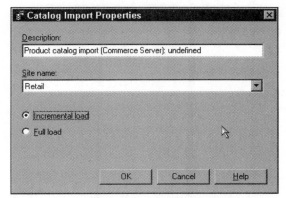

Figure C-41: Product Catalog Import task properties

Building a Package

After you've become familiar with the basic tools of the DTS Designer, connections, and tasks, you can start building DTS packages. Follow these steps:

1. Add data connections.
2. Add tasks.
3. Define the workflow between these objects.
4. Modify the properties of the package.
5. Save and test the package.

Create connections

You can create new connections by simply dragging the connection icon from the toolbox, or by selecting the appropriate connection type from the Connections menu. Every connection object that is not the destination of a task is considered a starting point in DTS. Typically, connections attach to each other by Data Transformation tasks, and each starting point represents a parallel path. DTS attempts to execute up to four parallel paths at once.

For example, suppose you need to copy information from your live database server to a reporting server. From the reporting server, you need to copy a subset of the data into a text file. You also need to retrieve a text file from a partner via FTP and import that data into the reporting database. You start by defining the four connection objects, as shown in Figure C-42.

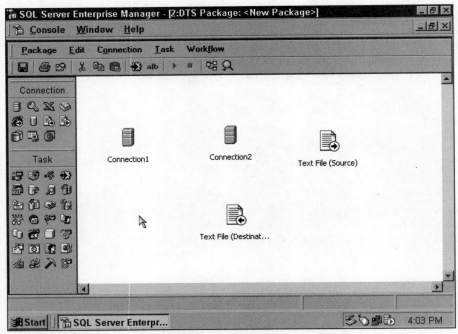

Figure C-42: Defining the connections

Add tasks

After your connections have been added, you can begin adding the necessary tasks. Following the example, you need to add two Data Transformation tasks — one task to move data from the live database to the production database, and another to transform the data into the text file. You also need to add an FTP task to take care of transferring the file. After adding the necessary tasks, the DTS Designer workspace appears, as shown in Figure C-43.

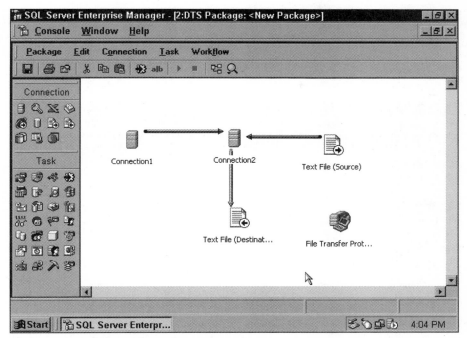

Figure C-43: Adding tasks to the workspace

Define workflow

Workflow helps SQL Server understand what to do if a specific task fails, succeeds, or completes with failure or success. Follow these steps to create workflow:

1. Select a starting object.

2. Hold down the Ctrl key and select the next object in the workflow.

3. From the Workflow menu, select the desired action.

In the example, the text file import into the reporting database should not begin until the FTP task completes, because the FTP task is retrieving the file. You may also want the DTS package to place messages on a special application message queue for a management application. These messages can be used to inform an administrator of a failure in the package. The revised DTS Designer workspace is shown in Figure C-44.

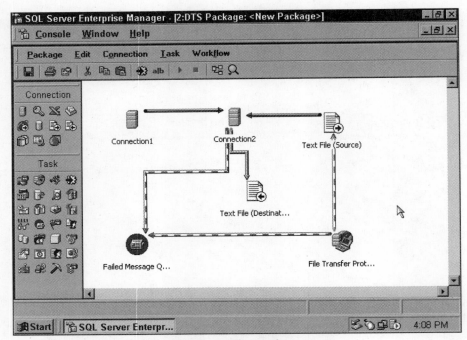

Figure C-44: Adding workflow arrows to the workspace

Editing package properties

The downside to the DTS Designer is that it executes completely on your computer, but the final DTS package executes on the server. This can complicate the creation of packages that use files. For example, specifying a source file of `c:\data.txt` refers to that location on your local computer, not on the server. When the package executes on the server, however, it looks for the file in the root of the server's C: drive.

To help work around this condition, DTS features a *Disconnected Editor*. This editor allows you to make changes to package properties, but doesn't validate that you enter correct data. This means you can configure a data source with a file location that isn't present on your workstation and DTS will trust you by allowing you to save the package. DTS returns an error if the file is not found when the package executes on the server.

The Disconnected Editor is shown in Figure C-45.

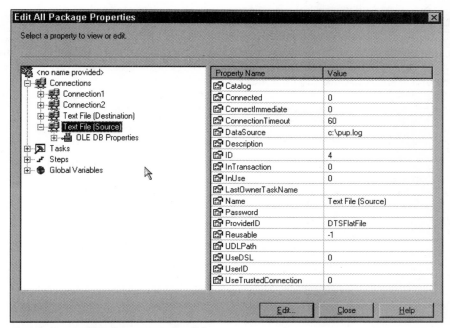

Figure C-45: DTS disconnected editing

Save and test

After you finish creating your DTS package, save it either to the local SQL Server, to the Repository, to a COM-structured file, or, in SQL Server 2000, to a Visual Basic .BAS file. You can specify a password to prevent others from editing or executing the package.

Tip Saving the DTS package to a .BAS file allows you to open the package in Visual Basic, and further extend it using the full VB development environment.

If you are creating the package on your workstation computer, I recommend against executing the package from the DTS Designer. Doing so causes the package to be executed locally on your computer, rather than from the context of the server. Instead, schedule the package to run from the server to perform your test, or log on to the server console to execute the package.

Summary

Working with DTS can be very easy with the DTS Designer, even though DTS' functionality and flexibility make it a complex set of technologies. By simply dragging the correct objects onto the Designer's workspace and connecting them with tasks and workflow indicators, you can build robust, modular DTS packages that greatly simplify most data manipulation and data maintenance tasks.

✦   ✦   ✦

Writing Pipeline and COM+ Components

In this age of scripting languages like VBScript and Jscript, many programmers wonder if compiled executable components are still necessary. The answer, of course, is "absolutely!" Scripts are still interpreted "on the fly," meaning that they can never match the performance of a pre-compiled component at run time.

Understanding how the Windows operating system treats components enables you to write more robust, better-performing components for your e-commerce site. You need to understand how Windows handles *threading*, which is the basis for the operating system's multiprocessing capabilities. You should also know the specific requirements for COM+ components, and more specifically, for Commerce Server pipeline components.

Threading

Every component or application running under Windows represents a *process*. In Windows NT, Windows 2000, or Windows XP, you can view most currently running processes with the Task Manager. Microsoft Word, for example, represents a single process.

Each process can create multiple *threads*. Each thread is responsible for executing a particular task, such as printing a document or waiting for user input. Windows is capable of running multiple threads at the same time, and can even run different threads from the same process on multiple processors. Therefore, threads represent the smallest unit of execution that Windows can work with, and threads form the basis for Windows' multiprocessing capabilities.

ASP+ = Compiled Scripts?

As this book goes to press, Microsoft is completing development of the next generation of Active Server Pages, currently called ASP+. In addition to a completely new programming model, ASP+ offers a significant performance advantage over the current version of ASP by using *compiled scripts*.

If you think that sounds like an oxymoron, you're partially right. By definition, scripts are interpreted line-by-line at run time. ASP+ compiles the script into a "pseudo-DLL" executable, transparently and on the fly when the script is first processed. Every time the script is accessed, ASP+ checks to see if the script has changed; if it has, ASP+ recompiles it into a new pseudo-DLL.

Although the compiling process results in a short delay, the resulting "compiled script" executes much faster than an interpreted script. Unfortunately, this script does *not* execute as fast as a completely compiled, traditional executable, so compiled components still have a place in the world of e-commerce development.

In addition to threads, processes can own specific resources, such as open files, blocks of memory used to store variables, and so forth. Threads generally need to access these resources in order to perform their work, and this is where complications arise. A process can have multiple threads running on completely different processors. Each of these threads, however, may need to access the same resources, such as a document file or an area of memory. The threads may also need to pass data to each other. Handling this interplay between threads is the challenge of a multithreaded, multiprocessing operating system like Windows.

Threading models

Windows supports several different *threading models* for different purposes. Each threading model sets rules and parameters that a process' threads must operate within, and each model provides specific advantages and disadvantages to the software developer. Most programming languages, such as Visual C++ and the languages in Visual Studio .NET, offer the ability to create components in one or more of these threading models, so the first step in authoring a component is to understand which threading model you should use.

Single-threaded

Single-threading represents the simplest form of threading and results in a component (or application) that is not multithreaded. All processing takes place on a single thread of execution, and the application is incapable of internal multitasking.

The early versions of Microsoft Word are an example of single-threading. When you tried to print or save a document in one of these early versions, the entire application was "hung" until the print or save operation completed. This happened because those operations occurred on a single thread, which was also the same thread used by the main application. While this single thread was busy printing or saving, it couldn't do anything else.

COM+ components and pipeline components must *never* be written as single-threaded because they will suffer a serious degradation in performance and will represent a bottleneck in your site's execution.

Note All Visual Basic applications were single-threaded until Visual Basic 5, Service Pack 2, in which apartment-model threading was introduced. This multithreading model was improved in Visual Basic 6.

Free-threaded

A *free-threaded* component is almost the exact opposite of a single-threaded component. Each new task within the component can be launched on a separate thread, allowing the component to perform better — especially on multiprocessor systems. Unfortunately, the operating system doesn't provide any help with this threading model. Each thread is essentially "on its own." Threads are unable to pass data to each other without using complex programming methods (called *marshalling*), and they are unable to safely access the same resources unless the programmer takes special precautions in memory and resource management.

Tip If you're interested in learning more about data marshalling and cross-thread memory and resource management, find a good book on advanced 32-bit Windows programming.

For example, imagine that the main thread of an application has stored the value "John Doe," representing a customer's name, in a specific location in memory. The main thread then launches two new threads to perform separate tasks. Both threads read the customer's name from the memory location and get the same result. Both threads also determine that the letters in the customer's name need to be uppercase (for whatever reason). The first thread makes the modification by changing the memory location to "JOHN DOE." The second thread attempts to change the memory location, but encounters an error because the memory location has already been changed by another thread.

This lack of synchronization between threads makes for great multiprocessing capabilities, but requires complex code to make sure that threads don't "walk" on each other, thus changing data that other threads need to work with. This is complicated by the fact that free threads have no "natural" way to communicate with each other.

If two components each need to create instances of a single free-threaded object, additional threads are created to run each new instance of the object. Therefore, special steps are necessary because none of the components' threads are assuming any special capabilities in communicating with the other threads in the process. This results in big savings in memory and processor overhead, because the original components aren't taking any special steps to ensure communication with the other threads.

Apartment-threaded

An *apartment* is a concept used to simplify multithreading for the software developer. All of the objects created in an apartment share a contiguous logical space created by the operating system. An apartment can contain a single thread or it can contain multiple threads. The operating system provides two abilities to all of the threads within an apartment — the ability to communicate with each other and the ability to safely access shared process resources. This makes creating multithreaded components much easier because tasks running on different threads can essentially assume that they're part of the same overall application.

Unfortunately, this convenience comes at a price in performance. Multiple threads can only communicate with each other and access shared resources if they are provided with some means of synchronization. Because apartment-model threading doesn't require the developer to provide this synchronization, the operating system must provide it.

When two applications need to create an instance of the same apartment-threaded component, two complete copies of the component must be created in memory. These two apartments aren't able to communicate with each other, but the threads within each apartment can still communicate freely. Although this creates a significantly higher amount of memory and processor overhead, this technique is necessary to maintain the internal logical processing space of the apartment-threading model.

Both

If a free-threaded component needs to call another component, that component must also be free-threaded. Likewise, an apartment-threaded component can only make calls to other apartment-threaded components. Of course there are exceptions to these rules; for example, a component created to use one threading type can call a component created to use the other threading type. These exceptions require that the components use special Windows programming techniques to communicate with each other.

Fortunately, components can be created and marked to support both free-threading and apartment-threading. This allows the components to be called by components that use either threading model, although the developer must take steps to ensure that the "both" component has all the necessary code to support free-threaded operation.

Mixing terminology

Microsoft's terminology for threading models has undergone many revisions, and will almost certainly continue to do so. For example, single-threaded components can support a single apartment-model thread because the components can have only one thread, which can communicate with itself quite easily.

Free-threaded components can support multiple single-thread apartments. That is, they can have multiple threads, each of which is a law unto itself (unless special steps are taken to synchronize them).

To summarize the available threading models in this context:

+ **A component can have one, single-thread apartment.** This can also be referred to as a *single-threaded component*.

+ **A component can have multiple single-thread apartments.** This can also be referred to as a *free-threaded component*.

+ **A component can have one multiple-threaded apartment.** This is the traditional definition of an apartment-threaded component.

Threading in Visual Basic 6.0

Visual Basic 6.0 uses a single multi-threaded apartment. This makes it unsuitable for use in some highly scalable applications because each new instance of a component created in Visual Basic requires a complete copy of the component in memory, which can create a great deal of overhead.

Imagine, for example, that you create a credit-card processing component by using Visual Basic. Then 100 customers try to check out on your Web site at the same time. Your server must be capable of running 100 copies of the Visual Basic component at the same time. Although this is certainly possible, imagine scaling the number to 200 customers, or 500, or even 1,000 customers.

On the other hand, a free-threaded component can create a new thread to handle each new customer. Because this requires significantly less overhead than is required to create an entirely new copy of the entire component, the free-threaded component offers much better performance and scalability than the one written in Visual Basic 6.0.

Unfortunately, creating free-threaded components in Visual Basic 6.0 is impossible because the language doesn't offer the necessary built-in functionality to handle thread synchronization and marshalling, and because Visual Basic 6.0 doesn't offer sufficient access to the Windows API for a developer to manually create the necessary functionality. In the world of Visual Studio 6.0, only Visual C++ 6.0 coupled with Microsoft's Active Threading Library (ATL) is capable of creating truly free-threaded components.

Component Theory

COM+ components provide robust, scalable functionality to applications. Components created with a single-thread model don't support this requirement. To make the creation and management of multithreaded components easier, COM+ takes on the responsibility of managing a component's threads — leaving the component author free to concentrate on basic functionality.

Threading models

COM+ also introduces a new threading model, called the *neutral apartment*. In the neutral apartment, components follow the same rules for creating a multithreaded apartment, and COM+ handles thread synchronization and interlocking resource access. Neutral apartments are the preferred threading model for COM+ components because they offer the greatest flexibility. However, only components with no user interface can use neutral apartment threading; any components that present a user interface must continue to use another threading model.

Note   The neutral threading model is unique to COM+ and isn't available in earlier versions of COM.

COM+ offers the following threading models to components:

+ **Main Thread Apartment.** This model is used for components running on the main thread of a process.

+ **Single-threaded apartment.** Also referred to as a *simple apartment model*.

+ **Free-threaded apartment.** Also referred to as a *free thread model*.

+ **Neutral apartment.** This model is used for components that don't implement a specific threading model, and run on the same thread as the process that instantiates them.

+ **Both.** Supports either type of apartment model.

Data requirements

For performance reasons, developers like to keep (or *persist*) application data in memory. It's obviously faster than searching through the database every time you need it and, after all, persisting data in memory is the whole point of variables.

However, the last thing that a COM+ component should do is persist data in memory. In a COM+ cluster, clients may "hit" several different servers with the same component; these components have no effective way to communicate with each other except through a back-end database. Therefore, any data that needs to be persisted has to wind up in that back-end database or it won't be available to the next copy of the component that needs to work with it.

Even if you don't implement COM+ clusters, a typical e-commerce site has multiple identical Web servers in a *server farm*. Load balancing is usually implemented on these farms, which results in clients almost randomly cycling between Web servers.

COM+ components on those servers must persist all of their data in a back-end database, where it will be available no matter which server takes a client's next request.

The basic workflow for any COM+ component should be:

1. Receive all necessary data from the calling component or script as parameters. If that isn't possible, receive enough data in parameters to look up the rest of the required data in a back-end database.

2. Retrieve any necessary data from the back-end database.

3. Perform processing tasks.

4. Save any persisted data to the back-end database. Not all components will create data that needs to be persisted, so this step isn't always necessary.

5. Return any necessary data to the calling component or script.

6. Destroy all objects and data that were created during processing. This frees up memory and processing cycles and ensures that the component's next instance starts "clean."

Location assumptions

COM+ components should never assume that they are running in a particular physical location because they may be installed on several Web servers, or they may be installed on middle-tier servers in a COM+ cluster. The component developer should always assume that the component is running in an undetermined physical location, and then carefully perform the following tasks:

✦ **Always refer to *all* resources by a complete, absolute path (either a URL or UNC, as appropriate).** This includes resources that are supposed to be located on the local server. Use environment variables to retrieve the server name and specify a complete path to the resource.

✦ **Always save all data to a centrally accessible data store by using an absolute path.** This path should either be hard-coded, or (even better) centrally configured so that all copies of the component use the same absolute path. This ensures that data created by one component is accessible to other copies of the component.

✦ **Make no assumptions about the availability of local resources.** For example, the first phase of a middle-tier COM+ cluster may include physically identical servers, so it may seem safe to assume that they all have a local DVD-ROM drive or some other resource. However, subsequent expansions to the cluster may use physically dissimilar hardware, thus creating problems for components that assume the availability of local resources.

COM+ components should always make use of centrally available resources, addressing them with a centrally configured absolute path.

COM+ and Visual Basic 6

Visual Basic 6 was specifically designed to take advantage of COM and Microsoft Transaction Server (MTS) technologies. Prior to COM+, developers had to make a conscious choice to write components to the COM or MTS specifications because the two were essentially separate (although related) technologies. COM was included with Windows operating systems by default, whereas MTS required an additional step to install the actual Transaction Server.

One major goal of COM+ was to unite these two technologies (as well as uniting Microsoft Message Queue Server, or MSMQ) into a single, built-into-the-operating-system set of technologies. COM+ components must be registered with the operating system in a special way, as part of a *COM+ Application,* which defines the operating characteristics of the COM+ component.

Although Visual Basic 6 wasn't designed specifically to take advantage of COM+ (in the way that Visual Basic .NET is), it can still take advantage of the underlying legacy technologies that make up COM+, such as MSMQ and MTS. The primary disadvantage to a Visual Basic 6 application as a middle-tier language is the restricted threading model, which requires creating a completely new image of a component in memory for each instance created by a calling application.

Visual Basic 6 pipeline components

The threading model of Visual Basic 6 is the primary reason that the language is unsuitable for creating Commerce Server pipeline components. Because pipelines are intended to run quickly and, essentially, "between" Web page requests from a client, it is essential that pipeline components support free-threading to enable them to work from a single in-memory application image.

By contrast, Visual Basic .NET supports a variety of threading models and gives the software developer the ability to spawn separate processing threads on command, thus providing greater control over the multiprocessing capabilities of a component.

Summary

Although writing your own pipeline and COM+ components may seem to involve a lot of complex rules, learning those rules can allow you to create very high-performance, highly scalable custom software for your site. The investment of time to learn how to program these components can allow you to extend and customize your site's operation far beyond Commerce Server's original capabilities.

✦　　✦　　✦

Index

Continued

Continued

Continued

Continued

Continued

Continued

Hungry Minds, Inc.
End-User License Agreement

READ THIS. You should carefully read these terms and conditions before opening the software packet(s) included with this book ("Book"). This is a license agreement ("Agreement") between you and Hungry Minds, Inc. ("HMI"). By opening the accompanying software packet(s), you acknowledge that you have read and accept the following terms and conditions. If you do not agree and do not want to be bound by such terms and conditions, promptly return the Book and the unopened software packet(s) to the place you obtained them for a full refund.

1. **License Grant.** HMI grants to you (either an individual or entity) a nonexclusive license to use one copy of the enclosed software program(s) (collectively, the "Software") solely for your own personal or business purposes on a single computer (whether a standard computer or a workstation component of a multi-user network). The Software is in use on a computer when it is loaded into temporary memory (RAM) or installed into permanent memory (hard disk, CD-ROM, or other storage device). HMI reserves all rights not expressly granted herein.

2. **Ownership.** HMI is the owner of all right, title, and interest, including copyright, in and to the compilation of the Software recorded on the disk(s) or CD-ROM ("Software Media"). Copyright to the individual programs recorded on the Software Media is owned by the author or other authorized copyright owner of each program. Ownership of the Software and all proprietary rights relating thereto remain with HMI and its licensers.

3. **Restrictions On Use and Transfer.**

    (a) You may only (i) make one copy of the Software for backup or archival purposes, or (ii) transfer the Software to a single hard disk, provided that you keep the original for backup or archival purposes. You may not (i) rent or lease the Software, (ii) copy or reproduce the Software through a LAN or other network system or through any computer subscriber system or bulletin-board system, or (iii) modify, adapt, or create derivative works based on the Software.

    (b) You may not reverse engineer, decompile, or disassemble the Software. You may transfer the Software and user documentation on a permanent basis, provided that the transferee agrees to accept the terms and conditions of this Agreement and you retain no copies. If the Software is an update or has been updated, any transfer must include the most recent update and all prior versions.

4. **Restrictions on Use of Individual Programs.** You must follow the individual requirements and restrictions detailed for each individual program in Appendix A of this Book. These limitations are also contained in the individual license agreements recorded on the Software Media. These limitations may include a requirement that after using the program for a specified period of time, the user must pay a registration fee or discontinue use. By opening the Software packet(s), you will be agreeing to abide by the licenses and restrictions for these individual programs that are detailed in Appendix A and on the Software Media. None of the material on this Software Media or listed in this Book may ever be redistributed, in original or modified form, for commercial purposes.

5. **Limited Warranty.**

    (a) HMI warrants that the Software and Software Media are free from defects in materials and workmanship under normal use for a period of sixty (60) days from the date of purchase of this Book. If HMI receives notification within the warranty period of defects in materials or workmanship, HMI will replace the defective Software Media.

(b) **HMI AND THE AUTHOR OF THE BOOK DISCLAIM ALL OTHER WARRANTIES, EXPRESS OR IMPLIED, INCLUDING WITHOUT LIMITATION IMPLIED WARRANTIES OF MERCHANTABILITY AND FITNESS FOR A PARTICULAR PURPOSE, WITH RESPECT TO THE SOFTWARE, THE PROGRAMS, THE SOURCE CODE CONTAINED THEREIN, AND/OR THE TECHNIQUES DESCRIBED IN THIS BOOK. HMI DOES NOT WARRANT THAT THE FUNCTIONS CONTAINED IN THE SOFTWARE WILL MEET YOUR REQUIREMENTS OR THAT THE OPERATION OF THE SOFTWARE WILL BE ERROR FREE.**

(c) This limited warranty gives you specific legal rights, and you may have other rights that vary from jurisdiction to jurisdiction.

6. Remedies.

(a) HMI's entire liability and your exclusive remedy for defects in materials and workmanship shall be limited to replacement of the Software Media, which may be returned to HMI with a copy of your receipt at the following address: Software Media Fulfillment Department, Attn.: *Microsoft .NET E-Commerce Bible*, Hungry Minds, Inc., 10475 Crosspoint Blvd., Indianapolis, IN 46256, or call 1-800-762-2974. Please allow four to six weeks for delivery. This Limited Warranty is void if failure of the Software Media has resulted from accident, abuse, or misapplication. Any replacement Software Media will be warranted for the remainder of the original warranty period or thirty (30) days, whichever is longer.

(b) In no event shall HMI or the author be liable for any damages whatsoever (including without limitation damages for loss of business profits, business interruption, loss of business information, or any other pecuniary loss) arising from the use of or inability to use the Book or the Software, even if HMI has been advised of the possibility of such damages.

(c) Because some jurisdictions do not allow the exclusion or limitation of liability for consequential or incidental damages, the above limitation or exclusion may not apply to you.

7. U.S. Government Restricted Rights. Use, duplication, or disclosure of the Software for or on behalf of the United States of America, its agencies and/or instrumentalities (the "U.S. Government") is subject to restrictions as stated in paragraph (c)(1)(ii) of the Rights in Technical Data and Computer Software clause of DFARS 252.227-7013, or subparagraphs (c) (1) and (2) of the Commercial Computer Software - Restricted Rights clause at FAR 52.227-19, and in similar clauses in the NASA FAR supplement, as applicable.

8. General. This Agreement constitutes the entire understanding of the parties and revokes and supersedes all prior agreements, oral or written, between them and may not be modified or amended except in a writing signed by both parties hereto that specifically refers to this Agreement. This Agreement shall take precedence over any other documents that may be in conflict herewith. If any one or more provisions contained in this Agreement are held by any court or tribunal to be invalid, illegal, or otherwise unenforceable, each and every other provision shall remain in full force and effect.

CD-ROM Installation Instructions

To install Commerce Server 2000, simply insert the CD into your server computer. The Setup program should start automatically. If it doesn't, use Explorer to locate the Setup program on the CD and double-click it.

Commerce Server 2000 requires SQL Server 7.0 (or a later version) to be present in the environment when it is installed.